The Selected Letters
of
ROBERT BRIDGES

An etching of Robert Bridges, 1898, by William Strang. See letter 26. Courtesy of the Lord Bridges.

The Selected Letters
of
ROBERT BRIDGES

With the Correspondence of
Robert Bridges and Lionel Muirhead

Volume 1

Edited by Donald E. Stanford

NEWARK: UNIVERSITY OF DELAWARE PRESS
LONDON AND TORONTO: ASSOCIATED UNIVERSITY PRESSES

© 1983 by Associated University Presses, Inc.

Associated University Presses, Inc.
4 Cornwall Drive
East Brunswick, N.J. 08816

Associated University Presses Ltd
27 Chancery Lane
London WC2A 1NF, England

Associated University Presses
Toronto M5E 1A7, Canada

Library of Congress Cataloging in Publication Data

Bridges, Robert Seymour, 1844–1930.
  The selected letters of Robert Bridges.

  Includes index.
  1. Bridges, Robert Seymour, 1844–1930—Correspondence.
2. Poets, English—19th century—Correspondence.
I. Muirhead, Lionel, 1845–1925. II. Stanford, Donald E.,
1913– . III. Title.
PR4161.B6Z48 1983   821′.8 [B]   82-6885
ISBN 0-87413-177-4   AACR2

Printed in the United States of America

For Maryanna

CONTENTS OF VOLUME 1

Abbreviations   8
List of Illustrations   9
Acknowledgments   11
Biographical Table   15
Introduction   19
Editorial Practices   75
Letters, 1865–1907   77
   Part I: Oxford and London, 1865–1882   79
   Part II: Yattendon, 1882–1904   135
   Part III: Chilswell, 1904–1930   463

ABBREVIATIONS

BBC	British Broadcasting Corporation
BL	British Library
BN	Biographical Notes
BP	Bridges Papers
DNB	*Dictionary of National Biography*
GMH	Gerard Manley Hopkins
GR	Gordon Ray
HAM	*Hymns Ancient and Modern*
HEW	Harry Ellis Wooldridge
LM	Lionel Muirhead
RB	Robert Bridges
R.S.L.	Royal Society of Literature
S.P.E.	Society for Pure English
TLS	*Times Literary Supplement*

LIST OF ILLUSTRATIONS

An Etching of Robert Bridges, 1898, by William Strang   *frontispiece*
Robert Bridges at Philae, Egypt, March 1868, after a watercolor
    by Lionel Muirhead   92
Map of Lionel Muirhead's travels in the Near East, 1868–70   102–3
Robert Bridges, date unknown   126
The Manor House at Yattendon, 1886   156
Monica Waterhouse, wife of Robert Bridges, summer 1888   178
Title page of *The Yattendon Hymnal*   302
The cast of Robert Bridges's masque *Demeter,* June 1904   457

ACKNOWLEDGMENTS

I wish to thank Thomas Bridges (the 2d Lord Bridges), grandson and literary executor of Robert Bridges, for his help and encouragement during the past several years and for his permission to publish the letters of his grandfather, and I wish also to thank Sir Patrick Thomas, grandson and literary executor of Lionel Muirhead, for his permission to publish the letters of his grandfather and the pictures of the Muirhead family.

For much of this edition I have drawn on the Bridges Papers recently deposited by Thomas Bridges in the Bodleian Library. These papers were collected by Edward Bridges (later the 1st Lord Bridges), Robert Bridges's son, and, until their deposit at the Bodleian, were housed in his home, Goodman's Furze. Edward Bridges had planned to edit and publish his father's correspondence, and for a number of years he collected and arranged the poet's letters and papers for that purpose. The tremendous pressure of public service (recording the affairs of Winston Churchill's War Cabinet, of which he was secretary, was only one of his many duties) prevented him from finishing the edition before his death in 1969. I am heavily indebted to his labors as, indeed, any other scholar will be who engages in serious research on the work of the former poet laureate.

Elizabeth Daryush, the daughter of Robert Bridges, gave me much factual information about her father, his family, and his friends, and after her death in 1977 her husband, A. A. Daryush, has given me similar assistance, as have Robert Bridges and Mrs. Hilary Corke, grandson and granddaughter of the poet, and Hilary Corke.

Pamela Diamand, the daughter of Roger Fry, made a transcript of her father's letters to Bridges, which are in the Bodleian Library and were used by Denys Sutton in his superb edition of Fry's letters; I too have found them of great help.

David Middleton made transcripts for me from microfilm of a large number of the letters and John Finlay gave me research assistance in the biographies of Bridges's correspondents. My research assistant, Francine Landreneau, tracked down many recondite allusions in the letters and was of great help in compiling the explanatory notes and in solving textual problems.

I wish especially to thank Catherine MacKenzie for establishing with the aid of infrared analysis the correct dating of the sequence of letters describing the painting of Bridges's portrait by Sir William Richmond. Several of the letters had been misdated in manuscript, apparently by a hand other than Bridges's. She also gave me valuable research assistance at the University of Cambridge Library and the Bodleian Library, when I was in the States and could not do it myself. Also, she called my attention to the important collections of Bridges letters in the archives of the University of Reading and in the archives of the Royal College of Physicians.

Muriel Bradbrook gave me information concerning the activities of the composer Cyril Rootham and his relationship with Bridges, and Mrs. O. E. I. Bonfield of Great Haseley gave me her personal reminiscences of the Muirhead family and of Bridges's association with them, and she allowed me to duplicate pictures of the Muirhead family in her possession.

I wish also to acknowledge the use I made of James Sambrook's *A Poet Hidden: The Life of Richard Watson Dixon* in annotating Bridges's letters to Dixon, and the assistance of Chris Mattox in establishing the Greek readings.

D. G. Vaisey, the Keeper of Western Manuscripts at the Bodleian Library, and his staff gave me invaluable assistance, especially Serena Farrant, who expedited the Xeroxing of the letters selected from the Bridges Papers.

Miss Jennifer Scherr, in charge of the Worsley Chemical Library at the University of Bristol, gave me valuable information concerning Tyntesfield and Bridges's visit there in 1886. Mrs. D. M. Goodall of Yorkshire gave me information from her family papers concerning Bridges's household at Yattendon and Chilswell.

Richard J. Finneran supplied me with the holograph of Bridges's letter to Yeats (no. 274) unavailable until recently. I also wish to acknowledge the use I made of the notes and text of his edition of the Yeats-Bridges correspondence, although my text of the Bridges letters was finally established from holograph copies in the Bridges Papers.

Gordon Ray of the Guggenheim Foundation allowed me to examine Bridges's letters to A. H. Miles concerning the editing and publishing of Hopkins's poems, and I learned much background material about Bridges from conversations at Oxford with Simon Nowell-Smith.

The ever-courteous assistance of the staff of the Troy H. Middleton Library at Louisiana State University has been of great help, especially that of Sandra Mooney in gathering material for the biographical notes.

I wish to acknowledge the typing assistance provided by the English Department of Louisiana State University. I also wish to acknowledge the cooperation of the librarian of Worcester College, Oxford, and of Lady de Villiers, archivist of Somerville College, Oxford, and of Pauline Adams, librarian of the college.

Michael Bott, assistant archivist of the University of Reading, made the collection of Sir Hubert Parry's letters available to me. The librarians of Worcester College, Oxford, gave me access to the collection of Bridges letters to C. H. O. Daniel; the archivist of the Royal College of Physicians, London, helped me to examine the papers of Dr. Samuel Gee.

My thanks are also due to the National Endowment of Humanities for a summer grant that enabled me to enlarge and complete this edition.

Finally, I wish to acknowledge the help of my wife, who acted as my research assistant in England and who helped me prepare every page of this volume.

A number of the letters in this edition have been previously published, as follows—those to Henry Bradley in *Correspondence of Robert Bridges and Henry Bradley 1900–1923* (Oxford: Clarendon Press, 1940); those to William Butler

Yeats in *The Correspondence of Robert Bridges and W. B. Yeats,* edited by Richard J. Finneran (London: Macmillan, 1977); those to R. C. Trevelyan in *XXI Letters: A Correspondence between Robert Bridges and R. C. Trevelyan on "New Verse" and "The Testament of Beauty"* (Stanford Dingley: The Mill House Press, 1955) (an edition limited to less than sixty copies); some of those to Samuel Butler in two articles by Donald E. Stanford—"Robert Bridges and Samuel Butler on Shakespeare's Sonnets: An Exchange of Letters," *Shakespeare Quarterly* 22 (Autumn 1971): 328–35 and "Robert Bridges on His Poems and Plays: Unpublished Letters by Robert Bridges to Samuel Butler," *Philological Quarterly* 50 (April 1971): 281–91; some of those to Stanley Morison in two volumes by Nicolas Barker—*The Printer and the Poet* (Cambridge: University Printing House [privately printed], 1970) and *Stanley Morison* (Cambridge, Mass.: Harvard University Press, 1972).

The pictures of "Robert Bridges and Aldous Huxley, 1928," and of "Robert Bridges and Carl Dolmetsch" were taken from *Lady Ottoline's Album,* by Lady Ottoline Morrell, edited by Carolyn Heilbrun, published by Alfed A. Knopf, Inc. Copyright © 1976 by Julian Morrell Vinogradoff. They are published here by permission of Alfred A. Knopf, Inc.

BIOGRAPHICAL TABLE

1844	October 23	Robert Seymour Bridges, eighth child and fourth son of John Thomas Bridges and Harriet Elizabeth Bridges, née Affleck, is born at Walmer, Kent.
1853	May 10	RB's father dies.
1854	September	RB enters Eton.
	October 31	RB's mother marries the Reverend J. E. N. Molesworth and the family moves to Rochdale, Lancashire.
1863	July	RB leaves Eton.
	Michaelmas	RB enters Corpus Christi College, Oxford.
1866	February	RB's younger brother, Edward, dies.
1867	July	RB strokes Corpus boat in Paris Regatta.
	December	Takes second in Literae Humaniores.
1868	January 12	Sails with Muirhead from Southampton on trip that takes them to Egypt and Syria.
1868–69		RB and William Sanday spend eight months in Germany.
1869	April	Death of RB's sister Harriett Louisa (Mrs. Plow)
	November 6	RB enters as student at St. Bartholomew's Hospital, lodging at 35 Great Ormond Street, London; M.B., 1874.
1870	August–October	RB in Paris
1872		Moves to 50 Maddox Street, Hanover Square, where he lives with Harry Ellis Wooldridge.
1874	January–June	Tours Italy with Wooldridge.
1875–76		House physician to Dr. Patrick Black at St. Bartholomew's Hospital
1877		Casualty physician at St. Bartholomew's
	April 21	Death of Dr. Molesworth. RB moves to 52 Bedford Square and makes a home for his mother there.
1878		Assistant physician, Hospital for Sick Children, Great Ormond Street, and physician, Great Northern Hospital, Holloway

Publications are not given in this table. See select list of books by Robert Bridges, below, for a chronological table of publications.

1880		Meets Canon Dixon (after previous correspondence) at Hayton.
1881	June	Suffers a near-fatal attack of pneumonia.
	December–March 1882	Retires from medical practice. Tours Italy with Muirhead.
1882		Moves with his mother to Yattendon and meets Monica, elder daughter of the architect Alfred Waterhouse, R.A.
1884	April	Becomes engaged to Monica.
	September 3	Marries Monica.
1887	Summer	Visits Canon Dixon in Northumberland.
	August	Gerard Manley Hopkins visits Yattendon.
	December 5	Birth of RB's daughter Elizabeth (Mrs. Daryush)
1889	January	RB and family in Italy
	June 8	Death of Hopkins in Dublin
	October 10	Birth of Margaret, RB's younger daughter
1890	December	Maurice, Monica's brother, dies.
1892	August 4	Birth of Edward Ettingdene (later 1st Lord Bridges), RB's only son
1893	December	RB's portrait painted by Charles Furse
1894	November	Vacation on Isle of Wight. Elected honorary fellow of Corpus Christi College
1895	Summer	Withdraws candidacy for Professor of Poetry at Oxford.
	July	Wooldridge appointed Slade Professor. Served until 1904.
1897	March 27–29	Meets William Butler Yeats for first time as he visits Yattendon.
	December 14	RB's mother dies.
1898		Muirhead paints picture of RB. William Strang does etching of him. Muirhead moves into Haseley Court.
1898	December or earlier	Meets William Johnson Stone and begins interest in classical prosody for poems in English.
1899	October	Outbreak of Boer War
1900	January 23	Dixon dies. Monica is seriously ill.
1901	January	RB moves family to Oxford for three months.
	February 28	Stone dies and RB begins time-consuming experiments in writing poems in classical prosody.
	August	With Monica engages in experiments in phonetic script.
1902–3		Monica and Margaret seriously ill, probably with tuberculosis
1903	August	Vacation on Isle of Wight

	September	Edward's first term at preparatory school (Horris Hill, near Newbury)
1904	June 11	*Demeter* performed at Somerville College
	Summer	Both Monica and Margaret are in sanatoriums.
	September	RB decides to move from Yattendon.
	Autumn	RB and family living in Gloucester
1905	February–June	Family lives on Foxcombe Hill and Boar's Hill near Oxford.
	June 30	RB and Monica go to Switzerland. Edward joins them for a time in August.
	July–March 1906	In Switzerland
1906	March 28	Returns to England. Moves to Bleak House, Boar's Hill, to await building of Chilswell.
	May 4	Edward enters as Oppidan at Eton.
	September	Moves to Whitebarn on Boar's Hill.
1907	July 23	Family moves into Chilswell.
	August 25	RB's friend Mary Coleridge dies.
1908	August	RB and Elizabeth travel to Scotland and visit Thomas Hodgkin, Monica's uncle.
		Demeter performed three times in Liverpool
	November 18	*Eton Memorial Ode,* set to music of Sir Hubert Parry, performed at Eton.
1910	December	Edward wins Demyship at Magdalen College, Oxford.
1911	March–July	RB's portrait painted by Sir William Richmond
	July	Vacation in Dunwich, Saxmundham, Suffolk
	Michaelmas	Edward enters Magdalen College, Oxford.
	Autumn	Elizabeth vacations in Berlin.
1912	June 26	RB receives D. Litt. from Oxford University.
	June 27	*Achilles in Scyros* performed at Ladies College in Cheltenham in presence of RB
1913	January	RB founds Society for Pure English.
	April	Edward tours Italy.
	July 15	RB appointed Poet Laureate
	September	Visits Lord de Tabley's sister at Tabley Hall and tours Cheshire and Wales.
	October	First S.P.E. brochure circulated
1914	July	Edward takes first in Greats.
	August 4	England declares war on Germany.
1917	February 6	Fire at Chilswell. RB and family move to gardener's cottage.
	February	Edward wounded in fighting in France

	March	RB and Monica in London tending Edward
	April	RB moves to Oxford for term.
1918		RB edits Hopkins's poems.
	September	Edward goes to Italian front.
	November 11	Armistice with Germany
1919	June–September	RB and Monica at Postmaster's Hall, Merton College, Oxford
	July 3	Margaret marries Horace Joseph.
	October	S.P.E. begins publication, which had been delayed by war.
1920	October	Oxford Letter of Reconciliation (with German intellectuals) composed by RB causes controversy.
1922		Edward marries Katharine Farrer.
1923	May 23	RB's close friend Henry Bradley dies.
	November	Elizabeth marries A. A. Daryush and goes to live in Persia.
1924	March 22	RB and Monica sail to America for three months' stay at University of Michigan.
	October 23	RB presented with Dolmetsch clavichord on eightieth birthday
1925	January 25	Muirhead, RB's closest friend, dies.
1926	April 25	Margaret, RB's younger daughter, dies.
1927	July 2	Gustav Holst directs concert of RB's poems set to Holst's music in presence of RB.
1929	June 3	RB appointed to the Order of Merit
1930	April 21	RB dies at Chilswell.

INTRODUCTION

I

Regarded superficially, Robert Bridges's life-style (1844–1930) was that of a late Victorian gentleman with an independent income—refined, intellectual, hedonistic. He had the benefits of an excellent Oxford education, which included a thorough knowledge of Greek and Latin literature; travel as a young man in Egypt and Europe; marriage at the age of forty to Monica, twenty years his junior, daughter of England's famous architect Alfred Waterhouse; residence in the large manor house of Yattendon,Berkshire—one of the most charming of England's rural villages—and later residence in Chilswell, designed by himself, on Boar's Hill, Oxford. He had three children: Elizabeth, who herself became an important poet, writing under her married name of Elizabeth Daryush; Margaret, a musician, who married Horace Joseph, a well-known author and senior philosophical tutor at Oxford; and Edward, friend of Winston Churchill, secretary of Churchill's War Cabinet, head of the Civil Service, and one of the last of the hereditary peers to be created in England. It is little wonder that many of Bridges's finest lyrics radiate with a feeling of serenity and joy and that his last poem, *The Testament of Beauty,* published the day after his eighty-fifth birthday, repeats and maintains much of the hope and happiness of his earlier poems.

However, the late Victorian age, the Edwardian period, and the reign of George V were a time of intellectual, religious, aesthetic, and political ferment, with the political turmoil culminating in the disaster of World War I. Bridges was not immune to any of these troubles, as a number of his poems and many of his letters abundantly show. Beneath the calm surface of his life there were grave problems, religious and philosophical, common to his times, and he resolved them in his own fashion. Furthermore, there was an unusual amount of strain brought on by the constant illness of his family (less frequently, of himself), which is for the first time revealed in these letters and which sometimes affected the tone of his work—as in a few despondent lyrics and in the last part of his masque *Demeter,* written when he became aware that his wife and his daughter Margaret had contracted tuberculosis. Bridges knew and consulted the best doctors of England, including the most famous of them all, Sir Thomas Barlow, and Bridges himself was trained as a doctor at St. Bartholomew's Hospital after taking his degree in Greats at Corpus Christi College, Oxford. But medical practice, even at its best in those days, appears to have been primitive when compared to modern standards. Bridges's outlook on life, then, was somewhat darkened in his last years by these personal problems. He never was, by temperament, the cheerful bouncing optimist that we find, for example, in the mid-Victorian Browning; on the other hand, he successfully resisted the neurotic gloominess of the fin de siècle and the cynicism of the Edwardian and Jazz ages. Taken as a whole, his letters have the tone of a man who has understood the basic difficulties of his time and has mastered the problems of his own life as well as the craft of his chosen medium of communication with the world, the art of poetry, to which he had a devoted and lifelong commitment.

The letters in these volumes are only a part of Bridges's extant correspondence, and only a small part of all the letters he wrote during his long life, many of which were destroyed by himself, including, unfortunately, his very important letters to Gerard Manley Hopkins. Of these only three survive. They have been included in this edition.

Those letters printed in the following pages document Bridges's long and interesting life from the time he was a young, relatively unknown student at Corpus Christi until his last years, when he had gained worldwide fame. There are many references to the details of domestic life that give us a memorable picture of the day-to-day routine of an educated man of literary tastes during the late Victorian period and the early twentieth century. But there are also important discussions of poetry that will throw considerable light on his own verse, particularly his prosodic experiments. His discussions of the problems he faced when writing his essay on Keats are of special interest, as are his comments on his notorious essay on Shakespeare. And here for the first time are published all the extant letters to members of the Hopkins family, which give us Bridges's side of the much-discussed delay in publishing his edition of Hopkins's poems. But perhaps the most important group of letters are those he exchanged with Lionel Muirhead, for they cover a period of sixty years and in them Bridges discusses almost every subject that interested him, from the quality of Muirhead's smoking tobacco to the most abstruse problems of classical and English prosody.

II

Truest-hearted of early friends, that Eton
Long since gave to me,—Ah! 'tis all a life-time,—

Robert Bridges began his close and lifelong friendship with Lionel Muirhead (1845–1925) when they were at Eton. Lionel's parents, James Patrick and Catherine (née Boulton), lived at Haseley Court in south Oxfordshire, to which they had moved in 1848 when Lionel was three years old and where in 1898 Lionel established his own home. After Eton he attended Balliol College, Oxford, where Gerard Manley Hopkins was a fellow student and where Robert Bridges was also an undergraduate at nearby Corpus Christi College. In the winter of 1867/68 Muirhead and Bridges went to Egypt at a time when travel there was uncomfortable and hazardous. Muirhead kept a journal of this expedition that appears to have been lost, but there is still extant a charming watercolor dated March 1868 that he painted, showing Bridges working at his writing-table in their tent at Philae on the Nile. The letters of Muirhead to Bridges describing his adventures in Mesopotamia a few months later have survived and are published for the first time in this edition. Bridges went for another trip abroad with Muirhead in November or December 1881,[1] soon after he had recovered from a near-fatal attack of pneumonia. They spent most of their time in Italy, returning to England in March 1882.

There are over four hundred letters extant (all previously unpublished) that Bridges wrote to his best friend, dating from 1865 to 1925. They reveal many aspects of the poet's career over a long period of time; they are the most intimate and informative source we have of Bridges's life. In them Bridges writes about his personal life, his marriage, children, domestic affairs, gardening, successes and failures in his literary endeavors, periods of ill health suffered by his family and himself—some of which sickness we know now was caused by a tubercular cow that Bridges purchased about the turn of the century at Yattendon. Muirhead was a gentleman of independent means, a good classical scholar, and a man of refined tastes. At Haseley Court he had an elegant library and he surrounded himself with works of art collected on his travels in England, on the Continent, and in the Middle East. (The picture of him in this edition in his drawing room at Haseley Court gives an accurate impression of his life-style.) It is natural, then, that Bridges should discuss in his letters their mutual interests in classical literature, modern literature, philosophy, art, and architecture. Muirhead himself was a painter, usually in watercolors, and he frequently included in his paintings examples of fine architecture, a major interest with him. He was, like Bridges, a good athlete. He rode with the South Oxfordshire Hounds, and for several seasons he hunted on an Arab stallion named Montessariff, a present from a Mesopotamian notable whose portrait he had painted while visiting him in his native country. But most important, Bridges wrote about his own poems in his letters to Muirhead, to whom he frequently sent his manuscripts. There is in Bodley a beautifully bound manuscript of "Now in Wintry Delights," a poem dedicated to his friend, which contains also several of Bridges's letters and the manuscripts of other poems, including "To L. M.," which begins "Truest-hearted of early friends."[2]

Muirhead married Grace Ashhurst in 1887, three years after Bridges married Monica Waterhouse. Muirhead's two children, Charis born in 1888 and Anthony in 1890, arrived at approximately the same time as Bridges's three children, and they are frequently referred to in the letters. Haseley Court was within a convenient distance of Yattendon and of Chilswell and the families frequently exchanged visits. They were all avid gardeners, as we quickly ascertain from the correspondence, with Monica frequently expressing thanks for flowers and shrubs arriving at Chilswell from Haseley Court. Haseley Court, although a house had stood there in Norman times and part of its present structure dates from as early as Edward II, is mainly Queen Anne and Georgian, with gardens reminiscent of the eighteenth century. It is well known for its topiary work, one section of which is still clipped in the form of chessmen set on a chess board. According to friends of the family, Muirhead used to play chess with a man named Somerville and the two of them designed and clipped the chess garden, which has been maintained for almost eighty years until the present day.

Muirhead died January 25, 1925, after just completing his eightieth year. Bridges and his wife attended the funeral at Haseley on January 27. Bridges's visits to Haseley Court continued even after Muirhead's death, and friends of the Muirhead family still remember the frequent attendance for the next several years of the poet laureate at dinners there.

III

Bridges has left us a graphic description of his first meeting with Canon Dixon (the elder of the two men by eleven years) in the summer of 1880 at the How Mill Station, Hayton, near Carlisle in the county of Cumberland:

Emotion graved the scene on my memory: a tallish, elderly figure, its litheness lost in a slight, scholarly stoop which gave to the shoulders an appearance of heaviness, wearing unimpeachable black cloth negligently, and a low-crowned clerical hat banded with twisted silk. . . . His face, I saw, was dark and solemn, and as he drew near I could see that the full lips gave a tender expression, for the beard did not hide the mouth. Nothing further could be read, only the old mystery and melancholy of the earth, and that under the heavy black brows his eyes did their angelic service to the soul without distraction. His hearty welcome was in a voice that startled me with its sonority and depth; but in its convincing sincerity there was nothing expansive or avenant.[3]

Bridges also commemorated this first meeting in his poem "Eclogue I," which begins "Man hath with man on earth no holier bond," of which Bridges says "The sentiment there is from life, but the incidents and scene are fictitious."[4] The poem was written and first published in 1899, just a year before Canon Dixon's death. In his letter of August 7, 1899, Bridges addressed Dixon as "Dear Basil" and enclosed a draft of his new poem—a pastoral dialogue between two poets, Edward and Basil, in which they celebrate their friendship by repeating a poetic contest that they had held twelve years earlier when each poet rivaled the other in praising the months of the year, so that by praising time they are thus defeating its effect on them. Each poet attempts to recall and repeat the lines that the other poet composed twelve years earlier. Hence what Edward says in this poem is a recollection of what Basil (Dixon) had composed. In his letter of August 7 Bridges wrote: "I thought that you might like to touch up some of the stanzas which I put into your mouth—for it is you, though I lie about Somerset, and I hope you will be amused at my fiction. You will see that your stanzas are those which EDWARD repeats. All very dodgy!!" Dixon in a replying letter (missing) suggested some changes in the final lines of the poem, but the suggestions were rejected by Bridges.

In 1899 Bridges's poetic powers were at their height. He wrote his fine "Elegy from a Summer House on the Mound" this same year. "Eclogue I" is not a major poem, but it has some very beautiful passages descriptive of the months of the year. Here is the description of April:

Then laugheth the year; with flowers the meads are bright;
The bursting branches are tipped with flames of light:

The landscape is light; the dark clouds flee above,
And the shades of the land are a blue that is deep as love.

Bridges had first heard of Canon Dixon about two years before his trip to Hayton. In 1878 Hopkins told Bridges of his poetry, the same year in which Hopkins, remembering Dixon as his master at Highgate School, wrote to him praising his poetry, which had undeservedly fallen into neglect. "Many beautiful works have been almost unknown and then have gained fame at last. . . . And if I were making up a book of English poetry I should put your Ode to Summer next to Keats' on Autumn and the Nightingale and the Grecian Urn."[5]

Bridges was very favorably impressed by the poetry, and even more by the man. He invited Dixon to make his flat at 52 Bedford Square his London residence while Dixon was engaged in research for his monumental six-volume *History of the Church of England from the Abolition of the Roman Jurisdiction*, the first volume of which was published in 1878. Dixon was presented to the vicarage of Warkworth in Northumberland in 1883, a living he held until his death. Bridges in his *Memoir* tells us:

> There I visited him many times, and have spent so many days that the dilapidated armchair and Severn's little drawing of Keats by the study fire seemed to belong to me.[6]

The available letters from Bridges to Dixon run from 1882 through 1899. Poetry was their chief mutual concern, and those letters which comment on the verse of their contemporaries as well as of themselves are of greatest interest today. Although they admired each other's work, they were not reluctant to point out each other's faults. Bridges at times wrote detailed critiques of Dixon's poems and made specific suggestions for improvement of style that Dixon frequently followed. Bridges persuaded Dixon, in his letter of September 7, 1882, to delay the publication of the long narrative poem *Mano* for one year so that he could undertake the revisions that Bridges was urging.

Dixon, long before he met Bridges, had gone up to Pembroke College, Oxford, where he matriculated in 1851 and where he graduated after reading classics in 1857. He was a member of a brotherhood of poets and would-be clergymen and artists that included William Morris and Edward Burne-Jones. His first volume of poems, *Christ's Company* (1861), was written in a style that owed much to Keats. The descriptive passages that Bridges called "pictorial Pre-Raphaelite" show Dixon at his best. His odes "On Conflicting Claims" and "On Advancing Age" and his poem "The Spirit Wooed" are considered to be among his best work. His verse was praised not only by Bridges and Hopkins but by D. G. Rossetti, Swinburne, and Mary Coleridge, the last of whom wrote the preface for Dixon's *Last Poems* (1905), in which she says of Dixon's "The Feathers of the Willow": "It would be hard to find among the lyrics of our own time—or indeed of Shelley's—one more exquisite."

Dixon's parents were Methodists. His father, Dr. James Dixon (whose biography his son wrote), was a famous Wesleyan preacher, but the family never relinquished membership in the Church of England and the poet never had any reservations about becoming an Anglican divine. Indeed, his *History of the Church of England* became his life work, and there are a number of references to it in the correspondence with Bridges.

Many of Bridges's poems and plays are referred to in these letters. In the first, dated July 1, 1882, Bridges replied to an objection that Dixon had raised concerning *Prometheus*, Bridges's first masque, the unfinished manuscript of which Bridges had sent him:

> It rather frightens me. What you say about the Prometheus being too finished. You must mean that there isn't much in it. But I still hope that you will be really pleased when you see the whole. A poem cannot be too finished? If it can pray let me revoke all my criticisms of yours.

The objection and the answer point up a difference between Dixon and Bridges. For Dixon the emotion expressed is of paramount importance; for Bridges, craftsmanship, the mastery of form. In subsequent letters Bridges referred to most of the plays that occupied his attention during the eighties and early nineties: *Nero I* and *II*, *The Christian Captives*, *The Feast of Bacchus*, *Palicio*, and *Achilles in Scyros*, and he states his intention of doing plays on Henry I, Henry II, and Cromwell. However, the neglect of his dramas by theater managers, critics, and the reading public discouraged him and he never carried out his intention to write more plays. Of *Nero II* he wrote to Dixon on July 29, 1892, "I find people like *Nero II* so that I hope my vein is not quite extinct." By "people" Bridges means friends to whom he had shown the manuscript, for the play was not published until 1894. After its publication Bridges wrote to Dixon about it in a very different vein: "I have been surprised that none of the critics have thought my Nero pt. II worth notice, and, considering that it completed a series of which they have never condescended to utter even the meanest utterance, it seems to me that they owed it to themselves to seize this occasion. I am rather sold, because I had looked forward to amusing myself with their remarks."

The seriousness with which Bridges took his critical essay on Keats is evident in his letters of 1894 and 1895 to Dixon as well as to Mrs. Woods, A. H. Bullen, H. E. Wooldridge, and others to whom he sent the manuscript of the essay in progress. He wrote to Dixon on February 20, 1895, concerning his essay: "I expect that my fault is pedantry. I hate it so much that I am not afraid of it, and therefore am liable to slip into it."

Bridges was a severe critic of his own writings—and of those of others. There are a number of stinging remarks on the work of his fellow Victorians as well as on writers of other periods. He was especially frank in these letters to Dixon. Of Carlyle he said: "He, qua mortal, is beastly, vulgar, smart, self-conscious, rude, one-sided, prejudiced, jaundiced, impatient, fretful, uncharitable, contradictory, all that is opposed to sweet and lovely. I should think that he must vulgarize his readers while he pretends to elevate them." Of Swinburne as a critic he wrote, "I have no opinion of his judgment. He goes swashing at a thing in the extravagant language of his momentary delirium, and thinks that it must be heaven inspired wisdom because Theodore Watts assures him that it is so," and of Dante Gabriel Rossetti, "I am quite sure that his sonnets bore me profoundly. . . . they are sensuality affected to dullness." In 1895, the year of the famous trial, he wrote, "I am quite glad that Oscar Wilde is quite shown up. No one has done more harm to art than he in the last 20 years." Bridges admired much of Shelley's verse, but of the man he said to Dixon, "Dowden [Shelley's biographer] will not allow the reader to think that Shelley was mad. If you may not sometimes laugh at Shelley you soon lose your patience with him." With reference to Huxley on Darwin's *Origin of Species* he said, "I think for rotten philosophy and poor rhetoric it would be difficult to match his performance." As for the poet Robert Herrick he asked Dixon, "Do you not think Herrick was an ass? I can't see why he should be thought so great a writer." Bridges's contempt for Herrick is difficult to understand, for Herrick's skilled use of conventional meters, so like Bridges's own, should have won his admiration.

Bridges's and Dixon's mutual friend Gerard Manley Hopkins died suddenly and unexpectedly on June 8, 1889, a few weeks before his forty-sixth birthday. Two letters written by Bridges to Dixon on June 14 and August 10, 1889, record Bridges's grief and shock. They are among the most interesting letters extant by Bridges and they give us a fuller understanding of a famous friendship that began in undergraduate days at Oxford. In the first of these letters, after speaking of "the terribly mournful tidings of Gerard's death," Bridges mentions the last poem he had received from Hopkins, "a sonnet to me, explaining some misunderstanding which he thought existed." The sonnet, dated April 22, 1889, was enclosed in Hopkins's last letter to Bridges, dated April 29, 1889. It ends with these lines:

> Sweet fire the sire of muse, my soul needs this;
> I want the one rapture of an inspiration.
> O then if in my lagging lines you miss
>
> The roll, the rise, the carol, the creation,
> My winter world, that scarcely breathes that bliss
> Now, yields you, with some sighs, our explanation.

In a letter dated March 20, 1889, Hopkins had sent Bridges one of his "dark sonnets," beginning "Thou art indeed just, Lord. . . ," and it is probable that Bridges had complained of what he considered the excessive melancholy of this and other poems by Hopkins in that period. Hopkins wrote his final poem as an explanation. The postscript of Bridges's letter is most revealing:

> That dear Gerard was overworked, unhappy and would never have done anything great seems to give no solace. But how much worse it would have been had his promise or performance been more splendid. He seems to have been entirely lost and destroyed, by those Jesuits.

In the next letter, two months later, Bridges mentioned a misunderstanding between himself and Hopkins, "very like a sort of quarrel," and two letters from Hopkins written near the end, which "were rather bitter, so that I put them in the fire." Bridges also says "I have proposed to edit some of his verses—Daniel to print them—*with a short memorial life.*" We know from Bridges's letters to the publisher Daniel (included in this edition) that Bridges entertained this project for about a year and then postponed it until 1918 for reasons discussed below in the comments on Bridges's letters to Hopkins's family.

IV

The publication for the first time of Bridges's letters to Hopkins's mother, Mrs. Manley Hopkins, and to Hopkins's sister, Kate Hopkins, throws considerable light on the still controversial issue of the nature of Bridges's attitude toward the publication of his friend's poetry. Hopkins died in 1889. The first comprehensive collection of his poems was edited by Bridges for publication in 1918, almost thirty years after Hopkins's death. Bridges was a key figure in this matter of publication, for Hopkins had entrusted his manuscripts to him. As early as 1921 Edward Sapir was saying, "From our best friends, deliver us, O Lord!"[7] And during the next four decades, as the importance of Hopkins's poetry became increasingly recognized, the reputation of his friend and editor was under attack. Bridges, according to his detractors, was quite aware of the value of Hopkins's verse. They claimed he delayed publication out of professional jealousy. According to them, it was not until 1913, when he was made poet laureate, that he felt his own reputation to be secure enough to risk presenting his friend's poems to the public. The facts of the case as we know them today point to a different conclusion. Jean Georges-Ritz, who had access to this correspondence and who quotes from it in the final pages of his book on Bridges and Hopkins,[8] has given a fair appraisal of the matter, and he concludes that Bridges's "strictures had brought and would bring more friends to Hopkins than bland eulogies would have done. For he *was* Hopkins's best friend."[9]

The facts of the situation are these. Shortly after Hopkins's death, Bridges began considering the best way to introduce the poetry of his friend to a late Victorian public whose taste had been formed by Browning and Tennyson and, for the more daring souls, by Swinburne and Dowson. In his first letter to Hopkins's mother, dated September 16, 1889, a little more than three months after the poet's death, Bridges told her that he was getting in touch with Hopkins's "Roman Catholic friends" concerning the proper use of the poet's literary and artistic remains. Bridges expressed the hope that "they will be more communicative than they are at present." This is the first of several ironic remarks by Bridges concerning what he considered to be Jesuit recalcitrance in cooperating with him on an edition of Hopkins's poems. (In all fairness we must keep in mind that Bridges had a lifelong Protestant bias.) Also at this time Bridges was writing to C. H. Daniel of the Daniel Press about the possibility of printing privately a selection of Hopkins's poems. Four of these letters, dated August 20, October 11, October 14, and November 19, 1889, appear in this edition. Bridges also mentioned his projected memoir and edition of Hopkins's poems to his friend Bishop Creighton, who replied in his letter of October 15, 1889, with an illuminating comment on Hopkins's character:

Your Memoir of Hopkins will indeed be an interesting and difficult piece of work. I had some correspondence with him when I was at Embleton about the birthplace of Duns Scotus which a vague tradition, arising from a desire of Merton College to claim him as fellow[,] assigned to the hamlet in my parish. I remember that Hopkins stuck to it because he thought it rested upon the earliest tradition; he was neither willing to leave the matter doubtful, nor to submit tradition to criticism: his point was "Find out the earliest tradition; that must be true."[10]

The project was delayed for reasons given in the fourth letter to Hopkins's mother. Later the project was abandoned altogether. Bridges wrote to Mrs. Hopkins on August 4, 1890, stating that Daniel's planned edition of the poems should be delayed until a memoir or at least a short preface could be written that would "put the poems out of the reach of criticism." I interpret this to mean that Bridges himself wanted to forestall what he rightly thought would be severe criticism or ridicule by readers unused to the prosody Hopkins was employing and unused also to Hopkins's highly original imagery and (at times) mannered diction by writing a brief critique explaining the prosody, admitting what he considered to be flaws in style, and stressing the beauties of much of Hopkins's verse, the kind of critique that he in fact did write almost thirty years later as a preface to the notes of the 1918 edition. Bridges sincerely felt that some of Hopkins's verse was overwrought and marred by excessive employment of stress prosody, that is, sprung rhythm. He made this clear in this letter when he said:

> I should myself prefer the postponement of the poems till the memoir is written, *or* till I have got my own method of prosody recognised separately from Gerard's. They are the same, and he has the greater claim than I to the origination of it, but he has used it so as to discredit it: and it would be a bad start in favour for the practice we both advocated and wished to be used. Readers would not see that the peculiarities of his versification are not part of his metrical system, but a freakishness corresponding to his odd choice of words etc. in which also his theories were as sound as his practice was strange.

Bridges was far from being jealous of Hopkins's talent. His chief concern was to protect his friend's interest by "preparing" the public for his highly original and unusual verse and to protect his own interest in the new prosody developed simultaneously by both of them. He thought he could do this best by publishing his own milder experiments in stress prosody first. Once the readers of poetry became accustomed to it they would be better prepared to appreciate Hopkins's original (and sometimes excessive!) use of it. We should keep in mind that Bridges sincerely believed, and plainly stated in public and private, that Hopkins, however talented, was not always successful in some of his metrical experiments.

One poem that especially fascinated, baffled, and irritated Bridges is the now famous "Wreck of the Deutschland," Hopkins's first experiment in sprung rhythm and his first attempt to return to the writing of poetry after his entry into the Jesuit order. The poem was inspired by Hopkins's reading about the death of five Franciscan nuns, exiled from Germany by the Falk laws, who drowned off the Kentish Knock in 1875. The poem has passages of powerful, sometimes frenzied rhetoric, of vivid and frequently bizarre imagery, of sonorous and sometimes deliberately harsh sound effects and unforgettably vigorous rhythms enhanced by Hopkins's descriptive and symbolic use of the storm at sea that killed the nuns and also by the challenge of the new prosody, which Hopkins successfully exploits to achieve lines of unusually heavy beat. There are a few passages that Bridges may have admired. But most of the poem shattered his sense of decorum. He wrote to Kate Hopkins in March 1918, when he was about halfway through the printing of the Hopkins edition: "That terrible 'Deutschland' looks and reads much better in type—you will be glad to hear. But I wish those nuns had stayed at home." Writing in his notes for Hopkins's poems at about the same time, he warned the reader to beware of the "Deutschland":

> the poem stands logically as well as chronologically in the front of his book, like a great dragon to forbid all entrance, and confident in his strength from past success. This editor advises the reader to circumvent him and attack him later in the rear; for he was himself shamefully worsted in a brave frontal assault, the more easily perhaps because both subject and treatment were distasteful to him.[11]

The poem nevertheless held Bridges's interest for years. Bridges's daughter Elizabeth tells of her father reading the first stanza and commenting on the accenting of the final word in the last line as Hopkins scanned it

Óver agáin I féel thy fínger and fínd thée

which, if we didn't know Hopkins's prosody, or rather his own scansion of this particular line, we would naturally read as a five-beat line without the accent over *thee*.[12]

But on the whole, in these letters as elsewhere, Bridges emphasized what he considered to be the beauties of Hopkins's verse. In his second letter to the poet's mother, dated October 23, 1889, he sent her a scrapbook of her son's poems and commented on "the melancholy sonnets which are very powerful and less odd than most of Gerard's work" and on "The fine delight that fathers thought," which he called one of Hopkins's best. All of these poems (written toward the end of Hopkins's life) are in prosody and diction less extravagant than the "Wreck of the Deutschland" and fairly close to Bridges's own style. In the fourth letter, August 4, 1890, he has "given up the notion of notes, and with them the poems." Two-and-a-half years later, on February 24, 1893, he asked Mrs. Hopkins for her opinion of the "notice" with which he is prefacing his selection of Hopkins's poems for the anthology edited by Alfred H. Miles, *The Poets and the Poetry of the Century*[13] or rather for what he hopes will appear in Miles's anthology. He says, "I can't tell whether Miles, when he sees them, will not shy at them as everyone else has done." It is evident that Bridges had met with several refusals to publish Hopkins's poems. In the following letter[14] he is delighted to report to Mrs. Hopkins that Miles has accepted the poems and says "I really now hope that Gerard will at last get the recognition which he knew he deserved." But Bridges was still apprehensive, for he went on to say "It is of course possible that the editor may shy at the last moment, but that would be very bad luck." He assured Mrs. Hopkins "I will take great pains to get the notice as good as I can make it." Bridges's letters to Miles written at this time reveal the painstaking care that he took in presenting the poems accurately and in an attractive format. He showed the same care in 1917/18 when he was preparing his edition of the poems. Bridges printed in Miles's anthology the complete text of seven poems and the partial text of four more.[15] As he feared, the reviews were not encouraging. "Curiosities like the verses of the late Gerard Hopkins should be excluded," wrote the anonymous reviewer in the *Manchester Guardian*.[16] Another anonymous reviewer, whom Bridges in a letter to Mrs. Hopkins enclosing the article identified as "the man who looks after Swinburne," that is, Theodore Watts-Dunton, mentioned Hopkins's poems "without censure," which Bridges indicated was the best one could expect from that quarter—"He would have sneered if he had dared."[17]

Bridges also deserves some credit for the inclusion of five of Hopkins's poems in *Lyra Sacra* (1895), compiled and edited by his friend H. C. Beeching, vicar of Yattendon, a relative of Bridges by marriage.[18] The vicar also published Hopkins's "The Blessed Virgin Compared to the Air We Breathe" in his *Book of Christmas Verse* (1895).[19] In 1899 Bridges called Mrs. Hopkins's attention to the printing of her son's "Thee God, I come from" in *Prayers from the Poets*,[20] and three years later he asked and received permission from her for Elizabeth Waterhouse to include "Heaven-Haven" in her anthology *A Little Book of Life and Death*. The poem caught the attention of Francis Thompson.[21] It was not until seven years had passed that the publication of Hopkins's poetry was mentioned again. On September 6, 1908, Bridges sent Mrs. Hopkins a letter from a person unnamed requesting permission to publish two poems. However, nothing came of this.[22] In 1909 Bridges sent to Mrs. Hopkins a copy of the January issue of *Catholic World* containing an essay by Katherine Bregy, which Dunne describes as "one of the first substantial critical essays" on Hopkins.[23] A few weeks later Bridges was expressing his irritation upon hearing the rumor that Edmund Gosse had considered publishing an edition of Hopkins's poems. He considered Gosse lacking in both taste and competence.[24] Bridges's ire and anxiety were even more aroused when he discovered that Father Keating considered the Society of Jesuits to be Hopkins's literary executors and that they might wish to edit their poet's works. "I am sure they would make a dreadful mess of the whole thing,"[25] and in his next letter he said "I certainly should not trust the Rev. Father with anything of importance."[26] In the same letter we find Bridges considering a private printing of "The Wreck of the Deutschland," but nothing came of it. In an undated letter, perhaps 1913, Bridges referred to Mrs. Hopkins's inability to prevent an "American from printing whatever she chooses," a bitter reflection on American and British copyright laws frequently repeated in other letters.

A few months after the outbreak of World War I, Bridges (who had a son in the trenches) was prevailed upon by the publisher Longman, who had lost his son early in the conflict, to compile an anthology from the philosophers and poets designed to appeal to readers distressed by the war. Bridges published his anthology, *The Spirit of Man*, in January 1916.[27] It had a selection of six poems by Hopkins (three with full texts) and Bridges hastened to ask the publisher to send an advance copy to the poet's mother.[28] This anthology marked the beginning of Hopkins's reputation. It was widely and favorably reviewed. Bridges made a point of sending to Mrs. Hopkins favorable notices of her son's poems. Of the two he sent her on April 26, 1916, the one in the *New York Times Review of Books* referred to Hopkins's "Habit of Perfection" as the "best poetry ever written about the religious life."[29] The following year Bridges wrote to Hopkins's sister Kate, "Gerard's poems in 'The Spirit of Man' were very well received, and I had some MS poems sent me the other day for inspection which showed strong traces of his influence,"[30] and in his next letter to Mrs. Hopkins he quoted Sir Walter Raleigh's favorable opinion to emphasize his statement "I have had lately some very authoritative appeals for the publication of all Gerard's poetical remains." He expressed the opinion that the Oxford Press would probably take the book if offered to them. This date marks the beginning of Bridges's task of presenting a comprehensive edition of his friend's poems to the public. In the next letter to Kate Hopkins[31] he made it clear that (with Mrs. Hopkins's permission) he intended to include all of Hopkins's poems. "Every scrap that he wrote should be published"—even the dreaded and dreadful "Wreck of the Deutschland," which "will no doubt please his real adversaries." The next sixteen letters are a record of Bridges's painstaking efforts to produce an attractive, readable book with an accurate text and informative notes that would aid a baffled public to understand and appreciate the poems. "I worked very hard at the book—about 7 or 8 hours a day," he said in his letter of February 18, 1918. Mrs. Bridges helped with the ornaments. Monica Bridges was, incidentally, unusually talented in design and also in handwriting. Her specimen cards for teaching school-children to write well were issued in 1896. Her *A New Handwriting for Teachers* (1899) reintroduced the italic hand. She contributed to *S.P.E. Tract XXIII* on handwriting and she copied a number of her husband's manuscripts in her clear and attractive script, several of which can be seen in the Bridges Papers. A revised edition, with eleven engraved plates, of her *A New Handwriting for Teachers* (Oxford, 1911), was on display at the International Penmanship Exhibit at the Victoria and Albert Museum, London, in the summer of 1980. In her introduction she explained that she consciously altered her hand after "making acquaintance with the Italianized Gothic of the sixteenth century."

On May 18, 1918, Bridges asked for permission to dedicate his collection of Hopkins's poems to Mrs. Hopkins. The dedication in Latin was composed by A. E. Housman. On December 8, 1918, Bridges sent a postcard stating triumphantly: "I am posting you advance copy of the book." The collection was officially published on December 19 in a small edition and sales were relatively slow. Dunne's note, which is worth quoting in full, tells the story:

This book was published in an edition of 750 copies. Of these, 50 were given away; 180 were sold in the first year; 240 in the second year; then an average of 30 a year for six years, rising to 90 in 1927. The last four copies were sold in 1928. The price was 12s. 6d. It is now scarce, and the few copies which appear for sale or auction command very high prices.[32]

Its eventual success must have exceeded even the expectations of Hopkins's mother. It certainly exceeded those of Robert Bridges. It exceeded also the expectations of another distinguished poet, A. E. Housman. Housman's response to a gift copy of the Hopkins edition, which the editor had sent him immediately after publication, is indicative of the "establishment" attitude that confronted Bridges from the beginning. Housman wrote:

> I value the book as your gift, and also for some good condensed lines and an engaging attitude of mind which now and again shines through. But the faults which you very fairly and judicially set forth thrust themselves more upon my notice; and also another. Sprung Rhythm, as he calls it in his sober and sensible preface, is just as easy to write as other forms of verse; and many a humble scribbler of words for music-hall songs has written it well. But he does not: he does not make it audible; he puts light syllables in the stress and heavy syllables in the slack, and has to be helped out with typographical signs explaining that things are to be understood as being what in fact they are not.[33]

V

William Sanday (1843–1920) went up to Oxford in 1862 as a commoner of Balliol College. In 1863 he gained a scholarship at Bridges's college, Corpus Christi, and graduated in 1865 with a first in Greats. Bridges's friendship with him dated from their Oxford days. In 1868/69, after Bridges's trip to Egypt with Lionel Muirhead (January–May), Bridges and Sanday spent eight months in Germany studying German.[34] Sanday upon his return from Germany took orders, and after holding several college livings he was recalled to Oxford in 1882 as Dean Ireland Professor. He subsequently became fellow and tutor of Exeter College and Lady Margaret Professor of divinity and canon of Christ Church. Bridges in his letters to him frequently discussed religious matters and this correspondence is a helpful source of information concerning Bridges's religious beliefs.

On December 14, 1898, Bridges wrote that he was reading St. Paul and had come to the conclusion that "St. Paul mistook the teaching of Christ." In an important letter twenty years later (June 16, 1918) Bridges indicated a growing interest in psychology: "it seems to me that our hope lies in getting into better intellectual relations with what the philosophers so hate viz. 'the unconscious mind.'" He was now beginning to believe that knowledge may be "implanted in us" and not attainable by "intellectual reasonings." "I know that my will is free, and all the reasoners assure me that it is not." There are also occasional literary discussions in the letters, and when Bridges was commissioned late in 1914 to compile the wartime anthology that became *The Spirit of Man,* Sanday was one of the first of his friends he turned to for advice.

VI

Sir Henry Newbolt (1862–1938) has left a vivid account in his autobiography[35] of his first meeting with Robert Bridges late in 1895 or early in 1896:

It happened that at this moment my wife and I went for the first time to Yattendon Court to stay with Mrs. Bridges' parents, the Alfred Waterhouses. At dinner that evening almost the only guests besides ourselves were Robert and Monica Bridges, who walked up from the Manor House below. It was a day to remember—probably no one ever forgot a first meeting with those two. The general talk after dinner turned for a time upon a charge of idolatry recently made against those who were for placing carved figures upon a church screen. After several opinions had been heard, Bridges came suddenly out of his silence and argued decisively that no human beings, not even the heathen, could in any true sense of the word worship wood or stone. I asked him if that implied approval of all ornaments or ritual. "It would," he said, "if they were in good taste, but they are generally hideous." "In this country, perhaps," I replied, "but you wouldn't say that of ancient Greece?" His face lit up at this and he answered with a slight stammer of eagerness, "V-very good! then the Greeks were not idolaters! But we can't go on talking here—let us meet again to-morrow morning."

A few months later the Newbolts were living at Pargiters, a house in Yattendon close to Bridges's Manor House and communicating with it by a door in the garden wall. On a warm April day Newbolt, on an invitation from Bridges, walked through the garden door with a copy of his own verses in his hand:

I found Robert Bridges lying in the sun on his own doormat, with his spaniel Ben beside him. There were some six or seven steps up to the entrance and dog and master were both stretched comfortably against the front door, where there was just room for me to join them. Bridges was dressed with the most elegant shabbiness, in an old grey felt hat, an old but well-cut lounge coat, and narrow lavender-grey trousers of nankeen, a material then so obsolete that I never saw it worn by any other man, except, I think, Mr. Wyndham of Clouds.
   "Now," said Bridges when I had settled down opposite to him, "you've got some verses for me—is that fat book full of them?" "No," I said, "there are only a few, and I think they're quite legible." To make sure of this point I had handed him first a slip of card on which I had pasted *Drake's Drum*—the version printed in the *St. James's Gazette* had been rearranged by the Editor so as to alter the order of the stanzas and spoil the rhythm, and I had used the scissors and paste to reduce it to order again. I mentioned this to R. B. but he was silent and absorbed. At last he murmured, as if unconscious of my existence, "Awfully swell, awfully swell." I held my breath while he read it again with great deliberation. Then he looked at me and said, "You'll never write anything better than that—it isn't given to man to write anything better than that. I wish I had ever written anything half so good."[36]

Bridges also expressed approval of the other poems Newbolt showed him and from that time until Bridges's death the two were friends, exchanging many letters. (Bridges's side of the extant correspondence runs to about one hundred and seventy-five to one hundred and eighty letters.) The friendship was almost disrupted in 1925 by a difference of opinion concerning American participation in the Society for Pure English, but it survived even this disagreement. It was Henry Newbolt who wrote the fine obituary of Bridges in the *Times*. One more account by Newbolt of a meeting with Bridges, this one of a dinner party that he gave for Bridges and a few friends at his London home in Earl's Terrace in 1898 or 1899, deserves quotation:

> One party we made for the Holroyds and Dickinsons, in order to revive in London the unfinished symposium of our Venetian Nights. Another was inspired by the hope of seeing Bridges as the Londoner he had once been, years before we came to know him. This was a complete success—he was a new man, a resplendent figure and a gay and confident talker. He discovered by some instinct, during dinner, what I did not myself know, that Basil Levett, who sat near him, was an expert in English Hymns, and they became so thick together over their wine and their church music that we were very late in reaching the drawing-room. There, to my astonishment I saw Bridges take possession of a stool and seat himself at Lady Margaret Levett's feet for the rest of the evening, flashing wit and humour from every facet, with the ease and quickness of the Elizabethan drama.[37]

Newbolt and Bridges, who had both been educated at Corpus Christi College, Oxford, had a number of mutual interests, which included the personality and work of the poet and fictionist Mary Coleridge, great-great-niece of Samuel Taylor Coleridge. She is mentioned in a number of Bridges's letters to Newbolt. Newbolt, a close literary and personal friend of Miss Coleridge (they founded a small writers' group they called the Settee) from about 1888, was probably one of the several friends who introduced her poems to Bridges. "Mary Coleridge's manuscript books had come under his [Bridges's] notice by accident—an accident carefully planned by intimate friends on both sides."[38] Bridges liked the poems and he persuaded his friend Daniel to publish a selection of them in 1896 entitled *Fancy's Following*. Bridges continued to be fascinated by Miss Coleridge and by her verses, as she was by him. In a charming letter to Newbolt dated September 9, 1896, she mentioned her recent visit at Yattendon with "Ponte Vecchio" (old Bridges!) and told of Bridges's enthusiasm for Yeats, whose work he had, evidently, just recently discovered. "Mr. Bridges was full of excitement about Yeats. Directly Mr. Binyon arrived, he flew upon him with questions. 'Do you know him? Have you seen him? What is he like?'" She went on to say that Bridges thought some of the lines in *Oisin* as good as Homer, but he "carefully noted the fact that the dew falls on almost every page, and he gets lost among the roses." She continued, "I think I have grown fonder than ever of that Faust-like study. If only Ben (the spaniel) were a black poodle . . . the picture would be complete."[39]

In another letter to Newbolt dated "The Manor House, Yattendon, March 4th, 1897," Miss Coleridge wrote of the Bridges family, "Now here they live artistically, not demanding of life what it cannot yield, but drawing out all that it can. Nothing is wasted, and they are not self-conscious nor restless, they are true North, South, East and West. I am down on my knees for knowing them." She and Bridges collaborated on a bit of translation:

I can't tell you how I enjoy it. The words come swarming, buzzing round, like bees—the smoke curls up from his pipe—the eternal possibilities of every little tiny paragraph bewilder and stimulate me so that an hour goes like a moment. Monica joins the dance when she has time; she is astonishingly good—I'm nowhere beside her—that makes it better still. Of course he does all the work really; but even to sit by lets one into the heart of the thing. It's a magnificent lesson in style—if only I were good enough to profit by it.[40]

Nine days later Mary Coleridge, still at Yattendon, began another letter to Newbolt "Feb. ? They don't observe the days of the month here."[41] She showed Bridges a new poem by Newbolt, and after he had expressed his admiration for it, "he got out a little thing by Gerard Hopkins, to show how stressed verse would have taken the matter, if you had chosen that instead of the Old Ballad form. At first I couldn't make head or tail of it, but after five minutes I began to perceive that it was extraordinarily fine."[42]

Shortly after her sudden and untimely death in August 1907, Bridges published an essay on Mary Coleridge in *Cornhill Magazine*,[43] for which he asked Newbolt's help, and Bridges in turn advised Newbolt on his editorship of the collection of Coleridge's poems, which were also published late in 1907.

A quite different matter of mutual interest was the British Navy, with which Newbolt had a long involvement. His paternal grandfather was a naval officer; and some of Newbolt's earliest poems, including the famous "Drake's Drum" and his book *Admirals All*, were concerned with the navy and led to Newbolt's being called a nautical Kipling. He served at the Admiralty and Foreign Office during World War I. In 1923 at the request of the Committee of Imperial Defence he undertook completion in two volumes (four and five) of the official *History of the Great War: Naval Operations*. Bridges, too, was always fascinated by ships of all kinds. His childhood was spent in Walmer, Kent, overlooking a part of the channel that was anchorage for the British fleet, and one of the finest passages in all of his poetry occurs in his poem "The Summer House on the Mound," written in 1899. In it he recalls his vision as a child of Napier's fleet bound for the Baltic in 1854:

> Cloudless the sky and calm and blue the sea,
> As round Saint Margaret's cliff mysteriously,
> Those murderous queens walking in Sabbath sleep
> Glided in line upon the windless deep.

This magnificient passage is followed by several lines that refer to individual ships by name:

> But chief, her blue flag flying at the fore,
> With fighting guns a hundred thirty and one,
> The Admiral ship *The Duke of Wellington*,
> Whereon sail'd George, who in her gig had flown
> The silken ensign by our sisters sewn.

Bridges was a stickler for correct detail—for example, he wrote to a number of naturalists to verify Hopkins's descriptions of birds, trees, and flowers, and he wrote to seamen to verify details of "The Wreck of the Deutschland." In his own poem he had described the flag of the Admiral ship as blue, as he had remembered it; but he wished to check his memory, so he naturally turned to Newbolt in his letter of July 17, 1899, to verify the color of the Admiral's flag in the Baltic operations of 1854. Newbolt promptly turned the question over to an officer who had been present in this fleet. The officer replied that he was positive that Napier wore his *proper* flag but would have to engage in further research before ascertaining the color. Evidently Bridges was eventually informed that his own memory was correct, for he retained his original description. The reference at the end of the passage is to George Bridges, the poet's brother who was an officer on *The Duke of Wellington*, and their sisters.

As we have seen, Newbolt, like Bridges, was a practicing poet; in the late nineties, with the publication of "Drake's Drum" and *Admirals All,* he became very well known, and Walter de la Mare tells us[44] that Sir Henry considered the writing of poetry to be his most important pursuit. Naturally, he sent a number of his books of verse to Bridges, who became increasingly noncommittal as to detail but who usually expressed general approval. In discussing *Mordred,* however,[45] he takes the trouble to examine serious flaws in this Tennysonian tragedy in blank verse.

From 1900 to 1904 Newbolt was editor of the *Monthly Review,* to which Bridges contributed five poems: "Peace Ode," "Recollections of Solitude," "To the President of Magdalen College," "To Robert Burns," and "Epistle II: To a Socialist in London," as well as his essay "English Music." Several of these contributions are discussed in Bridges's letters to Newbolt, and a year later Bridges commented on Newbolt's poems that he had chosen for Alfred H. Miles's anthology, *The Poets and the Poetry of the Nineteenth Century* (1906).

The Society for Pure English (S.P.E.), founded by Bridges in 1913, was another important mutual concern to both men and was a frequent subject of discussion in their letters of the twenties. Newbolt was not a member of the founding committee that drew up and signed the original manifesto (this committee consisted of Robert Bridges, Henry Bradley, Walter Raleigh, and Logan Pearsall Smith) but he was among the first to become a member in 1913/14.

For the story of the formation of this society, which lasted until 1948, we go to *Robert Bridges: Recollections* by Logan Pearsall Smith,[46] who tells us that a few friends (not named) were discussing Remy de Gourmont's book *Esthétique de la langue française* wherein the French writer, in arguing for the necessity of maintaining standards of "purity" in the French language, maintained that by "purity" he did *not* mean the exclusion of words derived from foreign sources. Bridges and his friends agreed that "our speech also was being injured by the prevalence of the same fashions, and would benefit equally by the establishment of a sounder ideal of the purity of our language." "Few things," Smith continued in his urbane prose, "are pleasanter than to spend a leisurely afternoon in congenial company, deploring the taste of one's contemporaries and the evils of the age one lives in; but 'flabbergasted' is the best word I can find to describe my sensations when, as our little conclave was about to break up, I became aware that Mr. Bridges took it for granted, in his swift peremptory way, that we were to engage in an active and practical campaign to combat the evils we had been so complacently denouncing."[47] Thereupon, according to Smith, Bridges announced that a committee would be formed that was to become the Society for Pure English and that Logan Pearsall Smith would be its secretary.

Bridges's widow, in a letter in the Bridges Papers written after her husband's death, had a slightly different recollection of this meeting. She said that Bridges remarked that if he could only find a secretary, he would be willing to form a society or a committee to uphold proper standards of English usage. Smith immediately volunteered his services and, according to Mrs. Bridges, her husband was stuck with his promise.

In any event, the committee of four drew up their manifesto and published it, and by 1914, when war broke out and the society had to be temporarily discontinued, it numbered almost a hundred members.[48] The society resumed its work after the war, in 1919, and as Bridges's letters to Newbolt show, Newbolt took an active part in its work. It was Bridges, however, who was considered the founding member and its leader from its beginning until his death in 1930. As Smith has written:

> Mr. Bridges was the founder of our Society; from the beginning he planned its policy, chose its collaborators, and guided its destiny, and wrote its most important papers. If it was his "private Academy," its members were content to have it so.[49]

One major problem faced by Bridges from 1920 on was the danger of absorption by other societies of a similar nature, and Smith describes in his *Recollections* how Bridges successfully fought off or, as Smith put it, prevented their "being swallowed up by one or another of these academic bodies."[50] Bridges's letters in the twenties to both Newbolt and Smith are frequently concerned with polite but firm maneuverings to keep the S.P.E. completely independent. Most embarrassing and dangerous of all was the "American Invitation" to make a "concerted effort throughout the English-speaking world to maintain the traditions and foster the development of our common tongue" and to form "a permanent international body of scholars and men of letters representing the principal English speaking peoples." Bridges welcomed American interest in the S.P.E. (he refers with pride, for example, to his contacts with H. L. Mencken and Vachel Lindsay as well as with scholars of the establishment such as John Livingston Lowes) but he didn't want the Americans taking over his S.P.E., and he succeeded in preventing them from doing so (if this indeed was their conscious intention, which it may not have been). His victory, however, nearly cost him his friendship with Sir Henry Newbolt, who seems to have taken more liberal views concerning the participation of the "Yanks" in their society.

VII

Bridges probably met Logan Pearsall Smith for the first time at Yattendon in 1902, perhaps just after Smith had sent him a copy of his charming informal sketches and observations entitled *Trivia*.[51] Bridges must have been favorably impressed by his new friend, who arrived at Yattendon about a year after Bridges had started his long and arduous experiments in writing poems in classical prosody. Soon after Smith's visit he set to work on a new poem in quantitative verse entitled "On Receiving Trivia from the Author." A copy of the poem written in brown and red ink in phonetic script is in Bridges's Manuscript Book,[52] with this comment at the end: "Summer of 1902 corrected Sept 1903 The trysyllabic[53] feet all marked with quantity marks—when I made my experiments in 'Stone's Prosody' I attempted the iambics last knowing their great difficulty; the above lines to Logan Pearsall-Smith were my first adventure in them, and I remember being satisfied at the time. But when I wrote DEMETER in 1904 I managed much better, and now I condemn the above and do not wish it to be published 1905." Bridges sent a copy of the poem to Smith, but he never published it in his lifetime. Smith kept the manuscript and in Bridges's final three letters to Smith (the last two, dated April 1 and April 4, 1930, are among the last he ever wrote) Bridges gave permission for the publication of the poem and instructions as to its printing. The poem was issued about two months after the poet's death, on June 19, 1930, by Kyrle Leng and Robert Gathorne-Hardy at The Mill House Press. This poem, then, marks the beginning and end of a long and congenial friendship. Its first line "When I imagine your select society" is indicative of the esteem in which Bridges held this distinguished American expatriate who was descended from a wealthy Quaker family that had spent much time in England and had established at its home, Friday's Hill in Sussex, a meeting place for scholars, writers, philosophers, and artists. Logan Smith settled eventually in High Buildings, which was near Friday's Hill. His sister Alys married Bertrand Russell; his sister Mary married Bernard Berenson. It was through Smith (as well as through Roger Fry) that Bridges kept in touch with the distinguished art historian and his circle. Smith was also the friend of another famous expatriate, Henry James, and it was to Smith that James sent his extraordinary letter praising Bridges's memoir of Digby Dolben, a letter that Smith lost no time in copying and passing on to Bridges. Bridges never claimed James as a close friend although he expressed admiration for him. They first met in the 1870s and on at least one other occasion, when they received honorary degrees together at Oxford, June 26, 1912. Another famous expatriate, George Santayana, was a friend of both Smith and Bridges; his name appears several times in their correspondence, and Bridges wrote a favorable review for the *London Mercury*, August 1920, of Smith's *Little Essays Drawn from the Writings of George Santayana*.

Logan Smith, like Bridges, was a man of independent means who devoted his life to the pursuit of culture. They had common tastes and interests and discussed and corresponded about Bridges's poems as well as other literary undertakings such as the wartime anthology *The Spirit of Man* and the edition of Hopkins's poems, along with French literature and music. One of the most interesting of the letters was a result of their plan to collaborate on a selection of Shakespeare's sonnets. Bridges, in his letter dated January 28, 1907(?), makes a selection of a few of Shakespeare's best sonnets and explains why he has chosen them. Smith did not agree with his choice and the project was abandoned. In later letters, considerable attention was paid to affairs of the S.P.E. for which Logan Smith, as we have seen, was secretary until he resigned the office in 1922. Perhaps the greatest value of this group of letters, however, is the insight it gives us into Bridges's literary tastes. He wrote frankly to Smith on this subject, frequently disagreeing with him, particularly in Smith's favorite period, the seventeenth century, for Bridges couldn't abide the poetry of John Donne and Robert Herrick, and he was not very enthusiastic about another favorite of Smith's, Sir Henry Wotton, whose *Life and Letters* Smith had published in 1907. And Smith in his turn was perfectly frank in mentioning *his* differences of opinion, and could on occasion be severe with Bridges's own poetry. When Bridges sent him a section of *The Testament of Beauty* in trial text, Smith reported his response in a letter to Robert Gathorne-Hardy: "I . . . have just stuck a whole pincushion full [of pins] into Robert Bridges, who however asked for it, as it were, when he sent me some proofs and asked for my comments. This was more than human flesh—even redeemed human flesh like mine—could resist. But he is well equipped with weapons of retaliation, and I dare say I shall get the worst of it in the end."[54] Smith's letters to his friends and relatives contain a number of vivid glimpses of Bridges. To his sister Alys he wrote in 1913 after a visit to Chilswell: "The Bridges were very nice, full of leisure and talk about books, and the leisurely atmosphere of the house is charming. . . . Bridges is full of his fads—classical metres, and the way the psalms are sung in churches—he sat a long time this morning with his feet way up over his head, singing me the Psalms of David, while I tried to do a little work."[55] And to his sister Mary in November 1914: "The Professors at Oxford, Walter Raleigh and Gilbert Murray and others, drill every day and Robert Bridges (who is 70) drills with them. They go through regular training and march through the country and crawl about through the hedges and ditches on their old stomachs in a heroic fashion. They think that the Government will give them rifles and khaki, and that the invading Germans, if they come, will recognize them as regular combatants."[56] And finally to R. C. Trevelyan in 1927: "I had a pleasant visit to Bridges, who is full of life and energy and indignation. It is pleasant to see energy in the old—it makes the prospect of old age more reassuring."[57]

VIII

Bridges met Henry Bradley (1845–1923), the philologist and senior editor of the *Oxford English Dictionary* (succeeding James Murray in 1915), at Oxford in 1899, and soon thereafter formed an intimate friendship with him that lasted until the end of Bradley's life. Writing to Mrs. Bradley after her husband's death Bridges said, "I loved him very deeply and reckon him among the few men with whom I have had full friendship without any intellectual or moral reserve." Bradley's first visit to Yattendon to stay with the Bridges family took place in September 1901. The second letter by Bridges in the long series of letters to him and to his widow that ran from 1901 to 1928 began with an answer to Bradley's apology, "I feel guilty of having bestowed my tediousness on you":

I enjoyed my talks with you immensely. I wonder how many of those who talk etymology with you have read Spinoza. It is delightful too to meet with anyone who reads both Spanish and Greek. Your general "erudition" amazes my small faculties: and I look forward to more chats. So much for your "tediousness."

Bradley, a professional philologist, was usually diffident about discussing broad subjects beyond his field of expertise, such as literature, philosophy, and religion. Bridges, however, soon discovered that Bradley had, as well as wideranging knowledge, literary tastes similar to his own. "In talking of literature," wrote Bridges in his Memoir of Bradley, "I do not know that we ever disagreed."[58] Their correspondence covered a great variety of topics, which included Bridges's own poetry. Bridges said that Bradley, for professional and economic reasons from 1896 on when he was installed in the North House of the Clarendon Press in Oxford, "sold himself to slave henceforth for the *Dictionary.*" Actually, Bradley devoted forty years of his life to this project, for he first began work on it at the invitation of Sir James Murray when Bradley visited London in 1883 and reviewed the first installment of the *Dictionary.* Probably Bradley did not regard his final years at Oxford as slavery, one reason for not so regarding it being his friendship and correspondence with Bridges.

Because Bridges respected Bradley's literary judgment, he sent him examples of his own work in progress and asked his opinion concerning poems he was considering for his anthology *The Spirit of Man* (1916). Several informative letters of 1902 and 1903 deal with Bridges's experiments in Stone's classical prosody and should be read with the letters to J. W. Mackail on the same subject. In 1907 he expressed the wish to send Bradley his ode on the Oxford pageant. In 1915 he asked for Bradley's comment on four selections from *Charitessi,* the first book of poems, published anonymously, by Bridges's daughter Elizabeth, with a view to including them in *The Spirit of Man.* He decided to include all four, after Bradley had commented favorably on three of them. In the early twenties he showed Bradley his "Poor Poll" and other experiments in Neo-Miltonic syllabics.

There are also interesting and informative references to two of Bridges's poetic dramas—the mask *Demeter* and the play *Achilles in Scyros. Demeter,* first produced at Somerville College, Oxford on June 11, 1904, with music by Sir William Hadow, was written on the invitation of Margery Fry (first cousin to Mrs. Bridges), who was then librarian at Somerville and later principal of the college. The occasion was the opening of the school's new library. She wrote to Bridges January 21, 1904, saying "we are anxious to celebrate the opening day as perfectly as possible" and adding "Under the library is an open loggia supported by several pillars, which I think would make a very pretty stage for a formal masque." Bridges accepted the invitation with some misgiving, but he completed the masque in a few weeks, faithfully attended rehearsals, and wrote out an elaborate set of instructions for the guidance of the actresses. The performance, which was attended by an audience of seven hundred, which included the prominent statesman John Morley and the vice-chancellor of Oxford, had a good press, and on June 13 Margery Fry wrote to Bridges about the "triumphant success" of the masque. "Even the grey weather was not a drawback, as too bright a sun would make the actors grimace."[59] Fifty years later the masque was revived and produced at Somerville June 26, 1954. Bridges's daughter Elizabeth was present at both performances. In a letter to Dame Janet Vaughan, January 19, 1954,[60] Margery Fry, recalling the first production, said that the stage was "fringed round with grasses and wild-flowers" and she described the costumes she had created: "I invented a way of twisting 'art' muslin into ropes." When wet it "produced quite a good Elgin marble crinkle. The cast were draped on the instructions of Lady Evans' book on Greek dress."

In May 1904 Bridges sent Bradley the manuscript of *Demeter,* asking for his opinion but requesting that he not show it to others because a good deal of the interest in the performance depended on "a suspense in the last act." This last act had caused trouble. In its original version, according to Margery Fry,[61] the masque ended in complete gloom. "All that seems good," she wrote "is but a scum upon the surface of evil." She objected that this was not proper for young ladies on a festive occasion and insisted that the ending be rewritten. "He retorted that I was like those who would put a happy ending on to Romeo and Juliet." But Miss Fry persevered and Bridges finally agreed to let their mutual friend Harry Ellis Wooldridge arbitrate the dispute. Wooldridge decided in favor of Margery Fry and Bridges rewrote the ending. Bridges admitted to Bradley that perhaps "a bit of my feeling may have strayed into the play." It was a gloomy period in Bridges's life. His wife was ill and neither she nor her husband was able to attend the performance. She and her younger daughter had contracted tuberculosis and Bridges was distraught with anxiety. It was this illness that broke up the home at Yattendon. The next year Bridges took his family for a nine-month vacation in Switzerland and then removed to Boar's Hill, where he built Chilswell House.

Bradley attended the performance of *Demeter* and wrote the next day to its author, "The masque bore the test of representation splendidly. I heard only one opinion—that the performance was a thorough success." He had equally high praise for the quality of the poetry, although he expressed reservations about the Cave of Cacophysis because of its ambiguous presentation of the problem of evil. We know, incidentally, from Bridges's letters to Dr. Gee and to Lionel Muirhead that *Demeter* was acted three times at Liverpool in 1908, which means that it was more frequently produced than any other play or masque by Bridges.

Achilles in Scyros was first performed at the Ladies College in Cheltenham, with incidental and choral music by Cyril Rootham, Fellow and Organist of St. John's College, Cambridge, a distinguished composer who was at the center of musical activity in Cambridge at the beginning of the century. Bridges and his wife attended the performance and were disappointed. In his letter to Bradley of June 30, 1912, he wrote: "The fact is that the girls could not get near masculine personation of any kind, and their little shrill argumentative voices would have dispelled any ocular illusion if it existed."

Chaucer's prosody, simplified spelling, phonetic spelling, and phonetic script (the latter two dear to Bridges's heart!), Latin pronunciation and its correct teaching in the schools, and a talk with Henry James in 1912 when both Bridges and James received honorary degrees at Oxford on the same day are a few of the subjects discussed by these learned correspondents. They usually agreed with each other, although sometimes with polite reservations. Their most serious disagreement was on the matter of Bradley's removing his signature from the letter of reconciliation sent in 1920 by the Oxford professors to the professors of Germany. (The letter was actually composed by Bridges.) In his letter of August 23, 1920, Bridges expressed his disagreement with Bradley's action more forcefully than usual. "As for your withdrawal of your name from the German letter. I am afraid that the Devonshire climate has had a relaxing effect on you. The fear that one's action may be misinterpreted does not seem to me any reason against doing one's duty."[62]

Henry Bradley was in at the very beginning of the Society for Pure English, which by 1914, when its activity was interrupted by the war, had made a fair start. It was resumed in 1919, and the letters from then until Bradley's death frequently refer to S.P.E. activities. In his *Memoir* Bridges tells us that "he had joined unreservedly in the scheme when it was first proposed in 1912, and from its practical inception in 1919 he was its mainstay. Though he never wrote any entire article for it, he passed and censured all its publications."[63] Bridges gives a charming description of the so-called committee meetings of this society, which began with "lunch in the little drawing-room overlooking the garden at C.C.C. [Corpus Christi College]. Curried chicken, apple-tart, and a bottle of claret were the regulation fare at those social repasts. No other Committee meetings were known to the S.P.E., and if all Committees were like ours in united purpose and mutual confidence, without chairman, secretary or book of minutes, there would be something to be said in favour of Committees. There we would sit chatting by the open windows till 3 o'clock and wishing the hours were longer."[64]

The concluding series of letters in the correspondence are to Mrs. Bradley, and are concerned with Bradley's death and the requiem service for him in Magdalen chapel and with the beautifully written and moving *Memoir* Bridges wrote in honor of his learned and beloved friend.

IX

"It is always pleasant to hear from you," wrote Bridges to his good friend Dr. Gee on October 28, 1893, "and I sit down very willingly to give you a little return chat." Such was the tone of his letters to the distinguished and highly literate physician, Dr. Samuel Gee (1839–1911), whom Bridges came to know early in his medical career. Bridges mentions him in his "Carmen Elegiacum" (1876). When Dr. Gee married Sarah Cooper in December 1875, Bridges was his best man. Gee was considered to be one of the first physicians of his time. He was one of the chief authorities on children's diseases. He was assistant physician at St. Bartholomew's Hospital in 1868 and physician and later consulting physician there from 1878 until his death. In 1911 he was appointed physician to the Prince of Wales. Among his publications were articles on Abraham Cowley and Andrew Marvell.

To him Bridges wrote many letters, of which sixty have survived dating from

1883 to 1909. Bridges wrote to Gee in an informal style on any subject that happened to come to mind—but most of the subjects fall into four categories: Bridges's own poetry; observations of a general nature on politics, religion, philosophy, and literature; domestic affairs; and medical problems pertaining to himself and his family.

"I like praise from friends," Bridges said in an early letter of March 2, 1885, and Dr. Gee was quick to give discerning acclaim to the poetry sent to him, including the two Nero plays, the *Humours of the Court, Eros and Psyche*, the *Yattendon Hymnal*, the book on Milton's prosody, and the Keats essay, with reference to which Bridges wrote a highly interesting "medical profile" of John Keats in his letter of July 16, 1894. Bridges was particularly eager to get the favorable opinion of Gee and his wife on his plays, for he was having trouble selling them to readers and critics alike. To Gee Bridges expressed his literary hopes and disappointments more frankly than to any other correspondent, with the possible exception of Lionel Muirhead.

Two other prominent physicians were among Bridges's friends and corre-spondents—Sir Thomas Barlow (1845–1945) and Sir Rickman John Godlee (1849–1925). Barlow, the first baronet of Wimpole Street and the most famous doctor of his day, held court appointments under Queen Victoria, Edward VII, and King George V. Bridges knew him well and wrote a poem in scazons to him in 1902 beginning "It's all up, I may tell you, good Thomas Barlow." Only one letter from Bridges to him is available, that of January 20, 1901, written on the occasion of Bishop Creighton's death and with interesting comments on Creigh-ton. Godlee, nephew and biographer of Lord Lister, was a prominent surgeon who in 1884 performed the first operation for the removal of a brain tumor. He too had court appointments under Queen Victoria, Edward VII, and King George V. The two letters to Godlee deal with Godlee's illustrated lecture and with the medical treatment of Bridges's son, Edward.

X

It was natural that Bridges and Samuel Butler (1835–1902) should become acquainted early in their lives, for one of Bridges's elder brothers, George L. Bridges of the Royal Navy, was married to Butler's sister Harriet; furthermore, one would expect this acquaintance to develop into a friendship. Bridges ad-mired Butler's *Erewhon* and considered the chapter on the musical banks the best satire he had ever read; he sided with Butler in his attacks on Darwin; he treated with respect Butler's argument that a woman wrote the *Odyssey* wrongly attrib-uted to Homer; he admired Butler's classical learning and pitied his hard-working, solitary life. Butler on his side admired Bridges's classical scholarship and respected, although he did not really like, Bridges's poetry—but this, as he explained to Bridges, was because he was indifferent to almost all poetry in English. However, they did not in fact become long-standing friends. Bridges, in a letter to his sister Mrs. Caroline Glover dated August 22, 1903, explained why. He mentioned his first meeting, just before Butler went to New Zealand in

September 1859, when Bridges was fourteen years old and Butler twenty-three. Bridges wrote to his sister:

> He was a very strange fellow. I met him first at Rochdale just before he went to New Zealand, and we made friends. He had then a good deal of charm about him, being always clever, earnest and kindhearted—When, on his return to England he came to London [autumn 1864] I met him there, and used often to go in and sit half an hour with him in his chambers. He was a very interesting talker, and I learned a good deal from him. I had a sort of pity for his solitary hardworking life. But one day when I was with him he revealed to me a side of his nature with which I had no sympathy, but rather a strong disgust for it, and from that day I avoided him. We met at times, now and then in the British Museum chiefly, and never had any open break. . . . But S. B. was both vain and ugly in mind. There was a meanness in his general mental attitude towards humanity.

Nevertheless, in spite of Bridges's reservations about Butler as a person, they continued to exchange letters on subjects of mutual interest. Butler was one of the arch heretics of the learned world, and this side of his nature undoubtedly fascinated Bridges. Butler's three greatest heresies were: (1) Darwin was an imposter and a fraud, and his wrong-headed theory of natural selection removed Mind from the universe. Butler promulgated his own views on evolution in a series of books—*Life and Habit* (1877); *Evolution Old and New* (1879); *Unconscious Memory* (1880); *Luck or Cunning* (1886); and *God the Known and Unknown* (1909, first printed as a series of articles in 1879). Of these, Bridges had the first three in his library, according to his letter to Butler of February 5, 1900. (2) The *Odyssey* was not composed by Homer but by an unknown woman poet. He presented his arguments in *The Authoress of the Odyssey* (1897). (3) Shakespeare wrote his sonnets not when he was middle-aged but between the dates 1585 and 1588, when he was a young man aged twenty-one to twenty-four years. He gives the evidence for his theory in *Shakespeare's Sonnets Reconsidered* (1899), which he sent to Bridges shortly after publication.

Bridges had considerable sympathy for all three of these heresies. In a series of letters exchanged between the two men from November 26, 1898, to October 27, 1900, the problem of Shakespeare's sonnets plays an important and interesting part.[65] Butler in his book tells us that he first committed all the sonnets to memory and in so doing he came to the conclusion that they had been published in incorrect order. He then proceeded to rearrange them so that they told a coherent story of the relationship between the poet, the dark lady, the rival poet, and Master W. H. He identified W. H. as William Hughes, who eventually became a cook in the navy. As for the dating of the sonnets, Butler was convinced that they were the work of a young poet in his early twenties because of weaknesses in style and structure. He believed their main theme to be the disastrous love of the poet for William Hughes. Furthermore, Butler found what he considered to be evidence for early dating by identifying the "mortal moon hath her eclipse endured" of Sonnet 107 with the defeat of the Spanish Armada in 1588, and he advanced other arguments based on topical allusions. Bridges, in thanking Butler for the gift of his book, agreed with the early dating of the sonnets but objected violently to Butler's hypothesis of Shakespeare's homosexual love for Hughes. Bridges considered the best of the sonnets to be the highest expression of spiritual and idealized love, a view that moved Butler to scorn. "I seem to hear Venus laughing from the skies," he wrote Bridges in response to Bridges's letter of December 31, 1899, a letter that should be read in conjunction with Bridges's letter to Logan Pearsall Smith dated January 28, 1907(?), evaluating Shakespeare's sonnets, and his letters to A. H. Bullen concerning his essay *The Influence of the Audience,* in which he expressed the unorthodox view that Shakespeare's plays suffered from the necessity of their being written to please a corrupt and depraved audience. In this essay Bridges was as much a heretic as Butler. It shocked the community of Shakespeare scholars, few of whom agreed with Bridges.

Another major topic of interest in the Bridges-Butler correspondence is the discussion between the two men of a number of Bridges's plays that Butler had asked be sent to him, and of *Eros and Psyche,* and of the essay on Keats. Butler admired the poetic craftsmanship displayed in *Eros and Psyche,* but he could not take Bridges's verse seriously any more than he could the work of other English poets. As he explained to Bridges, he rarely read poetry. Nor did he like the plays, although he tried to be discreet and tactful in thanking Bridges for sending them. But Bridges's side of the correspondence gives us some valuable statements as to what Bridges thought of his own plays and of what he thought of his essay on Keats. He considered this essay to be his most important piece of criticism and advised Butler to read it as an introduction to all his work, for it was his "treatise on poetic forms."

XI

The essay on Keats (completed in 1894), which Bridges was commissioned to write by the publisher A. H. Bullen as an introduction to the poems of Keats in the Muses' Library series, is a major topic in the correspondence with Bullen and with Margaret Woods the poet, wife of the Reverend Henry Woods, president of Trinity College, Oxford. Bridges's younger daughter was named after Mrs. Woods. President Woods was a fellow student with Bridges at Corpus Christi College, where he matriculated in 1861, two years before Bridges.

We learn from the letters to Bullen of April 16 and April 18, 1894, that Bridges was hesitant about accepting the invitation to write on Keats, and he asked for a fortnight in which to reread all the poetry and come to a decision. His love and admiration for Keats were profound, but he foresaw difficulties in solving certain scholarly problems such as the influence of William Browne of Tavistock on Keats. Bridges overcame his doubts, however, and by July 21 he was well along with his planned essay of ten thousand words, a "criticism of all Keats' work considered by groups." "The more I study him," Bridges went on to say, "the higher I think of his best work and the more I find to praise, but a good part of the Essay will be definition of his faults." By September 1 Bridges apparently had completed the first draft, for he wrote, "At present I have sent it away in batches for friends to read." And on October 9, 1894, he said to Bullen, "I send you my essay by same post as this letter. I am glad to get it out of the house."

One of the friends to whom he sent all or part of the essay was, as we have seen, Canon Dixon. Another was Margaret Woods. In a series of letters running from July 7 to October 9, 1894, Bridges discussed several problems of interpretation and evaluation with Mrs. Woods in considerable detail. He queried her about matters such as the unsoundness of Keat's notion that the bird is immortal but man is not in the "Ode to a Nightingale" whereas in fact man is just as immortal as the bird in the sense Keats intends. He was also concerned about the awkardness of addressing the personified Autumn in "Ode to Autumn" with the words "Think not of them," (that is "the songs of Spring"), and he asked her if she shared his doubts concerning the poetic value of "Ode on Indolence" and of the first four stanzas of the "Bacchic Ode to Sorrow" in the fourth book of *Endymion*. He also expressed his displeasure with Keats's inappropriate figures of speech, such as "green robed senators" to describe trees, although he told Mrs. Woods he would not include this particular objection in his essay.

But the principal problem for which he requested her help was one of interpretation of the allegory in *Endymion* and in both the original and revised versions of *Hyperion*. He became impatient with Keats in this aspect of his work. "As for allegory I hate it, it always bothers me and I think that if I had known there was so much of it in Keats I would not have embarked on the business." He was determined not to overinterpret but to simplify and clarify the allegorical meanings and to present only those about which he was certain. He told Mrs. Woods that he had the main lines of *Endymion* well in hand but was still not clear in his mind about the two versions of *Hyperion*, the poem that had given him the most trouble in writing a satisfactory essay.

Throughout the correspondence Bridges paid tribute to the aid given him by Canon Dixon and Harry Ellis Wooldridge. The help from Wooldridge came from conversations with him as well as by correspondence. Unfortunately, there is only one letter about Keats available in the Bridges/Wooldridge correspondence. It is dated September 21, 1894, and is included in this edition.

Bridges was also commissioned by Bullen to write an essay on Shakespeare as an introduction to volume ten of the Stratford Town Shakespeare, edited and published by Bullen 1904–7. As with the Keats essay, Bridges at first showed considerable diffidence in accepting the assignment, and after accepting it he offered twice to let Bullen withdraw it, first in his letter of October 15, 1905, and again in his letter marked *Private*, written from St. Moritz January 15, 1906, in which he told Bullen that there were certain things he had long wanted to say about Shakespeare's plays, but he had come to the conclusion that the results would be a highly controversial work—that it would shock the Shakespeare Establishment, which in fact it did:

> My lucubrations have not at all changed my opinion of Shakespeare nor do I think that I should be able to solve the problem which his extraordinary mixture of "brutality" with extreme, even celestial, gentleness offers, but the examination supposing it to be successful would define the brutality (the word is not mine) and that would be unpleasant to most readers.

Therefore, Bridges continued, "I think, after reading this you will not wish for my essay." Bridges had for a long time found offensive material in Shakespeare's plays. In the projected essay he would try to define the nature of this material and inquire into the reasons for its presence in one of the world's greatest writers. However, Bullen urged him to proceed, so Bridges persevered and finally sent him the completed essay on May 12, 1906.[66]

XII

Bridges's lifelong interest in music was frequently reflected in his letters. To Lionel Muirhead, Sir Henry Newbolt, and others he mentioned the numerous musical evenings at Yattendon and Chilswell, where he and a few of his friends sang madrigals and hymns and played chamber music. There are frequent references to his heroic attempts (sometimes successful!) to improve the singing of the Yattendon Church choir. Music and musicians are often the subjects of his poetry, including passages in *The Testament of Beauty* and the fine sonnet "To Joseph Joachim." For his eightieth birthday his friends presented him with a clavichord designed by Arnold Dolmetsch.

Shortly after World War I the Bishop of Winchester suggested that the words to the English national anthem should be changed. Lord Stamfordham, private secretary to the King, wrote to Bridges on March 24, 1919, stating that it was the general opinion that the present national anthem was lacking in poetic merit, and he added that the soldiers were tired of the repetitive references to the King in all three stanzas. Stamfordham wanted the poet laureate to try his hand at a revision of the words, but he warned him that the tune and meter must remain unaltered. In the correspondence that followed (in the Bridges Papers), Bridges made a heroic attempt to overcome his own dislike of both the tune and the meter. He eventually sent Stamfordham two new stanzas to replace the second and third stanzas of the original version. The secretary showed them to the King and to the Bishop of Winchester. The stanzas were rejected as being "not simple enough."

It was Bridges's dislike of the tune of the anthem that, at an earlier date, had led him to suggest to his friend Sir Hubert Parry that he compose a song to be set to words from Blake's "Milton" to replace the national anthem, the tune of which was of German origin. Parry composed a unison song for the poem, which begins "And did those feet in ancient times. . . ." Under the title "Jerusalem" it became a great national success during and after the First World War, but it did not replace the national anthem. It was sung at the Leeds Festival of 1922 with the accompaniment orchestrated for the occasion by Elgar. "Jerusalem" is still sung today at Anglican church services.

Bridges himself composed a number of poems to be sung, including four odes, set to music by Sir Hubert Parry: *Invocation to Music (An Ode in Honour of Henry Purcell)*, 1895; *A Song of Darkness and Light*, 1898; *Eton Memorial Ode*, 1908; and *Chivalry of the Sea*, 1916. Bridges took the task of writing words for music very seriously indeed. There are thirty letters to Parry (of which this edition publishes seven), dated 1894–95, that deal with just one of these compositions, the *Invocation to Music,* and there are other letters to Parry concerning *A Song of Darkness and Light.* In his letter of October 10, 1894, on the *Invocation,* which was to be performed at the festival of Leeds, he was first of all concerned with the problem of "requisite inspiration to order, " yet he was willing to undertake the assignment, for he said, "I see a splendid opportunity for something new, and popular. My idea is to show music in its various relations to the passions and desires of man: as something supernatural, mysterious and consolatory: which it always is to me." By April 1, 1895, he was deeply involved in writing and revising his poem to suit Parry's needs. Bridges took the attitude that composing a poem for a musical setting was very different from composing one without musical accompaniment in mind. He was willing to be very flexible in his dealing with Parry. "If it would make it any easier for you to alter any line yourself pray do so. Don't let me hamper your music when it has a will of its own." Bridges felt that it was necessary in a collaborative effort between poet and musician to have frequent consultation, and in his letter of June 12, 1895, he expressed his disappointment at not being able to meet with Parry more often than he had. He added, "As for any alteration made in my poem, you need not scruple." In his letter of August 28, he sharply disagreed with Parry, who had suggested that the "original" ode be printed in the program as it existed before being adapted to the music. Bridges wrote, "This ode has really never existed—and I don't know that it ever will except in the form in which you have set it."

As he explained on October 4, Bridges was unable to attend the performance in Leeds (Wednesday, October 2, 1895), but "I had to content myself with buying all the penny papers as I came up in the train yesterday, and reading what the critics said. I gathered two things, 1st that the Ode had really been a success, and 2ndly that the critics are a poor lot." Bridges himself wrote to Dixon (October 5, 1895) that he thought the "Dirge" the most successful part of the composition— "as good a thing as I have written."

A wide-ranging series of letters (1888–1925), of which this edition presents a few representative selections, from Bridges to the distinguished music antiquarian G. E. P. Arkwright, tells us something of Bridges's musical tastes over a period of thirty-seven years. Some of the correspondence is taken up with the subject of the *Musical Antiquary,* the magazine that Arkwright edited from 1909 to 1913, which Bridges in his letters insisted on calling the "Magger." He contributed three articles to it: "A Letter to a Musician on English Prosody," "English Chanting," and "Anglican Chanting." In an early letter in the series (November 17, 1889) Bridges commented on his own musical tastes. Besides Purcell he liked earlier composers: Palestrina, Vittoria, and "all of the madrigalians—Dutch, English or Italian." About Campion's music he was tentative; he had not found much he really liked. "If you would send me your Campion music I should be extremely interested to see it." But in later letters he expressed his satisfaction with Campion's mask as well as his delight at receiving a six-part Kirby madrigal that he planned to have sung at Yattendon. He also promised Arkwright the performance of a double chant by William Byrd (which he sometimes spells Bird) when Arkwright visited him at Yattendon. Bridges was also devoted to church music of various periods and on January 29, 1918, he wrote triumphantly to Arkwright that "there was a solemn and advertised performance of 4 Psalms on my method of pointing in New College. . . . The experiment was an unqualified success, and everyone was convinced and delighted."

There are references in a number of Bridges's letters to the *Yattendon Hymnal*, which Bridges published in collaboration with H. E. Wooldridge in four parts from 1895 to 1899. It presents music and words of one hundred hymns. Of these Bridges translated, adapted, or wrote forty-seven.

Bridges's musical interests included Bach, Beethoven, and Brahms, as well as lesser composers. With twentieth-century music he was not completely at home; yet it was characteristic of him to attempt to keep up with recent developments in the art. He welcomed the setting of Gustav Holst (1874–1934) for a poem by his friend Digby Dolben, and in the summer of 1927 there was an informal concert at Chilswell by Holst's pupils, who sang their master's settings of seven of Bridges's lyrics. Bridges expressed his appreciation to Holst in his letter of July 4, 1927. Imogen Holst, the daughter of the composer, described the recital. "It was one of the happiest days he [Holst] ever spent. There was a delightful informality about the way the rehearsal joined on to the performance and the performance happened all over again as soon as it had ended. The garden was dazzling with flowers and sunshine, and the Paulinas in the choir were speechless with excitement at being in the same room with so many distinguished poets. Bridges himself enjoyed it, and after the third hearing he found that he liked the songs."[67]

Holst had followed the poetic career of Bridges from the mid 1890s. In 1898 he set as songs for voice and piano "Awake, my heart," "My spirit sang all day," and (perhaps in the same year) "The birds that sing on autumn eves." A few years later he set "Thou didst delight my eyes," "I will not let thee go," and in 1925/26 the seven songs performed at Boar's Hill, and shortly thereafter two anthems by Bridges. In 1930, the year of Bridges's death, he composed *A Choral Fantasia* for the "Dirge," originally a part (the *best* part in Bridges's opinion) of the *Ode to Music*, which Bridges wrote for Sir Hubert Parry. *A Choral Fantasia* was published in 1931 and dedicated "In Homage, Robert Bridges." The first performance was in Gloucester Cathedral near the monument to Parry, which bears a poetic inscription by Bridges.[68]

Holst was also impressed by *The Testament of Beauty*. Although he set no part of it to music, he was inspired by it. His daughter wrote that it "was possibly his favourite poem. He 'lost his head' over it when it first appeared, and he used to take it about with him on his walking tours finding that it made an ideal companion."[69]

Mention should also be made of Bridges's *Eden: An Oratorio*, which was set to music by C. V. Stanford and published in 1891. Bridges discussed it in his letters to Muirhead, in which he said the libretto was finished June 25, 1890. It was performed at the Birmingham festival of 1891 and is generally considered one of Stanford's better works, but Bridges in his letter to Canon Dixon of September 12, 1891, was discouraged with the final results. "I had a letter from Gosse . . . damning it to my face! . . . Well it's not worth much."

XIII

In 1902, when Bridges was hard at work on his poems in Stone's quantitative prosody—his poems in longs and shorts, as he liked to call them—J. W. Mackail was one of the friends he naturally turned to for criticism and encouragement. Mackail (1859–1945), who graduated from Balliol College with a first in litterae humaniores, was according to the DNB the most brilliant undergraduate scholar of his day. He was the author of a number of books, including *Latin Literature, Lectures in Greek Poetry,* and *The Springs of Helicon.* He translated Virgil and Homer. He was professor of Poetry at Oxford 1906–11.

All of Bridges's letters to him of 1902 and 1903 are concerned with Bridges's experiments in Stone's prosody and relevant problems in English prosody. The next group of letters, 1909/10, continue the discussion of prosody and are also concerned with simplified and phonetic spelling. In 1913, when Bridges was occupied with his new experiment, his poems in Neo-Miltonic syllabics, he wrote again to Mackail with particular reference to "Noel." "God bless you for liking my poem" he wrote in his letter of December 27, 1913. In 1914/15 there was an exchange of letters on *The Spirit of Man,* and from 1919 on, the correspondence was usually taken up with S.P.E. matters. The Mackail series is of great value as a source of information for the study of the technical aspects of Bridges's poetry.

J. A. Stewart (1846–1933), classical lecturer at Christ Church and Professor of Moral Philosophy at Oxford, author of two volumes of notes on the Nicomachean Ethics of Aristotle and of *The Myths of Plato* and other books, was another Oxford don whose critical judgment of literature Bridges trusted. In 1923 Bridges sent him his poem "The Great Elm," to which Stewart responded on August 17 with enthusiasm:

> The lesson which "metaphysicians" have to learn from you, in the "Great Elm" and other pieces like it, is that the "ultimate problem of the universe" can be sighted and approached only by way of the Creative Imagination—that, in fact, it is not a problem for the Scientific Understanding at all.[70]

Two and a half years later Bridges sent him a copy of his *New Verse* (1925) and Stewart replied February 21, 1926, with renewed enthusiasm for "The Great Elm," expressing also his admiration for other poems in the volume:

> *The Great Elm* I shall re-read every time I take down the book. I think that you never wrote any thing greater: and Kate's Mother—I had not seen it since you let me read it in manuscript: but reading it now, I find that the walk is quite familiar—every stage comes exactly as I saw it two years ago. There is a stroke of poetic power in the last 10 lines which I had not felt however till now, and when we meet next I hope you will let me have a talk with you about it.
> *Come Si Quando* was one I saw two years ago—under another, or no, title— and I remembered most of the things in it when I read it yesterday.[71]

Earlier, Bridges sent to Stewart his striking sonnet on Democritus, explaining in his letter of late June 1919 that, becoming convinced of the "independent existence of ideas," he ventured to address Democritus, the founder of materialism, and express his reservations about the theory of atoms. To Stewart he wrote, "As you lean to the Platonic notion of ideas, you should have more sympathy with me than most people will have." These and other poems Bridges sent him led Stewart to write on December 15, 1923, "You are, indeed, composing the ancient difference between Philosophy and Poetry."[72]

The correspondence with Sir Herbert Grierson (1866–1960), which began with Grierson's offer to send Bridges a complimentary copy of his two-volume edition of John Donne (published 1912) is of interest chiefly for Bridges's comments on the metaphysical poet, which until the time of this edition had been unsympathetic. Bridges explained in his letter of August 26, 1914, the reasons for his reservations—"ugliness" of some of the poetry, the school of versification developed by Donne (Bridges probably had in mind the irregular meters and the bizarre diction and complicated conceits), Donne's psychology of sensual love, and his "'learning' which seems to me pestilential." But he promised to study Grierson's edition carefully and Bridges's annotated copy, still extant, indicated that he did so. It is evident, however, that his attitude changed little if at all. On January 6, 1922, he wrote to Grierson, "I also dislike the Phallic tribe, wherefore I have little sympathy with Donne as a human."

George Saintsbury (1845–1933) and Sir Edmund Gosse (1849–1928) were two other distinguished scholar-critics and men of letters with whom Bridges kept up a correspondence for many years. About Gosse, Bridges had reservations, and his remarks concerning him in several letters suggest that Bridges considered him to be a somewhat untrustworthy opportunist. Bridges seems to have been on more cordial terms with Saintsbury, although he disagreed with him on matters of prosody. In his undated letter to Henry Newbolt he gave directions on how to destroy Saintsbury's theory of equivalence, that syllables long in quantity in English verse and prose may be considered equivalent to stressed syllables, and he concluded, "I really think that the average ass would understand this form of demonstration." On the other hand, Saintsbury gave Bridges favorable notices of several of his books, praise that Bridges appreciated. The first letter to him in this edition, October 13, 1890, thanks him for his favorable response to the *Shorter Poems*, and in several subsequent letters Bridges expressed his gratitude for Saintsbury's reviews of his books. On July 6 and 13, 1891, Bridges asked him to review *Eden*, and on June 14, 1916, he thanked him for praising his sonnet on Kitchener. In S.P.E. Tract No. VI Saintsbury expressed himself too strongly (in Bridges's opinion) on the subject of Henry James, and Bridges felt it necessary to chide him for it in an editorial, but he hastened to make amends in his letter of November 13, 1921. In 1928 the two friends found themselves allied against Max Beerbohm in the affair of Beerbohm's criticism of Andrew Lang in an article in *Life and Letters*. "It is a pity that dueling has gone out," remarked Bridges. During the last four years of the correspondence Bridges made mysterious comments on a "somewhat superhuman" project he was working on, which piqued Saintsbury's curiosity. Bridges also referred to it as a "pretentious poem of unlimited length" and as a "heroic gymnastic" and an "inexhaustible occupation." The references were of course to *The Testament of Beauty*. In his last letter to Saintsbury (December 7, 1929) Bridges told him he was sending him a copy of the fourth impression of his unexpectedly popular poem. Toward the end of their careers the two friends discovered that they had the same birthday (October 23) and thereafter they sent each other annual birthday greetings.

In his letters to Gosse, Bridges was usually polite in spite of his real feeling about the man, which he expressed to Saintsbury on June 17, 1928, a month after Gosse's death:

> The world hasn't done with Gosse. His private diary or journal or whatever he called it will make a great splash in "Littrisher."—The only question is how far E G will have sacrificied himself by a total absence of scruple.

Bridges engaged in rather acrimonious debate with Gosse on at least two (and probably more) occasions, for his letters of March 2, 1879 and December 7, 1911 were written in a somewhat apologetic tone because of what Gosse might have construed as rudeness on Bridges's part. The most interesting conflict occurred at a meeting of a literary society near the end of the year 1911, in which Gosse supported the project of a centennial celebration of Robert Browning's birth. Bridges backed George Bernard Shaw's proposal that the society should associate itself with rising movements rather than dead poets and, as for Browning, Bridges wrote in his letter of December 7, "A Browning centenary would be in my opinion an advertisement with nothing behind it."

In another noteworthy letter (November 22, 1879) Bridges defended the book of poems *Wet Days*, by A Farmer (1879), which he considered Gosse to have criticized too harshly. The "Farmer" was Bridges's brother John Affleck Bridges, and Robert Bridges had had a hand in getting the book published. The author in a prefatory note to the volume states "these poems are plain things, written in such language as men are accustomed to use in my neighbourhood." The poems are second-rate, but with occasional authentic descriptions of the rural scene. Bridges in his letter made the best defense possible: "One of the most important, I think the most important of the qualities of writing must be directness, unbroken connection between thought and expression. This I think is very rare indeed, and to me it constitutes a great merit and the charm of 'Wet Days.'" Bridges then went on to attack the "gibberish" and "bosh" dispensed by the circulating libraries that no reviewer dared to criticize, his point being that, relatively speaking the poems of his brother that Gosse had handled so severely were superior to the general level of British taste.

XIV

Bridges carried on a sporadic correspondence with a number of writers of varying reputations, including Mrs. Humphry Ward (1851–1920), A. C. Benson (1862–1925), G. K. Chesterton (1874–1936), George Bernard Shaw (1856–1950), and Francis Brett Young (1884–1954). Mrs. Ward wrote many novels popular in her day, the best known being *Robert Elsmere* (1888). She was a niece of Matthew Arnold and this fact led to an interesting exchange of letters between her and Bridges. He explains to her in his letter of April 16, 1907, that after a conversation at tea with Warre-Cornish of Eton concerning the famous tree at the top of a hill near Hinksey that Arnold describes and refers to several times in "Thyrsis," Warre-Cornish had published a letter in the *Morning Post* saying that he had it on the authority of Robert Bridges that the specific tree Arnold had in mind could not be identified. However, Bridges had not stated such a possibility as a certainty, and before commenting in print on the letter, Bridges wanted to ascertain the truth if possible. Mrs. Ward replied on April 25: "We have never been able to identify the Tree, and Humphry says that he once walked over the Hinksey fields with Uncle Matt [Matthew Arnold] and he himself was uncertain."[73] Bridges replied on April 26, "I incline to think that it is better that the mystification should be complete. The fault of the poem is the ethical importance of the tree: and if the tree is imaginary, the fault is in a manner dissipated; for a purely poetic intangible object may better bear the burden."

Mrs. Ward in the same letter had queried "I wonder if you saw the use I ventured to make of your long poem, in *Fenwick's Career*." The poem is "Elegy on a Lady Whom Grief for the Death of Her Betrothed Killed"; the lines quoted are from the fifth stanza:

> And then the maidens, in a double row,
>   Each singing soft and low,
>   And each on high a torch upstaying:
> Unto her lover lead her forth with light,
> With music, and with singing, and with praying.[74]

Mrs. Ward, in her prefatory note to the novel, said that "any lover of modern poetry will recognize" the lines. In the novel, the entire poem is read by a lady friend to the struggling young painter, Fenwick, who thereupon paints a picture of the torchlit scene, which is viewed as "a sort of Mantegna Triumph—with a difference!" Bridges in his reply to Mrs. Ward said that the entire family had read the novel, but he was politely evasive as to the effect on himself of the book and of the scene in which Mrs. Ward made use of his poem: "it is impossible for me to recall all the natural delicacy of my actual emotions." The prose of the novel is sentimental and effusive; it is far inferior to the poetry Mrs. Ward quotes.

Arthur Christopher Benson, poet, novelist, and essayist who became master of Magdalene College, Cambridge, 1915–25, began sending his volumes of poems to Bridges in 1892, receiving replies couched in the vaguely polite language Bridges customarily used on these occasions. There was nothing vague, however, about the language he used concerning one of his own poems, "The Eton Memorial Ode," which was set to music by Sir Hubert Parry and performed at Eton on November 18, 1908—to the great disappointment of Bridges, who wrote December 27 to Benson, an Etonian, that it was as a performance "a mere failure." Bridges commented on another poem of his, "Noel," his first official utterance as poet laureate, which at the command of King George V appeared in the *Times*, December 24, 1913. Dr. Gollancz made the mistake of explaining the meter of "Noel" (which is in Neo-Miltonic syllabics) in a letter to the *Times*, stating that Bridges had written the poem in "the old English metre" of "Piers Plowman," though somewhat modified. "Nothing," Bridges wrote to Benson on December 30, "could have been funnier: it was the supreme justification of pedantry." But Bridges's sharpest language in these letters is reserved for his criticism of the methods then in practice of the teaching of Latin and Greek to schoolboys. On December 8, 1906, in his letter thanking Benson for two educational pamphlets, Bridges launched into an excoriating attack on the teaching of Latin and Greek in England. "It seems to me absolutely inhuman to set boys of 10 and 12 to learn the grammar of two dead languages, which their teachers cannot themselves speak or even pronounce." Bridges took the view, now commonly accepted, that modern living languages such as French and German should be taught by ear by native speakers in the language, with more emphasis on pronunciation and less on grammar, and that such teaching should begin at an early age—about ten years. The study of Greek should not begin until the age of sixteen, although Latin might be undertaken earlier.

In his first letter to G. K. Chesterton, December 5, 1917, Bridges mentioned that they had met only once and said that if it had not been for the partial burning of his house he would have tried to get Chesterton to visit him for a few days. Two years later a visit was successfully arranged in May 1919. Bridges, in preparing him for his stay at Chilswell House, assured him that "everything is quite easy and informal and we could have a meeting of pleasant company at dinner both Saturday and Sunday. . . . Walter Raleigh and John Masefield are quite handy—and will both be eager to come." It is quite evident that Bridges liked the man as well as he did his work and that he sought Chesterton's company. In his first letter to him he praised highly Chesterton's drinking song of Noah and also the poem entitled "The Grocer," as well as his *History of England.*

In the last year of his life Bridges found an ally in Chesterton for his fight against excessive standardization not only in English pronunciation but in man's life-style in general. On October 3, 1929, he sent Chesterton his S.P.E. Tract No. XXXII, in which he criticized the findings of his own BBC subcommittee on the pronunciation of English with special reference to broadcasting, and he asked Chesterton's help in his next tract, in which he planned to expose not only "the absurdity of pursuing standardization [of language] as in itself an ultimate Desirable" but also "the horrible absurdities of the Standardizing of *Man.*" Chesterton replied from Rome November 1, offering to join the crusade: "On the matter of the stupidity of standardization as a principle I would certainly do my best, if only as an attempt at an apology."[75] Bridges on November 6 thanked him for his offer of help and commented on his trip to Rome, saying "surely there is no man on earth fitter than you to compose the serious differences between Mussolini and the Pope! I wish you God Speed."

Bridges and George Bernard Shaw served together on the Committee of English created in 1921 by the Academic Committee of the Royal Society of Literature and on the Advisory Committee of Spoken English formed by the BBC in April of 1926 with Bridges as chairman. Bridges's letters to Shaw reflect their common interests in simplified spelling, phonetics and phonetic spelling, and the pronunciation of English. Of the letters to Francis Brett Young, novelist and poet, the most significant is that of October 4, 1914, in which Bridges thanked him for the complimentary copy of Young's book *Robert Bridges: A Critical Study.* Bridges referred to the title as "dreadfully appalling," but he expressed his satisfaction that Young had mentioned his friendship with Hopkins and had quoted Hopkins's sonnet "Look at the stars." Bridges went on to say "I wished you had been able to say more about his influence on my writing." As to a possible edition of Hopkins's poems he stated, "What I have printed are just the very few things that people would stand (at least such is my opinion), and a further revelation of him would provoke only adverse criticism and ridicule."

XV

Throughout his career Bridges carried on considerable correspondence with his fellow poets, some of whom, like Bridges himself, also made reputations as scholars—such as G. Lowes Dickinson and A. E. Housman.

Bridges became acquainted with Dickinson (1862–1932), a friend of Roger Fry, when Fry sent him a copy of Dickinson's "Jacob's Ladder" in 1890, the year in which the correspondence began. The two became better acquainted when Dickinson spent a few days of the Christmas season of 1891 as a house guest at Yattendon. Dickinson, like their mutual friend R. C. Trevelyan, was a poet and a scholar with whom Bridges could exchange criticism and discuss technical matters such as prosody and the proper construction of plots for verse dramas. We find Bridges sometimes on the defensive about his own poetry, sometimes severely critical of his own efforts. In his letters of late November 1890 and of December 24, 1892, he defended himself against the charge of being a mere antiquarian and of being archaic in his poetic diction, but in January 19, 1892, he was rigorous in his comments on his own plays: "The chief mistake I made was that I thought I could get more in than possible. The plot cannot be too simple and the general lines too clear." In this same letter there were references to Bridges's Parisian experiences—interesting because he so seldom wrote about his vacations in France. We learn that in Paris he went to the theater every night and that he frequently attended lectures at the Sorbonne and at the Collège de France.

In the criticism of Dickinson's poetry, Bridges warned his friend against imitating Browning—a practice he called *detestable,* and in their discussions of prosody he assured Dickinson that Coleridge's "Christabel" was not in the new stress prosody at one time advocated by himself and Hopkins because Coleridge's stress marks were often purely conventional and not indicative of the way a line was actually read aloud.

A. E. Housman (1859–1936) and Bridges probably met for the first time at a dinner party given by Sir Edmund Gosse on December 10, 1913. Prime Minister Asquith was also present. Of this occasion Housman wrote to Gosse, "Never before have I seen, and never do I expect to see again, a Prime Minister and a Poet Laureate composing a Missive to a Monarch."[76]

Bridges seldom mentioned Housman in his letters; therefore his opinion of Housman's poetry is difficult to ascertain, although it was probably favorable, for he included five of his poems in his *Chilswell Book of English Poetry*. There is no doubt, however, concerning Bridges's esteem for his scholarship, for he approached the author of *A Shropshire Lad* on at least two occasions to help him polish his Latin prose—once when he was composing his combined epitaph in Latin for his mother and for himself to be placed in Yattendon church or churchyard.[77] Housman explained to Bridges's widow that Bridges wrote the epitaph and asked Housman "to trim it for him."[78] Another time, when he needed advice in writing the Latin dedication to Hopkins's mother of his edition of Hopkins's poems, Bridges wrote to Housman (May 25, 1918) saying, "I am writing to ask a great favour. I want you to write me 3 or 4 lines of Latin," explaining that he wished to dedicate the volume to Hopkins's mother, who was in her ninety-eighth year, and that he would "make a mess of the numerals" if he wrote the Latin himself. He gave Housman the English version of what he wanted to say in the dedication. The letter is of considerable interest for Bridges's brief portrait of Hopkins, whom, he apparently assumed, Housman had never heard of:

> I am editing the poems of an old college friend, my contemporary at Oxford, Gerard Hopkins—a Balliol man and a fine scholar—became a Jesuit very foolishly—"pervert" before he took his degree, and died 30 years ago at Dublin—rotted with melancholy, because, being a patriot, he could not stomach the treason of his spiritual associates and directors—perishing of Typhoid fever.

As he wrote these words Bridges probably had in mind some of the last letters Hopkins sent to him, two of which Bridges destroyed. Hopkins's state of mind in his last years may be judged by an excerpt from his private diary dated January 1, 1888:

> What is my wretched life? Five wasted years almost have passed in Ireland. I am ashamed of the little I have done, of my waste of time, although my helplessness and weakness is such the wise man warns us against excusing ourselves in that fashion. I cannot then be excused; but what is life without aim, without spur, without help? All my undertakings miscarry & I am like a straining eunuch. I wish then for death & yet if I died now I should die imperfect, no master of myself, and that is the worst failure of all. O my God, look down on me.[79]

In the fall of 1923 Bridges was busy preparing a volume of "poetry for schools" which became *The Chilswell Book of English Poetry* (1924). He asked Housman's permission to include two poems from his *Last Poems*, which was granted. He did not ask permission to include three poems from *A Shropshire Lad* because he knew that Housman had instructed his publisher that there should be no permission ever given to reprint selections from this volume. Nevertheless, Bridges let it be known that he intended to include three Shropshire poems in his anthology in any event. Housman's letter to Bridges concerning this matter is not extant, but Bridges's reply of September 25, 1923, indicates his pleasure at receiving it. "A cinematograph picture of me reading your letter would have been of some use in revealing my delight. Your generosity really overwhelmed me." What Housman said to Bridges may be surmised from his letter to his publisher dated September 23, 1923:

> I had better also tell you that I believe that he (being Poet Laureate, and an unscrupulous character, and apparently such an admirer of my verse that he thinks its presence or absence will make all the difference to the book) intends to include three poems from *A Shropshire Lad,* though I have not given him my permission, because he thinks he has reason to think that I shall not prosecute him. Well, I shall not; and you will please turn a blind eye too.[80]

The anthology was published March 1924 and when Housman's publisher raised again the question of permissions, Housman urbanely replied:

> I have never laid down any general rule against the inclusion of poems from *Last Poems* in anthologies. The rule regarding *A Shropshire Lad* still holds good. It is true that the Poet Laureate has printed three poems from it in his recent anthology, but he does not pretend that I gave him permission to do so.[81]

The two poets remained on good terms until the end. Housman was several times a house guest at Chilswell. When Bridges received the Order of Merit in June 1929 Housman congratulated him, saying: "If the Order of Merit gives you pleasure, I shall share it; and no one can dispute your title to it. I hope you do not mind having Galsworthy for a yoke-fellow as much as I should. If ever there was a man without a spark of genius, that man is he."[82] Bridges replied, "Thanks! I liked your letter, all of it, and might have written much the same to you if, as I think would have been more suitable, our positions had been reversed." The correspondence ends with Bridges sending Housman a copy of *The Testament of Beauty* on November 24, 1929, after Housman had already purchased a copy. In thanking him Housman wrote, "I thank you for your friendly gift. As you will have surmised, it comes too late to save my pocket; but I shall now be able to keep it uncut and so enlarge the fortune of my heirs."[83]

Bridges was introduced to the poetry of William Butler Yeats (1865–1939) by his friend J. W. Mackail when he called his attention to Yeats's *Poems* (1895), which had appeared when the Irish poet was thirty years old. The volume, which was still in Bridges's library when Richard J. Finneran recently examined it, has written on the fly leaf "I never saw any of Yeats' poems till I bought this book recommended to me by Mackail."[84] Bridges was strongly and favorably impressed. He wrote to Yeats on June 1, 1896, praising his poetry. A few letters were exchanged, and Bridges invited Yeats to visit him at Yattendon. The visit and their first meeting (Saturday, March 27, 1897) are vividly described by Sir

Henry Newbolt in his autobiography. Newbolt, at that time a next-door neighbor of Bridges, had been invited for dinner, and when he entered the dining room he found that Yeats was also expected. Yeats arrived exactly on time. "Bridges sprang up and ran to the outer door; when he had dispatched the guest to his bedroom he returned to us, pleased and excited: 'He is very good-looking: he is tall: I like him.'"[85] Newbolt excused himself after dinner because, he said, "I knew he [Bridges] had a great deal that he wished to say, with a view to Yeats' metrical education."

On Sunday, Bridges confided to Newbolt, "I sat up hours and hours with him: I'm done up—not with talking, but with smoking so many pipes while he talked." And on Monday, just before Yeats left, Bridges said to him, "You must come again and stay longer—stay a week—but look here! you must bring some work to do: I can't have you talking visions to me like this—I won't have any more visions, they exhaust me."

Newbolt explains Bridges's reference to the "visions." On Sunday afternoon the conversation turned to Yeats's special interest, the occult. Yeats produced a pack of "magic cards" ornamented with symbols from William Blake, and persuaded Mrs. Bridges to press one to her forehead and await a vision. She did so and, to Yeats's delight and Bridges's consternation, the experiment succeeded. "She reported almost immediately that she saw a green tree of unfamiliar shape—it was increasing rapidly in size, like a banyan tree, by sending down shoots on all sides which took root in the ground and sprang up in fresh stems, filling the whole field of vision."[86] Bridges expressed the opinion that there must be a scientific explanation for his wife's experience and suggested they spend the rest of the afternoon playing cricket, which they did. However, although Yeats's obsession with the occult bored and irritated Bridges, Newbolt was careful to note that at the end of the day Bridges said to him, "But he's a great poet: a better poet than I am."

It was a mutual admiration for each other's poetry that kept the friendship alive. Bridges in his letters continued to praise Yeats's verse and he included eight selections of his poetry in *The Spirit of Man*. Yeats wrote a very favorable commentary on *The Return of Ulysses* and expressed his admiration for Bridges's other verse dramas as well as for *Eros and Psyche* and the *Shorter Poems* in *The Bookman*, June 1897.

Bridges several times expressed to Yeats the hope that he would look on Yattendon and (later) Chilswell as a rural retreat where he could relax and write among beautiful surroundings and have the company of congenial friends. Sometime in 1911 or 1912 he put his invitation into verse. He never sent it, but he copied the poem into his manuscript book with this note at the end: "When I wrote this I was not satisfied with it, and sent my invitation in prose. I keep it now because of its premonition of the European [?] war." The poem (hitherto unpublished) reads as follows:

> Invitation to W B Y
> 1911 or 12 never sent
> Copied. Aug. 1916.—[Orig. Kept]

I have a home where happy seasons pass
In golden leisure, whereof poets tell
And busy folk sheltered fr. folly dwell
Like insects neath the tall luxuriant grass:

Yet lacks it honour until thou have seen
The revenant graces of its woodland ways:
The solemn pines are sighing for thy praise
And proudlier wd stand where thou hadst been.

Come then, dear poet, where thou dost belong
And wilt be glad, so shall soft brooding peace
Enwrap thy spirit in its "gentle fleece,"
And make thy welcome above speech or song.

The far hills gaze in silence and give heed
To silvery belfreys sleeping in the vale:
Within the friendly house doth never fail
The magic mirror where is sooth to read,

How many tender hearts of future time
Who have out liv'd *the sorrow that shall be*
Will among graver poets honour thee,
And feed their pleasure on thy gentle rime.[87]

The "invitation in prose" probably refers to Bridges's letter of April 20, 1913, in which Bridges tried to convince Yeats of the pleasures of being a guest at Chilswell:

Will you never come and see us again? You are not always attended, I take it, by your company of players. Term begins today, and there are sympathetic souls who would be rejoiced to meet you: above all Walter Raleigh—and my house is retired on a hill, and has a large room, library and music room, where you could do what you liked. Really you would not do badly—I, though I am getting very old, am still alive. . . . Do come and see us this Spring before the hyacinths are over. The Spring is very beautiful in our woods. We are quite in the country, but can walk across fields and ferry to Oxford in 40 minutes.

Yeats finally accepted for the weekend of June 19, 1915, at Chilswell. Later, when Yeats lived in Oxford, intermittently from 1918 to 1922, Bridges was a frequent visitor at his house.[88]

From 1907 until 1913 the correspondence appears to have lapsed. In 1915 letters were exchanged with reference to Yeats's contributions to *The Spirit of Man*. In this correspondence Yeats repeated his admiration for the poems of Bridges's daughter Elizabeth, which he had seen in her first book, *Charitessi*, published anonymously in 1912. Yeats's praise undoubtedly influenced Bridges in his decision to include five selections from her poems in his anthology.[89]

Bridges, in his letters of 1915, sought Yeats's aid in helping him to persuade Rabindranath Tagore to accept Bridges's revisions of Tagore's poem "Thou art the sky," which Bridges wished to print in *The Spirit of Man*. After considerable discussion involving Sir Frederick Macmillan and Sir William Rothenstein, Tagore (persuaded by Yeats) allowed Bridges to make the revisions, which amounted in fact to a rewrite of the poem. The two letters to Tagore, May 10 and June 25, 1915, present in detail Bridges's reasons for desiring to have the poem for his anthology and the reasons for revising it. Three of the letters to Rothenstein, April 19, July 26, and October 7, 1915, also deal with this matter.

John Masefield (1878–1967), who succeeded to the laureateship in 1930, became a neighbor of the Bridges family when he established his home, Hill Crest, on Boar's Hill in 1917. Edmund Blunden eventually set up residence close by, and Robert Graves at one time rented Masefield's cottage near Hill Crest. Bridges took a great personal liking to Masefield; Masefield was always somewhat in awe of the older poet, whose Oxford education was so much superior to his own. Masefield and Bridges's younger daughter Margaret became close friends during the war years. Only one letter from Bridges to the future poet laureate (undated) is available. In it Bridges gives permission for his poems to be read at Masefield's recitations. Hopkins's "Felix Randall" was also included in these performances. Two letters to Walter de la Mare (1873–1956) express Bridges's satisfaction that de la Mare is including a poem by Canon Dixon in an anthology, and inform him that in answer to his enquiry about the out-of-print Keats essay, Bridges's old proof copy is being sent to him.

It is greatly to his credit that Bridges was always on the lookout for young poetic talent, and he made considerable efforts to advance the careers of those young poets he admired—a group that included Lascelles Abercrombie, Robert Graves, Maurice Hewlett, Mary Coleridge, Laurence Binyon, Edmund Blunden, and Harold Monro.

Bridges's friendship with Lascelles Abercrombie (1881–1938), a poet thirty-seven years younger than he, is typical. In a series of letters from 1910–30 Bridges gave Abercrombie detailed suggestions for improving the style of his poems as well as offering general opinions of approval or disapproval. In his first letter to Abercrombie in this edition (October 30, 1910) he said, "Thank you also for the poem . . . you might castigate it into being one of the best poems in the language," which was good advice for this relatively young and rather facile poet. Bridges persuaded Bruce Richmond, editor of the *Times Literary Supplement,* to assign Abercrombie books for review and he recommended him for various positions. He also sent him his own poems for evaluation and asked him to make specific suggestions for improvements in the trial text of *The Testament of Beauty.* He eventually brought him into association with the Society for Pure English and published in Tract XXXVI his essay "Colloquial Language in Literature." He invited him to be a guest at Chilswell where the criticizing of each other's poetry could be accomplished more easily than by correspondence.

Robert Graves (1895–   ) was also befriended by Bridges, who admired his poetry early in Graves's career and published his articles in the correspondence sections of S.P.E. Tracts VI and XV. In 1925 he recommended Graves for a teaching position in the States. When Graves received a three-year appointment to occupy the chair of English at the University of Cairo, he wrote to Bridges on January 2, 1926, "I diverted the letter of introduction which you so kindly wrote me for America to Egypt: so in part I have to thank you for this appointment."[90]

In the same letter he said, "I am taking your new poems [*New Verse*, 1925] for the voyage: they are very fine and fresh, particularly the first group. Do you remember Skelton's Parrot? . . . He is true ancestor of your parrot"—a reference to Bridges' poem in Neo-Miltonic syllabics entitled "Poor Poll."

Maurice Hewlett (1861–1923), whose "Song of the Plow" inspired Bridges's "Hodge," became acquainted with Bridges when he wrote to him in 1894 asking permission to send him his verse drama *Theseus* for a critique of its metrical form and stating that he had found his book on Milton's prosody of help in his own versification. Bridges agreed to give his opinion of the play; when it was sent him he became so interested in it that he read it twice and then, in his letter of August 29, 1894, he invited the author to visit him for a few days at Yattendon. Hewlett accepted the invitation and Bridges used the opportunity to show him Canon Dixon's poems as well as his own essay in progress on Keats, for which he solicited help from Hewlett on the interpretation of the allegorical elements in *Hyperion*.

Laurence Binyon (1869–1943) and Edmund Blunden (1896–1974) were also noticed by Bridges when they were relatively young men and were helped in various ways. It was quite natural, too, that Bridges should be attracted to Harold Monro (1879–1932), editor of *Poetry Review* and *Poetry and Drama* and founder of the Poetry Bookshop. Monro was a poet, but it was through his magazines and bookshop and publications by the bookshop that he had his most important influence on Anglo-American poetry from about 1912, the year of the founding of *Poetry Review*, until the closing of the Bookshop in 1935, three years after Monro's death. In his magazines and chapbooks he published Pound and Eliot when they were considered avant-garde; he published the Georgians and he published, as well, established writers such as Bridges. His bookshop was a meeting place for the best poetic talent of the time. He held poetry readings and recitals that included Bridges. Through Monro, Bridges could keep track of what was going on among the younger generation. In the first of the extant letters by Bridges to him, dated October 6, 1913, he offered to send his new experimental poem, "Flycatchers," to Monro, and in a postscript he added, "You said something about fees. We shall not quarrel over that." Monro undoubtedly welcomed both letter and postscript from the man who had so recently been appointed poet laureate. The poem, the first Bridges published after being made laureate, appeared in *Poetry and Drama* for December 1913.[91] It is a highly interesting experiment in what Bridges called "free rhythm" in his holograph copy in his manuscript book, and it attacked one of Bridges's favorite targets—dry-as-dust pedantry in the teaching profession. The dead flies in the library window "stiff-baked on the sill" remind him of the schoolmaster of his childhood:

> A dry biped he was, nurtured likewise
> On skins and skeletons, stale from top to toe
> With all manner of rubbish and all manner of lies.

In the third letter to Monro, October 25, 1913, Bridges called attention to

Willoughby Weaving, a young poet whose fortunes he was trying to advance. In several subsequent letters Bridges granted permission for the reprinting of his essay in the September 1914 issue of *Poetry and Drama,* an essay that first appeared in *The Musical Antiquary,* and he accepted an invitation to give a poetry reading at the Bookshop.

XVI

Beginning with his first book, *Poems,* 1873, Bridges developed an expertise in typography and design that made many of his volumes (often issued in limited editions) works of art. He created the flowers for the title page of his 1873 volume (published by Pickering) that attracted the attention of Stanley Morison. (They are reproduced on the title page of Nicolas Barker, *The Printer and the Poet,* [Cambridge, 1970].) He also designed the flowers on the title page of the memorial to Digby Dolben and the title page and headings of the first edition of Hopkins's poems. Several of his earlier volumes of poems (including the first) were printed at the Chiswick Press in close collaboration with Bridges on matters of type and design.

Bridges's association with C. H. O. Daniel began in 1881, when he contributed a poem to *The Garland of Rachel* printed by Daniel in Fell types, types that Bridges frequently used in later books printed by Daniel and most successfully, perhaps, in the *Yattendon Hymnal,* printed in the Fell types that had been acquired by the Oxford University Press. It was Bridges who persuaded Daniel to use these types. John Johnson, in his *Robert Bridges and the Oxford University Press,* said in 1930 that Bridges was one of three men who had done most to encourage the taste and accuracy of Oxford printing in the last thirty years.

But probably Bridges's greatest success was *The Tapestry* (1925), printed in modified Arrighi type and designed by Stanley Morison, in very close collaboration with Bridges. Bridges first met the distinguished typographer Stanley Morison (1889–1967) at Chilswell November 8, 1923, when Morison was invited to call as a result of writing to Bridges asking him if he designed the title pages of his own volumes and complimenting him on the typography of several of his books. Morison was forty-five years younger than the poet and a Roman Catholic socialist. He had religious and political convictions different from those of Bridges; yet they both had an intense interest in typography and in design, and they soon became friends. Besides *The Tapestry,* a beautifully printed limited edition that contained eleven of Bridges's twelve poems in Neo-Miltonic syllabics, he also designed the quarto edition of *The Testament of Beauty.* The correspondence between the two friends centered on these two volumes. The entire story of the printing of *The Tapestry* is told in Nicolas Barker's *The Printer and the Poet.* Almost all of Bridges's letters to Morison in 1925 deal with the difficult problems that arose in getting *The Tapestry* printed with the type desired and in time to precede the publication of *New Verse,* which was supposed to "reprint" the *Tapestry* poems. There was also the matter of Morison's omitting "The West Front." The delay in publication and the omission of the poem strained the friendship to the breaking point. But eventually *The Tapestry* was printed in time to precede *New Verse* (but without "The West Front"). Bridges was very pleased with the final result, a triumph of design and typography.

R. C. Trevelyan (1872–1951), a close friend of Roger Fry and a friend also of Robert Bridges, was well known as a poet and scholar. He published many volumes of original verse and translations from the Latin and Greek as well as critical essays including his *Thamyris or the Future of Poetry* in 1925, the same year in which Bridges was collecting his experiments in Neo-Miltonic syllabics for *The Tapestry* and *New Verse*. Bridges admired his knowledge of the classics and his knowledge of prosody.

He welcomed Trevelyan's letter to him of December 15, 1924, in which he said he was sending Bridges his article in *The New Statesman* on Bridges's "Come se quando," a poem in Neo-Miltonic syllabics with twelve syllables to a line that had first appeared in the *London Mercury*. Trevelyan wished to know if he had analyzed Bridges's metrical method correctly, raised questions about an extra-metrical syllable in one line of the poem, and expressed admiration for the poem as a whole. Bridges replied that the line in question was a misprint and added "Your stumbling at that verse shows that you had understood the prosody." He said that he had written six poems in the new verse in 1921 and commented, "People are now all running after 'free verse.' I say that this stuff is free verse. There is no syllable in the line which need be accented or not, or long or short— and yet the prosody is very strict." At the end of the year Bridges sent Trevelyan his book *New Verse* and in his letter of thanks Trevelyan commented in some detail on matters of style and versification. Bridges's reply of January 4, 1926, explained the rhythm and prosody of several of his verses and stated: "I agree with the Free versifiers that the old humdrum is worn out: but I am quite orthodox in believing that freedom must be within prosody not without it." These letters demonstrate clearly that Bridges had been following the imagists and the experiments of other writers of so-called free verse and that he felt that he too should be numbered among the experimentalists but not at the cost of abandoning all prosody. We have seen from his letters to Harold Monro that Bridges was interested in the experimental work of the younger generation, and we know that he had met Ezra Pound on at least one occasion, for the publisher Charles Elkin Mathews wrote in his journal "Mr. Bridges lunched that day [February 27, 1914] with Ezra Pound (a Cork Street poet) and in the evening he dined with the King. Mr. Bridges told me he considered 'The Personae' and 'The Exultation[s] of Ezra Pound' unquestionably his [E. P.'s] best work."[92]

First references to *The Testament of Beauty* (which Bridges usually called his "long poem" or "the poem" or *De Hominum Natura*, its original title) began in the letters of late summer 1926. Documents recently made available in the Bridges Papers at the Bodleian library now establish with certainty the date and circumstances of the genesis of this poem. *The Testament of Beauty* was published on October 24, 1929, one day after the poet's eighty-fifth birthday. A few days later, on November 11, 1929, Bridges wrote a note in pencil on two sheets of paper concerning the beginning of the poem, in which he said, in part, "After our daughter Margaret's death in Ap[ril] 1926 my wife happening to find the begin-

ning of a poem dated incipit Xmas 1924 lying on my writing table in the corridor—& liking the manner of it urged me that I might find distraction in
carrying it on."

The first page of the manuscript of the *Testament* (also in the Bridges Papers) is
a rough draft of the opening of the poem. There are fourteen lines written on
Christmas Day 1924. In this passage the last seven lines have been crossed out;
the first seven are retained and are with minor differences the beginning of the
poem as it stands today. It is evident in the rest of this draft page that Bridges
resumed his poem (according to the note quoted above) in April of 1926, adding
two more lines to the original seven. And then he stopped work on it until (as he
also informs us in his note) he had returned from a vacation at Bognor. He
resumed writing on July 8, 1926, and worked steadily at the first book for the
rest of that year.

The most substantial discussions of the poem are in the correspondence with
Trevelyan, Morison, and George Santayana. As Bridges finished each of the
four books, he had printed a trial text that he distributed to a number of friends
asking them for criticism and suggestions for improvement.

In the latter part of June 1927 Logan Pearsall Smith sent (at Bridges's request)
a copy of the trial text of Book I to Trevelyan, who immediately noticed the
similarity of the verse to that of the poem in Neo-Miltonic syllabics "Come se
Quando" but, he said, in his letter of July 1 to Bridges, "with perhaps even
greater mastery of the difficult metrical technique." He noted a flaw, however, in
one line, which was thirteen syllables instead of the twelve required by the
prosody and asked for further time to study the text. Bridges in his letter of July
2 expressed his delight in Trevelyan's interest and admitted that Trevelyan had
spotted an incorrect verse. From this point on until the *Testament* was completed,
the two exchanged letters on the trial text of each book, Bridges outlining his
intentions to Trevelyan, Trevelyan praising those elements in the work he admired and criticizing passages about which he was doubtful. The series is a
valuable source of information about the composition of *The Testament of Beauty*.
From the beginning, Trevelyan strongly expressed his admiration for the work
in progress. At first he was somewhat disconcerted by what appeared to be a
random sequence of ideas, but he soon came to the conclusion that a more
coherent design would not do for what Bridges wished to say. And he never had
any doubts about the meter; of it he wrote, "there can be no doubt that it is
admirably suited in movement and emotional effect to the subject matter" (July
13, 1927). It should be noted that most of Trevelyan's critique, apparently,
consisted of detailed notes written on the trial text itself, and for these notes
Bridges was grateful. He repeatedly expressed his thanks for the help, and
toward the end of the correspondence he wrote: "My sense of indebtedness to
you is so overwhelming that I do not know how to express my gratitude or my
shame for having imposed this task on you" (March 6, 1929).

Stanley Morison also received a trial text of all four books of the poem.
Bridges wrote to him January 17, 1927, urging him to visit Chilswell: "Come as
early as you can. . . . My poem is in type so that you will be able to take it away
with you—and you will be interested in it if nobody else should be." Morison was

in fact interested, for he sent Bridges the most substantial critique (with the exception of Santayana's letter) that the poem received during this period. It was his letter of March 10, 1927, to Bridges that may have suggested the poem's final title, for he said, "I found the new poem intensely interesting. I read it as a testament and I have derived much religious consolation from it." Book IV prompted two letters. Morison wrote on April 16, 1929, that "he much enjoyed the Poem" and was "greatly helped by several portions of it" but "found difficulties in the lines which treat of Good Disposition" and he took Bridges to task for dealing harshly with the incident of Hopkins's refusal to accept a peach from Bridges because it would give him too much pleasure.[93] On April 19, 1929, Morison wrote to Bridges again, a long and serious critique[94] that is almost entirely favorable in its judgment of the nature and operation of *conscience* and *duty* of the individual man: "your account of the development of Conscience stresses the view that it is Reason functioning in Morals & isn't a sense . . . . the truth as it seems to me," but he objects to Bridges's treatment of socialism, which apparently Morison (a Catholic Socialist) also believed to be an example of reason functioning in morals. Bridges had argued that Marxian socialism is dependent on class hatred. Morison said "I think the criticism of Socialism is harsh. . . . Marx does not desire class hatred." Bridges's reply to this long letter was to quote his wife, "What a shame, said my wife when she saw your letter, to hav made the man write all that." Bridges's side of this correspondence is disappointingly meager, although be obviously appreciated Morison's intelligent evaluations.

Bridges began reading the work of George Santayana early in this century, beginning with *Interpretations of Poetry and Religion*. By 1915 the two had met in Oxford and had become friends. Bridges continued his reading of Santayana's works and was paticuarly impressed with the *Life of Reason*. In 1920 he reviewed Logan Pearsall Smith's book *Little Essays Drawn from the Writings of George Santayana*.[95] By then a correspondence had developed between the poet and the philosopher. At least thirteen letters from Santayana have survived; they appear in Daniel Cory's edition of Santayana's letters.[96] Only one letter from Bridges, an important one published in this edition, has come to light. The letter, dated August 25, 1929, was sent to Santayana to precede the gift of *The Testament of Beauty* a few weeks later. Bridges explained that he did not send the philosopher the trial text because he feared he would not want to read it "in scraps." He then went on to acknowledge his heavy debt to Santayana: "For my attitude is so much like yours that it might be fairly said that I had borrowed all my system from your books." And he also said "I . . . shall be more interested in your criticism than in anyone else's." Santayana after reading the poem responded from Rome on November 4, 1929, in a beautifully written letter in which he made perfectly clear the contrast between his own profound skepticism and Bridges's semi-Christian theism. A careful perusal of Santayana's letter[97] shows his thought to be much closer to Wallace Stevens's doctrine of the Supreme Fiction than to Bridges's concept of the Ring of Being as developed in Book IV of *The Testament of Beauty*. Bridges saw spirit as pervading and harmonizing the entire universe. Santayana made a sharp distinction between the world of the spirit and the world of nature. He said "I should therefore agree with you completely if it were understood that you were traversing the life of spirit only, and leaving out all physics and logic." But of course Bridges was *not* leaving out the physical universe, nor logic.

An apparent influence of some interest (unnoticed before) on *The Testament of Beauty* was that of Bridges's soldier friend Jan Christian Smuts (1870–1950) and of the philosopher Alfred North Whitehead. Bridges's son, Edward, recalled the first meeting of the Poet Laureate and General Smuts, at which he was present. In 1917 Edward, while recuperating from a war wound in Millbank Hospital, read Smuts's speeches and writings and called his father's attention to them. At that time Smuts (who had fought against the English in the Boer War) was a general in the British armed forces and was later to become Prime Minister of the Union of South Africa and Field Marshal. Bridges wrote to General Smuts asking for a meeting. Smuts invited him and his son to his rooms at the Savoy Hotel in London. They got on well together, exchanged letters and books, and Smuts later visited Chilswell several times.[98] Bridges and his contemporaries admired Smuts as a striking example of the Renaissance "whole man" who had been successful in the world of action and of intellect. In dedicating his *October and Other Poems* (1920) to him, Bridges addressed him as "Soldier, Statesman, & Seer," and in his letter of November 19, 1926, thanking him for his book *Holism and Evolution* (1926) the poet laureate, without a touch of irony, salutes him as "Most Puissant and beloved Seer." In this same letter Bridges mentioned his long poem, *The Testament of Beauty,* which he had been working on "for the last six months" and added with reference to Smuts's new book that his poem was "the poetical adumbration of an almost identical thesis. Indeed I have already inadvertently exposed myself to the charge of plagiarism from your work, especially in the matter of Personality." And, he continues, "I have just read Whitehead's new metaphysic."

Smuts replied in a letter dated December 15 from Irene, Transvaal:

I am deeply interested to hear that you are reading Whitehead and busying yourself with the Odyssey of the Human Soul. Nothing is more fascinating than the rise of the soul from the dust and its progress through the geological ages until it reaches the spiritual world. It is the real Pilgrim's progress, not to be contemplated without the deepest emotions. . . . Whitehead and I seem to have approached the same problems and to have reached conclusions which have singular affinity."[99]

It is obvious from this exchange of letters that Bridges was reading both Whitehead and Smuts as he was writing his philosophical poem, and that an investigation of the possible influences of these two important thinkers on the *Testament* might be fruitful.

XVII

Robert Bridges touched, somewhat gingerly we may presume, the Bloomsbury circle by his acquaintance with Lady Ottoline Morrell, to whose salon at nearby Garsington he was an occasional visitor, and by his closer friendship with Roger Fry, art historian, art critic, painter, and translator of Mallarmé. Fry (1866–1934) was at the very center of the Bloomsbury group and, with the possible exception of Virginia Woolf, its most distinguished member. He was a cousin of Monica Waterhouse; it was natural, therefore, that Bridges and he should meet fairly early in Fry's career and become friends even though they were of different generations and held differing aesthetic theories and tastes, a fact that temporarily disrupted their friendship when Fry painted pictures of Bridges and of Bridges's daughter that the poet laureate thoroughly disliked.

In the fall of 1886 (when Fry was twenty years old and a student at King's College, Cambridge) Fry wrote to his fellow student the future architect C. R. Ashbee from Failand House near Bristol, the home of Fry's parents:

> There is a standard of beauty somewhere, and if there is not, the sooner we chuck the whole business the better. Just as to a morally-minded person it is inconceivable that there is not a right and a wrong absolutely, to which we constantly approximate, so to the artistically-minded man it is inconceivable that we have not yet something at which we constantly aim. This is the result of some discussions with a certain poet Robert Bridges who has been staying here, a most delightful man. It was great fun hearing him uphold the standard of Beauty against my sceptical parents, and it cleared my views much. He (R. B.) is very great on the severity of art and the necessity of enormous study in the technical parts without the least subordinating the higher aims to technique. I have learnt much from him.[100]

This aesthetic absolutism, "there is a standard of beauty somewhere . . . at which we constantly aim," was maintained by both men throughout their careers; yet in its application to individual works of art and literature they were sometimes led to very different views.

Furthermore, there developed over the years differences in opinion concerning the relationship between art and life, between aesthetic and sexual response, and between art and morals. In a most interesting exchange of letters, Bridges wrote to Fry January 20, 1924, concerning certain points raised in Fry's *Vision and Design*.[101] Bridges argued that "beauty is the quality in sensible objects which provokes spiritual emotion" and it cannot ever be divorced from those sensible objects as they appear in the real everyday world. Thus any so-called purely aesthetic responses to a painting of the female nude, for example, is certain to involve sexual feeling if the observer is a normal male. "I have to allow it [sex] almost as strong an aesthetic position," he continued, "as it claims in common life," adding "our faculty for seeing beauty may depend on the juice of some gland." Furthermore, Bridges appeared to be attacking the effectiveness of purely nonrepresentational art when he wrote "my argument would be that the resolution into planes and lines can be of no philosophical use." He went on to say that there is a definite relationship between art and morals: "if as I think, Beauty is that which provokes spiritual emotion, you have to admit that the school doctrine of its being amoral implies blindness to its essential quality." Bridges believed that that which awakes spiritual emotion is by its very function moral.

Fry responded by agreeing that "aesthetic apprehension is preeminently a spiritual function," but he differed from Bridges in what causes the aesthetic response. For Fry, the fundamental aesthetic response is brought about by the contemplation of pure form—and therefore the farther this pure form is divorced from the concrete particulars of real life, the better. "I set to work by introspection to discover what the different elements of these compound elements [in response to a work of art] might be and try to get at the most constant unchanging and therefore, I supposed, fundamental emotion. I found that the 'constant' had to do always with the contemplation of form. . . . I therefore assume that the contemplation of form is a peculiarly important spiritual exercise."[102] Fry went on to argue that "there are spiritual functions that are not moral: and that the contemplation of form is one of them. And he attempted to dispose of Bridges's argument that aesthetic response may involve sexual feeling as follows: "As to sex, it, like the endocrine glands, may be a predisposing cause, a stimulus (like Mozart's smell of rotten apples), but surely is no part of the aesthetic apprehension . . . as regards painting, I think you are quite wrong in thinking that the preoccupation with the female nude is a result of sexual feeling. It is simply that the plasticity of the female nude is peculiarly adapted to pictorial design."[103] The basic difference between the two correspondents would appear to be this—Fry believed that there is an aesthetic emotion or response that is independent of all other emotions and that it is motivated by the contemplation of pure form completely divorced from the particulars of real life. Bridges believed that the so-called aesthetic response does not exist independently of the other emotions but is rather a refinement of them, and that these feelings are primarily motivated by and inexplicably involved in sensible objects, the particulars of the concrete, everyday world.

In his reply to Bridges's letter, Fry was supporting arguments advanced in his essays "Art and Life" and "An Essay in Aesthetics," which Bridges had read as the lead articles in *Vision and Design* (first edition 1920). In these essays Fry did not completely divorce art from life, but he stressed the differences between them and argued the case for nonrepresentational art. "The usual assumption of a direct and decisive connection between life and art is by no means correct."[104] And in describing the principles of the new movement in modern art he said "We may summarize them as the re-establishment of purely aesthetic criteria in place of the criterion of conformity to appearance."[105] As for morality in art, Fry rejected it entirely. "Art, then, is an expression and a stimulus of this imaginative life, which is separated from actual life by the absence of responsive action. Now this responsive action implies in actual life moral responsibility. In art we have no such moral responsibility—it presents a life freed from the binding necessities of our actual existence. . . . Morality, then, appreciates emotion by the standard of resultant action. Art appreciates emotion in and for itself."[106] Fry used the word *beauty* with reluctance and was less Platonic in this respect than Bridges. Rather than "beauty" in art Fry wished satisfactory aesthetic response, and as we have seen, aesthetic response is of a kind different from that of the other emotions. Fry also believed that our response to what we call "the beauty of nature" is of a different kind from our response to what we call "beauty" in art. In *Vision and*

Design it is obvious that Fry's ideas had changed and developed since his conversation with Bridges, as reported in Fry's letter of 1886 quoted above. However, Fry still appeared to believe that there is an absolute standard of excellence by which individual works of art can be judged.

A few years later, in his letter to Bridges of September 28, 1929, Fry, in commenting on Bridges's broadcast lecture "Poetry," wrote "I wonder, of course, whether this word Beauty isn't too dangerous to use. . . . I feel sure that beauty as applied to natural objects, men, animals is quite distinct from aesthetic satisfaction."[107] (It should be noted that Fry was one of a small group of friends to whom Bridges sent his trial text of *The Testament of Beauty* and that the letter quoted above was written after *The Testament of Beauty* was completed and that Fry had read the entire poem, probably, before writing this letter.) A few weeks later, in his letter to Gerald Brenan, Fry spoke of "the simple aesthetic essence which is what we are after."[108] Earlier in 1921 he had remarked to Marie Mauron that he enjoyed "above all pure art . . . art which expresses a sensation without wishing to impose it." Fry's doctrine had affinities with Ezra Pound's theory of the image and James Joyce's theory that a short story should express an "epiphany." And it also has affinities with Hopkins's notion of "inscape." Bridges, of course, did not agree with Fry's reductive aesthetics and a few weeks after receiving his friend's letter of September 28, he published his *Testament of Beauty* with its frequent illustrative references to beauty in natural objects, men, animals, *and* works of art.

The exchange of letters early in 1924 is of particular interest to students of *The Testament of Beauty*, for the fundamental notion that the function of Beauty is to awaken spiritual emotion in the mind of man is constant in that poem which Bridges began eleven months later, on Christmas Day 1924. Although he abandoned the poem (after writing fourteen lines, of which he retained only seven) until the summer of 1926 for personal reasons, chiefly because of the illness and death of his younger daughter Margaret, it is clear from his letter to Fry that he had much of the philosophical substance of the poem in his mind as early as the beginning of 1924.[109]

Furthermore, Bridges's concept of beauty probably received some stimulus from Fry's *Vision and Design* and perhaps also from his *Transformations* (1926). In the lead essay of *Transformations*, "Some Questions in Esthetics," Fry further developed his notions of autonomous art and literature: "Literature is the creation of structures which have for us the feeling of reality, and . . . these structures are self-contained, self-sufficing, and not to be valued by their references to what lies outside."[110] In this essay, Fry also had more to say about his notion that the autonomous work of art provokes a response, the *aesthetic*, which is different in kind from all other intellectual or emotional responses. "We should regard our responses to works of art as distinct from our responses to other situations."[111] Bridges, it seems to me, in his letters to Fry and in his *Testament of Beauty* thought quite differently. For him beauty awakened spiritual emotion in the mind of man, and beauty as he understood it may be present in the landscape, in a bird song, as well as in a work of art. Fry's theories may have acted as a stimulus to which Bridges reacted negatively; it was a stimulus that helped him crystallize his own thinking in *The Testament of Beauty*.

Bridges's letters concerning Fry's aesthetics marked the resumption of a friendship that almost blew apart, according to Pamela Diamand, Fry's daughter. In 1923 Fry painted portraits of Bridges and his elder daughter, Elizabeth. The pictures were sent to Bridges, and Fry awaited what he was confident would be a favorable response. When no response was forthcoming, he wrote to Bridges inquiring about his opinion of the portraits. Bridges replied in his letter of July 10, 1923, which began:

> Your letter about the portraits—I will tell you what impression I had of them. About mine I thought that if I died without any other later record it would be supposed that I had suffered from acute melancholy, and my flesh had undergone a visible adipocerous decomposition before death.

He enclosed with his letter two passport photos done after he received Fry's portraits "by a cheap photographer in Oxford" and which "had not been touched up in any way" to show the painter what he really looked like. Bridges also expressed his dislike of the portrait of Elizabeth: "We would none of us like that record to go about." Pamela Diamand said[112] that the letter exploded at the family breakfast table like a bombshell. The friendship was almost impaired permanently, but Monica, acting as a go-between, smoothed things over and by the beginning of the next year the Bridges-Fry correspondence was resumed. Bridges could never understand why Fry should let honest criticism of his painting interfere with personal relationships.

One point the two had in common was their admiration of the poetry of Gerard Manley Hopkins. Evidently, Bridges showed Fry some of Hopkins's poems in manuscript, for as early as 1896 Fry wrote to R. C. Trevelyan, a poet with a serious interest in prosody, "I've got some manuscript poems of Gerard Hopkins which would make you tear your hair," and he quoted the opening lines of "The Windhover."[113] Fry's language was somewhat ambiguous, but there was no ambiguity in his admiration for Hopkins in April 1919, when he received a copy of Bridges's edition of the poet. He wrote to Bridges:

> I have for years been a fervent admirer of the pieces you had let out here and there, so you may judge of my delight when I found it at the Omega [the art workshop founded by Fry]—after all a most suitable place for I find myself curiously in sympathy with all the scraps I have yet found of his aesthetic—his "inscape"; that's what we are after, however much we miss it. . . . I feel so rich in the possession of all this new world of beauty that I don't know how to thank you enough for providing it.[114]

Pamela Diamand in a letter to Edward Bridges[115] and in conversation with me said that Fry frequently read Hopkins's poems to his guests at 7 Dalmeny Avenue and on one occasion created a sensation with his beautiful rendering of "The Leaden Echo and the Golden Echo."

XVIII

As we have seen, Bridges downgraded the cult of personality in vogue among the poets and artists of the period. Yet, from the beginning to the end of his literary career, his own personality obviously made an impression on all who met him. In the recently published account of A. C. Benson's diary there is this description of the poet laureate as he attended a conference of writers in September 1914:

> R. Bridges a glorious sight, wavy hair, black coat, huge red tie, light trousers, white socks, patent leather shoes; he sat in a tilted chair, looking at ease, calmly indifferent, every now and then craning his head backwards out of an open window.[116]

A few years later, in the summer of 1923, Mario Praz visited the Bridges family at Chilswell:

> one Sunday, not knowing what to do, I climbed Boar's Hill, through the meadows made classic by Matthew Arnold and dominated by the Scholar Gipsy's tree, and presented myself to Bridges. He has a face that looks as though taken bodily from a predella by Duccio di Buoninsegna; and what with his untidy hair, his woolly beard, his flashing eye and his warlike frown, I imagined myself in the presence of a holy anchorite or an old buccaneer, or a sort of Count of Monte Christo such as you see in popular illustrations to that novel. Even his hat has something adventurous about it; it looks like the hat of Robinson Crusoe. Bridges has no restraint in giving his own opinions, and he deals sword-thrusts left and right: of all living men of letters I do not know who escapes.[117]

XVIX

After the triumphant success of *The Testament of Beauty*, the career of Robert Bridges drew rapidly to an end. About two months before his death on April 21, 1930, he wrote to the widow of his old friend Lionel Muirhead:

> Monica writes all my letters for me but I must send a line myself to thank you for your prompt response to my request for Lionel's Italian Cape. I felt sure that you and he would both like me to use it: and it is not only a great comfort to me, and exactly what I needed to throw over me when I can sit out in the verandah: but it consoles my spirit with abundant memories. When it is returned to you it will carry memories of me—and who knows who else may be warmed by its historic wrappings.

Among his abundant memories he should have recalled with some satisfaction his varied poetic achievements from his first volume of lyrics in 1873 until the publication of his spiritual autobiography in verse in 1929, as well as his unceasing efforts as editor, essayist, anthologist, musicologist, scholar, printer, host, and friend to promote and maintain the life of the civilized mind.

Notes to Introduction

1. According to Jean-Georges Ritz, *Robert Bridges and Gerard Manley Hopkins 1863–1889: A Literary Friendship* (London, 1960), p. 168, the trip started in December; according to RB's brief account of his life (Bodleian MS Don.c.79, fol. 127–29), the trip started in November.
2. Bodleian MS Eng.poet.c.22. For the text of the entire poem see letter 366. A revised version was first published under the title of "The Fourth-Dimension" in RB's *Poetical Works* (1912).
3. Robert Bridges, *Three Friends: Memoirs of Digby Mackworth Dolben, Richard Watson Dixon, Henry Bradley* (London, 1932), pp. 121–22. (Reprinted by the Greenwood Press, 1975. Page references are to this edition.)
4. *Three Friends*, p. 120.
5. Claude Colleer Abbott, *The Correspondence of Gerard Manley Hopkins and Richard Watson Dixon*, (London, 1955), pp. 2–3.
6. *Three Friends*, p. 142.
7. See Edward Sapir, "Gerard Hopkins," *Poetry* 18 (September 1921): 330–36.
8. Ritz, *Bridges and Hopkins*, pp. 156–65.
9. Ibid., p. 164.
10. The entire letter with its entertaining account of undergraduate days at Oxford is in Appendix A.
11. *Poems of Gerard Manley Hopkins*, 2d ed., p. 104.
12. See Elizabeth Daryush's commentary on her poem "Air & Variations," in which she adopted the stanza form of "The Wreck of the Deutschland," *The Southern Review*, n.s. 9 (Summer 1973): 645.
13. (London, 1893), pp. 161–70.
14. March 8, 1893.
15. For a list of these poems see note to letter 827 and also Tom Dunne, *Gerard Manley Hopkins*, (Oxford, 1976), p. 6.
16. August 29, 1893.
17. October 1, 1893.
18. Beeching married RB's niece Mary Plow. For a list of these poems see letter 827 and also Dunne, *Hopkins*, p. 7.
19. Under the title "Mary Mother of Divine Grace Compared to the Air we Breathe."
20. Laurie Magnus and Cecil Headlam, eds., *Prayers from the Poets: A Calendar of Devotion*, (London, 1899), pp. 234–35.
21. Elizabeth Waterhouse, *A Little Book of Life and Death*, (London, 1902), p. 70; Francis Thompson, in his review "The Preferential Anthology," *Academy and Literature* 63 (July 1902): 88–89, described "Heaven-Haven" as "a very quiet and restrained little poem" and then quotes the entire poem. See RB's letters to Mrs. Hopkins for May 16 and May 21, 1901.
22. Dunne, *Hopkins*, p. 11.
23. Ibid., p. 167.
24. RB's letter March 28, 1909.
25. May 7, 1909.
26. October 11, 1909.
27. It was very successful, having been reprinted many times, most recently with an introduction by W. H. Auden, who said, "My own generation . . . is eternally grateful to *The Spirit of Man* because it printed for the first time poems by Gerard Manley Hopkins. We were enormously impressed and when, a few years later, Bridges published a selection from his work, we rushed to buy it." *The Spirit of Man*, (London, 1973). n.p.
28. January 18, 1916.
29. Dunne, *Hopkins*, p. 13.
30. March 26, 1917.
31. September 13, 1917.
32. Dunne, *Hopkins*, p. 14.
33. Henry Maas, ed., *The Letters of A. E. Housman*, (Cambridge, Mass., 1971), p. 158.
34. See RB's own account of his life in Bodleian MS.Don.c.79.
35. *My World As in My Time: Memoirs of Sir Henry Newbolt 1862–1932*, (London, 1932), pp. 184–85.
36. Ibid., p. 187.
37. Ibid., pp. 216–17.
38. Ibid., p. 184.

39. *The Later Life and Letters of Sir Henry Newbolt,* edited by his wife Margaret Newbolt, (London, 1942), p. 98.

40. Ibid., p. 100.

41. Ibid., p. 101.

42. Ibid., pp. 101–2.

43. "The Poems of Mary Coleridge," *The Cornhill Magazine,* n.s. 23 (November 1907): 594–605.

44. In his DNB article.

45. As reported by Newbolt in *My World As in My Time,* pp. 190–91.

46. S.P.E. Tract XXXV (1931).

47. Ibid., p. 484.

48. The membership list is reprinted in S.P.E. Tract I (1919), pp. 12–15.

49. Smith, *Recollections,* p. 500.

50. Ibid., p. 494.

51. The date of the first meeting is uncertain. John Russell in *A Portrait of Logan Pearsall Smith,* (London, 1950), p. 76, says that Smith's friendship with RB began in 1902 with the publication of *Trivia.* Smith himself in *Unforgotten Years,* (New York, 1939), p. 218, says that RB invited him to Yattendon after reading his short stories (which were published in 1895). Smith does not state the year of the visit, but RB's first extant letters to Smith, dated June 23 and July 17, 1902, and his arranging for a visit to Yattendon suggest that this visit may have been their first meeting.

52. Pp. 40–42. The Manuscript Book is in the Bridges Papers.

53. RB's spelling.

54. Smith, *Recollections,* p. 5.

55. Russell, *Portrait of Smith,* pp. 90–91.

56. Ibid., p. 95.

57. Ibid., p. 122.

58. *Three Friends,* p. 170.

59. The letter is in the Bridges Papers.

60. In the archives of the Somerville College Library.

61. In the letter to Dame Janet cited above.

62. See below for a further account of the Letter of Reconciliation.

63. *Three Friends,* p. 204.

64. Ibid., pp. 206–7.

65. RB's side of the correspondence is published in its entirety in this edition. Both sides of the correspondence, with minor excisions, will be found in Donald E. Stanford, "Robert Bridges and Samuel Butler on Shakespeare's Sonnets: An Exchange of Letters," *Shakespeare Quarterly* 22 (Autumn 1971): 329–35, and in Stanford, "Robert Bridges on His Poems and Plays: Unpublished Letters by Robert Bridges to Samuel Butler," *Philological Quarterly* 50(April 1971): 281–91.

66.See RB's letter to Bullen of that date. However, RB dated his essay "St. Moritz, Jan. 1906" when it was printed in June 1907 in volume ten of the Stratford Town edition.

67. Imogen Holst, *Gustav Holst: A Biography,* (London, 1938).

68. Information concerning the musical compositions is taken from Imogen Holst, *A Thematic Catalogue of Gustav Holst's Music,* (London, 1974).

69. Holst, *Holst: A Biography,* p. 164.

70. The letter is in the Bridges Papers.

71. The letter is in the Bridges Papers.

72. The letter is in the Bridges Papers.

73. The letter is in the Bridges Papers.

74. *Fenwick's Career,* (London, 1906), 1: 209.

75. The letter is in the Bridges Papers.

76. Maas, *Letters of Housman,* p. 133.

77. This epitaph led to a quarrel between RB's family and the officials of Yattendon Church. See the comments of RB's daughter, Elizabeth Daryush, in Bodleian MS Don.c.79, ff. 114–16.

78. Maas, *Letters of Housman,* pp. 303, 310.

79. In the Bridges Papers.

80. Maas, *Letters of Housman,* p. 216.

81. Ibid., p. 128.

82. Ibid., p. 282.

83. Ibid., pp. 287–88.

84. Richard J. Finneran, ed., *The Correspondence of Robert Bridges and W. B. Yeats* (London, 1977), p. 60.

85. Newbolt, *World As in My Time,* p. 192.

86. Ibid., p. 193.

87. The poem is on pages 166–67 of the Manuscript Book, which is in the Bridges Papers.

88. Finneran, *Bridges and Yeats*, p. xiv.

89. Yeats also wished to include poems by Elizabeth (Bridges) Daryush in his anthology *The Oxford Book of Modern Verse*, but she declined to give permission. See correspondence by Richard Finneran, Roy Fuller, and A. A. Daryush in TLS, February 3, March 10, and April 14, 1978.

90. The letter is in the Bridges Papers.

91. The standard bibliography of RB's works is George L. McKay, *A Bibliography of Robert Bridges*, (New York and London, 1932). It has been indispensable for this edition of RB's letters. However, McKay fails to mention this publication of "Flycatchers."

92. MS. 392/2/8 "Notes" in the Archives of the University of Reading Library.

93. Transcripts of Morison's letters together with some holograph letters are in the Bridges Papers. Letters by Morison concerning *The Testament of Beauty* are in Nicolas Barker, *Stanley Morison*, (Cambridge, Mass., 1972). The letter of April 16, 1929, is on page 255.

94. The letter is in Barker, *Morison*, pp. 256–57, and in Donald E. Stanford, *In the Classic Mode: The Achievement of Robert Bridges*, (Newark, Del., 1978), pp. 200–201.

95. "George Santayana," *The London Mercury* 2 (August 1920): 411–19.

96. *The Letters of George Santayana*, (New York, 1955).

97. Cory, *Letters of Santayana*, pp. 243–45.

98. The account of RB's and Smuts's first meeting is in the Bridges Papers.

99. In the Bridges Papers.

100. Denys Sutton, *Letters of Roger Fry*, 2 vols., (London, 1972), pp. 109–10.

101. *Vision and Design*, (London, 1920), and several later editions.

102. Sutton, *Letters of Fry*, p. 547.

103. Ibid., p. 548.

104. *Vision and Design*, (New York, 1947), p. 6.

105. Ibid., p. 8.

106. Ibid., pp. 14;18.

107. Sutton, *Letters of Fry*, p. 643.

108. Ibid., p. 645.

109. See "The Genesis of *The Testament of Beauty*," Appendix B.

110. *Transformations*, (London, 1928), p. 8.

111. Ibid., p. 2.

112. In a conversation with the editor.

113. Sutton, *Letters of Fry*, p. 165.

114. Ibid., p. 450.

115. In the Bridges Papers.

116. David Newsome, *On the Edge of Paradise: A. C. Benson, Diarist* (London, 1980), p. 312.

117. Mario Praz, *The House of Life*, (New York, 1964), p. 257.

EDITORIAL PRACTICES

Editorial emendations of the letters have been held to a minimum consistent with the principle of establishing a text that is easily readable. Conventional abbreviations such as sh^d for *should,* frequently used by RB, have been spelled out. The infrequent misspellings have been noted except that RB's consistent misspelling of *Deutschland* in the title of Hopkins's poem "The Wreck of the Deutschland" has been silently corrected, as has his occasional misspelling of the name of the publishing firm of Elkin Mathews. RB's punctuation and capitalization have been retained, with these exceptions. Series of two or more dots were frequently employed by RB, usually as substitutes for dashes. In all cases these multiple dots have been omitted and single periods or dashes substituted. The only use made of multiple dots in this text is to indicate material omitted by the editor. RB's frequent use of dashes and of dashes combined with other punctuation has been retained. Inside addresses and dates have been regularized. Dates have been spelled out and placed in the upper right corner, although RB frequently placed them elsewhere. RB's infrequent use of lowercase letters to begin a sentence has been corrected, as has his infrequent use of periods instead of commas. RB's occasional omission of the apostrophe in possessives and contractions has not been corrected. His occasional use of simplified spelling (*hav* for *have* for example) has been retained.

LETTERS
1865–1907

Part I

OXFORD AND LONDON,

1865–1882

R obert Seymour Bridges was born October 23, 1844, at Walmer, Kent, where he spent his childhood so beautifully described in his "Elegy: The Summer-House on the Mound." He was the fourth son of John Thomas Bridges and Harriett Elizabeth Affleck. In the brief account of his life dictated to his wife in 1928[1] Bridges speaks of his family and early life: "My family lived in Kent as far as registers go back. They were yeomen, lived in Isle of Thanet, Harbledown. Many of them are buried in the church of St. Nicholas, I[sle] of Thanet. Most of the family property came into the hands of my grandfather and was sold under the will of my father who for some years lived at Walmer, where I was born, the 8th of 9 children. My father died when I was 8 or 9 years old: and my mother married again, the Reverend Dr. Molesworth, vicar of Rochdale, where I used to go home for the holidays from Eton."

Bridges's father died May 10, 1853; in September 1854 Bridges entered Eton and on October 31 of the same year his mother married the Reverend J. E. N. Molesworth and moved with him to Rochdale, Lancashire. Bridges stayed nine years at Eton, where he formed his lifelong friendship with Lionel Muirhead and where he became a member of an ardent High Church set under the leadership of Vincent Stuckey Coles, a set that included Muirhead and Digby Dolben, who died by drowning in 1867, and whose memoir, so much admired by Henry James, Bridges wrote years later. Bridges entered Corpus Christi College, Oxford, Michaelmas term, October 1863. By the time the correspondence with Muirhead opens in April 1865, Bridges had become friends with Gerard Manley Hopkins, who had entered Balliol College in April 1863. In February 1866, his younger and favorite brother, Edward, died. In his memoir of Dolben, Bridges speaks of "an understanding between my younger brother and myself that we would always live together; and such was our affection that nothing but his early death could have prevented its realization."[2]

Bridges was an excellent oarsman. He rowed stroke of the College Eight in 1867 and in July of that year he went to the Paris Regatta where, according to Sir Henry Newbolt, "he had to make a dramatic choice between stroking his college boat or that of his old school. He naturally refused to desert the former, and heroically lost to the Old Etonians by half a length."[3] As he was preparing to go to Paris to fulfill this engagement, his friend of Eton days Digby Dolben was drowned June 28, 1867, in the river Welland. Bridges was unable to attend the funeral.

In September of this year he visited his family in Rochdale and then returned to Oxford for Michaelmas term, taking his viva voce examination on December 4 and receiving a second in Greats. He was now free to carry out his plan for an extended trip to Egypt and Syria with his friend Muirhead. They sailed January 12, 1868, from Southampton.[4] The two friends traveled together for several months in Egypt and Syria. By June 24 Bridges had returned to England, according to Hopkins's Journal,[5] and (again according to the Journal[6]) he was still in England August 25, 1868. Sometime after this date he and William Sanday spent eight months in Germany. In the meantime Muirhead had continued his travels in the Middle East, describing his adventures in a series of letters to Bridges, letters that are included in this edition.

On November 6, 1869,[7] Bridges entered as student at St. Bartholomew's Hospital, taking his lodgings at 35 Great Ormond Street, London. During his medical career he, to quote his own words, "held post of casualty physician at hospital in 4th year, was assistant physican of Children's Hospital at Great Ormond Street and at the (then) great Northern Hospital."[8] In July 1870 Muirhead returned to England and in August Bridges went to Paris, returning in October to continue his studies at St. Bartholomew's. By April of 1872 he had moved to 50 Maddox Street, Hanover Square, where he lived with H. E. Wooldridge. His fist book, *Poems,* which Bridges later claimed was written in two weeks at the seaside,[9] was published by Pickering of London in 1873. Almost all the copies of this edition were subsequently destroyed by the author. From January to June 1874 Bridges toured Italy with Wooldridge. He was graduated M.B. (Oxon.) in 1874. During 1875/76 he was house physician at St. Bartholomew's to Dr. Patrick Black, for whom he wrote his Latin poem *Carmen Elegiacum,* issued by Edward Bumpus in December 1876, and in this same year Bumpus published the first version of the sonnet sequence *The Growth of Love.* In 1877 Bridges was casualty physician for the hospital and in that year, after the death of his stepfather April 21, he found lodgings for himself and his mother at 52 Bedford Square. In 1878 he became assistant physican, Hospital for Sick Children, Great Ormond Street, and physician, Great Northern Hospital, Holloway. He was introduced by a letter from Hopkins to the work of Canon Dixon in June.

Bridges's "An Account of the Casualty Department," which caused a stir among his colleagues, appeared in *St. Bartholomew Hospital Reports* in 1878. *Poems* by the author of "The Growth of Love" was published by Bumpus in 1879 and another volume with the same title was issued in 1880. In the summer of this year he met Canon Dixon for the first time at Hayton. Bridges suffered a near-fatal attack of pneumonia in June 1881. By autumn he had recovered. He retired from medical practice and toured Italy with Muirhead from December to March 1882. In August he and his mother moved to the Manor House, Yattendon, in Berkshire, where he met his future wife, Monica Waterhouse.

Notes

1. The account is in Bodleian MS. Don.c.79, fol. 127–29.
2. Bridges, *Three Friends*, pp. 66–67.
3. Obituary of RB, London *Times*, April 22, 1930.
4. Humphry House and Graham Storey, eds., *The Journals and Papers of Gerard Manley Hopkins*, London, 1959), p. 159.
5. Ibid., p. 168.
6. Ibid., p. 187.
7. Ritz, *Bridges and Hopkins*, p. 167.
8. Bodleian MS.Don.c.79, fol. 127–29.
9. Ibid.

1: TO LIONEL MUIRHEAD

Corpus Christi College
Oxford
April 28, 1865

My dear Muirhead

I suppose that some one will save you the trouble of reading this, so I shall not spare your eyes by writing hugely. I hope that you are really getting on satisfactorily. It must be very slow work however at best, and your doctor's prohibiting Switzerland must be very provoking. I am ashamed of myself for not writing to you before, but (here follow the usual excuses) I am rowing in our College eight *and* reading for Moderations, and as I am very much behindhand in my books, not having even read them all yet, I cannot make up my mind whether I shall be able to go in for a class or not. I want very much to get through this term, and do not care at all about honours myself (especially as they probably would be such inferior ones) but the dons, and several other people, among whom of course Coles, urge me on provokingly. If I do go in for a class this term I shall at any rate be able to 'scratch' if I do badly—and in that event have to read for next term all the 'long'!!

You must conclude from my saying so much about the schools that I am anxious about them.—Concerning the legacy which you left in my rooms, it is the prettiest and most ornamental thing that I have got, and puts all the rest of my possessions to shame. My only complaint about it is that it is far too good for me. My conscience would not allow me to leave up the list of Books and lectures, for my reading reputation would not at all match such pretensions to work. I hope that you will soon come back to Oxford to claim it, when you shall also have the notes which I hope I shall read before 'Mods'. Unfortunately in the Vacation my sister was ill at home. 2ndly we had an election, of which you must have heard the disgraceful result. 3rdly, I was gettting up a petition—4thly my brother was at home, from which premises naturally follows the conclusion that I did not open a book.—I hope that you will come up here for a day or two soon, (though I am afraid that I should be able to see very little of you.) The Merton services last Sunday: Octave of Easter Day, were splendid. I never heard anything better—Liddon is up I suppose. He is to preach and lecture on Sunday. Glen has probably told you about Dolben. I will write again soon but ought to be retiring now, for the benefit of our eight oar—do not trouble yourself to write when you have no scribe—I congratulate you about the Ball: success.

Ever yours affectionately
Robert Bridges

2: TO LIONEL MUIRHEAD

> Corpus Christi College
> Oxford
> November 2, 1865

My dear Muirhead

I ought to have written before—a fact that I need scarcely have told you. Why did not you wait a few minutes longer in my rooms the other day? I should have been in from lecture. I was very sorry to miss you, though at the time I thought that you had come up. So I went to your rooms at Balliol only to find somebody else's arrangements where yours should have been.

I am very busy this term, my occupations being coaching on the river—as usual, football, which is more or less a necessity as we mean to beat Cambridge this year—and last but not least reading. You know that I went in for a pass in Mods last term in order that I might have all my time for Greats. I have begun to read in great style, but do not know whether I shall be able to keep it up or no.

The 23rd was my 21st birthday, so if my studious habits receive strength I shall attribute it to my wisdom teeth.

I was at Eton yesterday. We had a first rate game of football. But I saw very few people that I cared to. Gosselin was in London, which I knew beforehand. Walford, ditto.—James has grown a beard. Dom Stevens a moustache. Stephen Hawtrey a beard.—The Head was very gracious. We had a pleasant day on the whole, though it was a miserable day to spend best of All Saints in.—I hear better reports of your eyes. I hope that they are true (—the reports). Dolben as you know is ill though it is time he was well again now. He is not coming to Hors[e]path; his Father thought the domestic arrangements uncomfortable.

I am in great haste! So you will let me conclude.

> Ever your affectionate
> R. S. Bridges

3: TO LIONEL MUIRHEAD

> Oxford University
> Boat Club
> November 25, 1865

My dear Muirhead

I can trust to your knowledge of human nature and Oxford life to excuse my having been so long neglectful. (I have not begun a letter for more than a year now without an excuse.) I write now waiting for a Captain's Meeting in the Barge Club, and the arrival of the president may at any moment put an end to my letter. You were right in thinking Nihill belonged to the BHT. (It is almost as unmistakeable a name as Hillhouse Buel.) I was at the service at St Stephen's Manchester which was the ultimate cause of the row. The Bishop was I think very unfair, as he had never given Nihill, nor his rector, any sign of disapproval, and they had always obeyed all his wishes. Sedgwick, an Oxford M.A. and Br. Nihill have worked for some years in the poorest part of Manchester. They only had a schoolhouse for some time, which held 250 people I believe, and at that time they had 300 Communicants.—A large church was built and the land given by Lord Derby—who was afterwards scandalized by seeing the B^r Ld Cross on Nihill at a certain interview—there was an unavoidable hitch with the trustees and the Church has never been consecrated though in full use. All the proceedings there have been thoroughly satisfactory. A very large offertory:—well last vacation the English Church Union went to Manchester and a certain well disposed Rector lent his church. High mass was very ritualistic certainly, but neither lights vestments nor incense used. The elevation was what offended the Bishop though really it was fear that Nihill was about to establish a monastery in Manchester for which there was fair foundation.

I must end hastily.

your affectionate
RSB

Nihil[l]'s plans I do not know.

4: TO LIONEL MUIRHEAD

Etonian Club
Oxford
February 26, 1866

My dear Muirhead

You will excuse my long silence when you know its cause. I was summoned away from Oxford suddenly to the deathbed of my younger brother, the one whom [sic] you will remember always so looked forward to joining us in our Monastic scheme. He was always very delicate, but we never expected that he would be overcome by such a short illness, as his complaint is what usually ends in decline and gradual loss of strength, and he himself, till 6 or 7 hours before his death, had no idea, or rather could not believe that he would not recover. It was very fortunate that all of us who were in England were in time to be with him at the last and we have every comfort that we possibly could have, as he was very nervous and sensitive, and a long illness which always seemed inevitable (unless he had quite overcome his weakness and disease which was almost impossible) would have been a great trial to him.

I was very sorry to hear that your eyes were no better. You must not write such long tidy letters to me if it is bad for them, though you will soon get in the way of writing without looking much at the paper (if your eyes do not get stronger) and do not be afraid of sending scrawley looking epistles to me.

Have not you heard the whole history of the late Church movement at Eton. A motion was passed at the fellow's meeting last founder's day that there should be weekly celebration and intoning. Some discontent which the minority mani-

ested awed or was shared by the fellow in residence at the beginning of the
chool time—he gave no orders for change and nothing has yet been done.—
Excuse my breaking off suddenly   *the post*

Ever your affectionate

R. S. Bridges

5: TO LIONEL MUIRHEAD

Corpus Christi College

Oxford

June 5, 1866

My dear Muirhead

It is a long time since we have written either one to the other—and I am afraid
that you will be abroad. However I take the chance of your not having gone, or
having come back, or your not going at all, to ask you how you are now, especially with regard to your eyes. I hope to go down on Saturday, but where I am
going I do not know. I ought to go into Kent but do not know how to manage it. I
am to read all Herodotus in the Long Vacation, therefore think that the more I
am at home the better. You heard if you have been at home lately of the great
success of our College Boat in the races. We lost the head ship very foolishly but
were a good second, which surprised everyone. My Mother has been up here, to
my delight. By the bye she admired that watercolour of yours, (which you gave
me a year and a half ago) so very much. It gets a great deal of praise. Is there
any chance now of your coming up? I do hope that you will be able to. It seems
such a pity. Shall I send you that Calendar and frame that you lent me? Please *let
me know if you want it,* as I can easily transmit it.

I go out of college this term, but feel that the loss of my luxurious rooms will
be made up for a good deal by the fact that I have got rooms with Knight. A very
poky little house but convenient and cheap. If you are in England and able to
write let me have a line soon to tell me how you are and if there is any chance of
my seeing you if I go to London.

I am yours affectionately

RS Bridges

6: TO GERARD MANLEY HOPKINS

Rochdale Vicarage

September 12, 1867

My dear Hopkins

As it was so difficult to fill up your letter it was doubly good of you to write to
me—I was very glad to hear from you and had been expecting to for some time.
I should have written myself but was afraid that I might have said something that
I should not have done about Digby Dolben—perhaps I did? Thank you for

telling me what Dr Newman said of him. I do not think his words at all measured Dolben, though of course he cannot have known him at all. I should not dare to criticise what *he* said but agree much more in what you said for yourself. It is a thought that I have only known for the last 2 years or less that any thing one actually sees is the best, or as good as the best of its kind that has ever been in the world and perhaps that ever was or will be any where in the material universe and I especially appreciate it in art, and to me it is almost the only attraction in heroism. You will understand what I mean without my prolonging this into a schoolgirl's letter—but did not you think that there was an entire absence of strength in Dolben? It always seemed to me so in spite of his great moral courage as people would call it, in carrying out his "views".

I wish that I had time to write you a decent letter. My Mother is very ill indeed and has been now for some time. It is a nervous illness which is very distressing to her and to us, but the doctors all assure us that it is not dangerous though tedious and that we shall only have great difficulty in keeping [?] quiet enough after she gets well. I have consequently a good deal to do besides my Great work not the least tiresome of all being the playing of backgammon every evening with the D^r—in the little oven called the breakfast room. This with the time taken up by the exercise, which you know is necessary to keep me from deteriorating into some outlandish animal and upsetting all the received theories of species etc. completely absorbs my letter writing moments—I wish I could give you a good report of my work. I have got through almost all my Grecian history and hope to do the Latin before the term. I feel to be a good deal in your society for every now and then I look into one of your notebooks which thanks to your style recall you very vividly. I had a curious dream the other night in which your Dr Newman, Dolben, and a strange Roman Catholic priest and myself had the most wonderful discussion possible. Please write when you feel the least inclined, and even sometimes when you don't, if you think that a little self mortification would be timely. As long as my Mother is so ill I have a great many family letters to write, and people to think about which altogether makes it an effort to begin a letter to any one on ones own hook—Does Southey's Doctor (if you ever read the book) amuse you very much? Have you read any or all of George Eliot's works? What do you think of them. I have just (at least this vacation) read them all.

I am yours affectionately

RB

P.S. I have referred to your letter for your address and find that you ask me one of 2 questions. I do not know about Dolben's verses being published. His father is a sort of literary man.—Dolben was buried at Finedon, in the family vault under the altar of the famous church there. When you go I should be glad to go with you. We might make an arrangement possibly for some time next year, and then you might go all over the house etc. Remember you *stay with* me next term when you come up if you do not get rooms in college, and mine are to spare.

RB

I know what a stupid letter this is.

7: TO LIONEL MUIRHEAD

74 High Street
Oxford
Sunday, November 17, 1867

My dear Muirhead

I was very sorry to miss you when you were in Oxford I can scarcely say a *few* days ago as I wanted particularly to see you. I have not time to write a long letter, but want to know whether you will be able to have an evening with me some day soon. The schools begin on Thursday. Any day after that day I will entertain you at dinner and get up a whist party, or what I would rather do have some conversation. I have a good deal to talk about generally—at least so it appears to me at present, and in particular I want to ask you if you are disposed for a good long excursion abroad next summer. With me the only difficulties are funds and a companion. The first I think that I can get over, and if it is at all what you are inclined to do I should like a regular good and not hurried trip. But whether you refuse this, or think it improbable, I should like to talk it over. Please come in some day—but let me know beforehand. Thursday would not be a good day, but any day after that.

I am ever yours affectionately
Robert S Bridges

8: TO LIONEL MUIRHEAD

74 High Street
[December 4, 1867]

My dear Muirhead

My brother is coming up on Saturday evening so I do not know what to do about asking you to come in to Oxford, which I look forward to. I will write again.

I have a double barrelled breach loader which is in good condition, and would serve well I have no doubt, but it would be tiresome perhaps to take many cartridges out, in which case one of my brothers could change guns for a year I have no doubt.

The minutia of our outfit I scarcely feel settled enough to consider. I will write to you on Sunday when I know how long my brother is going to stay in Oxford, and on what day I am going home. I hope that you will come North with me, but I leave persuasion to when we can talk about it.

Ever, your affectionate friend
RS Bridges

Wednesday evening
I was in viva voce today and did not do badly, but the dons did not seemingly consider my position critical, and therefore I augur ill.

9: TO LIONEL MUIRHEAD

Etonian Club
Oxford
Saturday evening
December 7, 1867

My dear Muirhead

You must certainly have expected an answer before, and I should have written, but having some strangers dining on Thursday evening they prolonged my entertainment further into the night than I had intended, by making up a whist party. On Friday evening Oxenham came in, and we talked till quite late.

First I hope that you are better, and thank you for your invitation. I shall hope to make use of it some day next week, if you will let me know what evenings in the week you have disengaged. I say this as you said something about a ball which I would rather avoid—. I shall try and persuade you then to come with me on the 18th of this month and stay till Christmas. May I be successful.

Again I must thank you very much for the picture. As a test of its likeness to the original, Brooke, who does not know even the mature Knight, well recognised directly that it was meant for him. I was very sorry however that you had tired your eyes by drawing it, as I am sure that you had better take all possible care of them.

Today I have rowed down to Newham to see the trial eight rowed *and* all the way back, which considering that I have not rowed at all this term was calculated to fatigue me. I am just off to dine at B.N.C. but have to change first. I heard from MGK this morning. I had written to ask him to join us. I knew he could not, but thought he would wish to, and might possibly get over the apparent obstacles. He says he could not anyway manage it.

My old brother is coming up to Oxford tonight. I am afraid that he will not do more than stay over Sunday.

I am ever yours affectionately
R. S. Bridges

The possibility of my brother staying up makes it uncertain on what day I shall be able to see you—could you not, if you are better, come into Oxford on Tuesday?

10: TO LIONEL MUIRHEAD

74 High Street
Oxford
December 18, [1867]

My dear Lionel

I had a letter from my Mother by the last post in answer to one that I wrote the day I left you disclosing our plans. I find that my Mother enters fully into the idea, and is very much pleased with it, but I will show you her letter which is entirely satisfactory.

This being so I suppose that I may reckon on your coming into Oxford on Tuesday evening or Wednesday morning as I shall be going North by the 1.15 train *London and North Western*. I am sorry that I could not give you longer notice. I have heard from Phelps who cannot come, and have heard of someone who is described as 'a cub' who wants escort. I have asked for particulars, as it is possible we might find him desirable. My mother writes "bring Muirhead, we shall be very glad to see him, I must know your travelling companion."
If you come into Oxford tomorrow evening I could put you up.
With kind regards to your father and mother I am

yours affectionately
R. S. Bridges

Class list should be out now.
P.S. I am in 2nd

11: TO LIONEL MUIRHEAD

Rochdale Vicarage
Saturday morning
[December 28, 1867]

My dear Lionel
Thank you for your two letters and their information. I hope that you will be able to get berths. I enclose a crossed cheque for 30 £. I have made it payable to you as it seems doubtful whether you will get the places. Do not return it. You can either burn it or keep it till we meet. In case you cannot get berths shall we go by Marseilles or by a Liverpool boat? I will be making enquiries about the latter and let you know terms etc., and if you decide to go by one of these will see about the booking. —The best way to manage about the cheque if you want to use it would be for your father to cash it for you, as except in Oxford and at Praeds, or I suppose your banker, you might have some difficulty in getting it changed.
—In greatest haste to catch the morning post.

yours affectionately
RB

I shall go to town on Saturday.

12: TO LIONEL MUIRHEAD

Woolwich
January 7, 1868

My dear Lionel
I wish that I saw any way of avoiding spending a day at Southampton. My brother says that there is no reason to attend to the Company's regulation about

Robert Bridges at Philae, Egypt, March 1868, after a watercolor by Lionel Muirhead. Courtesy of the Lord Bridges.

the shipment of baggage. He has been by their boats often enough, and says that it only applies to heavy baggage, and that he shipped all his baggage heavy and light an hour before starting, but I should fear that they would tyrannise over a civilian, and it would be no joke to have to pay for it all as extra. I am sorry that you cannot dine here on Thursday—which is the guest night—but I think that on Friday we will take our meal at Southampton. —I shall expect to meet you at Radley's Hotel. I am paying a few parting visits in town, and completing the necessary arrangements.

I meant to have asked you before whether you are provided with a good waterproof Cape or Coat. I believe it is very necessary, and am going to invest in one. I could get one for you. I am writing in an armchair with the paper on my knee, in my brother's quarters here. He is making a military map of 'country marched over' some days ago, and is very much disgusted at having to do it.

I shall be at 23 Manchester Square if you write—I have as yet failed to make an appointment with Hopkins, but mean to see him—have numberless formal and other calls to make, and could have seen very little of you had you been in town. I am going to Praeds the lst thing this afternoon to arrange with him about my cash. I hope that your ball will go off well. It will be a very satisfactory farewell to home and the neighbourhood I should think—I know that I had more important communications to make, but I cannot think of them now.

Take out a lot of cartridges for your revolvers as we shall find amusement in 'potting'. Don't forget the Chessmen or Gibbon—I will give you a list of the books I have packed up. —Shakespeare—Browning-selections—Milman's Latin Churches—Max Muller's languages—Golden Treasury—Ellicott's notes to S. Paul—Riddle's Plato i Apol—Soph Ajax (this for your benefit)—Stanley's Sinai —Grk Test—Bible—and another book or two that I have forgotten. I shall take some more camphor, and if I have any room will fill up with the things you asked me to get.

Yours Ever
RB.

13: TO ROBERT BRIDGES

Beyrout
July 1, 1868

My dear Bridges

I have been here for 10 days encamped on the sea coast with the fine range of the Lebanon in front of the tent door and the little harbour as well: it is a pleasant place and one gets a breeze all day: A great consideration I assure you as the therm is 90 shortly after breakfast. I shall not give you much account of my journey up from Jerusalem, as it is all chronicled in the journal for your edification: it was very enjoyable and pieces of the country are really beautiful, and much more fertile than that parched limestone about Jerusalem. M^t. Carmel and Banias were the two most pleasant spots: the latter is not overpraised when

Stanley compares it to the celebrated Italian Tivoli, though of course Tivoli bears away the palm. The great plain of Esdraelon is a fine stretch of the richest soil but from end to end there is neither a tree nor a house of any sort that I could see. The guide book says there is one tree: I quite failed to see it though from the spurs of M^t. Carmel along which I rode past Mejiddo, and also from the summit of M^t. Tabor the whole plain lies at your feet. The site of Capernaum is also on a rich well watered plain miserably cultivated. I forgot to add that about a 4th at the outside of the plain of Esdraelon is cultivated for the excellent reason that any fine morning the Arabs may come across the Jordan with their flocks and herds and pitch in the middle of your best patch of barley; the Turkish government af[f]ording no assistance to the inhabitants for the protection of their crops. The muleteer (the same man you took to Jaffa) proved much more obstinate than any of his mules, and on the road we had two grand rows about camping at certain villages: he wishing to dictate the places I was to stop at. At one place where I had expressly told him I did not intend to stay, on my arrival I found the mules unladed and the tents pitched: I wished to pitch 3 miles further on and so pulled up all the tent pegs and told him to reload the mules: he utterly refused: Mohammed was furious and caught him by the throat wishing as he said afterwards to have "kill it him"—The Sheik of the Village separated them somehow. M. then demanded of him other horses to take me on. The Sheik said he had none. M. told him I had orders from the Pasha to get horses wherever I wanted them! "He be afraid" thereupon, and 7 camels made their appe[a]rance!! I selected 2 and the process of loading them commenced, when the muleteer seeing this unexpected turn of affairs, said he would proceed. The whole scene was very fine indeed and the noise was so great that I believe all the village had turned out on hearing of it, and stood round. On two or three other occasions M. thought you would have 'broke it his head' if you had been there. I have not found it at all dull as yet alone, except at meal times: at present there is a gunboat lying in the harbour and the officers on board are very pleasant. I often pay a visit and in turn entertain in my tent with coffee and Turkish tobacco. Last night I dined with the Captain and Viceconsul and we had splendid rubbers of whist afterwards as you may imagine when I was not in bed till about 2:30. You will be happy to hear I won on every rubber.

I feel ashamed at having got so far in my letter without congratulating you on the splendid success of Corpus, of which my brother writes: I suppose Balliol is nowhere, but I know nothing more. I am devouring a store of Saturday reviews which the Captain has kindly lent me. I wonder whether you have seen or will see in London H. Hunt's new picture from Keats: Isabella with the pot of Basil: I hear it is very good and it will probably interest you much as an illustration of your favourite poet. The pipe-box is all right and nothing shakes about inside which is very consoling. I sketch dilligently [*sic*] now I have so much spare time: I purpose going to Antioch shortly, though I hear fevers in that part of the country abound during Summer and Autumn. Still with Quinine I shall run the risk. My Father was greatly surprised at our economy, and much pleased at it also; he apparently thinks us most

[This letter, from Lionel Muirhead, is incomplete.]

14: TO ROBERT BRIDGES

Her Majesty's Consulate Aleppo-
Oct. 21st, 23rd 24th. 27th. 28th[1868]

My dear Bridges—

You seem to have had most exciting adventures on your homeward bound voyage and I heartily congratulate you on escaping safe with the books and the Bethlehem ware: I regret you could not summon up courage and Spanish enough to run over to Madrid where the picture gallery has no superior and few equals. I am going—after the fashion of Frederick with old Stevens at Eton—to outdo your story; mine indeed can only be half told as yet, the finishing touches which may also be the most important for me not having yet been given by the . Turks.

I had a glorious summer trip all up the coast, Sueidiah and Antioch being two of the loveliest places I ever saw in any country: I pass over all antiquities etc. At Aleppo I had a sharp attack of fever and was laid up for a month: 80 leeches were applied and I got through it and recovered so much that I started off into the Desert for Palmyra. The Sheikh who usually escorts travellers asks at least £80 for a single Traveller—a terrible item in our account book—. So Mr. Skene kindly undertook to enable me to reach Palmyra without any backshish, or very little. A party of Engineers had landed at Tripoli 3 months previously to make plans for a line of railroad from Tripoli to the Euphrates: the head of this expedition Colonel O'Reilly being a great friend of Mr. Skene's, and I started from Aleppo with a letter of introduction to him. Their camp was then pitched in the desert amongst the Arabs, with whom they were on good terms, at no great distance from Palmyra. As soon as I got once into the desert and as it were could be formally introduced to an Arab Sheikh by Colonel O'Reilly I was told a visit to Palmyra would be easy. 5 days journey brought me to Hamah on the borders of the desert—Most interesting ruins were passed every day, of cities built in the 4th or 5th century, and of rich Byzantine architecture. At Hamah I applied to the Pasha for an escort to Hassan Bey's camp, and after much delay was refused. So I hired a common Arab and set out to take my chance without escort. All night under the clear moon we travelled over the stony tract and at day break reached a small collection of huts, the farthest civilized settlement eastward till one arrives at the Euphrates. 40 Mowali a marauding expedition passed us in the night about a mile off; two men met us who had been robbed, I fortunately escaped. From this village I went on to Colonel O'Reilly's camp. Here I stayed 5 days enjoying myself mightily galloping about the great plains with quaintly shaped hills bounding them and seeing Arab life unadulterated. The great Sheikh Suleyman Ebn Meerched who rules over 60,000 Anasçh spent a day or two at the camp negotiating an escort for Colonel O'Reilly and Company to the banks of the Euphrates. Before I arrived at this camp the Engineers force 100 men in all Circassians, Hungarians, Syrians etc. had a fight with a tribe and came off victorious. The beaten tribe happened to be under the wing of the Turkish government while Sulemyman Ebn Marshed who defied the Turks was an outlaw. Suddenly on the morning of the 5th day 1100 troops appeared at 4 A.M. before our camp, with 8 pieces of rifled cannon. Colonel O'Reilly rode at once over to the Pashas and said he was quite willing to surrender without resistance if they would agree to allow him and his Engineers to keep their private arms, to make no one a prisoner, and to touch no private property. The Pashas agreed instantly. So all the camp was struck and away moved men, horses and camels on the way back to Hamah: I and Mohammed and my muleteers going with them. We all halted to encamp the first night near a spring of water. No sooner had we dismounted than the Pashas' conduct changed entirely. Colonel O'Reilly, his officers and myself were made close prisoners in a tent 14 armed sentries being placed over us. That night the Pashas had very little to eat apparently and sent to ask us for dinner as we had potted meats and other savoury messes in tins; I need scarcely add that after the scurvy treatment we had received, it was refused. Next morning at 3 A.M. by moonrise we started for Hamah, the muleteers and camel drivers being manicled [sic] two and two. After a long march over desert hills we reached the town: a grand procession was then formed, the Pashas riding in front and military music playing "Cut off their heads! Cut off their heads" as I afterwards heard. Having arrived at Hamah after looking as innocent and unconcerned as possible while the crowd were hooting us, and crying in Arabic "Vive le Sultan! à bas les Infidèles" we were all clapped into close confinement in the barracks. I cannot tell you all our little adventures while therein immured but generally we got next to nothing to eat as our servants (Mohammed included) were all in quad like ourselves. Here I remained for 2½ days. The second day I was summoned to open my boxes as all papers which seemed suspicious were to be taken. My journal miraculously was unmolested: our account book Alass! which had been kept with such scrupulous exactitude up the Nile by you and with quite as great care by me ever since, was supposed to be treasonable and was snatched up by the Bimbashee; besides this they took half of an old letter and 6 or 7 London bills for boots and clothes and spectacles which I had paid just before leaving England! The account book I tried hard afterwards to recover but could not: if the Sultan or Grand Vizier sees all these suspicious documents I hope they will be edified to learn how much we paid for turkeys and what our vegetables cost us a month with many other items of things not generally known! *I* was at length let out, Mr Skene having written to the French Vice Consul at Hamah strongly, but for 5 days I was detained within the walls of Hamah. During these days I learnt that the Turkish government suspected Colonel O'Reilly and his engineers of being engaged in a plot for the subversion of the government, rather a serious charge. At the end of this time I was ordered to Damascus, and the engineers were to go too. On my especial enquiry the Pasha told me I was not a prisoner and need not travel with the other prisoners' escort. So off I set with Mohammet, and the two muleteers for the 5 days journey. Awefully [sic] hot days they were, all spent in crossing parched stony wastes to the East of the fine range of Anti-Libanon [sic]. I have not had time to describe several amusing incidents which occurred, how the Pasha stole my dinner and my breakfast twice etc., but one little episode I cannot deny myself the pleasure of narrating. Not being handed over to an escort of soldiers as the Pasha had told me I did not go to Damascus as a prisoner. I intended to enter Damascus by myself to avoid a second triumphal entry! For two days I had traveled alongside of the cavalcade going to Es Sham (Damascus) and about 4 hours before entering the city we all stopped for lunch near a ruined village. I went up to the Pasha and told him of my intention, through Mohammed and his own French interpreter. With an astonishing mental facility he contradicted himself and said I was a prisoner and must enter with the others. "Eccelency" I said "hand me over to an escort of soldiers as you have done the other prisoners" 'No I will not." "Then Eccelency I shall set off at a gal[l]op for Damascus and you may retake me if you please, but until you do this I shall consider myself free to enter Es Sham as I like." Having repeated this twice, I *did* set off at a gal[l]op. For some minutes the Pasha did not notice my absence and thus I got a little start. Soon however he found I had gone and instantly 6 irregulars, 8 Albanians and lastly His Eccelency himself with some soldiers set off after me. For an hour and a half the chase continued until a large batch of camels, slow coaches very, stopped the way and the irregulars caught me. The Pasha swore roundly in Turkish, and flourished his cane in my face (all of which has been duly reported in my protest to the government) and was obliged to hand me over to an escort thereby putting himself entirely in the wrong. At Damascus we were all put in solitary confinement with 3 sentries keeping guard over each of us. Mercifully Mr Skene wrote very strongly to the Consul at Damascus that if I was not set at liberty instantly he would telegraph to the Embassy and after 24 hours of this intolerable thrawldom [*sic*] I again saw blue sky and society! I was detained for 10 days however to give evidence. As I knew nothing about a plot, my information must have been highly servic[e]able to the council I fancy. Fortunately I stayed at the consulate at Damascus and spent a very agreeable time. The Feast of Tabernacles took place while I was there and the Consul went to pay visits to his Jewish friends. As the Jewish houses, ladies, dresses, eatables etc. are all famous I was most lucky in seeing the 'tout ensemble' during a festival. The diamonds were gorgeous and together with the dresses and lovely faces nearly extinguished both my eyes, and the sweetmeats threatened utterly to devour my teeth: I cannot give you a more forcible resumé of my morning calls at Damascus! Each house had its tabernacle erected in the court, and all meals are eaten in it while the feast lasts, 10 days altogether.

I returned to Aleppo by way of Baalbec, but only spent one day at that most interesting place. The ruins much exceeded my expectation and the whole mass of building (the temple of the Sun and the temple of Jupiter) with the fine range of the rocky Lebanon red with the noonday glare and heat and thrusting its snowy peaks against the opaque blue sky, formed a picture not easily equalled. It so pleased me that I hope to find my way there again when I return from Tarsus to Damascus—To revert for a moment to the subject of the conspiracy; I have addressed a long protest to the Governour General of Syria and I intend to ad[d]ress another to the Embassy at Constantinople demanding heavy damages for all the annoyance expense and ill treatment to which I have been put. Mr Skene the consul here says I certainly will get them so at least it is worth while trying. I shall drop a line to you to tell you the size of the golden egg which the

Turkish government, after much cackling no doubt, may lay, but I shall not foretell you the size I demand partly for fear of making you envious and partly because it may not be so heavy as I expect. Here at Aleppo I am supremely happy, and draw very diligently: the town is full of Saracenic remains: a great castle with a noble gateway: walls full of delicate details in windows etc: and gateways of Khans which are my favourite subjects because of the crowd and bustle and camels in all sorts of groups and attitudes. The early Christian remains in several deserted cities amongst the hills, dating mostly from the 5th century are well worth visiting because so totally different from any other architecture I have seen: the elaborate and beautiful church at Jebel Simaàn where the huge Pagan altar of rock which served as the base of the Style of S. Simeon Stylites still remains intact under the octagon, is of surpassing interest. Though only two days' journey from beautiful Antioch and classic Daphne it stands in the midst of bare featureless limestone wastes without a tree in sight for miles. To live amongst such a country on the top of a column, must have been the most terrible penance conceivable. I do not think Tennyson's poem can be at all overdrawn.

I find the tobacco pouches are not made at Damascus, but at Constantinople which is world-famous for its needlework: I could not find any at Damascus when there, but if I come across any I will pick them up for you.

I have not told you that amongst the packet of letters I found at Damascus was one from Mr Moore at Jerusalem, saying that he had recovered my revolver from the Jerico thieves!

I am very glad you find your sister even so well as she is: if you fix on Wantage for a home I think you will like the place, there is a splendid ride along the downs to Newbury. I hope also you will come to know the Wroughtons, very pleasant people. Pray give my kind regards to D^r and Mrs Molesworth when you see them or write home. You have a just prejudice I know against lengthy letters and I don't think you ever can get through this torrent of black ink which has flowed from my pen, perhaps you may by skipping and jumping here and there

Your affectionate friend
Lionel B.C.L. Muirhead

P.S. I hear from good authority that no plot has been proved against the prisoners at Damascus, but still they are to be sent to Constantinople.

15: TO ROBERT BRIDGES

H. B.M. Consulate Aleppo
May 12, 1869

My dear Bridges

I saw some time ago in the papers that you were coaching Corpus but the result I missed, as you know one's newspaper reading in Syria is of the most fragmentary sort. Since I last wrote I have been wandering about drawing ruins and mosks but have not got into prison again. Much of the winter I have spent here enjoying myself greatly and a few days ago I returned from an expedition amongst the Druzes of Jebel el Ala who were most hospitable as they always are to Englishmen, to concoct a plan with Mr Skene of going to Palmyra which I do hope may turn out successful this time. All spring there has been fighting between the Arabs and Turks, the most amusing warfare. I will give you one or two little incidents. The military Pasha set out from Aleppo, and another Pasha from Hamah the latter taking a friendly tribe of Arabs to guide him about the desert. The Aleppo troops one day found an Arab camp with no one in it but women and children and flocks and herds and carried off every sheep and goat they could find, amounting to 25,000, and even more, bringing them back to the town. This camp belonged to the Arabs who were with the Hamah troops. Of course a great row was made and the af[f]air went to Constantinople where judicious bribes sent by the Pasha of Aleppo procured the recall of the Pasha of Hamah who was really in the right, and the Arabs of course were never listened to. Again, the Aleppo troops had been out 3 weeks and could not do anything against the Arabs who had sacked between 30 and 40 villages on the desert side when one day they found an Arab lying by the road side very ill and unable to move. Accordingly, they cut off his head, put it on a pole and brought it back in triumph to Aleppo saying it was the head of Jeddān a great chief who is all the time "alive and kicking" miles away. There have been numberless other things quite as good but I am afraid they will not have the interest in England which they have here. Last week I went to a Greek wedding a very elaborate ceremony: the robes of the Bishop and Priests were more gorgeous than I ever saw robes yet, thick with beautiful embroidery of gold and silk and pearls. The whole ceremony from the Bride's leaving her Father's house to the conclusion took 13 hours, so I hope you will applaud my patience in waiting to the end, and I also hope never to have to undergo such a prolonged ordeal. I am afraid you will become impatient for your pipe sticks, however, the box is safely lodged with the Consul at Bayrout and I will send them off at the first visit I pay there.

After Palmyra I wish much to go down to Bagdad if the heat is not too great to see Babylon and to return by Mosul and the Mounds of Nineveh, so you see I have a charming little tour cut out. My last purchase is of a fine Arab mare, really a thoroughbred and very beautiful. Mr Skene says I could not find a better bred mare in Syria. She was taken in war from the Anazeh and sold by auction. She now has a charming little foal, a chestnut colt. I hope they will both do well and reach England somehow.

Please tell me how your reading goes on and what you are doing, and if you have made up your mind to take orders. Has your proposed idea of living at Wantage been put into practice, it sounded very well; at least I hope your sister has found a comfortable home. If you are at Wantage and care to ride over to Hazeley (7 hours I believe) to spend a night my people would be much pleased to see you I am sure. 7 hours will seem a long ride perhaps but out here I did 15 hours the other day over the most detestable rocks too. Remember me to Montagu, Noel and to Hopkins when you write.

and Believe me

Your affectionate friend

Lionel Muirhead

16: TO ROBERT BRIDGES

Orfa
July 5, 1869
July 20, 1869
August 2, 1869

My dear Bridges

I left Aleppo finally I suppose about a fortnight ago and since then have been wandering over the desert among lawless Arabs and uncooth Koords to my great content and I hope their own also. I will give you one specimen of the sort of beings one finds in these camps and of their way of going on. Sheikh Tummor (a great man in his way though little known in England I imagine) was my host at Mumbutch (ancient Hierapolis though few ruins remain) and after I had spent the day with him he escorted me on my way towards the Euphrates, being himself bound for Abougalgal, and I for Kalat en Nedjm an old Saracenic fort on a lofty hill with grand views up and down the Euphrates. On descending into the valley of the stream I found a camp and having travelled all night stopped there and was soon fast asleep. On waking I enquired who the Sheikh was? There were two Tabdichs with me sent by the Pasha and they said the Sheikh a certain Abou Benné was a robber notorious everywhere from Aleppo to Orfa, and altogether a consummate rascal. It was with much relief that I heard he was away from home and was not expected back for some days. I mentally resolved if ever I got away from this precious 'home' it would be a great many days before I found my way back again. The next thing I heard was that a murder had been committed two days before at a camp at Abougalgal a few miles down the river. The victim was none other than the younger brother of Sheikh Tummor who accompanied me last night and who was on his way to avenge his death with 17 of his tribe as the keeping up of a blood feud is a point of honour with the Arabs. It did in no wise mend matters to be told that the murderer was brother in law of the man he had killed, and that he was the young handsome Arab of not more than 19 or 20 years old sitting on my right hand in the tent. He was in hiding, going about from one friendly camp to another to elude search. I thought if I had wished to find a tent throughout the whole desert where I should be likely to lose both my purse and my life I could not have selected a more likely one than that in which I was staying. However I trusted to my general appearance which presented little to attract the eye, to escape molestation; my grey coat being scorched into tints of yellow-ochre and my bedford cords which once presented a rich creamlike surface being worn into holes and generally ragged. Your invaluable money belt outside looks as though it were in its dotage, though within it perpetually renews a golden youth.—One of my Tabdichs was a Nubian who had come over with Ibrahim Pasha when he conquered Syria and has never returned like many other Egyptians whom one finds domesticated in the different villages. I am bound to say he did not present a warlike appearance, and it was perhaps fortunate that my travelling was all done by night when if evil folks met us on the road, his flat nose, thick lips, and unsoldierlike mien might pass without notice and criticism. He came to me one day when I was going to leave a camp to say that I must start at 2 P.M. at least, as the road lay along the river bank for several miles and they said there were lions on the way! I steadily refused to set out till 4 P.M. as during the heat if one rides in the sun fever is the inevitable result. I need scarcely add that the Lion must have been horribly frightened at the aspect of the black man, as he took care not to come near us: they probably regarded each other mutually as the "bête noir." Just as twilight was fading into starlight that same evening we came on a long stretch of shining river watering a rich little plain and low broken bluffs of rock for boundary, and 3 glorious white swans came sailing noiselessly down the bright grey rapids. My gun was in its case, but they looked so stately and beautiful that I don't think I could have fired if it had been with me. The Nubian Cawars hallooed horribly (perhaps thinking these were the Lions!) but they took no notice of his barbarous noises and floated away into the dim shadows behind us. As for Lions on the Euphrates they are undoubtedly to be met with, but I think lower down the stream only: a year or two ago two Arabs were riding along the desert near the river (one of them being a celebrated warrior Batràn) when they spied a Lion and tried to kill him with their spears: they managed only to wound him and the beast turned to spring. They evaded him and gallopped [*sic*] away on their fleet mares as fast as possible. The Lion followed for some time but at length they lost sight of him and night coming on they lay down to sleep. Shortly after this the Lion sprang on Batràn with a roar and tore him to pieces: the other Arab escaping. He had followed them doggedly all the time. The morning that I arrived at Birijik I saw a splendid flight of 41 fine wild geese who rose from the beds of sedge by the river, and plenty of noise they made, but I recollected the little result our wild-goose chases at Edfoo had, and did not attempt to go after them. Birijik is a picturesque little place in awful ruin as every town out here is, with broken towers of a fine old castle of the 12th century perched on a steep rock overhanging the stream and solid ramparts round the town. I had several amusing little incidents there but I shall weary you if I spin endless yarns, and so reserve them for my journal which I keep diligently. I believe that the art of journal keeping like everything else improves with practise, not that I intend to cast a slur on our youthful attempts in Egypt!

I dont know whether I told you that I am stamped for life as having been in the East by two great Aleppo buttons on my right hand and one on my arm. They are a sort of boil which natives have almost invariably on the face and are often fearfully scarred in consequence. Europeans generally have it on the arm or hand. It is a boil peculiar to Aleppo, Orfa, Mosul and Bagdad, at the two latter places it is very bad, sometimes as many as 300 breaking out at a time I hear. I really think Job must have had Aleppo buttons! Ill-luck to them they have come on my right hand and are painful enough, having already lasted 6 months and having according to popular tradition 6 months more to run their course. The hand is accordingly swathed up like a mummy, and it is awkward enough to have to present this great white paw to a Pasha, when as is often the case he insists on shaking hands to show his great civilization and familiarity with European manners and usages.

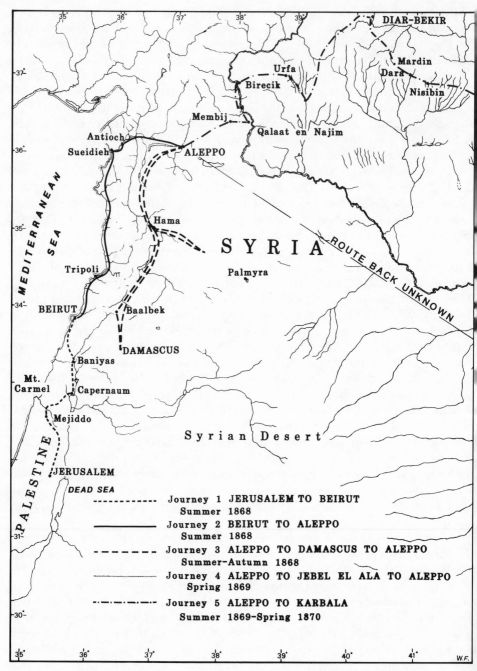

The travels of Lionel Muirhead in the Near East, 1868–70. Map by Will Fournerat.

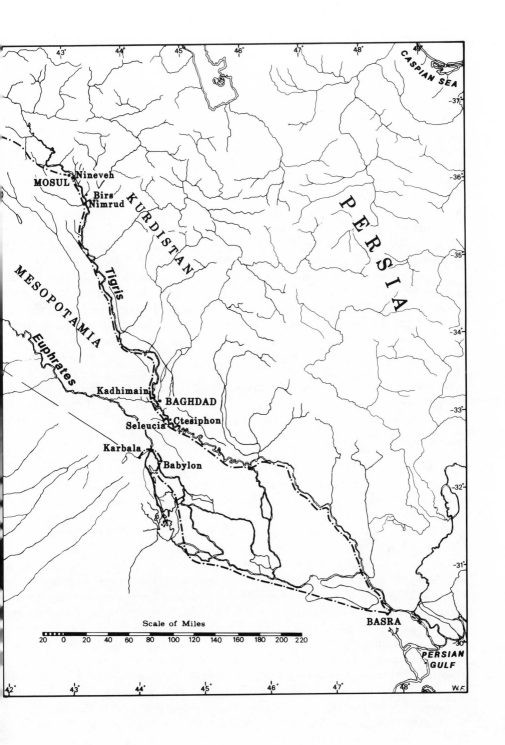

CASPIAN SEA

PERSIA

MOSUL Nineveh

Birs
Nimrud

KURDISTAN

Tigris

MESOPOTAMIA

Euphrates

Kadhimain

BAGHDAD

Seleucia Ctesiphon

Karbala

Babylon

BASRA

PERSIAN
GULF

Scale of Miles

20 0   20 40 60 80 100 120 140 160 180 200 220

W.F.

Orfa a city round which as Ur of the Chaldees and principally as Edessa cluster innumerable interesting facts in history ought to be a very pretty place. It is charmingly built on rising ground just where bare hills of red and purple rock slope into a rich plain of gardens vineyards and corn fields, which stretches miles away and is lost in glowing Suns Light. It is still surrounded by walls of massive stone partly of Christian partly of Saracenic work and a picturesque castle stands high up on a steep rock at whose base issues the lovely stream in which are preserved the sacred fish. They are ugly beasts, dark grey and of much the same sort as the sacred fish at Tripoli and elsewhere and owe their good fortune in being petted and fed without ever being fed-on to the lucky accident of the Patriarch Abraham having been born here. Many a more queenly trout and kingly salmon in the highlands of Scotland has cause to regret that the untoward accidents of birth and place have lost them the favour of the great Patriarch. These preserves of sacred fish are interesting in their way, because Derceto the mother of Semiramis drowned herself in the sea, and was fabled to have become a fish under which form she was worshiped as the principal Goddess of the ancient Syrians.—Probably fish were kept sacred in her honour at different places and out in this conservative East they have preserved their sacred character through Roman, Christian and Mussulman times long after the religion which sanctified them has perished. (N.B. *This does not come out of the guide book!*) The castle is in lamentable ruin and a single decrepid old man now keeps the key of the gate the possession of which has caused such torrents of blood-shed from time to time. Finally Orfa is really pretty from a distance but when one is inside the walls everything is in such a state of mess, ruin and general chaos that no stretch of imagination suffices to picture it as the beautiful city it must have been.

July 20th 1869

Your letter from Dresden turned up this morning covered with German post-marks which are refreshing in this sultry atmosphere. I am truly sorry it contains so much bad news, at least you have done your best not to give way to melancholy thoughts by going to Germany and studying the uncooth but fine language. I shall feel horribly afraid of you when you are perfect in German grammar, as hitherto I have regarded it with distant awe. You ought to come back tolerably perfect after so long a series of lessons, and I envy you the power of reading Goethe in the original. I am now going to tell you of my recent triumphs in the way of art. The Pasha here (who is a Mutasĕrif and a great man) hearing I was a draughtsman sent for me and begged I would do his portrait. I evaded the unpleasant necessity by saying I never had done such a thing, and if I had it would be impossible for me to do justice to a head like His Excellency's! This outrageous compliment (which I think however had a true oriental flavour about it) slipped off my tongue and down his Excellency's throat like melted butter, but he still insisted and begged so hard that I gave in. A few days after I went on a reception Friday and told him I had brought pencil and paper. He instantly cut short all his receptions, and sent for his black slaves who brought his uniform and decorations and got him up regardless of expense. He was then made to sit on a hard bottomed straight backed chair, with his legs on either side to represent sitting on horseback, that being the position he wished me to take him in. I kept him in this comfortable posture for an hour and a half during which I think his great wish for a portrait considerably cooled down, but he kept up his fainting spirits by smoking about half a dozen chibooks and drinking hard at iced sherbet and cups of coffee. Finally he sent me his most beautiful black Arab mare a very fine and lovely animal, whom I drew with far greater interest than her master. The saddle was a magnificent piece of Stamboul art and taste, being of magenta velvet and so bespangled with silver lace and ornaments that it almost dazzled the Sun to shine on it. After some days I produced my picture which I really think was a good piece of drawing: the likeness of the Pasha was good (you must know I have been working hard at heads) and the mare I think faultless. The Pasha was enchanted with the production and purred over it as he sat cross-legged on his divan, and had he possessed a tail I dont think it would ever have done wagging. He begged me to do a copy of it which also I finished and sent him. The same afternoon to my great astonishment and delight he sent me a beautiful purely bred Arab horse, 2½ years old and of a fine chestnut. He has a lovely outline of head and nostril, a tail well set on, and a famous pair of strong knees. Of course he is too young to ride except very gently at present, but he carries himself superbly and yesterday when I rode him to the great pool of Abd-er-Rahman to bathe he was much admired. He came a short time ago from the Shammar tribe. I think I shall send him off to England directly as it is useless dragging him all round by Bagdad. It seems to me that when all other trades fail I must take to drawing Pashas as the most profitable thing to do. If you had been here and he had heard that you were a poet (I am thinking of the Ode about the cigarette!) who knows but you might have had to extol His Excellency in metre, and have come in for a like share of good fortune.—Talking of cigarettes you must know that I think my thumb and fingers must have got new joints as they twist cigarettes beautifully; they are of this 𝑔 form and I am thinking of advertising them as the only genuine Malakof cigarette. (Malakof being French for crinoline as perhaps you know).

Aug 2. 69

I have just come back from a tour amongst the villages where there was precious little to see in the way of ruins and a great deal less to eat. Boorgool and Lebben and Lebben and Boorgool may serve as a formula to express the variety or monotony of my meals. I have been trying to pick up a little Turkish as in this land Turkish Armenian and Koordish are the only languages spoken and Arabic is not understood much, least of all my Arabic (though my vocabulary consists of 317 words.) 'Pechi' all right: 'Bir az dahav' wait a little: 'Bakallum' I will see about it and 'Saura' afterwards are my invariable Turkish answers to all questions which I don't understand, and mean politely that I dont intend to stop smoking or otherwise trouble my head about mundane matters till dinner time arrives. In Armenian I did pick up two words but regret to say that I dropped them both on the road back to Orfa and fear they are irrevocably lost. In Koordish I have got only one word by heart for certain which accordingly I fondly pet and cherish as my solitary ewe lamb, and the more so as I don't much think I shall ever have any more ewe lambs. Now I have come back I am rejoicing in a careless ease and the luxury of doing nothing and having nothing to do. I eat lots of grapes and plums and figs all of which are now plentiful in the market here. At midday I cling like a bat to the cushions of the divan in the darkest corner of my room and smoke perpetual narjiles and casual cigarettes. It amuses me to think of our first infant attempts at smoking narjiles in Egypt, I often smoke 5 and 6 and at Aleppo one day when I paid many visits I smoked 10.—Dont lecture me on this vice because you know you taught me!

You ask about "my domestic affairs" as though I were going to wed, which I certainly am not just yet. My Navy brother who got into the Britannia first place, came out second and is now a middy on board the Royal Oak cruising about the Mediterranean: he came in for the gayities of part of the Prince of Wales' tour in the East. My second brother who left Eton some little while ago took 6th into Woolwich and both he and The Minor have gone together on a hunting expedition in Sweden and Norway. As they are both great Nimrods and quite delighted to walk all day after game in the hottest days of September or the bitter cold days of December, I think they will enjoy themselves after a barbarous and uncultivated manner in the north. I should like to see them carrying home two bears, I think that would cool their ardour: I should only wish to look on and by no means to help. My Father and Mother and Sisters are all on a tour and round of visits in Scotland, so that Haseley must be quite deserted.

I have no longer Mohammed with me: I sent him back to Egypt at the beginning of the year: his honesty was not first class as he several times tried dodges which I found out but I gave him a fair character saying he was attentive and that he required looking after in the matter of accounts though not more so than any one else to be found in the East which I believe to be true. My present servant is an excellent fellow as far as I can discover from 4 months trial and talks French capitally, much better than M's English. I think he must be good as a German savant who has been routing out antiquities, etc. etc. in Persia during two years kept him all that time. My expenses are most moderate; horses are much cheaper up here than in Palestine: Beyrout being the dearest place of all.—Now that I have two riding horses of my own (besides my mare and the Pasha's horse whom I am sending to England tomorrow) I hire only two baggage horses and a muleteer at 30 Ps. a day (not 6/) My feeding comes to 5/ a day at the very outside. My servant wages are 360 Ps. a month about 2/a day. Corn for my horses costs about 2½^{d} a day each, and then there are incidental expenses such as horse clothes and halters and pots and pans. But since I left Aleppo my average per day has been 13/ exclusive of purchases but including two Tabdiches at 2/ a day each as a guard and if I chose I could decrease this but as long as I keep about £ a day I dont care.

Believe me My dear Bridges

Ever your affectionate friend

Lionel Muirhead.

Please remember me most kindly to Knight and to Hopkins. I much regret he is a Jesuit as I feel little love for "the Company—"

P.S. I intend D. V. to be at Constantinople next April or May: the intermediate time I shall spend somehow: Much of it I expect will be taken up in writing another letter to you!

17: TO ROBERT BRIDGES

British Consulate
Aleppo
April 18, 1870

My dear Bridges

Be not startled at the blushing complexion of this note paper; I have by me various hues—yellow, blue, green, etc. all of which I discarded for different reasons, choosing this instead so that some of the 'couleur de rose' which has pervaded the seven months since I last wrote to you, might be shed over the terse account I am going to give you of my doings—

I wrote to you from Orfa a sort of chronicle, which I daresay you looked on as a government despatch, but perhaps it amused me to write it more than you to read it: it certainly was of unpardonable length and I could not even plead Dr. Johnson's excuse (which perhaps you have heard from me before) that he used to write a long letter whenever he had not time to write a short one. Soon after its despatch I went to Harran and visited some old places near Orfa which look today as though they had long ago forgotten the Patriarch Abraham, and even the more modern 'Crusades' which just reached up to and included in this piece of country, and then I crossed over the high stony land to Diar-bekir. Here I found myself in the midst of the Armenians a people who have much selfishness, some wealth no principles (unless cunning you call a principle) and the longest ungainliest noses you ever chanced to see. They have as bad a name in the towns out here for rascality as the Greeks, though perhaps they are less obnoxious in other ways, being in no wise troubled with 'amour propre' while the Greeks are full of inordinate conceit and snappishness. As for the town of Diar bekir I think it must be unique in its way; it is wholly built of black basalt, and the walls being very high, old, and massive have a most sombre appearance as you ride towards them over the sunny plain: the race of pariah dogs in the streets is black: the scorpions (for which the city is more infamous than any other out here) crawl about the houses everywhere, and are black also, and lastly an Arabic proverb has it that the hearts of all the inhabitants are black. Please don't draw the conclusion that I left the place a nigger, because I must claim the same privilege as the Ethiopian in the matter of not changing my skin. I am not going to rave about the old Greek architecture of the splendid building now used as a Great Mosk because I have some of that down in colours, which I hope you will consider the next best thing to 'black and white', but the portraits of old Saracenic towers along the walls also grace my folio. It was a glorious sight—the autumn afternoons to wander along the slopes on the east of the city built on a solid plateau of rock and watch the clear beautiful Tigris flow through the rich gardens, while the ragged chain of Mt. Taurus fringed the Northern horizon. I should weary you if I were to drag you down the long journey to Baghdad, though there are lots of interesting places on the way, Dara, Nisibin, Mardin and Moosul with the famous Mounds of Niniveh opposite. From Moosul I floated down on a "Kelek" to Baghdad and had great fun on the way down. Two young Mussulman merchants were on the kelek with me and during the 8 days I was on the river I seldom found time hang heavy on my hands. I had the queerest little hut on the raft and at night fall we used to halt and light huge bonfires to keep off wild boars of which there are a great number in the tamarisk underwood which lines the river bank. Old sites of Ninivite cities met us at every turn and one place (the mounds of Nimrood) proved vastly interesting. A great number of the sculptured slabs remain unremoved from their original position and even where they have been carried off the forms and size of the chambers are distinctly trac[e]able—floating down the broad Tigris into Baghdad at Sunrise was one of the most fairy-like scenes I have met with out here, the slender minarets and fine domes rising amongst the waving Palm gardens with which the city is girt, and so calm was the water that all was reflected on its shining surface. The long bridge of boats which crosses the river, just served to connect the two sides of the city, for some portion of it stands on the right bank, and formed the whole into a lovely picture of the East. I stayed 6 or 7 weeks in Baghdad sketching Mosks and bazaars and coffee-houses, and orange gardens and seldom enjoyed myself more thoroughly. There are many Englishmen there and pig-sticking is in great vogue. I went out thrice: twice into the desert amongst marshes and forests of reeds on an average 10 or 12 feet high, and once during a whole week at Seleucia, the site of an old Greek city of that name. —We killed 5 boars and a sow. I fear I only managed to stick one boar and then I was not first spear, but it requires a little practice to use one's spear properly, and the first time I went out I did not take one. But it would be difficult to imagine jollier hunting expeditions than we had, and I am bringing back some fine boar's tusks. I also spent 10 days at Ctesiphon where there are ruins of the famous palace of Chosroes, taken by the Arabian Caliph Omar, and which is of astonishing interest architecturally, as containing (possibly) the first specimens of a pointed arch known. There was plenty of shooting there and glorious ground for riding. Bassorah [Basra] (where I spent 3 days) is a wretched place, but the creek running 2 miles or more from the river to the town is like a scene that you might expect to see in a theatre, such magnificent gardens on either side Palm, orange, pomegranate and Plantain tree hanging over the water while lovely kingfishers and a bright blue jay dart and gleam in the Sunlight. —Of course I went to Babylon and the wonderful Birs Nimrood with its astonishing store of Babylonian bricks, and such bricks too, far more compact in texture than many kinds of stone. —I picked up several fragments with inscriptions on them, but without excavating it was impossible to find a perfect one, and eventually I obtained two or three perfect specimens from a man at Baghdad of the genus 'Antiquary'. I went also to Kerbela where is the famous Persian shrine at the tomb of Hassan, and whither every Sheik who is able gives directions that his body shall be sent for burial after his death. The whole place in consequence is a vast graveyard and besides is surrounded with swamps so that it is notoriously unhealthy. The great mosk is one blaze of enameled Persian tiles from basement to cornice and supports a grand dome covered with gold. The Minarets are also covered with gorgeous tiles and gold, and the effect of the whole building under the deep blue sky is beyond description magnificent. There is another mosk of the same kind at Khazemun with two gold domes and four minarets. You who remember how delighted I was with the few tiles I saw in the mosks in Egypt may imagine how I reveled in this wealth. I am happy to add that I escaped any 'Balylonish Captivity'. I am now on my way to Constantinople by Smyrna, thence I hope to go to Mt Athos, Athens, Corinth and Corfu. My Father, Mother and Sisters are travelling for 3 months in Italy and want me to meet them at Venice about the middle of June, but I don't see much prospect of my being able to do so: I shall probably arrive in England in July not much later than they will. —And now after all this egoism I should much like to know what you are doing. You gave one or two mysterious hints in your letter from Dresden, and said you would have engagements for 2 or 3 years from last October, but you never told me if you had made up your mind to take orders or not. So how to address you I don't know and shall therefore stick to 'Esqre': if you are Reverend, why I shall be irreverent: but only for once in a way. You must wonder when that Egyptian box is going to be sent to you; nay, don't chide me any more because I have just sent it off, having painted my Father's address in great letters on it and I hope it will go safe. I did not open it. Write to Haseley how's yourself and where's yourself, and put on the letter 'to await my arrival', otherwise I shall never get it, and Believe me my dear Bridges

Ever your affectionate friend
Lionel B. C. L. M.

18: TO LIONEL MUIRHEAD

35 Great Ormond Street,
W. C.
June 24, 1870

My dear Muirhead

Your last letter dated Aleppo, April 18, reached me early in May, and I beg that you will observe that my paper's as good a colour as yours was. The chief objection to your letter was that it was no use answering it, as you were not to be at home for so long, and now I am almost afraid that you will have reached Hazeley before this gets there, for when once people begin to travel home speed increases about in inverse proportion to the square of the distance: observation on myself induces me to believe that I follow the law of the cube of the distance.

Well thank you very much for your letters, which being much more than I deserved did more than amuse me. I have to the best of my ability followed you in the spirit, but look forward still to having long descriptions, and many vive voce entertainments. You also will have a good deal to learn about your mother country, (and if your father is a conservative, and is your first informant you will think that we have all been going to the bad) and I can tell you a good deal of my personal history, which I hope may still interest you. I am not parson as you thought, but must protest that I thought I had told you that I had taken to medicine. —I can't honestly boast of having written very regularly or very frequently to you, but it is possible that a document containing information to this effect miscarried. I am pretty permanently settled here, and doing my professional study at S Bartholomew's Hospital. You will be bound to come to London soon after your arrival, and I can put you up in this house, if you will accept the offer of my 3rd room, but I am afraid that if, as I intend, I go abroad in the 1st week in August, and you do not return home till the end of July, we may miss each other till October. However please remember that I am most anxious to see you, and that I am really going out of England for 2 months beginning from the 1st week in August, and that I shall be definitely tied here till that time.

I am ashamed to close this letter with a request, but I am rather in want of the portfolio which you kindly took charge of for me at Hazeley—it is a good big one, has 2 lithographs of the cherubs in the Madonna di San Visto and one or 2 other prints for a schoolroom which never journeyed to their destination. This you might bring up to London if you come, or send it here by carrier—all times before October are alike to me.

Your letters made me wish very much that I was out with you, sharing the delights of that idle strange life, and that perfect sky. One never enjoys a drink of water in England as one can hourly in the East. I shall hope to see you very soon, and see you well. With very kind regards to your Father and Mother believe me ever your affectionate friend,

Robert Bridges

19: TO ROBERT BRIDGES

Haseley Court
Tetsworth
July 21, 1870

My dear Bridges

Here I am at home after my manifold wanderings, having just slipped by through Prussia before the railways were taken by the Government to convey the troops to the frontier. Half of my luggage and amongst it my box with all my sketches from Palmyra, has gone missing either at Darmstadt or Cologne and such was the confusion of peoples luggage and ideas in that region when I passed that I have little prospect of getting it back.

You will be happy to hear that the long box from Egypt has arrived and ought to be at Haseley this week: as soon as I can I will send on to you all your valuables carefully packed: I am anxious to see the box opened to find how ostrich-feathers and specimens of fossil wood from Cairo have managed to agree during so long a time, and I will report to you forthwith. I daresay you will send me the little box of Bethlehem ware which was so nearly lost on your memorable voyage home, if you have it by you. Please address it to me here

Haseley Court.
Oxford.

To be forwarded thence per
Wise Carrier

You must write me a line about yourself, and in a few days I will send you a longer letter having just now to drive into Oxford.

Ever your affectionate friend
Lionel Muirhead

20: TO LIONEL MUIRHEAD

35 Great Ormond Street,
W. C.
[July 26, 1870]

My dear Muirhead

Welcome to what I hope one may dare to call terra firma. I got your letter a few minutes ago—mine does not seem to have impressed you with the idea that I am really a permanency in London, and as you do not in any way refer to my new profession it is just possible that you have not yet come into possession of a letter which should have awaited you at Haseley.

Any how I grieve deeply for the loss—I hope only temporary—of your sketches—but one must expect them to turn up as I remember another portfolio of yours was supposed to be doing some time ago, which you had also left to travel in Germany on its own account—I am not exciting myself about the few possessions I have in the little long box which has been so thoroughly seasoned since I last saw it. I shall enjoy a cool pipe however if this weather lasts—you must find it almost as hot in England as the temperature you have accustomed your-self to—.

About your box of things—not knowing you were returning home when last I was at Rochdale I did not bring it up to London—it is tied up at home with some books of yours. No one is at home just now but my mother returns this week and shall have direction to send it to you in a hamper.

And now—in case you have not got my letter—I must tell you that I am reading medicine in London, living at the above address.

item 2. that I am going to France next week—Deo et mortalitas V-ibus and shall not return till October—when my term begins.

item 3. that it would give me indescribable delight, pleasure, vitality, amuse-ment, satisfaction, honour (I forget that you are accustomed to Oriental peri-phrastic compliment which I cannot attempt to vie with) if you will condescend to beam upon me with the refulgent rays of the too much removed sun of your shining presence through the foggy clouds of the sulphurous exhalations of this carbonicoxidised metropolis. —Seriously I am writing in a hurry and if you would come down for a day even to town this week or the few first days of next week—Sunday or any other day, I can put you up in my diggings, and make you comfortable I think. I know that you will be fast bound at home, but really it will not take you many hours, and you *must* want to do some London shopping soon, and I shall be away after next week—besides the National Gallery has been so very much and worthily replenished since you last saw it. Think of an express train up in the afternoon, a comfortable supper, chat—late retirement, proper and suitable breakfast, necessary shopping, luxurious and well adjusted express—dinner again at home.—

This programme is too artistic not to touch you—to move you—Yield yourself and come.

Yours ever

RB

Tuesday evening

21: TO LIONEL MUIRHEAD

35 Great Ormond Street
W. C.
January 30, 1871

Unto Abracadabra, the much travelled and magnificent, the perspicuous and perspective. In the name of the prophet and of all his followers from Aboo Behir the son of his mother, to Mohamed Salem the son of Salem. Greetings.

Considering the perpetual combustion and flux of all things let no change or revolution of the material, or of the mental which is in no little dependence thereon, ever awake to admiration or astonishment the mind of him who still commands a mutton chop for his breakfast and joint and potatoes for dinner. But the spirit of wonder has touched with her caustic rod the diseased and inflammable mind of the writer.

With much more deferential greeting and in the name of the prophet he would therefore suggest to the aforesaid muchtobebeéepitheted Abracadabra esquire that the following questions arising in the light of his mind lead to the inextricable labyrinth of the shadow of darkness

(1) Where *is* Abracadabra?

(2) Has he visited the exhibition of old Masters?

(3) If he has not done so, does he know how good it is?

(4) If he has done so is he still in London?

(5) Is it possible that he should be in London and not have called on Mrs. Crowhurst?

(6) Has he given up his plan of being in town this spring?

(7) or has he put off his visit?

(8) or is he involuntarily confined to the house?

(9) or has he wounded his right hand?

(10) Can he have come to London and taken any temporary lodging other than in the house of Crowhurst?

Let the blessings of health always pacify the stomach and mind of A.B.C.! and may his diligent pen guided by the light of truth convey the eyes of the humble writer to the spark of knowledge in the Pharos of hope-!!

———

Should doubts concerning the sanity of the writer arise in the soul of the addressed let him take the wings of a vehicle and hasten to the relief of the imbecile.

Who is only at home in the evenings.

RB

22: TO LIONEL MUIRHEAD

7. Fort Parragon, Margate
[February 22, 1871]

My dear Muirhead

Thanks for your card—and for your visit to Turner—I did not expect that he would accept my invitation down here. —I am not so miserable as you painted—the weather is lovely, and I don't find Margate at all bad. At any rate it is clean. — I paid my first visit to Mr Mason's, since your departure, this morning and procured a shoulder of mutton, which I attacked this evening. I have read Robertson's Charles V, am rather disappointed with Robertson, but much more with Charles. He appears to me a fit father to Philip. On the whole though I am pleased with the book. My literature being rather solid I sent down to the landlady to ask her if she could lend me any books. There turned up a motley group. Burns' works in 2 vols. Dr Cummings' great tribulation. A book of wonders of nature and art from the last century, containing full accounts of sea serpents, domesticated robins, murderers, and crimes etc. together (of course) with a full account of the Lyttelton Ghost—then a novel called 'The Jesuit,' and Southey's Curse of Kehama. —I daresay that good Mrs Saunders looks on this assorted variety with as much satisfaction and pleasure as I own I sometimes feel in regarding a shelf in my own room, whereon worthier authors present as detached an apparition as this teatray of—(Burns saves them from an epithet-). — Really I think that Dr Cummings has some eloquence. —On dipping into his book I don't wonder at all at his popularity, and I am convinced more and more that the one thing which must be taught before all others in religious education is the right estimation of the "letter"—without the implicit faith which people have in the text of the Bible, and its inspired authority no such nonsense as this of Cummings' would be possible.

I would write you a good letter had I a good pen, but there is no quill in the house, and I cannot do anything legible with this, so that I feel you will be glad when I leave off. I am much better, and will tomorrow send you a xxx. Wait till it comes.*

If it would suit you to come down at the end of this week send me a line. I shall not get to town till next week. —This I fancy is Ash Wednesday.

I am your affectionate friend

Robert Bridges

Ash Wednesday/   71

*Not a shoulder of mutton. No, nor a chili.

23: TO LIONEL MUIRHEAD

Marlow
[April 15, 1871]

My dear Abracadabr*a* (R.A.)

I meant to have written to you before, but have nothing to send you in the way of intelligence but a flourishing account of my health. I spend my days as days are spent in the country—rowing, archery—walking and lunching and loitering and feel much the better for the change of habit.

I have many more indefinite relatives here than it is possible for the most sanguine man ever either to desire or to deserve—and their friendliness is equally beyond and above the merit and expectation of so ornary a mortal as i. which will come back to town a new man near the end of this month. Complete idleness is the root of all energy. Rest is embryonic activity. Sleep is the ovarian unconsciousness of the chick thought. Taman taosher! What wisdom underlies these simple expressions.

I hope you are quite well. If so be will you please go to my rooms, extract the onevolumed calf bound Lyell's elements of geology and pack it up carefully in a little box which Tilly must find for you, and send it by parcel delivery prepaid— instruct Tilly—to RSB. Care of Owen Peel Wethered Esq:

Marlow

if you are so good I will write to you again. Meanwhile am ever yours affection- ately

RB
Saturday afternoon Easter/71

24: TO LIONEL MUIRHEAD

St. Bartholomews Hospital
E. C.
[July 18, 1871]

My dear Levional

I ran down on Friday morning to Seaford for 3 days at the seaside. If the weather had been fine I should have paid a visit to some of my friends in the country, but I thought that it would end in being confined to the house, so I went where a preponderance of water is normal. The first day I had a splendid sail, and got drenched with salt water. The second day I walked 25 miles and got wet to the skin with aerial showers. The third day, today, I lay and basked in the sun on the beach: and I came home by the evening train—

You are too cosmopolitan in your taste—it is a consolation to me that if you like sour crout (or Kraut) you like pyramids of Turkish rice also. I take vinegar with my cabbage, and think the red pickled sort excellent, but metaphorically at least, roast beef is better than any kind of cabbage; and a German cookery book is an abomination. My ode is extremely rough and illiterate, but I think I can make something of the notion.

I think a Norwegian brigantine is the finest looking vessel built now a days.

My friends at Seaford are very well. The head boatman has taken (I heard) to drink. A friend of Bismarck's has been staying down there. (The Germans are indeed everywhere—) he must have been a queer fellow for he was 6 f^t 6 in. high, and had a hole in his head where he had been trepanned, over which he wore a silver plate—He was paralyzed in one arm from the accident, and was engaged to be married to the daughter of the German chancellor. He was studying all the sciences and 7 languages at once, and worked everyday from 9 in the morning till 4 the next morning. He had been to 6 universities—A Russian letter that was sent after him had been to Prussia, Austria, Italy, Holland (Scheveningen) and Paris before it got to Seaford—and then Mr ——— was in London. Now he is at Orleans—

If there was only one German in the world it would be difficult to avoid him.

I am yours ever
R. Bridges

25: TO WILLIAM SANDAY

50 Maddox Street,
Hanover Square West
[April 28, 1872]

My dear Sanday

I have this day, Sunday, April 28, 1872, read your book through from beginning to end, bar one chapter that appeared to me to contain little but references. It came to me some 10 days ago, but as I intended to read it—you will remember that I promised to do so—I thought it more graceful to defer my thanks, which I now take the opportunity of expressing, till I could tell you also what I think of your work.

I do not I hope do wrong in taking for granted that you will care to hear what I think of it, and therefore (if I can avoid putting my sentiments in the form of a review I will) I shall proceed to give you my solemn judgement on the matter.

First of all, I think your style very good, and I wished very much that you had oftener found occasion to launch forth (as you did in one passage about in the 2nd ¼ of the Book) into something more general than the line of your criticism involved.—An excellent piece of English that—

Secondly. Your book doesn't quite convince me, but I think it very strong—the first half of it especially. You seem to take for granted the first part in the second, and suppose that the conviction established will carry readers over obstacles in the 2nd part. That I don't quite like.—I think you attach too much importance to *ordinary* minutiae in making them evidence. Try any 6 lines of Homer*. I think your treatment of the long Johannean discourses very good, and your method of making the Synoptists contradict themselves in the matter of the day of the Last Supper and Crucifixion has my sincere admiration. (Is that original?) Also you are very good in your expression of the opinion that the Synoptists contain a great deal of the doctrine supposed to be peculiar to Saint John. I think you always make your points exceedingly plain and are incapable of misinterpretation. I hope and expect that your next work will be less of a summary and that it may be translated into German to the utter confutation and extinguishment of all people who have such horrible names as Bauer, Weisächer & Co.—

I long for the pleasure of seeing you in town. I shall be up for about 3 weeks longer, when I intend taking a month's holiday in the country. I write now in haste, and thanking you very much for your book, which it gave me great pleasure to read, (especially as I recognized your capacity for writing English which at Dresden you used to be non-confident in) and apologising for whatever may seem uncourteous or stupid in my remarks.

Am yours ever
R. Bridges

*he seems to me a better example than De Foe.

26: TO LIONEL MUIRHEAD

Green Bank Cottage
Liverpool
Monday morning [January 1874]

My dear Lionel

I have just sent you off a telegram. This letter is to give you further explanations.—It seems that Wooldridge cannot get off till the 3rd week in January, and though I am very sorry indeed about it I think that I cannot put off my own starting any longer. So in accordance with what I told you in London I propose making tracks. I shall go up to town by the night train this evening after a dinner party here and shall breakfast with Wooldridge in town and tell him my plans, (Tuesday morning) and arrange for him to follow. Then I shall go on to Marlow in the evening and you can come over either on Wednesday or Thursday (Wednesday for choice) and arrange with me.

Then on Thursday evening I go back to town and breakfast with all the party—Wooldridge included—who are concerned in our trip. (I will give you the address of the breakfast room).—You are specially invited. I shall spend Friday in final preparations and shall start off on Saturday morning for Paris.—This is a list of the party.

> Philip H. Rathbone Esq.
> Mrs. Rathbone
> Miss Rathbone
> Miss Müller (her friend)
> Lionel Muirhead Esq.
> R.S.B.

a
maid
NOT a German

[You will like these people *very much*] and our plan is train from Paris to Nice on Sunday night getting to Nice on Monday night. Then start by carriage from Nice to Genoa. And take the train again at Genoa.

The advantages of this scheme will be very apparent if you study them and I beg of you to be ready in time, for I wish (in the absence of H.E.W.) to travel down with the Rathbones very much—as they too seem to wish it—and I shall not do so if *you* are not able to come, but shall defer again and come with you and H. E. W. This is a postponement that would be very awkward for me, as I have no place to sleep at in London—unless I ask the Monroes to put me up—and the postponement I cannot but think would be indefinite.

—Come over by train to Marlow on Wednesday—and talk it over.—If you can't come then a letter directed to me at Owen Wethered's telling me you will be in London on Thursday evening will be sufficient—in haste

yours affectionately
Robert Bridges

My kind regards to your Father and Mother and Sisters. I am sorry I cannot accept their invitation this time.

RB

27: TO LIONEL MUIRHEAD

50 Maddox Street,
London W.
June 19, 1874

My dear Levional

(If I may approach thy mysterious entity with a conventional endearment) I hope you are quite well. I write to tell you that I am coming North tomorrow, so that if you are in the neighbourhood of Rochdale you can pay me a visit. There will be very good cricket and that will be my amusement: I am afraid it will not be the same attraction to you, but you can read Dr. Molesworth's manuscript sermons if you like when I am playing. He is an eminent divine—the sermons are not very interesting but on the other hand they are nearly illegible so that they wouldn't bore you much. Wooldridge and I are very comfortable here. He amused me by telling me what your people are reported to have thought of your second style. I liked his sketch of Ravenna pine woods very much indeed. I wish he had done other good sketches, and today I saw some new plan of his at Powells, first class—big figures of saints with a plain dark back ground. I should have admired them at Arezzo, even at Arezzo. I wish I had been to Vallombrosa: but it was quite time I came home when I did. I was thoroughly tired of seeing things I had never seen before. By the way I have finished up Wooldridge's sonnett, taking advantage of your suggestions. I will send it to you. Here it is.

> This man if he be lost is quickly found
> By qualities not common to the many.
> Yet would he blush if I should mention any
> Though he is thirty, bald, and somewhat round.
>   On what he covets he will spend a pound,
> Rather than haggle much to save a penny.
> He would climb mountains easily, but when he
> Gets half up he returns to level ground.
>   Playing the game he does not understand.
> To take the small card of his adversary
> I've seen him play his right bower second hand:
>   So little is he versatile or wary:
> His mind is fixed and stable as the land,
> Which God has set so that it shall not vary.

Show this to Rathbone. I see you walked off with your Florentine books. My Boccaccio is certainly a forgery, an Italian one, but still a good book. I find the edition was also reprinted in London, in French type with a facsimile title. It is a sell, but the book is worth nearly what I gave for it in the English market.—You left Guisti behind—It would be great fun to find you in the North country express tomorrow, but I don't expect to.—Remember me very kindly to all the Rathbones, please, and thank R for his letter. I am very much hurt at his not taking any notice of my sonnett on you, which I sent him. I think he considers you too sacred a person to be treated in so strange a manner. I have taken down from my walls your picture of Friebourg, or Freibourg or Freiberg or Frieberg— and elevated the Nile. Meredith Brown suggested the other day that the latter would do as well upside down. I saw Stainer today. He is very well. I miss a private music evening at his house next week, with string quartett etc. by coming north, a great bore.

    I wish that Wooldridge hadn't worn out this pen by writing music, but he has, and I fear my writing is illegible. It doesn't much matter. W. sends his kindest remembrances to the Rathbones, and hopes that when he finds time to pay his promised visit to Manchester he may come on and make them a visit, *and please ask R from me if he will make arrangements for me to see the collection of Rosetti's pictures in Liverpool* if I may come and see him in about a weeks time. A line to Rochdale Vicarage will 'oblige'—in ten days I must be back in town. Remember the cricket. I am yours affectionately

Robert Bridges

P.S.

    Think of this when you've nothing else to do. Dr. Johnson said that Milton wrote a "babylonish dialect." Let us say something of Dr. Johnson.

28: TO LIONEL MUIRHEAD

St. Bartholomew's Hospital
June 21, 1875

My dear Lionel

I was very sorry to hear from Wooldridge that you had got the shingles. The classical name is herpes zoster—and I am rejoiced to hear that you are better again, and able to get about.—I am ashamed of receiving a letter from you when I should have been your correspondent, but I am rejoiced again on the other hand to hear from you. My occupation must be the excuse for my neglect, and though I know it to be a very insufficient reason for not writing to a friend when he is ill, I know that you will make me abundant allowances.

Wooldridge and Burke were thinking of starting on their water party this morning. They were to take Mrs Burke some hampers, and start from Oxford.— They depended a good deal on the weather, and as it is not promising this morning have very likely put off. They thought of asking you to join them at Goring. Whether they have done so or no I cannot tell.

They had some doubt about your being able to come. I am engaged next Sunday to go down to Canterbury so that I cannot make any promise or arrangement just yet. If I should come at all I think it would be the Sunday after. Considering the weather I am pretty well. I wish I had time to come down and eat strawberries. If I should be able to manage it I will let you know.

I have nothing more to tell you as you have I think heard lately from Wooldridge who will have told you of his visit to the reredos.

By the way if you have the address of the man of whom we bought our busts in Rome I should be glad of it for a friend of Dr. Gee's who wants 'one like it'.

Yours affectionately
R. S. Bridges

29: TO LIONEL MUIRHEAD

Library
St. Bartholomew's Hospital
July 5, 1875

My dear Lionel

Thank you for your letter received this morning. I sent off the address to Dr. Gee. I have nothing to say to you except that I went to Epping Forest the Sunday before last and heard a German band. This is the cause of the enclosed verses which I think will amuse you. I have just written them off. Le temp ne fait bien a l'affaire, la'ffaire, l'a ffaire, l'affaire, but it must excuse the weak lines. If it is amusing enough I will improve it.

If your sisters want a book to read. "The life of Ulrich von Hutten" Translated from Strause by Mrs. Sturge.—Very good and interesting, valuable etc. etc.—

yours

RB

30: TO LIONEL MUIRHEAD

St. Bartholomew's Hospital
London E.C.
August 16, 1875

My dear Levional

The milk cans and I got to London quite safely. Today the weather is very hot. A man who has been practising medicine in New Zealand has made me the offer of taking my work for a fortnight. I am thinking of closing with him—as it is a very slack time in my wards, and the weather will probably suit him better than me. I made a journey down to Maddox S^t today and remembered to bring home Corelli, which I will pack up and send to your sister. I am afraid that it is a very dirty copy, and I wish you would tell her that the manuscript additions, I think there are some, are not mine.—I shall probably go down to my brother in Worcestershire. If I have anything to say I will write again. Vesuvianus' direction is care of Archibald Briggs, Stanley Hall, Mr. Wakefield.

I am yours ever

RSB

My kind regards to all your party.

31: TO LIONEL MUIRHEAD

St. Bartholomew's Hospital
London
October 5, 1875

I send Dear Levional these sonnets 1st to you because I think that you have time to read them. I want them criticised.—2 of them are imperfect and one or two other lines want alteration.—With this preface what I want you to do is this—take a pencil and mark at the side any thing that you like—or dislike, or don't understand,—any thing especially which *grates* in the *wording*—And I want you to read them in this manner. 1st *neglect all the prose* and see if you can make any thing of the verse. I mean if you see enough argument in it to induce you to go on rather than leave off. Don't even read the suggestive headings. This you can do by always doubling the book back on itself. Then having followed my instructions so far go back and read all the prose, and see if that gives you a notion, a new notion, or none at all—Then read the verse again and send it me back—

(These are my instructions.) If they *do*, I shall print them, but only a few copies.—Please scratch at the side with a pencil any thing that strikes you. I suggest some marks.

> ? = what does this mean
> C = how does this run
> D = don't like this at all
> A = I like this very much—

and put these marks both against the number of the sonnett for the whole sonnett or against any line, and if against a word, underline the word.

Please do all this to oblige your extravagantly demanding friend.

RB

> There are *only* 24
> and some you've seen before
> about some I can't tell—
> But some run very well . .
> Only please scratch and strike
> Wherever you don't like—
> Your interest I shall judge
> By blot and scratch and smudge
> And your affection count
> Exactly from the amount
> of lines that underline
> These hundred and 36 verses of mine—Amen

32: TO LIONEL MUIRHEAD

S. Bartelmy's Lud's Town
October 11, 1875

My dear Levional

Thank you very much for your prompt industry. Had you put more A's I should have assuredly thought you an Ass. This is a joke, for I wanted you to be drawn into as many expressions of opinion as possible. That you do not understand Sonnett VII is a wonder to me. 2 or 3 people have seen it and liked it—and what is more, found a notion new to them in it, and approved it. It must have boarded you on an unfortunate day, when something had fixed the notion of some necessary word wrongly for the conception. All your other remarks are I think much to the point. That the 1st Quatrain of the Sonnett "Tears of Love" does not "scan", is plain enough. I don't know whether it is not better in its broken rhythm than it would be if it were polished. This is a question further criticism shall decide.

The remark I chiefly thank you for is that Wellington's and Nelson's heroes were 'exiles' in burial. I confess it never struck me, and if the sonnet is to stand it must be on the chance of its never striking anyone else. It is an accident, but an unfortunate one. Naval glory to be sure implies it. Military does not—and Nelson and Wellington, who are the types, were buried in England, and I suppose for that matter the greater percentage of their men also. I must go to Chelsea and Greenwich hospitals for information. I shan't add any more now about your remarks. You haven't heard the last of the sonnets yet—

One thing I was anxious to know was whether the whole had an effect as whole—on the *mind*.

Do they seem to be about anything in particular?

I wrote a poem of 300 lines last night! and I have a swelled face today. I don't know whether this is cause and effect.—I need not tell you that the 300 verses want a good deal doing to them.—I think it will amuse you. It is <u>very</u> serious.—I shall also have one or 2 lyrics to show you. That you liked my Shakespeare sonnet was great praise—*great*. I didn't expect any one to and thought I should have to omit it. I wrote another, before, which was too flimsy.

With my thanks. yours ever

RB

I have found rather a nice person.

I was amused about one thing, your objection to the end.—I am afraid it does "the heart, as they say, more credit than the head", but what amused me was the fact that the 1st transcript of the sonnet had this sestett

> "Step down, my fairest image, Oh step down!
> Take on thy final glory, do! for this
> The patient hands whereunder thou hast grown
>   Are outstretched to receive thee—Thou art his
> Who formed and fashioned thee. Awake and crown
> Thy sculptors labour with a living kiss."

But as Vesuvianus would tell us Pygmalion was but a maker of waxworks, and no artist.

RB

P.S.
> "Damn it" I said—alas! I spoke
> In haste the word that I should not—
> When I perceived my maid had broke
> The lid of my tobacco pot—
> But when I found the senseless slut
> Had thrown away the broken bits
> Then was mine anger stayed! ?. Tut! Tut!
> I damned and damned her into fits. . ."

EXTEMPORE ODE ON THE LOSS OF A TOBACCO-BAG-COVER
Dedicated with tears to the donator rei . .

by RSB

33: TO LIONEL MUIRHEAD

S. Bartholomew's Hospital
London E.C.
December 13, 1875

My dear Levional

Thank you very much for your letter. It is a great pity if you are not coming up to London again soon.—There has been lots 'doing' in Mad[d]ox Street—and there are several things on: Amongst others a play in which Bateman, Burke and Wooldridge are to act. As for the chair many thanks for it. I think it was in a weak moment that Wooldridge consented to the notion. My wishes were much more severe, and I think he agrees with me. Anyhow he gives in. I am sorry that you are doing St. Cosmo and Co. instead of something new, but I shall be very much interested in it. My sonnets are nearly ready "with additions and corrections." I have spent one evening over them already, and am now writing them out again. I am going to publish a preface with them, and print them anonymously. I am very busy with my medical work and get on well. I like Dr Black immensely. Dr Gee was married the other day. I stood as his best man and made a speech at the wedding breakfast. I took in the chief bridesmaid who gabbered to me about Max Muller, Ruskin and Sir James Paget—and I was ill the day after. Gee's wife is I am sorry to say older than himself. This is a great pity—I have been reading lots of new books lately. New to me but nothing of the hour—Get your sisters to tell you what Browning's inn album is like and let me have an opinion. No one I know is thinking of reading it. The Pole has gone a-way thank heaven. I got a letter from him in Paris this morning. Wooldridge has done a very good head of him. I lent him a very large sum of money—Talking of money I will repay you your 30 £ before the year is out if that will suit you. I am to have a great treat this evening. I am going to eat chops off Japanese plates with Chutnee made by Bateman at 6. this evening at Mad[d]ox St.—The gourmand pleasures of the rich are foolish compared to such an entertainment.

I have other letters to write so must shut up this—One thing more I heard from Marlow the other day. Owen and the family are very well.

ever yours affectionately
RSBridges

34: TO LIONEL MUIRHEAD

St. Bartholomew's Hospital
London E.C.
January 1, 1876

My dear Levional

I send you my very best wishes for the new year, and hope that you will enjoy many, and always receive my congratulations.

I wish to tell you that I can pay you your 30 £ whenever you like, but if you are coming up to town I will put off till then. The Pole got me to lend him such a lot of money that I was obliged to borrow 200 £ of my banker at 5 percent till better times should come. This enables me to pay my Xmas debts and I can acquit myself with you whenever you choose.

I hope that you are coming up again soon, I shall be busy till the end of January after which time I hope to be almost quite free. I am very tired of my way of living but must stick to it yet a little longer.

I think I owe you a letter, but don't quite know. Vesuvianus has told me of your letter to him. He has done several things to the portrait of my mother which now has quite lost all the hardness that made it so disagreeable. He is working very hard, and no longer requires stimuli—Is not this a change! There will be much to amuse you when you come up—The exhibition of old Masters par excellence.

With my kind regards and seasonable wishes to all your party I am yours ever

RS Bridges

35: TO LIONEL MUIRHEAD

St. Bartholomew's Hospital
March 16, 1876

My dear Levional

There are two other houses in Bedford Sq. on the S side: 51 and 52. Will you see them if you can and report to Wooldridge?

No. 52 is 185 £ per annum and is ready to be entered.

No. 51 is in the hands of the Duke, I do not know the terms. It is the house I am most in love with at the present moment. Enquiries are on foot.

I met Mr Mills in the Square this afternoon and we saw all the houses together. He is delighted with them, but he says that I had better do them up myself—not them exactly, but the one of them that I fix on.

Let me know if you think of eating beefsteak with me. . . .

Yours ever
RSB

36: TO LIONEL MUIRHEAD

52 Bedford Square
December 17, 1877

Dear Levional

I am delighted that you are thinking of beginning painting again; as it must mean that your eyes are much better.

I have had great difficulty about the Westminster Play. I have as yet only one ticket sent to me. That is for Thursday: the days being Tuesday and Thursday it is unlikely now that I shall get any more.

About coming up. Come when you like. I suppose that you must keep Xmas at ʒome otherwise we should be very pleased if you could spend it with us. Come ʒoth after and before Xmas if it suits. I know of no especial reason for any ʒarticular day on this side. In great haste (at breakfast)

yours ever
RSB

57: TO LIONEL MUIRHEAD

52 Bedford Square
April 3, 1878

ʒear Levional

Wooldridge tells me that he has heard from you. I write because I think you may care to hear an unprejudiced opinion concerning the picture. It was not ʒone in time for the academy, indeed though the Grosvenor is 14 days later here is some doubt whether it will be in time for that, but—it is a success. ʒecidedly, very decidedly. One unfortunate circumstance, viz, that Aeneas we ʒiscover, should be in armour, and though it would very much improve the ʒicture to put him into armour, yet there is not time.—W[ooldridge] got an old ʒrame for the picture, which is beautiful, and suits it admirably. It is a remark-ʒble production, and its excellence cannot escape the notice of the veriest fool: ʒor it has a sort of mysterious simplicity about it that makes one look at it, as I ʒound out when it was put in its frame. For to tell the truth I was sick of it—and hought I should never want to see it again.

So much for the picture. Bateman has 3 for the Academy. One he has sold and ʒne is a commission. H. E. W. clears out of here next week. He told you I ʒuppose the sort of thing he thinks of doing.

The Reredos is finished and has gone in. It is a most gaudy "pulticacious" dish.

When shall you be coming up? I suppose not before Academy is open. I am ʒoing off for a day next week, and for a month as soon as spring sets in. At that ime *I hope we may meet in Oxford.* We failed to do so last year.

yours affectionately
RB

ʒindest regards at home.

58. TO LIONEL MUIRHEAD

52 Bedford Square
August 10, 1878

ʒy dear Lionel

I am, this being a wet afternoon, sending all my neglected correspondents a ʒundred thousand apologies.—To the tribe of Muirhead were sealed 100,000.—

Robert Bridges, date unknown. Courtesy of Robert Bridges, the poet's grandson.

Thank you for your invitation. I should certainly have accepted it, or should now do so, and come to see the moon from Haseley Terrace, but—I must always get back to town on Sunday evening, and your railway does not offer facilities—or only such as I might term deterrent opportunities, or difficulties. This is the whole matter.

I had a very pleasant Sunday at Sandhurst, a fortnight ago. It seems a year and a half already, and the tribe of Sturt is on the eve of having its 100,000 sealed to it.

I had never met your brother in law before, and liked him very much. We had an easy Sunday! no religious exercises. Indeed we played lawn tennis without a boundary to the court.

Gerard Hopkins is in town preaching and confessing at Farm St. I went to hear him. He is good. He calls here; and we have sweet laughter, and pleasant chats. He is not at all the worse for being a Jesuit; as far as one can judge without knowing what he would have been otherwise. His poetry is magnificent but 'caviare to the general'. Stuckey preaches at St. Pauls. He is very fat—as ever—and his left eyebrow has gone a snowy white, which embarrasses one a little till one gets used to it.

Edgell has been to lunch. He is stiffish—there is an exclusive pushiveness in his Catholicism I take it.—H.E.W. is well. He no doubt has written to you. My mother is well. I am well. Other things seem pretty well. My mother sends kind regard. I am yours ever

R Bridges

39: TO LIONEL MUIRHEAD

52 Bedford Square

December 27, 1878

My dear Lionel

I wish you a happy New Year, and as many of them as you can get. Thank you for your letter, the chief effect of it was astonishment (to me reading it) for I thought that you were copying pictures at Perugia. We are getting on very well in London, and hope very much to see you on your way to Italy. Except for the pang of envy that it will shoot into my medulla. You had better take lots of great coats and tobacco however for I remember Perugia North Wind very well. I have an *unfinished ode* to A, which I intend to amuse myself by completing if we ever have any overpoweringly hot weather. It makes me shiver to think of it. Talking of odes, I have got about 20 pieces <u>ready for the press</u>; they are on the eve of being sent off. One or two lines still remain in a state which does not quite satisfy me. An hour or two—when I can get it—should set all to rights. They will be *better than anything I have done*, and 2 of them are I hope <u>successful in a new metrical system</u> of which I hope great things. I don't know if I ever spoke to you of it. This brings me to *Gerard Hopkins*. It is useless my telling you where he is, as by this time he is not there. He never can be according to presant [*sic*] arrangements, but when last I heard of him he was <u>converting Pater at Oxford</u>. Whether he is actually sent to undermine undergraduates steadily or not I cannot say Then *The Heautontimorumenos is finished,* at least we have come to the end, and I have copied it out, and all that remains is touching up.—'Asphaltium—to bring it together.—Then my famous *paper on the Casualty department is creating a furore* among my professional friends. I will send you a copy of it when I am supplied with them, or rather I will make your Father a present of one, hoping that his admiration for *rare tracts* will get it into a binding. Then I am going to begin *a series of medical papers for one of the med journals*[,] I think, as I am going off some of my outpatient work for a while.—Then I have made a complete <u>intelligible</u> theme for "The Growth of Love" which will be my next verse affair. <u>Much</u> <u>enlarged</u> and in every way more taking. <u>Entirely new system of rhythm in-</u> <u>troduced into sonnett-writing.</u> See what excitements we have. My mother joins me in kind regards to your people. I am yours ever

R Bridges

Thursfield has returned from a fortnight of *Cairo bazaaring.* Fancy these excitements. *A bazaar is to be held in his house in Montague Place.*—

40: TO EDMUND GOSSE

52 Bedford Square
March 2, 1879

My dear Gosse
    It will give my mother and myself great pleasure if you and Mrs. Gosse can dine with us next Saturday. The Thursfields have accepted our invitation to come and meet you. I think there will be no one else. We dine at 7.
    I have sent a copy of my verses to "the Academy". It was foolish of me to say what I did to you in the Savile the other day: and it would have been rude had you not been more author than critic, but I think I could explain myself to your satisfaction. However till I can do so I apologise.
    I am quite willing for the book to be reviewed by "the gentleman" you mentioned. And I see that if it should please him his opinion may strengthen the kind judgement which you and other friends have always held of my poems. On the other hand I see there remains something, to say which I had better not say lest I should stir up strife between the spirits of truth and contradiction; between idiosyncracy and taste. Even this much must be private, and I only say it that I may say it beforehand and not be credited for making it up afterwards. I have an exceedingly high opinion of his talent, and shall be amused and interested to (as

ladies say) the last degree. You had a 'new poet' when last I saw you. I have one now.

Yours very truly,
Robert Bridges

My kind regards to Mrs. Gosse in which my mother joins.

41: TO EDMUND GOSSE

52 Bedford Square
November 22, 1879

My dear Gosse

I have poisoned my hand, which in consequence lives in a sling, and you must therefore make some excuse for my long silence, and for any inadequacy in this letter, which I am writing of course to thank you for your delightful book. I saw that you had a long review in the Athenaeum, but I confess that I did not read those columns with great perseverance. As far as I have got in the book I like it very much, and you will be pleased to hear that my mother took a great fancy to the verses on your daughter. I should have read all the book long ago but a friend who found it on my table carried it off when I had, with the exception of plunges while I cut it, only read the two first idyllic pieces.

These however if I were a critic would amply suffice for the purposes of analysis and panegyric but I must content myself with remarking that I was very glad to find you making use of the idyllic form as you do in "The Sisters". It seems to me that the Idyll has a future in English poetry. All that has yet been done on the Theocritean and Virgilian models seems not to hit the mark. And I thought that you were quite successful. A difficulty to me lies in the Greek names. I should like English Idylls to be independant [*sic*] even of them, perhaps you do not think them a disadvantage. At any rate the important thing to get is the poetic landscape with the utmost elaboration of beautiful language. We agree about that.

When I get the book back which I hope to do as soon as possible, I shall read the rest of it with the same pleasure as I did the beginning.

We are very sorry to miss you and Mrs. Gosse, especially as you live so far off. I hope when Mrs. Gosse purposes in the morning to call in the afternoon she will send us a postcard, as it would often make all the difference.

I want to tell you that, though I agree with what you said about my brother's book in respect of its inartistic qualities, which offend me I am sure as much as they do you, yet I think you judge the book very hardly. One of the most important, I think the most important of the qualities of writing, must be direct-ness, unbroken connection between thought and expression. This I think is very rare indeed, and to me it constitutes a great merit and the charm of 'Wet Days'. When art becomes elaborate the triumph is, not to burden or weaken the natural expression in beautifying it, and since this is a danger even of simple rhyme and rhythm there is little of our everyday verse that is not ruined.

From this view I think my brother's verses are a success. They are very direct and genuine: and I think that you would like them better on a 2nd or 3^d perusal which however I don't expect you to give them as I certainly shouldn't myself But the novel reading public might well take to them. What are all the inelegan cies of Wet Days to the unintelligible gibberish, (quà language) of 'Theophrastus Such'? And this is the 'ne plus ultra' the 'desideratum' 'the Zoedone' the 'Reva lanta Arabia' and 'Cocktail' of the circulating libraries, and there is not one reviewer honest enough to say that it is bosh. As in my opinion, humble but plainly spoken, it is—clever bosh but profoundly damned bosh. From which I would deduce a moral that you should be kind to Wet Days.

I have a letter this morning from an accomplished poet of the Keats school (!) who praises it.

Believe me with kindest regards to Mrs. Gosse,
and many more thanks for your book.

yours very truly
R. Bridges

42: TO LIONEL MUIRHEAD

52 Bedford Square
June 9, 1881

My dear Lionel

I had discovered your absence from town, having called at your rooms to get you to come and meet two specimens of the genus 'Homo sapiens' variety architectonica—I deferred answering your letter till today thinking there might be a change of wind, but there is not. Now I have an engagement for Saturday, and another on Tuesday. If the weather should change I should like to come towards the end of next week. At present farewell.

yours ever
R Bridges

43: TO GERARD MANLEY HOPKINS

52 Bedford Square
June 15, 1881

My dear Gerard:

I destroy the comic verses sent and beg for no more. I am sure that they are not natural to you and they will do you no credit. In haste

Yours affectionately
RB

44: TO ROBERT BRIDGES

Haseley Court
Tetsworth
July 30, 1881

My dear old Robert You must really try to gain
A little strength to set you up and right again,
And meanwhile I have sent you in a biscuit tin
A posy thinking it quite safe to risk it in,
If only railway porters will take care of it
And guards will have the goodness to beware of it
It may escape untimely demolition
And should arrive in Fairly good condition.
Revolving many things within my cranium
I put not in a single red geranium,
Nor a petunia nor a calceolaria,
Nor (For there was'nt space) an araucaria,
Nor any plant termed bedding is there set in it,
And there's no scrap of 'grass-like' mignonette in it.
Only such things I gathered as Harpalium
And clematis and silver-leaved Graphalium
And Commelina and a Few such oddities
As are'nt like Covent-Gardening commodities,
Flame coloured Dahlias too (that is the best of them
They're scarcely out as yet) are with the rest of them.
I would add many things but that the phrases Fly
To right and left and make the thoughts to blazes Fly
And words won't Fit but get into a whirligig
Just like a dry-bob sculling in a burly gig,
I'd write 1000 couplets but my Muse's brain
Threatens a softening shortly and refuses plain
To find more rhymes though I should make her try on all
Her artful dodges:

Ever yours
Levional

45: TO LIONEL MUIRHEAD

Bedford Square
Saturday July 31, 1881

My dear Lionel
   The flowers are most beautiful. Many thanks for them. They are by far the
most varied selection I have had sent me since I fell ill. You will want to know

how I am getting on. This is the second day that I have been told to sit on the sofa in the evening, and here I am. It is also the 3rd day that I have passed without morphia. The doctors say I am doing well, but will not suggest any limit of time as possible or probable. The fever has not left me yet, and I do not expect to feel any better till it does. I am the worst possible patient, but I think really I could not have had a much worse time of it—I incline to think I am better as I could not have written this some time ago. Finally I look very well, and have all through—I have a thick black beard—I have *no* legs—but can stand for a moment, or walk across the room. I should be glad to see you. If you come to town, Liddon called thanks to you, and cheered me much. He was very kind.

My mother sends her affectionate regards—and was much moved by the flowers. However she said she never took so little pleasure in them or thought them so much wasted.

Such is our condition

your affectionate friend

RB

46: TO LIONEL MUIRHEAD

52 Bedford Square

August 27, 1881

My dear Lionel

I should have written before but am not always up to it—and there is very seldom anything especial to tell. I do not make flying leaps, and if I am a little better than when you were here that is all that can be said. I still have fever, which is a bore, and my cough is no better. On the other hand I now dress in the afternoon and sit in the drawing room, my bedroom being the back drawing room. My beard still grows. We think of going to Hampstead in a day or two if we can get a house—which is difficult. We are in treaty for one at present—

If I don't get better then, you may write my epitaph with that of poor General Garfield.

I hope you are quite well. If not at home this will no doubt follow you.

yours ever

RB

If at home kindest regards to all.

47: TO RICHARD WATSON DIXON

52 Bedford Square

July 1, 1882

My dear Canon Dixon

I have just got your letter. I mean your post card. It rather frightens me. What you say about the Prometheus being too finished. You must mean that there isn't much in it. But I still hope that you will be really pleased when you see the whole. A poem cannot be too finished? If it can pray let me revoke all my criticisms of yours. I shall not like meddling: but cannot help thinking I am right. Of course it's no use polishing a bad thing—or a poor thing.

I am going down to Pangbourne again today. I think we shall take the house there: and I shall not think it is thoroughly home till you have paid us a visit. About my coming to see you, I will come if I possibly can, and if you can have me. Of course the arrangement of the new house and the moving will occupy me very much and make it difficult. We ought to be moving by the first week in August.

I am within 100 lines of the end of my poem. I wrote 100 yesterday, which was a good 2 hours work. It ought not to be too finished, that? I am going down to Gerard on Sunday and will send on the MS of the beginning of Prometheus the first 1000 lines. Work you at Mano. Don't be afraid of finish—and say the worst you can of the part already sent. Think of Aeschylus.

Kindest regards to Mrs. D.

your affectionate
R. Bridges

I have seen "sand-wich men" in Bond Street.—"Day = Boarders" as I call them with this advertisement.

> SOMEBODY'S
>
> ART
>
> ·TILES
>
> !

This morning advertisements are sent me of *Art = books*.

48: TO RICHARD WATSON DIXON

Bedford Square
August 4, 1882

My dear Canon Dixon

Did I write to you to say how sorry I was to get your telegram? I am afraid that I shall not have another chance of seeing you for I don't know how long. On Monday moving begins in earnest and this day week I hope to be at Yattendon. The full stop which is put to my London life is smudged in a most unsightly manner by the processes of removal.

When I read the long list of, to-me-uninteresting (as the Germans would put it) engagements I made up my mind that I would never become a clergyman. You know the slight natural hankering I have after St Peter's crook—unless indeed I could be ordained a Dean, but there is no service in the prayer book for this improbable special occasion. Not that but a nice one might not be framed. A sort of ordination for such as are of riper years. I imagine it. The archdeacon presenting me and my fellow candidates saying, "I have examined these persons and find that they are well disposed and willing to become Deans". Bishop: "Thou hast enquired into their titles offices and emoluments, and fully acquainted them therewith—dost thou envy them from thy heart, and wish that thou thyself wert even as they??" Archdeacon: "I do". Then the Bishop shall turn to the candidates and say, "Ye that come hither to be ordained unto the holy office of Dean, have ye well considered that ye seek, and do ye earnestly and solemnly desire to be ordained Deans?" Candidates: "We do". Bishop: "Will ye faithfully and punctually receive the several stipends and salaries henceforward appertaining unto you, and will ye regularly and decorously perform all the duties and functions of your sacred stalls whensoever it shall not be in any way inconvenient for you so to do?" Answer: "We will". etc. etc.

Gerard has Prometheus. It is all written out. Wooldridge wants me to keep it awhile. He thinks very well of it, so that he thinks it would be worth while to be very careful and even rewrite some parts. I do not wish to interfere with your work, but should be glad to send it to you whenever you can spare it some leisure—I shall give it to Wooldridge when Gerard has done with it, which will be this week. I think well of it myself. I will take Mano whenever you like, if indeed you care for me to see it again before it is printed—I am afraid now that you will not get it out before the winter. Printing etc. takes such a time—e.g., Lang, who has a book to come out in October has had it all in print some months—I doubt if yours can be ready so soon. Do not let me delay it—either by having it, if you think you have done all you wish to do to it—or by sending for my work.

Could you manage to come to Yattendon for a week any time between now and the end of Autumn? I saw Gerard last Sunday. Those Jesuits do bully their men dreadfully. He shuns even his Jesuit fellow creatures—perhaps though these more than others. With our kindest regards to Mrs Dixon.

Yours ever

Robert Bridges

After next Sunday address me thus

       R. B esq^r.
       Manor House
       Yattendon
       Newbury
          Berks.

Part II

YATTENDON,

1882–1904

The next twenty-two years, which Bridges spent at Yattendon, were the happiest and most productive of his life. His long association with the private press of C. H. Daniel began in 1883 with the publication of *Prometheus the Firegiver,* his first masque, and the first of a series of ten dramatic pieces. The next year Daniel published *Poems.* In April Bridges became engaged to Monica Waterhouse, the daughter of the architect Alfred Waterhouse. They were married September 3, 1884. By June of that year he had finished his first verse drama (as distinct from the masques) *Nero,* Part I. The year 1885 saw the publication of this play and of the first version of the narrative poem *Eros & Psyche.* By April Bridges had almost finished his play *The Return of Ulysses* and had completed the first two acts of his "Menander-like" comedy in verse, *The Feast of Bacchus.* By the end of 1886 Bridges had three unprinted plays on hand—*Palicio, Ulysses,* and *The Feast of Bacchus*—and had planned with Lionel Muirhead the proper staging of *Ulysses.* By the end of January 1887 Bridges was at work on the fifth act of another play, *The Christian Captives* (but it was not completed until the spring of the next year.) By May of 1887 still another play, *Achilles in Scyros,* was almost finished. In the summer he spent a fortnight in Northumberland with Canon Dixon and in August Hopkins visited Yattendon for several days, and at this time Bridges and Monica were planning a light comedy in verse, *The Humours of the Court.* By October *Achilles in Scyros* was completed. "On the Elements of Milton's Blank Verse in *Paradise Lost*" appeared this year and was later several times revised and enlarged. This essay was the first extensive published evidence of Bridges's serious and profound interest in prosody, which had begun in the 1870s when he and Hopkins were formulating the principles of stress verse ("sprung rhythm"). It was to result in a number of further important experiments in the writing of poems according to various prosodic principles, modern and classical. Lionel Muirhead married Grace Ashhurst in the spring and went to Italy for an extended honeymoon. Bridges's first child, Elizabeth, was born December 6.

In April 1888 the last scenes of the *Humours of the Court* were written and in August Bridges completed *The Christian Captives,* which had been laid aside unfinished "for now 2 years." Charis, Muirhead's daughter, was born in the summer. By Christmas, Bridges had completed his revision of his sonnet sequence *The Growth of Love,* calling his first version "a mistake." Bridges and his family went to Italy for a month immediately after Christmas. Gerard Manley Hopkins died in Dublin June 8, 1889, and by August Bridges was planning with Daniel to issue a privately printed edition of his poems with a memoir, a plan that was abandoned some months later. Margaret, Bridges's second daughter, was born in October. This year saw the publication of another study of Milton's prosody, *On the Prosody of Paradise Regained and Samson Agonistes,* and also *The Feast of Bacchus* and the revised version of *The Growth of Love.*

The year 1890 was a decisive one for the reputation of Bridges as a poet. By February he was at work on the oratorio *Eden.* Four more plays: *Palicio, The Return of Ulysses, The Christian Captives,* and *Achilles in Scyros* were published in this year and also the *Shorter Poems,* Books I–IV, on which Bridges's reputation as a lyric poet rests. Anthony, Muirhead's only son, was born November 4. Maurice Waterhouse, Monica's brother, died in December.

By January 1891 Bridges had, except for minor revisions, completed *Nero,* Part II. *Eden,* set to the music of C. V. Stanford, was published in July and performed at the Birmingham Festival in October. In January 1892 Bridges and Muirhead were discussing once again the staging of *Ulysses* and Muirhead supplied his friend with line drawings illustrating the set for the final scene, drawings that would be suitable for including in a reprint of the play. Edward Ettingdene (later Lord Bridges), the only son of the poet, was born August 4, 1892. In March 1893 Bridges prepared a "notice" and selection of Hopkins's poems for Miles's anthology *The Poets and Poetry of the Century. The Humours of the Court; Founder's Day, A Secular Ode on the Ninth Jubilee of Eton College* (in black letter); *Shorter Poems,* Book V; and another rewrite of *Milton's Prosody,* in limited and regular issues, all appeared this year. In December Charles Furse finished his portrait of Bridges.

From June through September 1894 Bridges was hard at work on his essay on Keats. In November he took a brief vacation on the Isle of Wight, visiting Coventry Patmore for three days on his return home. In November he was elected honorary fellow of Corpus Christi College. *Nero,* Part II, the last of Bridges's poetic dramas (as distinct from his masques), and a revision of *Eros & Psyche* were published this year. In the summer of 1895 Bridges received strong support for the professorship of poetry at Oxford but withdrew his name from consideration. His essay on Keats, written as an Introduction for the Muses Library edition of Keats's poems (1896) was separately and privately printed in 1895. With the support of Bridges, H. E. Wooldridge was appointed Slade professor at Oxford in July. In April, work begun previously on *Invocation to Music,* set to the score of Sir Hubert Parry, was resumed. It was finished in August 1895 in time for the festival at Leeds October 2 and was published the same year. Part I of the *Yattendon Hymnal,* edited by Bridges and Wooldridge, was published in large handmade paper, limited issue, and in regular issue in November. In 1896 Elkin Mathews in the Shilling Garland series brought out the *Invocation to Music* (renamed *Ode for Henry Purcell*) together with other poems and a preface on the musical setting of poetry by Bridges.

In 1897 Bridges brought out in quarto and in folio his collection of *Chants for the Psalter,* with a preface by himself and ornamentation by Muirhead. Bridges composed some of the chants and rewrote others. William Butler Yeats paid his first visit to Yattendon March 27–29. In June Part II of the *Yattendon Hymnal* was issued. Manley Hopkins, the father of Gerard Manley Hopkins, died August 26.

In November Bridges began work on *A Song of Darkness and Light* to be set to Parry's music. On December 14 Bridges's mother died.

Early in 1898 Muirhead moved to a large and sumptuous estate, Haseley Court, not far from Oxford. It was to be his home for the rest of his life. *Yattendon Hymns,* containing the English words of twenty-three hymns from the *Yattendon Hymnal* that were not in the *Hymns Ancient and Modern,* appeared in February. In March Muirhead finished his picture of Bridges, and William Strang had by then completed an etching of him. *A Song of Darkness and Light,* which was performed at the Gloucester Festival, came out this year and the first volume of Bridges's *Poetical Works* (which eventually ran to six volumes) was published by Smith & Elder. In January 1899 Part III of the large paper *Yattendon Hymnal* was issued. By May Bridges had met William Johnson Stone, son of a master of Eton College. Their friendship had an important effect on Bridges's poetry for the next several years. In June, Daniel printed in black letter *Hymns by Robert Bridges,* which contained the words of those hymns which had been written, translated, or adapted by Bridges. In addition, Daniel also issued in limited and regular editions *The Small Hymn-Book,* which presented the words only of the larger *Yattendon Hymnal.* Bridges showed a sharp interest in the Boer War, which commenced in October. "It is difficult," he wrote to Muirhead, "to think of anything else." In December the fourth and final part of the large paper *Yattendon Hymnal* was published.

In January 1900 Monica became seriously ill. Richard Watson Dixon died January 23. At the beginning of the next year Bridges moved his family to Oxford for three months. William Johnson Stone died suddenly and unexpectedly of pneumonia on February 28, leaving Bridges bound with a promise to continue Stone's experiments in writing English verse in classical prosody. Bridges eventually wrote over two thousand lines in what he called his "longs and shorts." In November he started his first long poem in quantitative verse, an epistle to Muirhead which begins "Now in wintry delights. . . ." Another revision of *Milton's Prosody,* bound together with Stone's *Classical Metres in English Verse,* was published in December. During the year he read philosophy (with particular attention to Santayana) and Fraser's *Golden Bough.* In August he returned to his "old scheme of phonetics." Every night he and his wife practiced writing their phonetic script. In November Monica became dangerously ill. She appeared to recover but was ill again late in 1902 and had a serious relapse in 1904. Margaret was also ill during the latter part of 1903 and into 1904. The disease was probably tuberculosis contracted from the family cow. Eventually it drove the family from Yattendon to seek healthier living conditions.

During 1902 Bridges continued his experiments in phonetic script and in Stone's prosody, finishing his epistle to Muirhead in November. In the summer he wrote his poem in classical iambics to Logan Pearsall Smith, entitled "On Receiving *Trivia* from the Author." In February of 1903 he began his second epistle in Stone's prosody—which he referred to as his "anti-socialist tract." The Daniel Press brought out in March his first epistle, *Now in Wintry Delights* which included a facsimile, printed in red, of one page of a manuscript of twenty-three lines from the poem, written by Bridges in phonetic script. The Daniel Press also issued on June first, for the first anniversary, his *Peace Ode written on the Conclusion of the Three Year's War*. After a vacation in August on the Isle of Wight, Bridges corrected and finished his "On Receiving *Trivia*." Also in September Edward entered school. Toward the end of the year Margaret was ill with tuberculosis.

Bridges, at the request of Margery Fry, librarian of Somerville College, began his second and last masque of *Demeter* about the end of February 1904, finishing it by the end of March. By the time it was performed by the students of Somerville on June 11, Monica was in a Sanatorium in Bournesmouth. Margaret joined her in August or early September. By September Bridges had decided his family must leave Yattendon and, after vacationing in England and Switzerland, seek a permanent residence elsewhere.

Yattendon
Nr Newbury
September 7, 1882

My dear Canon

I have read through all the 6 tomes sent, and have come to a decided opinion which I think I ought to send you off at once. That is that I shall try and dissuade you from publishing Mano this year.

First my reasons. I think a great deal wants doing to the canto on the Normans and to that Canto of correspondence. I find them both rather dull, and the Norman one *long,* and they are in a critical place, just where the reader wants fixing rather than putting off. I will not trouble you now with what I should suggest in the treatment of them, but I shall not flinch from this opinion. Then there are one or two other matters which if I am right entail work and consideration e.g. I am not sure that the 1st mention of Vilgard is not too long. The statement of his opinions in that place takes off from the interest which is required to carry off the whole canto in which they are afterwards stated, and there (as I think) in a more interesting surrounding.

I shall have a good deal to say about the introductory canto.—But it is absolutely necessary that we should meet over this work. I think really that if you consider that it is worth another plunge (which I do) that I could shorten your labour.

But my question is this. The opinion I have to offer being now before you—what do you think?

1. Will you instead of getting Mano out get out a volume of shorter poems?

2. Or will you decide to leave Mano as he is, and wish me only to make textual criticisms?

There is one other thing I should mention. Though a good deal of the poem is now in the Dantesque stanza—especially the introduction—the variations your previous writing indulged in are *not* Dantesque, nor are they mere exaggerations of the liberties which Dante allowed himself. They are to my ear absolutely heretical: so much so as to forbid some of the expressions in the introduction.

I think it would still be well to get rid of these where you can do so easily. Also I think there is still left in the poem a good deal of diction (Gerard puns on this and says you should have a Dixonary) which crept in in slack moments and wants the hoe.

Of course my opinion of the whole poem is what it was. I find it extremely interesting, and am sure that (when it is in print) it will repay study. It is full of noble reflection, and fine imagination. Write and tell me what you think, and above all whether you could spend a fortnight here at any time. If not and you

would wish it I will try and manage to pay *you* a visit—Unless indeed my interfer-
ence is not mere conceited impertinence.—Still I think if we were to talk the
poem over we should agree as to whether it were worth while to dig over the
ground again.

—With our kindest regards to yourself and Mrs Dixon, who I hope is happy in
the quiet vicarage. I am

yours ever
R S Bridges

I think a fortnight would do it.—In which case perhaps if we met soon Mano
might get into print this year—

50: TO LIONEL MUIRHEAD

Yattendon
October 18, 1882

My dear Lionel

Many thanks for your long letter. I had heard of your cold. Nay in the person
of Wooldridge I may say that I have seen it, and I almost think, in my own
person, felt it.—I hope that you the great Author of all our colds are now
yourself recovering.

I wrote you a long letter once and tore it up because it contained a warm
invitation to you to come down here—which I could not honestly at that time
honour, and cannot I fear now. Unless you should like to come down for a day
or so when the weather is finer. For so short a visit you can come just when you
choose. If you come from Oxford the journey is easy, changing at Didcot out of
one of the right trains you will find a train waiting to go to Newbury. You go as
far as Hampstead Norris, which is not more than 2½ miles from us on the West.
I can always meet you at the station if I know in time, but if you came without
writing you might easily walk that distance on a fine day and we could send for
your things.

From London the best station is Pangbourne, some 6½ miles or 7.—Goring,
Theale, Aldermaston, Midgeham, Thatcham and Newbury are all within 10
miles also, averaging about 8, most of them offering lovely drives.

HEW has been here, and has worked very hard at Prometheus. In spite of all
the great searchings the MS remains delightfully tidy, and somewhat gives the lie
to a triolet in which I dedicate it to Wooldridge. (But I shall not print this) it may
amuse you.

DEDICATION
to
H E W

If any part of this is mine
This makes it yours. I claim the rest.
That you gave me: and so the best

—If any part of this—is mine.
But here and there so poor a line
Remains, that that 'twill soon be guessed
—If any part of this—is mine,
This makes it yours, I claim the rest—

Much good and I think no damage has been done. I now send it to Canon Dixon. After which I think its purgation may be considered over. It went on getting better right up to the end—I am now doing tragedies. With what success remains to be seen.

Leaving London seems to be a sort of desertion of you. You must make up for it by coming here. One day is as good as another, but fine days are best.

The country is lovely—

Take this letter as an invitation. Come in a shooting coat and thick boots. *When your cold is well.*

yours ever
R Bridges

Later on we might arrange for a regular long visit.

51: TO RICHARD WATSON DIXON

Yattendon
November 20, 1882

My dear C. Dixon

You will see how I think Mano ought to be printed. Only of course the initial line of the stanza not advancing so far beyond the others as in my M.S. but protruding a little and having the stanza number attached if you like. I should think not. That may be reserved for future editions for school use with notes *and Glossary.*

I return you the Latin verses which I am sorry to say I thought were a present to me. I liked 2 lots of them very much indeed, and am sorry to part with them.

I did not take much interest in them at first because I had been exposed to the disappointment of finding that they were not by you. Do you think the author would make me a present of a copy? There is a friend of mine who would very much like a copy also. Rev. C. B Hue. Cottage, St Lawrence, Isle of Wight. He might send them to him—Thus far I write on November 17th 82 picking up two ancient threads out of old letters of yours, awaiting to hear how you take my "version of Mano"—By the way shall I send Calypso?

———

Monday morning

Your two kind postcards arrive. It is very good of you to take my meddling so well. But I did not think that you would get any notion of my idea of the metre and what I consider your offences against it unless I wrote it out in some such manner. When you write tell me especially if you have a different notion of the stanza when you see it written thus. Some few of my emendations I know you will accept at once, because they seem what you intended. Of the rest some should I have no doubt be rejected—but I really urge those which point to a reconstruction of the periods—and also the rewriting of weak passages, a line here and there and sometimes as much as 3 lines together. Where I have rewritten myself it was merely to indicate the sort of thing I thought was wanted—e.g. in the description of Blanche. I thought my sketch would be of use, but did not for a moment think it final.—Again in the description of Gerbert I think I ventured to suggest a rearrangement.

Then there are one or two mistakes—at least I think you could consider them that———

Now I will go on willingly in the same manner if you think it worth while. Or I will attend to any branch of emendation you wish—But do not you see how convenient it would be to talk the matter over. If you are inclined to leave the periods as you wrote them—(and your judgement must decide this nor should I oppose it—except so far that if the alteration is not made I should think you should omit your introductory canto, and not mark the stanzas in printing—) there will of course be very little to do—

—But about the greatness and the letters. I have not the text but my chief objection is that it was unpoetic, and poor in diction. e.g., exagitate, I remember with some similar words rhyming, sanctificate etc. You may remember in rewriting that there is a good deal about the Normans, their manner of fighting etc. later on, when there is a battle with the Normans,—and as for the letters, the account of Vilgardus subsequently is so splendid that it would be a pity to say much about him before.

I would not put in anything which might be read in a history, as the beginning of a chapter could. But make some of your fine reflections on the history the knowledge of which may be taken for granted.

It is folly writing this to you, but I am remorseful at having given you so much trouble.—Yet I know you will do it all easily.

I should like Mano to be as fine and masterly from end to end as your history promises to be.—I shall expect a letter to give me your final judgment. But I shall be in no hurry and shall do no more to Mano till I hear.

In the meantime I may return the 2 other fasciculi which I have copied. Though their safety is now a matter of two strings, and I should not grieve over the loss of "the greatness".—I should smile maliciously.

With our kindest regards.

Yours ever

RB

52: TO RICHARD WATSON DIXON

Yattendon
January 29, 1883

My dear Canon

I send you some account of our trains from the latest Bradshaw.

leave Paddington.	10.20	1.0	3.30
change at Reading,	11.18	2.10	4.25
arr. at Pangbourne	11.41	2.23	4.54

The train after this arrives by night, but you can get a conveyance at Pangbourne. I should not drive both ways in the dark while the roads are so bad. It leaves London at 5. and gets to Pangbourne at 6.9 and another leaves London at 5.30 and gets to Pangbourne at 7.53.—

I shall not know what train to meet if you do not send word. If you are driven to telegraph, telegraph to Bradfield. I get a letter posted in London in the afternoon the next morning in time to meet the 11.41.

Manage to stay a good long time.

The Waterhouses will be away I am sorry to say.

Kindest regards.

yours ever

RB

We shall of course be very glad to see Mrs Dixon if she is with you. If she should come it might be convenient if she so arranged the baggage that if there was an heavy or large baggage it might be sent for the next morning.

We shall be absolutely alone and rural; thick boots and a slouch hat are the chief necessaries.

63: TO LIONEL MUIRHEAD

Yattendon

July 3, 1883

Dear Lionel

I am glad to hear that you are at home. I am afraid that I cannot accept your mother's very kind invitation for Thursday etc. as we have people constantly here and I am not sure that we shall not have a visitor. Why will not you come here? Besides which I am very busy. Come here after your yatchting [*sic*]. I never saw a bigger thunderstorm than we had last night, not much rain but incessant lightning for 5 hours, and 3 of them directly over our heads. The bedrooms were lit up by light under the doors from the passage and staircase windows—a splendid sort of thing in its way.

T. Π. has been a fortnight "in the binder's hands", so that he should be out any day. As you know the delay has been solely the printer's. I think it will be a pretty book.

With our kindest regards

yours ever

RB

It is nearly all sold.

54: TO LIONEL MUIRHEAD

Yattendon
September 7, 1883

My dear Lionel

I welcome you to the shires, and thank you very much for your letter and enclosure. If you do not want both the copies I can take one back. I think it was my doing that you were put down for two, I did not know that your father had ordered a copy, as his name did not appear, and I thought that you and he would each want one. He sent me some very amusing postcards. Your letter is by far the best and nicest that I have had on the subject. The flatteries are sweetly culled, and the fragrance of your pleasure is hot wafted in its full gush and flush to my exacting nostril. Well I am of course very glad that you like it. If one's friends did not like one's verse one would have little encouragement.

I am indeed glad that you were not cast away on the inhospitable shores of Ireland, though it would have given me an excuse for a 'Lycidas'. But I hope to show you that I am not hard up for subjects, nor likely to regard your salvation with any regret, if you will get into the train for Didcot, and disbark yourself at Hampstead Norris. Come any day, and, if you will, bring some sketching materials. If you can only stay a short time it would be very convenient to me if your visit included next Friday and Saturday (not this F. and S. but next week) as on those days I have invitations I want an excuse out of. Bring any number of herbacious perennials. Or if more convenient I will drive and meet you half way on the road. I have a light cart which I have borrowed while I am having one made. I found my dogcart too heavy for my mare in this country. But the weather just now looks rather unsettled,—however for my part I do not mind the rain, and the seat of a dogcart is I fancy not more exposed than the deck of a yatch [*sic*]. I shall await tidings of your approach.

yours ever
RB

55: TO RICHARD WATSON DIXON

Yattendon
Saturday September 15, 1883

My dear Dixon

I have not yet seen the Saturday. Gosse likes Mano better than Lang. Most people are very stupid. I have I think prevented Lang from reviewing Prometheus. As you say he is all sold. I have not seen the Academy on Mano. It is impossible to expect a modern reviewer to consider that any thing can be very good. Lang was wrong no doubt in finding difficulty in the story, but he is ill and languid. I do not see why you should expect good of reviewers. 'Love is the only praise' and they may not love. The quotation is from the Growth of Love unfinished poem of obscure poet: affected, forbidding, crabbed, quaint, elizabethan, miltonic, etc. etc. (in form cryptic, scrappy, outlandish, mysterious) simple, sensuous, passionate, true, picturesque, disregardful of form, (all epithets from my critics which I think of quoting on my next title.) I will try and write you a letter soon.

yours ever

RB

56: TO LIONEL MUIRHEAD

Yattendon
April 30, 1884

Dear Lionel

I write to tell you that I am engaged to be married to Miss Waterhouse. This is enough for one letter at least.

your ever

RB

57: TO LIONEL MUIRHEAD

Yattendon
May 22, 1884

My dear Lionel

Many thanks for your very kind and friendly letter. I am glad that you approve of my conduct.

I have plenty of letters to write, including one to my betrothed daily—and you will not expect me to say much on a subject so difficult.

You must of course come and pay us a visit in the Autumn, if as I begin to hope there is a possibility of our being married in July. I hope the reredos is getting on well. I saw Wooldridge in town the other day as he will have told you.

Ever your affectionate friend

RB

58: TO RICHARD WATSON DIXON

[Yattendon]
June 18, 1884

My dear Canon

I have had to tear off the other half sheet owing to incautious remarks. I am sorry that you are losing Creighton, especially as you had just got to know him a little. It is difficult to get near a man who talks so wildly. But he is really very sensible and warmhearted, and has been such a good friend of mine that i should have liked you to know him. His main deficiency is a sensuous artistic one, which he is mainly unconscious of, and this leads him very wrong in the subjects which we care most for. We shall get up a new prayerbook between us. Your parliamentary Litany, and my ordination of Deans. I think I inscribed also something concerning the "Houses of Parliament" for the P. B.—I think the clergy should refuse to pray for them in church on the ground of its being *of no use.*

—I should have sent you Nero, but I scarcely like to bother you with anything so full of corrections,—and I have not known what to do. I cannot write it out again. It is quite finished except a last verbal revision which will take a few days only when the time comes. It might be printed and acted as it is.—My plans are rather unsettled. I do not fancy that I shall be married before September, which is 2 months later than I expected and wished, but the Waterhouses seem to desire this delay for some reason, for one that the bride will then be of age. You will like her very much.—How do you think I shall get on as a married man? The interval is not beneficial to my work.

I am very sorry about Gerard and have treated him as badly as I have you—I must send him a letter.

I hope the Church history is going on well. I have great notions of that book.

I have bought none of your Daniel volume as I have been waiting to see if it sold of itself. If any are left I shall buy some and send them about.

Coventry Patmore has been very civil to me since Prometheus. He talks of paying me a visit. I am glad that you liked his son's poems. I hope that you wrote to tell him so. The praise which I was most ready to give them pleased him I think very much.

He has also seen Gerard's poems and has disliked them, admitting the genius.

I wonder if I could get a visit to you before September. I should like to and to bring Nero. Could it be? If so when so?

With our kindest regards to both yourself and Mrs Dixon.

yours affectionately
RB

59: TO LIONEL MUIRHEAD

Yattendon
[August ? 1884]

My dear Lionel

False reports concerning your voyages have prevented me from writing to you.

I called once in London. If you are in England will you come to the wedding—on September 3rd and be my best man?

Let me have an answer to this. As for present, you gave me my wedding present 🐱 years ago and I do not want another. If you wish to give Monica a present you could either give her a small *easel,* or have a few volumes of music bound (as I could show you) for us. But do not think but that we had rather not be presented. This is my 7th letter today. Excuse haste.

yours affectionately

RB

I was at Streatly reach all this morning—
I am too much occupied and going away to ask you down here, but if you should find your way here you would be welcome Monday.

60: TO LIONEL MUIRHEAD

Yattendon

August 15, 1884

My dear Lionel

I do not gather from your letter whether you will bestman me on the 3rd or no. I hope you will, but if it is left uncertain I may be in a fix. Please respond.

If you are at Hazeley I should get your letter in answer to this by Monday morning here, but as I shall most likely leave here on Monday on a visit north. Please, if there is any doubt about the letter being in time send a line also to me at care of Theo Waterhouse Esq. 4 Chester Place Hyde Park Square London W. where I can find it passing through London.

After next Tuesday my address will be for some days

c of. Rev. Canon Dixon
Warkworth
Northumberland.

I am going there on a Nero cleaning expedition and he is coming back with me here to marry me.

Fancy being really married!

I hope you will come.

yours ever

RB

61: TO LIONEL MUIRHEAD

Yattendon

January 28, 1885

My dear Lionel

Thanks for your letter and flattering enclosure. I am sorry to hear that you have been laid up, as everyone has, but glad you are recovering and that your illness has not taken so bad a form as some folks. I have so far escaped this pernicious season with occasional malaises. My wife has had to be in bed for 3 days, is now well again.

I hope to despatch Nero in a few days now. Printer and binder have been very long. But I think the printing will be done very well. As I am writing now I will not write again when I send it but will tell you now that I hope to go on printing in this double column form and this year to bring out Psyche and Ulysses continuing the pagination. Nero only cost me 15£ which I should get repaid. At least I hope that Psyche will make me rather more popular.

Pardon Nero if he is not pleasant. I chose the subject because it gave me incident and character and did not expect to succeed well enough to print with my first full drama.

I wish you if not too late all good wishes for this year. I hope you will be down here as soon as spring begins and join our singings. I think I shall be in town for a week next month.

your affectionate
RB

62: TO SAMUEL GEE

Yattendon
March 2, 1885

My dear Gee

Thank you a hundred times for your kind generous letter. I like praise from friends—indeed I need it for if I do not please them I am disappointed. That you think so well of Nero is a great happiness to me. I must tell you first how much I owe to Wooldridge's criticism. I may fairly say that though he did not write a word of the play it would not have come to any good but for him.

As for being *famous*. I do not know what it means. And though I am glad to have your warning I think neither part of your prophecy likely to be true—I take it as a measure of your praise only. I have written a sonnet on praise which I will transcribe on the opposite side. Judge from it my temper of mind—You know how I like Marcus Aurelius and Bishop Butler too—and may rest assured of my spiritual well being in this matter.

yours ever
RB

It would interest me to know if Mrs Gee found Nero readable—

————

Love the only praise

Who praiseth? If the poet have not known
His work is beautiful, who shall persuade?
And doth our time, that so wrongs Handel's shade,
Contrive his condemnation or its own?

The comment writ on Shakespeare hath not shewn
The perfect judgment that alive he laid
On his own work, which taketh, since 'twas made
Grace not disgrace save but of Love alone

And love in Loving nothing that is vile
Knows not the error of the mind, nor fears
To set his seal in secret with a smile.
But O, could one, as Purcell, win the tears
Of Love, such praise were more than to beguile
The learned fancies of a thousand years.

63: TO LIONEL MUIRHEAD

Yattendon
April 15, 1885

My dear Lionel

Thanks for your letter and nice little Bunyan. I am glad that you liked the get up of Nero. It was very good of you to read him all through again. I am afraid that very few persons will tolerate his coming up fresh at the end. But I have D. V. 5 acts of torment in store for him far worse than death in a 2nd part, which I hope too will not be so cumbrously long as First part is. In my own judgment it does not much matter his not being killed at the end. Everybody knows that he has been dead a long while and his name held in execration for 1700 + years.

We are longing for spring to come. I am sorry to say that my wife has been laid up. I hope she is not ill, and that we are taking more care of her than is absolutely necessary, but we wish to use all precaution. So we do not get any music. I have done no work this year except preparing Eros and Psyche for press. It will go I think in a week or two. I have not yet overlooked my final corrections. Also Ulysses is in a more or less complete state. I am inventing a comic metre and writing a Menander-like play on the lines of the self tormentor. I do not like the work: but it will be amusing I hope. I have done 2 acts nearly.—I want a good subject, as I do not mean to attack Nero II till July and might work at something else. My Mother is very well. When my wife is about again I hope you will come and see us.

yours affectionately
RB

64: TO LIONEL MUIRHEAD

Yattendon
Newbury
October 23, 1885

My dear Lionel

I do not know whether you are at home but if you could pay us a visit soon we should be very glad. My wife has not been well enough—I should say strong enough—to have visitors in the house this summer, but I think that she is herself again now, and we have just returned from a short stay in the Isle of Wight which was intended to complete her recovery. You know what you will have to expect if you come. No attractions whatever except a political meeting. We are as hard up as that, but if you could put up with it for a few days we should be very glad to see you. If you are in town you might come down for a Sunday—or at least come on Saturday and stay a little into the next week. If you are at home I would meet you either at Hampstead Norreys or on the road half way twixt here and Haseley.

"Awaiting your response"

yours affectionately
RB

You will like our new rector and would not like to miss one of his sermons if you knew what they were like.

65: TO LIONEL MUIRHEAD

Yattendon
November 24, 1885

Dear Lionel

Thanks for your letter, and for the tobacco which you so magnificently left behind you.

I wish you all happiness in your affairs, and a speedy commencement of new regime. I am myself very busy with endless occupations, such as training our choir, which is making vast strides. I have found a good tenor, and I think a male alto. Excellent voices and earnest learners. You shall have Psyche before Xmas. I hope.

yours ever
RB

66: TO LIONEL MUIRHEAD

Yattendon
December 9, 1885

My dear Lionel

I was in town for 2 days last week, called on you the first day, was told that you would be up on the 2nd—left a note to say that I would bring wife to tea if I had word at New Cavendish St that you had arrived. did not hear, so did not come. Suppose that you turned up after date. Now I send this in explanation of anything that may have puzzled you. The ice bears. I hope the weather will hold. We shall have but little opportunity for skating here but will make the most of it. Our man got in at the Election you will have seen. The biscuit baker was so sick that

he would not come forward after the declaration of the Polls to thank his supporters. There is a poor prospect I fancy for the affairs of the country with this
new parliament. I wish the radicals had had a good majority for, as one of them
said, the rustics are bound to be disappointed and will vent their rage on the
conservatives.

If you see Wooldridge do constantly remind him that he is due here at Xmas. I
shall have no work for him—

your affectionate
R Bridges

67: TO LIONEL MUIRHEAD

Yattendon
[Late December], 1885

My dear Lionel

Many thanks for your present of the Hamlet—which will be very useful as my
edition of the folio Shakespeare is too small print for my wife to read with
comfort, and it by far the most pleasant edition to read. Also thanks for your
good wishes which I reecho—I am delighted too with the kind things you say of
my poem. I am glad for the sake of your eyes that it is printed in such clear type.
I am not kindly disposed towards the poem, but I took pains with it and am very
fond of Psyche. She was a good creature, and Apuleius did not do her justice.

HEW is here. Of course he has a bad cold and cannot sing. He leaves tomorrow. We managed a little music however and sang a 7 part madrigal. And
mottets [*sic*] of Palestrina, and part of the Missa brevis. Our altoes have been
strengthened so that we do ordinary music very fairly now. You will find us
monstrously educ[ated] when you come.

With kindest regards and seasonable wishes to your people

your affectionate friend
R Bridges

H. Lunocentiday   85

P.S. I would have sent you and your father copies of Eros and Psyche but have
none to give away. The Publisher presented me with a single copy.

68: TO SAMUEL GEE

Yattendon
March 30, 1886

My dear Gee

I am glad that you think well of Eros and Psyche. Apuleius being the only
authority for the story his account of the offspring of the marriage of Eros and
Psyche is no doubt the "original." He says that there was one child ʿΗδονή by

which no doubt he intended merely Pleasure. But as Coventry Patmore said to me Apuleius was a sort of "Golden Ass" himself and did not see the meaning of his own story. To shift "Pleasure" to "Joy" seems a slight change but it makes all the difference, and though I expect most Christian renderings of the story would have, I do not think that J. M. was in his happiest vein when he made *Youth* the twin of *Joy* and a child of Eros and Psyche. But you may see a better meaning in it than I can.

This sort of difference between me and Apuleius runs all through for in my story Psyche is a charming character. All the persons in Apuleius are nonentities—and Psyche is silly.

I have not lost my cough I told you I had but something provoked it to make its reappearance, and it has been (except for the three days on one of which I wrote to you) as troublesome as sin. Still I feel much stronger in myself and hope that some day it will be gone again.

I had a letter from Barlow by same post as yours—and have sent him the same account of my cough. If you think I should take care of it or go seaside for a bit I hope you will say so. I thought of waiting to see what the spring weather would do. It seems like a chronic catarrhal state of upper part of trachea or perhaps it may extend to the larger bronchi—It is never quite absent, and rather troublesome.

yours ever

R Bridges

69: TO RICHARD WATSON DIXON

Yattendon

April 10, 1886

My dear Dixon

I don't think Daniel can be waiting for he was to spend the Easter vacation in Italy. That was one reason why I did not apologise more for my delay.

I don't like your title but am no judge of titles. I don't like "pieces", nor "including", but your reason for it seems good enough. I should call 'The spirit wooed' an ode, but if you have the alternative of 'Lyrical piece' that would probably take it preferably.

What you say about the descent of Jupiter in Cymbeline astonishes me. Tell me more. I don't like it and never did.

Criticism.   *Dickens*

"White precipitate".

You are welcome to 'precipitate' but people will think you got it not from me but found it at the chemists'.—'White precipitate' is a salt of mercury which is made up into a common ointment called 'white precipitate ointment' used to destroy lice.

"from their grey mysterious cave"
"hotly bayed"
are Shelley-isms
ditto next line

———   ———

2nd stanza. *See* how wintry are the *sounds* that come. Remember! you must call this an ode to a pig on the death of D.

I object to your writing any ode or anything else on the death of Dickens. I have a contempt for his father, and regard him merely as a very amusing writer in a vulgar style. In that inimitable and unsurpassed. Your reflection is that he said how near sorrow and joy were. The smile and the tear. I don't think he knew what joy was. Perhaps I wrong him, but query, if he did know, is he the man who told us this first, or better than anyone else? Thus RB.

Advancing Age

I don't like meddling with this which is one of the most fearfully sad things ever written: too sad.

But I think perhaps *step* would be better than *foot* 4 lines from bottom of p. 1. Crashing as epithet of foot seems to introduce the notion of hugeness and stamping.—The end of the top stanza on p. 36 is very fine.

The stanza on death of the dog I query whether you might not with advantage omit the word *die* in the 2nd line.

Read *fain reject.*
Next line *?The pitying hand*
for *the pity of the hand* metis gratia?

———

wearying sighs.

I don't know why wearying. Whether they wearied you or the dog it seems wrong. *?Wearied* is full of weariness.

———

N. B. Write never-moving.

yours affectionately

RB

If you write during next few days address c/o Creighton, Worcester.

70: TO RICHARD WATSON DIXON

Yattendon
August 5, 1886

My dear Dixon

The enclosed is I think very like a poem by Gerard Hopkins. It is quite an accidental parody being merely occasional lines or words written on a loose sheet

The Manor House at Yattendon ("The Sleeping Mansion"), taken when Robert Bridges lived there, 1886. *In right foreground:* **Mrs. Robert Bridges, Robert Bridges, Harry Ellis Wooldridge. See letter 956. Courtesy of the Lord Bridges.**

of paper for the purpose of trying pens. The paper was used as an outside to a copy which Monica is making of the Feast of Bacchus and it received quite accidental contribution as you will see. The poem was therefore some months I may say in construction, which accounts for its perfection. If it amuses you as much as it does me you will agree with me that it transcends mere ingenuity. I have finished my Psalter. I have been very sorry not to have sent you any contributions for your Birthday Book. But you said when you were here that it had to be ready so soon that I rather despaired. It is the sort of work which should be a long time on hand.—I have had registration of voters also to do, and many things which have distracted me.—Especially as I have been trying hard to get to work again. We leave for a visit to the sea in end of September and before that time I want to get the extremely obstinate Palicio into better order. The work is tedious because I have to be so concise. There is too much stuff in the plot.—If I can get this done before I go away I shall have a clear field to finish something new before Xmas. My mother has been away for a holiday and has just come back, and is I think glad to get home. Our schoolmaster is away and all the choir training etc. falls again to me—Our rector leaves tomorrow for his holiday, and this will add to my burdens a little.—The choir goes on very well. Their performance is sometimes admirable. We always sing now on Wednesday evenings without the organ. I give the key note from a pitchpipe and they sing by the book and give no trouble. Last Wednesday the chants were very difficult and they went without a hitch. It is very nice to have one's work so well repaid. On Monday last too the organ music for the anthem which they had to sing was left behind, and they did the anthem perfectly without accompaniment getting much that day from 2 or 3 London visitors who were present.—I shall be very busy copying music and finishing Palicio for the next month—but I hope to hear from you and send you a line now and then. I fear I cannot mend that sonnet. I cannot get at it. Could you do it?

yours ever
RB

This is written on "butter paper" which costs only /5 a lb. I buy it for scribbling and overseer's work.

71: TO LIONEL MUIRHEAD

Goodwick
Fishguard Bay
Pembrokeshire
Thursday, September 23, 1886

My dear Lionel

It seems good unto me to write unto you hence, because it hath struck me that when you are reading Ulysses you may amuse yourself by doing a picture (diagrammatic as you please) in perspective, of the hall of Ulysses, to be printed from a wood block when I print Ulysses, to serve for frontispiece and stage directions. If the sketch at beginning of MS is not explicit I will send you any details that you want. The important one is the relation of the outer court to the hall. It is necessary that the audience should see enough through the doors when they are open to be aware that there is a good congregation of suitors without. Then the threshold is raised going down at least 2 steps into the hall and as many or more into the courtyard. So that a section from behind forwards would be thus

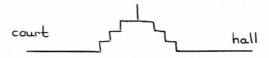

The stairs on the left must be practicable for the descent of Penelope, and connected with the balcony at back on which the maids appear in a row leaning over the balustrades (which as Ulysses made them by hand may be all different or fantastically varied)—At the bottom of the step is a good "landing" and this continued with the "dais" which runs all around, and on the left is broadest, sufficient to hold Penelope's chair when she sits to receive the gifts.

If you will do a pencil scheme and submit it for alteration I shall be so much obliged. I should also ask HEW to put in the scene where Telemachus introduces Penelope to Ulysses. The 3 figures would do well.

The Homeric house is a disputed question. The construction required for my play is not probable, but not at all objectionable. It would fit all Homer except the one fact which the drama forbids i. e. that all the suitors should be slain in the banqueting hall.

I hope you will do it. If you are not disposed never mind.

We are enjoying ourselves immensely, the weather being perfect. I think the deep sea bathing is what I enjoy most. I brought Palicio down here and have nearly cured him.

With our kindest regards

yours ever
RB

Size of drawing should be the size of the letterpress of Nero—*full.*

72: TO LIONEL MUIRHEAD

Yattendon
October 14, 1886

My dear Lionel

I was very sorry to hear that your eyes were giving you trouble again. I hope that you are by this time freed from the anxiety as well as the annoyance which it must have caused you. I should have written before, but have been wandering, and only got home a few days ago. Your letter followed me about, and turned up much after date.

We had a very pleasant time at Goodwic[k], and being in quiet I got to work again a little, but returning home found so many little things to be attended to that I am in my usual do nothing condition.

Of course I do not wish to bother you with drawing out Ulysses' house. If you feel inclined after reading the play I shall be much flattered as well as obliged. If I print it I shall want a descriptive frontispiece. Please also make as many suggestions as may strike you in a critical way. I am always glad of such remarks.

Come down here any Sunday you like. Our choir had a "harvest thanksgiving" last Sunday, and acquitted themselves very well. I asked Stuckey Coles to preach, but he couldn't come. Neither was he disengaged for any one Sunday through Advent.

I have heard from H E W who told me that he had seen you. He seemed in the same procrastinating mood as far as visiting us was concerned. I hardly think now that he will ever come. When I left Goodwic[k] I went to stay with the Frys near Bristol, and made a pilgrimage to the Gibbses at Tinsfield to see the Wooldridge windows. I thought them extremely good, though the people there hate them, and the old archdeacon whom they keep as a private chaplain could not imagine why I should think them worth looking at. They are in every respect but one successful, but the workman who did the faces was evidently incompetent and has spoiled the effect by making rather silly and ugly saints. The colour is excellent and the whole decorative effect the best I have ever seen in stained glass.

yours ever
RS Bridges

My kindest regards to your folk.
(We shall want a bulletin from you).

73: TO LIONEL MUIRHEAD

Yattendon
November 6, 1886

My dear Lionel

I was very glad to hear that you are so much better, and set that against the somewhat discouraging tone of your oculist. Nettleship I should think is not an optimist. I hope that he has not given you any very strong poisons to drink. I feel more disposed to encourage you than to express sympathy, although of course I know that in looking forward to possible ills the prospect is equally disagreeable whether the evil ever comes or no. But you have plenty of philosophy of your own—if you want any of mine come and pay us a visit. Any day. I am writing and shall always have busy mornings till Xmas, but if you do not mind that we can fill the rest of the time pleasantly enough. It is delightful your having a cassock here. It has not come, but when it does it shall take possession of a bedroom for you.

If you are at home (Your letter saith not where you will be) and can get any of your familia to read Ulysses to you I should of course be very glad that they should read it. I can warrant it free from stumbles—I should not wish any one who is likely to be going to translate the Odyssey to get hold of it. When you come down here I shall be delighted to read it you to get your criticism.

I hope you will get better every day. I am sure Nettleship is right about minute work. I used to think that you did too much. We will invent something for you to do. A new art. I think that Wooldridge may come for Xmas but I do not know.— I am selling my mare today. Do you know of a horse that would suit me?—must be strong and amiable.

—with kindest regards to your Father and Mother and sisters both.

your affectionate friend
RB

Come and see us soon, as soon as you like. You are of course always welcome.

74: TO LIONEL MUIRHEAD

Yattendon
December 7, 1886

My dear Lionel

I am glad to hear that you are going on well. I think a good deal about you. I have not written partly because I suppose it cannot be good for you to read letters, and partly because I am bored, and have nothing much to write about.

You will be glad that your surplice has arrived. I do not know whether it would fit Wooldridge or no, but it is pretty certain that you will wear it before he does.

He is now arranging to stay in London all through Xmas—and talks of coming to see us when his work is finished in January, by which we know he means June or July, and then will probably put off again for 3 months.

He is however coming down for one night (the 23rd) to sing in a concert.* But we hardly expect him, though his name is printed on the programme—he will probably miss his train—

The concert is a nuisance invented by our rector—

I will write again soon—

your affectionate
RB

*He won't want to wear your cassock then I should think.

75: TO LIONEL MUIRHEAD

Yattendon
December 26, 1886

My dear Lionel

It was delightful to get a letter from you again, and to have such good news about your eyes. Wooldridge has actually come here for Xmas, and was dressed in your cassock yesterday (which fitted him well enough) and he told me also about you. I feel sure that if you take care of yourself that you will go on getting better. At least I am certain that you need not be depressed by what oculists say, as they not only confess to you that they have little or no knowledge of that which is wrong with your eye, but they are I know extremely liable to make false deductions from what they see—let alone the difficulty and uncertainty of the interpretation of the actual appearances.

When your Xmastide is over I hope that you will come and see us, and feel disposed to stay for a good time. Please write and offer when convenient. HEW is going away on Tuesday. He is most amusing and entertaining and as usual instructive. He seems too in fairly good preservation.

I am glad that you liked Ulysses. As for the dog—there was no chance for him in the drama. Nor did I admit Theoclymenus, who is otherwise interesting. Nor the old nurse—I think that the audience would be intolerant of what you suggest the reader misses, a tender speech between Ulysses and Penelope. In such cases one line which admits of the tenderest interpretation is enough for the actor. The sentiment once arrived at, there is nothing more to be done. If the tears do not start, it's no use pumping, and most people would get up and look for their hats.

We shall be glad to see you any day. Only mind you stay some time. We will do our best to make you comfortable.

Now with best Xmas wishes to your Father and Mother and Miss Muirhead if she is with you

your affectionate friend
R Bridges

76: TO SAMUEL GEE

Yattendon
December 29, 1886

My dear Gee

I usually write a few letters at Xmas tide to friends whom I have not heard of for an undue length of time—and you may think that I should have this year included you—But though I have not heard from you for a long while it has not seemed to weaken my imagination and your very welcome letter today assures me that you are the same. Except that I think you want your inside stirring up a bit.—That there is to be no "real improvement in mundane affairs to the end of time" is a heresy and I fear you have been indulging too much in the stoic meditations that you are so fond of to the neglect of the more poetic and cheerful sayings to be found elsewhere. I believe—O the wilfulness of poets—that the meek shall inherit the earth, and I do not know that unless one thought that one could help them to that desirable position there would seem to me to be any reason for existing. Science certainly teaches us that man has improved and literature on the whole I think testifies to improvement since historical times.— But I won't preach.—The impending democracy is not likely to be a final step, nor in my opinion will it last very long if it should actually establish itself at all.

I was sorry to hear of your mother's death. My mother is getting on in years but though she is not of course as active as you remember her, she has excellent health—except for her chronic rheumatism—and looks as well as she ever did since I can remember her.

Legg has then taken my advice. It is not too late. With that appearance he might be a bishop yet if he will get ordained at once.

My wife is very well. We had a jolly time at the sea last autumn. I am sorry that you have sold your house at Hythe. I am thinking of leaving here and going somewhere less dear. This house is too expensive to let us travel as much as I should wish in the winter, and I have got now so many things to do here, that though they leave me plenty of time for writing, yet they distract my thoughts too much. At least I set it down to this that I wrote nothing last year. It may be that my vein has run out: for though I am well I certainly feel older than I did.— I have 3 unprinted plays which I hope to print soon, but there is no hurry about that and when I do print it will be privately. Nothing on earth would persuade me to pose as a poet or even a member of the literary profession. Without pretending to superhuman virtue I can say that I despise the whole thing as much as I loathe the vulgar [?   ] the crowd receives from journalists. Should the public demand my poems I know that I should do wrong to withhold them—But that is fortunately impossible owing to the reserve of my style. So I feel safe—as long as I do not court the beast of many heads.

I hope to be in London for a day ere long and will come and see you if I am. Now I send you my best Xmas wishes and for the new year, (to Mrs Gee and yourself) and may you live happily together through many—

your affectionate friend
R Bridges

Wooldridge was down here for Xmas. He thinks as you do (and most Londoners) about the prospects of the world.

77: TO LIONEL MUIRHEAD

Yattendon
January 22, 1887

My dear Lionel

Thank you for your last letter. I am on the 5th act of the Christian Captives and writing a vision of judgment so I can feel in key with your present reflections, and at the same time congratulate you on the probability of your being married soon. May I be there to see?

I am afraid that we must put off your visit. Monica and I are going away now for a bout of 3 weeks——After which any day you come we shall be delighted. I hope that your eye will go on mending. It is a good thing that you know the Psalms or you would scarcely use your cassock here. It is hanging up waiting for you. I hope that you will come as soon as we are back.

your affectionate
RB

78: TO RICHARD WATSON DIXON

Yattendon
January 22, 1887

My dear Dixon

I am so grieved to hear from my mother that you have been laid up in London, and I am afraid that you must have been rather bad or else you would have written to me. I hope that it was merely inconvenience and discomfort that kept you from writing and not incapacity—as I hope that there was nothing in my last letter which you did not like.

Perhaps you have been busy on history or lyrics. My brother John is down here. He does little literary work that I know of now but for magazines and newspapers—Lang is bringing out a little book on the Eros and Psyche myth. With a reprint. He writes to me occasionally.—Lord Justice Fry liked your history very much I hear, but thought you somewhat clerical—I am now finishing the Christian Captives. I think I shall get them right. I have since New Years day read a lot of Spanish comedies—chiefly Lope de Vega—They are not up to their reputation—but there are some good things. They are dreadfully alike—and without characterization. I return to Aeschylus—I read also the 2 large volumes of Shelley's Life by Dowden. I 'rose from the perusal' sickened with Shelley. That is his biographer's fault. D will not allow the reader to think that Shelley was mad. If you may not sometimes laugh at Shelley you soon lose your patience with him.

Did ever any other man take to himself a woman in the lifetime of his wife, and ask his wife to accompany him in his travels with his new love?

A family tree of the Godwins and Shelleys should be published showing the suicides etc.—I hope you are now getting better. I was comforted to hear that Dr. Barlow was attending you.

your affectionate

RB

79: TO LIONEL MUIRHEAD

Seaford. (Marine View)
February 12, 1887

My dear Lionel

I do not know how often you wish to be congratulated, but I suppose that I need not spare you now. It is amusing to hear of your engagement from so many quarters.

Very soon I hope to have the pleasure of felicitating you face to face, and I can only hope that the weather may be more reasonable when you come to us than it is now. I fancy from the accounts in the paper that we have had much severer cold than has visited you. There is snow on the beach, and the salt pools are frozen thickly. I will tell you all that has happened to us when we meet.

On Wednesday next we go to Hastings to stay a day or two with the Patmores. We hope to be in London on Sunday (that is tomorrow week) and get home on Monday or Tuesday.

I am sorry that our choir will not be in a very good condition for you: as both our altoes are away and our chief and best boy singer, not to speak of Paul and Morris W. both being absent, but I daresay you will make the best of it, and we can extemporise another 2 altoes.

If you will come in time for Wednesday evening service at 6 or 7 p.m. we shall sing In Exilis Israel together unless I miscalculate.

yours ever

RB

I will write to HEW.
Wife says she knew all about it long ago and won't write specially to you as you have been drawing so many compliments from other ladies of the family.

80: TO LIONEL MUIRHEAD

Yattendon

March 25, 1887

My dear Lionel

Thanks for your letter telling me of your marriage feast. I was going to write and ask you about it. I understand that you do not so much withdraw your invitation as display the obstacles to my good will—and that therefore if I can find my way over and back that I may put in an appearance. Should the wedding be over-furnished with guests I might get a chop at the village inn. As the time draws nearer and the weather declares itself—and most of all when I have clearly made out the best route and the travelling facilities I can then write and tell you whether I see my way to being present—as I hope to be.

Wooldridge is here. I think that he is decidedly better than when he came, but he is very easily fatigued. and I think did too much one day (of his own accord—I was at home with a cold) and rather threw himself back. He has great muscular weakness and queer pains. I should think he will get all right with food and care. He has recovered his spirits which astonishes him extremely. He doesn't seem to know where they come from or go to. He interrupts me to send his love to you, and to say that the sheep which you sent him will do very well, and he will drive some of them into your picture. He is doing me a careful watercolour of Gerard Hopkins. But it has not got to the colour stage yet. We have great music times; he sings alto in the choir wearing your cassock. Unfortunately I have not yet been in church once since he came having a bad cold, which is I suppose going away by degrees. Lunch is just coming up (and going down) so I conclude.

yours affectionately

RB

81: TO MACMILLAN & CO.

Yattendon

Newbury

April 22, 1887

Gentlemen

I am afraid that I did not definitely thank you for your offer concerning the Terence, as I should have done. The matter no doubt may appear to us in different lights. I cannot imagine a more thankless task. Terence's Language is more faultless than Virgil's, and does not offer the escape into elevation which Virgil allows. Then, when all is done, the best modern equivalent brings one into very rough contact with Latin manners. It was for these reasons that I recommended the reprinting of Cooke's version: because the colloquialisms of his date being now out of vogue one is removed from everyday life without effort or affectation.

I do not know for what purpose you need a translation but I should think that if Dr Holden (for example) were to accompany your reprint with notes on the scholarship, that the book would serve any turn which you could desire, either as an aid to students or as a book for English readers.

Englishmen who do not know Latin should read Plautus and Terence in the French.

I should not have ventured to offer any opinion had not your letter to me implied some confidence in my knowledge of the subject.

While obliged to decline your offer I yet send you my best thanks for it.

yours truly
Robert Bridges

82: TO LIONEL MUIRHEAD

Yattendon
May 8, 1887

My dear Lionel

I hear you are at Venice, and till yesterday we have all wished ourselves thereabouts. Now the weather has changed, and summer has come. Though we have had no spring things don't seem much the worse for it; and I fancy nature has made up her mind to show Spring that we can do very well without her: in hopes of getting her to make some step towards reformation. I am a thousand-fold ashamed of myself for not having written to you before: and what with the impossibility of finding you a wedding present I hardly dare write now. I must shuffle off with the consideration that it would be no use to send you anything out in Italy; so that if I wait till you come home I shall still be in time. Then I am godson to Marsden's last baby, and have the same difficulty there. If I write a jubilee ode I shall reproach Victoria Q: on the disgrace to her reign from the discomfort to intelligent folk produced by the bad taste, of which she has a share and has done nothing to obviate. Why, it would be like heaven to live in a country where one could go into the shops and see things that one could buy. The latest silver mugs seem to be decorated with fern leaves, like fashionable wine-glasses and suburban windows.

I hope that you are enjoying yourself. I have had 2 kind letters from your brother which lead me to suppose that you are. They were partly about a proposed visit to Hawkesley. But Monica is forbidden to march about this summer: and we are taking great care of her in the hope that our precautions will have the desired result. It was after your visit that Wooldridge came here—I hope he went back the better for his longish stay: I was dreadfully sorry to see the sort of condition which he seemed to have got into, mind as well as body. He was past my stirring up and only produced a fearful despondency and fretfulness of temper in me, which I was some time in shaking off. Lately I have been well at work. Achilles in Scyros is nearly finished and is I think something more in your taste than some of my work. Directly it is done I am going at a very amusing romantic comedy. I am sorry to be writing on two half sheets but when I got to the end of the first I lamentably and hopelessly blotted the second and had not time to rewrite. Our choir has improved very much indeed. I think Wooldridge singing with them must have taught them something which I *can't*. Sometimes the service is quite pleasant musically. My brother Tom's widow died suddenly the other day. Two of her younger children have come here for awhile. They are sweet creatures. Everybody very well. Monica sends her kindest remembrances etc. and with my love

your affectionate
R Bridges

Count this better than nothing, although poor.
My best compliments to Mrs. L. M.

83: TO ROBERT BRIDGES

Hotel Victoria
Venezia
Sunday, June 12, 1887

My dear Robert

I got your letter yesterday and read it seated on the steps of the Post Office with the Canal lapping the marble step where my feet rested and beautiful old windows with veined shafts and carved capitals looking over my shoulder, and having taken in all its welcome news from Yattendon I was the better able to enjoy all Tintoretto's frescoes in The Scuola di San Rocca and the wonderful collection of Venetian pictures in The Accademia, after which Gracie and I threaded our way through the labarynth [*sic*] of alleys to the north of Venice and back home by gondola. I forget whether you have ever been here, but if not you really must manage to come some day for a short time and enjoy the beauty and picturesqueness of the place though the want of elbow room in the streets would probably prevent you from delighting in the odd nooks and corners and the many coloured crowd as much as one who is of much more humble stature can do.—It is difficult to tell you what a happy time I have been spending and I should have written to you before but for the difficulty of finding leasure [*sic*] during the day with so much to be done, whilst at night I make a rule of not reading or writing anything. You will I am sure be glad to know that my eye is really much better, and I am again able to tell colour with some exactness, and have even ventured to do a little drawing, and if only it will continue to mend however slowly I shall be indeed contented.—I have found pale blue glasses invaluable, and with them can brave the glare of full sunshine without any inconvenience.—We started with the Italian lakes, and enjoyed Lugano greatly as the chestnut woods were all coming out and the great purple Irises were in full glory: but on the Lago Maggiore the weather got bad, and we therefore came down to Milan where we stayed nearly a fortnight making expeditions to the fine old city of Pavia and to Monza. The Certosa of Pavia was I thought on seeing it again after 20 years the most wonderful place I know in Italy. It is a grand building of brick and marble and is filled with treasures of mosaic fresco and sculpture in marble and bronze, most of it 'first rate' and scarcely anything that one could wish away. The Monks have all gone and the whole place has been made a monument of Italy, and is kept up by the government in capital order. Perhaps Monte Cassino near Naples may be as good, but in the north of Italy I know of nothing that can bear comparison with this Certosa.—The effect of the interior of Milan Cathedral who shall describe? You know it I think so I shall say no more except that I wish you were Precentor there.—Do not go to Monza— Bergamo is a fascinating spot notwithstanding that it owes none of its fascination to its Inns. The old town stands on a hill with the magnificent plains of Lombardy to the South, and behind it rise the Alps as fine a piece of mountain background as could be desired. I would have given much to spend a couple of months there drawing, but I did not dare to do so. Brescia has good things too, notably a very fine bronze Victory one of the best antique bronzes extant, and both there as at Bergamo there are a lot of delightful pictures which are in a light where you can see them as well as a lot which are in places where you can't.—As to Verona we stayed there a fortnight and only came away because we feared it would get too hot for Venice. It is full of beauty and I should like to live in it and draw for months: indeed I should prefer drawing there to drawing in Venice. And now I have given you some sort of outline of the places we have seen, all the charm of detail in which these old cities abound must be left to your imagination, that which Shakespeare has supplied is in its way as good as the real thing.—And now for your home news. It grieves me that you should vex your soul about a wedding gift and that your eyes should ever have looked at silver plate scrawled with fern leaves. It seems indeed a pity that fern seed cannot somehow exert its mystic power to the happy purpose of rendering the leaves invisible. If you are bent on giving me something perhaps at The Arundel Society's there may be a chromo which would please us both. Anyhow I venture to make the suggestion in order that you may be no more tormented by the silversmiths.

I shall be *most* anxious to hear good news of your wife's health by and bye. I hope you will write me a line however short; though at present I cannot give you an address a letter will always be forwarded from Haseley.—That your play writing goes on successfully is also very good news and I shall look forward much to reading Achilles as well as the amusing romantic comedy you hint at.—I have as yet seen no good books on the stalls, and I much fear that Venice has been ransacked over much. In the Ducal Library there are things that might cause one to break all the locks as well as all the commandments. Luckily neither is possible as the month of June is too warm to make an attempt which if it succeeded might make Venice altogether too hot—

Ever your affectionate
Lionel Muirhead

Oh! I have got such patterns for embroidery! They are too good to describe——.

84: TO ROBERT BRIDGES

Hotel Victoria
Venice
July 31, [1887]

My dear Robert

I have not altogether got over the sense of strangeness in being abroad and not seeing you anywhere about, but I suspect this year that you have had it as hot at Yattendon, as we in Italy, and hope it has agreed with you both.—We got into such very comfortable quarters in Venice that we made up our minds we would spend the summer here where there was abundance of lemons and ice and luxurious gondolas at hand always rather than go up into the mountains, where all these comforts might be absent, and hitherto we have done remarkably well.—Many days it is too broiling to go out much until the evening, when a row on the lagoons in a delicious sea breeze either under the starlight or a Venetian moon is one of the most enjoyable things imaginable. My eyesight is much more comfortable, and I do not find that the strong light does it any harm which is a great blessing. We worked very hard when we first came here, and saw most that the guide books told us of, and a good many things they did not, and now we can afford to take life easily with quiet consciences, and know pretty well what we care to go and see again and what we do not. The Tintorettos at Venice are certainly most splendid: there is a huge one in S. Maria Del Orto of the Worship of the Golden Calf with Mt Sinai robed in great clouds and a long desert valley below full of the tents of the Israelites and in the foreground a number of splendid Venetian women taking off their gold ornaments and casting them on a great heap round the golden calf, which 'fetches' me greatly. Unluckily it is too dark to photograph, and I do not suppose it has ever been engraved and I am quite disconsolate at having only my treacherous recollection to trust it to.—You really will have to come here on your next foreign expedition.—We made three journeys to Torcello an island some miles to the north of Venice where once was a town which has dwindled down to certainly not more than half a dozen houses, but the old Cathedral and Baptistry of the 7th century still exist and are most curious and beautiful. I made a large drawing of the place which I hope you may see some day. We are meditating a voyage by steamer to Chioggia a very picturesque fishing town to the south of Venice, where all the boats have gorgeously coloured sails and queer little Madonnas and Saints perched on the top of the masts. Gracie is hard at work doing embroidery, one of the patterns I got from

S. Antonio at Padua. I hope your Cricket and Choir go on well, and I wish you were Precentor of S. Marks. I hope too your wife is well.

Your affectionate friend
Lionel—

85: TO LIONEL MUIRHEAD

Yattendon
August 7, 1887

My dear Muirhead

We were delighted to get a letter from you. I should have written before, but never imagined that you would be spending all this hot summer at Venice. I suppose that it can't be hotter there than it is here: but no doubt your other correspondents have described the baking season to you. I have been for a fortnight in Northumberland with Canon Dixon, a very pleasant visit, and now I am at home again and shall remain, except for a visit to London next month. Do you see the papers? There was a cheering account yesterday of a Liberal Unionist's 'Ministerial' dinner at Greenwich!! The point of it was that it seemed to seal for ever their united determination to oppose Gladstone. Bright was in the chair, and made one of his best speeches dead against Gladstone, speaking of the grand old silly billy just as you or I should and Hartington who followed said some of the severest things that have ever fallen from his temperate mouth against the men who have left the Unionists for the Radicals. It was altogether the most hopeful business that there has been in politics since I can remember.

Gerard Hopkins, whose family now live at Haslemere, is just going home for his holiday. I am looking forward to going to spend a few days with him. We shall have a great deal to talk of. He writes to me that he has restored the mutilated choruses in the Coëphorae!! What next? I have not done much, but things go on. I should like to be in Venice for a week especially to see the Tintoret's—but the older I grow (and there's no mistake at all about my growing older) the more I prefer the earlier schools. It's a great pity that as art develops, 'taste' so generally declines.

It seems the same in other arts besides painting.—Monica has still to take care of herself, and is not allowed to walk about much. The consequence is that I don't see many people, and a 'corollorally' is that I have nothing to write about except myself. Achilles I am sorry to say is not finished, though he draws to a close. Monica and I are amusing ourselves with scheming the plot of a light-comedy in 3 acts, which should be good fun. "The Humours of the Court" is its name. I mean to get it done by Xmas. At present I am hardly ever inclined to work. Dixon kindly read *Palicio* for me and approved of it.—He has it to work on.—If you had heard the singing at Yattendon P. church this morning you wouldn't wonder at my echoing your wish that I was Precentor at St Marks. I wish I were. The village boys here with one practice a week do not arrive at great things. However this evening they have to sing the Psalms without the organ, and let it come in at the Gloria, and if they've got ever so little flat they'll get no pay. They point very fairly now. Did you hear of my army brother's widow's death? My nieces have been here, some of them. It is a large family of orphans in some senses not "unprovided for" but less prepared for independent or home rule than the sister Isle.

With kindest regards to Mrs. L.

yours ever

RB

Glad to hear the pages behave well.—Don't try them too much—

86: TO LIONEL MUIRHEAD

Yattendon
October 20, 1887

My dear Lionel

I was very glad to get your letter this morning and to hear the details of your delightful wanderings. Sorry that your eye had given you any trouble, but ready to give you credit for more philosophy than most mortals carry about with them—I hope that your wife reads your letters for you. With that surmise I will apologise to her if my writng is not all it should be, for I know by experience that my good intentions of writing plainly visibly decay in any letter that I ever write. I was sorry to hear of your mother's illness. It was the first news I had had of it. I fear it must have given you many days of anxiety. We are well here, Monica especially. And as the time is now approaching when she hopes to have a child to look after you will I hope find one here when you come back. We are going up to London next month for her confinement. At least these are our plans. We have been in the spirit a good deal in Italy this year, having been reading chiefly Italian history, and fighting all over your country with the Colonne and Farnesa commanders and the indomitable Swiss adventurers. I should like to see Urbino immensely but of all the places you mention Marostica tantalises me most. We should I think have been in Italy last winter had not a friend of ours used up all our spare money, and now we talk of going next year: but cannot tell. Perhaps one's duty is to lay up money in gold to meet the threatening exigencies. If Gladstone lives much longer there will be something very like civil war. He foments disorder now openly, and in consequence the London mobs now come to blows with the police and defy authority. It is best to take no interest in politics. There is nothing to be done but for the people to learn by experience I fear, and that must cost something. The sooner it comes the better.

I have done but little work. I finished the play I told you of—(Achilles in Sycros) this year, and if I had a few days good disposition I could write a comedy which I have drawn up but I have been sadly out of gear for writing. I wrote a paper on Milton's prosody, which is being printed by the Clarendon press as an appendix to one of their school books. It is a fair piece of work I think, and should set the example in a field where incompetence has reigned. I am busying myself too with hymns, in an attempt to do something for church music. This you must see before you can judge. I think it would interest you. I have seen few friends. Sanday came here for a day from Oxford, and Gerard Hopkins paid us a visit; he is more of the Jesuit priest than ever. His last poem too is if anything less intelligible than usual. Wooldridge stayed about a month with us; he is better than he was. He gets lots of work to do and wastes more time than ever over it. He brings books on music—and writes old fashioned music. I can't make anything of him. He does not take much interest either in my work. The same post which brought your letter brought a long one from Mr. Shadwell, the old clergyman who was at Venice and Florence with us. He recalled the Florence days. And I wondered whether you would call on Wilson of Tornabuoni S^t and have more whist, whether Captain Herbert still patronises Paoli's. You will see Stanhope no doubt. If so please remember me to him.

Today I am to go to the consecration of a chancel in the church where your wife's cousin's husband Mr. Preston Atkins is church warden. Yattendon is unchanged. I think my library is more interesting. And we have a good deal of interest going on. But I have not been up to much this year and have had one week in bed with rheumatism. I had however a very pleasant visit at Canon Dixon's in Northumberland and enjoyed sea bathing. The year will now soon be over. My choir goes on fairly well—It is generally a pleasure to sing with them. I paid a visit to Windsor and Eton this year. The latter looked more like enchanted land than any place I had ever been in. Just now we are buying a great lot of music. The weather is delightful, and the country looking its best. The trees this year are better than I have ever seen them. All is light golden browns and light greens, the skies every day cloudless blue, and the air sharp and brisk. Just now we are in fact much better off for weather than you can be, but that will not last long. I shall see Wooldridge again when I am in London, I hope he is not so bad as you think. He has seemed very comfortable when I have seen him, and has lots to do. With my paper I end my ragged letter with all our kindest regards and mine to Mrs. L. I am

your affectionate
R Bridges

I don't forget that I never sent you any wedding present. I shan't till you come home. Then we will see what can be done.

87: TO ROBERT BRIDGES

Hotel Paoli
Lung Arno, Tecca Vecchia
Firenze
December 11, 1887

My dear Robert

Here I am in the old diggings only at the other end of the House where we have got 3 comfortable rooms looking out on the Arno. Paoli himself whom I never much liked is not improved and 3 sets of people have left the place since we have been here in consequence of his sharp dealing, and if I came to Florence again I should not patronise his house; however as our rooms are just what we like we shall stay probably till the middle of January next, and quite possibly longer, as my wife has been rather unwell since we have been in Florence, and accordingly we have not done much sightseeing. Old Wilson is attending her and is a most kind and attentive person, and now she is much stronger and I hope in a short time will be quite herself again. We have had the most vile weather for the last month with the exception of 3 or 4 lovely days, and just now the fog is so thick all round that the hill of San Miniato is nearly invisible from our window, and the air is as raw and damp as it could be in Great Britain and Ireland. The facade of the Cathedral is the chief alteration since we were here a few years ago. The Italians are very proud of it, though all that is good in it is copied from the old work, and what is amiss is when the old work has been badly copied, as in the inlaid work round the windows which is so poor that it scarcely tells at all, and the carved figures beside Giottos lovely little works on the Campanile close by will not do at all. The column in the Mercato Vecchio with a statue of Donatello's on the top has been carted away, and a great part of the tall old Houses around are in process of demolition. I do not know what is to be put up in their place. Otherwise I think things remain just what they were. On one of the few lovely days we have had we drove round by Fiesole and Vinciliata where I remember so well we took a long walk: I had quite forgotten how very beautiful it is the whole way. The little 9th century Cathedral at Fiesole too has been restored by the Government, and all the rubbish cleared out of it: I cannot tell you what a beautiful building it now is. So soon as the traditional Italian climate begins to reassert itself and my wife is strong we purpose making several expeditions to mediaeval walled towns and fortresses in the mountains where the Zeit-geist who cannot travel much except by railway has not yet been.

Stanhope is very busy painting and I am to go and see his work next Saturday: he enquired much after you. He is very little changed himself, though Mrs S. has got a good deal stouter and her hair is quite grey. Their villa seems to me to be the perfection of beauty and comfort combined.—Your long letter to me of October 20. was highly appreciated, and I wish you success with all my heart in your hymn writing. The recollection of your choir is an especial pleasure in a land where the finest Churches ever built echo to the sound of the vilest music ever written, and the sound of an organ now will generally drive me dancing out of any of them. I do not know whether Dante has any specially hot circle for Italian organists, I am afraid organs were not invented in his day.—Your essay on Milton's prosody too I much long to see, but you do not say what school book it is that is to have it as an appendix. You will perhaps be interested to hear that the "Vyne" book is out at last and is a pretty publication and some of the text of much general interest. I have only just had a copy sent me—

We have seen the Times most irregularly and I do not in the least know whether all has gone well with your wife, but I earnestly hope so. I hope you will send me 'a line' as soon as you can as I feel very anxious to know. My Mother you will be glad to hear is very much better: I do not know whether she will ever be quite well after her attack, but she has latterly gained strength so fast that I hope she may quite recover.—My own sight is at present less troublesome:

Your affectionate friend
Lionel Muirhead

Pen   Ink   and Blotting paper all very bad

88: TO LIONEL MUIRHEAD

care of A. Waterhouse Esq.

20 New Cavendish St.
London W.
December 16, 1887

My dear Lionel

Monica has been blowing me up for the last 3 or 4 days for not writing to you—and all the while there was the letter from you travelling towards me—which I was waiting for. When last you wrote you had not reached Florence and I expected a line from you or a post card when you settled down. Now I fancy you at Paoli's. You will be glad to hear that I can answer your enquiries after my family affairs satisfactorily. Baby is now eleven days old. Monica had not much trouble, and is I trust getting well. It is a girl, and a fair sort of creature, not big but well shaped etc. We have had to stay already more than a month in London, and expect to have quite two months of it altogether.—It is rather hard to know what to do with oneself—the dirt is so dreadfully filthy and the reading room at the British Museum has in the interest of the lower classes been made impossible for gentlemen.—A jug of French dirt with germs from Soho 20 billions to the square millimetre.—However there is a concert now and then and there are old friends whom I am glad to see.

I was glad to hear that your eyes had been behaving better. I hope that your wife will get quite strong again, and that Wilson rose above his reputation. I thought well of him and he was very kind and painstaking.

I send you the Miltonic prosody. It may possibly (?) amuse you to have it read aloud to you ??? I think if you care about the subject that it is interesting.

It is a very bad afternoon for me to write to you, for I have got wet through once, and splashed with mud past identification twice, and coming home there is no room in which I can smoke except my bedroom which is at the top of the house and cheerless. Then it poisons one's soul to look at the mud colours with which this house is 'decorated'—eternal dinginess aimed at—and I confess successfully hit off. That is one thing one may say for the school, that they can do what they attempt.—There are 3 families now in the house, counting my own as one—for Paul Waterhouse married this year and lives here on the 2nd floor. We have the first floor—a suite of rooms to ourselves, on a level with the chief drawing room and the dining room.—As the ground floor is all office I do not know where the rest of the people live and all the sets of servants but there seems no difficulty in placing anyone who comes. I am very glad you wrote to me. I will write again when I am in a better humour.

yours affectionately

R Bridges

89: TO LIONEL MUIRHEAD

Yattendon

February 23, 1888

My dear Lionel

We were delighted to hear from you and rejoice at the prospect of seeing you home in April. On the whole I did not envy you your Ash Wednesday at Siena. But the Grand Hotel may be more accommodative than the black eagle. What funny times those were! Pisa, too—which struck you as drearier than ever—and to me blasted by scenes of disorder and discomfort in the lives of Shelley and Byron. I always imagine them wildly parading the Lung' Arno and talking their nonsense.

As for weather, we have had a queerish time, and are having, full accounts of which you no doubt have duly received from Haseley. To say that there has been a lot of snow would give you no notion of it. Everybody is snowed up. We have got the road to Pangbourne more or less open to rustic traffic; but the Lanes are in many places full from one hedgetop to the other 5 and 10 feet deep—and over all an incessant northerly and north easterly blast raging, which makes it a matter of indifference to the traveller whether snow is actually falling or no, for what has fallen does not remain on the ground but blows about like sand in a simoon or whatever they call the wind that brings the sand storms in the desert. Still I enjoy the bracing quality of the weather well enough, and the sun was shining brightly this afternoon between the snow showers—and I had after sunset a beautiful moonlight walk.

I think I have never seen such fine winter nights as we have had this month.

We have no news. Elizabeth grows apace and promises to be a hearty child. Monica is very well. We are both of us going up to town next week if all is well to the Bach concert, and shall stay a few days with the Gees.

Your mother has kindly asked us to pay her a visit at Haseley this summer which we very much hope to do. And we don't forget your promise to come and see us here. Wooldridge has not been down lately. He now does nothing but music. Yattendon choir goes on well. We sing Palestrina and Marinoni this Lent—which is a great advance, and of course without accompaniment. I have 4 tenors and 2 male altoes!! And though we are still very rough there is constant improvement.—I have as usual a lot of things on hand which are too difficult for me to do, but I get on slowly with them.—Some of them are quite new irons, which will interest you. Your attempt to read my paper on prosody aloud amused us much—such a passage as this would read well

§§ (2) A I xiii 59.
See xxx A (c) Y. and Cf PL. 11.89

—Strange to say, so far the paper has met with welcome from writers who confess that it supplies a "desideratum" and all seem to think it clear and simple. But no doubt there will be an outcry from some one soon.

Marsden is going to Jamaica as resident magistrate there.

My wife said that this was a good pen. I can't make it write as legibly as I wish. If I knew that M^rs M read your letters to you I shouldn't mind, but I am afraid of giving you trouble in making out my scrawls. I envied you when you were at Florence. I always enjoyed being there—but I am tired of Rome and I expect that you will want to get home again before you have been there long. Will you see the new Pope (at least new to me as a Roman)? Perhaps he makes St Peters more interest[ing] than the old one did. Will you go and drink rum at that Cafe in the High? I mean the Corso.—And look at the lemon trees on the Pincian and the bust of Ugo Foscolo? And hear the band play Verdi?

I can imagine you—Amen
yours ever
R Bridges

90: TO LIONEL MUIRHEAD

Yattendon
March 29, 1888

My dear Lionel

If I were to wait till I thought I could write you 2½ penn'orth you would never get a letter from me. I am sitting down to this little sheet now at 8. p m while Monica goes to church. We have had services at that inconvenient hour all through Holy week and I have held out so far. Tonight general indisposition and a slight sore throat keep me at home. Fancy services at 8 p m (with a sermon) in March! And a rainy March! Our rector is certainly inexperienced.—Your long letter, chiefly about the desecration of Rome, was very interesting. But how sad it is! We were, as it was, a generation too late for Italy. Railroads began the mischief: and now there can never be any end to it. Still what is new to us nowadays will be old fashioned very soon. The streets of London seemed an abomination when they first sported gas lamps and omnibuses. The tramways and electric light have thrown those innovations into a respectable antiquity. The destruction of beautiful things is however irreparable—another matter altogether. We must rejoice that we have even in our 19th century seen some beautiful things made.

Among these I should not perhaps reckon Mr. Browning's "Blot on the Scutcheon"—which is at present being acted for or by the B society in London. I am sorry not to have an opportunity of seeing it, but I could never get on far into it reading, which does not promise well for the stage. Elizabeth (not BB) thanks you for your kind messages and is very much looking forward to seeing you. She is not a bad little creature, but not old enough yet to praise very much. We have had the most awful weather possible. Having myself a belief in special providence, I have great difficulty in not connecting it somehow with the sins and vanities of the Meteorological Department. The fools said that we were to be plagued with a long drought this year, and wrote to all the newspapers saying it would not rain in March. Well it hasn't rained much, but then it has snowed every day, which counts for rain in the rain gauge and wells—and is the most wretched accompaniment to E wind that you can imagine. We had some 4 feet of snow in February—and no sooner had that disappeared from most places when snow began to fall again. Today it has rained for the first time.—The rooks who began to build at the usual time left off in despair. But they were at work again today. It will be a most miserably late spring. Do not be surprised at Wooldridge's not writing. He is quite inexcusable—it is strange to see a man of so much good sense flattering himself that he has fairly good manners, when he behaves in so many ways as badly as is possible. He's more or less of a Darwinian too! He *is* a queer fellow—I don't know how he manages to keep up his spirits. I fancy he must be very low at times, but I think he is brave and faces the physical and spiritual discomforts which he creates for himself with great intrepidity. Mrs Bateman is coming on to us next week from Lockeridge. At Yattendon the Antiquarians have discovered by hearsay that there used to be a very large chalk angle which is now closed up. So they are determined to open it. I don't know where they come from nor what they expect to find, but they employ what men they can get to dig—unfortunately they cannot hit the old shaft off. The caverns are I believe very extensive. In the imagination of the antiquarians they extend for miles around. But I cannot think what they hope to find. Creighton came here for 2 or 3 days last week. I have not been well for some time. Lots of rheumatism and I want to get away. I should like to let the house for 3 months. But we shall perhaps get away without that. With kindest regards to Mrs. L M

yours affectionately
R Bridges

Pray imagine Monica's messages. She enjoyed your letter.

91: TO RICHARD WATSON DIXON

Yattendon
April 19, 1888

My dear Dixon

Many thanks for returning Achilles with such signs of affectionate chastisement. I will pay the greatest attention to all your remarks. It came yesterday. I am extremely glad that you like it. I think that with exception of the Christian Captives it is perhaps nearer poetry than anything I have done.

This morning I have written the last scenes of my new Comedy, and am in good spirits with that. It is chiefly fun, but has I think a strong point or two. I hope you will read it down here some day this summer.

If you can't exchange with Beeching during your holiday could not you come *some other* time? Is it impossible for you to leave your parish except during your short holiday? Could not you I mean exchange work for some other Sunday or 2 Sundays? I wanted to ask you this. I am rather headachy this afternoon as I have copied a lot of music besides working all the morning and it has been too wet to go out. Besides it is a damp headachy day, and we are going 5 miles out to dinner this evening!! We are otherwise all well. I am full of selfreproaches at not having written to you oftener of late. I have not been in at all a corresponding mood.

Did I tell you Creighton had been here? I have been reading Darwin's Life and Letters. I don't think he does himself justice in his autobiography. I suppose he got dull enough in his later years. His correspondence about the best of his time shows a far better man than the account of himself written later. There is in the 2nd volume a piece of Mr Huxley's writing inserted in which that gentleman thinks to give an account of the reception the Origin of Species met with. "Instead of that" he philosophises, and I think for rotten philosophy and poor rhetoric it would be difficult to match his performance. I mean (if you have the book) where he argues that there is no such thing as chance, and asks you to go down on the beach.

Hoping to write again soon

yours affectionately

R Bridges

92: TO LIONEL MUIRHEAD

Yattendon
July 2, 1888

My dear Lionel

We congratulate you and hope all is going on well. Your letter followed me about and I have brought it home with me from a round of visits to Oxford, Cambridge, London and Seaford in memory of my old host at Seaford. I enclose a publication which I found for sale there, announcing his death.

Fancy 20,000 people at his funeral.

We are settled at home again, at least as far as the weather allows anyone to be settled. I am reading and living in "Arabia Deserta".

I will try and get your chant book finished before your wife is again at the piano. Send us just a line someday.

With our affectionate remembrances

yours ever

RB

Now we are both Papas

Monica Waterhouse, wife of Robert Bridges, summer 1888. Courtesy of Elizabeth Daryush, the poet's daughter.

93: TO LIONEL MUIRHEAD

Yattendon
August 8, 1888

My dear Lionel

I hope things are going on well with you. Your daughter's name is certainly fully calculated to serve the chief purpose of nomenclature, that of distinction. May Fosca have other distinctions!

I have finished copying the Psalter for you, and if you have any use for it I will send it as it is. It will want one or two places to be filled in—which I shall not be able to do for perhaps another month or so—I will either keep it back till it is completed—or send it you now, and have it back from you to finish when the material is ready—

I don't know where you are. I shall send this to Hazeley—We think that when you arrive there then will be a chance of your coming on to pay us a visit or of our coming to see you.

yours affectionately
RB

94: TO RICHARD WATSON DIXON

Yattendon
August 16, 1888

My dear Canon

This is to tell you that I am making a present of your history to Miss B—Jones who is going to be married on the 3rd of September to a man whom I know. I tell you lest you should by any chance be thinking of making her a present—in which case you might have sent the same gift, though I fancy that your modesty would prevent.

Now I have nothing more to tell you except such small news as you will never miss—I saw your Eudocia reviewed in the Athenaeum. The reviewer smote it as I thought.—A Londoner was down here and brought his Athenaeum with him. He was reading it in my garden on Sunday afternoon.—I said I wonder you waste your time reading that dullest of dull journals.—He said, I always read it— it tells one what's going on.—Does it? said I. He, to justify himself thought to entertain me and began reading to me from it the opening of Eudocia—Is not that about the worst verse you ever heard? he asked—And who is Canon Dixon?—Does not the Athenaeum tell you?—No.—"He is a great friend of mine; I can't defend his Eudocia, but the reviewer is a muff if he treats it as "the work of a 2nd rate man". So I fetched him some of your poems, and that evening we could not detach him from your history.—He sent to Daniel for your poems and was much disappointed to find one lot out of print. But why inflict on me the onus of explaining the paradox of your authorship of Eudocia? Daniel and you ain't to be trusted.—

———

I finished my Christian Captives and am beginning a mask.—Christian Captives had been laid aside unfinished for now 2 years.—Edward VI still in his grave.—I can't get at him.

———

Read Doughty's *Arabia Deserta,* Cambridge University press—
What a horrid summer it has been!! And as many earwigs and lice as if it had been fine.—I thought insects did not thrive in rain.

yours ever
RB

95: TO ROGER FRY

Yattendon
October 30, 1888

My dear Roger
Thank you for writing to Mr Wollaston. I did not wait to hear from you, but wrote to Doughty in Palestine and had a letter from him. He is to return in the spring I believe.
I did not know where you had been and I don't know Archer, and we shan't be able to come to Cambridge this term (to answer all your questions at once). I heard that you had been bribed to go on investigating cell tissues. Is that so? Tell us what you are doing when you write and what you are interested in.
All well here.

yours very truly
Robt Bridges

I don't like being Mistered.

96: TO RICHARD WATSON DIXON

Yattendon
November 6, 1888

My dear Canon
I was away from home yesterday. Today we expect "A Farmer". About the Stalls, what is my opinion worth? I remember being at Truro shortly after it was raised to a See, and laughing very much at the nomenclature of the new stalls, by which the old parish church chiefly asserted its dignity. They were all called after Cornish saints. Did you ever hear of them—O their outlandish names, and incredible legends of folly. It seemed to me most mistaken to burden the souls of

our agnostic brethren with such fables. I am an agnostic Christian myself, and would most willingly reverence anything either work or faith that came down to us from those ages; but I cannot away with their being remade.—Your Northumbrian fellows are I take it a better lot, but even with them I should say it would be much more lifelike, historical, real, and interesting to a future age, if there shall be any, to name your stalls after the most important places in the diocese. If your prelates or canons have no salaries it seems it would be impossible to keep to correct use. Unless it were made a rule that the incumbents of certain places held the stalls exofficio.—Still I should say that the most notable places, either for present industry or worthy unforgotten history would give the best names.— That's my opinion.

I am glad you are getting on so well with your history. You seem to have settled the Philip and Mary question pretty straight. I am in a happy condition of having no unfinished work on hand.—I have put an end to the Humours and the Captives and am meditating some new work.

Our kindest regards—

your affectionate

RB

97: TO LIONEL MUIRHEAD

Yattendon
December 13, 1888

My dear Lionel

I have been a brute not to have written to you, but have been dreadfully busy: more than I can describe, or than the particulars thereof could be read with patience by you. Also we have been staying in London. But now I will send you the Psalter, which has been lying about unheeded. It is in no respect final,* but will in some parts please you. Singing goes on very well here. But again the details are not worthy of the storic pen.—You seem very busy with Fosca. We find no time for our infant,—who however flourishes apart after her own fashion. She is tremendously strong and fat, too fat.—We are now making preparations for a month in Italy, and hope to start immediately after Xmas. Wooldridge "is coming" for Xmas. I am glad your eyesight is better, and that you rest it. The book you ask for is *Doughty's Arabia Deserta*. Cambridge University press this year. Other books—you will like *Dixon's History of the English Church*, now 3 volumes. Of course you have read *Voltaire: Peter the Great* which occurs to me because I have been reading it lately, the *biographical articles in Groves Dictionary of Music*—at least those which are not written by the Editor.—I can't think of any others just now. About my own work you ask at a most convenient time. I have never before been in such a happy condition. All the work I had about is finished up, the best play being a comedy "The humours of the Court". No 8 of my "dramatic works" counting *Prometheus* for one. Then I have put "The Growth of Love" together— 80 sonnets cutting out all the inferiorest ones, and finishing with sonnets in the

Shakespearian form. The other thing was a mistake: but I did not know any better. We have been in London all day today and have just returned and dined. Mr Waterhouse has ordered an organ for the Church here, which should improve matters. But since you were here we have advanced a good deal. We have also a reed band in the village, but this is not in a very forward state yet. I hope when we return from abroad that, if all is well, you will come and stay with us for a bit.

Did you hear of Addis's leaving the R. C. Communion? I wrote to him and met him in London, and had a long talk with him. It is a great delight to me that he should have relinquished the untenable. He is as zealous as ever but now very much on my lines, but would not come under any formularies—so is not a member of our communion. He saw the reasonableness of becoming one, but could not after his experience burden his conscience again and I think he was wise.

I wish you would tell me that your wife reads your letters to you. Then I would write more. Now fare well.

your affectionate

RB

*In fact we have already altered it much.

P.S. The village boys act the Merchant of Venice here on Boxing Day. I wish you could see it. We would try and persuade you to come for Xmas, but as we leave for abroad on the 28th my wife would not be up to entertaining and making her preparations.

98: TO LIONEL MUIRHEAD

Hotel Molaro

Rome

January 7, 1889

My dear Lionel

I was sorry not to have a moment to write to you before we went away. Your photographs came, for which we thank you very much. But you know I don't care for pho[to]graphs, and of babies!! Well, you *are* a married man. You won't catch me having my baby photographed. We came via Calais stopping at Arles, where we were detained by tremendous storms, part of the line giving way. All the country between Toulouse and Nice under water. We drove from Nice to San Remo. Train to Genoa. One day there. He intended to drive to Spezzia: hadn't time—one night at Pisa. Saw all things again well, found nothing improved. Lovely weather. Thence to Rome today. We think of spending a fortnight here—Are in pension au 4eme at this hotel, with very sunny rooms, a wood fire and Roman tobacco. My niece Mary Plow is with us. Rome seems a good deal altered. But it was lovely as ever on Pincian this afternoon.

I am sorry I never got the chants off to you. Oblivion. You must come and fetch them. We shall really hope for a visit from you when we come back if fortune gives us a happy return, and to make the acquaintance of Mrs Lionel. We don't intend to be satisfied with the photograph.

I wonder what sort of a house you have. In summer we must come and see it— I did a fairish amount of work last year spite of the abominable season, the worst I remember at all, and we have lived through some baddish ones. There are more abominable Swiss touters than ever about and they have worse manners than ever. Italy it strikes me viewing it superficially has not much prospect of good. There is not much in any of the people we have seen. They lie and cheat and play the fool and mismanage your luggage worse than ever—

With my love and my thanks for picture

Yours ever
RB

99: TO LIONEL MUIRHEAD

Yattendon
February 19, 1889

My dear Lionel

Here they come. It was a sad oversight that they were not sent before, but I hope you will like them now you've got them. Worse than being photographed is the trouble of sending copies to people (like yourself) who complain if you don't and when you think you have done it all beautifully and satisfied every one, up comes another claimant. My sister Mrs Glover has discontinued her correspondence with me because, I think, we omitted her by some accident. I thought that living in an out of the way part of Sussex she would never know anything about it.—If I had realized all this I certainly would never have consented—. I hope that you and "all" the family are well. I have a touch of the liver complaint, which I never had in my life before but once—and that was at school shortly after making my first acquaintance with sardines. Now this has come upon me without as far as I know any provocation whatever. We came home some 3 weeks ago. I hope that you will be able to pay us a visit soon. I can't make out what kind of a winter Providence intends that we should have this time. It is mild enough today.—When I am recovered I will write and see if we cannot manage to make some arrangement—I am doing nothing. Our rector is engaging in theological controversy in the county newspaper—this is out of my line.

Absolutely no news, except that when we meet we shall have much to talk of concerning the evil doings in Rome etc. I saw Wilson and Stanhope at Florence. We had a pleasant trip. I disliked the Italians more, and thought them dirtier than ever.

With our kindest regards for Mrs Muirhead

your affectionate
RB

100: TO GERARD MANLEY HOPKINS

Yattendon
May 18, 1889

Dearest Gerard

I am sorry to get a letter from one of your people telling me that you were ill with fever. And yesterday I sent you off a budget of notes on Milton's prosody. And when I last wrote I never mentioned your ailing though you told me in your letter that you interrupted it to lie down. What is this fever? F. Wheeler says that you are mending. I hope you are recovering properly. Let me have a line. I wish I could look in on you and see for myself.

You must send me a card now and then, and one as soon as possible to let me know about you.

Meanwhile I must be patient. I think that if you are really mending Miltonic prosody will be just the sort of light amusement for your mind. I hope you are well enough already. And will make a quiet recovery and complete for which I pray.

Your affectionate
RB

5 minutes before the letter came I was writing your name for the binder of the "Growth of Love" to send you a copy.

101: TO LIONEL MUIRHEAD

Yattendon
Monday, May 27, 1889

My dear Lionel

We also are housecleaning, and my wife is at her father's. I think however that things will be straight in a few days, and if it suited you and M^rs L to come on Thursday for 2 days we should be delighted. I am sorry that I cannot say stay over Sunday as I fear our room—at least the only room we can well offer you, is engaged on Saturday and Sunday to Lang, who is troubled with insomnia and cannot be put within range of the church clock or the farm yard. It is possible that L. will not come, in which case you could do as you liked about staying on.

If it suits you to come on Thursday and leave on Saturday—do so. If not put off till we can fix a Sunday. I will send the Victoria to Pangbourne to meet you if you let me know what train.

With our kindest regards
yours affectionately
RB

P.S. I wish you wouldn't brag about the weather. See what you've done!

102: TO WILLIAM SANDAY

Yattendon
June 11, 1889

My dear Sanday

Thank you for sending me your "sermon." I read it with the greatest interest and put it in the drawing room for my wife to read, and for some days forgot all about it. Whitsuntide brought us visitors and distractions. Now they are out and gone.

I want to know what the Magnum Opus is, and whether the Commentary on Ecclesiasticus is a book to get. I will try and discover some of E's contributions in the Christian Geography, which I possess. I never heard his name before.

These are mostly questions—but you need not answer them: I was very glad to read your protest against the 'decay of learning'. Certainly the universal smattering which is become fashionable makes a bad show: and the sort of commentator that the Clarendon Press is contented to get for its school classics does not figure well. As I remember Stubbs—and by the way I have been reading Mark Pattison's essays after all. They came here through our rector and my respect for M P is I think now raised to the proper level. I find the Essays very interesting indeed. It is difficult to imagine any one spending so much labour over the details which he has brought together but I can be grateful to him, and he seems to have done the work once for all. Pattison seems to me the ideal Quarterly reviewer. Reviewers would be valuable to literature if all the contributors knew their subjects as he seems to have done. Still as far as I have gone I do not see any great qualities of mind—but he manages to spend his emotions on everything, and his very careful writing is generally successful.

Perhaps before I have done the book I may think otherwise. As far as I have gone, not the least interesting thing to me is the development of the writer. Hoping you may have a pleasant holiday in Devonshire, and with many thanks for your sermon and kind regards to Mrs. Sanday

Believe me yours very truly

R Bridges

103: TO RICHARD WATSON DIXON

Yattendon
June 14, 1889

My dear Dixon

How can I tell you—the terribly mournful tidings of Gerard's death reached me two days ago. It is possible that you may not have heard. I hope you have. I should have written to you at once, but heard that you were from home. This morning I got your letter from Warkworth.

I had had only favourable reports from Dublin. In fact the people who wrote to me described his illness as a slight and not dangerous attack.

Still he was of course too ill to write himself. I do not know whether he died suddenly, or as is more likely in a relapse, and when the worst was feared chose deliberately not to see any one in his prostrate condition. One can only guess. Still I had no message of any sort from him after the last favourable one.

His last letters to me and the two last poems are if not a foreboding of it, yet full of a strange fitness for the end.

The last poem but one was an address to God, most powerful and plaintive. The last was a sonnet to me, explaining some misunderstanding which he thought existed. You will be anxious to see them and I will, when I am more in the mood for writing, copy them out and send them.

In answer to your letter. I am sorry that you are so overworked and have not been well. I hope you will get through all right.

Did I ask you to correct two misprints in the Growth of Love?

Sonnet II line 1. *and* for &

    XIV. 1. 13. *my* for may

We were very sorry not to see you.

I will write again soon—

With love from us to you

your affectionate
R Bridges

That dear Gerard was overworked, unhappy and would never have done anything great seems to give no solace. But how much worse it would have been had his promise or performance been more splendid. He seems to have been entirely lost and destroyed, by those Jesuits.

———

I send you the sonnet.

———

104: TO MRS. MANLEY HOPKINS

Yattendon
Newbury
June 19, 1889

My dear Mrs. Hopkins

I have not written before because I did not wish to add to your distress by intruding on it, and now that I do wish, I hardly know what to say. Since I got the sad news I have thought very much of you and Mr. Hopkins, and of the great sorrow which this sad sudden end to Gerard's strange life must be: though you have of course all the spiritual consolation which it is possible to have from the consideration of his singlehearted devotion.

To this and your own love for him I know that I can add nothing: but I have thought that I may possess writings of his which you would like to have copies of: and that it would particularly interest you to see his last letters to me.

I wrote to Father Wheeler to ask him to return to me any of my letters to Gerard which might still be kept among his papers: and he in his reply promised to do so, and said that Gerard had given instructions about his papers etc. From this I think it very likely that whatever there is of personal interest will be sent to you, in which case I should not have much to add. But I shall hear of this perhaps later on from Mr. Hopkins, and he will tell me what you would wish.

I will add nothing now but the expression of my sympathy with you both, and all the family, and I beg that you will not think it necessary to answer this letter before it is quite easy for you to do so.

My mother is away from home and would join me in sympathy and good wishes. With my kindest remembrances to Mr and Miss Hopkins believe me yours

Robt Bridges

P. S. I expect my mother will have written to you hereafter.

105: TO ROGER FRY

Yattendon
Newbury
July 24, 1889

My dear Roger

It was jolly of you to write me such a good chatty letter. I often have wondered what you were doing, and how you were getting on. The pity of it is that you do not say. Cannot you come down and stay with us some time this summer? The end of August would suit us very well: Now in ten days we are going away, at least I am, for a fortnight, and Monica to stay with her people. Next Sunday we have visitors so that we cannot ask you at once. Will you come then? You shall have as much music as we are capable of. I am no enemy to the moderns: I enjoy nothing more than hearing a Beethoven Symphony, and your friend Chopin is one of my favourites. But the old music is a more sacred thing. It knows nothing of composers' moods. It is pure art without any affectation or apparent effort, mostly vocal and sacred of course.

I have not seen Fitzgerald's letters—I look forward to making the acquaintance of a most agreeable man. But his literary work I don't much care for. As for the Persian poem is it not a peaceful prelude to delirium tremens? Pessimism is always nonsense: though it charms many people both as logic and poetry. Chiefly those I suspect who least believe it. Now by that I should like Omer Khayyam

better. As for his Calderon he praised him as blindly as he translated him, and H
wrote about as bad verse as ever was.

The New College American seems to be one of the half dozen who pretend
that they want to buy my poems. Is there any vanity like that? The sonnets he
spoke of to you are not published at all. So it is unfair to me to say that I
published an edition of 22 copies. 3 of my books are in the market and do not
sell. Still I would print more if it were not for the trouble, or the fact that after all
your trouble you get such a mean result.

The oil paints are Ludwig's Petroleum Colours. I send you a prospectus. Very
shortly there will be an English translation of the German "Directions for use"
The new thing is the medium, the secret being the solution of varnish in Petroleum (which was known to the old Masters). This gets over all difficulties of
manipulation, being as easy as watercolour. You can write a letter with it or paint
on common paper like this.

With our love to all your people and yourself

yours affectionately

Robt Bridges

106: TO RICHARD WATSON DIXON

Seaford

Sussex

August 10, 1889

My dear Dixon

I have not been able to write you a letter about Gerard.—If I knew how much
you had heard, I could supply the rest of the details, at least as far as I have
them, but there was nothing that you would particularly care to know that I can
think of, and the sad fact makes all else beneath consideration. You will however
like to see his last letters and verses. The last letter he wrote to me I have, but
very strangely it happened that the only two letters of his which I ever destroyed
were the two which he wrote me preceding that. I will tell you all about it when
we meet, but it was very like a sort of quarrel. He said in his last letter that he had
been joking, and he added a sonnet (very sad) in "explanation" but it did not
read like joking, and the letters were rather bitter, so that I put them in the fire—
of course I wish now that I had not done so. I shall like to talk to you about him

I have proposed to edit some of his verses—Daniel to print them—*with a short
memorial life of him.* I should be very grateful to you, if you would write your
recollection of him as a boy at school, and also some account of your subsequent
friendship.

I have after some delay succeeded in getting back from his friends in Dublin
the majority of my letters to him—which he had kept. I have written to his
parents to ask their wishes about the memorial—and I hope to see a friend of his
in town on my way home—

I came down here to get 10 days change of air, and if possible a change of refreshment of mind—so far without much apparent benefit, as the weather has been dreary and the solitude rather heavier than I looked for. I left wife with her people. She is well, as is also the young Elizabeth, whose name is Ish. She does not talk much yet, but is an intelligent original and good creature. I have learnt a good deal about psychology by observing her. What strikes me most is [the] miraculous ease with which she arrives at abstract notions or general conceptions.—It is quite incredible, and she brings her feelings, which are unusually tender, to bear upon them without hesitation. Also she is very quick at understanding all that is said.

I hope you are well. I have not got over my disappointment at missing you when you were in Oxford. With best remembrances to Mrs Dixon

your affectionate friend

Robt Bridges

107: TO CHARLES HENRY DANIEL

Yattendon
August 20, 1889

My dear Daniel

I have revised F[east] of B[acchus] 16–32. I fear I have suggested the alteration of a great many stops. I send the proof in another envelope "Not to be forwarded"—

In place of Felix I suggest putting your name in. It will be great fun, and there is no objection to it. As Chremes must have known some Jews if there were any about. I don't mean that you are a Jew, though we may be all of us Israelites for that matter.—If you object to the apparent slur cast on you by the line

"Just the last thing Daniel has disappointed me"

you may change places with Phanias. I merely record

"My old Friend Daniel has gone from home today."

And then it will be *Phanias* who has *disappointed* me. I think perhaps this is quite unobjectionable. You may make it allude to your visit to Frome (this is not so funny or mysterious).

I am requested to write a memoir of Father Gerard Hopkins, to be printed with a selection from his poems. Now are you willing to undertake that? You suggested it. If so will you make agreement to take it in hand the next thing after the Feast of Bacchus? I should fancy that there might be *about* 40 pages of verse—lyrical—and I cannot tell how long the memoir is likely to be, but certainly not so much as this. It will be a unique volume, *privately* printed only, but I think that need not exclude you having a few copies for private sale—at say £1 a copy.

This is all I have to say. When you are back at Oxford I should like to visit you one day before I go to London.

With our kindest regards.

yours very truly
Robert Bridges

108: TO MRS. MANLEY HOPKINS

Yattendon
Newbury
September 16, 1889

Dear Mrs. Hopkins

Thank you for your letter—of course I must see Arthur and Everard. I am very glad that they think that Gerard's sketches or studies may be made use of. can see them* very well when I am in London.

I shall not begin to do anything till I have seen as many of Gerard's Roman Catholic friends as I can. Some of them will be in London, and I hope when have had an interview with one or two of them that they will be more communicative than they are at present.

Arthur need not fear that I shall do anything without his knowledge. I have a present no notion at all as to the sort of thing which the 'memoir' will be.

I am sorry that it is too involved a matter to write on—but I shall be coming to see you as soon as I am in town.

I am with kindest regards

yours very truly
Robert Bridges

*I mean Arthur and Everard.

109: TO CHARLES HENRY DANIEL

20 New Cavendish Street
W
October 11, 1889

My dear Daniel

Since I last wrote we have a new daughter. All is satisfactory.

I was sorry not to see you in town; as we might have talked over matters. Viz what should be done about selling the Feast, and 2nd the Gerard Hopkins memoir.

About the Feast. I do not think that we need trouble to advertise or do any thing further than put it in the shops especially at Oxford, and perhaps have a "flyleaf" or better *print something on a post card* to send to a few people.

I think a post card covered with your black-letter type would be most excit-ing—only mention the price and state that you will not send without receiving money therefore.

About Gerard Hopkins' memoir—I shall not have written anything till *after* Xmas. But there is no reason why you should not print *the Poems* whenever you wish. My scheme for the book (I do not know how far it will be adopted) is something of this sort

1. *Title*
2. Portrait. aet. 38*
3. Memoir pp. i-xlviii.
4. Early poems as part of and same type as memoir. pp. xlix-lx.
5. *Portrait* aet. 20*
6. Title of poems
    and poems   1–50pp.
6.B a long note by G. H. on his own poems 51–55
7. Facsimile of handwriting*
8. Reproductions of Studies*

Nos. 2, 5, 7, 8-will be on loose sheets and supplied to binder with your work. I do not yet know who will undertake them. Perhaps no one.

You see this is arranged so that you might begin No. 6 anyday. Only your fascicules of "poems" must include their title.

I expect that you will not want to do any more before Xmas. In case you should—I would hurry up, but if the poems are ready by then, would that do—

If you are in Oxford I wish you would ask Blackwell if he doesn't send proofs of that paper on Samson Agonistes—I have enough new lyrics for a new volume whenever you wish—

With our kindest regards

yours very truly
R Bridges

PS I suggest italics for memoir and early poems, and common type for POEMS.

110: TO CHARLES HENRY DANIEL

20 New Cavendish Street
October 14, [1889]

My dear Daniel

At a week's notice I can send you Hopkins' poems whenever you want them, but I shall not be able to promise you the memoir before Xmas: and perhaps not till the end of January—and I cannot be sure of it then: so that you must not rely on getting the printing all done in the Xmas vacation.

I should know in a few days what number of copies the family would like printed. What do you say to 100—

If you want to be busy at Xmas and the poems are not enough for you what do you say to beginning something else for me? I could send you "Achilles in Scyros" or another lot of lyrics. My other plays would be too long for you I am afraid. I should fancy that Gerard Hopkins' poems would be enough, and then the memoir at Easter, but I should of course be delighted if you found time to bring out something of mine. Things are going well here the doctor says. Is there any chance of your being in London for a day?

yours ever
R Bridges

111: TO MRS. MANLEY HOPKINS

20 New Cavendish Stree
W
October 23, [1889

Dear Mrs. Hopkins

I send you today by registered post the scrapbook of Gerard's MS. You will be able best to read No 1-on page 1

3 —— 5
an admirable lyric
4 on page 6
in very beautiful rhythm
5 on page 7
five stanzas complete and sequent
6 on page 8
one stanza
8- B 2   and C

No. 9. and No 10. 11 and 12. pp. 12–16.
   contain the melancholy sonnets which are very powerful
   and less odd than most of Gerard's work.
No 28 (on p 33-)
   the 4th page of this
     O Deus ego amo te.
The rest are less interesting or more difficult to make out
No 15
   the first sonnet
   "The Shepherd" I do not like, but on the 4th page is
   "The Fine Delight" of which he sent me a copy which is one of his best-
I have a fair copy of all these MS[S] except No 2, the ode on
Everard's marriage (unfinished)
   I would copy them for you if you wish. We can speak of this when we meet.
In haste

yours very truly
Robt Bridges

112: To G. E. P. ARKWRIGHT

Yattendon
Newbury
November 17, 1889

Dear Sir

I am very much obliged to you for your kind present. I only returned from town yesterday and have been too much occupied to look it through—but it seems to be a very useful edition: and I hope it may help to make the work popular. I wish that all editors would now use these smaller forms. Our Purcell Society folios are a nuisance, but I cannot convert any one.

You ask me if I am interested in Elizabethan music. I should perhaps say that I am not a musician at all. That I should be on the Committee of the Purcell Society is a measure of the small esteem in which Purcell is held, not of my capacity. As a matter of fact I am very fond of old music; Palestrina and Vittoria are the sort of composers whom I like best, and of course all the Madrigalians, Dutch English or Italian.

As for Campion I do not know that I ever saw any music of his to make me think very highly of him. I remember I once copied out a tune of his in 4 parts intending to sing it in Church here—but it is still waiting with a lot of others until we get words printed for the congregation to use.

If you would send me your Campion music I should be extremely interested to see it, but do not you think that I had better buy it? I shall be most happy to do so if you will tell me the price (supposing it to be reasonable). You can have but few buyers I should think.

I am writing in haste, not to miss another day without thanking you for your present.

I hope I may some day have the pleasure of meeting you. If you are fond of old vocal music we should have a good deal to talk about.

Believe me yours sincerely

Robert Bridges

I know a good many brethren who would be most interested in the sort of work which you are doing.

113: TO CHARLES HENRY DANIEL

Yattendon
November 19, 1889

My dear Daniel

I know that you will have been expecting an answer to your letter: but since we got home I have been so busy that I cannot now believe that I am not neglecting some more urgent duty in writing to you. I hope that your London seller will turn out all right and send you the money for the copies which he had. The sale seems to have gone well. I hope it will continue. Your estimate for the printing etc. of the Growth of Love convinces me that I have been much deeper in your debt hitherto than I imagined. I hope the Feast will, with the balance before allowed me, wipe out the present score.

About recasting type. I cannot say. I should think it would not be worth the cost.—About Gerard Hopkins' poems I have come to a conclusion i.e. that they *must* be printed, so I will get them ready some day. The memoir will be a disagreeable difficulty, but I must manage it. At present I am occupied in sending all my plays to press. They will come out (like Nero) at Bumpus' as fast as they can be printed. "Palicio" is gone. "Ulysses" follows then "Christian Captives" etc. etc.—and my pamphlet on the Samson Agonistes prosody is out at Blackwells—I dare say you have seen it-1/- is its price.—How wrong of me not to have acknowledged return of Feast ms. Its safe transmission now is a matter of no moment. It came all right. Many thanks.

Would you send a notice of Feast to Miss Langley, Lovejoy's Library, London Road, Reading. I can send for more buyers' addresses when you want them. Your amended notice of Feast is lovely. How well the Growth of Love would look in that type!—I don't mean to give any Feast away. I want it to pay my bill with you. But I would go shares with you in a presentation of ONE to Canon Dixon. I think he would have one. Will you?

I will remember you have still some Dixon lyrics and will help to work them off.—I must come to Oxford soon to see your musical prints.

yours ever
RB

Kindest regards from us to you

114: TO G. E. P. ARKWRIGHT

Yattendon
November 23, 1889

Dear Sir

It is very kind of you to accept my invitation here. As you say you will be at home for some time I think it would be better in every respect as more convenient also to me to put off for a week or ten days. I am very busy just now, and shall then be less occupied, and I expect a friend from London to be staying with me, for a few days most likely in next week to whom I should like to introduce you.

It would be a pity when you come if you did not stay the night as we might have some music, and if you would accept a bed it would be more of a visit. I will then tell you of the people I know who are interested in Elizabethan and other old music. They are few but there is no doubt the sect is increasing—I will write to you again as soon as I hear that my friend is coming.

I liked the Mask. I think the Campion would sing better in harmony, and we will use them here.

yours sincerely
Robt Bridges

115: TO LIONEL MUIRHEAD

Yattendon
November 23, 1889

Dear Lionel

My wife is I am glad to say very well and you would not give her any trouble, but we don't understand why you write like a bachelor and say nothing about Mrs. L coming with you. Only we must fix a day for this as we have knocked 2 of our 3 spare bedrooms into one and use the sumtotal for a night nursery. It is possible to convert my dressing room into a bedroom but we *could not* take you *both* in if we had other visitors. So please let us know whether Mrs. L would come with you, if so we will fix a day. If not of course you may come over when the fit seizes you, and I need not write to you again. There is a carrier from Reading on Saturdays who could call for your bag at Pangbourne on his way home. But what a walk!!! Don't do anything rash, and get in exhausted, requiring hot baths and brandy and water.

Send me a line to tell me whether as we hope you will both come. (If so will you fix Sunday 15th?) or whether you will "drop in". I am sure it will be a case of dropping if you walk all the way.

We also are befogged. I never knew such weather.

your affectionate
RB

If you come alone you might come for the 8th. Basil Champneys may be here. Palicio is gone to press. I am in the midst of the punctuation of Ulysses. If you come on 15th you will hear my version of "Hear my Lov".
Let Mrs. L read this scrawl for you *please!*

116: TO ROGER FRY

Yattendon
December 17, 1889

My dear Roger

I am afraid that Wednesday is an impossible day for me, though as you say the programme is inviting. I must enjoy it with your ears. The coming of Xmas keeps me at home.

I hope you are getting on well. I am engaged correcting proofs, the most distasteful of all the occupations for which I am unfitted.

We have read Fitzgerald's letters, at least some of them. He was certainly a delicate spirit, but why should he have spent all his life in remaining an amateur. He might have known a good deal. It seems as if he lived shyly towards knowledge, believing that it might destroy for him the charm of beauty. As a result the older he grew the duller his letters—

I am glad that you found the metre of the Feast of Bacchus readable. I think it would be all right on the stage, and there it must go. Would not the Greek dresses with the "Persians" as Parsees all in white backed by the myrtle hedge be a good sight?

With kindest regards to all your home party

yours very truly
RB

(Now can I do it?)

117: TO SAMUEL GEE

Yattendon
Newbury
Sunday, December 22, 1889

My dear Gee

Xmas is coming and I thought of writing to you to send you our best wishes for the season and new year. Time though it never seems to be going very fast gets over the ground, and to recall our old St Bartholomew days is like looking into a past existence. I wish we met oftener, but our lines seem now far separated— however I hope that my wife will be on her legs all this year, and that we may be awhile together in London, in which case we might see something of you.

Xmas 'muddles,' as Monica calls them, are come about us like bees, but I—like the wild ostrich—have plunged my head into a thicket of printers' proof. I am publishing 4 or 5 of my plays, in the same form as Nero. The first is already through the devilish ordeal and I hope being published. 500 copies of each. I

Oh! think of having them done up in bundles of fifties and depositing them at some
Eh! friend's house or chambers in London, whence my publisher, the now famous E
Ah! Bumpus, may draw them, a bundle at a time as he wants them. I will honour you
Ha! by making you the first offer. They will help to gut your house should it catch fire, but I do not know of any other advantage on this side the grave. Before you consent consider. 30 or 40 bundles of Neros, 50 in a bundle. It struck me that you might have storage room. If you have not I will seek elsewhere. I don't like to ask Bumpus to devote so much room to me, and the plan I propose has the advantage of my knowing how the sale goes.

I will send you copies (no fear! I hear you say) of them as they come out. You will find them all light reading enough, not like the sonnets.

Are you going to have experience of an influenza epidemic? We have had everyone suffering from colds; I myself have quite escaped hitherto—and I have been on the whole very well—but the country has been wet and dull.

I shall be interested in the result of my publications. My brother, who has given up farming, has 2 books in the press. You or Mrs Gee may come across them.

I am afraid you will think this letter all about the storage. It wasn't—though that may have had something to do with precipitating my sympathies.

Kindest regards to Mrs Gee

yours ever
RSB

I hope the children are well—I may say now, as well as ours—

118: TO LIONEL MUIRHEAD

Yattendon
February 4, 1890

My dear Lionel

We hope you are well. I begin this letter just 5 minutes before the post goes remembering that I wanted to ask you a question. Now it is just such a question as you would like to answer.

Supposing the seasons were represented by 4 precious stones. Which should they be?

Winter.	frost.	snow.	diamond.
Spring.	young	green	emerald
Summer			ruby?
Autumn	?	?	?

(fruit and corn)

Now just you answer me this

RB

119: TO LIONEL MUIRHEAD

Yattendon
February 7, 1890

My dear Lionel

If the ruby goes for autumn it must mean wine. I want rather to represent earth appearance. Winter and spring are all right, and every one knows the diamond and emerald or thinks he does.

The ruby is a well known stone.

Perhaps Jacinth and Topaz are better for Autumn, but they are so like the ruby.

Is there a fine yellow stone to represent summer heat?
Sapphire would be the summer sea.
I think at this stage of

> Diamond
> Emerald
> Sapphire
> Jacinth

When you write tell me the typical colours of the stones from a Jeweller's point of view. I find in museums that all stones are of all colours. Also their importance.

yours ever

RB

Many thanks for last favour.
Wooldridge has gone back to London.

120: TO RICHARD WATSON DIXON

Yattendon
February 22, 1890

My dear Canon

I *do* congratulate you, and shall be impatient to see the work—but fear that the printers will keep us waiting a long while. What a trouble printing is!! Now will you not be taking a holiday, and if you do will you not come and see us? That would be delightful, and what a lot we should have to talk about!*

I am now at a piece of work that I much wish to discuss with you. Also I am reading early English history. Henry I and II etc. If life lasts I hope to make plays out of all those people. They were fine beings: and had something to do.

But we live in far better times. Your view of my work is very friendly and splendid, but though it is delightful that you of all men should think as you do of it, I am not self-pleased—only I think I add something to the literature that good people may read in after times with pleasure.—You say my "destiny." Just so, but no one ever thinks of it in that way. It is all fuss—

I am not in a letter writing mood today, nor have the leisure, but just this line of thanks and congratulation—and hope now to hear oftener.

Shall you go anywhere for a change where we could come too, if you don't go to London and come here? If you have not had influenza at Warkworth I think it wise to keep away from it. It should all be over in another month.

your affectionate

RB

*old Hayton times—

Our love and kindest regards to yourself and Mrs Dixon.

I caught a glimpse at a house the other day where I was visiting of a Review and in it an article by Gosse on Browning's profundity etc. ! ! !

121: TO LIONEL MUIRHEAD

Yattendon
April 1, 1890

My dear Lionel

We are very sorry to hear of your sore throats. I hope you are both better now. The throats and Easter with its weeks made us put off our visit: as no doubt you meant we should. After Easter we should like to come. In May we are going to Cambridge: and we shall be away from home then for some weeks. So that if we do not come before might we come to you for a week in May either before or after our visit to Cambridge. I am pestered with all manner of flies. I mean printers publishers critics and book makers come about me like flies: and I wish that for 48 hours I lived in the old time when one might have gone forth and destroyed them in the name of the Lord, and hung their scalps. . . . on the barn door. But one must sit and suffer like a Quaker.

hoping you are both better, with
kindest regards etc. from us both

yours ever
RB

122: TO LIONEL MUIRHEAD

Yattendon
[May, 1890]

My dear Lionel

I hope you are both better. T. O and send me an answer.

RB

If you are at the sea you can easily find out if you don't happen to be "au fait."

————

Imagine the steamers to have shut off steam, and to be coming on with their acquired speed. Let the opposite half sheet be the open sea. If there is any wind let it blow from the North
Let B be a rowing boat with course from W to E.
Let it be a foggy day
Let s s s be steamers

—

Let the steamers be suddenly
sighted by man in B—

—

What is the correct word for man's
description? Are the steamers
"bearing down" or "bearing" "athwart
his course"—or what is it?

RB

123: TO LIONEL MUIRHEAD

Yattendon
Newbury
May 24, 1890

My dear Lionel

I did not get your letter containing the bad account of your Mother's health till yesterday when we arrived home from our holiday. Of course if I had had it before I should not have written proposing to visit you next week. Though in your 2nd letter, which answered mine, you say that you think we might come, yet I think it would be better to put off. I should be very glad to be of any use I could be in the ways of consolation: and do not feel a frivolous incapacity: but it happens that it is on our side also rather unpropitious time for us to be away. My niece Miss Plow—I did not know it when I wrote—has got engaged to be married to the rector here. The excitement and necessary business is a great nervous trial to my mother, and I think I should do wrong in not remaining at hand till it is all over, to be of any use I can be.—So we must defer again.

I have a great deal to tell you, but I will not write more today. I have all kinds of things to attend to and a cricket match. After the match Shakespeare's Julius Caesar will be enacted by the boys of the village.

With our kindest regards

yours affectionately
RB

I have not exactly in words said how extremely grieved we were to hear of your mother's condition. I knew that she had suffered extreme weakness ever since her bad illness, but hoped it might be alleviated in time rather than have this conclusion. I had always a strong affection for your mother, whom I well remember from the first of our acquaintance.

fare well

If kind messages from me to her might reach her, I should be very glad.

124: TO MRS. MANLEY HOPKINS

Yattendon
Newbury
May 28, 1890

Dear Mrs. Hopkins

I am glad to say that I can at last fulfill my promise and send you the rest of Gerard's letters. I had tried several times to read them: but always had put them down again without much progress: till yesterday, when having returned home after a month's visiting among friends, and being unsettled and in the low spirits which I find generally accompanies this change of surroundings, I thought of them: and was surprised to discover that I was in the congenial mood; in fact they cheered me up altogether.

You will read them with great interest. I have taken out only two or three and those only because they narrated family events etc. and though I might just as well have left them with the rest, I thought it better,—in the absence of any reason to the contrary—to respect the understanding on which they were written.

I have erased a name or two—these merely of persons to whom I should not wish to give any right to have their say.

I hope you are all well at Haslemere. It may interest you to know that my niece Mary Plow is going to be married to Rev. H. C. Beeching, the rector of Yattendon. He is a scholar, about 30 years of age. We like him very much.

Keep the letters as long as you wish. I found among them more distinct references to Gerard's state of mind than I remembered. One in particular is very plain. I always considered that he was over nervous about himself, and exaggerated his symptoms—which I think he did. In fact I think his mental condition was of this sort. I may say that I have come round again to more my old state of feeling with regard to his memory.—

It happens that Bell is now publishing my poems. I thought that if I could make the occasion I would introduce some of Gerard's verse into the notes of that book and see if the critics noticed it. What would you think of that?

With kindest regards to Mr and Miss Hopkins

your very truly

R Bridges

P.S.
I have 5 £ offerred [*sic*] me for a copy of the Growth of Love, by a bookseller. So if you ever want to get rid of your copy send it to me. But I had rather you would keep it if you wish to.

125: TO LIONEL MUIRHEAD

Yattendon
June 14, 1890

My dear Lionel

We were very sorry to hear from M^{rs} L that you were not well.—No doubt your anxiety and sorrow will account for it: but I cannot quite exculpate that wretched Influenzaical winter, which has meddled with most people's physical status, and, among its many devastations, has ruined 2 of the best voices in my choir, a great practical annoyance.

I am still busy with proofs etc. The printers have been very slow. This morning I am making a clearance of accumulated debris of dramas etc. It is a strange thing how all one's affection for a poem departs as soon as it is printed in modern style. "Manuscripts are cheap today".

We expect HEW next week. When he comes we might come over to you for the inside of a fine day. Our 'visit' must be postponed. Meanwhile you and M^{rs} L might come here again for a day or so if family arrangements permit.

On Tuesday is the bridal of Rev H. C. Beeching and Mary Plow. Perhaps you never heard that it was coming off. If so you will scarcely believe it. A great change at the Rectory since the old Loveday times. These are the true love-days, (to rob you of a joke too obvious I fear for your refined skill.) Among the guests are 5 Aunts of the bride!! and 7 bachelor friends of the bridegroom. Will not they pair well? Now I don't "enter into" this sort of thing at all well. I wish you were coming.

I hope you will send us better news of yourself—

your affectionate

RB

Very kind of M^{rs} L to write about servant. Wife is too busy to be courteous in her replies just now—will no doubt write as things clear up.

126: TO LIONEL MUIRHEAD

Yattendon
June 26, 1890

My dear Lionel

I am sorry that we have not been able to get away any day yet, and now it cannot be this week. Still we hope to come. In confidence of which I will not write more.

One thing which has sprung up and promises to be a drawback is that I promised Professor Stanford his libretto about now, and I was not able to take it up again, to finish it, till yesterday.

But I have now got my lyrics off, completing the book with 40 new ones. I hope you will like it. You will see it announced on the cover of Achilles.

Hoping you are well now, or much better—

with kindest regards

your affectionate

RB

127: TO RICHARD WATSON DIXON

Yattendon
Newbury
July 30, 1890

My dear Canon

That Oxford book is not worth postage backwards and forwards. It will keep till I come, but if we do not come I will send it as you desire. I write now to ask whether it will be convenient to you to take us, and if so when.

We are going to the Worcester musical festival from September 9th to September 12th. Therefore our visit to you must be either just before, or just after that. If we put it off longer it would be too late, and now we have engagements which will last till about 2nd week of August. Thank you for your letters. I am glad that your new curate does. Our parlour maid is going to be married and we are also anxious about a new groom. I have been reading Cowper's letters again the ones Hayley did *not* publish. How admirable they are! And what a contrast to Pater's appreciations: in which I seem like a creature of black misgivings, moving about (for I cannot read straight on) in a world not realized. Wordsworth should have written 'a world' not 'worlds'. The sense is as in *this* world—not in a number of infinities—But Pater says that Wordsworth's expression is always right. This morning in a London 2nd hand catalogue I saw my Nero advertised at 20/. It was a rubbishly dishonest catalogue: but the joke was none the worse. How pleased it must be after struggling for 3 years at 2/. to find itself at 20/.—having magnificence thrust upon it. Achilles will not come out. He mistakes Clay's printing house for his Trojan tent. Wooldridge still with us. Leaves tomorrow. By the way Daniel is going to print "the Growth of Love" in black letter. It looks fine. 100 copies. At about 12/6.

We all wish you the best of everything.

your affectionate
RB

128: TO MRS. MANLEY HOPKINS

Yattendon
Newbury
August 4, 1890

Dear Mrs. Hopkins

I am very sorry that my indolence should have caused you trouble. I supposed that you would trust the post: and at worst the miscarriage of a copy is no great matter.

The real reason why I did not write was that I nearly determined to return you the book. It will not quickly come again to such an honoured place, but since I last wrote to you the printer Mr Daniel has been here and has persuaded me to allow him to print another 100 copies (this time in black letter!! and now I fancy already done), and I thought that you might prefer a copy of the new edition which will be the handsomer book. In this indecision I did nothing.

The new edition will soon be known of, so I think I should offer the copy of the old one to the bookseller who wanted it, together with the crabbing information.

If he does not take it I will return it to you if you still wish to possess it.

I am glad that you are keeping Gerard's letters. I hope there is nothing in them but what will give you happy thoughts.

I asked you about printing a poem or two of his in my new volume, coming out in October.

I intended to bring them into notes at the end of the book, but now, for irresistible reasons, I have given up the notion of notes, and with them the poems.

Mr Daniel says that he will print a selection at any time, free of charge—up to 150 copies. Yourselves and friends to take a certain number, and the rest for private sale among interested outsiders. Perhaps you will like this plan. The memoir must I think be given up for the present, but perhaps a short 'preface' might be written which should put the poems out of the reach of criticism.

I should not like the poems to be printed without some word of that sort, and it is a difficulty which a memoir would have got over.

I should myself prefer the postponement of the poems till the memoir is written, *or* till I have got my own method of prosody recognised separately from Gerard's. They are the same, and he has the greater claim than I to the origination of it, but he has used it so as to discredit it : and it would be a bad start in favour for the practice we both advocated and wished to be used. Readers would not see that the peculiarities of his versification were not part of his metrical system, but a freakishness corresponding to his odd choice of words etc. in which also his theories were as sound as his practice was strange.

In this I am not considering myself, but the prospect of introducing this new way of writing, in which if there is any reputation to come to him, it will be from the recognition of the principles which I think his own verse would damage.

I have no doubt of the adoption of the system, and when once it is recognised his verses will establish his claim to foreseeing (not to say outgoing) the limits of it.

A year or 18 months is all the delay which I expect will be necessary for this, and I should like it for the reasons I give I hope not unintelligibly.

With kindest regards to you all

I am yours sincerely
Robert Bridges

129: TO MRS. MANLEY HOPKINS

Yattendon
September 26, 1890

Dear Mrs Hopkins

We returned home yesterday after a month's absence and I found the packet of Gerard's letters returned. I write to acknowledge them at once.

Also I send you back the book of Sonnets which I am very glad that you should keep. I intended sending it before but never got so far as packing it up. My wife had a bad attack of jaundice, and that and other matters diverted my attention. She is now well again. Part of our holiday was devoted to getting her a suitable change of air, part to the Worcester Musical Festival.

Today excuse a hasty letter. The black-letter edition of the Growth of Love (100 copies) is now out and can be had of Mr Daniel—in case you know of any one who would like to buy it. He charges 10/ or 12/ I think but his books can always be sold for more a few months after they are 'exhausted'.

With kindest regards to Mr Hopkins and yourself

> yours very truly
> R Bridges

130: TO GEORGE SAINTSBURY

> Yattendon
> Newbury
> October 13, 1890

My dear Saintsbury

You may be sure that I never had a kinder or pleasanter letter than yours: and I must ask you to excuse my having sent you my book so baldly without accompanying words, but I could not tell how you might take it.

I knew that you had once said certain nice things about something of mine, and I hoped that you might look kindly on this volume, and that if you did, you would be willing to do it a good turn some day. So I numbered you among the half dozen friends to whom I ventured to send it. It is, you will admit, a harmless production, and it has gone out to all the reviews to receive their literary judgement. Bell tells me that he has made a very good start with the sale already.

It is most agreeable of course to get at the poetic side of a critic, the human side, so to speak: and finding you in this natural countryfied humour I am tempted to ask whether you cannot forge a little further Westward one of these fine days and pay me a visit here. If you have so few days that there is no time for precommunication you can train to Pangbourne, and there get a fly which would take you over to us, a pretty drive, in ¾ of an hour. You will be sure to find me at home. We could put you up, or you could return the same day. If you come later than this assumes and would write I would send to meet any train.

The country is very pretty here and no one knows it. Still much depends on the weather, and it would be no disadvantage to come on a fine day, rather than chance the weather by a fixture. I fear however that the engagements of such a busy man as you are will prevent your accepting an invitation at such short notice.

In any case accept my thanks for your very kind letter, and warm friendly reception of my poems, and believe me

> yours very sincerely
> R Bridges

131: TO LIONEL MUIRHEAD

> Yattendon
> October 20, 1890

My dear Lionel

Thank you for your letter. I am very glad that you like my work. We have been sorry never to have seen your home, but I hope that your wife will keep quite quiet and be the better for it.

We were at Windsor and Eton the other day: everything was as bright as it should be.

I was amused comparing your letter with one I received by same post from George Saintsbury. He wrote as warmly as possible in praise of the book and especially noted 5 or 6 poems as what he liked best. Among those few were two, which were known to me as the worst in the book, and which only just scraped in: and a third which he said he liked best was one which had a strong critical objection urgeable against it.

You on the other hand with natural good feeling put your finger on the best things.

And Saintsbury has been 20 years and more a professional critic.

The weather has been as you say charming.

Daniel has brought out a black letter 100 copy edition of the Growth of Love. It sold off at once and the demand does not cease.

What a man Daniel is!

And everyone swears that they never saw anything so difficult to read. The poems are selling very well. The handmade copies are up at 15/.

This sort of thing promises to provide us with amusement during the winter.

I am doing the 2nd part of Nero, and am just going at it now.

With our love X

your affectionate

RB

132: TO GEORGE SAINTSBURY

Yattendon
Newbury
November 1, 1890

My dear Saintsbury

I am much obliged to you for the review in the Saturday which I could not mistake for any one's but yours. I do not know if it is decent to thank the angelic impartiality of a critic, but I hope you do not mind.

I shall be in town next week, and away from home too the week after, but shall be here on Saturday and Sunday. In fact Sunday is the best day to come, except as I told you, there is a difficulty about sending to the station. So to come on Saturday evening and stay till Monday morning is what my friends generally do. But then I must warn you that I go to church on Sunday at 11, and again at 6:15. The services are short, but they are musical, and that is what engages me, as the villagers do their best. This leaves me free for an afternoon walk, and unless you want to walk all day there is really no inconvenience, as you need not sing yourself.* We hope you will come.

your truly

Robt Bridges

*Nor hear. (which is worse)

133: TO LIONEL MUIRHEAD

Yattendon
Newbury
November 7, 1890

My dear Lionel

I have a list of 8 letters to write today so I will do no more than congratulate you on the 'happy event' and thank you very much for writing. In all felicitations my wife joins, and we are very glad to hear that you have no cause for anxiety. You must have been in a "state"! And for the other matter your Father is too kind.

your affectionate
RB

134: TO G. LOWES DICKINSON

Yattendon
Newbury
November 13, 1890

Dear Sir

Ever since Roger Fry sent me a copy of 'Jacob's Ladder' I have owed you a letter: but how neglectful you have thought me I cannot tell, as I do not know how far I am indebted to you for the present of the book. If you sent it you will at least know that I asked for it: and as I had read it well before I asked for it, I have really paid you the only formal compliment which strict manners would allow, except my thanks for letting me have it: to which, as I said, I do not even know that you were party—on the chance however of your expecting to hear from me, and of your misconstruing silence, I venture to write to say how much I like your performance; and hope that you will write more. N° III seems to me full of a promise of poetry of original and rare character, but I do not wish to write a critical letter—nothing is more difficult than to express one'self to a stranger in such matters without peril or misinterpretation, and I hope that we may meet and talk over the subjects in which I see we have a common and strong interest.

Let me protest against your occasional following of Browning's manner. To me that is *detestable,* and whether you agree with me or not pray consider two axioms. 1ˢᵗ that it is the function of art to beautify. And 2ⁿᵈ to quote another who has expressed my meaning well: "Rien n'est plus vite banal que les hardiesses de mauvais gout".

I do not know what chance there is of our meeting, but if you should be ever in London, and inclined to pay me a visit here I should like that very much, and I hope that you will find it possible. We should have a great deal to talk about.

I am yours truly
Robt Bridges

135: TO G. LOWES DICKINSON

Yattendon
Newbury
[Probably late November 1890]

Dear Sir

I quite agree with what you say as to the relation between literature and contemporary Thought. But that seems to me a necessity of life: and its truth is a natural outcome marred by effort. I take it the poet has to show the emotional result, so to speak—of this intellectual contact: which latter being the measure of his head it is a case of μὴ μεριμνᾶτε We will talk of these things. I only write this to cast off any suspicion that I am an antiquarian. I find that it is rather my belief in progress and my looking ahead which puts me out of sympathy with much modern work. At any rate, even if it is held that *art* is concerned in the product, it should disguise itself as much in this as in its other efforts.

It was very kind of you to take my letter so gently and gratefully. And it gave me much pleasure to learn that you liked any of my work. I shall look forward to seeing you here at Xmas, if as I hope you will find time to come, and will send us a line. We should have much to talk of—especially rhythm.

Yours truly
Robt Bridges

136: TO GEORGE SAINTSBURY

Yattendon
Newbury
December 8, 1890

My dear Saintsbury

Pray accept my thanks for your kind and most acceptable present—it is such a handsome volume that it makes me ashamed of mine. I have not even time to look in it this morning, but I fancy that I must have read some of the earlier part of it somewhere before.

I should have called on you in Reading if I had had the opportunity. It happens that I am very busy now, anxious to get some work finished before Xmas.

You will be glad to hear that my 'shorter poems' sold out very quickly. At least there were only a few tens of it left some time ago, and it is being reprinted to be in time for Xmas.

The Athenaeum has not yet noticed it nor the Spectator so that their reviews will probably just do for the 2nd edition—

I was so glad to hear that Creighton has been appointed Canon of Windsor. It is a good place to be at, and near us. But the change of houses must be a trouble to a man who arranges his house to his own taste as Creighton does.

Excuse a very hasty note. I have a lot of letters to jam in between work and post time. We suffer from most inconvenient posts, coming late and going away early like Charles Lamb.

yours very truly

R Bridges

Is your house much this side of Reading? How is it best approached?

137: TO LIONEL MUIRHEAD

Yattendon
December 27, 1890

My dear Lionel

I hope that you are having a good Xmas. We have been in trouble. Maurice Waterhouse is dead, he got a chill skating in London, and died in 5 days. I do not know if you know how much beloved he was. The funeral is to be here on Monday.

yours affectionately

RB

138: TO RICHARD WATSON DIXON

Yattendon
January 4, 1891

My dear Canon

Very many thanks for your splendid present, the Vol IV of your History, which I have been enjoying. It promises to be at once a joy and a κτῆμα for ever. Writers of such books as you (and I) (!!) write deserve some thanks from people like ourselves. So let us thank each other. I fancy that your history is already in very general use. I wish myself that you would write a note to the first volume, on the morality of the monks. I understand that your point of view is that nothing should be said against them that is not proved, but the difficulty of proving the sort of thing that they were credited with is great. I find that the general sense of historians is against you in this: they say that you make an ex parte statement of the case. Now as for scandal, I am as convinced as it is possible to be that history is full of lies of that sort. Any spicy story once told was repeated and believed, and modern historians have a task before them to weed history of these things. I have been engaged lately in weeding the history of Nero. I am convinced that the *Sporus* business was all made up. Also he did not set fire to Rome—etc. etc. But to return to the monks. 1st. the probability is against them. Whether you make up your probability out of their universal reputation or from an a priori argument as to what must be the effect of getting such men as they were together under such rules. 2nd. I think evidence is to be had against them, in the antereformation visitations of the monasteries. I saw one which was awful. I should like you to guard yourself in a note from being misinterpreted to affirm more than you would yourself say that you do affirm.

I may be wrong in thinking there is really any necessity for this, but I remember that my impression after reading your account of the suppression was that the monks had been needlessly ill spoken of, and I am sure that historians think you are not fair in this matter. (What cheek!)

I ordered a book to send you as a Xmas gift, but it has not come. It is an American poet!! And I hope you will find him as good reading as I did. He is not first rate, but might have been so: or if not, still there is that about him which makes him worth studying. The book had to be sent for from America. You should have it in a few days.

I have finished Nero II and am setting to work at other things. Lang has a sort of favourable article on me in Longman, but it shows an ageing mind*. He likes the old things better than the better ones written since, and he is hopelessly out of it with the plays. He thinks Prometheus is a play, and speaks of the plays rather, I thought, as old fashioned; whereas their form and ethics are both new. Still he gives me more praise than I deserve, and should be allowed to lump it where and as he likes. The Athenaeum wholly ignores me, which makes me very cocky. This is the way *great* poets are served.

with our love

your affectionate

RB

*! See Appendix

Appendix

I did not mean what followed as justifying evidence, but if you see his article note how he talks of the poems which came out when he was an undergraduate, and his criterion of excellence is what remains by him, and it is just these things. Then he objects to my introducing modern ethics into Greek stories, but does not (= did not) object to Morris introducing Medievalism into them. I am half afraid he only likes my verses because my first volume was of that date or thereabouts.

RB

139: TO MRS. HUMPHRY WARD

Yattendon
January 9, 1891

Dear Mrs Ward

Thank you for your letter and the prospectusses. I think the lectures should be very interesting and should like to hear some of them, which is saying a good

Ieal. The subject's admirably chosen, though I rather wonder how the French heology will answer.

Maurice's death was a terrible misfortune. I never met a nicer fellow, great natural gifts of all kinds and a most gentle nature. He was intending to take orders, and would have been one of the sort in whose existence, you (not without reason) disbelieve.

Mrs. Waterhouse was most heroic, and though she must come to feel her sorrow more when the necessity for being brave is passed, yet she bears up wonderfully, and has been almost cheerful in her resignation. I saw her this morning and told her you had written. She begged me to thank you very much for your letter to her, and say that she will be writing to you soon. She finds the letters very difficult to write, and has many that she feels obliged to answer at once before nearer friends'.

As for Maurice he died bravely, though it was at the turning point of his life. But I think it is only the superstitious who are troubled in this way.

I am glad to hear that your boy is getting well. I had not heard of his illness. Certainly children are more of a care than the miser's gold.

Your kind invitation it would give us great pleasure to accept, but I am afraid that I cannot definitely close with it. May I write again? We were hoping to be in London in March for a day or two. Meanwhile do not reckon on us. When we do come, it will I hope be easy to arrange a meeting for a chat.

Thank you also for your kind words about 'Achilles'. My new dramas (I mean the ones in the new manner) must await their trial. Critics do not seem to know anything about stage plays and the public naturally do not wish to read them after the doses of—well I must not abuse my betters. It was very good of you not to laugh in silence about the 'libretto', but I hope when you see it you may be interested enough to help to draw attention to its neologies.

With our kindest regards, and to Mr Ward.

yours very truly
R Bridges

P-S

I should have thought that the "broad church" business had borne fruit. Things are much changed.

140: TO LIONEL MUIRHEAD

Yattendon
Newbury
January 22, 1891

Dear Lionel

Thanks for your letter. We are very well—and have enjoyed the weather immensely. But I am sorry to say that my Mother seems failing. She has felt the cold and also the shock of Maurice Waterhouse's sudden death, and has ailed a

good deal, and yesterday she had a little *stroke:* from which it did not seem as i
she would rally.

Today she is better again, but I have telegraphed for my brother and sisters t
come.

I know that you will be grieved at this, but my Mother is 83—and though
should wish her to live another 10 years I do not wish it unless she should kee
her health—and when the end comes it is so natural that one's chief sigh I thin
is for the thought that one will not end so ideal[l]y oneself. She is perfectl
happy, and to live through a series of half parryings of death would not be wha
I should wish for myself.

I will not write more now—you will know that I have lots of letters to write.

We were glad to hear such good news of you all, and that your house ha
proved comfortable through this cold weather.

If all is well we think of being in town for a week in March.

With our love to both

yours affectionately

RB

141: TO G. LOWES DICKINSON

Yattendor
January 24, 189

My dear Dickinson

Thank you for the verses. I send you my animadversions, and would apologis
for their illegibility, but I think that after what has passed I had better write as i
as possible, and I can do that as you will see—

I will send Roger his book.

Thanks for the notes of the prosody. I will attend to them. Have not had tim
to refer to it yet.

I deliberately abused the word elision, lest I might be interpreted to mea
something by it.

About the poems. I was surprised to find generally the diction etc. less goo
than in Jacob's Ladder. Are the poems earlier? In some of them e. g. Consola
tion, Apologia (?), Sechuman remus (?) Milton I do not know that I should hav
recognised the poet. On the other hand Desiderium and Haunted would hav
left me no doubt. Nor Dadossa, but that poem is (you will see I think), no
satisfactory as it stands. I would shorten it as much as I could.

I dare say you will read my notes—which I wrote as I read, till I broke off, as
show in the notes—

If these poems were written some years ago I expect that you have already go
over the chief fault which they betray—which is I think lack of distinction o
diction—you sometimes waste a lot of room.

If you don't see what I mean I will write and explain—but I think the verba objections to the verses will exhibit my meaning, and for my judgment you may attach what value to it you please.

We enjoyed your visit and hope to see you again someday.

Some of the places I like best have come under objection and some I do not care for much did not suggest criticism.

yours truly
R Bridges

PS You left /6^d on your dressing table.

142: TO A. H. BULLEN

Yattendon
Newbury
January 24, 1891

My dear Bullen

If my plays are to be acted it must probably be done at first in the way you suggest, and I shall be grateful to any friends who suggest it in the proper quarter as I cannot do so myself.

I think a woman disguised as a man always betrays herself, and it is ridiculous. Why Shakespeare was so fond of it was that *his women were acted by boys**. A lad can disguise himself as a woman perfectly, and Achilles would be a first rate part for such actors as you now see among the stage loving undergraduates.

Shakespeare was of course glad of any excuse to *get the petticoats off.*

Many thanks for your "kind expressions"

In haste

yours very sincerely
R Bridges

*The Epilogue to "*As you like it*" is spoken now by *women!* The *If* and *kind offer* were all right enough with a boy speaking.

143: TO LIONEL MUIRHEAD

Yattendon
February 1, 1891

My dear Lionel

I have been intending to write to you. Today's opportunity is that I am lying, or rather sitting up, in bed. I have a most ferocious cold; and I thought I would see if lying in bed was any good. My experience is that it is not. I could not have sneezed more had I been in one of the garden beds. I'll never try it again. Now it is 6 pm, and I shall go through with it for today, though I am very much disposed to get up and dress for dinner as usual. I have spent the day reading Byron, an author most neglected by me. This has not much cheered the time, and his Lordship can never have been so sneezed at or on before.

Nevile Sturt turned up on Sunday, with two friends in football caps and short pipes. I asked him about you—He seemed to think that your wife was not quite strong again yet. I hope you will be able to send us a good account.

We have had a bad Xmas as you know. My mother however is better again. She has my oldest sister staying at the Grange, and she looks as if she would get over this winter's attack. Children and wife well.

I can't imagine where I got my cold. It is a nuisance this fine weather. What lovely weather! It suggests beginning to make plans for summer, but probably in a fortnight we shall have snow again and all the terrors of spring. We talked of going abroad this year, but have had to give up the notion—I hope that we shall be able to pay you a visit—

We had 3 days in town last week, which we enjoyed very much, getting in 2 concerts, and 2 exhibitions. There are some good English pictures at the Old Masters. No doubt you have seen them.

We expect Wooldridge here very soon. I did not see him in town.

With kindest regards . . .

your affectionate
RB

P.S. When either of you write, let us hear of the family.

144: TO G. LOWES DICKINSON

Yattendon
February 18, 1891

My dear Dickinson

I was too busy to write to you when I should have done.—Today I have abundant leisure, granted by a diabolical cold in the head. I want Lanier to adjure the 'spring germs'. How ridiculous it was of him!

First to thank you for your notes on the Milton prosody. The passage about elision of something is indefensible, as is another just below, at least so they both seem to me now. That kind of thing is not in my way, and I got very impatient of it. I was lucky to be as intelligible as I was. I meant to misuse the term *elision*, but not to write such nonsense. Synaeresis is a bad word. A word is wanted that means nothing. The fact is that when two vowels come together the first is more like a musical appoggiatura than anything else—I think the Greeks abused their vowels: though I fancy it is wrong to come to any decided conclusion in their disfavour. Still as far as we can judge they pronounced them much alike, and cut them clean off. Both wrong.

In my private opinion the open vowels are not similar in their explanation to the "elisions" where a liquid occurs. These latter are more like trisyllabic feet. But I would have nothing to do with theory in my tract.

What your friend Wedd says about a fixed number of stresses in a line to make stanzas is new prosody, I entirely agree to. That is the way to make stanzas: and so I have made them, and will try to do so in future. Of course if one likes to set rule aside that is one's own affair. And I can only say that after writing some thousands of lines in metre it is an inevitable human failing to kick over the traces. Privately I think that the best verse is to be got at thus. But—one must of course have worked in the ruts a long while before one can know how to leave them—

You referred me to Christabel, whether it was not in new prosody. Certainly not. The author merely *states* that there are 4 stresses in every line. There are not always 4. The reader has to pretend there are, e.g. "Is fástened tó an añgel's féet" (4) would read in new prosody thus

Is fástend to an añgel's féet   (3)

and if "Why stares she with unsettled eye" (which would not scan at all in new prosody) has 4 accents why has not the following line 5?

Then Chrístabél knelt bý the lády's síde.

No statement in the preface can compel you to accent *with* in one line and slur *by* in the other. The point of the new prosody is that the rhythm is determined by the accents and not the accents by the rhythm, and though Coleridge meant the 1st he as often wrote the 2nd, and that is why no one has ever been able to make good verse on his model. It is odd enough that no critic has ever pointed out the simple fallacy.

By the way talking of Christabel did you ever think how much better stanza 2 of that poem would be if *cold* were written for the first *chilly*. Chilly is the distinction of perception and foolish in the questioner??? So I think—

I hope that *some* of my criticism was of service. I am afraid much of it may have been foolish.—The rector here asked me the other day if you were publishing anything. I told him you were looking for a publisher and he recommended Septimus Rivington. I was in S R's new offices the other day. They are splendid. In King Sᵗ Covent Garden. I think the firm is called Perceval and Co. R is not allowed to use his own name for a while. Some agreement with the old firm he has separated from. He is I fancy looking out for authors, and is said to be a very good fellow. He seemed so to me—you might try him if not yet suited.

yours truly

R Bridges

P. S. Thanks for all you said about "Shorter Poems". I am glad you liked "My spirit kisseth". As for the being of IV. 25, it is quite simple, but the poem seems to have taken the form of a riddle: to which I have had so many answers that I only wish to add to them—Some lady suggested Mʳ Gladstone!!

Thanks also for telling me Mr Raleigh's opinion. What a splendid name he has! It is something to please a man with such a name. I hope I may meet him some day.

Stephen's quatrain very fancy. I heard it again in town. The rest of the poem I fear not so good.

I just saw Roger for a moment in town before he was off to Italy.

145: TO LIONEL MUIRHEAD

Yattendon
February 28, 1891

Dear Lionel

The point about outrigging or half outrigging is to get more length and therefore leverage inboard. *Do not get a non outrigged boat unless it is very long.*—A short boat not outrigged must either be tubby and therefore heavy, or be too narrow for the oars, which is the worst labour of all in rowing. A full sized randan need not be outrigged except for bow oar, and that is what they call half outrigged I expect. (But I do not *know* whether this is what is meant. It may mean short outriggers.) The objection to a long boat is that in windy weather it must be well loaded, or will make very one sided rowing.

Both the randans and the outrigged gigs are useful boats. But I should not like ladies to go out alone in outrigged boats, as the outriggers are the source of accidents both in locks and collisions. This reduces you to the randan and if I were to buy a boat for general use I should buy a randan.

The old wherry is delightful, but I have not much experience of them—You will remember seeing that at Eton—

I suspect they are not built now. The randan being a big boat is not exactly light but you will remember how it travels. HEW you and I with 3 portmanteaus and corresponding hampers once raced an outrigged pairoar between locks with triumphant success.

If you buy a secondhand boat I think that Salter could not object to your having it on trial to change in the first season if you do not like it. Pay half only of the money down to keep him to his bargain.

East at Reading has now the reputation of being a much cheaper man than Salter. I do not know if you would think it worth while to write to him. East, boatbuilder, Reading would find him. You might ask him his randan prices.

I should think a mahogany boat is what you would like to possess.

Look at No 57 unless you decide for the randan. Remember of course if you get a randan that you will have a boat that is always bigger than you want for yourself and wife only, but on the other hand *quite safe* for 6 or 8 persons, and one that you might let your wife take the children out in without any anxiety whatever.*

yours affectionately

RB

My cold *is* in my chest and in my toes and hair and finger nails etc.

*except in windy weather

In any case see that your oars are of full length and the sculls racing sculls which over lap thus

146: TO LIONEL MUIRHEAD

Yattendon
March 3, 1891
4:15 [P.M.]

Dear Lionel

Wife begs me to write and ask you if you have any handwriting capitals that you can recommend, fluent but not scrolly.

She is doing some samples of handwriting which I hope will be facsimiled and published and is not decided about the most convenient form of some of the capitals.

If you know any good shapes would you send them. It does not matter to do them *very* particularly, as the *scheme* is the great thing, the "rhythm", and I think she could manage the finessing all right.

Thanks for your last letter

yours affectionately

RB

Post goes at 4.20

147: TO ROGER FRY

Yattendon
May 14, 1891

My dear Roger

It was very good of you to write us that long letter. To tell truth I had been somewhat jealous towards Dickinson, who has written to me once or twice, and always with news of you. He has even told me your judgement of places and things, with which I quite agreed. It will be very pleasant to talk of all these matters with you. What a delightful time you must be having! That first visit to Italy, and at your age, is the very cream of life. To be able to see it all with one's own mind, not through Ruskin or Hare. Thank heaven I never read Ruskin. I am glad you went through the Etruscan country. I drove. My friend had had an attack of fever and couldn't walk. I got sick of going into all those little tombs. I fancy that I managed to miss the best of them, but they were miserable after my Egyptian memories, and I am nothing of an antiquarian.—I often feel as Heine did toward the 3 Holy Kings—you remember? If not you will not wish to be reminded of that ill-mannered German Jew in Venice.—Monica and I had plans to be in Venice *now*, but all things have militated against it, and we are shelved here as fast as can be. I am sorry to say that my mother is very ill—distressingly so—and no reason to say anything about it to you, except that it makes it pretty certain that you will find us at home on your return. So come down any day, with or without notice. We shall be delighted, and M. sends you all sorts of messages. You need not defend landscape painting to me. I must have said more than I intended against it.—I do like "sketching" and have suffered from it.—This year there was an exhibition in London—you saw it before you left I expect—in which English landscape carried all before it.—The old Italians were poorly represented, and Walker in a square 6 inches licked a wall side of Florentines. Also another victory of England over Italy to my mind is the contrast, of certain portraits, Gainsboroughs and Romneys, with 2nd rate Venetian grandees. Our 18th century admiral with his background of sea sky and cannon was godlike beside those snuffy stolid musty councillors. It was plain that he could not only beat them at fighting or dancing but would strip much better, and there was an island breeziness about him much more poetic than the velvet business.

If you don't know Horatio Brown at Venice I think you should call on him and introduce yourself. I have met him and though I do not know him well enough to give you an actual introduction I know he would be glad to see you; he is said to be very hospitable, and his long residence in Venice should not fail to be of great use to you. He is sure to know Middleton well.

This is a dreadful scrawl, but it was this or nothing, and in a foreign country with lots of spare hours it may be better than nothing. Your last adventure was amusing. I can fancy you in the cafe. I remember many little Etruscan cafes where I was the only Englishman. I suppose that you have made lots of sketches. (Not of the sort I inveigh against, "subjects") and will bring them here.— Dickinson's book is out "From King to King." He sent it to me yesterday. I have not read it yet. I was delighted at your quoting Dixon's "*Spirit-wooed*"—I did not know that you liked him. A book has just come out representing the poets of his decade of this century.—There are some dozen and a half, and he not there! Lots of fellows, I never heard of. Pages of Garnett, and such like duffers, and no Dixon. He will be resuscitated like Blake.

No more of this penograph

yours affectionately
RB

148: TO RICHARD WATSON DIXON

Yattendon
May 16, 1891

My dear Dixon

It is too long since we have heard from you. Steal me half an hour from Halma or whatever you call it and tell me how you are. We have had bad times—My mother's decrepitude is cerebral, and what might be called softening of the brain. She is very seldom herself—and has all manner of delusions. Our aim is to keep her cheerful and discover what drug best promotes sleep when she is restless, and to drive as best we can the delusions into pleasant channels. This has been very distressing, and depressing. And I do not feel the better for it yet. You may imagine that I have not done a stroke of work all the year. I don't know what we should have done if it had not been for my sister (Lady Molesworth) who has been a great deal here, and has nursed and sat up with my mother. Today we expect a professional nurse, who with my mother's attendant should manage everything very well.—Having told you this I seem to have told you all I have to say, for naturally I have not taken an interest in anything—Things however have been going on—at least time has been passing, and I suppose that if you were here I should have lots to talk about. I very much want to know whether you are going on with your history, or are writing poems. Now Creighton is a bishop there is I suppose a chance for your getting a stall, but I do not know how things are at Peterboro? He will make an admirable bishop I feel certain.—I hope that you have not been troubled by influenza.—I think that both Monica and I had it some month or so ago, but if we did it was a very modified kind. We were both ill for a fortnight, first I and then she, with similar symptoms—headache and cough, but nothing distinctive except that it was quite unlike an ordinary cold. The children have been very well. Elizabeth is now very amusing. She is very observant and curious, and has a great memory, a timid child, obedient and careful. Margaret promises to be a good contrast. Monica is very well. I have never known her so strong as she has been all the winter. She is working very hard at music. Which subject introduces Wooldridge, who was down here for a month at the beginning of the year, and is coming now again (for another month)?) this next week.

Today we have a London visitor for Sunday.

A third edition of my "Shorter Poems" is being printed.—A man who is editing "the poets of the century" sent me a volume the other day containing his account of the poets born between 1830 and 1840. *You are not among them.* There must have been over a dozen in all, and ten of them I had never seen before, i.e., their poems, amongst others Garnett of the British Museum (I'll trouble you). Now I think I was joyful that I was able to congratulate myself I had refused him permission to put me into his book. He was very angry with me: but did I not do well?

You will have to be rediscovered after your death like Blake. Some officious Gosse will hang his hat on your tomb.

My choir is doing very well. Our young organist suddenly developed "the seeds of consumption." At least he began to spit blood etc. It was quite unaccountable. There was no consumption in his family on either side, and he seemed the picture of health. We had to send him off to get cured as speedily as possible, and I think, as I hope, that he may get over it. But the result has been that our choir has had to sing for a month without any accompaniment: and it looks as if they would have to continue to do so for 6 months more. This has improved the singing immensely, and the boys are growing up well.

The blossom on the fruit trees this year is quite incredible—and the next remarkable thing is the show of dandelions. The fields are golden with them. can't think where they came from, and each plant is prolific above example. A common plant will have 20 or 30 huge blossoms on it with stalks a foot long— Their magnificent colour makes the country look very rich.

Monica joins in love, and we hope that Mrs Dixon (to whom we send all kind messages) is quite well.

your affectionate

RB

P.S. Monica sends you a story of Elizabeth. She observes all the books in the study and enquired about your history one day. M said what it was, "and perhaps some day he will come here and you will see him". Eliz. "Or perhaps if I am a very good girl I may some day go and see him, Mama!" I vote you come—Eh!

149: TO GEORGE SAINTSBURY

Yattendon

Newbur

July 6, 189

My dear Saintsbury

I have told Bell to send you a copy of 'Eden' a libretto which I wrote for Stanford last year at his request, for the Birmingham Festival this October.

I have also told Bell to send it to the 'Saturday' for review. If on perusal you think it worth notice as a poem and have an opportunity of mentioning it should be very glad.

Stanford is very much in earnest about it, and I should like to help him. The music man of the Saturday will no doubt have his say. But I know that Stanford wishes the attention of the public called to the libretto.

You will understand that I do not wish to seem to ask anything which is difficult to grant or refuse—and that I really care no more about it than my wish to oblige Stanford—which I think I do by calling your friendly attention to the matter.

My wife joins in kindest remembrances to Mrs Saintsbury, and thanks for your hospitality that day of our visit.

Next Sunday we are fully engaged—could you come over the Sunday after? I forget now what you said your engagements are. We are at home till September 5th.

> yours very truly
> Robt Bridges

'Eden' should be announced this week for publication next week.

150: TO GEORGE SAINTSBURY

> Yattendon
> Newbury
> July 13, 1891

My dear Saintsbury

It is very kind of you to promise to attend to "*Eden*". I write to say that I hope you will not feel at all bound to say any thing more about it than just what you think it deserves—and if you think it does not merit a notice, do not give it one at all.

I think we shall be free *next* Sunday if that day suits you to come over.

> yours very truly
> Robert Bridges

151: TO RICHARD WATSON DIXON

> Yattendon
> August 10, 1891

My dear Dixon

I am very sorry for those your misfortunes: and that they trouble you. I hope that the disclosure of them was some relief! I feel rather inclined to chaff you about them: and think that you must be singularly free from real troubles just now: at which thought we rejoice.

But, I am sorry that you think that your last volume has not been well received. I have heard much praise of it. I did not care so well for it myself because of all that Eucharistic controversy—the heart- and hand-burnings.

We are just about rebuilding our school.

M and I go away in September with the children to the Isle of Wight. We are regretting the little likelihood there seems of our meeting with you again this year.

In haste with our love

> your affectionate
> RB

152: TO EDMUND GOSSE

Yattendor
Newbury
August 15, 189

My dear Gosse

I should have written before to thank you for your letter about Eden. I did no
send it to you because I thought that you would care for it. But I did not know
what to do about it. It seemed better to send it than not to send it.

I am very sorry to hear from various quarters that you are not well. I hope tha
there is nothing really wrong, but that you are only feeling the malaise which
think has been almost universal this year where there has been nothing more
serious.

The Waterhouses have been particularly unfortunate.

With our kind regards to yourself and Mrs Gosse I am

yours truly
Robert Bridges

153: TO RICHARD WATSON DIXON

Lower Nito
Isle of Wigh
September 12, 189

My dear Dixon

Your verses have come today I will give them my attention and hope to return
them in about a week. They came as a delightful surprise. I had forgotten tha
you had promised to send them. We are in most delightful quarters, in the mos
lovely part of the Island, and being close to St Catharine's point can observe the
new electric light, which is I am told the strongest in the world.—It has to
compete with cloudless sunsets, bright half moons, and the planet Jupiter, and
does not come off at all badly. It is a lovely effect just after sunset; there is a sor
of artificial purity about it which is magical and masterful.—When there is a mis
over the sea at night that is all lit up by the lighthouse, so that the sea is brighte
than the sky: a strange effect.—We of course are high above the sea, or we coul
not see this.

Have you read Sidney Colvin's edition of Keats' letters? It is a golden book,—
most charming,—most readable, and of course brim full of sad tragedy from th
knowledge of the fate overhanging the young poet. He was a most lovely soul—
just here and there a touch of London vulgarity, but nothing to matter.—
recommend the book most completely—it is cheap too—

I have also brought down here some Frenchmen to read—of them anon. The
are clever but depressing.

I guess from what you said in your letter that Eden was noticed in the Satur
day. I am glad of it. Unfortunately I never see the papers. The Saturday woul

not praise it: I had a letter from Gosse who is about 1/5 of the affair: damning it to my face! I had sent it to him. He said it should have been all in stanza!! Well it's not worth much, but in stanza it would have been most "tolerable and not to be endured".

your affectionate

RB

Monica sends love to you both.

154: TO G. E. P. ARKWRIGHT

Lower Niton
Near Ventnor
Isle of Wight
September 17, 1891

My dear Arkwright

I should have written before to thank you for the Kirby madrigals, which arrived the morning I was leaving home. At least a roll of music arrived which I took to be the Madrigals: but I had not time to open it, and did not like to bring it down here to risk its life at the seaside. I put it away to rejoice me on my return, and forgot all about it till this evening; when as I was walking along the top of the cliff after sundown, some 400 feet above the sea, it came into my head—I don't know if you know this part. We shall be here I think till the Birmingham festival, to which we hope to go, and after that shall return home, which will be the 2nd week in October. I hope that you will be able to come and stay a few days at Yattendon. I have heard how hard you have been working for Wooldridge: but have not had much news from him. Just before we left home Rockstro the "contrapuntist" was staying with us: and we had a good deal of music of one sort or another.

I am sure that I have nothing to tell you.—When we get home again I hope nothing will occur to prevent your coming to pay us a visit.

yours truly
R Bridges

My wife joins me in kind regards to your people.

155: TO LIONEL MUIRHEAD

Yattendon
December 15, 1891

My dear Lionel

Thank you for your long letter. I was delighted to hear that you had got an architectural commission and if you work on a good large scale I really do not see why it should try your eyes. But do not consent to make your working-drawings with fine lines on a small scale—let them be full size. I have no doubt that you will do a very good thing—and I wonder at the good sense of the vestry, both in seeing that you could do it, and then asking you—500 years hence it will stand high among the antiquities of Berkshire if you see to your foundations and material.

HEW is here—he will not send you any particular messages as he wants to write to you tomorrow he says. He is now sitting before the study fire in an armchair reading—it is a wretched wet morning.

Family are all pretty well. We are building a new school here—New school master is bad at the organ, but will come better I expect.

—Wife joins in love, and if we don't write again, Xmas good wishes.

yours ever

RB

156: TO LIONEL MUIRHEAD

Yattendon
Newbury
Xmas Eve, 1891

My dear Lionel

I am much distressed to hear that you have all had the influenza again—but rejoice that the demon seems to have so little power over you.

Thank you much for sending the chant, which is well composed and should sound solemn. No doubt we shall use it, it is above our average. I should think it was by Sir H. S. Oakeley, at least it is in his manner. We have not tried it yet. Our Psalter goes on improving and HEW has written 2 or 3 good double chants for it. He is with us still but this weather does not agree with him. He does not venture his nose out of doors, and sits in an armchair with his feet in the fender all day. In fact he never sits upright except to eat: and that is the only exercise he can be said to take, besides dressing and filling his pipe. I do not know whether he would be any better if the weather were warmer. He has written one good chant since he has been here, and been all through my Nero II and made valuable suggestions on it—and except his lethargy of body seems all right.

This letter was to bring you our Xmas greetings—a happy Xmas and New Year to you and your wife and children—and many of them.

yours affectionately

RB

157: TO LIONEL MUIRHEAD

Yattendon
January 7, 1892

My dear Lionel

Thank you very much for the illustration. It is very amusing. I have not seen much of the school, but a cousin of my wife's who is a clever fellow, has gone i for it: and his sketches rather justify his procedure, but sketching is one thing and painting another, and the method deprived of colour seems senseless.

We are all well, but how long we shall remain so it is difficult to prognosticate, because that magic scourge the Influenza has been encroaching on us steadily for the last fortnight and is now in the village and at our doors. We have established what quarantine regulations are possible, but I suppose we shall all come in for it. I hope we may escape as well and as quickly as you seem to have done.

Nevile Sturt was here last Sunday. We enjoyed his visit very much. He came alone. Perhaps that was the reason.

Do not you enjoy the weather? The sunrises (and after the sunsets) are most beautiful. HEW nearly killed me when he was here. I have more or less got over it, but not without passing through a sort of purification of bronchitis and neuralgia.—These are better. W was very good and obliging and clever, but O but—you know—

With our kindest regards to Mrs Muirhead, and all best wishes for New Year

your affectionate

RSB

158: TO LIONEL MUIRHEAD

Yattendon
Newbury
January 14, 1892

My dear Lionel

It was awfully good of you to take so much trouble with that drawing: I like it very much and it would make of course a very good ideal illustration of the scene, which I recognized at once, but if I am to have a picture *printed with the play*, it must serve to explain stage directions—first of all the picture should be the shape of the stage; if yours had as much again added on to the right, it would be about as it should be—some other points are these—The place for Penelope's chair, when Ulysses jumps up, when he declares himself must be a more commanding place: 2^{ndly} There must be lots of room for people to sit and eat—I supposed a bench against the wall all round the room with narrow tables in front of it; this would require the columns (unless table and all is behind them) to be much smaller things, merely gallery supports about a foot from the wall, which is more like what they would have been in Ulysses house which he built himself.—If you think of doing a picture, which of course would please me very much indeed, it would be better to sketch it first, and alter it till it answered all requirements.

I would not have the gallery more than ten feet from the ground.

I wish we could come and see you—we can't leave home. We have just heard of the Prince's death.

We hope that you have quite recovered from the influenza, and will keep wel
We have escaped so far.

yours affectionately

RB

Wife sends kindest remembrances and love to Mrs. M.

159: TO G. LOWES DICKINSON

Yattendo
Newbu
January 19, 189

My dear Dickinson

I was very glad to have a letter from you. I never had any particular reason fo
writing, or you would have heard from me before. We have had a good deal o
anxiety and trouble this year, and are now unable to receive visitors on accou
of the prevalence of influenza in the village and about, together with the redu
tion of our staff, consequent on the illness of their relatives in other places. An
this sort of thing has been going on most of the time since you were here. W
hope for better times.

I was very glad to hear that you are going to Paris with Roger, and that you ar
thinking of making your next work a regular drama.—Though you did not sta
it, I was, I suppose, not wrong in coming to that conclusion. I did not care for th
form of your "King to King" as I think I told you, but I do not wish to judge it a
useful literature. You may have something to say in history which you can on
say in that way. If you are really going to write a drama I feel as if I ought to b
able to give you the results of some of my experience. If you were here I have n
doubt I might be of some help. The chief mistake I made was that I thought
could get more in than is possible. The plot cannot be too simple, and th
general lines too clear, else the drama degenerates into mere intrigue, an
incident, and becomes only amusing. I am quite sure of this, that in a tragic o
quite serious play the main lines cannot be too simple. And this is the chie
difficulty of an historical drama—because history supplies you with such au
thoritative details that you cannot miss them out without being untrue—an
admitted they ruin your drama. Now from the point of view of the dramatist it
better to be false to history than to spoil one's drama. And as I suppose you
interest will be chiefly historical I do not know what line you will take.

When I stayed in Paris I used to go to all the literary and some of the classic
lectures at the Sorbonne. There is always a list of the lectures posted up insic
the walls, and I never had any difficulty in getting in—they are free. There wer
also lectures at the Collège de France that I attended (of course Theatre eve
night).

You refer to "Eden": I would have made it better if I had more time. Th
music is not for me to criticise. It is not simple enough for my taste. The pe

formance was very fine at Birmingham. Henschel worth hearing. I will try and see Butcher's book. Don't despair of art—What one turns out may be worth little enough, but art there must be, and let us do it as well as we can. Above all beauty and gaiety.—After this I shall expect some advice from you—

yours truly

RB

160: TO LIONEL MUIRHEAD

Yattendon
February 2, 1892

My dear Lionel

The drawing of the hall which came today is everything that I could desire, and for my purposes might be printed just as it is. I suppose however that you would wish to do some more to it. I return it with the other.

The following things strike me.

1st   that the drawing is still of the hall, and not of the stage. The stage could not I think be so deep. I do not in the least mind this, in fact I think it is better to draw the place than the representation of it.

2nd   There would of course be a lot more tables, but there's no necessity for showing them, and their most convenient position it might be troublesome to arrive at.

3rd   The fire-place. This must be a difficulty. You have placed it rightly if it is visible. I have written the play imagining the fireplace out of sight of the audience. It is behind the right wing, and Ulysses sitting towards it faces the audience, and has his face lit up by the fire. Also he is then back to the gallery when the maids come in tittering.—There are other conveniences in this plan, and I think it would be the stage arrangement. You could not show it in your drawing unless you did a regular stage scene picture.

4.   The *'landing* place' at the bottom of the stairs. This is well enough where you put it because the depth of your picture allows, I imagine that on the stage it would have to be prolonged in the same perspective in the stairs.

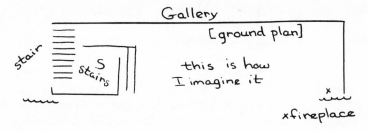

Yours is much better to look at.

Your picture is admirable and I would not alter it. HEW might decide which scene would be most pictorial to get figures from. The one you choose is good.

5.   Ulysses in his disguise was quite *thin* I take it. Awfully miserably scraggy.
6.   The arms. There should be enough arms where the suitors could have got at them if they had not been removed.

Glad you are well. We are—

yours ever

RB

161: TO LIONEL MUIRHEAD

Yattendon
Newbury
June 28, 1892

My dear Lionel

I have been so busy finishing my textbook that I have had no time for writing—I finished yesterday, after a vast amount of labour, looking up examples etc.—and am after all pretty well satisfied with my work—and am going to take an idle day. Having just done breakfast therefore and being seated at the open window I begin by attending to a few neglected duties, the first of which is a letter to you—I hope that you have been enjoying this weather. I never knew better. We are all well and only suffering from political threats—We are to have a meeting and dinner next Friday. I think we shall oppose a pretty strong front to the grand old humbug in these parts, at least it looks well. I hope your part of your county is all right.

When I came to you I intended to bring your copy of Thoreau with me. I will send it by post if you want it. I read it. I don't care much for it. Thoreau hermitizing with constant visitors from the town, and full liberty of retreat reminded me of your "night" on my doorstep in London when you tried the experience of the homeless one.—I was very glad to see your new home and your children. I congratulate you on having such fine sturdy offspring. We expect an addition to the family here some time this summer. HEW writes that he is thinking of visiting you soon and will look in for a day or two on us. I write today to ask him for Sunday the 10th including Saturday 9th when we open our new school: when Mr. Waterhouse wishes to have a function.

I have succeeded, I think, in getting some very good paper to print on. I shall not use it for Achilles—which should be out as soon as book season commences—but for all my subsequent books—at least if I go on doing well with the public. I hope to be able to mend Eros & Psyche now and get that out this Xmas in good form. Perhaps in the Autumn you will be able to pay us a visit if all goes well—With our kindest regards to Mrs. Muirhead—and many thanks from me for my pleasant visit—

your affectionate friend

RB

162: TO RICHARD WATSON DIXON

Yattendon
July 29, 1892

My dear Canon

Thank you so much for your letter. I wish I could announce the event. We are writing. Wife is very well. I am glad that you are busy. Don't put too much of our present condition into your revision, but I expect that you are getting all right: You looked much more like yourself when last I saw you. I called again once, and missed you. I have been playing cricket. Achilles is out at the Clarendon Press (Bell). I have told publisher to send it to all reviews, so we may get some fun out of him. But I fear that they will shirk their difficult duty under plea of its being a second edition. My poetry only makes me acquaintances. I did not send anything to Miles. Someone must make a stand against that sort of thing. Did you see the real Miles? and what kind of a sort of a Miles is he?—Your new poem ought to be worth something if you do not neglect your diction, which there is danger of in your present love for—which—what shall I say—You must guess. I have come to the conclusion that I was too happy to write lyrics. Now I am reading Carlyle's Cromwell.—I should like to talk with you about Cromwell. He puzzles me very much. I don't understand his face. What do you think of his face? Do you see the man or is it a mask? And if it is a mask is it only the mask of his religious delusions and enthusiasms? Or did he consciously make it? Anyway I like him better than Carlyle. He, qua mortal, is beastly. Vulgar, smart, self conscious, rude, one-sided, prejudiced, jaundiced, impatient, fretful, unchariable, contradictory, all that is opposed to sweet and lovely. I should think that he must vulgarize his readers while he pretends to elevate them. A very Miltonic limbo he lives in. "This is not a letter", as you would say. I think if I can get to understand Cromwell I will make a play of him. But Peter the Great's wheelbarrow stops the way. I must trundle that off first. I hope to make it rumble to some tune. I find people like Nero II so that I hope my vein is not quite extinct.

We are nothing now if not musical. A friend of mine has taken the Rectory—(Beeching gone into the wilderness for 2 months). He plays the violin and his wife is a pianist—and a pupil of Joachim's is staying with them, a wooden looking German. No end of trios and string quartets in the air—Choir singing pretty well. Our new schools finished. Such a heaven for the schoolchildren—Bobby Lowe dead too. He was an illustration of the futility of the don species, at least the Oxford-don species. I see in the Times that he warned the nation of the working man very early in the day. That was something, but then he took office under Gladstone instead of joining the Conservatives. The Commonwealth period suggests that we may be on the eve of a civil war. But that war was produced by the abuse of religious excitement. I think we are free of that. How the English cad does hate bishops! I have a lurking sympathy with him, Warburton for example. Nor did I love Sam that was. The bishop of Reading is a good sort—and no harm in Stubbs. I think the cad would like Stubbs if he knew him. Mitres and copes won't do. What will do? Our parish council takes no interest in these things. Between the love of liberty and of order who shall steer us? Not Beech ings I bet. Nor Samuels. No more time.

your affectionate

RB

163: TO A. C. BENSON

Yattendon
Newbury
August 3, 1892

My dear Sir

The present which you have made me of your book of poems gives me great pleasure, and I am very much obliged to you for it, and shall duly value it. Your kindly-meant request that I should not trouble myself to acknowledge it tells me at least that you do not wish for more than sympathy from your readers, and it spares me the always difficult task of writing an 'appreciation' to a brother poet but I hope I may say that I admire some of your work very much and like the spirit of it all.

To find that my own poems are read at Eton by anyone is gratifying, but that they should be the means of communion with Etonian poets is just what I should desire. I wish for your muse more success than has been the portion of mine and I shall hope for the pleasure of making your acquaintance. I see from one of your datings that you have been in these parts.

I am yours truly
Robert Bridges

164: TO LIONEL MUIRHEAD

Yattendon
August 5, 1892

My dear Lionel

A son born here yesterday. All doing well. Thanks for the catalogues and information. I will write soon I hope.

Our kindest regards.

RB

165: TO LIONEL MUIRHEAD

Yattendon
August 13, 1892

My dear Lionel

Thanks for your congratulations. Every-thing seems to be going on all right. My 'Milton Prosody' is now set up in type, and I am correcting the press.

made an extract from a book in your library, and should be glad to verify it. I would send the passage for you to collate, but as I cannot give the page reference, it would I think be less trouble for you to send me the volume by post, which as it is a small one I think I may venture to ask. I will return it. It is the first volume of your Tyrrwhit's Chaucer, the volume, that is, containing the account of Chaucer's versification. I should be very glad if you would lend it to me.

I have the greatest difficulty in getting my work in this grammatical department accurate—and the printers of course do not make it easier—It is necessary to verify all the references and quotations.

If you don't wish to send the book I will copy out the passage.

The weather is delightful, but domestic circumstances do not allow me to do any work. I am however in the 1st scene of Peter the Great, and feel interested.

with our love

yours
RB

166: TO G. E. P. ARKWRIGHT

Yattendon
September 13, 1892

My dear Arkwright

The Kirby 6-part Madrigals arrived safely yesterday. I send you my very best thanks for them, and hope that we may ere long get enough voices together to try them. By the way your Newbury musician Liddle Mus. Bac. has been over here, as he will tell you. Speaking of you he said that the Byrd Madrigal, which was sung at some concert was a great success, sounded better than anything else. He seemed to me a very accomplished musician but I did not see much of him. I have an invitation to an organ recital. I should like to go, but it contains an obligation to subscribe to those painted windows in the parish church—which are not to my taste.

We are fairly over our troubles I hope, and thinking of going to the sea for 10 days or a fortnight—When we return I shall pester you with an invitation. I hope that your house is painted to your satisfaction.

We have had extreme music here. A German fiddler, an amateur alto, and a pianist all at the rectory.

'Quavering and semiquavering care away' (as Cowper has it) all day and all night.

As they are thinking of settling themselves near by, you will come across them perhaps. I have got an attack of rheumatic neuralgia in the leg—which is no joy. With kindest regards to your people

yours sincerely
R Bridges

P.S. There was a letter in the Athenaeum about a month ago from a man who had been rummaging at *Lincoln*, and he stated that there was a lot of old Madrigal (English) music in the Cathedral library there which was worth looking up. I forget the names. Byrd among them. I told Wooldridge of it, but I think he took no heed. You should look them up and see if you can complete or add from them. Perhaps you saw the letter.

167: TO G. E. P. ARKWRIGHT

Yattendon
October 12, 1892

My dear Arkwright

I don't like receiving all these handsome presents from you and making no return. You will have in future to put up with taking copies of my poems in exchange. I found the two volumes of Byrd on my return home yesterday, from the Isle of Wight. On my outward voyage we met your sister travelling with her violin. I am better, but terribly knocked about. When will you come and see us? It will be better a little later, that is if I go on improving. I am no use yet; besides (if you come for Sunday) it is choir holidays and we do not begin singing till the 23rd—on which day there will be a *double chant* by Byrd!! Did Wooldridge ever show it you, written for the *Exeter Hymnal?* It is magnificent. To return to your Byrds. The volumes look excellent: and I hope that we shall manage this winter to sing most of them. Some of them do not look very interesting—but I expect that they would sing well.

What are you going to publish next? I long to know whether you get anything of a sale. This summer has been a very bad time for selling anything I am told. I believe cotton is at the bottom of it, and the Mackinlay tariff. Wooldridge is very busy, not only with this Chappell book but he has a big picture ordered. We have all the Chappell book proof here, so we know how that is going on. His settings are some of them most admirable.—My wife begs me to say that if you come over for the middle of a day she hopes that you will persuade your sister to come with you.—I am sorry that just now we cannot put you both up—our house is so small—at least we can very seldom manage it—and I am afraid that the days are getting short for such an expedition.—But if it suited your tastes it would be delightful for us.

With many thanks for the music, on which I heartily congratulate you.

I am yours sincerely
R Bridges

Our kindest regards to your people.
P.S. I am very much honoured by the place of my lines in your book. They seem to do pretty well.

168: TO LIONEL MUIRHEAD

Yattendon
November 21, 1892

My dear Lionel
I thought it would be waste of a letter to write to you while Wooldridge was with you. I hope that he told you all about us. I gave him to understand that I expected him to save me the trouble of telling you how we are. And he carried back your volume of Chaucer, which I hope you duly received. Now I feel as if W must have told you everything that I have to say. Indeed we have been very dull for ever so long: and this foggy weather does not help one to brace up. I am in hopes of being able to settle down to something before Xmas. Is there any chance of your wife wishing to come for a Sunday before winter sets in? We should be very glad.—I think that Dixon seems to be getting better. But he is not over cheerful yet. I have just sent off my last pages of the Milton prosody. I did not do anything at it for two months. It went about the country to be criticized, but no one did it much good.

I am very sorry that HEW has set so many of his tunes in 4 parts. The dance tunes suffer from it and I am afraid it is too late to alter them. I told him not to do it before he began. But the greater part of the book is excellent. One of my sisters is here looking after my mother.

Write and tell us if you will come for, say, the Sunday after next.

With our kindest
your affectionate
RB

We had pleasant visit to Oxford on Sunday. I am getting old enough not to mind visiting the haunts of my youth.

169: TO A. H. BULLEN

Yattendon
Newbury
November 22, 1892

My dear Bullen
Thanks for your letter. I did not mean that I wanted the line amended (heaven forbid) or that I wished it to scan. But the whole speech is (as you admit in your notes) corrupt or unfinished. I admired your respect for the text—and your one great emendation is famous. I only wished to know if you had any opinion on the subject.

As for the "old dramatists" I guess that you left off with much the same opinion of them that I have.

My little book of prosody is merely to establish once for all a sure basis fo English prosody, and that I humbly opine that I have done. I hate the gramma business, but no one else would do it. I have written 4 or 5 'papers' or appendice at the end which will I am sure interest you: and I have no doubt that you wil agree with them: as they are only common sense in plain English.

I will remember your invitation to translate Anacreon's 3 pieces, but I do no like translations unless the original is good enough to suggest an English form and not perfect in itself. When the original is perfect there is nothing to do because the translation of the perfection is impossible, the poet always makin the poetic best of his own language, which is *different* in another. Therefore the best translation must be alteration.

Will Beeching pass his vivâ voce?

yours very truly
R Bridges

Would you come down for a Sunday some day, any Sunday?

And then I advise you not to look at Lyric Love; it would set you back into permanent curvature.

170: TO LIONEL MUIRHEAD

Yattendo
December 20, 189

My dear Lionel

I hope you are all well. This brings you our best Xmas greetings. I hope yo will have a merry Xmas. The children no doubt will. I have treated you ver badly as regards letters. I must make some arrangement next year which wi enable me to leave home oftener. But this year has been exceptionally difficult.— I saw the other day a volume of the Kelmscott Press. I thought it very good. I might be better but there is a great deal to be thankful for. I think of writing t Bell to ask him to see if he could get something of mine done by Morris—

My Milton prosody should be out early next year. It had 2 months standsti for some reason, and then another 2 months by mistake. The last revise has no been sent in. They are going to do some 'handmade paper' copies. You shall b duly informed of them. We don't know whether we are to have HEW here fo Xmas or not. He does not tell us. I have been doing little or nothing—Nil an praeterea little—But a lot of tedious business just now. We have had a fe visitors. We are all well just at present. The baby has given some trouble—but h is a fine boy and should do well.

Amen and Amen

yours ever
RB

171: TO G. LOWES DICKINSON

Yattendon
Newbury
December 24, 1892

My dear Dickinson

Our best wishes for "merry Xmas", and thank you for your letter. Keep Nero as long as you can make any use of him, and show him to Roger by all means, but I had rather that you did not let it lie about or lend it to ladies.

I am of course very glad that you think well of it, but your adverse criticisms are what I am glad to get. And I hope that you will write as many remarks as occur to you (with a *lead* pencil please) on the MS. Anything which jars, or which you do not like, please to notify.

About Elizabethanisms. I think these are chiefly in 2nd person singular of pronoun and verb.—It must be remembered that Shakespeare is permanent and will never age. The diction of our time will in 100 years or 200 years be antiquated but not Shakespeare's diction.

Secondly, blank verse always requires elevation, and a remoteness from *common talk*. In proportion as you let the characters be perfectly natural in their utterances you require some artificial raising of their speech. This is easily helped by using the 2nd person singular for the colloquial plural.

Thirdly, the translation of the Bible gives it a familiarity and solemnity.

Fourthly, the difference of attitude between speakers is shown by the use of singular or plural address, and if the singular be given up a tremendous power is lost (Read carefully the prison scene in "Measure for Measure," III. 1 after Isabella enters—and see how the 2 numbers are used by Claudio and Isabella. Every change [of] meaning a change of attitude of mind.) Whereas if it is used at all it must be used pretty frequently. Also the plural is used in such a play as Nero for Royalty, and this distinction would also be lost.

You mention also *doth*, and probably would include the *th* ending of 3rd person singular of verb for the modern *s* as *writeth* for *writes*. I use this whenever I can as a means of getting rid of a sibilant. English is so full of them that with all one can do one has too many ss.

Consider these things and tell me if they weigh with you. I am abused by Lang for being "Elizabethan" but really my use of these Elizabethanisms is most reserved and intentional.

yours very truly
RB

172: TO LIONEL MUIRHEAD

Yattendon
January 5, 1893

My dear Lionel

Thank you for your letter with seasonable compliments which we return. Also for the Spectator. Mrs Waterhouse takes in the "Spec" as she calls it: and I always see the Advertisements in that and Athenaeum every week. She also told me of the quasi honourable mention of my name therein. There are now and then signs that my work is getting better known and more read: but the common critic is afraid of drama, and the pretentious critic only writes nonsense about it, so that I do not get much mention except for my lyrics, and they sell very slowly now—

We have had, except for the deplorable absence of skating near our house, a very good Xmas, but 2 days ago I had toothache, and yesterday a visit to dentist with extraction of a wisdom tooth. This morning I am comfortable again and am going skating. There is lots of small Yattendon news, but you must come and hear and see. We had a very good Xmas tree for the children, and a good concert. Our new schoolroom is most beautiful for singing, and we now propose to have music there every Saturday evening at 6.pm. Vocal music sounds most heavenly. Half or three quarters of the effect of music depends entirely on the τόπος . τόπος is everything.

I hope this year to go on printing my plays and shall be glad to have your picture for Ulysses printed with title to volume which should be by Xmas next. Perhaps you will seize an occasion to get the figures put in in time for this.

I have been able to do no writing, but shall try some soon. I wish we could get away for a change. My mother is very well.

yours affectionately
RB

If you want to know of books to order at Library, any tales by Q. e.g. "I saw three ships," or by MORLEY ROBERTS, e.g. King Billy of Ballarat, or by BARRY PAIN will amuse you.

173: TO LIONEL MUIRHEAD

Yattendon
February 10, 1893

My dear Lion

My Shabby scraps have been long on my conscience and I thought that I would write you a letter today. Out latest news however not of the best, that my wife has managed to import an inferior sample of influenza from London—at least she has been otherwise unaccountably in bed with fever for 4 or 5 days, is now convalescent.

We had spent last week in London and had not a bad visit altogether, crowding in many distractions, seeing pictures and hearing music, none of the best. The modern music gets to my taste worse and worse. The new concerted vocal music, part-songs by Brahms and Henschel, is extraordinary stuff, in my humble and stiffening opinion just intellectual rot. The pictures too were a melancholy spectacle. At least a gallery full of Burne Jones is depressing. At first sight of his best one is struck with admiration, but it is sad how the more one looks the less one admires. I never saw such badly drawn feet any where, his angels in the Creation have both gout and rickets, which is discouraging to the hopeful mortal who dreams of some day getting rid of deformities in heaven, and strange too it is that with his born artistic instinct and faculty he should cut off parts of his chief figures with the frame. Insanity is not as great an enemy to art as affectation and ill conceived mannerism. London itself gets more and more intolerable every year, and the aesthetic development of the average man is very lamentable. Every thing is self conscious. Even the poor coalscuttle, which used only to don the ornaments of trade, and had no ambition above the 51 exhibition, is taking hints from Ruskin. One thing is an improvement: the electric light indoors. The house where we stayed had it, and the convenience was immeasurable.

I should much like a long talk with you. We have had Stuckey Coles staying with us for a few days, and enjoyed his visit. He is just the same as ever, foolishly churchy, but excellently kind and good. He is even a sort of professional controversialist in the press, thinking it worth while to write and shut up incompetent low church men all over the country.!! He had to my surprise read my plays. He liked them, but did not care for my lyrics. Criticism from him was worth hearing. I am getting much spoken of in circles. I hope to print again this year: but the American copyright law makes it advisable for me to have some sort of American edition before I print again in England. As yet I have no sort of public in Americay.

I have seen the Kelmscott press books. I think they disappointed you: they did me. The paper is good, and the printing well done, and it is very easy to read. Otherwise I do not see that Mr. William Morris has cut much above Ye Leadenhalle Presse. It is wonderful why he so admires old work, when it is plain that he does not see why it is good. His printing is like his poetry. That he considers in the manner of Chaucer; but it lacks all that makes Chaucer admirable. Chaucer reminds me of my 'Milton's Prosody' which should be out now any day. There are to be good paper copies. I will give you early information. We were to have gone to Oxford this week (when I would have looked it up at the press) but the influenza has interfered. I don't know when we shall settle down again. We may all of us go to bed in turn, or out of turn. The baby is mad with vaccination, and schreeches [*sic*] like an owl. If the nurse gets it (the influenza) I shall be up a tree. I shall have to wash and dress the baby etc.—And the nursery chimney (constructed by A. Waterhouse R.A. etc. etc.) smokes awfully with this west wind. It blows wildly to be sure, and our house is exposed to the W. It is like a box of whistles, or as if all the Aolian harps of the Lake school had come to life. Did you ever hear an Aolian harp? I never met with one.

You may have seen that our Rector conceived the vain ambition of being Reader at the Temple in place of Ainger retired. He got influence and testimonials to put him among the selected 4 out of 500 or so, but could not push further. I won a box of chocolates over it, nothing more; I offered 20 to 1 freely, but no one would take me but Mrs. Paul Waterhouse, who superstitiously hedged against Providence.—She attends the Temple. If this is unkind it is mere humour or revenge or retaliation after many sermons suffered.

I wonder if you would come and see us when the influenza is over. I despair of getting abreast of the times in a letter. I seem to have made no way at all. I saw HEW in London. He has more or less done with Chappell's book, but his purse is full of spiders, as Catullus has it. His last trouble is a really bad throat which has alarmed even him. He is recommended a sea voyage. You may imagine how very low he would jump at that even if he could afford it. It is I fear no use asking him into the country because he feels the cold, and we are much colder here than in London. I hope he will stop smoking which is more than half the cause. I am waiting now to hear again from my friend Dr. Barlow, who goes to see him, (of course W would not trouble himself to go to a doctor) and will do his best.

My mother is very well, looking as cheerful and bright as she ever did. She has resumed her garden walks, and I found her playing hide-and-seek with the children. An extreme fiction however, difficult even for their infantile innocence.

With our love

yours ever

RB

I hope your eyes have been behaving well.

174: TO MRS. MANLEY HOPKINS

Yattendon
Newbury
February 24, 1893

My dear Mrs Hopkins

I send you what I have just written and selected.

As for the notice. I cannot tell what the tone of it is like. I hope that you and Mr Hopkins will call it by any names which you think it deserves, and I shall be glad if you will *pencil on the MS.* and draw a line through anything which you object to.

Remember that it is to appear in a book full of similar notices, and eulogy and not likely to be a distinction. I wrote in the humour that the reader had a right to know certain facts, and these I tell him as shortly as may be. Adding what seems to me I have a right to make him understand.

But if there is *much* more of the personal in it than you wish there is a real difficulty. Gerard's failure and melancholy seem to me essentials—And if you wish them passed over the best thing will be for you or Mr Hopkins to rewrite the notice (using as much of mine as you like)—which I will send to Mr Miles, telling him that it is not by me, but that I will be responsible for its correctness.

As for the poems. I can't tell whether Mr Miles, when he sees them, will not shy at them as every one else has done. I hope that you will think that the selection made is likely to please. If you can suggest anything better, pray do.

I am afraid that you may not like the Irish Sonnet being in.—I do not myself

,ee any objection to it, and it will be very interesting to readers from its reference
.o the affairs of the day.[X]

Was the Mermaid poem a prize poem? I do not know. Please correct me there
f I am in error, and do as you please generally with my MSS. I am in no hurry
:or their return.

With kindest regards

yours very sincerely
R Bridges

[X]I suppose "began"—must have some sense. I have written to an Irishman to
enquire.

175: TO MRS. MANLEY HOPKINS

Yattendon
Newbury.
March 8, 1893

My dear Mrs Hopkins

I write to tell you that I sent the little notice of Gerard and the selection from
his poems to the Editor of the "Poets of the 19th Century—" and he is not only
willing to insert them, but—as you will see from his letter which I enclose—
wishes to put Gerard alongside his recognised contemporaries.

I am very much pleased at this, for though it is not much of an honour to be
in—at least the company is not *very* select—it is for that reason an injury to be
excluded, and I really now hope that Gerard will at last get the recognition which
he knew he deserved. It is of course possible that the editor may shy at the last
moment, but that would be very bad luck.

I have the MS back from him and will take great pains to get the notice as good
as I can make it. I shall have also to send a few questions to you, about the
reading of one or two lines (—and shall ask you to compare the proofs with
Gerard's MS—) in the cases where you have the original MS.

I don't know what other poem to send. I will look again at the Poplars, but I
am afraid that its rivalry with Cowper is against it for this purpose.

With kindest regards believe me

yours sincerely
R Bridges

PS.
You kindly asked me a question in one of your letters about my plays. What are
printed are (except Nero I) still to be had at Bumpus' for 2/6 (or 2/ I forget
which) each. I hope to continue this series as soon as the ones already printed
have paid their expences. Achilles has done this—But the small edition of that
which I brought out at Bell's, uniform with Shorter poems, did not sell. It was

sent to all the reviews, but they did not notice it much. I expect to go on with the Bumpus series this year and include a volume of them with general title—

176: TO LIONEL MUIRHEAD

Yattendon
Newbury
March 13, 1893

My dear Lionel

I have been in town. Your proposal to come at the end of this week is most grateful. You say nothing about Mrs L. Monica begs me to ask you to try and persuade her to accompany you. We are sorry that we cannot extend our invitation to the children. I can't promise you that you will get any music next Sunday. We have had no choir for 3 weeks, but measles. 52 children all at once, but probably we shall begin again on Sunday. On acount of this my nursery has been at the top of the hill at the Court, the Ws being in Italy. If you have not had the measles I wouldn't come for next Sunday, though we have kept ourselves free of infection as far as we know. If you have had them of course it doesn't matter. Against your putting off is this, that we have any amount of invitations out for April and expect the house to be full.

Tell me what train to meet at Pangbourne and whether M^{rs} L is coming with you.

Hoping that you will come

yours affectionately
RB

L.M.

I must be allowed to say myself how delighted we are [to] think of seeing you on the 18th, and how much I hope Mrs Muirhead will be able to come too.

MMB

177: TO MRS. MANLEY HOPKINS

Yattendon
May 2, 1893

My dear Mrs Hopkins

The revise comes this morning. I send it on to you.

First may I ask you to compare Nos I and VII with the originals, which you have. It is possible that there may be some mistake in my copies. I do not wish any of the others compared, as I have originals in every case, and with the latest corrections, which corrections however I have not always used.

In the last line but one of I the word *ringing* seems to me possibly wrong.

Secondly. Though a good many friends have seen and approved the notice, yet Canon Dixon, who was here the other day, and whose judgment is better than any one else's on such a matter, said that he thought that the final sentence was too severe: 1.5. "miss some of those first essentials of beauty, which are attainable by all poetry alike." It was not the sense which he objected to, but the fact that the notice ended with such decided fault-finding. It would be of course very easy to soften this : and *I should be extremely glad to have Mr Hopkins' opinion, and yours, on the matter.* I would much rather have it <u>said</u> that I was unkindly severe, than that I allowed my judgment to be led astray by my personal feelings, and I do not wish to leave anything but good for the critics to say. The only damaging thing that they can say is that the poems are not good enough to justify Gerard's place among the 'poets'. Though this is absurd (if you look at some of the others) yet it is possible that the pedants might say it: and I think it is well to make it quite clear that those who hold the contrary opinion have their eyes fully open to the defects which the pedants might point to.

I expect the result of this publication will be a desire on the part of a good many persons to see more of Gerard's work. On this point I should like to take Mr Hopkins' opinion. Perhaps he would like to revise the sentence in question.*

I expect that Mr Miles would like the papers back pretty soon.

with kindest regards

yours very truly
R Bridges

*I shall take Canon Dixon's advice if I get no authority from Haslemere.

178: TO MRS. MANLEY HOPKINS

Yattendon
May 5, 1893

My dear Mrs Hopkins

Thank you for the corrections. The omission of *of* was very important and slipped my attention.

I have altered the sentence but not the sense of the concluding paragraph. I think it is better now.

I am very glad that you did not think the note at all unkind in tone. I hope it will do its work.

As for Sir or sir—As Gerard wrote a small s I think it better to print it. It may be more respectful than a great S. At any rate I am sure that he would not have written the small s carelessly so it is best to leave it.

with many thanks

yours very truly
Robert Bridges

Our kindest regards to all your party, in which my mother joins.
the paragraph stands now
"but very often, among verses of the rarest beauty, show a neglect of those
canons of taste which seem common to all poetry"

179: TO ROGER FRY

Bognor
Sussex
June 27, 1893

My dear Roger
   I have had bad opportunities of writing letters since you left. To find a lodging, get into it, suffer it—also the distraction of leisure by printers. Perhaps I
should have overcome the difficulties if you had not gone out of England. That
always chills correspondence. Will the universal 1^d postage do anything to destroy this prejudice? Now at last I write. I am very sorry if you were disappointed
about the picture—and I hope that when we see it again we shall like it better. Its
being only half dry was of course much against it—but I cannot help rather
wondering that you were satisfied with it as a likeness. I cannot, I know pretend
to be able to criticise painting properly—and I must also admit a special interfer-
ence with my judgment in this instance in favour of my offspring.—But allowing
for this the portrait does not seem to give a right impression of the child. It is
possible that what I most object to, the quality of the flesh tones, may dry off—
but when you left us the flesh seemed to me not to be that of a young child. I
mean definitely that the colour was not clear or strong enough, and if the sitter
should grow up into a plain girl, it would be an unfortunate record against her
that she had never had an infant's freshness of complexion. There is also the
question whether the head is not too large.—A fear has crossed my mind that
you may think that Wooldridge said something to set us against the picture:
though it is scarcely possible that you should imagine that we should not have an
independent judgment in such a matter. Still I wish to say that he is far too
cautious to commit himself in that way, and was careful I think not to express
any opinion till he knew ours.—My fear lest my parental prejudice might have
been too much for me was done away with by finding that all the relatives had a
similar but stronger feeling about the likeness.—The best thing to do will be to
let the matter rest awhile. One of us may come round. Meanwhile I am sorry that
you will not accept the cheque. Though very generous of you this complicates
the situation, for the money, though it could not have been considered as a full
payment for the portrait might have passed as a sufficient sum to cover your
expenses etc. However we shall not disagree I hope about that: you will no doubt
let us have another opportunity; and, as you say, all experience is of use. Your
visit was a great pleasure to us, and I hope that this adventure will determine you
to come again soon. I should like you to try a portrait of Monica.
   Our visit here has not been quite a success. None of us are I hope the worse for

it, but we have not got as much benefit from the sea air as we thought we had a right to look for. It is a dreary and relaxing place, only the sands, the attraction, have not disappointed the children.

When you were at Yattendon we talked of verses made in sleep. I had almost no experiences to relate. Strangely enough I have had two down here. The first time I woke with this couplet in my head

> Nor build thy palace with the mire
> That baketh in eternal fire.

In this case the satisfaction which accompanies such creations in sleep must have overslept itself, or something went wrong with the 2nd word in the 2nd line which does not seem quite right: *"baketh"* for *"is"* or *"has been baked"*. The notion was that health or happiness should not be built on what is morally damnable.—Last night the slamming of a door (in the S gale which has at last brought us much rain) woke me as I was examining, it seemed, a big dictionary which the Rector of Yattendon wished to get rid of. There were in all only a few hundred words in it—each having a long article on it—with an index at the end.—I looked down the index and seeing the word GELIKE which was new to me, turned it up. The article on the word began with the following quotation:

"Souls that gelike a single instant's pride." Then slammed the door.—I woke, and having to light a candle to go and see what door it was, and shut it. I wrote the line down on the end of Lord de Tabley's Orestes—which I had been reading till I went to sleep and which no doubt gave me the form of dream.—The only significance I can see in these two experiences is that the verses have both of them a moral turn.

With Monica's love

yours ever
RB

Sent to Failand to be forwarded

180: TO SAMUEL GEE

Railway Station
Gomshall. S.E.R.
Feldemore
Near Dorking
July 3, 1893

My dear Gee

I am afraid that you must not trust to me to detect solecisms in Latin verse.—I don't myself see any thing wrong in your neat transference of Lucretius' verses.—I did not know that Gallus was used for Gallicus. I will look that up when I get home tomorrow. It struck me that it might be in fashion now to write *inlustrans* for *illustrans* in Lucretius (but no doubt you have Munro's volumes at hand—) and I am not sure that it would not be prettier in this sort of inscription in *capitals* to write V for U.

We have been 3 weeks at the seaside for the children's sake, and to get our housecleaning done.—We are here with one of my wife's uncles for a few days, a luxurious house in beautiful country. We are all pretty well—and going home tomorrow.—My mother keeps getting better—at least that was her condition when I left home. I am bothering with printers. I am going on with my series of plays. I have been correcting proofs of "the Humours of the Court" this morning. Daniel also is printing another pamphlet of some 25 lyrical pieces—

I ought to have sent you a copy of the Prosody—but the handmade paper ones were so terribly expensive and the few copies given me by the Press were soon eaten up by friends on the spot—the small edition not being out yet.—If the big edition does not sell off I shall no doubt get some more copies of it.—I hope that the Appendices, and the treatise on the Agonistes will please you. I took great pains with the composition of these, and shall be glad if you think the writing both terse and easy—which was my aim.—I have found the weather *too* good.— Hoping that you are all flourishing and that you may be able to send me good news of the daughter who gives you so much anxiety

I am

yours ever
R Bridges

My wife joins in kindest regards to Mrs Gee, and sends you some for your own consumption—

181: TO ROBERT BRIDGES

The Cottage
Hambleden
Henley-on-Thames
July 25, [1893]

My dear Robert

Thank you very much for the beautifully printed black letter Leaflet of the Eton ode which was forwarded to me from Hambleden. I was very busy copying a couple of portraits in water colours and so waited till my return home before writing my thanks. I like the simple enthusiasm of the ode very much notwithstanding the fact that it banished sleep from my eyes the night after I read it, and I lay awake till 6 o'clock in the morning thinking of old Eton days.

I do not think in my last letter to you that I mentioned the arrival of Milton's prosody. It is an excellent piece de resistance where you can cut and come again and when I had finished the book I could only think of the line 'omne tulit punctum qui miscuit utile dulci'—the dulce emphatically applying to the form paper and nice red binding of the Little Quarto. I shall always owe the book gratitude for inciting me to read through Tamburlane the Great.

I am so glad you can come here next week: we have no engagement till August 10th so suit yourselves as to days, and we will make expeditions by boat:

your affectionate
Lionel Muirhead

182: TO LIONEL MUIRHEAD

Yattendon
August 17, 1893

My dear Lionel

I got home yesterday—but I nicked my leg at Pangbourne station and am consequently on my back with an attack of lumbago—which will prevent me from writing at once about the Ulysses. It seems to me all right. Shall I keep it and show it to H.E.W.? I have a great lot of things to do, and have no judgment while this rheumatism is on.

We had a most pleasant outing.

Bateman has sent some rather good sketches for Eros & Psyche. It promises well. HEW's picture is come, but is not hung—

yours affectionately
RB

183: TO ROGER FRY

Yattendon
August 22, 1893

My dear Roger

I am very much obliged to you for the Dante, which I am glad to possess, and read with real pleasure. I have only been home a few days so that I have not had time to do it justice: but I must not defer writing to thank you. I expected a translation by *you.* I cannot think that you have adopted such a very bold disguise as a false name and College, so I take it that the author is a friend of yours. Have you ever spoken to me of him? I do not remember that you have. As for the book I will tell you my first impressions of it. In primis I think it is in some respects the best verse translation of Dante that I have seen, (I do not know Langley's)—for it reads to me like Dante.—It gave me the same impression as the original. The writer has certainly justified his choice of metre, which I confess that I should a priori have condemned. For the beauty of the Spenserian stanza—is a certain smoothness, which is not Dantesque, and that 12 syllable line always begins to bore me after its frequent recurrence in a long poem. I am not sure that it is not the least well managed difficulty in the translation, and there are a few points in the prosody where I do not quite approve. But the whole effect is certainly successful.

I regard the task as impossible, and cannot imagine anyone attempting it. The last passages are untranslatable, and how anyone can toil through the rest with this fact before him I do not understand. It is however a good thing to do, and I hope many English readers will be grateful. The rendering seemed very correct, but the author is evidently a better judge of such matters than I am. I may perhaps say however that I thought his liberties of rhyme and strange words and coined words always like Dante, and in good taste. I doubt if the reviewers will appreciate this. When you write tell me something of the author.

When are you coming here again? Wooldridge is to be here tomorrow and will probably stay ten days or so. We have had a good holiday. The Waterhouses are all gone away. I am busy with printers. Monica sends her love.

yours ever

RB

184: TO MRS. MANLEY HOPKINS

Yattendon

October 1st, [1893]

Dear Mrs. Hopkins

There was a long article in the Athenaeum of September 23rd on Mr Miles' volume—by the man who looks after Swinburne. I was glad to see that he mentioned Gerard's position in the volume without censure of any kind, and went out of his way to praise my notice. As he is particularly and professionally my deaf adder* this was satisfactory.

With kindest regards

yours very sincerely

R Bridges

*He would have sneered if he had dared.

185: TO LIONEL MUIRHEAD

Yattendon

October 17, 1893

My dear Lionel

You have known me long enough not to be surprised at unreasonable neglect (postal that is)—so I won't trouble you with apologies, nor with an exact account of my rheumatics which are as Providence made them, neither better nor worse. I am sorry that you had 'a touch of it'—I have not seen the Duke of Argyll's book, nor anybody else's book, but I treasure your recommendations like new port. HEW was here when he painted that landscape. I think he overdoes his stippling business and takes all the fun out of his picture before it is done. I liked it much better before it was finished. I hope he will pay you a visit. I have had my portrait painted by Charles Furze; it is very good, but he was only a week here so that it is not yet glazed. But it is as good as it could be. We liked him and enjoyed his visit much. He is a tremendous worker.

Mr. and Mrs. Wellington Udal are coming to stay next week with us. I hope Providence will allow me to get about with him.

I have also asked Bateman to do me illustrations for Eros & Psyche. I have entirely amended that poem and it is now fit to print. I don't want to wait till his drawings are ready. I hope he may come here for a day or two.

HEW said that your Ulysses was all right, he suggested no alteration. I must return it to you, when I have energy to get out a piece of cardboard and string.

Humours of the Court is printed at Clays like the other plays and is coming out identically by the clock with an American edition, which last is accompanied by 20 new lyrics, which are I think as good as anything that I have done.

Daniel has also printed the lyrics and his book (paper wrapper) will be out with the others.

Having finished off these things I feel at liberty.—Nero II is all ready to print but must wait a little longer.

With our love

yours ever
R Bridges

Children well, also my mother pretty fit.
Monica's thanks to Mrs. L M for the post card.

186: TO JOHN LANE

Yattendon
Newbury
October 23, 1893

Dear Sir

I have to thank you for sending me the copy of Mr Benson's poems. It is a very pretty book.

Mr Daniel tells me that he has informed you that I objected to the advertisement of my book 'The Growth of Love' as it appears in your list which I saw at the end of Mr Benson's volume: and that you told him that you would be glad to know my wishes.

I quite see how the thing may have come about and that it was a convenience to you to put that issue of Mr Daniel's among your other books.

The objection which I have is this—that the advertisement might be used as evidence that "The Growth of Love" was *published*, in which case it might cost me the American copyright. It may seem needless to take such a precaution, but I think that you should make up your list so as to avoid the statement (which you make) that the book is either published by you, or is a purchased "*remainder*".

You could either put the words 'not published' or 'privately printed' after the book in question: or you might set all Mr Daniel's books under *his* name. But if you see my objection you will know best how to meet it.

I hope to see Mr Daniel tomorrow, and I will tell him that I have written to you.

I am yours sincerely
Robert Bridges

P.S.
I think also that perhaps my publishers might have a sentimental if not a businesslike objection to my name appearing in a list of your clients. You will know whether this would be so.

187: TO SAMUEL GEE

Yattendon
October 28, 1893

My dear Gee
It is always pleasant to hear from you, and I sit down very willingly to give you a little return chat. I feel inclined sometimes to grudge you the success in your profession which cuts you off so from human conversation. It is shocking that you should never have time to come and spend a week with us. I hope to see you however ere long, for we must manage to have a week in town before Xmas, and I dare say that you will find an evening for us to visit you. We are all well. I have had an attack of lumbago, but it is now gone off. My wife is stronger than I remember her to have been before. The children have given no trouble, and teach themselves (my wife says that they don't—). I can send you a copy of the book of which you sent me the Advertisement. I should like you to see it because it contains a notice which I wrote of Gerard Hopkins, and a selection from his poems. The essay on me is too laudatious. The volume has called forth a lot of criticism of me: I was told that besides that notice in Temple Bar, which you saw, there have been goes at me in the Edinburgh Review, Illustrated London News (Saintsbury), and Pall Mall Gazette. I have not seen any of them. I fancy they are most of them hasty ill informed affairs, but they must do me good, and eventually help to empty that cupboard of yours. As you say the old plays have almost stopped selling, but I am going to start them off again before Xmas. A new play of mine is coming out in England and America. In America the edition will be accompanied by some 20 new lyrics, which Daniel will bring out simultaneously at Oxford. The play will also appear in the 4th series and commence the continu-

ation of that, which I shall prosecute till the volume is fat enough. I think that you will like the new lyrics. The play is amusing—a comedy in 3 acts.

I am glad that you have been elected Censor at the College—I don't know what it means. I suppose that some day you will be President—that will be very good. The idea reminds me that I have had my portrait painted by Charles Furze. I think it is very successful.

I am interested to hear that you have bought the house at Midhurst. You must let us come and see you there some day next summer.

I wanted to tell you that I have entirely corrected Eros & Psyche, having rewritten a good part of the first two cantos. I am pretty well satisfied with it now. I should be printing it at once, but I have asked a friend (Robert Bateman) to do some woodcuts for it, and I don't know when he will be ready. I am now trying to persuade him to let me have an edition without any illustrations first. He does not seem to wish this.

I am also beginning to print the hymns which we have collected or set for the choir here. It will be one of the handsomest music books ever printed. The type is being cast for me at the Clarendon Press from some old matrices that were brought to England from Holland by Fell in 1670 or thereabouts. They have never been used. They are also recasting a contemporary word fount to match.—It will be very beautiful. I shall bring out some 32 pages at a time. If I do as I intend it will be the beginning of a lot of music printing. I am not writing anything now. We were away for 2 months in the summer and since then have had incessant visitors. They will end next week, and then I hope that I may begin again. I wish I could get this letter to you on Sunday instead of Monday, then you would have leisure to read it. My wife joins me in kindest remembrances to yourself and Mrs Gee.

I am

yours ever
RB

188: TO LIONEL MUIRHEAD

Yattendon
November 15, 1893

My dear Lionel

Your letter seems to be an answer to one of mine which I have forgotten all about. Today I send you a copy of the Humours which you will find amusing reading aloud when you get into it.—At least the originals amused me and I hope to have improved them. Please remember that it is *not* yet *published,* so do not let any one see it yet, lest they should enquire for it and complain that they cannot procure it. I understand your not feeling up to taking W in. He is a most expensive guest. Fortunately we have coals in plenty as yet, but other difficulties—one being water—I feel as if we might come out into "a wealthy place" if we could only be "brought through" the "fire and water".

Daniel's book should be out before Xmas. Bell tells me that the American edition is already printed, and is binding. It will be fun to see whether the Yankees buy me.

I will send you back the drawing but there is no hurry about it and HEW said that you had done all that the engraver would require.

We are now all very well, but I am in a sort of 'nervous' condition which frets needlessly about little things, and makes life rather a muddle: because there are always lots of little things to bother about.

We think of going to London for a week at end of month, and have an invitation to stay with your aunt Mrs. Robb, which we imagine will be very pleasant.

I hope you will like the Humours.

yours affectionately
RB

Our kindest remembrances to Mrs. L M.

189: TO SAMUEL GEE

Yattendon
December 2, 1893

My dear Gee

We are at home again after being in London 3½ days without visiting you, which requires some explanation. The fact is that we were summoned home by telegram as my mother was thought to be in a dangerous condition. Whatever it was, it had passed off before we returned. I am sorry now that I put off visiting you so long, but it was on the principle of "business first and pleasure after," and we were terribly busy, as indeed I am this morning—the letters I am writing are too many to count.

I saw my publisher Bell in town. He says that my books are now going to sell very well, and he has come round to liking the plays, and believing that people will read them when they find them out.—*He* is now going to take the old plays, and may send to you for them, but I do not know whether he will take the lot off all at once, or 50 at a time. I have told him how I have had my pamphlets by 50s in a case. I enclose you a leaflet of Daniel's. I don't know if I did before. The books are as a matter of printing worth having, and you will see from the leaflet that I could not give them away. The new lyrics will be printed in the usual form in due course. There is also an American edition of them, by Bell, in a small 8vo volume with the Humours of the Court, but I cannot recommend that book. I send you a copy of the Humours—I feel confident that it will amuse you. I shall go on printing now without pause till the volume is complete, unless there should be no sale at all. I am much disappointed not to have seen you—it was one of the pleasures which we most looked forward to. We are pretty well I would say very well, but I have sufficient indisposition, cold and lassitude, to qualify the whole family bulletin. Still I'm not very bad.

with our love

yours ever
RB

190: TO LIONEL MUIRHEAD

Yattendon
December 16, 1893

My dear Lionel

I don't suppose that I ever wrote any answer to your letter about Daniel's book, because I have spent about 2 s. a day on postage for some time without much effect, or sign of final extrication—and naturally friends have fared badly. I was very glad that you liked the book.—I think well of Daniel's black letter—a lot of people cannot read it, and more won't—but that does not signify. The thing is to get something nice produced. I fancy that Daniel's black letter volumes will look very well when bound. He sells them readily enough, and they command a fair price in the second hand market.

Furse has been here again for 3 days and has finished my portrait, which I suppose we shall not see again till next year's exhibitions are over. He also did a sketch in pencil of my wife, which we keep, and one of me which he wants to have lithographed.

The Waterhouses are all gone to the Riviera for the winter with Amyas, whom the doctors recommend to winter out of England this year.

My mother keeps pretty well. The Wooldridge news is interesting. Of course you will have heard of it. I have no late information. We have not yet got our large copy of his edition of Chappell. It is a fine book but the price enormous. It is owing to me that there is this large paper issue.

We had a very pleasant week or rather 3 days with your aunt in London. She was very kind and got up pleasant dinners. I hope that HEW will come and live down here. It was a vast mistake that you didn't, as it turns out. With our love and best Xmas wishes if I don't write again.

yours ever
RB

Bateman says he is coming here about the New Year time. The notion is to talk over an illustrated edition of Eros and Psyche which I think I must have told you about. I hope it will turn out well. He has been building or restoring a church. The 3rd edition of my shorter poems is just about exhausted and I am going to print the 4th (which will contain Book V) and all future books on handmade paper. I have got some that I like pretty well. I took up this second scrap of paper to tell you about Bateman, and there are a lot of little things which don't seem worth writing down.—Would you come over for a day some day before Xmas—or is the broken railway journey and the uncertain weather too much for you?

RSB

191: TO NORMAN MACCOLL

Yattendon
Newbury
December 18, 1893

My dear Maccoll

I am sending you a copy of my last printed play thinking that it may interest you on account of its relation to Calderon and Lope de Vega, and I take the opportunity of asking a favour of you, with regard to a book of mine which was sent to you for review.

The Delegates of the Clarendon Press asked me last year to write them a text book on Milton's versification. When it was printed they had a small edition printed on hand-made paper (as the fashion is) at an advanced price—and they witheld [*sic*] the cheap edition 'till this should be sold out. They sent it round to all the reviews etc., and the critics did not take any notice of it. Therefore the book is standing on their shelves.

The blame naturally falls on me, and I feel responsible for it unless I do what I can to get it <u>noticed</u>.

Though I am confident of the ultimate success of the book, which contains only matters of fact, and these hitherto unnoticed,—it seems my duty to do what I can to start it—and I would ask you to put it into the hands of some competent person.

If you would look at it yourself and read, say, one or two of the papers in the Appendix (the beginning of the book is too dry and technical for me to recommend it) I think you will see that it deserves attention.

I am

yours truly
Robert Bridges

192: TO RICHARD WATSON DIXON

Yattendon
December 21, 1893

My dear Dixon

A happy Xmas to you, and many thanks for yours to me and ours. Ours is to all of you—perhaps you have no one but your two selves at home. We also are alone. No stray vagabond shares our puddings. The Waterhouses are all away in

South of France on account of the youngest son who is delicate—this is a grief to us—his delicacy—their absence is a bore. It gives us such a lot of things to do more than our share, besides depriving us of the only society there is—I am busy-ish correcting proofs, and you will get the things whether you like them or no. It is extremely good of you to write to me just what you think—but you have become so terribly scrupulous of late that I wonder, if you really wish me well, how you can expose me to the peril of *neglecting* your advice!—Don't think that I am hopelessly trifling. If you had been reading Heine's prose lately, as I have been, you would think me an ascetic devotee.—I still think your measure rather a big one. But there is a chance for the hymns. Jowett once told me to write hymns.—But would the hymns that he meant be the same that you mean? Heine was very wicked, and I think I shall write a book Adversus Heinem. I suppose that is the right accusative case. I wonder what you would think of that? It would give me opportunity to say many things that ought to be said—It strikes me that you don't think it matters whether one is a R Catholic or a Protestant. No more do I.—I am afraid that this letter is "a thing of earth".—Now what Corporal Nym says and what Bishop Butler says is very good. It reminded me of what Chaucer's cock said. (Quoted in the Humours)

I read a lot of Rossetti lately. The full edition of him came down here. There is some shockingly poor verse got in especially a journal to and in Belgium.—Also I am quite sure that his sonnets bore me profoundly. You used to admire them. I doubt whether you could read them now without being of my opinion that they are sensuality affected to dullness.—I think *the White Ship* is the best of his poems—it is magnificent. *The Staff and Scrip,* which you liked best is nearly as good. It would be better if it did not betray a lot of affectations—it has splendid things in it, better than the ship—but the few blots put it in the second place.

your affectionate
RB

My own work appears to me dull and useless but just now it has a market value: and something may be done with the *Mammon* of unrighteousness.

193: TO LIONEL MUIRHEAD

Yattendon
December 27, 1893

My dear Lionel

Many thanks. I return the list. The plants marked are those which we *should* especially like to have (not, as you suggested I should mark, those which we have got). We find that all the rest are in the Waterhouses collection, which we can pillage. We should much like the marked ones, and will take care of any others that you may think it worth while to send—if you should have any very good trains.

I am sorry that I can't write you a better letter. I have been correcting proof, and preparing for the press all the morning and have a bundle of useless letters now to answer.

I expect Bateman here on Friday. I am sorry that you didn't feel inspired to come. But there is little attraction, and my tobacco is not very good. HEW's news is of a difficult nature to digest, but I am sorry that he talks of living in London. That is stupid.

I hear that there was a notice of my last lyrics in last week's Saturday Review, I suppose Saintsbury, and that the Eton Ode was praised.

our best wishes

your affectionate friend

RB

I wish I had time to describe a sermon which Beeching preached us last Sunday telling us that it was permissible to rejoice, i.e. at Xmas time. We had singing too a la fiasco.

194: TO RICHARD WATSON DIXON

Yattendon

January 29, 1894

My dear Canon

I return you the music. I am very busy. I read it at once and put it aside intending to write to you the next day, but it passed quite out of my mind, and I should never have thought of it again on this side the grave if my wife had not turned it up accidentally today.

To proceed at once to business. It is difficult to give any decided opinion without knowing how much instruction the youth has had. It is full of grammatical mistakes—but if he has never learned composition it shows that he has picked up a very good notion of the rudiments of it. It does not seem to me to contain any evidence whatever of original genius,* but the negative is of course not worth anything. There are things in the 2 hymns which could be really remarkable if it was the fact that he had never read or heard any Purcell. *And the structure of the hymns* is good,** but that again is on the Genevan model more or less—

—I don't think anything more can be said.—All depends on how much he knows, and what opportunity he has had.

As I began by saying I am very busy. I hope to send you the Feast of Bacchus in a few days, or perhaps there is no use in sending that as you have it, but I will send Nero Part 2 which is now just going to press. I have given a good deal of time to the correction of it.—I think it is now as I wish it. Wooldridge is going to be married. He has been engaged a good many years, but the engagement had to be kept secret as his marriage was deferred during the life of one of his wife' parents who died last winter. Perhaps this should be private, but Mrs Dixon may know the party, one Miss Olding, who lives in Russell Square.

Excuse great haste

yours ever
RB

*Judging it apart from unknown circumstances
**This would be remarkable if he was not familiar with various hymns. Did you see Gosse's cheeky article about me in a Saturday Review some time ago? I saw it yesterday for the first time. I was represented as a passionless almost inhuman creature who "coquettes" with prosody! There is a mischief for you. But the article was full of a certain praise.—Now Gosse of all men! For I make no doubt whatever it was Gosse, though I have no evidence but the internal.

195: TO LIONEL MUIRHEAD

Yattendon
February 18, 1894

My dear Lionel

My wife begs me to answer your card. We shall be glad if you would send the plants to Hampstead Norris. It is very kind of you to take the trouble. We shall be delighted to have them.

Binyon got mended and left us. We have got the children home. Baby has the whooping cough badly and keeps us in dismal misery. I hope he will soon be better, if not I shall have sciatica. The other children are in for it, but are not bad yet.

I enjoyed your visit more than I can tell you. I wish it could have been longer. I pray you come oftener, in which request my wife joins heartily.

I hope that you found your home party all better.

By the way, I am reprinting my shorter poems and am going to dedicate each book to a friend, putting merely

TO
M N

on back of subtitle.

I want to know whether I may dedicate BOOK IV to you, and if so whether you would be L M or L B C L M.

I am

yours ever
R. B.

Our kindest regards to Mrs Muirhead.

196: TO LIONEL MUIRHEAD

Yattendon
March 9, 1894

My dear Lionel

I don't quite know when I wrote last. We have had a bad month of it with the whooping cough. The baby worst, now they are getting better. Your plants are all flourishing. We look at them with pride whenever we go into the greenhouse. I am having a new kind of stage made. Our hyacinths have been very good. We shall arrange our house as soon as we get the summer things out, and I shall want your advice on the spot as to the building of pits.

I was at Oxford one day this week, and saw a good many people. My shorter poems are coming out in their 4th edition with Book V added. —That will be their final form. —Very good handmade paper.—The choir here has taken a holiday during Lent, no singing at all. I wish we could protract Lent for a few months longer. I can't make up my mind to go back to the servitude. I have been reading Parry's book on music. It is very good, at least all the part where he confines himself to his own art. His preliminaries, generalities and analogies are bad. But the music part is excellent: learned, concise, readable, and comprehensive.

During our whooping cough time when we could not get much away from home—the weather was most beautiful. Now that we are getting back to our routine it is awful. I have not heard from Wooldridge. I am doing nothing but correct proofs. 2nd part of Nero. It will be some weeks before it is out. I will send you a copy.—If you hear of a good parlour-and-upper-house-maid I wish you would let us know.—Ours is too stupid. What is the last modern book on whist? Do you think that you will be able to come down again soon? We shall send the children to their W grandmother.—No more today from

yours ever

RB

Wife joins me in kindest remembrances to Mrs. L. M.
Capital letters have not got on much, are being resumed.

197: TO SAMUEL GEE

Yattendon
March 27, 1894

My dear Gee

I was delighted to hear that you liked 'the Humours,' and it was most kind of you to sit down and tell me so. I hope that you will sometimes take up my plays and look into them, for there is a lot of stuff, with which I think you would sympathise, scattered up and down in them.

I fancy that when you wrote you had M^r and Mrs Marsh staying with you. It happened that I was entertaining their son, who is a very clever fellow with remarkable literary taste. I found him a most agreeable companion—.

I am busy correcting the revise of the 2nd part of Nero which you should therefore have in less than two months. Parts of it are quite the best things that I have done. Curiously it takes *longer* to get a play printed than it does to write it— and it is much more trying work, there being absolutely no enjoyment of any sort in it, and nearly as much application of a different kind. Printers now a days are miserable beings. They should be excluded from the franchise. They are mere adjusters of type, and controllers of rollers.

There was a long notice of my "Milton's Prosody" in the Athenaeum last week, seemed favourable from the glance I had time to give it. That book has I think now made its start, and will get on—

I shall send this to London as I guess that you will be back again at work. Excuse two 1/2 sheets and haste

yours ever

RB

Our united kindest regards to yourself and Mrs Gee.

198: TO A. H. BULLEN

Yattendon
Newbury
April 16, 1894

My dear Bullen

Thanks for your letter and the copy of Browne. I have never read him, but I remember taking up a copy in a library and reading a few pages as I stood, and being convinced that he was responsible for a great deal of Keats' manner. Looking into your volumes the impression is confirmed. I came on a lot of passages which I could not distinguish from Keats, and I do not think it a coincidence that Browne has the line

"Let no bird sing"

in one of his lyrics. I should not care to write on Keats without coming to the bottom of such questions—and they are very difficult of analysis, and also of definition, and I should not like to do the work when I was only half way through the study of it.

I have read your introduction to Browne—but I suppose that you would wish mine to be less bibliographical, and more critical, sending those who wish for his life to his letters and other books about him.

I think that, if you will let me, I will defer my answer for a fortnight, in which time I will reread Keats' poems from the requisite point of view, and see whether too many questions arise—

My notion of an essay on him would be to give

> The bare facts of his life and circumstances and how they influenced his
>   work.
> The models and development of his poetry, etc., etc.
> The faults of his work
> The special excellences

And I consider that a stiff job. As the essay is so short there would be no room for illustrations, nor for complete chronological treatment of the poems—which would have to be given in a table.

As a small return for your 2 volumes I send you 2 of mine, my last two plays. (I have not got the last but one).

yours very truly
R Bridges

If you do not wish to wait a fortnight do not feel bound to me in any way. With the time limit which you set I think it most likely that I shall not feel able to accept.

P S.

Of what character are the notes (said to be Miltonic) in Mr Hart's copy of Browne? I shall like to see those, unless they are geographical or such like.

199: TO A. H. BULLEN

Yattendon
April 18, 1894

My dear Bullen

All right—I will send you my decision in about a fortnight.—The more I think of it the more I like it. But I don't know if I can do it. Of course I think J. K. one of the highest gifted poets that was ever born into the world—and to give a worthy portrait of his mind, and at the same time a clear philosophical account of his ways towards nature and art etc.—may prove beyond my powers.

I should wish to get at more interesting and precise generalizations than the literary critics do. Otherwise Colvin's Keats is good. In any case I shall ask you to promise me that you will reject my essay if you do not like it.

On perusal I don't find much in Browne, but there must be something to account for so strong a first impression. I hope to discover it.—At best it can only be something very unimportant and one may find that there is no room for facts of this nature.

One thing I am clear about. I won't read Leigh Hunt. I will take him as read.

yours sincerely
R Bridges

200: TO G. E. P. ARKWRIGHT

Yattendon
June 27, 1894

Dear Mr Arkwright

I did not go and see "poor Wooldridge turned off." Now I think that Wooldridge's marriage will be a very happy thing for him. Shall I write him a prothalamion, and you set it to music in the mottet [*sic*] style? I heard from H E W in Cornwall, where he seems to be enjoying himself.

I wish also to tell you that we have had 2 good sings at your Kirbys and Birds. I told you that I had got enough copies to make it possible.—I was surprised at the excellence of Kirby's things. They went with us much better than the Birds; that was no doubt our fault. Bird seems rather hard. We only tried 4-part things but we had 5 or 6 voices and made a good noise.

Also, I was in Oxford for a few days and I found undergraduates singing Bird and Kirby from your books and—let me tell you—the tenors were complaining of the difficulty of reading the G clef. "Why did Arkwright take the trouble to transpose them into that horrid G clef." Those were the words.

Hart is now really beginning our hymn book. It took some time to get to work but the first batch should be out this summer, or at any rate before next term.

I wonder how you like the 1st lot of the Fitzwilliam virginal book? You are lucky to have your sister to play it to you. It wants to go too fast for my wife.

She begs me to transmit her kindest regards, and we hope that you and your sister will come and spend a day or two with us very soon.—We can put you both up if you don't mind being across the garden.

Write and say which days you will come *after next Sunday*.

I have temporarily glazed the screen in our church which has improved the singing immensely.

I am my dear sir

Yours respectfully
R Bridges

We profanely call your old English edition "Arkwright" e.g. Have you an Arkwright?

201: TO MRS. MARGARET WOODS

Yattendon
July 7, 1894

My dear Mrs Woods

Thank you very much for your letter. I will write fully in a day or two. Sufficient that Charles Furse is here, and other people besides. Yesterday we had a great cricket match.

I send you 2 batches—the tail of Endymion, of which I shall want to know what you think and the other a defence of Keats' Epistles against Colvin and others. This last seems yet only a sketch, but it contains all the matter and will probably have to be rewritten in connection with the Revision of Hyperion. This I have not in a legible or even very finished form: but I will send it in a day or two. Meanwhile please excuse this hasty note. My pens are all execrably bad. I will try and get a better one next time.

I hope you are enjoying your time on the coast, and that Woods has no rheumatism—I mean the President. Give him my love

yours very truly

RB

202: TO SAMUEL GEE

Yattendon
July 16, 1894

My dear Gee

You know that I am writing an essay on John Keats.

It used to be the fashion to say that he was killed by a review in the Quarterly.

This nonsense has now given place to the tale that he was a feverish hectic lad with the "seeds of consumption" in him, and that he died of an inherent malady aggravated by falling in love with Miss Brawne.

The true story has always seemed to me to be this.

(1) That his mother who after her second marriage had a very unhappy life, contracted "consumption" in a not unusual manner, and then (2) infected her youngest child Tom, as is very common. (3) After her death John Keats nursed Tom till he died and in doing this caught the disease. (4) So far from his being *especially* liable to it—though that he caught it shows him not to have been immune—he showed I should say a peculiarly long resistance to it. He had what I should conclude to have been a phthisical laryngeal affliction for nearly two years before he first spat up blood.

I should like to say this if it is the right impression, and have wondered whether in the next month you would have time to read *his letters* and see whether you agree.

I recommend them on their own merits as one of the most interesting books I know; they are perfectly straightforward and transparent. If you have time to read them you can get them for a few shillings—"Letters of John Keats edited by Sidney Colvin." Macmillan—

yours ever

RB

I have had a good deal of work on Keats, and shall I hope be able to write an interesting essay.

203: TO MRS. MARGARET WOODS

Yattendon
Newbury
July 17, 1894

My dear Mrs Woods

I am working away at Keats' poems. I think I told you that I had promised Bullen to write him an introduction for his Muses Library edition, when we met at Daniel's dinner talk. Your extempore solution of a difficulty then, and the knowledge which I have from your own poems of the direction of your poetic sympathies make me very anxious to ask you some more questions. I wonder if I may? I should like to write a sort of examination paper. I will send one or two questions now, but do not trouble to answer them unless you feel so disposed.

(1) In the Ode to Autumn, The "Think not of them"—Is not this awkward as addressed to the personified Autumn? It has always seemed so to me. If it could be taken as 'No thought of them' it would be all right, but this is impossible? And would be a bad colloquialism.

(2) In the Nightingale. The thought in the last verse but one "Thou wast not born for death" is unsound. Man being as immortal as Bird in this sense.—Can this be explained to make sense by making *Bird* mean the *song*? I do not think so.

(3) Do you see any poetic merit beyond the expression of mood in the Ode to Indolence?

——

You will see by the sort of question that I am feeling punctilious about expressing my own convictions where they quarrel with the fine stuff. I have got to think better of K for the study of him, and am getting rather lenient towards him I expect. I think that I have found out the main lines of the Allegory in Endymion without doubt. This is very interesting to me. If you care about Endymion, I would send you my notions for approval and correction. I should like also to know whether you admire the Bacchic Ode to Sorrow in Book IV and whether it would not be much better for the omission of the first 4 stanzas.

I hope that you and the President are well—and we both are still looking forward to the possibility of a visit from you this summer. We shall be at home till September. The President said he would offer if he could.

yours very truly
R Bridges

204: TO A. H. BULLEN

Yattendon
July 21, 1894

My dear Bullen

I have written down a lot of stuff now, and wish to ask you one question.

You said 10,000 words. Do you prefer *more or less?* I expect that depends or whether you have 2 volumes or 1.

I can't see how far I should naturally extend to, but it becomes evident to me that if you want a *short* essay I must pay attention to cutting myself down.

I think it necessary to have an *analysis of Endymion.* This in itself must be over 70 lines. Perhaps you would print that before Endymion and not as part of my essay. It will come well in the Essay.

I do not know if I am doing at all the sort of thing that you want. I am much interested.

My paper will be a sort of criticism of all K's works considered in groups—the more I study him the higher I think of his best work and the more I find to praise, but a good part of the Essay will be definition of his faults.

Give me your impressions especially as to length.

yours very truly

R Bridges

Have all the lines of the longer poems numbered in your edition—It will make i more valuable and useful.

205: TO MRS. MARGARET WOODS

Yattendor

Newbury

July 31, 1894

My dear Mrs. Woods

We enjoyed your visit very much and I was much heartened by your very kind approval of my work. I have not anything written out fair enough to send you but I have been going on fairly satisfactorily till today, when I am met with what promises to be a considerable difficulty. It is the meaning of the Revision of Hyperion. The more I read it the more there seems to be in it. 2 or 3 things seen certain. (1) that Keats was influenced by Dante when he wrote it (2) that all the new visionary part is intended to be allegorical. Much of it is of course quite directly and unmistakably so.

I confess however that I cannot yet make out what it all means. What is the fire of the rainfall—or rather what is it that is being consumed, and on the consumption of which his life depends? And what is that life? And what is the feast? And what the drink which when he has drunk he swoons away—and awakes in a temple? (3) This also is clear, that on the interpretation of the new part the signification of the old Hyperion depends. It was not like Keats to try to work up an old poem into an allegory when he had not originally intended it for one.

It would be a very good thing to settle the meaning of this Vision. The extremely direct and severe style forbids one to suppose that there was any muddling about it, or a meaning only suggested and not carried through?

I hope that you will feel interested enough to investigate it with me—or rather for me. I am sure we must come to the bottom of it.

By the way Endymion Book I lines 25–33 are a puzzle. One friend suggests a full stop after "passion poesy." (This does not signify.)

yours truly
R Bridges

206: TO MAURICE HEWLETT

Yattendon
Newbury
August 2, 1894

Dear Sir

If I can be of any use to you with respect to your play I shall be very glad.

I think that if you send it at once I may find time to read it this month.

I am very glad to find that my 'Milton's Prosody' has been of use to you. I understand from your letter that you wish chiefly for criticism of your metrical form etc. Any opinion worth having implies a good deal of attention, and I am very busy just now and unable to promise the time which it would take up, but if you like to send it on the chance I will take care of the MS and do what I can.

The easiest way is to pencil the MS. I do not know if you would allow this.

yours truly
R Bridges

207: TO MRS. MARGARET WOODS

Yattendon
Tuesday afternoon
August, 1894

Dear Mrs Woods

Your letter of Sunday has just arrived by the afternoon post and I have read it—in spite of Furse—I have sent you an envelope of my foolish remarks already today, and had begun to copy the notes on Hyperion etc. I find your letter full of new suggestions which I shall wrestle with at leisure, but I will go on copying what I wrote and send it just as it was for you to see. I have no doubt that I can much improve it with the help of your interpretation. I thought the feast was the books of the poets but came to change my mind. I wonder if J K knows what a lot of bother he is giving us. It strikes me that if you have only a volume II with you, I had better send you a small copy containing the early poems which I have written on. I post it with this.

I am very sorry to hear that the President is no better. I hope we are to have drier weather.

yours (with many thanks)

very truly

RB

208: TO MRS. MARGARET WOODS

Yattendon
August 14, 1894

Dear Mrs. Woods

Thank you very much for your letter.—First of all my wife has written to her uncle and sent him your address. I am sorry that it did not strike us to ask you if you knew him. We took it for granted—besides acquaintances in holiday places are sometimes a bore.—I hope that you like, or will like the tapestry of Justinian in his (our) library. I admired it very much.

About the Keats. Pray do not give yourself any more trouble than you feel inclined to take.—I have not disguised from you that I am seeking to make use of your wits instead of my own—and I am very grateful for any assistance that you may give me. I felt sure that the subject would interest you, and I know that you would like to help to get the right thing said, and though I had plenty of time yet the essay has to be "sent in" at a given date, and it is impossible to be sure that one will have made up one's mind on all points by any given time. Under these conditions the help of other folks' judgement is like an extension of time—and is a great consolation—

I have now talked over most of the difficult matters, but not the allegorical, with my friend Wooldridge, whose head is better than mine—and I have come to be pretty decided as to what should be said on most points. I am not writing it all down—your remarks and criticisms, both when you approve and differ are of great value—

I have not yet reconsidered the 'Vision' of Hyperion by the light of your remarks, because I have been at the other poems, but as soon as they are cleared off I will go at that again. I expect to find that you are right about the Temple: but I am glad that you agree about the feast etc.—

Shall I send you the other batches as I copy them out, or have you had enough of it?

I see from your remarks that I must make it clearer that I consider the revision of Hyperion worse poetry than the old version.—As you say, all the emendations are for the worse.—Do you think that K was right (however) in getting rid of *Senators?*

As a matter of fact it is fanciful and foolish to call the trees *'senators'*—the distinction means nothing, but I feel about it like Stevenson's man who was impressed by such phrases and said "Ah, sir! John Keats was a fine poet!"

As for allegory I hate it, it always bothers me, and I think that if I had known there was so much of it in Keats I would not have embarked on this business.—I have however a perfectly clear conscience and a determination not to go beyond what is quite plain and common sense and even with this limit there is plenty new to be said.

We have been in Oxford all day. I utilized the Scriptorium, and we lunched with the Warrens.—I hope the President is better. With kindest regards

yours very gratefully

R Bridges

PS

I see I have not answered your question about the life and letters. I do not think that there is any occasion to read Colvin's 'Life'. It is a good book but his edition of the *letters* is the book to read. That is quite a cheap book, and worth possessing. I do not know of any volume of letters which in my opinion equals it in interest. No one ever wrote himself down so frankly and lucidly as Keats, and his character and opinions are unusually full of sanities.

I think Lord Houghton's life is 'out of date'—

I doubt whether there is time now to go through the letters before I send in. My love to Daniel.

one addendum

Please mark as *obscure* or *doubtful* anything which seems to be so in my MS. I shall not have space to *extend* or amplify, but I can correct expressions. I will attend to that matter of the 'springy branches of an elm.'

209: TO LIONEL MUIRHEAD

Yattendon
August 16, 1894

My dear Lionel

I can't believe that your letter is 10 days old—when I have been intending to answer it every day. The fact is I am still busy with my Keats essay as I promised to send it in this month, and am conscientious about it, feeling very responsible, also knowing that I shall never have another opportunity; also hoping to meet Keats in the next world; where no doubt I shall find a complete celestial edition of my works printed in Aldine italics on vellum: and I should like him to smile on me for my criticism of his works if not for my own. Now to answer your letter. The children did very well on the Chilterns in spite of the rain. The baby (who is now a 2 year old) has not quite lost his cough, but they all seem to be very well. Wife and I had a pleasant visit to Fairford. I did not much care for the glass. I like earlier stuff much better. Some of it was good enough however for any body. The worst of it was that the church was not ventilated, as none of these magnificent windows are allowed to open. I complained of this, feeling that I must die of it and the verger told me that the complaint was general in spite of three gimlet holes which they had made in the tower. We spent 2 days in Oxford, and were over there again for the day 3 days ago. I went up about the printing of the hymn book, which goes on very slowly. We visited the Taylorian where some of Holman Hunt's (Coombe?) pictures are on view. I do not care for H Hunt. I wonder if he is a descendant of Leigh Hunt. The summer has been very bad, but is remarkable for your joke about coelum non animum mutant, which is the best that you ever made, to my knowledge—but the praise will be lost on you, as you make no distinction in jokes. I hold that there are jokes and jokes. HEW has been down here with his wife. Don't forget that she plays whist. He came to talk over some Keats questions with me, as prearranged, and gave me a good deal of help. By the way at Oxford all Burne Jones' drawings of Eros & Psyche are on now. They are excellent. I wish I could get them. Bateman has not written to me for months. Things are in status quo, which is a very fine indeterminate expression. You will now be at Shirburn Lodge. I shall send this there. I was sorry to hear of your uncle's death. You do not say whether your executorship is accompanied with any privileges. Your Aunt Mrs. Robb was to have visited us but has put off, as I have, writing to ask your sister here which I wish to do ere long. I hope she will come. I was much grieved too about Pater's sudden death. I had met him very seldom of late, but he was an old acquaintance.

I have been well this summer and have enjoyed cricket—at one time I had a batting average of 60 but it has now gone I fear below 20. I must knock it up again. We have had a great many visitors this summer. I have taken to glasses to read by, and this I think has saved me a good many headaches, which I began to suspect were due to my eyes. I discovered it by finding that correcting printer's proofs put me into a violent rage. For some time I could not imagine why. Then I guessed and certainly the glasses cured me of it at once.

No time for more now. Our kindest remembrances to your wife.

your affectionate

RB

210: TO MRS. MARGARET WOODS

Yattendon

August 20, 1894

Dear Mrs. Woods

I will answer your kind and very welcome and encouraging letter this evening. I am just off to a garden party 10 miles away.

I send by this post, as you permit me, the batch of verbal criticism. Tell me if it is too long, or what you think of it. I shall be able to send a lot more stuff in a day or two, but the introduction and summary (in which I treat of the blank verse of Hyperion—agreeing entirely with you) are gone off to a friend.

in haste yours very truly

RB

Kindest remembrances to the "invalids" but if you all walk 16 miles a day you can't be so bad.

211: TO MRS. MARGARET WOODS

Yattendon
Newbury
August 22, 1894

Dear Mrs. Woods

I hope that the invalids are doing well. I guess that the President is going on Joe Cross his yacht. I hope it may do him good. My wife and I expedited to Holy Isle from Bamboro' and were within an ace or two of being washed away by the merciless tide.

About aurists. The fact is that aurists divide maladies of the ears into two classes, those that can be benefited by syringing, and those which cannot. They keep the best kind of syringe, and know how hard to squirt, and how hot the water should be. I know an aurist whom I believe to be honest: I think he would give Daniel a straight opinion. My wife had one of the squirtable deafnesses once, and he squirted her into full possession of her hearing in about 3 minutes. He also knows all about smoking which is important, having smoked himself into the condition of what is called an ear-patient.—I hope that you will like the tapestry of Justinian in his library.

———

re Keats

I was really delighted by your last letter, because you seem to think that my essay will help Keats on. I would do anything I could to make him some compensation for the brutally snobbish manner in which he was treated by the honoured literary set of his day, and unless I had thought that I could do him a good turn I would not have undertaken it. I confess that I have been surprised to find the existing criticism leaves one such an easy task: but there is the danger of seeing more than is to be seen. Especially with those annoying allegories. I think your suggestion of how to treat them is the right way. That is merely to state what is certain. I have done this so far: but that does not prevent one's wishing to make out so much as one can. I began at Hyperion Revision again yesterday evening. I have not yet come to any conclusion about your criticism of my interpretation of the temple, but I see that I may get a clue from the 2nd book of Endymion. I have treated of the blank verse of Hyperion (and of other qualities in Keats' style) in the general remarks at the end. These, and the introduction have gone off to my friend Wooldridge. I will send them to you when he returns them. And in a day or two I will send you the Odes and Sonnets, which are finished. In fact I have now done it all, but not copied it out. I shall send it off before the end of the month.

I shan't say anything against "green robed Senators" etc. of course, but I think that I am right. I should say it was one of the expressions which just miss the mark—but you will see what I mean in my 'general' remarks. Such expressions are often in Keats more showy than the absolute hits, but this crowd of suggestion does not satisfy. Here is another good instance.

"How tiptoe night holds back her dark grey hood" They are delightful to read, and one is very grateful for them, but I feel that except for the versification of them (which carries them a long way) they are the sort of thing which Keats might have adorned his talk with.

Please find all the faults that you can with my paper. I shall be grateful in proportion. I sent a question to Lord de Tabley who is a Keatsian, but without any result.

Today we drive 15 miles to lunch.

yours kindly

R Bridges

What is a senator after all?

P.S.

It strikes me that I may as well tell you that my notion was that the steps to the altar in Revision of Hyperion are the same as the marble ways (whence at his prayer the flowers spring up) in Endymion Book II. Read (if you have time to enter into this mystery) End II from line 199

"And but from the deep cavern"

     to 364

"To seas Ionian & Tyrian"

———

How beautiful the verse is!

212: TO MAURICE HEWLETT

Yattendon

Newbury

August 29, 1894

Dear Sir

I have come to the end of the work that kept me from attending to your play, and have now read it twice through. I do not think that it would be a succes[s] if it was published as it now stands. I judge from my own impression—and I cannot quite understand your drift. No doubt your intention was perfectly clear to yourself, and I should probably get at it if I spent a little more time over it, but I am naturally stupid about allegory, and have no turn for it, besides which the work which I spoke of as occupying me was an essay on Keats' poetry to serve for an introduction to a new edition of his poems, which has necessitated a good deal of browbeating over his allegorical work: in consequence of which I am more than usually impatient.—Now I do not see how I can write you a satisfactory letter about your play unless I start with a fair notion of its purpose. It struck me that if you could come and pay us a visit here, say from a Saturday till Monday, we might talk matters over. I take for granted that you sent your work to me because you thought that I could be of some service to you. It seems to me from reading your play that there are a good many things that I could tell you, which from my way of looking at things are important, and which you do not seem to consider quite as I do.

I think that the chief defect in the work is want of directness and simplicity—but there are plenty of minor matters to talk of.

If you had rather that I wrote, or if for any reason you cannot come here, will you send me a line and tell me what the moral point of your play is? I cannot myself see why Theseus is driven off. I mean why he goes. If it is only the influence of Dionysus, this influence must be some human force which we recognise, and I do not see what the God is intended to represent.

Again what is his purpose with Ariadne?

Perhaps you have such a simple answer to these questions that I shall be ashamed of not having seen it, but then the question will arise why did not I see it? Which it will be my business to lay to your charge.

We shall be at home till the 24th or so of next month, when we shall be away for a fortnight, and return in October.—Any day would suit us for your coming. If you come from London Pangbourne is the most convenient station, but that is 6 miles off. *Hampstead Norris* on the branch line from Didcot to Newbury is quite close to us, but there are very few trains. This station is best if you come from the west, and you can use it from London, if you choose your train. If you cannot come till October you may like your play returned and you could bring it with you. I don't mind writing but I shall not of course be able to be of as much use as if we talked, but perhaps I should not manage to be of much use anyway.

> I am yours truly
> Robert Bridges

213: TO RICHARD WATSON DIXON

> Yattendon
> September 1, 1894

My dear Dixon

I am very much pleased that you like my notes on Keats. I write a few conversational remarks on your letter at once.

1. What I sent you is only a small portion of the essay which will be:

1. Introduction
2. Endymion
3. I stood tiptoe and Sleep and Poetry
4. Hyperion and revision of it
5. Tales
6. Odes
7. Sonnets
8. Epistles
9. Drama
10. Lyrics
11. General remarks

———

I shall be glad to send you any of these that you wish to see.

———

I want very much your criticism of the revision of Hyperion notes.

———

I have absorbed your remark about selection of man by moon.

———

As for Keats or Endymion nowhere saying that the moon was connected with his ambition: that is plain from many places in Endymion, especially the one I refer to iii, 132–188

> thou didst blend
> With all my ardours—thou wast the deep glen.
> Thou wast the mountain-top—the sage's pen—
> The poet's harp—the voice of friends—the *Sun.*
> Thou wast the river—thou wast *glory* won.
>   etc. etc.—

Any criticism is welcome.

———

President of Trinity, Oxford (ie Woods) and Mrs Woods* are at Bamboro'. I told them to look you up. She is the authoress, quite a charming person to meet. She has a lot of my Keats essay now.

I have finished it quite only will amend to order.

your affectionate

RB

*and Daniel

214: TO A. H. BULLEN

Yattendon

September 1, 1894

My dear Bullen

Marriage is honourable in all but in an editor it is abominable. I enclose you Colvin's letter. It is really an important matter to get these things well edited. I suppose that Mr. Drury's marriage would not be a sufficient reason for him to resign his work to Colvin. Could not you and Colvin do it together? Anyhow make use of Colvin. Don't show this letter to Drury.

As for my essay I am grateful to you for not wanting it recopied. It is more or less readable. As it cannot be fully printed till the text of the poems is set up, because of references to them, which must be to pages of the book, I don't suppose that you will want it yet.

At present I have sent it away in batches to friends to read and some of it is now in Northumberland and some at Brighton. I am only afraid that you may think it too long. If you have time to read it preliminarily, and wish to do so I will send it to you when it returns to me.

Please return Colvin's letter at your leisure.

yours truly

RB

215: TO MRS. MARGARET WOODS

Yattendon
September 4, 1894

Dear Mrs Woods

Many thanks for your letter and MS received safely and remarks which I will attend to. I will gladly send you the other parts of the MS if you care to see them. As you say that you are leaving Bambro' tomorrow I think it is scarcely worth while to post them to you there. If you will let me have your address I will send them.

I am glad that you think that we may feel comfortable about the allegory. Canon Dixon has the Hyperion papers, and I expect some help from him. He returned me the Endymion with some excellent suggestions and directions. He liked it very much. I shall send him the Odes, Tales etc. this afternoon which you can have when he has read them.

You say that there are too many quotations in the 'Diction and Rhythm' paper. You must refer to all lines which I quoted containing trisyllables. Do you think that it is worth while to enter into that question at all? Did it interest you? Did it convince you? I gave the quotations because I do not think that without them anyone would believe that there was such a pronunciation as I describe.*

I wish when you write that you would give me your opinion or impression on that matter.

I suppose that you will be going South with Daniel to Buscote, and I shall therefore direct there though I don't know exactly what the address should be.

yours very truly

RB

*And of course it would be quite easy to make a strong case for the other side. Rossetti has 'And mir'd my feet with quágwatèr,' which must be affectation only.

216: TO RICHARD WATSON DIXON

Yattendon
September 12, 1894

My dear Dixon

Hyperion arrived safe, and your notes which are of great value. I do not think that you will find any of the other papers give you such trouble. The fact is that this paper on Hyperion was a sort of first shot, and is the only one which has not been amended. I wrote down what I thought of the allegory to clear my own vision. And I think that I can do it much better now. I have had another turn at it since I wrote the paper which you saw. I was really indolent about it and tried to get others to work out the allegory for me, but I could not get any satisfactory solution so I had to do it myself after all.

Many of your remarks on Hyperion major, are excellent and I shall certainly use them. But when you say that this epic fragment is all machines, and 'grinding an empty mill' I do not quite know what you intend.—Do you only mean that these old divinities are abstractions and nothings? One word of explanation would help me, because you may mean something which I do not see.

yours ever

RB

It is most kind of you to work like this at my stuff. I hope you enjoy it as much as I do.

217: TO MRS. MARGARET WOODS

Yattendon

September 12, 1894

My dear Mrs Woods

Yet once again. Canon Dixon has returned my paper on Hyperion to me, and I am now going to rewrite the account of the allegory of the revision, according to the latest lights.

I find that in the interval I have forgotten a good deal of what I made out or thought that I made out, and I am writing to you to ask you if by any chance you have kept the last letter which I wrote to you at Bambro'. It was on a half sheet of foolscap written folio wise. I should be very much obliged to you if you could send it to me. This is of course indolence on my part: I do not want to have the trouble of looking it up again, and if I see the letter I shall remember exactly where I was on that morning.

Dixon's notes have so far been of great service, and I am using them, but he says nothing of the allegory. At least he accepts my interpretation.

I have also forgotten which papers of the essay you have not seen. The whole is in these parts

1. Introduction
2. Endymion
3. I stood tiptoe & Sleep & Poetry
4. Hyperion and revision
5. Tales
6. Odes
7. Sonnets
8. Drama
9. Lyrics
10. Diction & rhythm
11. General remarks

I will send you any of these that you wish to see, if you are not by this time tired of the subject. Dixon has most of them now, and returns them to me one at a time.

I hope you are well, and that Daniel is better, and that you have good accounts of the President. [Note: here RB scratches out two lines.]

With kind regards,

yours very truly

R Bridges

PS. My wife made me scratch out that sentence so do not try and read it.

218: TO HARRY ELLIS WOOLDRIDGE

Yattendon
September 21, 1894

My dear HEW

I send you Dixon's scribbles. I could not make much of them at first, but the sentence on page 4 opened my eyes. You remember that in your last to me you questioned whether Keats had any real passion. Now look here.

The passage in the ode to Melancholy is thus—

> "But when the melancholy fit shall fall
>   x   x   x   x   x
> Then glut thy sorrow on a morning rose,
>   Or on the rainbow of the salt sand-wave,
>   Or on the wealth of globèd peonies;
> Or if thy mistress some rich anger shows,
>   Emprison her soft hand and let her rave,
>   And feed deep, deep upon her peerless eyes!"

I, interpreting I suppose rightly, the *rich anger* to be in the same category as the *wealth of peonies* said that K here struck a false note. Dixon says no not exactly a false note. K's only notion of Love was as an inner sphere of natural beauty, and the anger of his mistress is a beautiful phenomenon, and regarded quite irrespective of its motive, or its meaning: or its effect.

This must be right, and it seems to me to throw light on the whole question. I have spent a good deal of time in considering the matter, and it helps much in the Endymion allegory: a few words of which I have altered (in my explanation) with excellent effect. Now I want to write a whole paragraph in the general remarks to give this most satisfactory explanation of K's mind. I want you to think it over and tell me your impression—

As for the rest of Dixon's letter, perhaps you may see more in it than I am able to. I don't mean to follow D in his advice to "enlarge". I wish to say straight what I have to say and then leave it.

What he says about epithets. This is true, and due to K's objective manner— not important (?)

About nature being the proper object of poetry I do not see this. If he means phenomena to the outward senses I don't see that it is true.—If he means more, then everything is Nature and Keats is merely a section of Shakespeare.

———

There is one point that I am not quite happy about in our collaborated general remarks about the fine imaginative phrases. We say that these satisfy the aesthetic imagination and reveal new aspects of truth—the intellect, and then the quotations hardly come up to the mark. Can you think of any that do? Or did you think that the quotations were good enough?

yours ever

RB

Wife's cough is very bad and gives me anxiety. She does not get better of it.

219: TO MAURICE HEWLETT

Yattendon
Newbury
September 26, 1894

My dear Mr Hewlett

I am glad to find from your letter that you have been busy, and cannot therefore have wanted Theseus. I am ashamed of having kept it so long, but my days for finishing my essay on Keats are numbered, and my conscience is far from satisfied. I had no notion when I undertook the work that there was so much to puzzle out. Only yesterday apropos of nothing a simple solution of the meaning of the Alpheus & Arethusa episode in Endymion struck me, so simple that I cannot imagine why I never thought of it before. It is possible that even 'that mysterious old man' Glaucus may don reason and fall into rank. You will understand that both for Keats' sake and my own I am anxious not to make mistakes through carelessness, and until the essay is out of the house I find it too much on my mind to settle to any other work. I am much obliged to you for your notes on the revision of Hyperion, and glad that you agree about the Dante in it. Your notes will be of great use: especially as confirming my judgment. I am glad to hear what you tell me of your chance of getting your play acted. I hope it may lead to your being considered a playwright, in which case the public may consent to receive something quite serious from you. I do not see much hope for English drama at present, because the theatregoers only want to be amused, and the acting companies have so few really decent actors a-piece, owing no doubt to the high rents and salaries. Also the demand for a lot of scenery makes it almost impossible for them to get profit out of any play that will not run for a long time: and that means of course a huge miscellaneous audience, to which in the present state of things such drama as is worth writing cannot appeal. I doubt if the greatest genius could hit this off. It would be possible if there were fewer theatres, so that the dramatic public were compelled to go to one or other: but with the companies themselves bad and unable to act a good play properly, it is not a wonder that the people run off to see the representation of a railway accident, or—as I saw advertised in Newbury—a lady being crushed in the street by a steam roller, of which there was a very realistic pictorial advertisement, with a statement below of the address of the firm who had made the steam roller. Will you send me a line to tell me really whether you want Theseus. I will go at him today and get on as well as I can.

yours truly
R Bridges

PS

In addition to my preoccupation my wife has had a sharp attack of bronchitis which has kept her in bed and given me some anxiety. It has prevented us from leaving home, as we intended last Saturday, for a change, and we have had to receive the plumbers and people who were engaged to come to pursue their avocations in our absence.

PPS. I have already done some Theseus. Send me address where to post him.

220: TO RICHARD WATSON DIXON

Yattendon
September 27, 1894

My dear Dixon

Many thanks for offering to send me Swinburne on Keats. As I have done my work I think it would be no use. Besides S. is sure to be wrong, and people might think that I ought to notice him somehow, which cannot be expected if I have not seen his paper. I have no opinion of his judgment. He goes swashing at a thing in the extravagant language of his momentary delirium, and thinks it must be heaven-inspired wisdom because Theodore Watts assures him that it is so. 'They say' that Watts does this in order to console S. for not being allowed any liquor. This is very funny. I once read very carefully, and with the hope of instruction and [line missing]

—My Keats paper is much improved. I shall be glad when I have to send it away. The last thing I hit on was the explanation of the Alpheus and Arethusa episode in Endymion. It is as simple as English cheese. I can't understand how K managed to hide things up so. I have however no lights on Glaucus. But the sea book is "*the secrets of death.*"

Does that help?

yours ever
RB

221: TO A. H. BULLEN

Yattendon
Newbury
October 9, 1894

My dear Bullen

I send you my essay by same post as this letter. I am glad to get it out of the house. When you have read it I shall be anxious to hear whether it suits you. It is longer than I intended but I should be sorry to cut it down. I have made it as definite and concise as I could, and owing to the generous help of 2 friends it is better than could have been expected of me.

About printing. Besides the cross references, which must be left blank, there are numerous references to the poems which cannot be printed till your book is set up—but they might be provisionally printed from the MS and altered after, if they did not correspond.

I send a paper of instructions to printer, which I should be glad if you would kindly look through, and approve or alter.

I hope the MS is legible enough.

The analysis of Endymion will take up some room, but I think it is absolutely necessary.

yours very truly
R Bridges

222: TO MRS. MARGARET WOODS

Yattendon
Newbury
October 9, 1894

My dear Mrs Woods

My wife has been ill for the last month with bronchitis, and this has been the cause of the interruption of my Keats correspondence. Everything has been in a muddle, the Essay however struggled on. Dixon came up to the scratch like his old self, and it is much improved since you saw it. I send it off today to Bullen, and am glad to get it out of the house. I found out a lot more simple things in Endymion which dawned on me suddenly from time to time, and the whole thing hangs well together.

We are going to the sea as soon as the weather permits us to travel. This sort of weather puts one out of sympathy with Keats' ceaseless adoration.

I see another book of yours announced. I shall be anxious to read it. You must have had some difficulty in carrying on your work these last two years.

I hope that the President is now much better, and that your time in the North and his yachting did him good.

I have to thank you for your help with my work, and I should like to mention your name with Dixon and Wooldridge at the end of my Essay if you approve.

yours truly
R Bridges

223: TO HUBERT PARRY

Yattendon House
Newbury, Berkshire
October 10, 1894

My dear Parry

Squire has written to me to say that you might be writing a Cantata or short choral piece for the Leeds Festival next year and that you would do an "Ode to Music" which might also serve for the Purcell Festival, and that you (would) like to hear my ideas on the subject،

I have yesterday sent in a piece of work to the publishers which has engaged me all the summer, so that I am quite at leisure to think this over.

I write at once to you to say how glad I should be to do it with you, lest you might think I was indifferent. Also to prevent there being any misunderstanding. I should wish you to understand that whatever passes between us I shall never consider you in the least bound but free to give up the notion at any time.

On my side I can't promise to have the requisite inspiration to order, but I see a splendid opportunity for something new, and popular. My idea is to show music in its various relations to the passions and desires of man: as something supernatural mysterious and consolatory: which it always is to me. Also it seems to me that something quite new might be done in the music by the blending of the different attitudes of mind or spirit, instead of their merely isolated contrast as in Handel's Alexander's Feast.

If you have any idea on the subject send me a line. I shall think it over and if I get any lights will write again in about a fortnight.

I could not get to hear Saul and the papers don't give one much information. I hope it satisfied you, and that you are not overdone.

yours ever
R Bridges

P S.   If a definite musical scheme presents itself to your imagination I could work my stuff to fit it, and this recommends itself to me as a satisfactory procedure.

224: TO RICHARD WATSON DIXON

4. St Catharine's Terrace
Niton, Isle of Wight
October, 1894

My dear Dixon

I have come down here with my wife to see if I can't get her well. (She is a good bit better.) I am not very fine either, and need mending.—I am writing to you today to tell you that I have written to my publisher to instruct him to send you a copy of my 4th edition of Shorter Poems. You will find one of the divisions or

"Books" dedicated to you. The whole volume is now printed on hand made paper, and I shall always use this in future. I can't think how I omitted to send the Book before. I thought I had sent off the presentation copies, but it seems that I never did any such thing.

The Keats Essay has gone off to Bullen.—I have not heard from him about it yet, except that he does not object to its length. It was much improved since you saw it, not only by the attention which I paid to your remarks, for which I cannot sufficiently thank you, but also for all Wooldridge's work.—I went up to London and had a long chat with him, in the course of which we settled some very important matters to our joint satisfaction. I intend to acknowledge your assistance in the concluding paragraph; for which I do not ask your permission, as I could not print your work without such a statement. I will not make you responsible for anything.

I have been surprised that none of the critics have thought my Nero P^t II worth notice, and, considering that it completed a series of which they have never condescended to utter even the meanest utterance, it seems to me that they owed it to themselves to seize this occasion. I am rather sold, because I had looked forward to amusing myself with their remarks. Eros & Psyche 2nd edition is in the press, and will soon be out. It is much improved, and will some day win its way to popular favour—at least such is my conviction.

By the way did you read Kidd's "Social Evolution"? I liked it. It settled a lot of questions with me or in me, though I do not follow him altogether.

With our kindest remembrances

yours ever

RB

225: TO MAURICE HEWLETT

Niton
Isle of Wight
October 17, 1894

My dear Hewlett

Thank you for your letter. I am glad that I was so wrong about your intentions as to Theseus. My strong impression is that you will have to reënvisage your idea. I will try and put my objection which is I think mainly this.

Dionysus could not possibly be unhappy because man did not love him. He is an idea, constructed without that notion in it. The failure (which might be the tragedy) of the Greek Gods was that *they did not love man*. Therefore they perished, and though this is the same thing as man's not loving them, yet the making them unhappy on that account is, I think, not only to bring in a modern thought, but to do it in a most awkwardly subjective manner—the idea being sorry for its own imperfection.

I think this is a twist which may be at the root of such an artistic inconsistency as occurs between the Chorus' complaint of the "chill remoteness of Gods" and the extravagant heat of Dionysus: which may logically be defended but very much hinders the clear force of any simple idea.—You will remember that I did not think Theseus simple enough.—Ariadne in Naxos would make a fine tragedy, but I do not think that, as you have it, it clearly presents any philosophical truth. I say this knowing that you must have a better head for such things than I have, and most likely have your ideas perfectly clear. I am only speaking of the presentation of them as offered to me in the play.

Do not trouble to answer this. I hope we may have an occasion to talk it over again. I shall know better what I am talking about next time.

yours very truly

R Bridges

Thanks for speaking to Dent & Co. I do not care about the matter except for its real inconvenience—

226: TO LIONEL MUIRHEAD

Yattendon

November 5, 1894

My dear Lionel

We have been home more than a week: and I thought I would send you a letter apropos of nothing. They are banging off fireworks in the village in honour of St. Guy. Of late years I have had much sympathy with that martyr. I ought to tell you that my wife is much better, and has lost her cough but she is not strong. I wish you would come over for a few days and have some whist.

I hear by today's post that they have elected me an honorary fellow of C.C.C. Ruskin is my fellow Fellow so to speak. "Colleges make one acquainted with strange fellows".—My new edition of Eros & Psyche is out. I am trying to write an ode in praise of Music for Parry, but I doubt if I shall manage it as he wants it off hand or out of hand, and I am not much disposed for writing. We hope to go to town for a few hours soon and if so shall see H.E.W. I spent a couple of days with them a month agone. They are very comfortably and conveniently housed and situated. I have given up the choir here—couldn't stomach the Rector any longer.—I went to church on Sunday morning and heard them. I thought them very good. I go on printing the hymns, but have been stuck fast for two months for want of paper. I am having some made. It won't be anything wonderful then.—We stayed 3 days with Coventry Patmore on our way home from the Isle of Wight. He introduced me to Mrs Meynell's little book of Essays called the "Rhythm of Life". One or two of them are tip top—really as good as possible. Order the book at your library and read it. You will find out the good ones.

Your chrysanthemums are coming on all right, but it is a very late year with us. Most of the plants are still only in bud, and they are near 5 feet high all of them.

I have heard nothing yet of my Keats Essay except that the Editor has received it. I begin to fear that he is afraid of it.

I haven't finished the Psalter yet. I have a chant of my own in after all for the 68th Psalm which I could not get anything to suit. Did I tell you that it has been raining here? We are going to ask our bishop to have the prayer and thanksgiving for fine weather altered for this part of the country, so that we may give thanks for a fine afternoon, and pray for a fine 20 minutes, and so on. I have seen nothing of Acland. I suppose he is back in London. We have been doing patterns out of your book. We happened to get some very fair silks at Ventnor. One is magnificent. I mean one pattern as worked. Come and see it. I heard from Knight the other day. His brother is ill. I never see him. By the way M[r] Waterhouse copied some patterns out of your book to put into his Architectures. I couldn't prevent him—Amen

Come and play whist

yours affectionately

RB

Hope Mrs L M and Xaris and Antonio are well

227: TO LIONEL MUIRHEAD

Yattendon
Newbury
November 22, 1894

My dear Lionel

I am delighted to hear that you can come: It was a fortunate notion. As you do not accept in the plural, or I should say the dual number.(—It is very odd that the Greeks who had no matrimonial sense should have elaborated and kept up a dual number, while we have nothing of the sort though we are always wanting it. How useful it would be for married men like ourselves, including the wife but excluding the nurse and children. I think I must invent a dual number). I am afraid that Mrs. M can't accompany you. My wife is afraid that she may imagine that she was not asked, and has written a note for me to enclose (I won't be bothered with any more ceremonies). I hope that she will be able to come.

Rather to business, fix trains etc. as your father delights to do. Well, Imprimis my mare fell down dead 3 days ago. If it was not 3 days it was 4 or 5, it may have been 6. She lies buried between two ricks half a mile off. Nor is this a wantonly wandering from the point: it constitutes the shadow of a reason for your coming to us via Hamstead Norreys rather than Pangbourne. If you come so, your trains, as I make them out in a bradshaw of last month, are

Henley	11.5
Twyford	11.15
Twyford	11.22
Reading	11.31
Reading	11.55
Didcot	12.35
Didcot	1.25
Ham Norr:	1.52

The worst of this plan is that you kick your heels for fifty minutes at Didcot. Otherwise no time is lost as we are an hour's drive from Pangbourne.

If you come this way, that is the only train, till evening trains. So that if it does not suit you, come to Pangbourne *and fix your own hour, letting us know.* We can borrow a very good horse for 4 shillings, and if Mrs. M is with you it will cost you much more than that to go round by Didcot; besides that we should have to horse the waggonnette to bring you both from H. Norris. So if you bothas come (Now for some duals) comeas by Pangbourne and please excuseas my not having sent my first invitation to youoin in this number. It was ill invented and I don't feel sure that it is successful now.

So as you come come any way

your affectionate friend

RB

Please to bring another volume of that needlework book.

228: TO MAURICE HEWLETT

Yattendon

December 12, 1894

My dear Mr Hewlett

I am sorry that you can't send a better account of yourself. I am sorry that you have been overworking. It is a fault to be 'studiously' avoided. Let things grow of themselves. I hope that you will soon be yourself again. I have been setting everyone a good example of doing nothing: and have felt more than usually occupied.—I am just getting through revise of my Keats article. Some of it I am pleased with: but the allegories are not more attractive in the reading (the explanation of them) than they were in the fidgetting out. I was in town last Friday, and caught cold driving home in the rain in a dogcart—our mare fell down dead about the time of the Tzar's death, and I have not got another yet.—In consequence of which I am invalided indoors with rheumatism and headache and other of nature's consolations.

The poet whose books you saw here was Canon Dixon. I don't know where you can get his best things, because they are all late works: and his early books— (Smith & Elder—) did not sell, so that he has only printed the later ones at the Daniel press, which means editions of 150—and those all taken up. But you will most likely find these at the Museum. One is called *Odes & Ecologues;* one is '*Lyrical* Poems.'—The early books would I think disappoint you though D. G. Rossetti spoke enthusiastically of them.

The Daniel books are so rare that I shouldn't like to send them out on loan by post—occasionally they turn up in 2nd hand catalogues—and always at reasonable prices because Dixon's name is not recognised by the critics as among the poets.

Excuse a letter written rather under difficulties.—I hope that you will be able to send better tidings of yourself.—I should have liked to have heard some particulars of how you got on with your stage play.

I am much disappointed with John Davidson's last book. I think he has more imaginative poetic power than any man of my time, and yet he can't put a thing together decently, and now has gone off on common claptrap fads, and mere flash. I am afraid he will never do well.

Hoping to hear better news of you

yours truly
Robert Bridges

The Clarendon Press have issued the cheap edition of my Milton's Prosody, in their usual mean form.

I have a piece of definite work on hand now which I must get done before Xmas.

229: TO SAMUEL GEE

Yattendon
December 31, 1894

Dear Gee

It was very good of you to think of sending me your salutations. Here is ours to you, with all manner of good wishes for the coming year, and may you have many years of happiness.—I have had a bad cold, a fearfully bad cold. Now this change to frosty weather seems to be driving it away.—My mother is well, and has had a really merry Xmas.—I take enough interest in medicine to be glad to hear all that you care to tell me. It is always *very* interesting—especially when you tell me what you are doing. You are certainly a very fit person to write an estimate of the power of antitoxin. I for one believe in the future of scientific medicine—and can be enthusiastic about it. Vaccination shows us that hope is not vain—and it seems only a question of time to discover a lot of these poisons and their remedies. Practitioners may perhaps be more sceptical.—Tomorrow I begin a new sphere of action, as District Councillor. I got myself returned for this place, as it is very uncertain what the result of popular election may be: and we do not want our model Union to have all its principles subverted. We have, by statistics, one of the best, if not quite the best managed Union in England. There will be a general attempt to reintroduce out-door relief. Did you ever read the literature of the years 1834–1875 on that question? It is most entertaining. Farmers used to discharge their labourers in order that they might "go on the Parish" and then come back to them at lower rate of wages, etc.etc.

I finished my Keats Essay. It is an entertaining piece of work. I don't know when it will be out, but I have revised it and got rid of it. It may come out any day I suppose.—It is to appear as Preface to Keats' Poems in "The Muses Library" Lawrence & Bullen. But there will be a small edition of 150 copies in de luxe form. I receive numerous recognitions now of my work from many quarters. I have as much "popularity" as I could want. Poets seem to be scarce. Excuse a

badly written letter—I am ashamed of it when you write so exquisitely to me.
Alas I am in an arm-chair by the fire.

Wife joins in kindest regards

your affectionate friend

RB

I see Saunders occasionally.

230: TO ROBERT BRIDGES

The Cottage
Hambleden
Henley-on-Thames
January 15, 1895

My dear Robert

This is the 365th day of my 49th year, an incredible but true statement which
seems to demand consideration but refuses to be modified in the least by any
amount that I can give. The half century has been very kind to me and has given
me great enjoyment in ways that I like best, and though worries of various sorts
and regrets have not been absent from time to time, they have left little impression in comparison and are mostly dry and withered whilst the happinesses are
alive and green. It is something to have built nests of pleasant thoughts in which
one may take shelter, and which one hopes no wild beast of despondency may
ever succeed in tearing to pieces, and my thanks are largely due to you who have
helped me to build them.—I hardly suppose this next quarter of a century or
whatever is to come can be equally pleasant, indeed I dont know what good thing
I can do in it comparable to that of getting married, but it is useless forecasting
imaginary good or ill and Horace is always whispering

Quid sit futurum cras fuge quaerere [et]
Quem fors dierum cumque dabit lucro
   Appone:
Permitte Divis caetera.

And tomorrow at Yattendon

Dissolve frigus, ligna super foco
Large reponens: atque benignius
Deprome quadrimum Sabina
   O Thaliarche merum diota.

and believe me

your affectionate
Lionel Muirhead

231: TO LIONEL MUIRHEAD

Yattendon
January 16, 189?

My dear Lionel

Thank you for writing to me on the occasion of your birthday, and for the kind things said. I thought that you had been 50 last year. I was, worse luck to it although I did not wind up the study clock for 8 months. I really do feel old in the limbs sometimes. On the other hand I feel as lively as ever when I am all right. I don't like this thaw. I got on well in the foot. I wish for the sake of my children and wife that I could look forward to 25 years more. I am afraid that my "cistern", as the poor folks say, does not promise to hold out so long as that. The older I get the more thankful I feel that I have not got to support my old age by manual labour—though I suppose that I should be now much stronger in body if I had had to gain my livelihood by digging. But digging in the rain would probably have made me even more rheumatic than I am. But then again I should have got more used to "the rheumatics."—I am now trying to write some lyrics. I am writing also an Ode to Music for Hubert Parry to set. Only he is so much overworked at the Royal College that he does not seem to be able to pay any attention to it.—Church, our man, is laid up, and we have had a more than usual amount of coughers and such things—but nothing serious. Wooldridge sent us a new hymn-tune the other day. 50 copies of the hymnal are to be printed folio size on best paper. They are magnificent. I have got only 8 pages printed yet but I think we shall get Part I, i.e. 32 pages, out this summer.

I wish you lived nearer and that we could meet oftener. But it's no use wishing With all good wishes for your ½ century and that you may have good health with content and much happiness, and that I may sometimes share some of it, I am your affectionate friend

R Bridges

Wife joins me in all my good wishes and we send our continued remembrances to M^rs L M—

Since I wrote this we have lunched and drunk your health very well in not bad wine. I must try and write you a birthday ode. My wife says that your philosophy is better than mine. So I think it is. I am afraid my poetic avocations have undermined my philosophy. By the way I often read Horace. I am thinking some day of printing some "Animadversions on Horace's Odes."

Our baby is getting amusing; he is beginning to talk some, and consequently repeats anything that is said to him or to any one else. He shows, perhaps it is only by accident, extraordinary artistic notions: so that I think that in some previous existence his soul may haply have inhabited the body of some swell Wife showed him a picture of the Pantheon the other day, and said, "Isn't that a beautiful building?" to which he replied "That is a beautiful building. Did I build it?" It is unfortunate that he has not a clearer notion of who he was.

RB

232: TO RICHARD WATSON DIXON

Yattendon
February 20, 1895

My dear Dixon

Thank you for your letter. I was delighted that you are writing again. I have to lament, as you do, that my schemes in that line become less and less magnetically attractive to my faculties. I have 3 magnificent subjects for plays now all waiting for my attack, and I dally, and do not even dig my parallels. However I have written some lyrics this last month.

It is very pleasant to me, what you say of our friendship. You have been a great deal to me ever since our first meeting. I owe a great deal to you and always remember with delight the pleasant hours which we have spent together in chat. Also my work is the better for its contact with yours. This you must reckon all in the balance when you are tempted to think remorsefully of the past: and do not forget how many men you have helped. For instance that parson who came into these parts from yours. He owes you a great deal, and knows it and speaks of you with the greatest admiration and reverence. I hope you are now in good enough care to do without such consolations.

As for the Keats Essay. I am very grateful for the criticism, and I wish very much that you would mark the things in the Essay which displease you as faults in form or writing. My aim was to be perfectly clear, and I am not sure that the "but first" form is not due to that. It is needful, very often, to remind the reader what your prefatory remark or qualification is intended to apply to: and it is very useful to clear away any obstruction which would prevent your putting a case simply.—Thus, "I am going to tell you the relation between A and B. But first I must explain that when I say A I do not mean a—etc," then follow with the statement of the relation. I do not see what there is to object to in this.

I wish that you would mark the objectionable things in the Essay that I may amend them. I expect that my fault is pedantry. I hate it so much that I am not afraid of it, and therefore am liable to slip into it.

It would be better to print the quotations from Endymion. But they would be of no use to anyone who was not studying the poem—and any student of the poem would look them up. To study Endymion means to work at it for many days together, and any such student would be "deeply grateful" to look up any hints. As a matter of form I find that long poetic extracts in an essay always put me off. I can read a poem or an essay on a poem—but a mixture of the two I find intolerable. The only use of quotation in an essay (to my thinking) is either to enforce a point beyond dispute, or by sudden introduction of a few verses in the midst of the prose to overwhelm by beauty. I have done both these things several times in my Essay.

I don't know what you mean by using nouns for verbal forms. At least I don't know my tendency, and should be glad to have that pointed out. (Which would be done if you would mark the Essay with red ink).

You underrate your contributions to the Essay in saying that I might have taken more of your hints. There is a lot of your work in it.

One or two things which you said were in my judgment not right, and I fancy in talking over these you would come to agree. Other things I may have omitted for sake of simplicity. But I have put in a great deal.

When I get a copy of the Essay I mean to mark the contributions of various friends, and initial them—as a memorial—and to identify my own work.

If you have the leisure some day to read the Essay again pencil to hand and mark objections I shall be glad. You shall have a large paper copy when they come out.

With our love

yours affectionately

RB

233: TO LIONEL MUIRHEAD

Yattendon

March 15, 1895

My dear Lionel

Thanks for Peter who came all right. I had no notion where he was. I wanted to begin his drama the other day, but could not do so for want of the book. Now I have got on other things. It didn't matter a bit, but I have got all the scheme now into good form and could begin any day when I have reminded myself of a few details.

Glad to hear good news of you. How similar uncles are. I had an uncle too like you—a maternal uncle like yours—who married like yours, and died as yours did—whose executor I was as you were of yours, and whose property was vast, as yours I believe; and whose solicitor was a swindler, as in your case, and as in your case decamped with a lot of money to South America after having failed for some 300,000 £.

I have still occasionally to sign a receipt for a dividend of $\frac{1}{4}^{d}$ or so in the pound.

The hymn book is getting on well. It promises to be most lovely. It is going on faster now.

We are going to print the Psalter chants this summer, though the collection is not complete. It will be therefore somewhat tentative and private.

Come here any day. We have influenza in the Village but none so far in the house, and we keep ourselves isolated.

In somewhat of haste

with many thanks for the book

yours ever

RB

234: TO HUBERT PARRY

Yattendon
April 1, 1895

My dear Parry

Your letter is quite clear as to what you want of me, and I will try and supply it.

On your part when you want it send me a postcard to say so, because I don't expect I shall hit off what will satisfy me very easily, and should in that case keep it by me till you needed it.

I have been trying to resume the broken threads this morning, and thought it useful to write out the thing as far as it has gone—both to get it into my head again, and because I do not at all remember whether I have made any corrections since I sent a copy to you. I have in this copy changed a word or two in No. VI which you say is to be given to a Basso.

I am very sorry for you. Your College and influenza, etc., examinations and all, and I will try and not give you more trouble than I can help. But I cannot expect not to give you a good deal—because if I ever hoped to write anything satisfactory for modern music it would only be with the expectation of being able to understand the composer's requirements when he explained them to me. I have thought that perhaps I might understand enough music for that. I am perfectly certain that my unaided efforts are not likely to be good, and therefore I deplore the circumstances which hinder me in this instance from doing my best.

I think that you should—before this fortnight of composition comes on—manage to have a talk with me about difficulties of detail—I cannot imagine that there are none which might not be thus amended. I would come and lunch any day when you are ready.

I quite understand that it would be risky for you to come here, because the atmosphere might not be congenial. But the notion of *interruption* would not occur to you if you had ever been in this remote place.

I send you the new copy.

Write and say when you want the Finale.

If it would make it easier for you to alter any line yourself pray do so. Don't let me hamper your music when it has a will of its own.

yours ever
RB

235: TO RICHARD WATSON DIXON

Yattendon
April 20, 1895

My dear Dixon

M^r and Mrs Daniel and their 2 children have been staying here, and I have had many thoughts about your lyrics odes etc. which he printed now years ago—

pleasant thoughts about beautiful things—and I wonder that there is not yet more sign of their coming to the high place which they will ultimately hold.

There is one interesting witness of their influence. Daniel is now printing a 2nd volume of lyrical poems by Binyon. I saw the proofs of these. They are not quite masterly, but are full of poetical beauty, and they are written mostly in a sort of new prosody, and show decidedly the influence of your best work. The book will be very interesting to you. The writer is a man who should do well, though he seems to grow somewhat slowly. He has good feeling a true mind and a wonderful visual memory—

Next week Monica and I hope to spend 2 or 3 days in London. We shall be up on Tuesday and Wednesday nights at least; we shall be staying with Wooldridge at 18 Hanover Terrace Notting Hill. W. In case you should be in town also I give you the address. He has the ode which I have written for Parry to set to music; I will send it you from there. I don't think that you will like it. The worst of it is that it is really my sketch of an ode for Parry to suggest upon, and he takes it as it is. At least I do not yet get any suggestions for alteration. It is an unsatisfactory business to write for these musicians. They are in such a dreadful hurry, and their ideas seem confined to what is presented to them. So my ode is a mere congeries of musical opportunities.

Last time you wrote it was about my Keats Essay. If when you have done criticising it you will return me the copy which I sent you, I shall be glad of it. I do not particularly want it, but as it is the only copy, and the book does not come out, it would be convenient sometimes for me to have it to show to enquirers, who think that I am the cause of the delay in the appearance of the book.

I am very glad that Oscar Wilde is quite shown up. No one has done more harm to art than he in the last 20 years. I did not know he was so bad, but I confess that I have a grain of satisfaction in the collapse of the traducer of idealism.

I hope that you are well. I have not been over fit since the weather changed—and now have a bad cold.—Otherwise we are all well. I am getting on with the Yattendon Hymnal. It should be a splendid book, and the Churchwardens want me to print the Psalter.—This is not of equal interest, but will contain some original stuff which has a future before it in some circles. I shall be always glad to have new words of hymns, if you know of any.

The rector here has published a volume of poems 'In a garden' or some such title.—I have not seen them yet.—Another versifying parson came over to lunch yesterday on a bicycle. He did not seem worth much. I suggested to him that his parish work would not leave him time to pursue his poetic art satisfactorily. He did not see the point.

Do not you think that Herrick was an ass? I can't see why he should be thought so great a writer.

With our united love and good wishes to you both

yours ever

RB

236: TO HUBERT PARRY

18 Hanover Terrace
Notting Hill W.
Friday, April 26, [1895]

My dear Parry

I am going home again tomorrow and will get to work at the Ode.

I am staying with Wooldridge who has seen what I had written and sent to you, and I find that his criticism coincides generally with yours.

He seems to think that a little work on the lines which you suggest will bring the Ode together and make it intelligible. This rather consoles me, for I had come to think it a hopelessly sketchy and broken backed affair.

He likes the 'Dirge' number best—as I do, and I hope that you will not find it necessary to weaken that by making 2 stanzas of the 3.

I will send you the amended edition as soon as I have done it. I have the copy which I sent to Wooldridge so that I shall not want yours again.

By the way Wooldridge agrees with me that the number "Thee fair Poetry oft hath sought" is too barefacedly Miltonic, but I do not think it worth while to alter it, as I at first suggested and you dissuaded.

I hope you are well. I saw a lot of the music people at the Wagner concert last night. The VII symphony sounded quite oldfashioned after Tannhauser & Siegfried, and I fancy the conductor rather overdid the expression in light and shade. But the whole performance was magnificent.

yours ever
RB

237: TO MRS. MARGARET WOODS

Yattendon
Newbury
May 18, 1895

Dear Mrs Woods

Your kind invitation for June 13—We are at present negociating a visit to the Warrens. They asked us for Sunday June 2, and we, not able to go then, offered for the 9th. We have not yet heard whether that suits them.

I can't answer your invitation till I have heard from them, as we told them our plans and they may have been fitting us in for the end of that week, which would clash with your proposal.

We hope to leave home next Monday (this Monday) for 3 weeks, and we must be at home again on June 14 to receive visitors who are coming for the Alcestis at Bradfield. By the way have you read Verrall on Euripides? Don't keep your days open for us. We will come if we can, and I will let you know when I hear from St Mary Magdalen College, and then you can tell us whether the time which you now offer would still suit. I know how precious the June days are and should be

very sorry if you put any one off for our uncertainty, which I am sorry I canno
prevent.

I am glad if you are not in any way discontented to have your name appearing
at the end of my Keats' prolegomena. I am curious to know how the professiona
critic will take my excursions.

with love to H. G.

yours very truly
R Bridges

I need not say how much we both thank you for your invitation.

238: TO HUBERT PARRY

Trinity College
Oxford
June 12, 189!

My dear Parry
   Your demands for poetry came at a most unfortunate time as I have been
travelling about visiting and have had absolutely no opportunity for the neces
sary leisure of mind. I shall be going home tomorrow and shall hope to manage
to do something. But we unfortunately have visitors till next Monday. Up here
have had some difficulty in dissuading my friends from running me for the
Professorship of Poetry. I do not want it at all and have had my name withdrawn
   About the Ode I am very sorry for the inconvenience and as you say 'critical
condition of your affairs.
   I hoped when I undertook it to have a good deal of consultation with you
about it; and am sorry that your original work is so driven into corners. The
result is I fear that neither of us will be pleased.—As for any alteration made in
my poem, you need not scruple—nor will it be worth while to print the original
Though if there is much alteration it might be as well to state that there is some
   When I get home I will try to do what I can and be more intelligible.
   Excuse a hurried note. I am going out with these people.

yours ever
RB

239: TO LIONEL MUIRHEAD

Yattendor
June 17, 189.

My dear Lionel
   I am very sorry about the whooping cough. When my children had it I wa
very anxious about them, but though they had it severely they seemed none the

worse for it, and that is the only consolation which I can offer. We tried many things and I don't believe that anything did any good—but it is useful to take regular doses of some alkali—bicarbonate of potassium is the usual thing given—because that really does always in cough tend to loosen the phlegm, and that is very important in whooping cough. The most important thing is that the children should keep their food down—if they bring up all their meals they pine.

We came back from a month's holiday in Cornwall and Oxford some 4 or 5 days ago—and since then we have had visitors who came to us to see the Bradfield Greek play—and I have had to try and write poetry for Parry to set to music. There is to be an ode of our joint contrivance performed in honour of Henry Purcell (tercentenary) at the Leeds Festival this year. Unfortunately Parry's occupation at the Royal College of Music has made collaboration rather a fiasco and broken the back of the poem, which will however still contain a little good stuff. At Oxford I found the people wanted me to stand for the Poetry chair. I was very strongly supported, but am not going in this time. It is plain that I can have it 5 years hence if I will. Now we are running HEW for the Slade Professorship. I think he would get it but that Herkomer—of whom the University is as disenchanted as it is of Professor Palgrave—will not retire *and* I doubt if we shall get enough devilry into the electors to kick him out. All this is good fun. Now my reason for not being able to write you a longer letter is that I have a long list of agenda—among them the revising of 8 pages of proof of the Hymnal, which is going on very well. The next 8 pages will bring the pages up to 40 and there we shall stop for the present.

The fuss about me at the University got me a good deal of very useful consideration, and has done much to establish me. When your coughers are a little more chronic should you be able to pay us a visit? I shall not be leaving home I expect again this summer.

I hope they will do well.

With our love and kindest regards to Mrs. L M

yours ever

RSB

240: TO ROGER FRY

Yattendon
June 23, 1895

My dear Roger

Many thanks for returning the 'Essay'. I am glad that you liked it, and sorry that I had not one to give you. I don't know when it is really going to be published. There has been a demand for it exactly in proportion to its extreme scarcity—inversely—

I hear fine things of your portrait of Miss Palgrave. I want to see it. I envy you your easy wanderings. I wish you could find us a good French sous-bonne in the lands whither you are going, but I suppose you have not much acquaintance with the gentry of those parts.

Please come to us, if you can, some time this summer. We shall be at home til
autumn, and with one short break till Xmas. Any time would suit us. Tomor
row—e.g.

I hope Wooldridge may get the Slade. But it is too good to hope. Leighton and
Poynter could get it him if they chose. But are they likely to choose? What a
Professor he would make! It would be actually possible for an undergraduate, to
say nothing of the dons, to form some opinion as to what the word art really
meant.

It would almost tempt me to go for the Poetry Professorship 5 years hence.

Come to us when you can

With love from us both

yours ever
RB

241: TO HUBERT PARRY

Yattendor
June 28, 189!

My dear Parry

I am sorry that one of the emendations gives trouble. <u>Please alter it to suit you</u>
or write the music which seems wanted and send me the bars and obvious words
or put in other words of your own.

There is no objection to the old 3 or 4 lines of No. IX. They will make no
difference and you can do just what you will with the Ist stanza of No. IX.

Of course in this Number I expect you to omit the 4 lines about Pain and Pity
But if you could cradle your declamation for 8 bars, the sense of the passage
would gain by their insertion. I left them on the bare chance: but you must no
let me interfere with your scheme. The music is the important matter.

About the title. 'Ode to Purcell' is of course ridiculous. My notion of it origi
nally was an 'Ode to music for the commemoration of Purcell's centenary', the
allusion to Purcell being in the two numbers—Sorrow's lament and the Dirge. A
the Ode stands now these allusions are even more obscure and remote, I think
than I made them—and it was impossible to get very near—so that your title o
"Invocation to Music" is I expect more correct. Still I see no objection to adding
"in commemoration of Henry Purcell". It would add interest, and do something
towards paying our debt—and the occasion cannot of course recur. Also if Pur
cell's name gets attached to your piece of music it will distinguish it from other
and be convenient and it might get used at the Abbey celebration if they have ar
orchestra there.

I was glad to hear from you, but do not let yourself be bothered with any detai
so much as you describe. There is nothing to be gained by it.

yours ever
RB

242: TO RICHARD WATSON DIXON

Yattendon
July 8, 1895

My dear Dixon

I wrote a great part of a long letter to you the other day, but I tore it up it was such stuff. Not the first time I have done that.—Today I am in a foolish irritable mood. I got up at 5.30 and am suffering for my folly. Not the first time I have done that—I know that I can't write a decent letter, but I can jot down a few gossiping notes. First of all about that professorship—I did not wish for it, and never meant to take it, but I did not mind my friends just doing as much as they did, because in the absence of recognition by London critics a little 'consideration' was useful to me, e.g. the Master of Balliol read my Milton's prosody and Keats Essay, and thereupon became my supporter, and a very warm one.

Binyon has just got out a new volume of poems with Daniel. It is not actually 'out' yet. The last poem, a long and somewhat reflective one, seems to me to do something to fulfill the promise of his earlier work. He is now in the Print room at the British Museum.

Wooldridge is a candidate for the Slade Professorship. I don't know if he has any chance. The only elector whom he does not know something of is one Erickson (Sir John I think) head of University College: London, I believe. If you should know him send him a word.

We had a fairish holiday and are glad to be at home again. It is our time for visitors.

My mother is worse than ever. Her bodily health is maintained and I am glad to say that she is cheerful and very seldom in any pain, and gets out in her bath-chair every day.—But her mind is almost a blank and conversation very difficult.

I have written an ode to Music which Parry has set to music, at least he has set part of the sketch and an altered version of the finished parts. I don't know what the music is like.—I naturally don't take much interest in it, because I had hoped to do a good thing, and have done merely a broken backed affair, through no fault of mine.—It contains some good things I hope—a dirge especially, which I have sent to be printed in the 'Pelican' a C.C.C. magazine. I will send it you when it comes out. Parry has spoiled it as a poem.

I have seen a lot of people. I am sorry to say that the reception which my work generally receives now has had the effect of making me thoroughly disinclined to write a word more. I could not have foreseen that.

My hymnal is getting on. The First part—40 pages, 75 tunes—will be out in the Autumn. I regard it as a satisfactory affair. The appearance of the book is excellent. I think it quite first rate, and I am sure that I am difficult to please—

Recent events have slightly aroused my interest in Politics.

I am unable to play cricket this year. Perhaps it is time that I gave up.

With our love

your affectionate

RB

Tell me all about yourself when you write—
Can't you pay us a visit this year???

————

PS   If you should happen to know the *present Dean of Lincoln* I should [rest of letter missing in holograph]

243: TO HARRY ELLIS WOOLDRIDGE

Yattendon
July 16, 1895

My dear HEW
Thanks for your letters—very interesting—I look forward to enjoying the Purcell anthem but have not had time today. I don't know what plans we shall have. We shall take the children away some time in September. If you come to Abingdon I shall hope to manage to see something of you. I can easily get over for the day. I don't know why you choose Abingdon or whether you may go somewhere else. I hope it will be within reach of us, and that you will be able to come to us on your way out or returning. Just now we are pretty full of engagements to visitors. Benecke and Binyon come this Saturday, and a niece of mine is coming for a fortnight. I am trying a new horse.—I was at the Board of Guardians today—tomorrow I must be in Newbury, and on Thursday in Reading, and here to take the chair at Mount's M P meeting in the evening. These details to serve you for some account of myself. But I am doing nothing worth writing about. I saw the Guardian notice: it amused me very much. I thought it was from the house of Bernard. I guess this lady has had her say about me before once. I took her for the wife of some Eton master. She means well.
    I don't know what I shall do about the stereotyping business. I have not heard from Hart.
    I heard that the Bishop of Peterborough wanted "Ark the 'erald Hangels" changed back to Wesley's original, and so I have altered the words to your hymn, much to its advantage. The "refrain" is not now mixed. It was rather mixed before because the old words made a bad beginning, but not a bad refrain. It now reads

> "Hark! how all the welkin rings
> Glory to the King of Kings!"

As Peterborough says, the Angels were not heralds, and they did not sing "glory to the new born King"—.
    That is the sort of thing I am driven to write about. My eyeglasses have lost their spring and wont stick on my nose. I have tried to read Scot's [*sic*] "Heart of Midlothian". O how awfully tedious he can be. Here's an amusing sentence "Those who love nature always desire to penetrate into its inmost recesses."—We rejoice that the Palmer[?] has got such a licking at Reading for all his People's

)arks and bronze statues. Bellairs is in for the post of organist at Lincoln Cathe-
lral. I expect he has no chance. Our dog Benedick does well.

yours ever

RB

Read the Saturday

Thanks for the ψεύδο Wordsworth.

P.S. July 17

Congratulations!

44: TO LIONEL MUIRHEAD

Yattendon
July 17, 1895

)ear Lionel
HEW is Slade Professor.
! ! ! ! !
am glad the children are
getting over their troubles.
Come then on July 29 as you
propose. In haste

yours ever

RB

P.S.
My wife bids me urge you to
bring M^rs M with you.
Now I guess this is
mpossible. But of course if
he could come so much the better.

45: TO A. H. BULLEN

Yattendon
August 20, 1895

Private

My dear Bullen
I have declined Mr Shorter's proposal. I did not see how confusion between
he two books could be avoided, though he wanted only a short biography.
Supposing that he persists—do you think that a short biography, which should
refer to your edition for criticism, would help or damage your book?

It would probably often sell in mistake for it.

I think I might do the Shelley for you if you gave me as long as you give Drury

I would rather have done Shelley than Keats in the first instance. What stand in the way of Shelley criticism is the childishness of his metaphysic. I believe tha it is bottomless nonsense—which Keats meant when he said "Poor Shelley!" Bu in face of Shelley's supreme other gifts it requires a metaphysical reputation to condemn him. It is possible that prolonged consideration might make something of it, but it is difficult. Though all advanced metaphysics are unintelligible to me I yet draw a line between the unintelligible, and the meaningless.

I once projected a critical essay on Shelley with a metaphysician, whom retained to tackle the 'idea'. I was to do the poetry of it. He soon withdrew in disgust.

I have even now a scheme on with a lady friend who believes in the content o Shelley's ideas.

yours very truly

RB

PS   I told Mr Shorter that I had sent on his prospectus to you. It seems it was : privately printed draft of a prospectus only.

246: TO HUBERT PARRY

Yattendor
August 28, 189!

My dear Parry

I never objected to the words of the Ode being printed in a book of words o programme. What you proposed was that I should supply a *different* version fo the programme from what you have in the music.

I really do not see how any one would profit by this—and if they would profit can't undertake to do it. This ode has really never existed—and I don't know tha it ever will except in the form in which you have set it. I think that, as you say, i you put a footnote in the book of words to say, what is true, that the words have been slightly adapted by the composer that will be sufficient. I should not sa anything about "the exigencies of the music", or give any reason. I should cal the programme

"The words of the Music
an ode by RB
slightly adapted by the composer"

That would be quite sufficient for me.

Then if you want any gloss why should not you supply it? You know what the public will want. I confess I do not. All Novello has to do is to reprint the word.

from the score in the usual manner, and it seems to me that you are the fit person to supply the gloss or heading to the stanzas, because 1st of all you would wish the gloss to interpret the music—and 2ndly, I do not think it is very satisfactory for an author to write notes or explanations of his own words (It is different with music).

You may do exactly what you like in the matter. It really does not signify to me whether you state that the words are altered or not: but if you do not state it you might be blamed afterwards for not having stated it. I hope this is all clear. I am sorry to give you any trouble by misunderstanding.

Novello may print at once.

yours ever
R Bridges

247: TO HUBERT PARRY

Yattendon
October 4, 1895

My dear Parry

I got home last night after a month in Somerset with all my family, and found your letter from Harrogate of the 1st. I had no idea when the Leeds Festival was, and the first intimation that reached me was a letter forwarded to me at Porlock from here, written by a critic after the rehearsal.

I am very sorry to have missed the opportunity, but I doubt whether if I had been home I could have managed to make all the prearrangements necessary to secure reasonable comfort. I enjoy things as much as ever but find myself less and less eager to seize opportunities. And as it happened this time that I was on Exmoor while you were waving your rod there would have been some difficulty, though I might very well have come home two days sooner. I rather expected to have had a line from you, but I know how busy you are.

I should indeed have been glad to have heard the performance.

I had to content myself with buying all the penny papers as I came up in the train yesterday, and reading what the critics said. I gathered two things. 1st. that the Ode had really been a success, and 2ndly that the critics are a poor lot. It is extraordinary that they cannot give one a better notion of what has taken place.

I should like a line from you some day if you have time to tell me how you thought it went. You say very kind things in your letter, but I am aware that I gave you a good deal of trouble. I wish we could have talked the thing over more. Still I expect it is a success. I should be very sorry if you were disappointed.—No doubt a second performance will help the public. Hoping that you are now getting a holiday before term.

I am yours ever
R.B.

I am sure that you will not think it was any lack of interest in your work which kept me away. I cannot imagine a greater treat than such a performance by such a Choir. But perhaps I ought to apologise for my absence.

248: TO RICHARD WATSON DIXON

Yattendon
October 5, 1895

My dear Dixon

Thank you very much for your long letter, which I had been looking out for. It is delightful to know exactly how you are spending your days. I wish I could work as you are working. I have done nothing for ever so long. I think sometimes that I shall have to take to coṁentating. My Keats' essay was so much 'appreciated'. You know that I always intended to write a commentary on Shelley's Prometheus—then the Keats Essay rather took its place in my schemes, and in that I said many of the things that I wished to say. But I have now had several direct invitations and exhortations to write on Shelley, and that has caused me to look over the Prometheus again. It would be not a bad thing to edit a critical edition of it. The more one reads it the more things one finds that require explanation—and which one is certain cannot be understood by the average poetical admirer. On the other hand the more one reads, the more hopeless is the philosophical entanglement. I have been away from home for a month—and took a Shelley with me. I am ready to make some "revelations" already. We went to Somerset—to 2 friends' houses, and then for 10 days to Porlock Weir, which is on the outskirts of Exmoor, where we saw some stag hunting and met with good company at the Inn.

It was a "Gentleman from Porlock" who called so inopportunely on Coleridge and broke off "Kubla Khan."—We returned on Thursday, which was I fear the last warm day. On Wednesday my "Purcell Ode", of which I sent you *the Dirge*, was performed at Leeds (my friend Hubert Parry wrote the music). There was a good account of it in the Times of Thursday. It seems to have been a success.— Some of the ode is good enough. I had no "collaboration" in a proper sense with the musician, and do not know how the music goes. Some of the accounts in the daily papers (all of which I bought at the railway stations as I came along) were amusing enough. One writer said that I showed the influence of Dryden and Robert Browning!!! Would it be possible to go further wrong?

I was rather disappointed at your having nothing to say about the Dirge, which I fancy is as good a thing as I have written. I guess that its Ecclesiastes vein was unsympathetic to you. But the point of it was to express that view of the matter— and the moral of it is that the poetical expression of it is *the* (or at least *a*) cure for the melancholy. This it seems to me is what art has to do. To satisfy by expression. In the ode Sorrow complains that art having left the country she has no expression for her soul—and she asks for comfort. Music gives her the comfort of this most melancholy dirge.—The next movement is more cheerful, and passes off into a sort of triumph.

I am glad to hear of the stereotype edition of the History Volumes I. and II. I am sure that you will have considered the various criticisms brought to bear on them. I understand your wishing to modify some of your judgments of men, but I should prefer the old unscrupulous or less scrupulous version. Still it does seem to me that one can believe nothing whatever of what contemporaries *say* of a man. When one has actual facts to deal with, facts that cannot possibly be questioned—as e.g. the number of Henry VIII's wives, and their ends—then one may say something definite, but when contemporaries narrate what *may* be mere scandal then I for one do not believe it. I read history with tons of salt not with a grain.

History and travel are my favourite reading.—I cannot write you a much longer letter today. Some day this month I shall be sending you the "first part" of our Yattendon Hymnal; the last 8 pages of the 40 which make the Part I are in the press. It will be a very handsome book and I hope it may do something to better church music in England. At present it is vulgar. At Wells Cathedral they had an admirable choir but sang the most rotten stuff.

The two gentlemen in the neighbourhood whom I know both said that the music was so stupid that they never went to the Cathedral. Now the clergy are much to blame for their ignorance of music. It should be recognised by them as the most powerful ally of religion.

Nordau (is that his name?) is I suppose about the best possible example of the "degeneration" which has moved his indignation. He is I should imagine very smart—but vituperation without insight or discrimination is poor stuff; one soon wearies of it. It is like the plague, which slays good and bad alike, powerful enough, but inhuman. This book is I suppose the market venture of a clever man, a book of the hour only.

Your "Hayton revisited" interested me very much. How well I remember alighting at that station, and walking up with you to the rectory, where we had such long evening talks over the fire. It was a delicious time to me, and to have to find it so far back in one's memory is very melancholy. But en revanche my wife has a scheme for us all to come to Warkworth or to Bambro' next year. I hope it may come off.

With our kindest regards and remembrances to Mrs Dixon,

yours affectionately
RB

249: TO LIONEL MUIRHEAD

Yattendon
October 20, 1895

My dear Lionel

Tomatoes have been very plentiful this year: you have therefore been much in my mind. Not that I think of you always associated with tomatoes, nor only when there are tomatoes; but always when there are tomatoes, and with the daily tomato daily. We have been away for a month this autumn children and all, eating tomatoes in Somersets. We finished up at Porlock Weir—where there is a good small Inn on the border of Exmoor, and there we assisted (in the true French sense) at the stag hunting, returning to our Yattendon tomatoes about a fortnight ago, with the tail of the hot weather. Now we are wondering whether you and M^{rs} M will not come and see us, before the atomatic winter sets in. We have visitors next Saturday-Monday and the Saturday-Monday after that (i.e. November 2 . 5). I have to spend in Oxford at a C. C. C. dinner which is apparently to last 2 days. Between these engagements or after would suit us. We have got a horse again at last; Elizabeth has christened him 'Simon de Montfort'—he is a grey horse, very tall, near 17 hands. I had to enlarge the lorre box for him, and now we are raising the garden wall. He shall fetch you from Pangbourne when you will. In a few days I shall be able to send you my presentation copy of Pt I of the Yattendon Hymnal. I have a specimen already. It is very good. I did not go to the Leeds Festival and cannot make out from the papers how Parry's cantata went off. I wish I could have heard it: but for one thing I was eating tomatoes then at Porlock, and for another the whole programme did not interest me, but if it had I doubt if I could have gone through with the nuisance of securing *seats and beds*. I don't know any one at Leeds, and had no invitation.

Will you both come and have some whist?

yours ever affectionately

RB

We hope you have all been well. Wife sends kindest regards.

250: TO MRS. MARGARET WOODS

Yattendon
October 26, 1895

My dear Mrs Woods

I was sorry that you were not at home when I called yesterday.

Binyon when he was here some time ago told me that he was going to try a shilling volume of poems—no binding—and moderate size. I thought it a good idea, and we projected a series of these shilling volumes, to be brought out by Elkin Mathews. (The solder which bound Elkin Mathews to John Lane is dissolved, and I have some pleasure in helping discarded honesty.) The series so far consists in a volume by Binyon which is not yet out—I have promised to supply the 2nd volume, and I expect someone will be found for a third—if not Binyon no doubt will have got another shilling's worth ready. He has absolute control of the series so far as admission to its privileges are concerned. Mathews is to give the author 3^d in the shilling. (I fancy 2^d to the trade 3^d for himself and 4^d printing.)

Woods said that you were thinking of bringing out some poems soon. I wondered whether you would join the shillingers. When Binyon's book is out I will tell him to send you a copy and then you can judge of the "Format". I like his taste in such matters, and I think the book is sure to be nice.

I write this at once in the hope of securing you for volume 3.

I was glad to hear that your eyes were better. My wife did not answer your letter for fear of your replying.

With kindest regards from us both

yours very sincerely
R Bridges

I shall be in Oxford on November 3rd.

251: TO LIONEL MUIRHEAD

Yattendon
October 28, 1895

My dear Lionel

I am very glad that you like the hymnal. I am very much pleased with it myself. I expect the folios all to sell, and if they do they will pay all expenses. Your handsome order of 3 copies will be a good start. I expect that we shall be going at the 2nd part about Xmas. It was such a trouble to get the 1st part done that we must take a little rest, but the printers understand it now and get on without giving us much trouble. I only gave away 2 copies of the folios besides one to the Bodleian, so that I have not drawn much on my capital. I think Mr Waterhouse will print the Psalter, but that is not absolutely ready, and we have not yet got an estimate which is in any way reasonable. It will be cheap and fairly nasty.

I am sorry that you have a cold. I hope the kitchen boiler gets on all right. You can come here any day except that I go to Oxford November 2 till 4, and next Thursday we go to London for the inside of the day.

yours ever
RB

You will see that the wrapper, preface and index do not form part of the book, supposed in a completed work.—Many thanks for your generous offer. I should like to associate you in some way, but hope we shan't need to come on our friends for "rhino." However we may meet with difficulties hereafter—but of these hereafter.

252: TO MRS. MARGARET WOODS

Yattendon
November 18, 1895

Dear Mrs Woods

It is all right about Elkin Mathews' advertisement. It was in itself really a sham catchpenny trick with nothing behind it, and he had himself withdrawn it in shame before he got my Binyon-born rebuke.

HYMNS

IN FOUR PARTS   WITH ENGLISH
WORDS FOR SINGING IN CHURCHES
EDITED BY ROBERT BRIDGES

Part I

Printed at the Oxford Univerſity Preſs

By Horace Hart, with the Muſic Types of Peter Walpergen
and the Roman and Italic of Biſhop Fell

I 8 9 5

The title page of *The Yattendon Hymnal*. See letters 233, 235, 248, 251, etc.

B. was here yesterday. He has a specially devised wrapper for this 1ˢᵗ series which is to be called "E M's shilling garland". Lane has already prospectused a shilling novel series, so there are excitements in Vigo St. W. B's Nᵒ· I will be out by Xmas. I am ready with Nᵒ· II but can't print till after Xmas, as I have sent one of the poems to the Pageant. I am writing today to ask Dixon to do a volume with a selection of his Daniel odes etc., which I hope he will let me make for him. If you join the company you will be IV. B will then want to edge in with another I expect, and I think I can get a worthy VI and VII and shall ask Lᵈ de Tabley if he will not make an VIII, and if all those come out next year we should be fairly successful.

In haste yours very truly
RB

I got an arrangement at the Abbey. Sorry I troubled you.

253: TO ROGER FRY

Yattendon
December 10, 1895

My dear Roger

Thanks for Dickinson on Democracy, which I took down in 2 drafts, and enjoyed. I hope it will reach the people for whom it was intended. It would do good. Such a lot of people only want to follow some display of intelligence, and half our great stride is done by people who would rather stand still, but do not wish it to be thought that they are behind the time. I believe that there may be a change in the common opinion that radicalism means intelligence.

Sorry to miss you at Cambridge—we were: but did not know where to hit on you. We had a fine time. One of your Kings' dons took us to chapel on Sunday afternoon, but the music was not of a high order. When we got home we went to Oxford and heard the new Slade Professor inaugurate. We thought he did it well. Good matter and all extremely lucid—the style both of composition and delivery very good. After his second lecture he came on here for a day on his way to London, and is going to Cornwall for Xmas. I suppose we shan't see you again till the Spring. We should be very glad if you cared to come, but the winds and the weather are not inviting.

I am afraid that I don't sufficiently admire the Pageant. I fear it must disappoint your artist friends, neither of whom come out very grand. It was kind of them to put in Millais' Sir Isumbras. I shall cut that out and frame it. The poem by Maeterlinck I thought as good as need be. Is he always as good as that? Can you tell me if there is a volume of lyrics by him? I should be glad to read some more like that one.

What am I to do with Democracy now I have read it? Send it about, or return it?

Monica sends love.

yours ever
R Bridges

254: TO LIONEL MUIRHEAD

Yattendon
December 17, 1895

My dear Lionel

Thanks for your letter. I am glad that you like Binyon's verses. I do, very much. The second number of the Garland will contain my Purcell ode, which you enquire after, and some 1/2 dozen new lyrics, which I hope will be among the best things of my Muse. The volume won't be out for another month, as the Purcell ode got into a dreadful mess with Professor Parry, and needs some leisure to extricate it.

I think the shilling idea is a very good one, and I hope that it will be appreciated by the public.

I was very sorry about Philip Rathbone's death. I had a quite affectionate regard for him. I wrote to Mrs Rathbone and have had an answer from her. His death was quite sudden, and I don't fancy that Mrs. R has quite taken it in yet. He used to be often away from home.

I never see anything of that family now.

I was also very much, more than by Philip Rathbone's death, distressed by the death of Lord de Tabley. I had made friends with him the last 2 years, and we kept up a pretty regular correspondence, enlivened by occasional meetings in town. He was a most delightful fellow, but very modest and shrinking.

I am glad that the Hymnal still pleases. I am afraid that you won't find the settings very good for the piano. It has been making things for the piano which has ruined vocal writing. These hymns must be sung unaccompanied. However the Jeremy Clark[e]'s are not in this class, and do well enough either way.

My Latin Hymns will in all cases have the Latin words also printed with them and the original tune in the old 4 line stave notation. At least this is our plan. The new 4 part settings will I think be a revelation.

When are you coming to us again?

yours ever
R Bridges

One blessing of Xmas is that our organist goes for a holiday. The unaccompanied singing in church was *very* good. I was quite proud of my old choir—I had not been inside the church for ever so long.

255: TO ROGER FRY

Yattendon
December 26, 1895

My dear Roger

Xmas Tree Day. The children all wild. Adults also much interested by your fascinating magnetic toy. I like the mechanical evolutions, the cross and spiral, best. Also good fun is to be got by arranging a fight between 2 needles and betting if necessary on one. A hairpin easily defeats a needle. It does it with great skill.

The children have had too many presents, but that doesn't matter much.

I am very much obliged to you for your present of Dickinson's book. I shall be delighted to possess it. I did not know whether it was intended for me to keep. I think I got one purchaser for it already. I liked it very much.

What fools the Americans are! Their economics and politics are worse than their art and literature.

Which leads on to Lane. Binyon told me about his publishing my namesake. I am really very sorry to be the cause of his making such a fool of himself; beyond that I don't care two straws. It cannot possibly do me any harm. And it is no business of mine. It is the business of a publisher (just as it is of any tradesman) to distinguish his wares, and not sell a different thing from what the purchasers ask for.

This is a new departure for publishers. It does not look to be a lasting game.

I hope that your father is better. We have had no accounts of him. We send our Xmas wishes and love to all the party.

yours ever
RB

256: TO MRS. MANLEY HOPKINS

Yattendon
January 29, 1896

Dear Mrs Hopkins

It was very stupid of me not to answer your letter at once, for I have now no excuse to give for my long delay, and cannot imagine how I can have let it remain so long. Time however does fly.

In your letter you said that you had a parcel of scraps of Gerard's music, and asked me if I should like to look through them.

I should of course very much like to see them, and I shall hope to do so some day when I am at Haslemere again, which I shall hope to be ere long, but unless you have any particular reason for sending them I am sure that I have not time just now to enter into their subtleties. Gerard had a notion of starting music, as everything else, on new lines, and I cannot without great difficulty follow his intentions so as to do them justice. Honestly I think that his ingenious inventions do not lead to anything, and I have not myself the delicacy of ear to fully understand them.

What little time I can give to music is taken up by a very practical concern in which I am now engaged, which is too long to give you the details of.

You kindly enquire after us. My mother keeps in good bodily health, but her memory has got so bad that it is very often difficult to have rational conversation with her. She is however very cheerful and quite free from serious pain of any kind.

All my household has been well, until at Xmas my wife fell suddenly ill. I don't exactly know how, but she had I suppose been doing too much, and had to go to bed for some time. She is now getting about again a little: but does not regain her strength very quickly.

This will account in great part for the better half of my silence. I think that my sister in law is going tomorrow to stay with the Redmaynes. Perhaps you will see her. I hope that you will: and you will then hear of us and we of you.

Hoping that you are all well, with our kindest regards to yourself and Mr. Hopkins, and to your daughter

I am yours sincerely
Robert Bridges

257: TO LIONEL MUIRHEAD

Yattendon
February 21, 1896

My dear Lionel

I want to hear that you are all right again. I shall envy you much in the matter of your third set of teeth. It is a good thing to have got that over. I have not many grinders of service now.

Whether you will come and see us? It is not the time of year to ask the children to accompany you.

My wife has been ailing ever since Xmas. She seems now to be getting slowly stronger, but she is not of much use yet.

The children are good fun.

I am translating Latin hymns for the 2nd part of our Hymnal which should be printed about June. I have done several, and will send them to you for your inspection and criticism.

Today I begin with the *Jesu dulcis memoria*. I like my translation, which you must sing in mind to the Latin tune.

The point in which I see it could be improved is that it would be better to keep the 3rd person in the first two verses. I could not manage this. I should be glad of any suggestions. Keep it a few days for that purpose.

yours ever
RB

Our kindest remembrances to M^rs L.

————

If you hold the sheet open you will have Latin opposite.

258: TO LIONEL MUIRHEAD

Seaford
March 30, 1896

My dear Lionel

I have never heard from you that you got all right again after that eye attack that you had. I was sorry not to meet you at Oxford, where I went to 2 of

Wooldridge's 3 lectures. Sir Henry Acland told me that he had sent you a special invitation to stay with him: and I was not without hopes of bringing you off to Yattendon by the evening train. We now have through trains from Oxford to Hampstead Norris, which I find a great convenience: though I was really less at Oxford last term than usual, owing to my wife being seedy. It is on her account that we came down here—last Wednesday till this next Wednesday—and I hope that we have got some good. Elizabeth is with us. HEW's lectures were very good, the last, which I did not hear but read at home, the best of all. He has now got out of the general history of the theory and that sort of thing, into the technique: on which his remarks are most illuminating. I suppose there has never been anything of the kind so good. He had poor audiences, but that was due to his deferring his lectures till just term-end: when everybody is engaged; he is however making his mark very surely. He came on to us for a week after the last, and arranged with me the 2nd Part of the Hymnal, for which the material had been collected. I think it will be more interesting than the first. I did nothing to press the sale of Part I, as I expect to be in so much better a position when Part II comes out. The correspondence is that we had only 20 £ assets, and are 37 £ in debt. Mr. Waterhouse is willing to pay this off, but I want to meet him about half way, and as you offered to help I shall make bold to ask if you have a sovereign or two to spare. Do not send anything but tell me if you wish to help. I shall not be sending in copy till June: and I think I shall not page for another month. My Mother will give 10 £. I think of getting subscribers beforehand for P^t II. P^t I has been adopted by the choir at St Barnabas Pimlico. We expect to be leaving home for a month in middle of June. Cannot you, I mean both, come and pay us a visit before then? It would be very kind of you. I have been getting rather melancholy. I am glad to see that Chamberlayne is advocating my doctrines of colonial free trade—which I have preached for 20 years to deaf ears. Our love to you all.

yours ever

RB

I had a terrible accident to my big grey horse. He fooled and fell in the lorre box and broke his ischium. He has been in slings since, and *seems mending!!*

259: TO WILLIAM BUTLER YEATS

Yattendon
Newbury
June 1, 1896

Dear Sir

I have been reading your poems, which my friend Mr Mackail introduced me to. I write to tell you how much I admire a great deal of them, and what pleasure they gave me.

I know that I run the risk of being considered impertinent, but I had rather you should think that than perhaps misinterpret my silence.

Hoping that you will excuse the liberty that I take in writing, and that you will write more and meet soon with the success which your work must ultimately reach,

I am yours truly
Robert Bridges

260: TO LIONEL MUIRHEAD

Yattendon
August 26, 1896

My dear Lionel

I said at dinner this evening that I would write you a letter. Wife was going to assist me to compile it, but now she has gone to bed early, having caught a bad cold the other day, and being in the thick of it. We got home about 10 days or a fortnight ago, after spending a month with the children in Somersets on the Mendips most of the time just outside Wells. Since we got home I have been very busy. We are now getting Part II of the Hymn book out, and it is astonishing what a lot of detail there is to attend to. They are abominably slow printing it too, so that it goes on wasting one's time much more than it need, though somehow it generally turns out that we make use of the delay. You will be glad to hear that this 2nd Part will be better than Part I. I hardly thought that we should keep the standard so high, but it is rich in fine things. I have got about 8 or ten plain song tunes in and most of them with new translations of my own. Also I have provided words for several fine tunes that had no words at all to fit them. I find that the book is getting to be pretty well known or at least acknowledged, and I hope that this 2nd Part will establish it firmly.

I hope that you are all well. I wish there was any chance of seeing you. If you could come down any time we should be delighted—especially if you could bring Mrs. L M with you. Our plans are that we shall now be at home indefinitely. *Next Tuesday* we hope to go over for the day to the Arkwrights the other side of Newbury. Mr. and Mrs. HEW are to be staying there, and I must have a talk with him before he goes abroad. I understand that he is starting for Venice in less than a fortnight. I don't know what he has been doing in the way of preparing lectures for next year. I fancy that he has been editing music for the Purcell Society.

Our parson is away for a holiday and his delirium tenens and his wife (d t i wife) are first rate whist players. Unfortunately we have not had more than one opportunity of making use of them. My wife has taken to the bicycle and I have ordered one for myself. It has not come yet. I fancy that when we both are mounted we shall be able to come over to your place in the morning quite easily. The roads however just about us are so bad that there is not much use in them till we get some 4 miles off. This is a bore.

I won't trouble you to read any more but sit down and write us a line to say how you are—and when you will come and have pipes and whist with us. You couldn't do better.

yours ever
RB

Our kindest remembrances also to Mrs. L. M.

I am reading Chateaubriand's "Mémoires d'outre tombe" D'you know'em?

261: TO LIONEL MUIRHEAD

Yattendon
Monday, September 21, 1896

My dear Lionel

I had a long letter from HEW yesterday, written before he can have received ours. I send it on to you for your perusal.

I hope you arrived all right. We have not yet heard of Jenny's arrival at Folkstone though she went off armed with addressed telegrams and postcards. I have just telegraphed enquiries.

We enjoyed your visit, as Bo would say, "too much": and regretted that you left so soon. I miss the Vandyck in the study too. I liked it extremely—it seemed to me to be a boon to men—and really in some respects more "useful" than the original can be. Except in a large hall those huge portraits dwarf everything.

With our kind regards to M^{rs} L

yours affectionately
RB

Send Mrs D. the Feast of Bacchus first, if you have not already posted anything to her.

P.S.

We have just heard of Jenny's arrival. By the way I don't at all like the notion of your riding the bicycle. The great point of it is the speed that you go and not seeing well on one side of you might give you a bad accident any day. It is impossible to ride them and not go fast, and that makes any accident dangerous.—I shouldn't be tempted if I were you, and there is no real fun in riding them.

262: TO LIONEL MUIRHEAD

Yattendon
October 21, 1896

My dear Lionel

The Psalter cover is lovely and we are very much obliged to you for it. We shall certainly use it just as it is except that I shall put an *L M desig. or del* at the bottom of it in a corner. Its being a little too large does not matter because the photographic process can of course reduce it as easily as not. I suppose more easily than not. The Psalter is at present at Cambridge being read over by the Professor there for errors of the pen. It should return in a day or two when it will go straight to Oxford for reproduction—all the preliminaries having been settled.

My wife will no doubt thank you for the curry recipe, and I shall hope to benefit by it.

To-day I have a touch of lumbago which I am trying to combat. I have been to the Board of Guardians on my bicycle and have got home without its being much worse. It came on just after I started.

On Friday we have a lot of people coming here to sing mottets [*sic*] and madrigals. We hope to have a really fine sing. If it succeeds it will be the first of a series of monthly meetings and will lead to a *Yattendon Mottet* [*sic*] *and Madrigal book* in the manner of the Hymnal. This would be great fun. I should think that HEW would resign the Slade Professorship or talk nothing but counterpoint at his lectures.

I have not heard from him again.

yours ever

RB

263: TO LIONEL MUIRHEAD

Yattendon
October 29, 1896

My dear Lionel

I am very sorry that you have been seedy with a cold. We have pulled through the change pretty well.

You will have got my post-card of yesterday which answers one part of your letter. I shall see Hart in a few days and will then write to you. I do not think that the reduction of one inch or 1½ inch will affect the size of the letters at all. It would be a great pity for you to have all the trouble of doing the page again. It could not be better, and I expect that the rubbings out etc. can be got rid of easily from the stone if they show too much. You shall hear what Hart says.

I am much obliged to you for sending me HEW's letter which I return—I had not heard from him since the letter which I sent to you.

We had a great sing here the other day 9 voices—all Palestrina and Lassus. Everyone could read well except me. I think we shall get some jolly singing here now. A new tenor and his wife are at hand. He is excellent.

yours ever

RB

264: TO SAMUEL GEE

Yattendon
November 4, 1896

Dear Dr Gee

I send you same post old proofs of all the pages of my hymn book so far which I think you would look at with any great interest—

The object of the book is primarily to set the music right, which at present is a disgrace to English musicians.

In the 1st issue of 25 hymns I kept to the words of the common hymn books in the churches, because I thought that would be most convenient, in fact that any attempt to improve the words also would wreck the chances of the music being used. Since then I have found that the people are more anxious for new words than to have their music set right. So I have taken the exactly opposite course of pushing the music by the attraction of new words.

These I hope you will like. It is going on now pretty fast.

I send you also a specimen "introduction" or advertisement—and list of tunes in Part I. The guinea book is very fine indeed—

———

In reading the words of the hymns you will see that where the verses are of 8 lines the first 4 lines of each verse are on the left side page and the last 4 on the right.

Also in the Latin hymns the first English verse is under the music on left page and the first Latin under the "Gregorian" notation on right hand side—the rest of the verses follow on right hand side parallel.

———

I have tried to get the mere antiquity out of the old hymns.

yours ever
RB

Part II hymns 26–50 will not be out much before Xmas.

265: TO HENRY NEWBOLT

Yattendon
November 25, 1896

My dear Newbolt

I return Yates & Drinkwater. I prefer the former and have bought a fatter edition. D I could not read—after much reading I am left with a strong impression of the perverse follies of man, especially of the paradoxical desertions from side to side, which appear to follow some law, like that of the unaddressed letters in the Post office, and of the waste of ammunition. I did not get to the interesting part, but I must return the book now. I shall look out for a 2nd hand copy of the earliest impression, and read the end some day when I am inclined.

Have you been writing any more verses? I don't think R K has been doing well to judge by the reviews.

"When Omer twanged his blooming lyre" etc.

Hoping you are all well

With our kindest regards

yours sincerely
R Bridges

266: TO WILLIAM BUTLER YEATS

Yattendon
Newbury
December 10, 1896

Dear Sir

Your letter is as great a surprise as it is a pleasure to me this morning—and as you date from a hotel I answer by return. When I wrote to you I purposely wrote such a letter as you could answer or not—for nothing is more tedious than admiration from people with whom one does not feel in sympathy—and had I said as much as I felt about your poetry you would have been constrained to thank me. As it was I was reconciling myself to the idea that you didn't care whether I liked your poetry or not. As a matter of fact I can read very little poetry so called—and your book is a great exception. It has given me a great deal of delight, and I find magnificent things and very beautiful things in it. And it is most pleasant to me to hear that you have cared for my verse—and will therefore welcome my admiration for your work—

I hope when spring comes that you will consent to pay us a visit here. The country is pretty enough, though as you date your preface from Sligo I must not boast—still I feel safe from comparison because all is so different here—

I wonder what you are doing in Paris, and whether French farce delights you. I do not like Paris in the winter, but they have become more musical than they were when I used to be there.

I ought to say that your letter to me is unsigned—from which I hope I may conclude that you are in the middle of some piece of work which has got hold of you—I cannot make a mistake however in recognising in it the answer to the only letter which I have written in the required sense.

Thank you very much for promising to send me your forthcoming book. I should greedily buy anything of yours on the strength of the poems—

believe me yours sincerely

Robert Bridges

I should like to write to you some day about your poems, or better talk with you.—I think you have hit off one form (and really a new one as you do it) perfectly—in Cuchulin and the bag of dreams. By the way let *bag* stand in last

line—why did you alter it? But I liked most of your alterations—
I saw the 2 editions—

267: TO LIONEL MUIRHEAD

Yattendon
January 15, 1897

My dear Lionel

It's very well to imagine us sitting at breakfast enjoying the prospect of beautiful collotypes! I'll tell you presently what has happened. But first of all I must send you my new year greetings, and my wife's, and to all your party. It is a great mistake that you didn't settle down somewhere nearer, so that we could have occasional sings and whistings. This awful Xmas is now passing by, and we are hoping to get settled down quietly again. This year has been worse than ever, though we have done less than usual; in fact we have softened only and scarcely acted at all. And the weather has been so abominably soft and unpleasant that there has not seemed even the usual customary reason for "keeping Xmas" at all.

The hymn book has been going on *very* well. Awfully slowly, but I can't make them go any faster at the press. When they have finished the 8 pages which they are now printing there will be only 8 more pages to finish this "part," which will come to end of 50th hymn and 80th page, and I shall go on at once without the intervalum temporis which I indulged in last time. There is a lot of my work in this 'part' in the way of words. Some of it successful I hope. It is a better part than P^t I, and I have got lots of material for going on with P^t III.

But as for the Psalter. They said that they could not print collotype on both sides of page, so we decided on photolithograph, and this looks very well at its best. But they did the first 4 pages first, containing the preface and heading, on which my wife had spent so much pains, and the photographer in order to bring things up to the utter possible blackness "touched up" the lettering! Can you imagine such villany [*sic*]? The man is a sheer fool, and the worst possible draughtsman. So the page is of course *ruined,* and has to be all written again.

We had worked very hard at the job, and got quite sick of it, so that it was only with the greatest patience that we finished it, and to have the thing wantonly destroyed was a pretty bad trial of temper. I used all the oaths that I could remember without much satisfaction, and there the matter stands now. I shall probably in a few days set them to work at the end, and by the time they work to the beginning going backward we may have got the work done again.

I told Hart that this sort of thing explained why he could not compete with Paris, if he employed such unintelligent workmen. But I am afraid that he has not the right sort of intelligence himself.

I wish very much to get an artist permanently employed at the Clarendon Press. I think that it will very likely be done—

I suppose that you cannot run down for a few days soon. It would be very jolly if you would come, and I know that my wife would be glad if Mrs. M came with you—but, she, my wife, was laid up last November, much in the same way as she was in December 1896. But she got better again much quicker. Still she has not been very grand: and she is not I fear really up to entertaining. Therefore while I do not scruple to send you a bachelor invitation, I think that just now would not be a good time for a *double* visit.

I am sorry to write so badly but Xmas has driven me wild, and now I put down my pen to—no I don't put it down at all.—I end this letter in order to begin another to concoct a courteous refusal to Canon Scott Holland who asks me to write a poem for 'the Commonwealth'—I *suppose* a high church socialistic magazine!

yours ever

RB

268: TO LIONEL MUIRHEAD

Yattendon
February 10, 1897

My dear Lionel

It will be delightful if you will come on Tuesday next. I am very sorry to hear about your sister in law's illness. I hope that she is now getting better every day.

Pray give her our kind regards and say how sorry we are to hear of her illness.

The Psalter is nearly repaired. We had a turn to at it the other day.

The Rector here wants to put up in the church a list of all the incumbents since the flood. My wife promised to do it for him. It was then to be painted or written.—Now he has changed his mind and will have it carved in oak. She thought she could manage the design for that by using the freer forms of the alphabet used in monumental brasses, but he wants something quite legible to rustics, so she is thinking of cutting herself clear of the business, as she does not know any good examples of such work and has not time to invent anything new, which would be likely to be really good—besides knowing nothing about oak carving. She asked me if I would ask you if you by any chance have any drawings of wooden inscriptions and if so whether you would bring them with you.

We shall be delighted to see the coronal.

yours ever

RB

Kindest remembrances to your wife please

269: TO WILLIAM BUTLER YEATS

Yattendon
Newbury
March 8, 1897

Dear Sir

Now that the weather seems to promise better I am writing to renew my invitation.

If a Saturday till Monday visit suits your work, that is convenient to us—but there is no objection to any other day.

The trains from London are

Paddington.

1.55 or 5.15

and *Newbury* where you change

3.48 - 7.3

and at Hampstead Norris (our station)

4.11   7.31

If the 2nd train happens to be late it is sometimes inconvenient for dinner arrangements.

I could meet you at Hampstead Norris by any train that you fix on.

We have only one spare bedroom in the house, so that unless we make a fixture sometime beforehand I cannot promise to be able to put you up exactly under my roof, but I have another roof, at the end of my garden, where my friends often stay, a sort of dépendance, and I do not think that you would object to it, though I should not like to ask you here without the warning, lest you should think your reception discourteous.

I very much hope that you will come.

You will be received in the name of a poet, and find others here besides myself who are friends of your work.

believe me yours very truly

R Bridges

In case you should choose a Sunday you may like to know that *Sunday clothes* are not particularly useful here, but evening clothes are sometimes convenient.

270: TO WILLIAM BUTLER YEATS

Yattendon

March 17, 1897

Dear Mr. Yeats

I am very sorry indeed that you are engaged in such a dull task—and I am afraid that you may not be in a particularly good humour with me when you come.—But let me reassure you on one point—i.e. that you need not be afraid of hurting my feelings, and are, as far as I am concerned, at full liberty to say anything that you wish. I lack that distinctive mark of the poet, the touchiness, which resents criticism. Honestly I am indifferent to these things: (and I don't mind if anyone should say that I am vain of being proud—) —But you would please me very much if you would in your review say two things, (1) whether the plays are *readable*—amusing, i.e. whether you want to put them down after you have begun them—because this is the main point, and (2) I should be glad of a plain statement that my plays are for sale at 2/6 each, because the papers always make out that they cannot be bought or are privately printed, or out of print, or all three.

Nero p^t II, which completed my volume of 8 plays, was sent to *44* papers or reviews, and so far as I know it had *no* notice whatever except in the Times.

I shall look forward to your coming and hope to do away with any bad impression left by your surfeiting on my old work—

Unfortunately the weather has gone back again—but I hope it will mend before end of next week.—We have had, as far as the weather goes, a most wretched year.

Send me a line to say which train you come by.—Our station is Hampstead Norris—change at Newbury—*from* Paddington—

yours very truly
R Bridges

271: TO WILLIAM BUTLER YEATS

Yattendon
Newbury
March 30, 1897

My dear Yeats

We enjoyed your visit very much and I hope that you will think of Yattendon as a place where you might some day run down for a week's country air and retirement in the Summer.

You left your dress shoes behind you. I sent them off by parcel post today. I hope that they have reached you safely.

I have read most of the book and come to a great deal that I like very much, but it is so very unlike anything that I know that I have not formed any judgment of it and shall not till I have reread it all carefully. I do not know whether you would care to have it criticised. This is of course merely a practical question, as to whether you imagine I might chance to say something which would be of use to you. If you wish for criticism you will let me know.

Today has been lovely. I wish Sunday had been like it. We took the children out into the woods and gathered fircones. You did not see any of our woods, or rather forests; which I now much regret as they are our chief attraction.

By the way I liked some of the lyrics in the Secret Rose, especially "O what to me the little room"—I hope that you will take care of your body and that the Saints or goddesses will preserve you from too much of your Rosa Alchemica. I am glad that Michael Robartes is dead.

My wife joins in kindest regards.

Believe me yours very sincerely
R. Bridges

272: TO LIONEL MUIRHEAD

Yattendon
March 31, 1897

My dear Lionel

Thousand thanks for the Post. Without it we should have missed Jameson's examination. It made me think much better of him. I only knew him through

Herkomer's portrait, it is a curse to be painted by Herkomer especially if as apparently in Jameson's case the soul is so much superior to the body. To omit the spirit and paint the flesh as Herkomer paints flesh is a dull kind of art. The saints keep us from "single vision and Newton's sleep"!! From which errors we have been providentially guarded during the last 3 days, having entertained a spiritualist of the first water, the young poet, W. B. Yeats. He is an extremely nice fellow, but wild in his mind, living with spirits and fairies. We liked him immensely, and he was excitedly entertaining. Still one can have enough of spirits—

You were not at HEW's last lectures. We went up for the night and stayed at Trinity. The lectures were better than ever and HEW got much more in touch with his audience, provoking murmurs from them when he said good things. So that I hope now that he will begin to be quite himself. He also gave a *very* good report of his health.—I hope that will continue, but he broke his regime a little at Oxford, and with us afterwards, and I have not heard his doctor's report since he got back to town.

We talked over 3rd part of Hymnal. I am becoming quite a recognised hymnologist; the Cowley Fathers applied to me the other day to give them something for one of their special occasions.

The Psalter is not yet in a condition to ask for your cover—I don't know indeed how they are getting on with it. I have left it entirely in Hart's hands being sick of the bother of it. I expect that he will do it all right.

The lovely yesterday we spent the afternoon of in the woods gathering fircones—

Hoping you are well, and that your sister in law recovers her health, with wife's and my kind regards to her and Mrs. L. M.

I am yours ever

RB

273: TO LIONEL MUIRHEAD

Marine Crescent

No. 12

Folkestone

May 8, 1897

My dear Lionel

I was very glad to get a letter from you. We are also spring cleaning—and took all the children away for some sea-air, after spending a week with one of my wife's uncles in Surrey. You know Folkestone and can tell whether you would like to join us—the run from Reading is very easy though they make you change carriages too often. We could give you a bed in the house, and we would play whist in the evenings. But I'll bet any money that you won't come when you hear that I have got a touch of rheumatism. I think it is passing off, and I am trying hot salt baths. But I am not really at all well. I can't do without exercise and can't take it with the rheumatics in my leg. I like the place. The town is really much better than the average English town: and I made the acquaintance of Allebone, and of Maestrani the first day. If my rheumatism allows of it we hope to make one or two excursions—We have got our bicycles with us—to Canterbury, and to my old birthplace Walmer, where it will delight me to see the old paths that I scrambled over when a small boy. We hope to get back to Yattendon before the end of the month. And not till then will the 2nd part of the Hymnal be issued. I expect it is ready now, but I had arranged to issue it before I left home, when some foolish and needless delay supervened and I had to go away before I could announce it. I mean to send away a good many copies and advertisements *simultaneously*—so that I can't work it from here.

Meanwhile the Cowley Fathers have applied to me through F. W. Puller, to provide them with a hymn to bury themselves to: and I have been modelling Prudentius to suit them. I must send you a copy of it. I suppose they will adopt it. But isn't it odd??!!

What you say about the portrait interests me much. I am truly glad that you have destroyed that hand. I hope that the work which you are doing will not hurt your eyes.

The lithographic plates are now all made for the Psalter, and it only remains to take the impressions. When I go next to Oxford I will take them your cover drawings.

What a mess this war has been, and what asses the Philohellenes have made of themselves! I am truly sorry for the Greeks, but more for the cause which they seem to be damaging by their wild incompetence. I have today read Lord Salisbury's speech at the Primrose meeting and was as much surprised at his confidence in European peace as I was delighted at his hits at Gladstone and Harcourt. They were inimitable. Dizzy couldn't have done it better.

If you want a week at the sea come here; but don't come expecting much of me, though I do hope to be better next week.

yours affectionately
RB

Wife's kindest remembrances.

274: TO WILLIAM BUTLER YEATS

Yattendon
June 15, 1897

My dear Yeats

I was at Oxford on Friday and Saturday, and on Sunday had two visitors here from London. One was Binyon, the other a man whom I had not met before, who was quite enthusiastic about your work especially the two volumes of tales. I had read the two books again with the intention of fulfilling my promise of writing to you about them, so I discussed with him the judgment that I had arrived at and found that he quite agreed with me. And this I confess makes me hesitate less in telling you the one criticism that I have to make without further consideration.

I think that the stories are artistically the worse for an apparent insistence on the part of the writer to have them taken otherwise (i.e. more seriously) than he suspects the reader would naturally take them.

Of course I know that it is your intention that they should be so taken, only I do not think that the intention should appear. The manner of presentation should be sufficient and I do not see that you need distrust the power of your presentation.

This is rather a subtle matter, because in looking again at the stories I don't quite see where I get my impression of this "insistence" from. I fancy it lies chiefly in your sometimes just overstepping the mark—e.g. in "Regina Pigmeorum." The sentence "I asked the young girl etc" will not fail to make readers wonder at the personality of the writer.—I should like to talk this over with you some day when we can refer to places in the stories—I should not have liked to offer the objection if my feeling about it had not been very strong, and if I had not found another admirer with exactly the same impression.

Reading the stories again made me admire the workmanship more than ever. The gentleman in question said that he thought the prose style better than any that he knew—and I am inclined to agree with him.—It is extremely beautiful.

Omitting the last story of the Secret Rose I don't know that I have any thing to mention that seemed to me below level. Some of the stories of course are more telling and interesting than others—I do not however fall in comfortably with the humour of crucifying the beggar. The accounts of the gleemen are splendid—and the humour all through is of the best.

I expect that while we agree absolutely about the necessity for mysticism, we do not take quite the same view of the value of the phenomena in themselves, but I can't write about this.

When I re-read "The Secret Rose" I marked a number of places where I thought a slight alteration of words would improve the flow, or where it seemed to me that you had made a slip. I should like to go over these with you some day in view of a new edition. It seems to me that these stories are an excellent proof that English "short stories" may be written in as good style as the best French ones. I hope you will do more short stories of Irish life—

I am not *in the least* overstating my admiration of your 'style'. I am *very grateful* to you for your presenting me with these two volumes, and I shall try and profit by them. The writing is (I should have said) too good for success in journalism. Is it not so?—No one has ever told me of it—Perhaps the somewhat bizarre character of the subjects puts people off the mark.

Please come and see us again before long and be assured meanwhile of my blessing and high esteem.

yours very sincerely

R Bridges

P.S.

Thanks for "the Bookman." I was forgetting about it. I was pleased that you quoted as an example of good rhythm the same lines that the Athenaeum quoted as an example of bad rhythm. This is as it should be. Also you amused my wife very much by numbering "The Yattendon Hymnal" among my original works. Many thanks for the trouble which you took with my things reading them etc.

275: TO RICHARD WATSON DIXON

Yattendon
Newbury
July 5, 1897

My dear Dixon

I am very sorry, but you are quite right. I have a list of all to whom I sent Part I and your name is not in it. I can't remember how it was but I suppose you were away from home at the time, and did not return till I had fabricated the idea that I had sent copy to you.

I am very sorry for the trouble which you have had in searching for it. But Part I doesn't much matter—and I only want to know from you about *words*, and only this about them, viz. what conclusions you have come to about hymn words from your recent engagement on the committee.

There is I think a peculiarity about my book in the suitableness of words to music whereby both gain a great deal—but that is a question not to be entered upon. To exhibit it every hymn must be sung through: and sung as intended.

I am going up to London. Next I think to stay 3 days with the Bishop. I will write to Burne Jones and see if he is at home, and if so whether I can see him.

I am pretty well, but not in very good spirits.—Monica joins in love to you etc.etc.

yours affectionately
RB

276: TO LIONEL MUIRHEAD

Yattendon
September 17, 1897

My dear Lionel

I was sorry to hear such a bad account of your sister in law. Acland, who was over here staying with the Gulls, told me about it. I had not met him before, and of course I could not help liking him, but I am sorry that I saw very little of him. We also had visitors, and we did not cross much. He seemed to be much pleased with the portrait. You ask about the Psalter.—I expect it may be another month before it is quite ready but I had proofs of it all nearly a month ago: the hand-printing of these things takes some time. We are busy just now with the third part of the Hymnal. HEW paid us a visit and I schemed it out with him. We planned nearly 40 tunes and a good part of them are done. He made some very fine settings: but I am sorry to say that he has got now entirely involved in his xt book on counterpoint, so that I doubt if I shall get any more settings out of 1m for a long while. These same settings set me a good task, for most of the 1nes had to be provided with words. I have diligently applied myself thereto ith a certain amount of success. I have certainly made some things which go to 1e tunes and are unlike the ordinary stuff. I have been much more successful eally than I had expected, and I am making use of the inclination or aptitude hich the effort has produced, and going on at them still. My impression is that 1e 3rd part of the Hymnal will be better than the 2nd. Anyhow it is as well to be 1nder that delusion while one is working at it.—We have had a good many isitors. Tomorrow the Bellairs are coming. Today we have suffered from the 'ouble and excitement of packing off a sick Swiss nursery maid, whose father 1me from Switzerland to fetch her back: she insisted on taking off one of my ortmanteaux and one of my wife's boxes—but even at that price I am glad that 1e is gone.—I don't like the Swiss. I'll never have another. Their only virtue is arly rising.

My wife has a bad cold, and has gone to bed early. We think of being at home ll about this time next month, when we intend visiting London and Cambridge, lso perhaps a visit in Cheshire. If it should suit you to run down here before 1en, so much the better. I should like very much to show you the hymnal work.)ne cannot get too much criticism. The 2nd part is getting 'appreciated'. The hildren are well, and I don't think that I have any news. Some one showed us an 1musing game which any one can play at. You might find it useful, but I expect ou know it.—It seems very well known. It consists in trying to discover a quota- ion (a line of poetry is best) from dots in place of letters. E.g. I think of "on haliced flowers that lies" and write down

```
..  .........  .......  ....  ....
To find it out you ask me for an E
..  ......E.  .......  ....  ....
```

vhich I put in there. Wherever I like it I have any choice. Then you ask for a T 1r for other letters, and if you ask for one that is not in the sentence it counts gainst you as one life. 5 lives is extinction.

It is amusing enough. It is not necessary to know the quotation. The one I give s a difficult one.

with our love
yours affectionately
RB

g.
. ..A. I. E.
...E RS T H..
 .I E S

Vhat is this?
..E. .O R D. T H..
 .I E S

What is this?
...E.   .O R D.   A N D
...I E.   .A

E

277: TO MRS. MANLEY HOPKINS

                                                                Yattendo
                                                                Newbur
                                                    October 11, 189

My dear Mrs Hopkins

I must write and send you my sincerest sympathy. It is difficult looking back t
those Hampstead days to believe that one is 53 years old: and that our fir
acquaintance was so long ago. I knew that Mr Hopkins had been failing i
strength for some time, and I was not surprised to hear of his death. I hope tha
it was easy and painless, and that you keep your good health. I am very sorry t
see you so seldom—and I am doing some work now which I think would intere
you, and in which I should much value your sympathy and criticism. But thes
are matters on which it is [as] difficult to write as it is pleasant to talk.—I shoul
like to tell you that when you once paid us a visit here we got very fond of M
Hopkins, and I am sure that my wife will never forget him. That visit was a grea
pleasure to us. Please some day when you have time write me a letter telling m
about yourself and family.

My mother is still living. She is in fairly good health except for the failure o
her memory, and a general haziness of ideas.—She would not remember eve
your name, and barely recognises her own children sometimes, though at othe
times she is more like herself. She is however generally free from pain an
cheerful or easily cheered.

We are all pretty well. My youngest is now 5 years old.

I am afraid that my wife's uncle [*sic*. See note.] Mrs. Redmayne, your neigh
bour is very near her end. It is a sad thing for that family. She is one of th
influenza victims.

With my kindest remembrances and sincerest sympathy to all your family

                                            I am yours most sincerely
                                                        Robert Bridges

278: TO LIONEL MUIRHEAD

                                                                Yattendo
                                                    November 24, 189

My dear Lionel

I know that I am knee-deep in owed letters to you, but I am afraid that it i
chiefly on the subject of the hymns that I ought to write, and I have been able t

to nothing lately in that department. So that I must again put off. I have got on and now rather a troublesome job for Parry, who wants me to provide him with a libretto for the Leeds festival next year, and I managed to persuade him to try some quite new form.—I have to provide something to help to carry it, and have a toughish job. Of course I have aimed a little higher than I find easy to carry out—if you will excuse this muddle of metaphor. Then there is another thing which I am engaged to write for, of which more anon. I don't know when I shall get back to the hymns. The last thing I did for them was to read through all the Wesley hymns—Perhaps you don't know (I didn't) that those two Wesleys, John and Charles, wrote 13 volumes 8vo of 400 pages each chock full of hymns without gaps or blanks.—Well I went through them and emerged with a strange notion of the Wesleys. I never made such a study of monomania. It seemed to be like that. It was awfully depressing, more depressing than the tunes in Sternhold and Hopkins, and they are death-dealing. I think I must show them up some day in an article thereupon.—To leave Psalms we have been well. Bo has been developing. He has now a passion for riddles; he makes up the most amusing nonsense and renders it impossible to eat at lunch for laughing. One of his riddles today was "Why was I born horrid?" The answer to this riddle was "I don't know"—and he really seemed to see the sense of it. When he was counting the other day, the nature of the decimal system dawned upon him, and he said, Well, it must have been a very clever man who invented that".—To leave Bo, we had an extremely pleasant holiday, which finished, as I think I told you, with 3 days at Eton. I did not like being so old there. Are you going up to Saints Club Hood portrait dinner? I may go but am not certain.

The Psalters may be out any day now, they have been some time at the binders—I will send you one. Rothenstein's portrait of me is out in the "English Portraits." I wonder what you will think of it. The "letterpress" about me is altogether too much. It does not quite compare me to Shakespeare, but it could not be more friendly and laudatory. I should be ashamed of it and sorry, but I am really rather amused to think how it will nauseate the London critics. It is enough to make F. T. Palgrave turn in his grave. It's a good thing it didn't come out in his lifetime. Now here's the end of the paper. I hope Monica wrote her thanks for the book.

with love
your affectionate
RB

279: TO LIONEL MUIRHEAD

Yattendon
December 1, 1897

My dear Lionel

I am glad that you don't dislike the portrait so much after all. It is really rather amusing to get a glimpse of what people will think of one after one is dead.—I don't suppose that one is much like what one thinks of oneself—and the impression that one makes on others is I suppose as truly what one is, as anything can be. Nothing amuses me more in this department of phenomena than that anyone should imagine that I am "goodlooking"—I think R's picture is flattering, though it can't be thought beautiful!

I have not heard the Professor's verdict. He and his wife are going to Bournemouth for a week or two at Xmas. Your letter came this morning. I was looking at your hymn for Van Eyck last night. I think with one or two amendments it will be very fine indeed, but I have not fitted it to any tune yet, and I won't ask you to alter it till I get the music. But if you like to work at it you may (if you wish) entirely discard the rhyme of the odd lines—the eights—and only rhyme the sixes. You will probably find that this will enable you to say better things—the choice of words being so much freer. Common Measure does not *read* so well when only the alternate lines rhyme, but the other rhyme is not at all missed in singing—at least most tunes do away entirely with the necessity—and I myself like hymns better without it. The freedom gained is enormous, and there is also a *general sense of freedom* given by the absence of rhyme which is difficult to explain. It may be in part due to the long association of rubbish with this metre.—As soon as I find a tune I will write. It wants a good one—and there are plenty—but I don't yet know the right one—and I shall not be able to leave my work for Parry just yet.

> In haste (as always)
> yours (ditto)
> RB

Since writing this I have got copies of Psalter. I send you a Large paper.—I could not get the finial ornament in the right place or cover of this size so omitted it.— It is on all the small copies and *inside* the large. The large are much the best.

280: TO LIONEL MUIRHEAD

> Yattendon
> December 15, 1897

My dear Lionel

My mother died yesterday morning quite suddenly, after eating a good breakfast.

I am extremely thankful that the end was so easy and painless and that we had not the trial of a farewell scene.

The funeral is to be on Monday at 3. Carriages will meet the down trains from Pangbourne, but I cannot offer to *put you up* as I expect we may be full of relatives.

If it is a fine day it is not perhaps impossible that you may come but I shall not expect you. If you wish to come let me know the train, that I may be sure to provide carriage.

> RB

81: TO HENRY NEWBOLT

Yattendon
December 15, [1897]

My dear Newbolt
   My mother died suddenly yesterday.
   I just send you a line today about your verses. I think they are not very suitable
or music. It would be good practice for you in this department to *translate them*
into musical oration. Imagine a choir singing them, and yourself one of the chorus,
and you will soon find the bad places you would not like.
   It is not that to begin with,
and all the grammar is too reflective in scheme.
chool is a bad climax being a prosaic metaphor—the sense of the word out of key
with the sentiment.
   All the stanzas begin badly—i. e. *weak* words. Every word should be interesting
or well sounding.
   Correct it and I'll send it to Parratt.
   He is getting on but I fancy there is time enough.

yours sincerely
RB

Any good hymn tune would serve as a test sung slowly.

82: TO MRS. MANLEY HOPKINS

Yattendon
December 28, 1897

Dear Mrs Hopkins
   Thank you very much for your kind letter of sympathy.—You will be glad to
hear that my dear mother's death was, after all her last years of failing strength,
quite sudden: so that we were spared all pain and sorrow, except that of losing
her—and her mind had latterly become so weak, that we had really gone
through the parting before.
   We had a very beautifully sung service in our little village, and I have chosen a
spot for her grave near the old yew tree, where strangely enough we found that
in our old crowded little churchyard no one had ever been buried before. I hope
over the place to set up a churchyard cross—
   I know these particulars will interest you. I should very much like to think that
you would come down and stay a few days with us this summer.
   May I ask your acceptance of the first instalment of my church hymn book.
With our united best wishes for the new year,

yours very sincerely
Robt Bridges

283: TO SAMUEL GEE

Yattendo\
December 29, 189'

My dear Gee

We both send you our best wishes (to you and Mrs Gee) for the New Year—anc thanks for yours.—My dear mother's death was a release from a most undesir able condition for as you know she had not been in any respect her-self for a long while and it was a great mercy to be spared at the end what might have been ; painful scene. She had taken a good breakfast, and was being dressed when she complained that she felt a pain.—The maid asked if there was anything that she could do for her, but she said it didn't matter, and she would go on dressing anc "not give any trouble". Then she fell back dead. I feel that I shall have to face the sorrow which her loss will be to us, when the old memories return as they will d(after the sad routine of these last years has faded away—

We are all well. I can't say how busy I am. The whole of the family busines really falls on me and it will be some days before I can wipe off the correspon dence of casual enquirers and relatives. This must account for the emptiness o this letter. I have too to finish a 'hymn of Nature' which my old friend Parry i going to set to music for the Gloucester Festival this next year. It is something new, and I hope you will like it. I am not sure.—I am not—in answer to youi enquiries—giving up poetry more than I can help. In some respects I am doing more than I have done—for what I write now contains pretty plain statements o the 'faith' which I believe is expressed in all my work. I feel to have grown to see clearly what is meant by what I believe—I am not sure that it may not be a pretty widely received expression of the thought of our time. What will you say to this; I should like to talk of these matters. I send you as an étrenne the 1st installmen of the Yattendon hymns, which if I have a few more years of life will be ; pretentious work. Did you see my portrait and puff in "English portraits" 2/6 published by Grant Richards?—I come in N° 7.

yours affectionately\
RB

284: TO LIONEL MUIRHEAD

Yattendo\
January 27, 1898

My dear Lionel

I am engaged in packing up all my mother's effects for distribution among the family. There is going to be no sale—So you may imagine that I am pretty wel occupied. We have had 3 days of it and shall not finish on Monday. This and the preliminaries have prevented my writing to you; also I have had a great bout a hymns, with a greater appearance of success than I anticipated, so I have been rather sticking to them at odd times, while I felt in the mood.

Else I should certainly have written at once to condole with you on your more serious packings. It will be a comfort however to you that you can put your things into vans at your door and not really risk any thing on roads. But what a trouble! And what a searching of heart to know how to dispose them at Haseley.—You must be very sorry to break up house, but I am not sure that you have not been there long enough. I hope you will be very happy at your own old home. I suppose it means that you will end your days there. Not a bad place if you have money in proportion to the house.

This wretched winter has not been very favourable to us. The children have all of them been indoors for more than a week with colds and coughs—and I had a great scare the day before yesterday, when I found that our under nursemaid (whom we had always supposed a strong healthy girl) was in the first stage of consumption. Fortunately she had been very little with the children; but I shan't be comfortable about them for a long while.

We have had musical visitors—

We have begun a governess. She is spending her first week in the house. Then she is going to lodge at the tinshop. She is a very quiet nice sort of girl. I hope she has not got consumption—I remember Goldsmith's "The dog it was that died". But really one's sympathies are not with the dog—Benedic is very well—I am pretty well—only occasionally desperately hypochondriacal.—I am writing (or rather have written) a new Cantata for Parry. The Purcell Ode is being performed at Newbury this spring.—My wife had a jolly long letter from yours the other day which I read with great pleasure.

—Bo is coming on very fast—

yours affectionately
RB

285: TO HENRY NEWBOLT

Yattendon
February 8, 1898

My dear Newbolt

I need not say how delighted I am with the success of Miss Coleridge's book. I am sure that she owes you a deal of gratitude for your bothering with the publishers etc. I have not had time to read the book yet, and therefore have not written to her. I am only just getting through the worrying business following on my mother's death. I think that I am getting to the end of it.

Thank you very much for doing the hymn. We will try it with a tune one day and tell you how it goes. I should be very sorry for you to waste your time on this sort of thing, but new stuff is dreadfully wanted and I don't despair of getting it. My own experience was thus. I thought it impossible to do anything decent till I

translated some old hymns to go to their proper music. Then having music tha
wanted words I got to free paraphrasing and correcting, and now I find that the
tune is generally sufficient in itself to make a hymn of. I have done a lot of thing
which people are quite enthusiastic about, and which satisfy me, as being goodish
stuff, almost quite free of the old ruts, and what I should be glad to sing myself. I
don't think that your hymn is quite out of the ruts.

Strangely enough I have done a hymn to a most magnificent stately old tune
for Coronation Days etc.—a sort of Jubilee hymn which is much on your lines
This is rather a pity as it preoccupies the place of yours. Next time you are down
we will talk of these things.

We have a plan for spending March in Cornwall. But we hear of the influenza
being very bad there: and if it is I doubt if we shall think it worth while to go so
far to meet it.

I hope "Admirals All" still sells. I hear that you and Phillips have given a Philip
to the Garland—I might add a new bolt to it, but it never showed any sign of
running away before.

yours ever
RB

P.S.
Please congratulate Miss Coleridge for us—and tell her I shall be writing. My
wife joins me in kindest remembrances to Mrs. Newbolt. I am glad that you are
nearly settled in. I hope that you will like your new home, and that it may see
much happiness and good fortune.

286: TO LIONEL MUIRHEAD

Glendurgan
Falmouth
March 21, 1898

My dear Lionel
Your picture gives immense satisfaction. It is certainly the best by far that
there is of me and there is now another, a 2 guinea etching by Strang, who
considers me a cross between Moses and an old lion.

I am too busy to write today, but have a lot that I want to write about. I am
passing Smith & Elder's volume I of my "Works" through the press. I have got
Prometheus and Eros & Psyche now set up and corrected, the 2nd item in this
volume I is "the Growth of Love". I was sorry to find that it wanted a lot doing to
it. I am getting on pretty well with it here, have made some great amendments.

There is one word which I thought you could help me to correct. In one of the
sonnets (No. XXV) there is a description of frost at Perugia and it ends

> nor their armour thin
> Will gaudy flies adventure in the air,
> Nor any lizard sun his spotted skin.

Spotted is no doubt a vague term which sounds very well, but is rather applicable to snakes than to lizards such as we see, and I wish to alter it without spoiling the line. I can't for the life of me remember the colour of Italian lizards. Can you help me? The epithet must be one of *sight*. *Mottled* would do. I don't recollect that they had any particular colour.

We go home on March 30 or 31 I expect. I hope to be writing again. Now I am very busy and am going out with the children in a boat.

With renewed thanks for the picture of which I hope to be able to buy copies

yours affectionately

RB

I wish we had got our measles! And congratulate you on Charis' having pulled through all right. What "troubles and adversities"!!

287: TO LIONEL MUIRHEAD

Yattendon
April 15, 1898

My dear Lionel

Thanks for your letter. I am glad that you managed your move so well. When the days get a little longer I must ride over and spend the middle of the day with you. It is not a long ride. I had to go to Sutton Courtney the other day, and got there in 1½ hour.

We had not a good time in Cornwall as we all got the influenza there. But the children are very well now. Wife is in bed, but is better today. When I got home I found the lizards in a book, and spotted will stand. Only I could not remember the spots.

I have not altered Prometheus at all. Only in *one* or *two* places I found that there was a word or two that I could easily amend. I was very much surprised to find it so good as it is. Eros & Psyche will be just as in Edition II. I found a slip or two which I corrected, but nothing either in Prometheus or Eros & Psyche which you would notice.

The G of L I have done a great deal with. It will not be *much* better. I cut out 10 sonnets altogether, and rewrote a good lot of places. I did not know whether I should be able to do it. But Cornwall agreed with me very well in that particular and I hope that all the work that I did was good.

It should shape as a very strong volume because the 3 poems are in 3 distinct styles and it seemed to me that they were (all the 3 styles) sufficiently mastered.

You will see that I am in a good humour with the book. It is not the usual mood, so excuse my indulging in it while I may.

We were 6 miles out of Falmouth on the Helford river.

Next month we begin printing at hymns. I hope I shall have 50 to finish the book with.

M sends kindest messages to your wife from her bed. My kindest remembrances and to your father, who I hope is well.

yours affectionately

RB

Strang's address is W^m S Esq. 17 St Georges Square, Regents Park N.W.

288: TO RICHARD WATSON DIXON

Yattendon

May 24, 1898

My dear Dixon

I was very glad to hear that you had been Rothenstein'd and melanolitho'd. I received a big package from Grant Richards this morning, and opened it with eagerness—alas! It contained only the final number and cover of the "English Portraits". Which reminds me to ask you whether you still have the number of that publication which I sent you as a sample for letterpress—as if you have, I should much like it returned; my series being incomplete without it. Perhaps you may accompany it with a copy of your portrait, which I "die to possess". I shall if it is worth having frame it and hang it at once.

I am glad that you liked R. He is a very clever fellow, with easy sympathies: and makes himself most wonderfully agreeable to his company, at least so I found. It seems unjust to suppose that a man is different from what he shows himself to be, and yet it is difficult to avoid the suspicion that R's nature does not always follow his intellectual convictions—or that they are not thorough convictions. I had a thousand hypotheses to explain [to] him. I did like him. He was quite successful here.

I am sorry that you have been ill again, but you say that you are recovered. I have not been grand for months, but get on much as usual. Today I am going with Monica to London for the night. A concert and a day at the British Museum.

I am going to finish off the Hymnal this year (if the printers will go so fast) with a set of 50 more Hymns making 100 + in all. The book will be, in its department, an important work. In the next 25 hymns (51–75) there are 15 sets of words by myself! Written for tunes which have no 'hymns' worth singing to use them with. The whole is nearly ready now.

I have read nothing of Gladstone. His vast pretentious idolised personality has been one of the dreary shadows of my life. There have been others. I suppose it is always so: especially in thickly peopled and democratic countries. The man whom the people venerate must be a humbug or else made up of a stuff with which vulgarity is familiar, unless indeed it should happen that a really great man won favour by some brilliant achievement. As for Gladstone he was exactly suited to the business. His intense earnestness and vitality pleased—and his power of convincing himself that he was always right (even when he took at different times exactly opposite views) is better than the cleverest imposture, while his immense memory, and his power of talking high flown periods about anything whatever were really unusual gifts. He should have been a mathematician or an astronomer or a bishop. I don't understand politics very well, but he seemed to me a mischievous politician.—Certainly in no other branch was he successful. Art, science, literature, religion.—In all these he was a painstaking dullard. But he was a wonderful man, for his strength of constitution—his memory, his love of applause (which was his pleasure) and his (not least) magnificent serious courtesy.

yours ever

RB

289: TO WILLIAM ROTHENSTEIN

Yattendon

June 2, 1898

My dear Rothenstein

I have duly received the completion of the English Portraits, and am most grateful to you for the presentation. The book will always be of value and interest. And this morning, with your letter, I have a copy of your portrait of Canon Dixon from him. I am framing it. I like it, but I shall not know how much, till I have had it by me for a while. It is certainly a good likeness, and one which I am extremely glad to possess. It seems to me that you are getting on well, and I shall expect you to become a master in a fine style of portraiture. Strang's portrait of me had the disadvantage of not being very like me. My friends prefer yours, though they all say that you hav given me too much nose.

Yeats I know. He has been here, and we want him here again; he is a true poet, and delightful company, but he is in great danger of fooling himself with Rosicrucianism and folklore and Esoterical spiritualisms. It is just possible that he may recover—some of his work is of the very best both poetry and prose.

I was in town last week for one night, for a concert. I saw the 'Milanese' pictures at the Burlington Fine Arts club. There is a *very* fine Leonardo (?), a woman, pagan, with a wreath of flowers, belonging to Charles Morrison, worth going to see, with some other good things among a lot of school stuff.

The weather is miserable. I am sitting over a good fire—but the rain is not unwelcome if it would only be warmer. If anytime this summer you can spare us a Sunday from London we shall be delighted to do our best to entertain you.

Excuse a hasty letter

yours sincerely

Robt Bridges

290: TO LIONEL MUIRHEAD

Yattendon
August 5, 1898

My dear Lionel

I am very sorry for your various troubles, but glad to see that your eyes must be much better again. I ought to have written long ago, but about a month or so ago and *more* I was expecting to ride over to Haseley any day. Then the Slade lectures came on: and one day after cycling to Oxford I found on my return that I had a boil coming on the nape of my neck. This proved the first of three, each worse than the last, and I scarcely got fit to leave home for our long prearranged visits. Now these are all over. I got home the day before yesterday, and have been correcting proofs ever since.

The most interesting batch of these is the next lot of hymn book, which is now fairly well started. When we were at Wells we heard 2 of our Yattendon hymns in the Cathedral, "Love of the Father" was one, and that was sung by the choirs of the diocese at the Choral Festival, and the words I believe found favour with the clergy.

We had a very delightful time at Wells. The organist there is very good in having things that we like to hear, and one afternoon we locked ourselves inside the Cathedral and sang the Missa Brevis straight through.

This afternoon I am sending off the final sheets of Smith & Elders 1st volume of my collected Poems. It was to have come out in October: whether it will or not I can't tell. The American war seems to have interfered. However I am glad that the Yanks gave the Dons such a good licking. I hope it may teach Englishmen to be more respectful to their cousins. As for the Spaniards, I should like to see them kicked out of both Americas. I hope the Pope is proud of his children.

I think nothing is duller than reissuing one's old work. It is bad enough bringing out new things, though it can't be said that I do too much in that way nowadays. But I have a "Hymn of Nature" publishing on October 26 in the September number of the Cornhill. It is the poem which Parry has set for the Gloucester Festival. It contains some queer words to sing in a Cathedral, but I hope it won't be the last time that such things are allowed. I should have told you that they sing "Blest pair of Sirens" for an anthem at Wells.

The children are well. Bo was 6 years old yesterday. He is much developed. We have a governess now. She is a success—so far. She can play whist.

My wife sends her kindest remembrances—and says that she is looking forward to your visit next month. I have caught cold somehow and have a sore throat—which I particularly resent, as it entirely prevents me from smoking.

I have not sent you either philosophy or consolations. Fact is I hadn't time. And you asked for news. But I imagine that your sister in law's condition must be very serious. I see looking through your letter that you ask about the Madrigals.—I don't fancy that they will be any good, but I wrote some words to please

Parratt who had his heart set on the scheme, a difficult task. I made one or two good hits I hope.

yours ever
RB

Please give your wife our kindest regards and sympathy. My wife especially wishes me to say how very sorry she is for the bad news.

291: TO RICHARD WATSON DIXON

Yattendon
August 13, 1898

My dear Dixon

I have had your portrait hanging up now for some time and I think I know what I think about it. It is a wretched piece of work. I hoped at first that something might come out in the portrait which would in a measure compensate for the faults of drawing—but I can't say that it seems to do you any sort of justice. I should be extremely sorry that I had persuaded you to sit to Rothenstein, but after all this portrait is better than nothing, for it gives a good deal of you, and it is evident that most of the work is only incompetent. I should think that R would do another gratis.

Bo's remarks upon it are amusing. He is developing very fast, and is altogether amusing. You would have been amused today if you had heard Elizabeth say to my wife, "I think Mother that Bo should learn 'from the clearness of heaven to the north'"—the children know a good many of your short lyrics, and like them.

I have not been very grand since last Xmas, and this hot weather seems to take the remains of one's strength quite away. I am however working pretty steadily now at the hymn book, which is practically finished, and what work remains to be done is mainly the printers. Still they won't get through that for another 18 months. I wish that you could have worked at the words with me. It has been uphill work, but writing words for fine tunes is really very pleasant, and I hope you will be pleased with what I have done.

I heard of your meeting with Mr. Longmore (of Hermitage) in Holland. I had a visit from Appleton one afternoon. He was most friendly and agreeable, and he is always delighted to talk of you.

My wife wishes me to ask you whether you will be at Warkworth in September. She wants me to take a solitary holiday by the seaside then.

It would suit me very well if I could get away from here. Meanwhile is there no chance of your coming to stay with us?

This life is so short that it seems to me worth while to arrange a meeting if possible.

It would do me good to have a little of your company. I had nearly said of anyone's company, for I get no society here except when a friend comes down from town for a day or two.

There will be an ode by me in the September Cornhill, set by Parry to music for the Gloucester Festival.

yours affectionately

RB

Our best to Mrs Dixon—

292: TO HENRY WOODS

Yattendon
Newbury
August 13, 1898

My dear Woods

I was very glad to hear from you and get your address, and to know that the place suits your wife. I heard of her at Oxford about Commemoration time, but did not chance to meet her.

It is very kind of you to ask us to come and see you, and if we can at anytime get away there is nothing that we should like better.

As for Calderon. I learnt what Spanish I know with the purpose of reading him, but, after all the fine things that I had read about him, was immensely disappointed. Reward however came to one in the enjoyment of Cervantes, at least his Don Quixote, which seems to me as good as Shakespeare, though not so various. But as for Calderon—I read about a dozen plays, I suppose, but unfortunately have no notes, and it is so long ago now, that I do not like to trust my memory for particulars. It would be better to consult an admirer. Mrs. Humphry Ward is one, and Maccoll, the Editor of the Athenaeum, is a still greater enthusiast.

Calderon is of course a master: and a good deal of pleasure is to be got from him. But his characters are very conventional. They have no individuality, and there is consequently a great sameness in his plays. Nor do I think him at all a profound writer. The famous play 'Life is a dream' seems to me very poor in significance, though there was a good opportunity. His good points however are great. First his faultless manners—using the word in its broadest sense—2nd his poetic skill—which is always prominent both in the constitution of his plots and in the extremely polished verse of his dialogues—and 3rd, what is I think common to him and Lope de Vega, the most perfect skill in narration. In pure poetry he only ranks high in the second class of the world's poets, and in Lope de Vega's more hasty productions there are sometimes scenes which for force and natural directness leave, in my opinion, Calderon far behind. But C took much more pains with his plays, and consequently escapes from fault-finding pretty well.

If you don't get sounder advice, I doubt if you would do better than begin with "El principe Constante" which I seem to recollect the best.

With our kindest regards to yourself and Mrs Woods

I am yours ever

R Bridges

293: TO LIONEL MUIRHEAD

Yattendon
October 8, 1898

My dear Lionel

I am very sorry indeed to hear the bad news which you send. It is of course impossible to say how far your Father may recover, but it seems from your account to be a severe stroke.

Even your philosophic temperament must I am sure have felt rather a strain of late, but I suppose it is not a bad thing to have one's troubles together, and you will be glad to be at Haseley now if these should be your father's last days.

Now that your wife's sister is so very ill, I really hope that your wife will give up some of her constant attention which, if it should not, as you fear, wear her out, must yet remove her usefulness from home, where it seems sufficiently needed.

I hope that the children are well. That should be a great comfort to you. I shall hope to hear from you again very soon.

And in a few days I shall be able to send you a proof of your hymn in the "Fell type". I would send it today but have only the one copy which I should keep to check the corrections of the press. We have now 15 of the last 50 set up, and are beginning to break the back of the undertaking.

Wooldridge has been here staying for 3 or 4 days. Today he has gone on to Oxford to make a visit to Hadow. He seemed very well and is satisfied with his progress in his music book. But he fancies that he *may* get it done by Xmas. He does not see that it is impossible, and at Xmas he must begin his Slade lectures (he read your letter).

My wife joins in condolence—Please do not think of letting your wife write when she is so busy. Meanwhile

I am yours affectionately

RB

294: TO CHARLES WOOD

Yattendon
Newbury
October 10, 1898

My dear Wood

I can today write you about the old hundredth. I am getting on with the printing, about 8 pages a month. I have got material almost entirely completed for the whole book and am writing the notes.

According to present scheme the "old hundredth" is No. 79, and will be printed in January.

Wooldridge has been down here, and I have got him to make his final revision of the setting. He has cut out the supertonic close in the second line (which sounds queer when the melody is in the top part) so that that leaves your fine second line (which otherwise was like his) quite free, and he has made other corrections, and put in the long initial notes of line 4.

The arrangement will be that his soprano setting will be on the left hand side of the page, and your tenor setting on the right, with the words of "all people that on earth do dwell" divided between the two settings. Over leaf will be one of Bach's 3 time settings of the same tune with the words "From all that dwell below the skies," 2 verses only.

I think that will do justice to the tune. I enclose Wooldridge's setting, and also return yours with my humble request that you will consider my weakness in the matter of that interval of a tenth between the soprano and alto. Of course I will put it in if you insist, which seems not unlikely if you think it more important to keep that jolly close, but it will be the only example in our book of such a thing, and is really contrary to our principles.

Secondly I think that you will agree with me that my suggestion of making a point in the last line with half time, only leads to trouble; and you will be glad to set the beginning of that line with all the voices together.

I send you Wooldridge's setting, (which I have just put together from various scraps of paper) that you may make your setting different from his* where you would wish to do so which suggests the remark that as he has used the same close as you have in the 2nd line, that is some part of a reason for your changing that piece of your setting. W. thinks the tune should be in G. What do you wish? I think it is rather high for his setting. Would A^b (in which I have transferred his setting in F.) do? They must of course be in the same key. I hope that you are now settled comfortably, and that you won't mind my bothering you again.

yours sincerely

Robert Bridges

I am having good fun with the notes.

*I was interrupted here.

295: TO RICHARD WATSON DIXON

Yattendon

October 14, 1898

My dear Dixon

I have just returned from Oxford—two very pleasant days staying with Sanday, and there I saw Miss Hatch, and they told me that all the while I was at Warkworth they were staying at a place in the Coquet Valley 15 miles off!!

I put 2 or 3 of your emendations into my "Salve caput crucitatem" so your work that afternoon was not thrown away.

Reading in St James the other night I came on θρησκεία —translated religion in that passage "pure religion and undefiled" etc. It seems to me a very good example of the sense of the word which you sought to establish as current in that time—viz, the forms rather than the creed—(I think θρησκεία is used for the *worshipping* of angels in Colossians.) On the other hand I do not find that Shakespeare ever used the word in the formal sense.—I thought I would write this to you tonight, but I have nothing more to say. Hymn printing goes on well and my notes promise to be voluminous and amusing.

Wooldridge, who has been staying here liked them—

My book is all ready to appear but does not appear.

yours ever

RB

I wrote to Bishop [of] Oxford, a strong letter about you, and received a very gracious reply. I attached others also.

P.S. "Religion" now includes Folklore and Fairytales etc. See Bodleian Catalogue raisonné.

296: TO LIONEL MUIRHEAD

Yattendon
October 17, 1898

My dear Lionel

I am glad to hear that your Father's end came to him without more trouble: and I feel sure that, after so severe a stroke as he had, the prolongation of existence is only misery. I am thankful that you are spared. You will be exercised as to your immediate future. I hope that you will not decide in a hurry.

I wonder whether you will accept my wife's invitation to Charis, sent yesterday.

I send you your hymn, which is being printed off today.—The correction in No. 63 was not an afterthought. I wrote in something quite wrong in my copy for Press and can't imagine why, and it as nearly as possible got printed.

My wife joins in all kindest messages of sympathy to Mrs Lionel and of course to yourself.

yours affectionately

RB

You must remember that this place is very damp in wet weather—otherwise I think it is healthy enough and we would take great care of Charis.

297: TO WILLIAM SANDAY

Yattendon
October 19, 1898

My dear Sanday

I don't like my own new line for the Wesley, and am glad of any suggestion. Especially from you. I should have missed the hymn but for your recommendation.

Stedfast is excellent—unfortunately contains two sibilants, which is expensive.

I can't see that *infancy* is sense, though I confess that you are not the first person who has defended it to me. It may dawn on my stupidity presently. If infancy means the age before we can talk—can you really take seriously a poem which appears to be founded on the recollection of that period, and speaks of the ideals of that period?

The first thing I remember is a recovery from pneumonia when I was between 3 and 4. Then again all is a blank till I got a bad fright.

If "walking a mile or two" does not mean walking, as you say it cannot, it is a very difficult description of the mental state of an infant.

That couplet seems to me to wear the curious nonsensical charm which I dislike. It is beautiful, and deserves to mean what it apparently does not mean.

Send me more suggestions* for in-ex-tin-guish-a-ble—there is room for much, but we must not pile adjectives.

yours ever
RB

*Any time in the next 3 months.

298: TO HENRY NEWBOLT

Yattendon
October 22, 1898

My dear Newbolt

I did not recognise the handwriting on your parcel, and it was a relief as well as an unexpected pleasure to come on your volume when I opened it.

I am very much obliged to you for your kindness in sending me a copy, which I shall value very much, though I shall always think the little shilling number of the Garland the more interesting book, your editio princeps. I hope that your public does not yet flag.

I see that you have printed the hymn which you so kindly wrote for my hymnal. It seems to me to read very well in print, but I don't think I can make any use of it. At least so far I have not been able to fit it. I have got to the end of my material for the Hymn Book and the printers are working away pretty well. The 3rd part should be out by Xmas and the concluding part with very voluminous (and I hope amusing interesting and instructive) notes by this time next year. It does anything but fall off, I think. I have 2 or 3 pages still unoccupied.

My first volume is out I believe (at Smith & Elders). Hart the printer informed me that after my revise he discovered "something wrong with the *a*'s" in the text, and had a new lot cast and substituted.—This was I fear a mistaken kindness for opening in the book I came on this word

Ftera.

There will be "something the matter with the a's" now if they have put them back in this fashion. The word above is

after.!

I hope you and Mrs. Newbolt and family are well. I have not heard lately from Mary Coleridge. I hope they are cheering up.

With renewed thanks for your book and kindest remembrances from my wife and self to you and Mrs. Newbolt.

believe me yours sincerely

RB

299: TO HENRY NEWBOLT

Yattendon
October 28, 1898

My dear Newbolt

I have been reading in your book off and on since it came. I don't think it fair to read all those things at once, because one insensibly wears out one's enthusiasm in any given direction, and these poems mostly call for the same kind, and a good deal of it.

This morning after reading the Bishop of Bath and Wells again I stumbled on your dedication. Really I might never had seen it at all, as modern books have such a lot of titles and half titles that (one being enough) I don't often turn them all over.

You must have been surprised at my saying nothing of it in my letter to you— and now I really don't know what to say, except that I am abashed by the compliment, but value it extremely. Thank you very much and also for the kind expressions in your letter which are in the matter of friendship and sympathy most warmly reciprocated.

As for the poems. You know that I knew most of them before, and what I think of them, and I like the new (to me) ones as well. They make a very good book.

I am just off to Newbury and write not to miss another post. Though really as I was filling up with your book the odd moments before starting I have not time to write properly.

yours ever
R Bridges

300: TO SAMUEL BUTLER

2 Royal Crescent Ramsgate
November 26, 1898

My dear Butler

Except for the occasional hushed réncontres in the British Museum I have heard or seen so little of you for so long, that I was very glad to get a letter from you. I heard occasionally some news from "Rocco" as our children used to call him—he was a great favourite and generally spent a week or a fortnight with us at Yattendon every summer, when we beat up a few pupils for him.—I knew of your kindnesses to him.

About the book that you send, I am very pleased that you should think of me as one willing to help in such a matter, and I hope that your intention of giving a little unexpected pleasure may be successful. You may certainly say for me that I have read some of the poems with great pleasure, and especially admire the directness and simplicity of expression in some of her little nature pieces—such as the first three and "The Lament" on p. 42—I do not know whether you will think this worth saying, but I can't in honesty go any further. However I will look at them carefully again and see if I can correct my judgment to be more like yours—which I guess at present to have been a little led by your feelings.

Your letter was forwarded to me here, where I have just come with my wife and youngest child for a little sea air. We have come in for a regular stiff blow.

I have spent what time I had in reading the poems, so excuse a hasty letter.—I am just going out again and have not time to ask you questions (which you could not answer) about Ulysses etc.etc.

I don't know what you are up to now—but if Ulysses is an opera I hope you will get it on the stage.

yours sincerely
Robert Bridges

301: TO LIONEL MUIRHEAD

2 Royal Crescent
Ramsgate
December 2, 1898

My dear Lionel

I hope that you are getting on all right. We have been here, Monica, Bo and I, for 10 days, and hope to go home on Tuesday. The idea was to benefit me. You know that I had a boil in the summer, and since then have generally had one going on. They remind one of the evolution of suns or planets. I have one now. I hope it is the last. Otherwise I am very well. I think that Bo enjoys the sea more than any of us. He has been in the highest spirits all the time. I don't know that I have much to tell you. I read the paper every day here, and usually buy the

Chronicle, which certainly is the liveliest and most amusing daily paper that I ever found in England. And on the whole it is not at all bad. I was very much prejudiced against it, but feel quite friendly towards it now. It is even advocating the decimal system, and I believe that I could get it to go in for my reformation in spelling. I know that you don't like that, and I feel inclined to write the rest of my letter in 'the new spelling.' Which last sentence would be—only this—"and I feel inclÿnd tu wrÿt de rest ov my leter in the niu speling." I had a pamphlet from a man yesterday who I think is on the brink of it. I have been watching smacks beating up against South Wester and strong tide all the afternoon.—We see all the Goodwin and French lights here very well, and all Pegwell bay between us and Deal, but I dare say that you know the place. Now I am going to have a game of patience or old maid with Bo. We have a lodging very like the Folkestone one, too big, but clean and fairly comfortable. I expected to get proof of the next batch of Hymns here, but they have not come. Still I feel pretty sure that Hart will have my Part III ready for Xmas—and I shall be very glad to have them to send round for Xmas boxes. Monica's book on handwriting should also be ready. We shall have only 100 copies of the first edition, and shall be sending round announcements of it.—I have all the material to finish the hymnal too during the coming year. Except that one or two of the tunes have as yet got no words to them, and I am getting exhausted. However I did one here last week.

When you write tell me something of your plans. If you don't stay at Haseley I hope that we might manage something which would enable us to meet oftener. I hope that Mrs Keene is better, and that you are well and in good spirits.

Monica sends her love to your wife and I my kindest regards.

yours ever
RB

302: TO WILLIAM SANDAY

Yattendon
December 14, 1898

My dear Sanday

Thank you for your letter and kind present, which I value very much. It is a great pleasure to have a book of your thoughts to read, and it ought to do me good. I began it at 10 p.m. last night, and finished it before I slept, and if I liked the first 3 sermons the best, you will say that I did not give the 4th so good a chance, and that 4 sermons at once is perhaps too much. But I read with unflagging interest. I think the book should be very useful, and your apology for the Roman Catholic is most telling.

I am of course sorry to feel quite outside all this, and I do not know whether I shall ever come inside again. I have not sufficient faith in man's inventions. What you say about the natural growth of the Christian institutions, and the absurdity of confining the grace of God to channels of man's invention and contrivance, (to give it the twist which it takes in my mind) appears to me so true, that it makes the whole clerical position a historical, developmental, opportunism; and the sort of question which arises in my mind is whether in our day the time has not come to throw a great deal aside for good and all.

I sympathize with what you say so well about St. Paul's Epistles etc.—that they are in themselves evidences of spiritual gift: though I do think that academic education and the habit of considering them as 'inspired' tends to exaggerate their greatness. But I think more and more that St. Paul mistook the teaching of Christ, and I wonder what some of the twelve thought when they saw the 'Church' getting into—(I don't quite remember how I meant to finish this sentence. I have been interrupted for 2 hours and my good intention of writing you a long letter is more or less frustrated.)

You will understand, without the trouble of reading my disquisition, that my difference is the less importance which I attach to the thought of St. Paul and the men of his time. No doubt a great many churchmen will think that you go too far, as it is, in "explaining things away": but this is all inside theology—and theology is, it seems to me, very much adapted to the opinions and beliefs of the time, and is unable to go further than you go. I should think that your book could do an immense amount of good.—It is impossible to imagine anything more Christian in tone.

Do you think "O, for a closer walk with God" a good hymn for singing in church? I have been very much pleased with the result of your first advice, and want more.

As for the "article", I doubt if I can write it, but I will try because—well partly because a good article by me on the subject, if I could write one, would help to call attention to my book.

ending in haste

yours ever
RB

303: TO LIONEL MUIRHEAD

Yattendon
May 1, 1899

My dear Lionel

I was glad to hear from you and to know what you will be doing this year. I will in turn tell you of ourselves, and probable eventualities.

We have had our outing, taking the children down to Seaton in Devonshire, where we spent a month, chiefly March.—We do not expect to leave home, any of us, till the autumn.

Until the end of the summer I shall be very busy.—Smith & Elder are bringing out the 2nd volume of my collected 'works' in October, and it is to consist mainly of the "Shorter Poems."—As these will make only some ⅔ of a volume I am going to fill the book up with chiefly new matter—some 80 pages—and I have been for the last two months writing for it. I didn't at all know what I should do, but fortunately had a sort of poetical spurt, and have done a good lot of things.— I shall have to work at this till the book *must* go to press: and they are now beginning to print.

Also I have arranged to have the Hymnal finished in October at latest. The notes will be very elaborate, and they will be beginning to print these in about a fortnight. They had no good small music type for the musical illustrations etc. in the notes, so that I am getting these electrotyped in Holland, where one of the printing houses possesses an old small lozenge type which is rather good. This work will require a great deal of attention. Also two of the hymns are unfinished.

Daniel is now printing my original contributions to the Y. H. in black letter. It will make a nice book. There will be 120 copies at 12/6 which may help to pay expenses of the Hymnal. The Hymnal is not dead on the market. It seems to be selling.

I have bought out a shilling edition of the Shorter Poems. It is a pleasant looking little book. It has been out a month. 700 sold already. So it looks as if it would go off well. Bell publishes it. It is only a reprint from the stereotyped plates of the old edition. There will be a 'fourth of June" eclogue (you have seen it) in the June number of the Cornhill.

———

I never intended to get as much on hand, but I shall not mind the work, especially if the weather is fine. HEW will be coming here for a few days, when his Oxford lectures are over; which will coincide with the end of summer term. I have lately met W. J. Stone a son of the Eton master. He is very nice.

I cannot find your letter this morning. I don't remember whether there is anything in it which I should especially answer. If there is I will write again when I find it.

Monica's book on handwriting sold out at once. She is preparing a larger and cheap edition.

yours affectionately
RB

304: TO LIONEL MUIRHEAD

Yattendon
June 27, 1899

My dear Lionel

I am glad that you like Daniel's book. I think it is the best to be got out of his type etc., but he should have kept to my design of having full pages. He has twice allowed gaps, which spoil the effect, and are inconsistent. Why cannot people see these things? Also his ornament p.l is no good, as he uses it. I had nothing to do with his titles, except to veto one horrible thing that he sent me at first.

I was delighted that you cared for my φῶς ἱλαρόν . The original is so beautiful that I think it is better to keep a little away from it, choosing some stanza which plainly necessitates differences. Keble's version (HAM) is horrid. The old prose one (Bishop Andrewes?) is very nice, but has no singing rhythm or measure. The tune which I have made the translation for is very simple, and sounds as old as the words. I did not set it to my translation, but wrote the translation for the tune.

I am getting the notes printed. It looks as if they would prove interesting. The music is not all printed yet, but I don't think that subscribers who expect the book in October will be disappointed.

When I was last in Oxford I made the discovery of some really good old black letter—must be early 16 century. They had not enough to work with, but told me that they could get more in Germany. I intend buying enough to print with, and having a good book at last. I know now how to get good paper. It will be delightful if after a lifetime of failures one gets a good book done at the end.— Still I am not altogether discontented with the hymnal, when it is not compared with a book of the best period.

It would be delightful to see you. I have often thought of riding over, but last year I got "run down" and had in consequence a mighty plague of boils and things, and am afraid of overdoing exercise, which I enjoy at the time. In this hot weather a long ride takes a lot out of one, if one can judge by exudations.

Wooldridge is coming next Monday. He is going to do some work with me. After that I shall be at leisure till August 3 or 4.

(I have not told you I think that I am bringing out in a Quarterly which is launched this autumn an article on Hymns—which will advertise my book, and I hope stir up the clergy. HEW is going to look over that before I send it in)—It is possible that at that date (August 11) we shall all go down to the seaside again, because a friend has lent us his house on the North Devon coast for that month. My second book with Smith & Elder is to come out in October. It is to be composed ⅔ of "shorter poems", and I am just now engaged in writing up the other 3rd, which will contain some new matter—a miscellaneous lot of things, some old and never printed, some from magazines and lesser publications. I hope you will like the new work. It is in some respects better, I think, than what I have done before, clear and simple. Wooldridge is coming partly to read these things for me, because I have no time to let them soak. If you could come any time after he left us you would be very welcome and would not interrupt me at all. Indeed your congenial society would assist my soul.

We are building, rebuilding, the main outhouse or barn here, and I am taking the opportunity of intercalating a fives court between it and the coach house. I have long had designs on my stable yard, and meant to build a jolly barn. BUT!! the kindness of Mr. Waterhouse stepped in. He would not allow me to have any architect or builder but himself. I couldn't get out of it—and now his gratuitous services are doing—you may guess what. Isn't it annoying? Besides he tells me it is to cost me 600 £. If he should come round at the end and pay for it I shouldn't be able to thank him. Worst of all is that he thinks that he is putting himself awfully out to please me. I had the very greatest difficulty with him to get the fives court rectangular! He gave way at last with "Well I suppose you will have your own way"—Such an idea of obstinacy!—My philosophy is at considerable strain. I don't venture near the scene of my trials. Bo looks after the bricklayer and keeps a pretty good eye on him I believe. Well my dreams of improving the stable yard are flown. Except I still hope that the fives court will be practicable.

With our kindest regards (MMB to Mrs. K and your wife)

yours affectionately

RB

305: TO WILLIAM BUTLER YEATS

Yattendon

June 30, 1899

My dear Yeats

I was very glad to get a line from you, and to hear something of your theatre. I take a great interest in it, but don't of course hear much down here.

I was fortunate one day, being on the railway, and buying a "Chronicle" to hit off your letter on the Drama, aimed at some conventional critic. I liked it extremely, and it seemed unanswerable. I hope that your Dublin plays will be a yearly thing, and that they will pay their expenses. As for London, it is hopeless at present—it is all scenery and low 'fun', with some fashionable rant. I expect it was never much better, but the conventions just now are the deadliest dreariness. Thanks for alluding to "Ulysses".—I don't expect (or really wish) to see a play of mine on the stage, but I feel confident that when the "Feast of Bacchus" gets there, it will stay. Still that is not much in your line.

A thousand thanks for "The Wind among the Reeds." I shall value extremely a copy with your inscription, but you do me wrong in imagining that I am not among your buyers. I got the book as soon as it came out. How then did I not write to congratulate you and thank you for it? I don't know where to write to you. And that uncertainty always prevents me from writing a letter. It's like talking to a man who may not be in the room—If you will send me an address whence letters are always forwarded to you I will trouble from time to time with my praises and salutations. It happens that you have never written to me twice from the same place. Now it is Galway.

This is a good place except in winter. Spring and Autumn are not bad, and I hope that you may come in Autumn. We are free of all hat and coat conventions, and you would find it quiet here and easy to work: and could stay on as you liked.

The new poems delighted me. There are things I don't understand, but that is all the better.—I am very glad that you have got so much recognition; it is really very lucky—though I don't suppose that you can have a very large sale. Still enough to pay a little I expect. To publish at a loss is most depressing.

I have a new volume of "Collected Works" (a sad sign of age) coming out in October. ⅓ of the book will be more or less new, and hoping there may be some among the poems that you will like I will send you a copy if I know where to send it.

Accept, as the French say, the tribute of my lofty and unimpaired esteem.

yours sincerely

Robert Bridges

I am glad the Papists went for you! They are very cheeky just now.

306: TO HENRY NEWBOLT

Yattendon
July 17, 1899

My dear Newbolt

I shall be sending some new poems to the press to print in Smith & Elder's second volume with my old "shorter poems"—one or two questions arise in an elegy of my youth—reminiscences, which I thought you might be able to answer for me.

(1) What is the anchorage in the Downs? Chalk? Do you know what the anchors hold in here?

(2) Sir Charles Napier's Baltic fleet in 1854 flew the blue ensign. Do you know any one who could tell you whether Napier flew a blue pennon at the maintop?

It seems that he would have done in 1850, and my memory is that he did, but I can't find out, and if he didn't I should alter a line.

———

I have sketches of Dundas' Squadron in 1855—he had a white ensign, and all his ships a long pennon at the main—but the sketch does not show the color. It was no doubt white.

———

But I only want to know about Napier's pennon or *pendant* on his flagship.

———

I don't think any one could tell you who did not at least *see* the ship. It seems that the custom changed about that time.

yours sincerely
R Bridges

Don't trouble unless your acquaintance with admirals makes the thing easy.

307: TO HENRY NEWBOLT

Yattendon
July 25, 1899

My dear Newbolt

A thousand thanks. I will gladly wait. Is it not odd how difficult it is to get a little piece of information of this sort!

I wonder whether Laughton came across my brother? I have lost touch with one or two of his shipmates whom I used to know. My wife wants to know whether you and your wife would be able to bring the children down here sometime in September to middle of it? Is it possible?

in great haste
yours sincerely
RB

308: TO LIONEL MUIRHEAD

Yattendon
July 27, 1899

My dear Lionel

Many thanks. It is thus: I am going to print 70 or 80 pages of new poems in my October volume, with the 'Shorter poems'. Some of these I have written for the purpose, others have seen the light, others are old. It is a very miscellaneous lot, and I thought of putting a bunch of Love poems among them.

The question arises whether the public will take for granted that they are to my wife, and whether in that case it is well to print them.

You will see exactly how the matter stands—and if you will look at them once or twice with this in your mind I shall be extremely obliged to you. I send herewith. I don't want them back at once.

yours ever
RB

We will arrange about your visit here later.

309: TO RICHARD WATSON DIXON

Yattendon
August 7, 1899

My dear "Ba*s*il"!

I am just making copy for my new volume. The enclosed is one of the poems to go in. I thought that you might like to touch up some of the stanzas which I put into your mouth—for it is you, though I lie about Somerset, and I hope you will be amused at my fiction.

You will see that your stanzas are those which EDWARD repeats.

all very dodgy !!

yours affectionately
RB

Please return in course of the next few days to *me* at

Cliff Cottage
Lee
Ilfracombe
Devon

any improvements welcomed

310: TO RICHARD WATSON DIXON

Cliff Cottage
Lee
Near Ilfracombe
August 18, 1899

My dear Dixon

Thanks for yours. I have no doubt that your suggested alteration of the end of the Eclogue would be an improvement, but the introduction there of three allusions in the place of two would set up a new balance which I have not leisure to consider. I feel sure that the thing runs off very easily now, and I am afraid that in attempting to make use of your suggestion I might overload it. Therefore I shall send it in as it is.

I think that tomorrow I part with the last of the copy, and then shall not have any work to do except correct proof. The notes to the hymnal are extremely long and elaborate and need a deal of looking to.

————

It is of course very wrong of Lang to write about things that he is not sufficiently informed on. But all the press writers do that, and they don't do *much* harm. It is disgraceful to Lang, who could really do so well—and might help the deserving: which I think he does when he knows of them. But the judgement of these London critics is sadly lacking, and really their personalities are incredible. Coming down here I bought a copy of the Chronicle—and found a good deal about myself in a review of some new poet. The reviewer apparently wanted to take the opportunity to write me down, and told all manner of lies about my *ethos*. I reminded these folk once of the 9th commandment, and I think that made me a good many enemies—it hit them hard.

I brought down here a volume of Carlyle's French Revolution. I had never read it, and am quite astounded with its skill. I dislike his manner of writing extremely—and think e.g. that his Cromwell is *very* bad, but this French revolution delights me—nor do I generally object to the manner of it. The subject is so overwhelmingly difficult, and his mastery of it so easy, that it excuses anything. Every now and then he goes over the boundary of what is tolerable.

Did I tell you that I had a paper in the new "Journal of Theological Studies" coming out in October, on "Some of the principles of Hymn singing?" I hope it may do good. It will amuse you to read. We are getting on well here, except that I am not sure that the place suits my wife. The children seem to be daily the better for it. They are bathing or "paddling" all day.

We expect to go back home before the end of the month.

Any chance of seeing you this Autumn? Could not you come to Yattendon?

With kindest regards from us both to yourself
and M[rs] Dixon
your affectionate
RB

311: TO LIONEL MUIRHEAD

Yattendon
September 21, 1899

My dear Lionel

I am so much obliged to you for the Latin books sent from Blackwells. I haven't had time to look at them yet: but I shall soon have plenty of leisure, and I think I shall begin teaching Spokes his rudiments at once. I have just come in from gardening, and have sat me down at my wife's writing table, and am making an unexpected and disagreeable experiment with her fountain pen. It's kill or cure with my handwriting, and I can stand it no longer, though I see that it is my own fault and that if I were to write very slowly I might make something of it. My hand aches already.

There seems too to be this objection to a fountain pen, which I never thought of, that is, there is no [use] in wiping it when you have done writing. You might go on wiping for ever. I was in Oxford yesterday. I have quite finished the Smith & Elder book now. I do not expect to see it again. The hymnbook is all in print and corrected except the directions to binder. We are engaged in correcting the proofs of the word-book. So things are clearing up.

We enjoyed your visit immensely. I was sorry that all your news was not good, but was glad to find that the contrarieties which are "out of our power" do not shiver your philosophy. We have got our governess back now, and are planning to go off in October to pay one or two visits. Then we come home to plant shrubs and trees.

The new building has now been roofed in for some time, and the carpenters are flooring the top room. You may walk up and down on it. It is about the biggest room in the parish, after the church and the school. No cement on the fives court yet.

Goodbye. I have another letter to write. Let us hear from you at times. No news from Wooldridge since, (did I tell you?) he wrote a pencil note to say that he was back in London and seriously ill with influenza. I am very anxious about him, but I think his wife would have written if he had been very bad—

Our kindest regards to Mrs Muirhead and Mrs Keene

yours ever
RB

312: TO RICHARD WATSON DIXON

Yattendon
Monday, October 2, 1899

My dear Dixon

It is most unfortunate that we have fixed to be away from home on the 18th. I have to be at the Corpus Gaudy on October 11th and on the 12th we are going to

Somerset to pay two visits and shall not be home again by the 18th. Three days later we should be at home—and I am expecting a visitor before the end of October whom you would have liked to have met, and who would delight to meet you—Cornish, the vice provost of Eton, and his wife.

Cannot you prolong your visit in London over the Sunday, and come to us for part of the following week?—I expect we should be home again by the 20th. It seems a great pity that we should miss this possible meeting and there is so much to talk of.

I am glad that you are getting on with the history. I have come to the end of my work, and look forward to resting from the labours of vanity, not that I am 'vain' of the vanity. Never can there have been an author who thought less of his work. I lack that note of the true poet. Though I have always taken the keenest pleasure in my work while it was a-making.

I hope that you will like my "new poems," and the end of the hymnal. The notes to the hymnal are 30 pages of close printed quarto; which are, I believe, a serious contribution to criticism. Now we are constructing a rock garden and a new barn and a fives court—and in November are going to engineer a new walk round the meadow, with a total reconstruction of the stable-yard.

I have taken to reading, but I find my old impatience of going on with anything that I dislike: and my old difficulty that I like so few things. Then I don't like this damp weather.

———

This Boer War will be a big thing. It looks to me as if it might be a great proof or trial of the country. I dreamed that it was all over in one great battle in which the Boers got utterly smashed. In my waking moments I see a very different sort of contest. I suppose the goverment [sic] know what they are in for, but they do not seem to be acting with sufficient force. It is to be a long contest for supremacy in South Africa: and an uphill one for us. Shall we show our old determination and power? I pray that we may. The hope is chiefly in English out there, who have the sense to hate Gladstone and Mr Stead, and know how to shoot straight. This peace conference business is all nonsense. "I labour for peace, but when I speak with them thereof they make them ready to battle" and as long as men like fighting, fighting there will be; and it is a better way of settling things than lying. Come and talk of these things—would not you like to fight?

your affectionate

RB

313: TO LIONEL MUIRHEAD

Yattendon
October 26, 1899

My dear Lionel

I have been away paying visits in Somerset and Hants. My wife was to have been with me, but got prevented at the last moment. I ended up with Chichester and the Isle of Wight—got back to the Manor House today. It was a most fortunately timed trip—never was better weather. Today the news of the flight of the Boers before the Dublin Fusiliers—but alas for the unlucky shot that slew Symons!! I fear there will be a good deal of that before all is over. I am very anxious to see the details on Monday. But I should have thought I had died well if I had been the man to give those scoundrels their first licking. I wonder how it will affect their subsequent fighting.

It is difficult to think of anything else, but I took pen to answer your long letter, which I found on my return.

Your description of your reentry into the swept and garnished house, whence you came out, was very amusing. I was delighted that you were in such good spirits, and revelled in imagination with you. You can't have enjoyed the weather more than I have.—I am, as it happens, devoting this autumn and winter to a series of necessary cares after house and garden, which promises to be pleasurable. The difficulty here is getting manual labour—every one seems to be employed.

You ask after the doings of my publishers. First, "the Journal of Theological Studies" (Macmillan) has just appeared.—A copy came to me yesterday. It contains my hymn article. I glanced over the pages of the journal and it seemed to me that my paper was somewhat a strange contrast to the rest. Secondly there will be rather a close race between Frowde and Smith & Elder for the second place. Both the Yattendon Hymnal and the Poetical Works Volume II are promised by the end of the month, and there is every probability of their being up to time. The word book of the Y. H., Blackwell, Oxford 1/6, should not be far behind. Indeed it is merely a question between the binders. It will be rather a pretty book. There is a list of the music at the end.

It is most delightful to have all these things behind me. I am writing to tell Smith & Elder to send you a copy of the Poems as soon as they are out, so don't trouble to order them.

The Cornishes ought to come to us next Friday.

What should make the Karnac columns fall? Have they had an earthquake? Kindest regards from us both to Mrs. M.—Goodbye—

your affectionate
RB

I had to read a lot of William Morris's life aloud last night. I found it very dreary stuff.

314: TO HENRY NEWBOLT

Yattendon
November 19, 1899

My dear Newbolt

Thank you for your kind letter. I felt that that poem rather invaded your department, but it was an accident. I have given up reading the newspapers. I ordered a daily paper when this war began, but it soon drove my peace away, and now I don't open it when it comes. Some one will tell me when there is a turn in the game. Meanwhile one may just as well sleep at night and enjoy one's ordinary faculties such as they are.

I am glad that you are coming down here. We are very busy planting shrubs: the rain came just the very day we wanted it: but every thing is getting into the usual forlorn November mess. The oaks and elms still hold their leaves, but I expect the coverts will be pretty open when you come with your gun.

We have had a few visitors—Mr. and Mrs. Cornish from Eton,—and Canon Dixon who left us this morning. Our kindest regards to Mrs. Newbolt and the Coleridges if you see them.

yours sincerely
R Bridges

315: TO HENRY NEWBOLT

Yattendon
Evening, November 27, 1899

My dear Newbolt

All right. I don't know who your man is, and I think that I had better not know: and as long as I don't know I think there can be no objection to your putting the facts before him, and seeing whether they do not make him withdraw.

The next 4 volumes will be 4 volumes of drama, the seventh volume would be miscellaneous—and I should think that there would be new matter before then. The 8th and 9th would be prose—essays etc.—S. & E. gave me to understand that they wanted to print the lot.—But they very soon changed their minds. If I got an offer from anyone to continue the series (which I should do on better paper) I would force S & E to tell me plainly what they mean. They could scarcely wish to *prevent* my publishing my own poems. One difficulty is that I should have to give Bell the option. I don't know if he would take it. I am not so bound to him but that I could take anyone else's offer if the terms were better than his. I was disappointed at S & E not going on. But there is an advantage in it, as I am relieved from correcting proofs etc. which I hate.

Yours ever (with many thanks for your interest)

Robt Bridges

I could find out at Oxford what the volumes cost to print. I have the first two stereotyped—or rather squeezes of them are ready for stereotyping.

316: TO LIONEL MUIRHEAD

Yattendon
December 4, 1899

My dear Lionel

We were afraid, when we saw your wife's handwriting, that there was something the matter with you, and are glad that it is nothing worse than a sprained arm. However, we condole with you upon this. I hope it will soon mend. I was glad to hear that you had your Parts IV, but I expect that you got them without their proper covers. It is difficult to get [c]over directions attended to.—But if you are going to have the books bound it will not matter. I am having all the spare copies bound at the press—so that there will soon be only complete books to buy. The binding is similar to the one on my wife's little book of Handwriting, and it looks very well. Also it is cheap. If you liked to send your copies to Hart he would have them bound in these boards like the rest. But you might prefer another sort of binding.

In *directions to binder* Hart has made an omission. There is one page (the last of Part I) which will have to be cut off—but I think it would be better to leave it to be cut off after the book is bound.

I have been up in London and in Oxford several days lately. I saw Stuckey Coles in Oxford; he looked very well. He is doing *very* badly in the HAM word committee. They are I fancy making a grand mess of it. I should think it most likely that among them they would destroy the book.

The Magdalen College anthem book now just reissued contains some of the Y. H. words—but I hear that they are thinking of issuing a hymnal!!

We have done all our planting, and are well, except that my wife is not allowed to gad about, which is a trial to her and to me.

I hope that all goes well with your party—

With kindest remembrances from us both

yours ever

RB

You shall have the word book in a day or two.—There are 100 copies on larger hand made paper price 5/-. I expect this little book will sell but it is impossible to tell—

317: TO LIONEL MUIRHEAD

Yattendon
December 14, 1899

My dear Lionel

I was just sitting down to answer your letter when the P. S. arrived, and now I can't find the letter which I thought I had in my pocket.—The war-news drives me wild.—I don't think there was anything special to answer in the letter— except that it contained a full and particular bulletin about your arm. That sort of thing is very painful and annoying. I remember your saying that you felt something of it when you were here—but everybody has a *little* of that kind of rheumatism sometimes and I did not suppose it was going to be worse. I expect that you set it off using it roughly. I am glad to hear that it is better.

I read Lucretius when I was at Eton, partly I suppose because we didn't do him in school. I had a beautifully bound copy which I remember carrying under my arm and studying at odd moments when I was 6th form prepostor. It is still as lovely and stainless as ever. The best parts of him are very beautiful.

As you go to Oxford so easily now let us arrange to meet there one day next term. I often go in my hours being from 12 to 6.

I have (with the children) made a conical snowhut on the lawn. I can stand upright in it though I can only just creep in through the door.

My racket court is finished, and the big wood-house with the long room over it, where I now find carpentry agreeable. I am making a bookcase for my folios. Did I tell you that I saw HEW in London one day. He is not well from his influenza, but says that he keeps his perpetual enemy at bay. He did not look well, though better than I expected to see him, as I had been anxious.

yours ever
RB

318: TO MRS. MANLEY HOPKINS

Yattendon
nr. Newbury
[December, 1899]

My dear Mrs Hopkins

I am writing to send you and Miss Hopkins our best Xmas wishes. We heard of you not very long ago from Miss Buckton, who paid us a poetical visit on a bicycle. She had written to me about her poems, and we were somewhat surprised, as much as pleased, to find her to be a hard working person.

I was reminded to write to you by a book which was sent me the other day, called "Prayers from the Poets" published by William Blackwood & Sons. It contains a poem by Gerard (whom they print Gerald) on August 22nd. "Thee, God, I come from". I do not know whether you were consulted about this, or whether it was merely bagged from Mr. Beeching's book. In any case I am sure you will be glad to see Gerard's verses finding their way into collections like this. It would have pleased him very much. Also I am glad to find that the manner in which I first introduced his work to the public has resulted in its serious acceptance. The book in question is not a very competent book but I suppose it is made for a particular public.

You may also have had some correspondence with Basil Champneys about Gerard's letters to Coventry Patmore. I found that Champneys was very much struck with them, and he desired to make them over to me when he had done with them. Would you have any objection to this? It seems to me a good plan—as they would go with mine—and it is possible that the whole might some day be printed. If they should be they would make a very remarkable and valuable book.

I often think of old times and my visits to you at Hampstead. I send you a memento of ourselves in the small word-book to our Yattendon hymnal.

With kindest regards and best wishes—at this most lamentable time

yours very sincerely
Robert Bridges

319: TO SAMUEL BUTLER

Yattendon
nr. Newbury
December 23, 1899

My dear Butler

I have long wanted to read your book on the Odyssey. I got it yesterday, and must write at once to say how delighted I am with it. You would be the last person to wish that any one should think that one day's reading is sufficient to master all the detail. But I used to know the Odyssey very well, and I think it the best poem in the world, so that first impressions of such a book as yours go for something: and I am sure that you will be glad to find that I like it extremely. There can be no doubt that it is one of the most valuable of the books on the Homeric question. When I was at college they tried to teach me Wolff's theories and I used to laugh at them, and scouted the idea that writing was not known at the time of the composition of such poems. Now of course it is known that it was invented.

There are a lot of things that I should like to talk about—and a *few* things I don't agree with.—I should like to take advantage of your reading to know what were the best books that you found on the Homeric question.

What conversations you must have had with old Rockstro! Was not he shocked?

There is no reason why the Odyssey should not have been written by a woman, only the woman was not like Mrs. Barrett Browning. It is of course difficult (in the absence of the works of those early poetesses) to imagine a woman having written the great καὶ τὰ φέρει of Book xviii 135 in the speech of Odysseus to Amphinomous. That always seemed to me the biggest thing in the Odyssey. One of the biggest things in the whole of poetry—and it is so quietly said that no one heeds it.

I like all that you say about pedants amazingly. I feel as if I had written it myself. They deserve it. I like your incidental appreciation of Jane Austen and Dante. But of Dante it must be remembered that his mere poetry is unique, and though he is lower than Virgil or Milton his *charm* is ineffable.

One thing more in my hurried note. You are still advertising your "Fair Haven." I should like to know the history of that work in the market.

I am delighted to see that you have tackled Shakespeare's sonnets and smitten Sidney Lee. I send for the book today.

With best Xmas wishes,

your sincerely
Robert bridges

320: TO SAMUEL BUTLER

Yattendon
nr. Newbury
December 28, 1899

My dear Butler

It is very good of you to think my scrap of a letter worth such a long answer, but you are a patient letter-writer which I never was.

Your history of 'The Fair Haven' astonishes me, so few copies sold! I have a copy—many thanks—and have almost all of your books, the only gaps being due to the over appreciation of borrowers. I always hold you up as one of our best stylists. You taught me a great deal.

I am disappointed that there is no book on Homer. I never came across one, no, and thought that you might have. A great deal of the criticism of the Iliad by the men who would divide the poem into separate pieces is of value, just as Verrall's book on Euripides (the Alcestis) though the thesis is untenable is full of lights. You did not tell me that you talked Homer to Rockstro. He had a Homeric dictionary on hand—but who was of course as feeble as you could desire on the subject, though brimming over with enthusiasm. Your admirable portrait of him hangs in my drawing room.

I was disgusted by the rubbish written on Shakespeare's sonnets. Have not seen Lee's book, and don't want to. What could a Jew make of Shakespeare's love? By the way I am glad that Holden liked your Odyssey—He was an old friend of mine—and with all his training in pedantry held the top of his head above it somehow. He was most free and genial. He liked a new idea.

I am interested to read your note on that speech of Ulysses. It is very difficult to believe that a woman (especially a *young* female) wrote it. Only of course one does not know what women could do then. The notion that man's 'unstableness' is best illustrated by the readiness with which he accepts ill after good-fortune seems to me most poetic and profound. As for its not being in character with Ulysses I think I differ—his character has just that shifty and wordy cleverness, which enables him to say anything. And the better the thing he says, the better is the use made of his various opportunities. I am sorry to have 'old Grimthorpe' as a fellow admirer.

I am very much surprised that the book has not had more sale. This I cannot at all understand, for there has been a good deal of talk about it. I will see if I can't get one or two persons to read it who I know would like it.

Xmas has intervened. I have not got the sonnet book yet.

yours sincerely

R Bridges

321: TO SAMUEL BUTLER

Yattendon

December 31, 1899

My dear Butler

I thank you very much for your kindness in presenting me with your book on the sonnets, which I shall value all the more for the inscription. I read it yesterday, and so can send you first impressions with my thanks. It is strange that you should have written on my two favourite poems. I do not like this so well as your Odyssey essay, but I agree with a great deal of it. I should think that Mr Lee must feel sorry. It is wonderful what wretched stuff English criticism is, and how especially bad the present London product.

I like your explanation of "The mortal moon hath her eclipse endured". I never could see how James I came in there. That puts dates back satisfactorily. I wish to agree with your early dating. The passage "Three winters cold etc." is of importance; but "That time of year thou mayst in me behold" is very difficult; still generally I believe that your explanation of extreme youth as accounting for these exaggerations of 'age' better than real middle age would is sound. (And yet it is Shakespeare.) Your whole envisagement I am inclined to reject. 1°. The mean personality of W. H. which disagrees with the hints that other poets wrote of him and to him, and that books were dedicated to him. 2°. The worthlessness of his character and conduct, which disagrees with the very frequent assertion of his reciprocal affection, which is so beautifully and passionatel[y] told. 3°.—The idea that Shakespeare would have disliked the publication of the sonnets, in face of his plain statement that they would immortalise the recipient; which implies that they were intended to be read. 4°. And what follows from this, That whereas you make the explanation of certain expressions to be shameful, it is impossible that they can have been so. 5°—Your assumption that the sonnets not addressed to W.H. should be put with those addressed to him. Surely by the nature of the case they cannot have been: and even if your contention that their order of date can be made out, (and I don't object to the idea that they may have been contemporary, and even have relation to events touched on in the W. H. series) it seems to me that they are external to the W.H. series, and damage it, and were *not* intended to form a part of the 'immortal' poem.

Why did S never edit his own works? Why did Socrates, Aristotle and Christ show the same indifference? Yet it is incredible that one who took such pains in *writing* and correction should have been indifferent as to the form in which his works got about. Did he retire to Stratford to revise and publish, and did his untimely death rob the world of something better than its best?

My own key to the Sonnets has been that S saw that ideal love could be heightened by dissociation from sex. And feeling for W.H. something of this ideal love he sought to give it poetic expression: and I think that it was the absence of sexual feeling which enabled him to use the sexual imagery. This sexual imagery is of universal application in metaphor, and could only be excluded from a treatment of ideal love by secondary considerations of propriety and the fear of a misunderstanding which S did not fear. This boldness here is quite logical, though it is unparalleled.

I don't like the passage in which you say that S *must* have *known* a Doll Tearsheet etc. implying intimacy. By this sort of argument what must he not have known? Prosperos Calibans and Imogens. As for the low characters the slightest contact would be enough, and attendance at the magistrates' and law courts would have been ample provision.

Generally as to your book, I should say that the condition of the problem which you have set yourself to solve is such that it is of its nature insoluble. Among the infinite circumstances in possibility, which are altogether lost and unknown, the only clue to which is an idealized and purposely veiled reference in poems which are written with a poetic intention, it is beyond the power of ingenuity to construct one hypothetical set with any approach to conviction. But I promise to read the sonnets again (I know them pretty well) in the light of your explanation, much as I resent it, and though I cannot do it without the prejudice that S intended his poem to be read, and felt himself quite proof against such an explanation.

I was sorry that in so elaborate a book on the sonnets there was so little exposition of analytical detail—for the poem seems to be full of careful "construction" (even to the point that suggests revision and intercalation of later work among earlier.) But this I see might have obscured your more general aim. Yet the absence of this, and also, as it seemed to me, the absence of rise and fall of feeling with the poem, give to your book (at first reading) an uncongenial dryness, almost like want of poetic sympathy.

I know that you would want me to say just exactly what I think. So I have jotted my thinkings down. Of course there is much that I like, and the humour of certain jokes. The foreign lady at the B.M. and the "initials".

yours sincerely
R Bridges

P.S. I am afraid now that I have written a letter which your animadversational mind will itch to answer. Pray don't give way: I haven't yet mastered your book.

322: TO SAMUEL BUTLER

Yattendon
January 5, 1900

My dear Butler

I am sorry that you have had an attack of the plague. I am engaged in nursing a household sickening of it.—My wife has it rather badly—so excuse my not answering your letter for a few days. Very kind of you to offer the books. I will write you may be sure.

yours sincerely
R Bridges

Dr Garnett!! Well!

323: TO SAMUEL BUTLER

Yattendon
Newbury
January 25, 1900

My dear Butler

I have been having a bad time—my wife has been dangerously ill, and though she is now apparently getting on well, she is still very weak and ill, and I shall not be free from anxiety for some time.

I am writing you a short letter tonight lest you would think that my interest in the topic which your last book raised has flagged—or that I did not, as I said I should do, study your book after the first reading.

I worked pretty hard at it—until in fact the subject began to sicken me. The more I read the stronger your position seemed to be—but yet I was not more convinced. It only seemed to me that the refutation was more difficult. I don't remember quite what my position was after a first reading, but I expect that I think pretty much the same now, viz, that the hypothetical reconstruction of facts which you have undertaken is impossible, and that you underestimate the (excuse the term) ideal, or poetic cast of the 'poem'. You said, I remember, that my notion of the sonnets as 'a poem' showed you that we could never agree about them. But I would undertake to prove that they are a poem in the sense in which I use the word, i.e. that they were composed with definite relation to each other: more relation than is implied by their being merely successive experiences or states of reflections. I cannot see that there can be any doubt about this, and I think that if you had worked your analytical genius more at the artistic construction than at the circumstantial explanation, you would then have convinced yourself. I am very sorry indeed that you have been so clever as to make up so good (or bad) a story—but I willingly recognize that no one has brought the matter into so clear a light as you have done.—You are always perspicuous—and nothing but good can come of such conscientious work as yours. Still you must remember that you proved Darwin to be an arch imposter—and there was no fault in your logic. It is not the logic which fails in this book— —It is no use writing this sort of stuff. I was afraid you might think I was shirking it if I did not write: so I took up my pen: but not with the notion of doing any more now than assure you that that was not the cause of my silence. I hope to write again when things are better with us here.

yours sincerely
R Bridges

324: TO SAMUEL GEE

Yattendon
January 27, 1900

My dear Gee

I have been having bad times here. We all got the influenza. This South African business distracted me: and for the first time since the plague appeared I relaxed my vigilance and we have paid for it. As for the children and myself, we did not make much of it, but my wife, who happened unfortunately to be much reduced in strength by 2 months of the sickness of pregnancy, has been dangerously ill. She has been more than 3 weeks in bed, and though Dr Barlow prognosticated recovery from the first, and she has been now a week without cough or fever, yet her restoration must be very slow if not precarious, with her double sustenance to carry on. She still has to be nursed, or at least attended, night and day. So much for our health. I am as you may imagine not very robustious, but I do not think that there is anything the matter with me, though one's muscular condition after influenza is I suppose never of the best, and I cannot get enough out of doors yet.

You say you have been reading the newspapers. As for me, when I found out that our military authorities had taken none of the necessary precautions and made none of the common sense preparations, which I or any intelligent layman could have told them of years ago; and that our generals were behaving in a foolhardy way: after about 3 sleepless nights I gave up looking at the papers, and never in my life I think have kept myself so studiously uninformed as to what was going on. It was no use worrying as one could not help. Now they tell me things look better, and I read the paper yesterday. But I do not believe in their advantage at this Spion Kopje: It seems to me that it was practically undefended, and that we lost any number of men as soon as we got there. It seems as if it might be another trap.

The behaviour of the country and the colonies and the private soldier has been splendid: no better sign of national life could be wished; 15 years ago no one would have thought it was possible.

It was the music not the words of the hymns that I published for the sake of. I wrote the words merely to enable certain tunes to be sung. The emotional element in religion is absolutely expressed by music—by nothing else. You are religious, but as Spinoza was I think.—I was reading him in bed last night, and thinking of you. I chanced to buy the 2nd edition of his Tractatus Theologico-politicus the other day. I was reading the chapter on miracles. How very excellent it is. And how strange it seems to one that his arguments are so neglected or forgotten that some of the best of them were quite fresh to me. Especially that consideration that miracles (the point of which is that they are infractions of the laws of nature) are used for the convincing of the vulgar, who do not know the laws of nature.

If you want a book to read get one of Samuel Butler's last two. Either his "The Authoress of the Odyssey" or "Shakespeare's Sonnets" (Longman).—I do not in either case recommend them for the sake of the thesis, but his extreme acuteness and perspicacity and criticism are a constant delight, and he throws great light on everything that he deals with. Besides he is most excellent reading. I think really his location of the scene of the Odyssey is most probable. My wife was very much distressed to hear of your wife's "valetudinary" condition. I hope she is a bit better. Excuse a scribble from your

affectionate friend
RB

325: TO SAMUEL BUTLER

Yattendon
February 5, 1900

My dear Butler

My wife is really I believe getting better. It has been an awful time and the mere wearisomeness of it is not over yet.

The Bishop of London is quite right about 'commonsense'.

I shall "If I am spared" have a go at you some day. That I know will be good news to you.

Some one lent us once a book (written for the public) on the private lives of the sovereigns of Europe. They were held up to admiration, the veil being lifted reverently to show that they were human. I recommend you to read it if you come across it. Several of these demigods were represented as employing their leisure in "supplying the lacunae of their education." As for my lacunae. Your books are of different <u>sizes</u> and I have (really I am ashamed of it) so many thousand of books that I could not be sure of finding out at once what volumes I had, though the same sized books of the same author are I think always together—and I should not have liked to send an imperfect list.

Indeed I am really ashamed of sending you a list at all, especially after your very kind present of the Shakespeare which has made even my selfish and grasping heart over flow with gratitude: nor do I presume to offer you volumes of my own.

I have been reading Long's history of the fall of the Roman Republic. There was one sentence of that stoic author which would I think amuse you. "The tribunate of Drusus was a year of wonders . . . In the country of the Vestini it rained stones and tiles for seven days; on which Scheffer has the instructive remark that you will scarcely find any where else than in Obsequens an instance of such rain."

yours sincerely
R Bridges

List over leaf.

I find
Evolution Old and New
Life & Habit
Unconscious Memory
Alps & Sanctuaries
Fair Haven
Odyssey
Shakespeare's Sonnets
My copy of Erewhon or Erewohn has I believe found a home in New Zealand. I don't care for any but the 1st edition of this book, which I may come across some day.
I don't remember whether there is a Darwinian volume missing. I can't remember any title.

326: TO SAMUEL BUTLER

Yattendon
February 7, 1900

My dear Butler

You are really too generous. I always enjoy reading your books and look forward with nothing but pleasure to devouring at my leisure the pile now in front of me. I shall be very glad to send you mine in return, but I have some scruple in doing so, for I thoroughly dislike the idea of anyone reading them for any other reason than the attraction that they may possess, which is of course the only reason which they can have for existing.

Therefore I shall ask you, if you intend to read any of them, to begin with such as I think are most likely to interest you; and then if you find any pleasure in them you can go on if you like. The books which I shall send you will be poetry— but I have written one or two 'essays', and you would perhaps find them a good manner of reacquainting yourself with an old friend whom you knew only in his salad days.

For this purpose I should like you to read my *Introduction to Keats'* poems in the edition of *Keats* published by *Lawrence & Bullen* in "the Muses Library". (I am not responsible for the editing of the poems). You could find that in the Museum. It is a treatise on poetic forms—in their external aspect—and is I think written in different manner of criticism from that generally used: the manner which I think sound and useful. I am afraid that, as it deals in externals chiefly, it will touch on matters which you may not feel much interest in, but I think it is really *generally* interesting not only for its method but its matter.

I will write to Bumpus by this post and tell him to send you the 2 first volumes of my 'complete works' now being issued by Smith & Elder. I should especially wish you in them to read my Eros & Psyche, which is intended for the poetry-reading public, and in the 2nd volume the later, especially the "New Poems".

With many thanks for your kind and generous present.

yours sincerely

R Bridges

I am sending for a fresh supply of books from which I will select some to try your temper with.

327: TO LIONEL MUIRHEAD

Yattendon
February 9, 1900

My dear Lionel

We seem to be going on all right. My wife now gets up for 3 or 4 hours a day. —She is very weak and we are not quite "out of the wood", but things look better.

You introduced me years ago to "Curzon's Monasteries". Have you a copy of his Armenia? It is worth having, and if you have not a copy I can send you one.

yours ever

RB

I hope you have been going on all right. —I shall like news of Charis. Our love from both to both.

in haste.

328: TO SAMUEL BUTLER

Yattendon
nr Newbury
February 16, 1900

My dear Butler

Though I could never be surprised by your kindness, yet, knowing also your antipathies, I think I am more gratified by your devotion in facing my poetry than by the interest which you tell me actually bore you up through the reading of my long narrative poem. However convinced I may be that friendship is strengthened by sorrows and pains, still I should not wish my friendship to be the cause of discomfort, and my hesitation in sending you my books, (as my neglect in not sending them before) was merely an unwillingness to inflict the lection of them upon you, and not at all any coyness, or that vain sensibility to others' opinions which might impose on you the necessity of coining compliments. So now, if you can tell that you find my play interest[s] you, I will send you more—and if you will believe that I ask for neither admiration nor praise, (and there were words in your letter which implied as much) they may be the less unwelcome; for there is scarcely any more distasteful task to an honest and gentle mind than that of concocting 'appreciation' to flatter the touchiness of an author. I am afraid that I totally lack that note of the true "poet". And I believe too that I have even a greater dislike than you have to what is called 'literature', i.e. the matter which is supplied to the literary market to suit the taste of the ordinary reader, or the fashionable critic.

But history, science and art will make an infinite library, and life is not sufficient for any one of the three.

If you should read my 'Feast of Bacchus' tell me if its broad humanities interest you, and if you will have the other plays.

I should like you to read my "Essay on Keats". Art is what I most care for, and that tract expresses or at least implies my attitude toward it. Part of it too cannot fail to interest your critical faculty.

Thanking you for your letter, and with sincere apologies to Mr. Jones I am yours sincerely.

R Bridges

329: TO SAMUEL BUTLER

Yattendon
February 21, 1900

My dear Butler

Thanks for your letter. In answer here are the other plays, except the first 'Nero P^t I' which is out of print—but that accident does not mean that the plays sell. Byron, Tennyson and Browning have ruined the reputation of poetic drama among sensible people. Booksellers sell my plays at advanced prices, pretending that they are out of print. I never could sell Nero I at 2/—but it was quoted in catalogues at 21/. So you need not fear that my gift will cost me anything.

Porcis comedenda relinquis.

The history of them is as follows. I always wished to write drama. I began at school. When I seriously set to the work I approached the difficulties through a masque 'Prometheus the Firegiver.'

Next I took a historical subject which gave me characters and plot, and used the Shakespearian form as that best known to me: and I wrote 'Nero Pᵗ I.' I never meant it for more than an exercise, else I should not have taken the cumbrous Shakespearian form, with its innumerable drampers and frequent changes of scene. This play was a good deal read and praised by historians—so I did print it.

After that I went on my own way and the other plays are such as I should like to see on the stage. Except that 'Nero II' which I was much urged to write in continuation of 'Nero I' has some of the difficulties of the first part, and though it is made for acting, yet it would need trouble and expense and a *very* strong cast to put it on the stage. I think perhaps it is the best thing that I have done.

If you like reading drama I think that you will find no difficulty in mine.

I expect that I do not quite agree with you about "Elizabethan English." I hate the sham of it, such as Lang writes. I can't read it. Your translation of the Iliad seems to me much more Elizabethan than his Odyssey. My difference is thus— The English of 1600 is the unalterable and familiar basis of our speech. It is fixed by Shakespeare and the translation of the Bible. Later styles, as Pope and Macaulay, age very quickly and have little behind them—good style must always have a relation to Shakespeare—Then poetry implies some idealization of language, and this is most aptly supplied by the old tradition. Again the frequent sibilants, which we slur over and soften in speech, have to be pronounced in recitation or acting, and they *must* be avoided as much as possible. Thus I find it convenient to use *hath* for *has,* and *doth* for *does* etc., and also the subjunctive mood where it is grammatically correct. In your Homer I do not like your saying

If Paris *kills* Ajax.

I should say if he *kill* or *should kill.* This will explain some things and my notes some others.

The introduction of Keats which I wish you to read is in *Lawrence & Bullen's Muses Library*—the edition of Keats published some 4 or 5 years ago.

yours sincerely

R Bridges

I like your Iliad—but I never thought the Iliad readable as a consecutive poem— it has magnificent things in it—and the Greek hexameter keeps one up—nothing else—

p xiv. Contents of Book VIII "Juno & Minerva set out to help the TROJANS"! ! !

330: TO LIONEL MUIRHEAD

Yattendon
February 22, 1900

My dear Lionel

I send you Curzon's Armenia. It is an excellent book, barring an ill-conceived episode which begins I think on page 11 about a previous voyage on the Danube. Of course the book is not as good as his Monasteries, but how could it be? Still it has some quite first-class things in it: and the description of the country is most lively.

We hear this morning of the relief of Ladysmith. I hope it is true, but I fear that Cronje has escaped! What are those Boers up to now? I suppose one may trust Roberts to see through their designs even if he cannot outwit them: but he is or has been a very lucky man, and I sometimes fear that he may trust, like Caesar, to his stars: and get away into difficulties. Anyhow things look better now.

I liked Lord Lansdowne's speech very much. His statement that the stream that was flowing would not cease to flow was well calculated in expression.

I am busy this morning with household affairs, of which the doing up of your parcel is one. Therefore excuse a short note.

Thanks for the news of your family. I wish it were better. We are now getting over our difficulties unless Providence has something fresh in store.

My wife wants to know if this time of year is favourable for rearrangement of perennial borders. She thinks that next week she might superintend it in a bath chair!!

yours affectionately
RB

331: TO SAMUEL BUTLER

Yattendon
March 4, 1900

My dear Butler

You brought it on yourself and that is my only consoling reflection.

In answer to your letter (1) I am very glad to have any objection to details, such as you make, as I shall very probably have to reprint these plays, and shall then consider most carefully any such objections, and try and profit by them in revision. (2) I am *very much* surprised and pleased that you like my version of passages of the Odyssey. These were the very last things I should have shown you with any confidence. (3) I quite agree with you about Lear and Othello. Still I think them *readable*. I don't think I could stand seeing them acted. Lear certainly would be too painful. My Nero is rather history than drama, and I have no liking for the subject. Though not so horrible as Shakespeare it of course has not the same power of passion to sustain it. On the other hand it is in a way more defensible as art on a lower level, making a picture of real history, which it is necessary to know.

(4) I am glad that you find versification easy. In "The humours of the Court" I have I think succeeded in making blank verse do a great deal of comic ordinary business without flatness which I don't think has ever been accomplished before. If I have succeeded it is merely by dint of technical devices of extreme elaboration though of course hidden.

After reading your letter I feel much more in sympathy with you than I did before: and as if I should like to have a long talk with you. I know that we are irreconcileable on some points—but I think that you are modified—and of course there are some essential main lines on which we were always agreed.

How could you (to go for one detail) speak with any respect of Gladstone? And his "Homeric studies"?

Don't bother to write—but believe that if you do I consider nothing of more value than fault-finding. If you would pencil all the things that most offend you as you read and let me see the pencillings, that would be a great boon (if there is any excuse for ever using that word).

yours sincerely
R Bridges

332: TO R. WILKINS REES

Yattendon
Newbury
March 7, 1900

Dear Sir

I am much interested by your letter and as an old friend of Canon Dixon I hope that I may some day have the pleasure of making your acquaintance. I am glad that you are preparing an 'article' on the Canon's work for one of the periodicals. It is of course very difficult to do justice to anyone in this manner without a thorough knowledge of his work, and a good deal of pains and labour. On the other hand it is better to do one's best than to do nothing: as I am doing, though I have been asked to contribute some "memories" etc.—I know nothing of the proposal to publish a small book at present. I will myself do something some day, if the day comes: but Canon Dixon (whom I think you should style Dr. Dixon in your paper) has left his work behind him, and its recognition will slowly grow. I do not think that any stir in the public journals will affect that, one way or another.

His most important work is a History of the Church of England from the time of Henry VIII. 4 volumes are published and the 5th was ready and will be published posthumously. It is a very readable book, and written throughout in a fine and imaginative style. It is already recognized as a text book and authority— and will in my opinion take its place among the best 'Histories' in our language.

Some account will be found of Canon Dixon in the 'Life of William Morris' written lately by Mr. Mackail. It is in connexion with Morris that Dixon's name is best known to the general public.

There is a short account of him in the Oxford Magazine for January 31, which I send to you, (asking for its return). It will tell you some things—The writer is I think mistaken in saying that I am his poetical pupil.

The little shilling book (Elkin Mathews) was got together by me in order to get his verses before the public, but it really met with no appreciation. I think it would be a good thing if in your article you would call attention to this, and plainly tell your readers that they can have a selection of his verse for one shilling. A good many of your readers would perhaps buy so cheap a book.

My opinion of his poetry is that it contains passages of the highest excellence. I think e. g. that the little song "the Feathers of the willow" is a gem which will find a place among the best things of the kind. On the other hand his poetry is very uneven, and his Mano is [?] by a heaviness which his historical sympathies inflicted on it, while the romantic qualities of his poem persuaded him to play fast and loose with the history in that poem so that it is neither one thing nor the other.

I willingly tell you what my opinion is, but though you are at liberty to use it as you will, I must beg of you *not to quote my words as my own*, or coming with my authority.

It seems to me that you may make a point which would interest the public in this way—viz. make use of their appreciation of William Morris and Burne Jones, and say that Morris' work is known, and Burne Jones' is known, but Dixon's—which is as great in its way—(his history I mean chiefly) has yet to win its acceptance. This might be connected with his extreme modesty and retiring nature: and his fate to work all his life devotedly for the Church (being one of the most gifted and brilliant of the clergy) without any recognition save that of an honorary Canonry.

He always did a great amount of diocesan and episcopal work.

I am much gratified by what you so kindly say of my poetry.

Excuse my writing in some haste.

I am yours truly
Robert Bridges

333: TO LIONEL MUIRHEAD

Yattendon
March 24, 1900

My dear Lionel

I was very glad to hear from you. You will be indeed delighted to have got all that business done. The house too is I suppose nearly or quite in order, and you can look forward to enjoying the spring. But how completely old Mother Nature has us at her mercy. Maybe there will be no spring at all. I am however inclined to think that the devil may have done his worst this winter. He seems even to be sick of Krüger: in spite of that old cad having maintained that he had a tail.

I have two nephews in the war, one with Buller's force has had narrow shaves, but has escaped so far. The other with Plumer we of course can hear nothing of. My Milton's Prosody has sold out! And I am writing an additional chapter for the 2nd edition and am trying to persuade the Clarendon Press delegates to reprint with it a tract by William Stone son of the E D Stone who was a master at Eton in our time.

Have you heard that the Rector of Yattendon is leaving? He has only a few weeks more here!! We are looking forward to his successor. There seems a chance of his being a gentleman. I have a very pleasant but quiet almost hermitic neighbour at the Grange one Mr Marchant who was a master at St Paul's London. He is not only a good scholar but a good musician, and plays whist well. Unfortunately he is lame and cannot help me with the game of squash racquets in my new court. My great loft over the wood-house makes me a fine carpenter's shop. It is a magnificent place, and will ease the house of a lot of lumber.

Thanks for the 'cutting'—I read it. I wonder if those critics know what rot they write: and how they contradict each other. Some of them, or their editors, are manifestly dishonest.

The Spectator for instance has taken no notice of my new poems at all and I do not think there has been any review in the Athenaeum. This is plainly ridiculous. It has on me the unfortunate effect of making me think that I must be really a much greater poet than I imagine. By the way have you read either of Sam Butler's new books? You should read 'The Authoress of the Odyssey'. The book on Shakespeare's sonnets I do not recommend. It is very clever and even useful, but it needs an antidote. We read Erewhon again the other day with much delight, and I am reading Clough and Charlotte Brontë.

With our love

yours ever

RB

334: TO HENRY NEWBOLT

Yattendon
May 1, 1900

My dear Newbolt

I was glad to see your handwriting, and much interested by the contents of your letter. I do wish that I was at Lynton. As for the new Magazine I should have thought that there was room for a literary magazine, but the general defection of the mags from literature of course means that the public don't want it: and if they did it is not easy to supply. Your task is to discover a Sainte Beuve.

The English writers on criticism with all their cleverness and smartness are so dull: and really I don't know that the English public would read a Sainte Beuve if you found him. I was reading the other day that Ruskin said that Pope was the most typical Englishman of all writers after Chaucer. Now Pope in his Dunciad wrote against dulness and never saw that his "wit" was only a kind of dulness: and to my thinking one of the worst forms. I am like the French editor who in the plethora of clever writers sighed for a man who should be absolument dépourvu de l'intelligence!—a man in fact like myself. But the public don't care for such stuff as I produce. However I shall hope to send you an eclogue or two or something versical if you think fit. Of course there is a fair audience for good literary work, but it is not as numerous as the conditions of a cheap magazine require, and I doubt if it is any use trying to sell at more than one shilling.

I am occupied today in revising my Milton's Prosody for the Clarendon Press.—It has sold out! The second edition is to have a long additional appendix on "stress-prosody and the English accentual Hexameter"—and the delegates have consented to my proposal to print Stone's treatise on "Classical Metres in English" with my "Milton's Prosody". Stone's tract is revised for the purpose, and will contain a full account of the true quantity of English syllables according to Latin and Greek prosody. He thinks that classical metres could be written. I don't quite agree with him, but it is certainly a most important thing for people to know about the true 'longs and shorts' on classical principles. I think that he is almost finally right about them, and no one yet has written any sense on the subject. The basis is of course phonetic, and some extraordinary results come from its application. It is all common sense, and convincing though revolutionary.

I do not mean to take the Oxford professorship. The idea of writing a series of papers on the subject of English poetry has often occurred to me, but I do not think that they would be suitable for a magazine. If I were engaged in editing such an affair I should depend a good deal on the interest of "occasional notes"—short paragraphs in which *smartness* might be indulged ad lib. I think the public will call for *smartness,* and I think it can be put without literary offense into gossip.

I have had the most miserable winter. No use to speak of it. It has left me a wreck. I hope what remains of the year will restore me. One thing is good, the rector of Yattendon is leaving, and his successor promises well. He sings, plays cricket and whist, and has other social qualities. Also I find Marchant a good neighbour, though owing to my wife's illness I have been able to make little use of his residence so far. My wife is now much stronger, and if all goes well we may get away to the seaside in October, and remain there till we wish to return.

She sends her love to your wife and kindest remembrances to yourself by salutation.

yours sincerely

RB

Writing in the garden in the sunshine!!!

335: TO ROBERT BRIDGES

Haseley Court
Tetworth
Oxon
May 31, 1900

My dear Robert

I must not let the first month of Summer quite expire without writing to enquire after your welfare and to beg that if you have any recipe for making summer days pass by more slowly you will of your charity impart it to me. We keep to our 7.45 o'clock breakfast most punctually and this has some effect in lengthening our days: I wish we had started it earlier in life, but we want the Cabalistic incantation for setting Joshua's sun in the heavens.—The paper has just come in with the news of the (practical) close of the Boer War; it is useless to write in a letter on this subject, but it is indeed a pleasure to have achieved this result in the teeth of the Jesuits, the Stead faction, and all the rabid jealousy of Continental nations. Did you see that the Reverend Stephen Gladstone would not allow his Church Bells to be rung on the relief of Mafeking? He will have a bad Purgatory. I can only conclude these paragraphs by singing the National Anthem in the celebrated verse of Victor Hugo (when he boasted that he could write English Poetry):

> Pour chasser le spleen
> J'entrai dans un inn
> Oh! mais je bus le ginn
> God save the Queen!

In your last letter you said that your parson was going: I suppose by now he is gone: may you get somebody better: is it improbable: the better ones are so seldom manufactured: ours is awful: he is not going: I adopted your counsel to give up going to Church as far as practicable: it has been a difficult business, but diplomatic revolt has carried the day 'at home' which is all I care about. Mrs Robert in this—as in all else—has I know an understanding mind.

You will be surprized to hear that all my family have taken to Bicycling. Anthony began it and learnt in 24 hours: Charis said she must do as her brother did: Gracie said she couldn't let her daughter run off in this way unchaperoned, and I naturally was compelled to try to keep an eye on my family, so by this time we all go about quite easily and effectually. It is not much fun, but is extremely useful. I have not yet invested in a bicycle but must do so; what do you recommend? You are sure to have genuine views on the subject, and I shall be most grateful for hints and warnings. E.G. How about a Free Wheel? You talked at one time of selling your old machine and getting something bigger: perhaps your 'Bike' would do for me if you still want to get rid of it.

I am awfully sorry that your domestic arrangements will postpone a visit here

rom yourself and your wife to which I have looked forward for many months: I
lon't know whether there is any likelihood of your being able to come over here
n any way at any time. We can always put you up if you can come whenever it
uits you, and if you Bike we can get any luggage over from Tiddington.

With my kindest regards to Mrs Robert

I am your affectionate
Lionel Muirhead

336: TO LIONEL MUIRHEAD

Yattendon
June 1, 1900

My dear Lionel

Your letter was very welcome. You would have heard from me before, but we
have been in great troubles and uncertainties, and just now are passing through
very critical days. Things however are not desperate. I can't write the details but
we have had to face one of those arrangements of nature which make it almost
impossible for a mother to live. I don't know how to put it, nor whether to be
more angry with the devil who got us into this hole, or grateful to a kind
Providence who coming mysteriously and as it seemed fortuitously to the rescue
at the very last moment has been a very Baden Powell to us. Still we are not
relieved' altogether. And it will be some days before I can write with confidence,
at the best.

I hope this news about Pretoria etc. is true, and that all is doing well. There
seem a great many of the ruffians about: and that Botha is the best general they
have had, and is capable of doing something surprising.

Excuse a short letter. I shall be writing I hope in a day or two.

yours ever
RB

About bicycles. I have not a free wheel on mine. It is a good machine by Lee &
Francis. I should have a free wheel if I were to buy a machine now—but I should
also have a tire break [*sic*] on the front wheel in case of accident to the free wheel
machinery. I have never ridden a free wheel, and take for granted that it is easy
to get to manage the break [*sic*] with the feet. Perhaps it would be worthwhile to
hire one to try first, because it must evidently be a source of danger unless it is
well in the rider's control. On the other hand it seems an admirable solution of
coasting for ladies, whose skirts are a source of danger in the old machine from
their coming into contact with the revolving pedals. Also they tire more easily
than men, and should have every convenience of this kind.

337: TO LIONEL MUIRHEAD

Yattendon
June 11, 1900

My dear Lionel

Things are going on well with us, and if so continue we shall be at the seaside all July. This is a nuisance. Many of Butler's books are the best possible reading. The title of the Darwinian books are

1. Life and Habit
2 Evolution Old & New
3 Unconscious Memory
4 Luck or Cunning
5 Selections from Previous Works

I remember thinking the first 3 of these very good. I do not know if I have read the other two.

I am myself quite convinced by Butler's *location* of the Odyssey. Excuse a scrawl. Our Rock garden is doing well.

yours ever
RB

P. S. The last war news has worried me very much. I hope we shall soon get better accounts. Louis Botha is a very good man. But Roberts is up to him I should think if he is not too old—I wish he were 15 years younger.

338: TO SAMUEL GEE

Yattendon
August 17, 1900

My dear Gee

We have been getting on pretty well. My wife made a good recovery and though still rather anemic, she is looking well and stouter than she has ever been. She was well enough to spend July at the seaside, and we were fortunate in hiring a friend's house which was very comfortable. I enjoyed bathing in that hot weather more than I have done for years. Now we are all at home again and I am trying to put this house tidy. I do not know that I can boast of being in very high spirits: I think this war has depressed me generally—and there seems no end to it. I am convinced that a good deal of the general disturbance is due to the absurd reason that it is the end of a century. You have been reading Philosophy. I have often tried to get a good set of Bishop Berkeley's works, but have been unfortunate. The books are not rare, but somehow I have never got them, and I have always put off reading him as I wish to till I get the books. The last philosophy that I read was in a little original edition of Spinoza which I picked up. I must say that I like contemporary editions of books —I have a vast lot of books now, and a good deal of my tidying is putting up bookshelves. I wish you could come here for a day or two before you go back to work. Is it quite impossible? I really think that you would enjoy this country—and it would be great pleasure to us all, and would do us good.

The children are growing up fast and are doing pretty well. They are not without promising gifts and they take a delightfully keen interest in everything.

I have put a churchyard cross up over my mother's grave. It looks well, and I was glad to get over the difficulty of a gravestone.

My wife joins me in kindest remembrances—and love.

yours ever
RB

339: TO SAMUEL BUTLER

Yattendon
October 27, 1900

My dear Butler

I am very much obliged to you for your kind present of the translation of the Odyssey, which I shall value very much. I am glad that you say that it is intended for those who do not read the Greek: for I shall probably only look up certain places in it. Certainly you are a very conscientious translator. I think I told you that I was quite converted to your localisation of the story. I think I should have doubted another writer's facts, but I quite trust your description of what you found and saw.

I am not at all surprised at your feeling estranged from my work. I am however surprised and really flattered at your having read the plays and getting them bound. At least I presume that you found them readable. All kinds of people read them, by which I mean that when they take them up they feel interested and go on and read to the end.

I was away in Somerset when your letter and book arrived here. I returned today. We are all going to spend November at Brighton. If you happen to know anything of any professional teacher of drawing there let me know. (I don't want the drawing master for young ladies.)

Thanking you again for your very kind gift.

yours ever
R Bridges

P.S.
I am very much delighted (as many of my friends will be) with the notion of a new Erewhon. It is a brilliant idea, except that till I see it I can't believe that it will be as good as the first. I never read any satire that I enjoyed more than the chapter on the musical banks.

340: TO LIONEL MUIRHEAD

28, Oriental Place
King's Road
Brighton
November 30, 1900

My dear Lionel

I enclose you Jackson's letter, and your approved line. I have told him that he may now go on, and that I suppose you will thicken your inscription at your leisure. There seems no hurry.

We go home on Thursday. I think my wife is a little stronger.

I am tired of Brighton though we have not had at all a bad time. Elizabeth has been to a studio kept by an old friend of Sam Butler's. She has made her first studies in serious drawing—carefully modelled heads and hands, and has also drawn from the live model. This is just what I wanted. She has done very well.

With our kindest remembrances to your wife.

yours ever
RB

341: TO ROBERT BRIDGES

Haseley Court
Wallingford
December 27, 1900

My dear Robert

I send you the inscription which I have had ready for some time but forebore to send earlier out of consideration for the long suffering postman at Xmastide. I have done my best to thicken the letters so that they may give the raised curved surface for the gold in the hollow when cut: I hope Mrs Robert will correct anything you may find fault with.

I hope your Christmastide has been a happy one: with 3 children in the house it can scarcely I think have been otherwise, such marvellous faculty have they of enjoying themselves until they get so tired there is nothing left but to fall asleep and recruit for the next day's pleasuring. I expect this is the arrangement Nature would like us usually to adopt, but somehow we [part of page torn out] all praise it unanimously.

Well Robert here we are (laus Disfaventibus) at the end of the century both having had a far larger slice of health and happiness than has fallen to the lot of many we have known. I dont understand life in the least and dont now seek to do so; the puzzles in it are quite insoluble and must be left to be cleared up in the saecula saeculorum of which my portion of the twentieth century is but th narthex. But it is a thing to be grateful for that the years have planted in one's mind a garden of clipped hedges and sheltered nooks where all sorts of pleasant memories of people and scenes and books and things that cannot be enumerated bloom perpetually. It is my hope that if sight should fail they will still be visible. You have helped me to plant this garden, and will I am sure accept my thanks. Please give Mrs Robert my kindest regards and Believe me

your affectionate
Lionel Muirhead

342: TO MRS. MANLEY HOPKINS

Yattendon
Nr Newbury
December 30, 1900

Dear Mrs Hopkins

My wife and I send our love and best wishes for the new year. I was very glad to see your handwriting again, and wish that I was able to pay you a call, and talk with you. We get occasional news of you from Mr Redmayne.

It is very pleasant also to find that you take an interest in my poems. I hope therefore that you saw my last volume in the Smith & Elder edition, Volume II— which contained some new poems that you might like. It was the publishers' fault that the 3rd volume did not immediately follow. I think they were disappointed with the immediate sale (or rather non-sale) of the first two—though as far as I can make out they should have amply paid their expenses. It was a bad time for selling poetry, and the most important reviews did not give me at all a good welcome. Indeed neither the Spectator nor Athenaeum took any notice what-ever of my 2nd volume, though it contained a lot of new stuff. I consider this a very high compliment—especially as some of these new poems were at once put into the new Oxford anthology. But it did not please the publishers I fancy. However now they have gone to work again, and 4 volumes of the plays are to come out without any interval. The first will contain that old Nero, and should be out by Easter.

My wife is getting much stronger now. She has nothing the matter with her so far as I know, I am glad to say, except weakness due to her severe illnesses, which may or may not have told you of.

We spent November at Brighton with all the children, and have come home for Christmas. We are thinking of going away again in January.

Please remember me very kindly to any of the family who may be at home, and believe me

yours very sincerely
Robert Bridges

343: TO LIONEL MUIRHEAD

Yattendon
January 2, 1901

My dear Lionel

Your thickened inscription came quite safely, and shall be duly transmitted to Jackson. I hope that the next time you see it, it will be in gilt on black marble.

Thank you for writing me such a good New Year's letter. I reciprocate all your kind wishes and pleasant reminiscences. I went with my wife to the 10:30 a m service in the church this morning, and during the quiet time thought over many old things. But it was very odd to hear "the full, perfect and sufficient sacrifice and oblation" and to think what one had been taught to believe.—The recollections of my life that are associated with you are all pleasant, and some of them among the most pleasant of my life. But I often think how bad and ungrateful a companion I have often been. Then I remember how philosophical you are—and I hope that it didn't much matter in the long run.

Looking back to the old days few things satisfy me more than the consideration and position which HEW has obtained. I owed more than I can say to his wits: and it would have been very sad if he had never been drawn out of his cave. I am still hoping that they will ask him to reside.

I do not know if I told you, but it is very possible that we of the Manor House shall all go up to Oxford for next term, if we can get a suitable home.

I hope that this year will do better for us all than last year did. I got very nearly tired of human existence. I am very sorry for your anxieties, especially about Charis. I trust that this year will lessen that trouble. My wife joins in kindest remembrances to your wife and we both send all good wishes to you both.

yours affectionately
R Bridges

344: TO THOMAS BARLOW

Yattendon
January 20, 1901

My dear Barlow

I was very much obliged to you for your bulletins. I did not hear of the poor Bishop's death till your letter on Thursday! I was glad that you got to like him. His was a very strange mind—at least I doubt if any one quite understood him, for he was evidently not a man to be readily classed: and an offhand classification would have done him great injustice. He was usually extremely reserved; and since he used freedom of speech as a cloak, no one liked him on first acquaintance. On the other hand he won everybody's heart very soon. His great gifts were sympathy kindliness and sociability and the exercise of these by a mind of rare power, acuteness and retentiveness. It is strange that a man made by nature to be a bishop should not have been allowed a little more time. He was by far the most philosophical of our bishops, and I looked to him for a Church policy: I was disappointed that he did not show more of his attitude in London; but supposed that he was waiting for Canterbury. I was one of his first pupils, and have known him for 33 years or more: but I do not venture to say that he was intimate with me. I doubt if he was with anybody, though he was to me undoubtedly sincere, and never shrank from question. I should like to talk with you about him some day.

We have virtually taken a house in Oxford for the term, and should go up, if nothing hinders on the 30 or 31st. You shall hear from me there, and come and see me and also if you will dine at high table at CCC.

yours ever
RB

The *Times* obituary notice, written probably by an *old friend* (!) was, I thought, very hard on Creighton. It took a great liberty in speaking of his sincerity as a sort of open question. But it shows how even his friends were puzzled.

345: TO LIONEL MUIRHEAD

17 Bradmore Road
Oxford
February 3, 1901

My dear Lionel

We are settled in here for the term. Elizabeth goes to draw at the Ruskin school. Margaret has violin lessons and Edward has found a small school. We are as you may remember just at the corner of the Parks—really very conveniently situated. The house is commodious and we have a good spare bedroom. I hope that you will run up and see us. Monica extends the invitation to Mrs. Muirhead: but I doubt if she would find anything to repay the inconveniences of travelling in this weather. If the weather should improve she might like to come. But in any case I think you would find plenty to do going about with me and seeing old friends and strolling round the galleries etc. Monica is not at all strong yet and does not walk very much.—She gets out once a day seldom twice: and is a good deal occupied in arranging the children's doings.

I do not know whether you can easily leave home for the night or whether you would just run down for the inside of the day. We shall be here till end of term, in fact till end of March—and shall be glad to see you at anytime. Stuckey Coles is in good form. If you come you should stay if you can especially if you have not heard the singing at the lovely Mission Chapel on the Iffley Road. It is a wonderful building for sound and they do the plain-song very well. I have little actual work besides correcting proofs. We are all pretty well.

yours affectionately
RB

346: TO LIONEL MUIRHEAD

[17 Bradmore Road
Oxford]
February 11, 1901

My dear Lionel

I am very much grieved to hear of Charis' illness. I was talking of her to Dr Acland the other day at Yattendon and lamenting the great anxiety which you must have on her account. I do not think that there is any trouble worse than that which one's children can give one in this way, except I suppose their moral obliquity. That must be altogether unsupportable. I have had a good deal of anxiety myself—but so far things have gone well with me. I am taking for granted that what is now wrong with Charis is some development of the symptoms that you told me of. Perhaps I am wrong. I will not write more of it. You will tell me when I see you.

So far I am enjoying myself more than I deserve. I have a great many friends here: and the society of people at once so friendly and accomplished, all active and interested in life is a great pleasure. Also there is plenty of music. I went to Magdalen Chapel & Hall last night: it was quite like old times. Only I did wish that Stainer or Parratt had been there.—Before our time is out I shall know whether I like the idea of settling at Oxford. There is another alternative—that of taking lodgings for the term—

I hope you will manage to come up. I was glad that you could write such a cheerful letter. There will be plenty to see and do here if you do come.

yours affectionately
RB

Next Sunday I dine in C.C.C. and have asked my guest. I can only have one—so don't come for next Sunday.

I hope Antony has got over his cold—we have had a turn at them.

347: TO LIONEL MUIRHEAD

Yattendon
April 12, [1901

My dear Lionel

"What shall I do with these wet racquets—you left them in the garden" said my wife out of breath after skurrying home on her cycle from tea with Lady Gull. "Why! is it raining?" "Pouring." So it is. It might be snowing—I was just sitting down by the fire to write you condolence on your laryngitis, after having had tea with Margaret in her bedroom, where she lies becolded. Oh! if I only had the arrangement of the weather! It seems to me that it might all be so simple an

atisfactory. Now the other two children have come into the room and are setting
ut the draught board.

I am thoroughly sorry for you, and hope that you are getting better. I have
een in better health than I deserve to be, considering how much I smoke, and
ow I indulge in afternoon tea, and keep myself awake by drinking coffee of an
vening. Any day that you come we can have a pretty good whist. I have been
ery busy getting a final edition of my Milton Prosody out. It had gone out of
rint, and is now coming out in a new and somewhat luxurious dress in the same
olume with an essay on "Classical Prosody in English" by William Johnson
tone, E D Stone's son. Did you hear of his untimely sudden death about one
nonth ago? He died of pneumonia after a few days illness. He was a most
elightful fellow, and exceedingly clever. Now I am working to get his Essay
hrough the press. His father and family have gone to live at Abingdon so we
nay see something of them. Lots of people have been asking me to sing Victoria
n excelsis, but I find that I have not much feeling for the old Queen; though I
an't help going on praying for her at family prayers, which the children observe
o me at breakfast. Our rockery is doing marvellously well. Even the Edelweis has
ome up thick. We brought some new things from the St. John's Gardens.

I have paid for the Y. H. Book. I paid about 130£ in all, but expect to get a
ood deal of it back. It has not sold badly, and I have had to reprint Part I.

I am now publishing my Hymn article (which you saw) as a pamphlet, with the
Hymn-book prefaces at the end as a sort of advertisement of the book. Blackwell
t Oxford is doing it at his own expence. It is a tidy little tract, and you shall have
ne from me as soon as it comes out. This reminds me of poor Stainer. I ought to
ave gone to his funeral the other day, but could not ascertain the hour, and did
ot like to give up a whole day. He was a most excellent person; as HEW said, his
ad taste was not his fault. But, my wig! how bad it was. I think that anyone who
new him loved him, in spite of it. Really I think I should have a good deal to talk
o you about if you came here: but this chat must suffice for the evening.

Hoping it will find you better

with our love

yours

RB

Vife joins in kindest regard to Mrs. Muirhead. How jolly everything ought to be
n a few weeks!

48: TO LIONEL MUIRHEAD

Yattendon
May 2, 1901

Iy dear Lionel
I am this morning going to stretch a piece of drawing paper on one of those
eautiful boards with which you presented Monica 17 years ago: with the inten-

tion of getting a water colour lesson out of you for Elizabeth. I will not let her bother you much, but she can sit and paint where we are and ask you what to do. Then it struck me that you might like to choose some simple subject for her to begin upon—and that if I wrote to you you might think of one of your own sketches, of which you would be able to say exactly how it was made.

She has got on with drawing but has no notion of water colour.

In any case do not bother, as perhaps there is no reason to have anything in particular. We want you to stay as long as you can, and if you can stay long you will I hope bring your cycle.

yours

RB

349: TO LIONEL MUIRHEAD

Yattendon
May 10, 1901

My dear Lionel

I want you to read the enclosed at your leisure. I read it aloud to you when you were here. I have now copied it out very legibly so that you may have no difficulty in reading it. I wish you to criticise it. That is (if you like the poem generally), to tell me what parts of it you do *not* like, any harsh line or doubtful expression etc. I shall value your animadversions very much as I want to get it as good as I can, and this heroic couplet is the most difficult thing to manage naturally. I don't want it back at all soon. I was at Oxford yesterday, and we had a good lecture from the Professor. I wished very much that you had been there. I am not going today, as the weather is so dreary.

Hoping that you found all well at home.

yours ever

RB

350: TO LIONEL MUIRHEAD

Yattendon
May 15, 1901

My dear Lionel

Very many thanks for going so carefully through my verses. I shall try and get out some of the offences.

I knew of the *whoms* and *whoses* and had marked them to consider what should be done with them. Of course the mere fact of a grammatical construction suddenly appearing and declaring itself for a time and then as suddenly disappearing is in itself good, and I was not sure that there were too many whoms etc., only it is reasonable to insist that they should have the same antecedent in the thought, which mine have not.

As for open vowels. I do not see the objection, but if any sounded unpleasant I must reconsider them and try and discover why they displease.

We are going to Oxford today, to hear the Professor. Perhaps we may meet you.

yours ever
RB

351: TO MRS MANLEY HOPKINS

Yattendon
Newbury
May 16, 1901

Dear Mrs Hopkins

I am sending you the reprint of an "article" which I wrote some time ago to advertise my hymnbook. It is republished for the same purpose. I thought that you might care to read it, and if not I should be very much obliged if you would give it or lend it to any one who is interested in the subject.

I hope that you are well. It seems a long time since I heard of you. I spent all last term in Oxford, with my wife and children. Now we are at home for the summer. My wife is getting stronger by degrees after her bad illness last year. She is not up to much yet: but I trust is slowly getting all right again.

Mrs. Waterhouse asked me if I could get permission from you to print one or two of Gerard's religious poems in a little book which she is making up for Methuen.

I do not know how to describe it, but it is supposed to be about "Life and Death" so that there is some latitude for Mrs. Waterhouse's fancy. I do not myself see any objection to her printing the verses: but it lies with you to decide. One of the things which she wanted was "I have desired to go".

My wife joins in kindest remembrances to you, and to your daughter or daughters at home.

Believe me yours very sincerely
Robert Bridges

352: TO MRS. MANLEY HOPKINS

Yattendon
May 21, 1901

Dear Mrs Hopkins

Thank you very much for your kind letter—with permission to Mrs. Waterhouse.

Your kind enquiry after Nero (Part I) is very touching—and I cannot neglect it. It is so very good of you to want to read it again. I am afraid it will disappoint you when it does come. They have been inexcusably long in printing it but really it is all in type now and I will get them to send me some proof sheets of it from the press which I will forward to you, as it will not be published till October—

Secondly may I ask you whether you or your daughters have ever read "Reminiscences of an Irish R. M."—if not order it from your library, or I will lend you my copy. It really is more like what a book should be than any of those painful masterpieces of our Thackerays & Co.

yours sincerely
Robert Bridges

What you say about Lionel is very interesting.
PS
It strikes me that I may as well send you my copy of the proofs.

It is possible that I may want them again. If I do you will excuse my writing to ask you to return them.

RB

353: TO WILLIAM BUTLER YEATS

Yattendon
nr Newbury
June 18, 190?

My dear Yeats

I am sorry never to have a chance of meeting you. Binyon was here the other day and brought some tidings. —I hope that you and the Muse are getting on well. Is it *possible* that you will honour us by another visit this summer? —Some Sunday when you have nothing better to do? I am writing today because by some accident I took up your 'Poems' yesterday, and I have been reading at them ever since. With the same admiration and delight, but all fresh because of my bad memory—the best gift that I have. —I forgot what time of year it was when you were here. I rather think it may have been about this time—it is not bad—a little over green—I think you would like the quiet if you could stay long enough to taste it. Do you think that you could come some Saturday till Monday? There is a very first class train from Paddington to Pangbourne of an evening. —It leaves Paddington at 6.10 and its wandering and milky smoke does not stop at Reading. You must get into the right carriage which is slipped after Reading for the little stations. We would send to Pangbourne to meet you. I suppose that Elkin Mathews will send this on to you. I don't know whether your old address is of any use. Please come if you can.

yours sincerely
Robt Bridges

354: TO HENRY NEWBOLT

Yattendon
July 9, 1901

My dear Newbolt
    The pens are all bad.
    I am much obliged for the review. It was very good of you to have that article in. I had seen it. In fact a copy of the MAG was sent to me and I had been intending to write and thank you. It was of course very flattering, and I was especially pleased to find that Mr. Symonds' previous praise had not worked remorse in him. I thought he had overdone it before—but he is too clever a reviewer to spoil the interest of his notices by half measures, which really never please readers. I have not seen you since you started the MAG. I hope it has established a fair pecuniary return—it has certainly been a success. I always hear it spoken well of, though I do not often see it. The Waterhouses take it. My wife was writing to Mrs. N yesterday, but I doubt if it came off. We were discussing the possibility of your coming down here some time in this summer. It would be very nice for our children. Then I have some things which you might pick from for your MAG if so disposed. Tomorrow we are going off for a 3 days' visit to a friend's. After that we expect to be at home. One of our children has been bad with a throat. Otherwise we are well. I am wrestling as usual with the Clarendon Press, having Will Stone's "Classical Metres in English" coming out in the same volume as my Milton's Prosody, to which latter I have added a fullish account of stress rhythm, and of the English accentual hexameter, which I think are both good reading for those who care for such things. Stone's paper is quite revolutionary and full of common sense and irrefutable truths. His lamentable death gives me trouble as well as sorrow.
    When we get home we must try and arrange for a visit from you. Perhaps you will be able to write and tell us whether there is any chance of your being able to come. I am unfortunately very busy now with all sorts of stupid affairs that I must attend to: entailing visits to people who live far away.—In this weather everything seems a long way off, if it's not on the lawn.

yours ever
RB

Our kindest remembrances to Mrs. Newbolt who I hope is well.

355: TO LIONEL MUIRHEAD

Yattendon
July 13, 1901

My dear Lionel
    All the things arrived safely this morning. I am ashamed of having given you all that trouble—glad that all the things were mine, so that wife and Spokes came

off creditably. I can't help sending you the postage—because I feel wronged in a similar matter myself if I am not recouped in stamps.—We got home quite comfortably. The rain did not get as far as us last night, but we share the coolness following the storm. It must have been London way.—We planted the plants—and are now entertaining a visitor—

I had to take a lot of exercise yesterday after my too idle days at Haseley—but the port wine agreed with me wonderfully—

We enjoyed ourselves much—and I was very glad to make the children's better acquaintance: and shall hope to see more of them—

We both send kindest regards to Mrs Muirhead and your aunt

yours ever
RB

356: TO SAMUEL GEE

Yattendon
July 18, 1901

My dear Gee

The Wooldridges are coming to us on the 30th for a fortnight. I write to give you the earliest information so as to avoid any risk of missing your proposed visit. It would be extremely pleasant if you would come and stay a few nights. If you can come for only one night then you know that you can be in London by 10. a m or a few minutes after.

Sunday 28th is free as far as we are concerned.

After the Wooldridges' visit we shall be disengaged.

I wrote you a very poor answer to your long letter to me, which contained some admirable friendly matter, which did me good. It was delightful to hear that you read my poems with any satisfaction.—I am beginning now to reap some of the compliments which the journalists bestow on the aged.

I read a lot of Locke yesterday and the day before together with Fowler's life of him. He would be very pleasant to read (Locke) if there was not something to pull one up in every other sector. My philosophy has somewhat matured. I shall yield to the temptation some day of writing metaphysics. I shall ask you for a commendatory poem.

We shall hope to hear that you are coming down. We have a lot of new trains. Pangbourne is still our favourite station, but we have good trains to Hampstead Norris, which is 4 miles nearer. The time is much the same allowing for the drive.

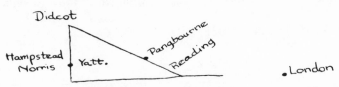

Some of the through trains run by Didcot and some by Newbury. If you come in the evening there is a marvellous train

Padd. -------------------	6.15
Pangbourne ----------	7.12

(slip carriage)

We could send to meet you either at Pangbourne or Hampstead Norris.

yours ever

RB

357: TO ROBERT BRIDGES

Haseley Court
Wallingford
July 19, 1901

My dear Robert

We were very glad you managed to get over here for a visit though the atmosphere in which we had to receive you rendered locomotion so uneasy: we have been stewing pretty well ever since and for the last day or two have taken to living in semidarkened rooms as being cooler than even under the shade of the trees on the back lawn: The country outside the grounds is so open and sun-burnt, that we feel enclosed literally by the flammantia moenia mundi. This afternoon I have promised to go with a water party on the river at Shillingford: luckily it has been postponed till 5 o'clock and I dont expect to get home till 10.30 but the river at Dorchester ought to be nice in the summer twilight.

"Santayana" came by second post yesterday afternoon: I am so much obliged to you for the volume which I am going to take out and read with care under the trees, as it must be sipped like good wine with attention and enjoyment, and I will let you hear again when I have finished the bottle.

You may be amused to hear that Anthony was observed to be specially energetic the other day and said that a great access of energy had come upon him since seeing Mr Bridges, and he thought if the Government would only send you out to South Africa that no Commando would stand against you!

I hope Mrs Robert was not overtired by her visit: I will send one or two more plants later on when there is more chance of moving them with success:

your affectionate
Lionel Muirhead

358: TO WILLIAM BUTLER YEATS

Yattendon
July 24, 1901

My dear Yeats

Thank you for your permission to Mrs. Waterhouse, which I will transmit to her. I do not warrant her book, in fact her taste is not as mine in anything. But these things have to be left to go as they will—and it is after all some sort of consolation that there should be people who 'appreciate' that part of one's work which one does not care for oneself. I have always said that if I had published what I had burned and burned what I had published I should have been a popular poet. Quite an echo of the age and a man of the day.

I am sorry that we have missed you but you must come in the Winter and make up—don't forget. And the dusk and fireside will be a better atmosphere for you to tell the children some of your Irish legends.

I am much interested in all that you say about your work—and very much pleased that you are able to carry out your scheme.—Your style in lyric and narrative is alike most *charming* (in the right sense of the word) to me and I should think that a combination of the two should show you at your best.—The trouble of lyric verse is, I fancy, that it needs a mood which is fitful and really impossible to sustain.—It is of its nature to exhaust itself and break off—whereas the narrative, though it may really be as full of imagination, or seem to be, when once started has a tendency to rush on of itself. So that with this to fall back on you need never be idle.

I agree about the recitation, I think. It is a very difficult matter. Setting *song* aside—which has several degrees—the mere reading of poetry, if well read, is full of melodious devices, which it is the art of a good reader to conceal, so that he gets his effects without calling attention to them. The word recitation—and the presence of an instrument—makes open confession of his art, and without becoming a singer he ceases to be a reader. The hearer has his attention called to the method itself—and as I have never had any experience of good chanting or recitation I do not know how I should like it.

There was a kind of recitation fashionable some years ago in London drawing rooms—satirized by Anstie—and it even crept into the churches.—I have heard the old Testament 'recited' in Westminster Abbey. This used to draw tears from me—tears of laughter. I shook as at a French farce.—This is the only sort that I ever heard. I can't really imagine a recitation which I should myself like so well as good reading (in which the same art would be disguised) but I think that there must be such a thing—and I hope you and the lady will discover it.

I will send you a book with some interesting poetic notes in it before the Autumn.

yours ever
R Bridges

359: TO ROBERT BRIDGES

Shirburn Lodge
Watlington
Oxford
August 25, 1901

My dear Robert

It is difficult to thank you enough for the Volume of Santayana's essays which are delightful: I envy the man his command over language which enables him to say just what one would wish to have said oneself, if only the jus et norma loquendi had been granted. 'Imaginative belief' was the phrase I had invented for myself, not perhaps a very good one, but combining chemically with 100 interpretations that I find in the pages of the book, and reading it has been like going through a process of crystallization.—Who is the author?

It seems a work of supererogation to praise your Lyric 'Along the meadows etc'. I do not know what magic it is that weaves common words into a song so beautiful. The Vision and the words and metre all seem so exactly right that they must always have existed so for you to discover. I really don't think you have written any more perfect lyric anywhere, and you must have had a happy time as the verses formed themselves to your imagination.

We are of course very sorry to hear of the dangerous illness of Mr Waterhouse, which must be such a source of anxiety and distress to his family. You said I remember that his health lately had not been good, but I had no idea when I saw him last at Yattendon that he was on the eve of so serious an illness as I fear this is.

We in various ways have all been knocked up by the heat, and are glad to be on the top of the Chilterns instead of down in the plain, though I am sorry to leave my garden. I went down yesterday and it looked quite beautiful: everything seems to have come into flower at once.

With my kindest regards to Mrs Robert

I am

your affectionate
Lionel Muirhead

360: TO LIONEL MUIRHEAD

Yattendon
August 27, 1901

My dear Lionel

I am glad that you liked Santayana as much as I did. He is, I am told, a Spanish American who was at Cambridge, a contemporary and friend of Roger Fry, and I believe him now to be wandering in Northumberland with Lowes Dickinson, who wrote those half historical half poetical books which you may never have seen. I think that S is all right, except that he seems to me to find fault with Shakespeare for doing exactly what he praises Jean Lahor for. People do not however understand S. because he uses Imagination for the active faculty which is above the understanding, what Coleridge e.g. called the Reason, and thus his book is really a thesis on Coleridge's dictum that 'Reason and Religion differ only as a two-fold application of the same power' though here as elsewhere Coleridge uses Reason for the product = knowledge of the whole—and though Coleridge used 'Imagination' for the diction or language of Reason, Imagination is used by Spinoza to mean merely 'opinion'—

I myself like Santayana's use of the word, and I consider his doctrines as really sound and fundamental—whereas Coleridge gets away into abstractions: the fallacy of which may, from our modern standpoint, be assumed. I have been reading a good deal in philosophy lately, and have been astonished to find how much everything is antiquated by our conviction of man's slow progress, and the consequent dependence of all true psychology on what one may call anthropology. A neighbour brought me the 2nd edition of The Golden Bough the other day—and I am now reading at that. Fraser's matter is good, but I do not find that his lucubrations are very illuminating.

I had been intending to write you for some time, but it happened that when I had as I thought finished with the book which I am editing for the Oxford Press, they took on them to want an index!! This was the devil, and I did not like to refuse them. I sent it off yesterday morning. Then when the finishing of this book left me a little leisure I fell into my old scheme of phonetics, and Monica and I spent a bit of every evening writing out something in the new script. I should have amused myself by sending you a letter in that, but I thought it would be a shame. The scheme however really works well, and the next thing that I do will be to bring out a pamphlet on it. The object of it is to have a script which shall be (1) purely phonetic. (2) more beautiful than the present script and (3) plainly intelligible to the eye, i.e. not much differing from our present mode of spelling. The reasons for it are (1) the absolute absurdity and inconvenience of our present spelling (2) the certainty that some phonetic system must eventually obtain—and that it will be both phonetically brutal, and horribly ugly. The rationale and justification are that I have imagined a lot of tricks which will get over the difficulties which have baffled etymologists, and believe that I can make a beautiful script.

I have great encouragement in this, that I surprise and convince the learned sceptic. I do not think that a specimen would be of much interest without a few explanations but here is one—

In this short extract there are 14 of my tricks. | Ⴀh and th (dh & th) | ᴜ̆ (for iu) | ꞁ̧ the new sign for the i sound in die- | R and r distinguished. | Ȼ for the ee sound- | E and e distinguished | ş = z | ⱺ and o distinguished (this last needs some explanation being the short o of horrid, which is short in or when or is before a vowel   long when terminal or before a consonant as for and ford) | a and ɑ distinguished. and | ꞩ the new sign for = ey = eh = a in fate [fᵹt may be spelt all these ways(= wey\$)| and ⌣ the short u in but, only known in English—

This is enough to give you an impression—

We had a pleasant and long visit from Wooldridge (and his spouse); he was quite recovered from his fatigue, having had a month at St. Ives, but he is even less elastic than ever, though he shows certainly no sign of mental deterioration. He has however quite lost his singing voice. He was fat and well looking—and kindly gave Elizabeth some very valuable instruction in drawing.

I was delighted that you liked my lyric. I had a letter from Grant Duff's publishers this morning asking me for one of my poems for a Victorian Anthology. I thought well of Grant Duff till his Diary came out. That shows him to be after all an aristocratical prig. I shall have nothing to do with him.

We are sorry that you have not enjoyed this summer without drawbacks. We have thoroughly enjoyed it. The other day we spent 6 hours on the river. Now it looks as if it were over, and the horse chestnuts are nearly ripe!!

Mr. Waterhouse is really bad, but he has made a slight promise of recovery. Dr. Gee comes to us tomorrow.

With our kindest regards

yours ever
RB

361: TO HENRY BRADLEY

Yattendon
October 2, 1901

My dear Bradley

I am very glad to hear that you liked Santayana's book. There are several things in it that I do not agree with. His explanation of the Platonic ideal for practice—his inability to find what corresponds to religion in Shakespeare—are points which first occur to me but I do not think that I have ever met with anything so much like my own notions as his general position. I always seem to see man as the center of concentric spheres, the nearest to him being the 'circle' of common sense and matter-of-fact, beyond this the circle of science and intellect, and beyond that, stretching out to infinity, the realm of imagination, which imagination, if it be present radiates from the center, and is related to everything, at least *if it be present* at all.

I enjoyed my talks with you immensely. I wonder how many of those who talk etymology with you have read Spinoza. It is delightful too to meet with anyone who reads both Spanish and Greek. Your general 'erudition' amazes my small faculties: and I look forward to more chats. So much for your 'tediousness'.

We have not had many spare evenings for phonetics since you left. But we had one—and I can announce that I think my ingenuity has conquered the ee problem. I like to brag of my ingenuity, for it is but a mean excellence, and I don't feel sure of it. Still for the moment this satisfied me.

What is wanted being an i that looks like an e; for instance I want to write swiit for sweet: the solution is to write a capped i. The cap answers the double purpose of making the i look like an e, and forming a ligature when the letter is doubled. The character will therefore be something like this— ꝑ ꝗ. I must take a steel pen. ꝑ ꝗ e.g. degree is degrꝗ the & thee are thꝗ thꝗ.

I think this gets over a lot of difficulties and I trust you will sufficiently admire it, but not feeling sure how you will receive it, I will not venture any further remarks.

I hope that you will be restored by your holiday. It is a good thing to get away from work whenever one is not inclined for it. Work done when one is not quite fit is of no use.

yours sincerely
R Bridges

362: TO ROBERT BRIDGES

Haseley Court
Wallingford
October 6, 1901

My dear Robert

Here we are at last settling down for the autumn months and making such provision as is possible against the cruelties of winter by piling up logs, getting our boots resoled (a capital ex-army bootmaker has settled in the village) and laying up a pile of bottles of chutnee and curry powder in the store cupboard. Thus having provided for warmth clothing and food I can sit down with an easy mind to thank you very much for Volume iii of your Collected Poems which I found on my table when I came home on the first of October. I expect the public will read the plays in this form, for the book is a very convenient and tempting one, though I like the old quarto edition best. I still think Nero's characteristics are more 'fascinating' in the 2nd Part than in the 1st—notwithstanding 'Hoo let us eat their Gods' which is in his best style—but as for Achilles whenever and wherever I dip into it I am obliged to go on reading to the end and I fail to imagine anybody being able to do otherwise. I wish you would do the coming of Demeter to the house of Celeus and the rest of the story as it stands in the (so called) Homeric Hymn. I cannot help thinking there is a delightful and beautiful play to be written which would afford you endless opportunity of allusion to all-sorts-of-things-in-general concerning human life in which I think you specially excel. Do please think about this, when you have finished your script which I think very ingenious and quite likely to do all that is wanted to simplify spelling for the unborn generations of the XXth century without making the written language look hideous. This latter quality in it is specially commendable, but the growth of English spelling is so like the growth of the British Empire an unpremeditated happy-go-lucky arrangement with surprizingly successful results that even its anomalies (not quite all) are dear to me. Alas! is this the inelasticity of old age, a literal ossification. I imagine that different counties by and bye will want different scripts: I am sure Monmouthshire where I have lately been will want something choice to express its tongue, and have you seen the conglomeration of letters in Erse??

Anthony has just gone off to school at Summerfields near Oxford and we miss him horribly: it brings home to one the fact that life is after all a series of meetings and partings, only the latter seem really to begin sooner than they need. Now we are starting a governess for Charis, who is certainly better than she was some time ago but still is not free, and must be taught with great care. We had 72 applications, whereas in 2 months we have only had 2 applications for a kitchen maid's place. I dont hesitate to say that we wish the numbers were reversed. Man does not live by cooking alone, but cooking he must have ever since Prometheus stole that unlucky fire from heaven. I fear the jealous mind of Zeus has at last imagined the device of destroying cooks, so as to render the theft of no avail. How absurdly like him to be sure, and ere my kitchen stove is extinct I must sacrifice a roast leg of pork shortly to propitiate his nostrils by its savour. The leg of pork itself he shall not have. I have not yet found out when the Slade lectures are to take place: if I go in by train I have in any case to spend over 4 hours in Oxford, but the last lectures were arranged for such an hour that I had to spend nearly 9 hours in Oxford which of course was out of the question. I must write to HEW. With kindest regards to Mrs Robert

I am

your affectionate
Lionel Muirhead

363: TO LIONEL MUIRHEAD

Yattendon
November 15, 1901

My dear Lionel

My wife has been dangerously ill for the last fortnight with acute pleurisy with effusion and all the rest of it. I cannot say that she is yet out of danger but the symptoms are mitigated, and she has held up very well. Also she sleeps well, and thinks that she is getting better, and can now take small doses of Middlemarch between her milk and brandies.

She has certainly had very bad luck. But she seems really to show a stronger vitality in illness than in health. I have been trying to write you a poetical epistle. But I do not get on very well with it. It is a great pity that there is no better metre for it than there is. Those heroics had to be kept up so high, and are therefore unsuitable for the case of an epistle. As soon as they lack absolute beauty they are dull in my opinion.

I have written a long ode to Burns, which I will send you. HEW has it now.

I am merely writing now to tell you of our troubles. I hope all is well with you and that Charis really gets better. Please tell me about her when you write.

With our love

your affectionate
RB

364: TO LIONEL MUIRHEAD

Yattendon
Evening, November 29, [1901]

My dear Lionel

I am glad to be able to send you very good news óf my wife. She seems now to be getting on as well as possible: so that I hope her convalescence may not be as tedious as I feared. I do not remember when I last wrote to you, but it is only the last two days that we have been altogether satisfied.

I am very anxious to hear from you about Charis. I suppose it is just the time with her when the trouble may pass or not pass—and I could not when I saw her feel that there could be any reason why it should persist.

I must condole with you on the death of your brother in law, who always seemed to me most agreeable. Of course I knew nothing of him, but I should think that he and your sister must have had a very happy married life. I suppose there is no thought of Mrs. Sturt coming to Haseley? All these things picture themselves to me as scenes in one of Miss Austen's novels—for at odd times I read aloud to my wife and she likes Miss A better than anyone else. But a few days ago we were reading Middlemarch. I had never read it and did not care for it at all though the story in itself makes one want to go on. But I am singular (I believe) in thinking that a defect. For why should one be stimulated to read a book which gives one no pleasure when one is reading it? What I dislike in George E is her careful analysis and dissection of monsters of her own creation. That Bulstrode, a beast, I don't believe there was ever anyone like him. And if an artist is going to invent, why invent beastliness, and beastliness without fun. Then she is so overserious in her exposure of the faults of foolish and young thoughtless persons, and does not see that they are only good to make fun of. Her very humour is generally stilted, and there are whole chapters of conversations in the public houses. Supposed to be very witty I believe, but as tedious to me as the smell of stale beer.

We also began a Trollope, not successful. It was all right enough, but it is not alluring, nor is there ever any temptation to make one take up the book a second time. One would rather go out and make a real call on some neighbours, and have it booked to one's credit.

My Milton's Prosody is out. I send you an advertisement of it. I have only 6 copies and most of them forestalled. Also I have finished the proofs of Volume IV of my "Collected works".

Send us a line soon. With kindest regards to your wife

yours affectionately
RB

365: TO LIONEL MUIRHEAD

Yattendon
December 16, [1901]

My dear Lionel

We have been getting on well. Today is not a good day with the patient, but she has been making steady progress for a fortnight. I know that you will be glad of tidings, but I am writing as much for my own satisfaction. I wish you were here to bear me a little company. It is getting on for 6 or 8 weeks since I saw anybody—and I am pretty tired of it. I read a lot of Nietzsche the other day. Did you ever read him? He is excellent amusement—a sort of Ruskin in philosophy. Style I fancy copied from Heine, very good—opinions extreme and paradoxical, but a lot of truth mixed up.—I didn't like the second part of Erewhon so well as you did. I don't think that half the things that Butler so patiently satirises are worth the trouble. I do not like any of his drampers—and I thought some of the things in bad taste. Nothing came up to the Musical Banks of the original book.—I have been reading Horace's Epistles critically—have nearly come to the end of them. I think I must some day bring out a volume of animadversions on Horace. I find many things which it seems to me that the critics have overlooked, good and bad. I took them up because I want to write some English stuff at about that level, and I thought I might learn something from him. My difficulty reduces itself to want of a metre. I tried a sort of Epistle to Burns on moral philosophy in the Scotch stanza which he uses so well. It ran to 20 stanzas, 120 lines, and I sent it off today to the Monthly Review. I do not know whether Newbolt will buy it. It has I think some original philosophy in it which I believe to be quite sound. Perhaps it is not original. I have however always missed it in books, i.e. since I came to think it. It will amuse you if nothing else. I bought a Baskerville "Shaftesbury" (his characteristics) a couple of months ago at Oxford. A fine book. There is a good deal in him—but I think few people would now read him to find it. I was surprised to find, as I thought, the model of David Hume. I mean in style of sentence, and attitude toward reader. The last few days I tried (after George Eliot and Miss Austin [*sic*]) reading Tom Jones to my wife. I had never been able to get on with it, and was surprised to find that reading aloud it was not at all bad. However before we were well half through we were sick of it chiefly I fancy from the persistence of the unnecessary coarseness. But to the last we found plums—but threw it, plums and all aside.

You would think from this that I was a great reader. Wife would join in kindest remembrances to Mrs. Muirhead.—She is I hope sleeping overhead. I am writing in the dining room.

yours affectionately
RB

I hope to go into Oxford the first fine day.

366: TO LIONEL MUIRHEAD

[Yattendon
December 23, 1901

To L. M.
My most faithful of early friends, that Eton
Gave me how long ago!—'tis all a lifetime,—
With my fortieth-and-odd auspication
Of Christmas 'happiness this idle item.
　Old Plato imagin'd his architypal
Ideas to possess the fourth dimension.
For since our solid is triple, but always
Its shade only double, solids as *umbrae*
Must want equally one dimension also.
(Could Plato have avoided or denied it?)
Thus Saint Paul, when opposing in Corinthians
To our earthly bodies celestial ones
Meant just those pretty aforesaid abstracts
Of four platonical divine dimensions.
　If this be not a holy consolation,
More than plum pudding or a turkey roasted,
Indeed I'm sorry; take it or reject it,
I can't find anything better to send you.

My dear Lionel

You will wonder when there is so much rime on the trees that I should have taken to the classical quantitative verse. If you miss the rime you will know where to look for it. The verses are on Stone's phonetic system. (See his tract passim) that is they should scan like Latin if written phonetically. But no elisions are allowed, and H is a consonant—also words in ion are contracted to a short vowel—and *one* is of course like *won*.

yours

RB

hendecasyllables

⏑̄ — — ⏑ ⏑ — || ⏑ — ⏑ — ⏑̄

P.S.　I reopen this to say our children are all going to a masquerade Dance on *Friday*. Elizabeth and Edward are disguised as Turks—and we dont manage the sashes very well. It strikes me that you may still have one or two of those long Egyptian sashes silk (mine are long since worn out) if so, and you could post them *on hire,* so as to reach us on Thursday at latest I should be very much obliged. Anything for turban or sash. But we shall manage anyway.

　Edward is splendid—with black moustache.

367: TO HENRY NEWBOLT

Yattendon
December 23, 1901

My dear Newbolt

I am sorry to hear that you have been ill. I mean since I saw you in London. You were not well then, but I understood that you had been ill and were better. We of course have had a bad time, but the patient came downstairs yesterday, and the nurse goes off tomorrow. So we are comparatively reconciled to life again. The children are well.

This brings you all our best Xmas wishes—not excluding an echo of your prayer for the New Year. This war is of course a terrible trial: but it has got to the bottom of a lot of things. Everything has however so shifted in the last 20 years that one can't pretend to foresee the future. I should never have imagined so much loyalty, bravery, determination and patriotism to exist—and it really looks to be good as such stuff usually is.

I was glad that the verses would do for your Mag. I think myself that there is something in them, though the limits do not allow detail in exposition. Mr. Hodge, Editor of Saturday, has got me to send him a lyric: and as he was willing (much to my surprise) to pay me what I asked for it, it suits me very well.

I have during the last fortnight made use of my broken times to accustom myself (as far as I can) to make verses in Stone's quantitative method. It always seemed to me impossible, for one had never regarded words in this way and again had no rhythms in one's mind to build on. One has to write a good deal before one finds what rhythms English gives one in this manner. This is such tedious work that I should never have done it but for the imposed heelkicking of last month.

What is this Bacon cipher? I do not see the papers—and really I don't want to read about it unless it is very ingenious or amusing.

With kindest regards to Mrs. Newbolt and all our seasonable good wishes

yours ever
RB

368: TO HENRY NEWBOLT

Yattendon
January 6, 1902

My dear Newbolt

Thank you for proof of the Burns poem. I will keep it awhile in case of any useful criticism. It was very good of you to accept it. Do you like it to be so spread out?

Crawley is a master at Bradfield, and lives in the fields between Bradfield and Yattendon. He has visited me several times. He is now publishing a book at Macmillan's on Primitive Marriage. He left the proof of the preface with me last time he was here, and it strikes me that I may as well send it on to you. I do not know whether there is any privacy about it. He seemed to me to be a very clever man. He seemed to know all about classic "quantity".—He said that he entirely owed to Stone's original paper a clear vision of the classic versification. He did some verses (English) in the classical prosody—they were some of them, I thought, very good.—There is something *extremely odd* about the man and his wife. If his paper is not *interesting* it would be a pity to choke the public off the subject with it. For it is a subject which can easily be made interesting by quotation and anecdotes.

I was much struck by Crawley's English quantitative verse, because whenever I had tried to write it, I had found it *impossible,* and his seemed to run off as if he had thought in it. During the last month I have had much idle time indoors, and have employed it in trying to analyse this difficulty, and to master it; with the result that I am able to write pretty freely in "William Stone's patent classical English phonetic quantitative versification," and have come to the point at which the pursuit is full of amusement. It has surprised me very much to find how the difficulties which seemed insuperable give way—and at the same time my wonder at other people's partial successes is mitigated. I should like to show you my efforts—but I shall not do anything with them till I have some more.

Your suggestion that I should write a paper for the Mag on the subject is rather tempting, but I do not think that the public will (or should) take any interest in it *until something has been* done. And it is not sufficient to do one or two things. A lot must be done. I do not myself know yet how long the resources of the language which I am at present drawing upon will last out. I may be working out a very small vein.

It is however good as long as it lasts.

yours ever

RB

Mr. C. is also publishing a Greek elegiac version of Omar K's quatrains (interp Fitz) in America—prospectus came to me.

369: TO LIONEL MUIRHEAD

Yattendon

February 1, 1902

My dear Lionel

I am awfully pleased at your liking the "Stone's Prosody"—and send you what I have done in hendecasyllables and scazons.—These metres are much more tractable in English, and I believe that hendecasyllables are as easy to write as anything could be of the kind.

The Hexameter is terriby difficult—I don't know whether it will go in English except as a tour de force. It is possible enough to write a few at a time, but difficult to continue saying what one intended to say. Also the rhythm seems so far to me to be repugnant to English.

I have however a lot of treats ahead which I shall arrive at in time. I have unfortunately got my right hand in a sling from a slight sprain of the elbow (at racquets) hence my bad writing, though perhaps no worse than usual. I hope Antony's cold is better.

your affectionate

RB

370: TO HENRY NEWBOLT

Yattendon

February 3, 1902

My dear Newbolt

I hope that you are better. The season is not favourable either to mind or body. It is odd how these transitions of the centuries bring hard times. I believe that it all actually depends ultimately on a disturbance of mind set up by the Kalendar, in the profanum vulgus.

I am returning you the proof of the Burns epistle—I have done nothing with it. Indeed I have not looked at it till this morning, when I made the few corrections which you will find.

I think they are all right except that I do not feel sure about the two colons which I have substituted for full stops at ends of stanzas 12 and 13 on page 5. I prefer them, but if you do not like them let the stops stand.—I am very much obliged to you indeed for printing this—I hope your public will like it.

We all send good wishes and kindest remembrances to Mrs. Newbolt and yourself.

yours ever

R Bridges

371: TO HENRY NEWBOLT

Yattendon

February 5, 1902

Please return

me these

things

My dear Newbolt

Thanks for your letter. It is very fortunate for my Ulysses that Stephen Phillips' play is on. It is possible that it may call some attention to it, and I am very grateful to you for your intention of making use of the occasion.

I send you two enclosures—one Yeats' dicta on the play—the other Samuel Butler's on the "translations" in it. I should like you to see what has already been said if you have time to read them.

_____

I was rather pleased with Palicio when I went through the proofs, which was more than I expected. I found it quite exciting.

_____

I hope that "Burns" will suit your readers. Impossible to say.
Sorry for your vaccination. We are all done but did not "take."

yours ever

RB

I have done a lot of classical metres in "Stone's Prosody"!! did I tell you—and I am still going at them. It works well, but the hexameter (for instance) is almost impossible.

372: TO J. W. MACKAIL

Yattendon

February 9, 1902

My dear Mackail
  I only sent you that volume in order to draw a letter from you. It is so long since we had any converse that I found it very difficult to write. I did write a letter, and I may have put it in the book, but if I had, you would have answered an invitation which it contained to promise to come to Yattendon in the Summer. Meantime I rejoice in your invitation to your house, and I will come and take tea with you before my evening train home the next time that I am in town. I shall be more than interested to see your children, for they promised to be excellent. I too have budding branches and both my girls 14 and 12 are practically grown up, though still in short frocks. We must see if we cannot all meet in the Summer.
  I wonder if you took any interest in "Stone's Classical Prosody." Perhaps you did not see it. I printed a revised version of it with a new edition of my *Milton's Prosody* at the Clarendon Press last year.
  First I would like you to see my new chapters on accentual or stress rhythm. They contain some interesting points.
  Secondly I wish you would write the history of our traditional prosody—which I call *syllabic,* to distinguish it from the other two kinds, viz *quantitative,* and *accentual* (or stressed). It seems to me quite an easy thing to do for any one who has any acquaintance with literature between Roman time and 1000 AD. and access to a library to quote from.
  Thirdly about Stone's prosody. Whether his system is actually the Greek system or the Latin or neither may be questioned, but if it is not, then those systems are lost to us, and his system is (as far as I can be a judge) the system by which we read and appreciate the Greek and Latin. (I have had some very interesting correspondence with Henry Bradley, of the Dictionary, on the subject. He is

extremely acute, indeed as acute and accurate and well-read as he is modest)— But as to the practical matter.—I have since Xmas been trying my hand at writing English in classical metres in Stone's system. It seemed impossible at first—but it came easier by degrees. And though there are difficulties which I have not yet mastered I have been very much surprised at the result, e.g. some of my elegiac distiches seem to me to have the charm of the good Greek ones!!! And I am convinced that they are the production of the prosody.

Fourthly. I want very much to show you some of these things. But of course it is not much use unless you have read Stone—and reasoned out his treatment of the indeterminate vowel, which is the main difficulty, and which, in spite of everything, will remain a difficulty, until so much verse of this kind has been written as to establish the actual English rhythms which are pleasing. Then the uncertain words will be allowed or disallowed. At present they are outside begging for admission.

Oh Jam satis est.

yours ever

R Bridges

What does Horace: Frigida curarum fomenta
mean?

Tell me if you know.

If you have not the 'Prosody' I will tell my bookseller to send you a copy.

373: TO HENRY BRADLEY

Yattendon
February 10, 1902

My dear Bradley

I am writing because I am sure that you will be thinking that I have treated you very scurvily. But don't think that your careful letters were ill-bestowed. I have been thinking over all the points, especially those that were new to me. In the mean while I am doing what I set myself to do and writing stuff in the prosody. The practice does teach one a good deal and I am afraid that just now I am *avoiding* the use of the doubtful words. Sometimes I think that I see my way to distinctions.—But I shall hope to talk over these things. I am trying to see if I can interest Mackail in the subject. My verses have pleased the only classicist that I have sent them to. But I must do more yet. I have done only about 250 lines, exclusive of a lot of experimental hexameters, which prove the most refractory of all, not to write bad ones, but to make the whole easy and fluent.

The great difficulty, that the writer seeks to "combat" the typical rhythm, and that the reader looks for it can never be got over. Nothing would induce me to make the feet show too plainly.

It occurs to me to say this, that if your explanation of Greek quantity is right, then (1) It is absolutely lost to us and unknown. (2) It is uncertain how nearly the

Latin corresponded to it (can it really have corresponded considering the nature of the elisions in Latin and Greek?) and (3) Our appreciation of Greek and Latin rhythms and scansion seems so complete in its *satisfaction,* that a system *founded on our interpretation* must be more satisfactory to us than a real rediscovery and adoption of Greek practice. Ergo, go on! I say to my Muse.

yours ever
RB

My results give me great pleasure now and then.

374: TO J. W. MACKAIL

Yattendon
February 12, 1902

My dear Mackail

Your long letter has given me a great deal of pleasure. I hope to answer it in a few days. Meanwhile I have asked Bumpus to send you a copy of the prosody. I should be glad if you would read my appendix on stress prosody.

I quite agree with you (indeed I feel it very profoundly) about the impossibility of writing letters on these subjects.

Also on the phonetic difficulties of English, considered as a medium for Greek prosody.

I was absolutely incredulous as to there being any possibility. But when Will Stone died I thought that I owed it to him to make a venture at his prosody.—It is of course impracticable to make any attempt even, until you have definite rules by which to treat (if only by way of experiment) the doubtful English syllables. Stone's rules are consistent, and—whatever the results may be—it is possible to apply his rules.

I began with Hendecasyllables, which I soon found easy enough, and then I went on to use difficult metres—and I have done Scazons—Elegiacs—Alcaics (!) and Sapphics. Hexameters I find the most difficult task, that is to make anything tolerable to the ear.

There is no one's criticism which I desire more than yours so you may be sure that I shall send you my experiments.—But I should like you to have Stone's essay by you when I send them.

I shall ask you not to show them to anyone—

I owe my knowledge of and acquaintance with Yeats to you. A long time ago you introduced me to his work, or recommended it, and I bought the book, and admired Y very much.—He came here on a visit. A charming fella if he wasn't so stuffed with mystic rot—but no doubt that is one reason of his poetic charm. Blake was stark mad—and Shelley just half mad—

By the way I don't think much of dramatic criticism in England—and I know very well that the dramatic critics don't think any better of it than I do. I may have an appointment in town next week—if so I will let you know.

yours ever
RB

375: TO. J. W. MACKAIL

Yattendon

February 25, 1902

My dear Mackail

I send you these things. I have got tired of them, and shan't do any more for awhile at any rate.

I think you may as well read them in the order in which I wrote them—viz:

1. Hendecasyllables etc
2. Elegiacs
3. Sapphics and Alcaics
4. Hexameters

There seems no difficulty in doing the Hendecasyllables up to the point which mine reach, and not much difficulty about 2 and 3, but the Hexameters I found very difficult, and I don't know that I have got over the difficulty.

But a good deal of it would disappear if one could find out what rhythms were pleasing. I kept (in the Idyll for example) much nearer to Virgil than I think desirable or agreeable.

If you find them worthy of any sort of criticism, I shall like to hear it. Only don't waste words on civilities. I don't mind what you say.

I kept to Stone's prosody, except that I found some words would not satisfy, and I had to reject whole classes.

I thought my original distich Elegiacs the best things—and was very much pleased with one or two of these. I don't think they could have been done any other way e. g. "When thou my beloved". I like that one very much.

Henry Bradley (of the dictionary)'s views on Greek prosody are most interesting—and quite new to me. I have had a lot of good letters from him.

I shall be very much obliged if you will *not* show the verses to anyone. Unless one does a lot they are nothing.

Sorry you get home so late, else I would call some day.

I told Bumpus to send you my book, and I hope you liked my appendix.

yours ever

R Bridges

I know how tedious and difficult it is to write a consecutive letter on these matters (with so many points of uncertain definition) so please jot down remarks anyhow, as it strikes you. I shall understand.

376: TO J. W. MACKAIL

Yattendon

February 27, 1902

My dear Mackail

Many thanks for your letter which crossed my amusing packet, for I am sure it is amusing if it is not anything else.

I am very glad indeed that you liked Appendix J. I took great pains to make it quite simple and clear.

I was most pleased myself with the explanation of Shelley's "Away the moor" which has been to me one of the most beautiful and affecting poems in the language, and has I feel sure been excluded from collections because the pedants (like Palgrave) thought that it didn't scan.

I agree with you about the versification of Sensitive Plant. It is no doubt abominably careless, but I fancy that Shelley never wrote anything which did not justify itself to his most admirable ear by some method of reading, in this case no doubt one which we do not approve of—a sort of sing song which over rode the syllables.

Your appreciation is very rewarding to the humble student.

RB

PS.   Read my new note to the Appendix on the *Extrametrical syllable*.
On Romantic realism.

377: TO LIONEL MUIRHEAD

Yattendon
Sᵗ David's Day
[March 1], 1902

My dear Lionel

I hope that Antony has been getting on well. I feel half inclined to send you the old temperature chart, which is lying about somewhere, of my wife's illness, to show you how able I am to sympathise with you. It was nearly 2 months long. We have in consequence to go to the seaside, and think of going to our old lodgings at Seaton in Devonshire, the week after next. This I tell you on the chance that you may be doing something of the same sort, and possibly might come to Seaton also.

I have heard two of H E W's lectures in Oxford. They were first class, but he has got into a strange naturalistic or realistic rut, and refuses to get out of it. One of the days I took both my girls up and we attended a very first class chamber concert the same afternoon. I am afraid that we shall be away from home before the next batch of lectures commences. But I must be in Oxford one day again before I go to the sea. I wonder if you would be able to come in the same day and prowl about with me.

I have a poem on Burns in the Monthly Magazine.

Write and tell us how Anthony gets on

your affectionate
RB

378: TO HENRY NEWBOLT

Yattendon
St. David's Day
[March 1], 1902

My dear Newbolt

I hope that you are better. We are getting on pretty well—are going to Seaton in Devon, if all is well, the week after next, for a month.

I hear that influenza is bad in town. There is a good deal about here, but it has not attacked us yet.

I am writing to thank you for the Review, which arrived at breakfast, with my Burns ode. It is a pity that it is St Davids day instead of St Andrews. I shall be much interested to find out whether readers like my new style of verse.

I read at breakfast Hogarth's article on Phillips' Ulysses. It interested me very much, and seemed to me to be well done. I can't imagine how Phillips has escaped Pantomime. Of course my Ulysses is a very different sort of thing, and never pretended to be anything more than a dramatisation of some of the scenes of the Odyssey, and the chief blame that I have hitherto had has been from Homer-lovers who object that I have altered Homer too much.

Such a scene as that between Penelope and Ulysses seems to me to be what I should like to see on the stage. Hogarth's article makes me wish to *read* Phillips' play. But I should be sorry to *see* it I am sure.

I am sending you my thanks by the early post.

yours ever
RB

379: TO HENRY NEWBOLT

Yattendon
St. David's Day
[March 1], 1902

My dear Newbolt

I wrote you a letter just an hour ago, and sent it off by our early post.

I had not seen your noble encomium in "on the line". I did not expect nor look for such a notice of my volume.

It is only too flattering, but it is very well done. The quotation from Yeats is magic. How well he writes—.

So I add this to thank you. I said in my letter that I can't imagine the return of Ulysses without that long interview with Penelope. I thought when I wrote it that I had converted the Epic into Drama with almost imperceptible touches.—The result is that no one sees the difference. This should please me—Even in the speech of Ulysses to Amphinomus the addition of "And now—thou seest me" strikes no one—and I doubt if any translator has ever seen the point of ἀκιδνότερον in that speech XVIII. 130. But I don't know the translation well. But Butcher & Lang have "*feebler*". Butler (with all his pretences) has "vainest", Pope "*vain*", Cowper "*weak*". All missing the point,—which is one of the biggest things in the whole of poetry.—

with many thanks

yours ever
RB

380: TO LIONEL MUIRHEAD

Yattendon
March 3, 1902

My dear Lionel

Certainly we remote Britons have had a bad time of it these last years. I found much encouragement in the society of a nephew who is home with a wounded arm from S Africa. He is a fine soldier, and is only afraid that the war will be over before he can get back to it. But you will think that it would be better fun fighting Boers than bacteria, which makes me quote from an Alcaic ode (to Evening, the spirit of) which you have not seen

> No hungry wildbeast rangeth in our forest,
> No lion or bear prowleth around the folds
> Keep thou from our sheep-cotes the tainting,
>   Invisible peril of the darkness.

I copy this hoping that it may amuse if not charm you towards the general spirit of consolation. But I hope that now you will be feeling relief without too much reaction. I can't say how sorry I feel for the terrible trial which you have been through.

Seaton is on the border of Devon and Dorset. The sea is a deep shingle bank, so that tourists actually in summer calms may walk off the packet by means of one plank on to the shore.

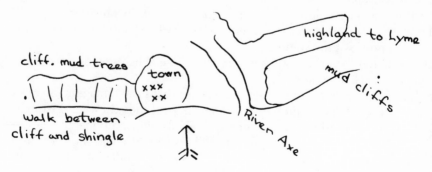

t is a warm place with plenty of basking under the mud cliff.

All the land is high behind except that the Axe comes down a pretty wide alley some mile away to E— lovely excursions in lanes and on downs and hills all bout but most of them a mile off. The attraction to us is the mile of asphate walk etween the cliff and the shingle, for it is always sheltered there, and you can sit ı places under fir trees on the mud cliff. A mile away to west is Beer, where here is a great fishing establishment, very busy, and the rocks and rocky cliffs egin.

It seems to me a very healthy place. My map is not a success, so I will make out better one on another sheet.

If there is any definite information that you want let me know. It is the land of he Stuckey's. If nothing should hinder us we shall be off there on Thursday veek.

My wife joins in messages of sympathy to your wife for all her troubles. We incerely hope that you will have no further troubles. There is influenza very hick here, but we have not got it in the house yet.

> your affectionate
>
> RB

enclose map. Kindly return in a day or two.

381: TO HENRY NEWBOLT

> Yattendon
> March 6, 1902

My dear Newbolt

I need not say that I am very much gratified by Mr. Murray's cheque. Not having seen Messrs. Smith & Elder's signature for several years increases my admiration. Thank you also for returning Butler's letter and Yeats' article, and for having sent me the Times article which I was delighted to see. I am sorry that Phillips has been mechanically boomed—I hoped that he had raised his bald pate above the waves by his native exertions only. However if Sidney Colvin is swimming round him he may hope for good times, which I most sincerely wish him— at least if it is possible to get at drama through the Pantomime entrance. I have seen several people who witnessed the play and of these one told me that he laughed outright at the gods, especially Zeus—and another that she did not care to stay to see it out.

I was in town the other day and saw the advertisement in the shop windows.— I did not give him credit for it. I am sorry that you had another bout of the plague. We are hoping to get away next week to Seaton. Everyone in the village has had the influenza almost except our household, and this morning one of the maids has gone to bed. So the cup may be dashed from our lips.

In the notices I see of the African war I miss 1/ the supposition that Kruger has *bought* the foreign press. I have no doubt of it—and 2/ the explanation of the conduct of Botha and DeWet in the fact that they like fighting better than not fighting. They will be *sorry* when it is over, as many of our men will be.

Excuse haste (with many thanks)

yours ever
RB

382: TO J. W. MACKAIL

Great Western Railway
March 19, [1902]

My dear Mackail

I was fearing that you must have succumbed to the influenza. I rejoice that you are all right.

My other surmise was that you were studying Stone.

I grieve that this was not the case, as the whole point of my experiment is that the prosody is fixed and certain.

E. g. I believe that it cannot be questioned that our aspirate is a consonant, and *must* assert by position. Thus the un of unhappiness *must* be long. The difficulty the ear has in granting this fact must be due to our pronouncing Greek and Latin aspirates as we do our own, i.e. as consonants, and *not* reckoning them to be such. Now Stone is very clear and is the first authority that I know of to put main difficulties such as this, right.

Before him I should never have guessed or imagined that onion was a trochee. But it is. The i is a consonantal y and the word is onyŏn. On the borderline there are all sorts of difficulties which practice might clear up.—E. g. Stone rules the modified tsh of much as short. This offends a good many and I fancy that practice would make the rule to be that it is short only when unaccented and long when accented, the accent serving to prop the vowel with some of the conso-nantal sound—

The question is, Can there be a system in English? And if so, is Stone's right? And if not, what is the matter with it?

Henry Bradley's objection to it is that he (in common I suppose with all scholars) has mistaken the principle of Greek quantity—and I confess it looks to me as if B was right. Only he maintains that the Latins must have been in the same box with the Greeks. I think they are in the same box with us: at least they would be if we could get into any box.

yours ever
RB

I am staying at Seaton—(Today am in Exeter)

83: TO LIONEL MUIRHEAD

Seaton
Devon
March 22, 1902

y dear Lionel

I hope that all has been going on well with you at Haseley. I know how tedious slow convalescence is: but I hope that you will not have had anything but steady covery in your patient.

We have been down here now for more than a week, and I think that the 1ange has already begun to operate on my wife. She is looking better. The 1ildren seem very well and enjoy dabbling about with naked legs among the 2cks in spite of the cold wind and water. On sunny days it is pleasant enough on 1e shore, and at all times fresh and bracing. I took Elizabeth in to Exeter the her day to be confirmed. The Bishop of our party having had to go to bed with fluenza, the confirmation was in the Cathedral. The organ there is lovely. I did 3t admire the ceremony. The service was ruined by the introduction of some of 1e most maudlin and washy hymns with their tunes out of H A M. I was 1rnestly praying the Preserver of Souls that my dear little girl might be safe-1arded through life from the unholy spirit that all the parsons seemed to be 1voking, and that she might have the Spirit of Wisdom, and understanding, and 1e spirit of might, instead of that spirit of bosh and ignorance, and weakness— hich sounded in the air and was apparent in nearly all the faces of the clergy.

I have nothing to do here. I had intended to bring down all Voltaire's corre-2ondence, which I wanted to look through for a special purpose, but Willert ho was lending the books to me, unfortunately sent the box to Newbury (which 3 you know is only our postal address) so that I did not receive it in time.

We think of going home again about the 15th of next month.

The children read music very fairly now and we amuse ourselves singing in 4 arts, for my wife puts in a tenor somewhere, now in one octave in [*sic*] now in 1e other.

Now it is a Latin lesson (Vulgate).

yours affectionately
RB

84: TO LIONEL MUIRHEAD

Yattendon
May 4, 1902

1y dear Lionel

If I had only known of your lamentable condition I would have written—and ad I known your address—but what a curious disease to have invented and how well you write with your left hand! My nephew of South African activities had a Mauser bullet right through his upper arm, severing the nerve which become the ulnar lower down. Fortunately it was not entirely severed, and when last heard of him he was recovering the use of his arm very fast, and impatient to go after DeWet again. He told me that all through his voyage home he had dreadful pain in the arm.

I suppose your complaint has been like Sciatica, of which I have some experience.

We got on very well at Seaton. Monica gained a pound a week, (I mean 1 lb. which was worth more to her than £1!)—But I wish I could make a pound of anything. When I wrote so far as above it was Sunday, and there was a piano flute and fiddle trio going on behind me, the flute getting sharper and sharper Now it is Monday: which I had arranged to spend in Oxford. But the train by which I intended to go was taken off this month, so that I had to come home again in a bad temper and despatch apologetic telegrams. We are full of silly but necessary muddles of various people's businesses just now. I hope to get more free in a fortnight. I want to go on with that "Stone's Prosody". People like my experiments. I have done nothing since I left home in February. I go to Oxford once a week this term. I suppose that your movements will depend a good deal on your arm. You say nothing of Antony in your letter, by which I suppose that he has got all right again.—I hope Charis is getting on well. The change of air will have been an experiment. We are really all of us very well now except that Monica has a little cold, which I think she must have caught from me. Very hard lines, as I haven't had a cold till just now for more than a year I think. I gave up smoking for a week or ten days but I was obliged to return to it.

I hope this letter does not show how bad my temper is today. I think cold winds in May are enough to make anyone wild

With our kindest regards to Mrs M. and best wishes for your speedy recovery

yours affectionately

RB

385: TO SAMUEL GEE

Yattendon
June 15, 1902

My dear Gee

Thank you very much for sending me a copy of your Lectures and Aphorisms It has been lying on my table ever since it came, and I have occasionally read in it: but, as you know, I do not interest myself in medicine now-adays. But I should have been very sorry not to have had this volume. I should have written to thank you for it before, but I relied on your not knowing whether I was at home. It is a long while since I heard anything of you. I hope that Mrs Gee continues to be pretty well. You were selling your house in the country when last we met. I have hardly been in town since, I had to come up on business once or twice. I dislike it

o much that I neglect things which I fear I ought to do. We are supposed to be
ll pretty well. My wife has got to look quite strong again. In fact she seems to me
o be above her usual standard. The children are also very flourishing. My
econd girl, who is about 12½ has quite outgrown her elder sister, and weighs
1early nine stone. Despite this rainy season they manage to get on merrily, and
he Peace has certainly lightened all hearts. The Coronation is a monstrous
1uisance, but we shall not I hope have very much of it here. I am busy in various
vays. We have now perfected our calligraphic phonetic writing and I hope that I
nay get my book on it done before Xmas. I have also a new style in poetry which
vill amuse you. Today we have Miss Coleridge staying with us. She and my wife
ire gone up to tea with the Waterhouses, and I am using the interval. M^r W can
;et about with a stick, but he cannot move his arm. He is out of doors all day
iriving or in his bath chair.

I wonder whether you will be able to pay us a visit of any kind this year. If you
:an do so I hope that you will write and propose a time. I am afraid it will be of
10 use my saying how much we should like it if Mrs Gee could come with you. Is it
ossible that she would be well enough to stand the journey and strange house-
<eeping?

By the way Wooldridge tells me that he has a complete respite (if not a cessa-
ion) of his dire disease, and is enjoying ordinary food with impunity.

Now I must close. I do not say anything about the excellence of your book for I
have not read it more than enough to recognize your clear style and full matter,
and indeed I doubt if my opinion would be of any weight.

With our kindest regards to Mrs Gee

> I am yours sincerely
> Robt Bridges

Dick Dennys at the Hospital is a great nephew of mine)

386: TO LIONEL MUIRHEAD

> Yattendon
> August 1, 1902

My dear Lionel

Thanks for your long letter. We have been going on as usual and have now
begun the Summer holidays, which means that the governess is off—and we are
left to ourselves. We had a pleasant visit from H E W who seemed very well, but
he, and other visitors have put off my work and I have not written a line for 3
weeks. Before I left off I had done a good lot, and am at the 140th line of my
Epistle to L M. The hexameters now go very well. I don't know when I shall get
on to them again. The Peace ode turned out a success, and I wrote a 28 line ode
in Iambics which went better than I expected. I think H E W approved on the
whole of the experiments. He evidently thought better of them than he had

expected to think. Of course he does not follow their scansion. I must send you the last batch soon.

I may have to go to Windsor for a day ere long; a distant relative of mine is ill there. I shall take the opportunity of calling on Parratt though nothing ever comes of him. Royalty ruins people—I mean any contact with it. I sent Cornish (the vice provost) a copy of my Latin pronunciation paper. I do not know whether it will be possible to force Eton to reconsider its ways. I should think that Hame (?) was hopeless. However the matter will not drop just yet. The new schoolmaster here turns out to be, as I hoped, a good voice trainer and teacher of boys, so that there is every chance that by Xmas we shall have a good boy choir of trained boys who can read and sing. If so I shall take the choir again. I have a class of 3 men—two tenors and a counter tenor, the last admirable. But the men who can sing and like it do not like going to church.

I wish we could get the Sunday services on weekday evenings. I am glad that Antony seems better and is regaining his strength.

With our love to all

your affectionate
R Bridges

387: TO HENRY BRADLEY

Yattendon
August 11, 1905

My dear Bradley

Let me first congratulate you with congratulations to be passed on to your daughter at whose success I am much delighted, for your sake as for hers. Canon Bernard's house if an orthodox will be a most comfortable home. I suppose he is the man whom I used to know at Magdalen—a very nice fellow, with all the amenities, and a grata persona everywhere. She will meet all the County people. You must play the Polonius to her before she goes. I am sorry that you can't run down here just now: but if you can spare us one day before term begins it will be very good of you. I think that we have rubbed all the corners off the phonetic writing now. There were one or two symbols that made the script look a little obscure—these we have got rid of. The chief thing was the e sound in the and thee. We have thought it possible to keep a very ordinary sort of e for this ɛ something like that—so that the innumerable words that contain it will look much as they did before. At the same time we have arranged for this e to show that it is a little self-conscious of its 'i-ness.

I took up with the longs and shorts again in June, and have worked pretty well at them since. The main thing that I wanted to do was to master the hexameter and I think I can pronounce or rather enounce—no I don't know how to finish the sentence with that word. I wanted to say that I have been in my own judgement entirely successful. I have written nearly 200 lines of the Epistle with

atisfaction to myself—and some 4 or 5 ladies who had none of them the least
notion of the rules, were all of them independently enthusiastic with the metrical
result: and said that they liked it better than any other metre that they had ever
come across!!!

I have put off iambics, as being the most alien and refractory to English; but I
have written one ode in them which readers approve of. Also I wrote a long (64
line) peace ode in Alcaics which pleased me—and I have finished the Hexameter
eclogue or pastoral which I sent you the beginning of. I find that Will Stone's
prophecies all come true and I am working out the margin of doubtful syllables
with a pretty convincing line of distinction. I shall want to show you all these
things, especially the Hexameters.

My notion is to write about 2000 lines. I do not think that less will be of much
use to convince people that the thing is not mere fooling: and I don't think that I
can yet have done more than 600. I should get on faster, if the subject of my
epistle did not land me in such difficult matter. I have done Geology and As-
tronomy, and some physics and am now at Chemistry. Then comes Biology, and
then I am free to let myself go.

We are all well. I was at Windsor all yesterday, and am writing this by early
post Monday, that you may get it before you leave Oxford. With our kindest
regards to all your family

yours sincerely
R Bridges

P.S. Mind you tell your daughter the absolute importance of being *strict* with her
pupil. My experience is that the want of discipline is the fault of the amateur
teachers.

88: TO LIONEL MUIRHEAD

Yattendon
August 20, 1902

My dear Lionel

I also am alone at home. My wife and children are on a short visit to their——
well—Waterhouses. No other word would finish the sentence. I am willing and
shall be grateful to receive Miss Dittany or any other visitor, of her sex. I have
been going on with the classical verses—and you may be interested to hear that I
have already done over 200 lines of my Epistle to L.M. People like it very much.
The total score of the side is over 700 which is not bad, considering how bad the
wickets have been, and that there are about 30 batsmen still to go in, while, as I
told you, *L.M. is 210 not out:* and I expect him to make another two hundred.
Sometimes he makes his runs a great pace, at other times he doesn't score for a
week while other batsmen come and go and add their ten and twenties.

We had a good day on the river last week—and are going to try and get another tomorrow. Spokes has rather a good schooner, which sails well—a toy one of course.—Ben has a bad ear, and he doesn't like my cauterising it. We have a few visitors engaged to come here next month, some of them musical. I went to a Funeral at Kensall Green come fortnight ago of an old lady in whose dining room used to hang a lot of family pictures. 2 of these, almost the best, will come to me. Elizabeth is doing water colour. Margaret nearly through Mozart's violin Sonatas. My wife has with my assistance about perfected the phonetic writing. I will end my letter on it.

The worst of it is that I have nothing to say. I may as well tell you therefore that I have done a lot of iambics. I put them off to the last because I thought them least like English verse, and on that account most likely to fail. I don't think that I have written enough yet to judge by. That last wonderful letter is a soft g. I don't know how to make it.

your affectionate
Robert Bridges

I should have gone away from home this week but we have a case of smallpox in the village—we are nearly out of quarantine.

389: TO HENRY BRADLEY

Yattendon
September 4, 1902

My dear Bradley

You wrote on August 10th that you were going away for a month. Is it possible that when you get back to Oxford you will be able to run down here for a night or two? We have September 13–15 disengaged.

If you are doubtful, please remember that *you will be of great use* if you do come. Not only have I many classical verses for your criticism, but our phonetics have I think reached an almost final stage.

By showing passages written out in our system to many different people we discovered what were the chief stumbling blocks to the ordinary man, and that has led us to remodel one or two matters.

I think it is more satisfactory now—but in the reduction of the u sounds to types some questions arise, on which we should much like your expert opinion.

I hope that you will come—

With our kindest regards to Mrs. Bradley

yours sincerely
R Bridges

I hope that your holiday has done you good.

390: TO HENRY BRADLEY

Yattendon
September 9, 1902

My dear Bradley

I am very glad indeed that you can come. I can't very well get on without a consultation. Hadow has been here, and he is keen about the longs and shorts. He hesitated about the right solution of one or two points which have I think cleared themselves up for final solution or at least decision one way or other, and I look forward to a consultation with you to come to a definite practical conclusion.

I have found out a lot of things about these doubtful syllables—by means of practice. Hadow also liked the phonetics. He read them off without key as fast as he could have read ordinary English—and then mastered the system in less than 10 minutes. That is very satisfactory. He liked the appearance of the script also.

I am glad that your Malvern trip was so successful. You will tell us all about it.

yours sincerely
R Bridges

P.S   Trains are I fancy unaltered.—The one which leaves Oxford at 2.25 and gets to Hampstead Norris at 3.23 is the one by which I suppose you will come. We will send to meet that on Saturday if we do not get any other injunction from you.

391: TO HENRY BRADLEY

Yattendon
September 22, 1902

My dear Bradley

A thousand thanks for your letter on the monosyllables, which is of great use. I send you the photograph, and shall await yours—any time will do—
I shall come up some day after term begins and tell you a lot of things, and ask a lot more.

———

Meanwhile I am troubling over what in your dictionary you call the ordinary vowel i *Psychi, riact.*

I find that in my practice I have written $\overline{\text{rec}\bar{\text{o}}\text{mp}\bar{\text{o}}\text{sd}}$ chlo$\bar{e}$ and I should certainly write r$\bar{e}$act but I have written Cr$\breve{e}$ation.—I had written Cr$\bar{e}$ation, but was dissatisfied with it, and I rewrote the verse in which it occurred.—Now I find Newbolt (who has been here) is inclined to make this vowel *always* long.

Do you see any difference between creation and react?

Stone points out that a vowel open before another has a tendency (before the

word accent) to lengthen itself—and this is most marked in react—I do not hea
it so plainly in creation.

I should like your opinion.

yours ever
R Bridges

In the verb create the e seems long, so I suppose it will be in the substantiv
unless there is some condition here which I do not know of.

392: TO LIONEL MUIRHEAD

Yattendo
October 3, 190

My dear Lionel

We have, for our sins, not for mine, Eve is at fault, to go to the sea in Novem
ber, and I am writing to enquire about Southsea. The finger of Providence seem
pointing strongly in that direction.

Whether there are baths in which children can swim, bath chairs, decen
lodgings, any useful information. We shall need a good deal of room with
governess and 3 children and a maid.

Except for this seaside plan we are all extremely well. My wife is vexed at ne
getting her strength back after her illness last year so quickly as she would like.
seems well to try 3 or 4 weeks at the sea.

We have had a lot of visitors and I am just going down to the station to brir
up another. Between times I have been working away at the prosody. The L. N
Epistle has now got 260 odd lines, and there are some 850 lines in all finishe
Our phonetic scheme is I think receiving its final touches, and it has been p
tronized in a quarter which will ensure its making its appearance in public e
very long. It meets with great favour.

I forget what you think of it, but I am rather proud to have got over insu
mountable difficulties and taken an inexpugnable position.

yours ever
RB

I have no practice in writing it yet, and make many mistakes.

393: TO HENRY NEWBOLT

Yattende
October 9, 190

My dear Newbolt

I have just written to Johnston, and sent him the new letters required
complete our alphabet. I expect that when he returns me these he will have son
suggestion about type.

I have been going on with the longs and shorts. I will copy out any that you ant for your Birmingham lecture, or send you my MS to read from, but I do ot want the verses shown to anyone.—I wish to keep them to myself till I have ot enough done. If anything put me out of humour with them, as a very little ight, I should shut up.

Also I will send you the Elegy which you read, and so kindly approved of, *if you ant it for the Monthly.* I don't really wish to print it: but I shall on the other hand e only too glad to let it earn a little money. But you must promise not to read it t the Café.—Perhaps you don't want it.

I sent some scazons to Barlow today, and told him to send them to the Lancet r other Medical Paper.—But as they indirectly praise him I am afraid he won't.

I was in Oxford yesterday. We are going to the sea—probably to Southsea—in ovember for 3 weeks. Do you know any good lodgings at Southsea?

I hope you are feeling better, and not overworked.

With kind regards from my wife and self to Mrs. Newbolt etc.

yours sincerely
R Bridges

94: TO MRS. MARGARET WOODS

Yattendon
nr Newbury
October 28, 1902

ear Mrs Woods

'Procrastination is the soul of business' has been the maxim which has gov- rned my life now for 2, or 3 months, and it has enabled me to get through a ood deal of work. I have really put off writing to you about your play with the otion that I should have found time to read it before this, but I am still too uch occupied in trying to finish off some work.

The copy sent to me bore the legend "with the Publisher's compts" but I do not now that it may not have been sent to me at your commands, so I must thank ou for the present, as well as for the honour done to me in your preface. I am oing to read the book, I need not say; meantime my wife has enjoyed it very uch, and I am sure that you would be pleased with the manner of this praise hich she gave it if you knew how 'difficult' she was.

Your preface will help my "Milton's Prosody" which needs a fillip now and en, but the main cause of common sense is gradually ousting the enemy—and really think that in a year or two, we shall have a really scientific treatment of ythm.

I hope that you are well. We have been going on pretty straight in spite of the retched season, but my wife seems just now to want a change, and we think of ending 3 weeks of next month at Southsea.

With kindest regards from us both to yourself and the DD

yours sincerely
R Bridges

395: TO LIONEL MUIRHEAD

Yattendon
October 31, 1902

My dear Lionel

We are very grateful to you for your letter about Southsea. It contained the only special indications that I have succeeded in eliciting.

I think of running down there *next Tuesday,* i. e. November 3rd to find lodgings. What I want is some guaranteed experience of cooking and cleanliness etc. etc.

Would the Colonel of whom you speak in your letter be likely to be of any use? I prefer to know something of a lodging house before I adventure in it.

Your poem is coming on. It is now 360 lines long. Another bout or two will finish it, and is almost all written out, as far as I have gone, ready to send to you in a large script easy to be read.

We should all go to Southsea about the 11th.

yours ever
RB

396: TO LOGAN PEARSALL SMITH

Yattendon
November 7, 1902

My dear Pearsall Smith

I have been in Oxford twice this term, or 3 times—and am sorry that I did not know that you were to be met.

Idly loitering in Oxford again "'Mong colleges and old libraries"—I had to get out my book to find that quotation. I have just finished my long hexameter poem. I hope to get it printed at Xmas by Daniel. I have written to him about it. We are all going to the sea on Tuesday for 3 weeks' change of air, so I am afraid there is no chance of my seeing you till after that. But if all is well I shall hope to be up in Oxford once or twice again before end of term.

Excuse my writing in great haste. I have a lot of letters and no leisure to write them in.

I would have sent you your iambics, but I think they want something doing to them. I don't fancy that much is to be made of that metre in English.

yours truly
R Bridges

397: TO LIONEL MUIRHEAD

Yattendon
November 9, 1902

My dear Lionel

I am sending you a copy of my Epistle and will just make a few notes concerning the Prosody in order to save trouble in reading.

1. The scansion is phonetic, but I have occasionally only modified the spelling in the phonetic direction, and this is neither complete, nor are the symbols which I have used always observed.

2. Note that h in English is when fully pronounced a strong consonant so that ŏf is long before ʽhis. I sometimes (where it seems most required for a reader) indicate this by a rough breathing thus ʽhis.

3. I put this rough breathing in some other places. E.g. to remind you thatʽone (or ʽonce) which looks as if it begins with a vowel really begins with a consonant— thus wunç.

And to show the consonantal y which often precedes our long u this combination (following a single consonant) will lengthen a preceding short vowel *if that vowel is accented,* thus ritual is really rit.yu.al etc.

4. This leads to the rule that no *accented* short vowel can be short before any two consonants, thus săcrămĕnt is sác-ră-mēnt etc., and this covers compound consonants e.g. our soft g is pronounced dg, which if the vowel preceeding be unaccented will not affect it, e.g. ēncoŭrăging has the a before the soft g short, but a word like bādger has the first syllable long.

The reason is that the accent splits up the compound consonant, and the words divide thus

en cóu ră-dging

bắd - ger

thus Gēŏlŏgў

but
Gēŏlógĭc

5. A new rule (just beginning to be perceived by Stone) is the refusal of accented monosyllables to be short, thus gŏd măn lŏve cannot be short before vowels, but in compounds where they are not accented they would be short.

6. me he she etc are all long unless enclitic or proclitic, thus gíve-mĕ has the enclitic me short—

7. Some syllables are pronounced either long or short at will.—Thus I use mĭnutely or mīnutely ăc.cretion or ā.cretion and such words must be pronounced as they scan. These are very few.

8. All Greek and Latin proper names I use with their original scansion. I think it barbarous to anglicise them, though some names in very common use might be exceptions. Thus I scan
Thēss ắ lĭ ăn Lărīssă
which in English would be
Thĕssálĭăn Lărĭssă
These names must be pronounced as a Greek would have pronounced them or a Roman.

9. You know well enough the doubled consonant fallacy; happiness is hăpĭnĕs. The doubled consonant cannot affect the quantity of preceding vowel *unless it is pronounced.* E.g. hăppў is like răpĭd.

10. I have taken (meaningly) no liberties except that I have once written omnipotential—whereas I make a rule that words in *ial* shall have this termination uncontracted. I will alter this line. Words in ion like nation always contract the termination—and obedience etc.—the i is almost lost. This is an example of the worst kind of difficulty which one has in enforcing classic rules.

11. Words in *ble* are considered to be as if—bael thus
                                    invisibael things

I have written large to save your eyes, not beautifully. We hope to go to Southsea for 3 weeks on Tuesday. Our address 1. Gladstone Houses, Clarence Parade. I shall want to hear both what your general impressions are, and what places seem to you most successful. You won't make it all out at once, for I have put a lot of stuff into it.

yours ever

RB

Wrote the last 6 lines this morning while the family was at Matins.

398: TO HENRY NEWBOLT

Yattendon
November 11, 1902

My dear Newbolt

We are all off to *Southsea* tomorrow—address *No. 1 Gladstone Houses, Clarence Parade*. I shall want to take the children to Portsmouth to show them things, and it struck me that you might be able to make it easy for us through one of your naval swells. If so we should be very grateful—But we do not want to give trouble.

You do not say when you want the Elegy. I have finished the Hexameter Epistle. It makes 430 lines.

yours sincerely

RB

I never expected that you would find that you could go in for type casting. Perhaps when some facsimiles are out I may find a millionaire who would like to do it. I think I shall get Daniel to print my "Epistle" in "plain English" with a facsimile page of phonetic MS. Meanwhile I will try and get Johnston to work. Please go and see him sometimes—and make him show you his MSS of various kinds.

399: TO HENRY BRADLEY

Gladstone House
No 1. Clarence Parade
Southsea
[About November 15, 1902]

My dear Bradley

I put my address at top not because I want you to write to me, but to account for my not having turned up at Oxford. We came here this week for my wife's sake, and expect to stay about 3 weeks, after which I may hope to visit Oxford. I hope that you are well. We have had miraculous weather down here so far.

Before I left home I finished my hexameter epistle. It ran to 430 odd lines, and it seems to me satisfactory. I had prepared myself some fine opportunities, and the verse seemed to me to take them very well indeed. The difficulty was to cut it off and end up. I made a fair copy of it and sent it to its destination and Daniel hopes to print it for me at Xmas. I think that I decided almost every question of rules of quantity, and I am now amusing myself by transcribing it in my phonetic. It has been an advantage running these two things together. I thought that we had nearly finished the phonetics, but now that I am beginning to prove them (my wife had hitherto done all the translation) I find a good many little matters which I think can be amended. I shall probably go on translating into phonetics for 2 or 3 weeks, and by that time I shall have found out what are the chief stumbling blocks. In writing oneself one finds out all the inconveniences. I am very much pleased with the general result and appearance: but I find things which I want if possible to get rid of. Daniel will of course print my poem in newspaper spelling, and I should like to have one page of phonetics facsimile'd and bound with his text, but I may not have got the whole alphabet in final order in time for him.

I have naturally no other news for you. My "Stone's Prosody" has now reached over 1000 lines. There are of course a few places that need correction by later lights. I am very much indebted to you for all the help which you have given me. I wish I could send you the poem to read: but have no really legible correct copy. I believe that you will like it.

This is a wonderful place for variety of noises. I have told my children to make a full list of them, and then I will see how they scan. I foresee an excellent poem, at least if they will scan. It is wonderful how things do scan with a little handling. I made several lists of things of various kinds in my Hexameter epistle—but enough of that. I am going to bed.

yours sincerely
Robt Bridges

400: TO HENRY NEWBOLT

Gladstone House
1 Clarence Parade
Southsea
[About November 15, 1902]

My dear Newbolt

I ought to have written to you before about your navy longs, but I have been very busy, and have only just read the book, and not thoroughly yet. It is of no use reading when one is full of other things. But (as you will not expect a detailed criticism of all its contents) I can just say how very much I admire "Commemoration". Also "the only son". These two I thought the best in the book, and both of them showing a peculiar mastery and gift of your own.—I am sorry that I do not know what "the hazardous pitch" is.—And I did not know that there was a "gran-ite pillar".

The sonnet 'Pulchritudo' I liked very much—and the last stanza but one of the first poem seemed to me to be of your best. As for the poem called Yattendon I am afraid that your readers will think you are a man of eccentric tastes. I shall enjoy the book at my leisure.

I am now doing at odd times a good deal of transcription into phonetic, and finding out the practical inconveniences which can be remedied by a little management and alteration. I have with my wife's assistance reduced the U s to 3—a great feat.

Don't bother anyone about our visit to the dockyard. A lieutenant here has introduced us to the Policeman which seems to be sufficient. We have also an invitation to go on one of the ships.

I suppose it will do if I send the Elegy when I get home again.

I am thinking of writing a short essay on the first elements of rhythm. I think that I have discovered something which makes it all pretty clear to the man in the street. If I write it I will offer it to you.

yours sincerely
Robt Bridges

401: TO LIONEL MUIRHEAD

Southsea
November 27, 1902

My dear Lionel

I was glad to get your letter about the hexameters: we knew that you would like the sulfurous Chinamen. Since I came down here I have been experimenting in phonetic writing, and have copied all the epistle in our latest script, which has revealed two false quantities: these I have corrected, and made a few other slight alterations. I should like to put them into your copy, so I am asking you to return it to me next week, when I get home again, which I hope may be on Tuesday: for I am tired of this place. The tea is bad, and I have a pain in my back. Margaret is practising double stopping in the room just behind me, and that may possibly have something to do with it. My curious writing is more easily explained: I am accustoming my hand to these characters that I may be able to demonstrate my phonetic system if it comes to anything—at present I am rather discouraged by difficulties. I feel inclined to give you an example, but a steel pen and an armchair by the fire do not give the best results.

I am obliged to you for your list of verses that you did not approve of. Babyhood is all right; the spelling is terribly deceptive: but I will not discuss the objections. Now I am called off to play a round game of word-making.

> your affectionate
>
> RB

402: TO LIONEL MUIRHEAD

> Yattendon
> December 13, 1902

My dear Lionel

The children are all going to a fancy dress ball on January 2, and two of them will wear the Turkish costume which was made for them last year. You said at that time that you had some odds and ends of Turkish things which would be valuable on such an occasion, and that you would have wished to have lent them. If you have anything which you think would be of use, and would send it we will take great care of it.

I returned the Epistle some days ago. I suppose it reached you all right. I am busy now in writing out a page of facsimile phonetic to bind up with Daniel's edition. He has begun printing. I may write out a short poem for you in the script. But as I want this to go by the early post tomorrow I will not wait for it.

> yours ever
>
> RB

403: TO LIONEL MUIRHEAD

> Yattendon
> December 15, 1902

My dear Lionel

Thanks for your letter. I am just sending off my page of phonetic for facsimile to Hart. As I have a copy which went wrong I send it to you that you may see what it is like. If you think well of it I shall be very glad. It is really the way in which I should like to see English written. I do not object to a few modifications.

I am sorry that my inexperience in writing forbids my doing more justice to the script. It should be extremely beautiful. My hand is too uncertain, but I am better at it than I was and can go at a good pace.

Keep any money that you wish to spend on it for a better opportunity.

yours ever

RB

Please erase the s in the line
Juices of plants
It should read *juice* of plants

404: TO HENRY NEWBOLT

Yattendon

December 17, 1902

My dear Newbolt
Thank you for your letter. I will try and put together my ideas on rhythm for you this Xmas. I really think I can make the matter very simple, readable and convincing.

When it is done you can have it or no as you like. I saw your kind article on Volume V Smith Elder, and was much gratified.

Daniel has already set up half my hexameter epistle, and thinks to bring it out this Xmas Vacation. The end of it is better than the beginning.

I have written out a passage in my phonetic script, and sent it to Clarenden Press to be facsimiled and bound up with the volume. It looks very well, and I think it will launch the phonetics most favorably. When people have seen them we shall know whether we have many supporters.

I could not get any work out of Johnston: so I did the thing myself.

I am going into Oxford tomorrow.

The weather is beastly.

yours sincerely

R Bridges

It will be very convenient for me if my Elegy comes out in your Mag about the same time as my hexameter poem. It will prevent people thinking that I am wholly given over to idolatry.

405: TO SAMUEL GEE

Yattendon

January 2, 1903

My dear Gee:
I have been intending to write to you for many days to send you our best wishes (to you and Mrs Gee and your daughter) for the new year. It seems a long

time since anything passed between us. We are all well, except that my wife has never quite got her strength back after her bad illness last winter, though she is supposed to be absolutely free from any other trace of her pleurisy. She suffers from fatigue; and is now trying to regain strength by moderately increasing her exercises. Tonight she has taken the two girls out to a fancy dress dance; I hope she will not be over tired by it. It is the first time that she has gone out in this way since her illness.—The children seem to be growing up strong.—But I must not write of them.

I have been working at odd times all this year in writing poems in the Greek manner. I have done a good lot of them. Daniel is now engaged in printing a 430 line long hexameter "*epistle*" on all things human and divine (medicine not excepted) and I hope it may be out before the end of the vacation. I am telling him to send a prospectus of it to you when he is ready, and I feel confident in it interesting you. I am not giving any away, as I hope to raise a little needful wind by the sale. It is to be accompanied by a sheet of facsimile of MS in my own hand in my new phonetic writing, the point of which is that it is really phonetic, and that anyone can read it easily, but that it is beautiful, and (as I think) artistically superior to the ordinary way of writing and spelling. When it is launched in this way I shall push it some time this year in one of the London monthlies. I hope it will meet with your approbation. About the poem I feel pretty sure. Just now I am sorting out the question of rhythm, and I have made I think some rather fundamental discoveries, especially about Greek practice, which (it appears to me) have been either altogether overlooked or mistaken, or unappreciated. Unfortunately I have not enough books here.—I hope that you will be able to send us a good account of Mrs Gee's health.—I still sometimes wish that you were thinking of retiring from the profession, and indulging your literary tastes for the rest of your life. Then I might see something of you. With our best wishes

> yours ever
>
> RB

406: TO HENRY NEWBOLT

> Yattendon
> January 8, 1903

My dear Newbolt

I am sending the Elegy back to printer by this post. I have corrected printers errors, and some punctuation—and altered two or 3 lines for verbal reasons.

If the corrections are clear to you there will be no reason for me to see a revise, if not it can come back to me.

If you want a title for it, it was called "Recollections of Solitude". I don't care whether or no it has a title, but I expect it is better for the Magazine.—People like a heading.

Did you see 3 Stanzas of mine in last week's Saturday? Daniel has had lumbago, but he is well on with my epistle and the facsimile page of phonetic is very successful. I hope he will finish before term begins, but I am beginning to doubt.

I hope you have all been well this Xmas. We were most flourishing till the children's parties began. Since then not so lively. The weather is as beastly as possible.

With good wishes for New Year

yours ever

RB

I saw your kind notice of my Volume V. I think your eulogies do the book much good. My distant relatives almost respect me—

I was quite forgetting about the Rhythm. It is developing.—Will be in 3 parts as I see it now. Part I. on the possible expression of "poetic" Rhythm—demonstrating the Greek position to be the one logical method.

Part II. Enquiry into Greek theory.

Part III. Other methods in use.

Part II Exercises me much. I have come at last to see my way to explain their behaviour so as to reconcile all the various things said about it by their writers. It is *amazing* to me to have to discover such things for myself. They are not in any book that I have found yet.

407: TO SAMUEL GEE

Yattendon

January 9, 1903

My dear Gee

Thank you for your letter (I was delighted to hear such a good account of your wife) and for the Plato, which arrived safely. I have already read one volume through, for as I have to *look* all through it, I find that it amuses me to read the dialogues again—and I shall come to some that I have never read. The first volume was all familiar. I have just put it aside, after going through *Phaedo*, which in spite of its beauty is I think as depressing as anything in this world. The folly of the Athenians in killing Socrates—and the illogical argumentations which Plato has put into his mouth make a picture distressing in all its main features. I never could understand why Plato could not see the glaring blunder in his own logic.

I gather from the tone of your letter that you will "highly appreciate" the philosophy of my Hexameter poem when you get it. I am sure it will both interest and amuse you. There is a lot about medicine in it—Daniel has been laid up with lumbago and it is impossible to say when he will get it done.

My eldest girl is very seedy with a depressed condition following a sharp febrile attack with sore throat. She does not cast it off, but it is still within the week and I hope she is getting better. She still has a little rise of temperature *in the morning,* not more than half a degree, but I do not understand it, and she seems very weak. Is it a symptom which you recognize?

I shall be writing again soon.

yours ever

RB

A letter is always welcome.—

408: TO HENRY NEWBOLT

Yattendon
February 1, 1903

My dear Newbolt

A thousand thanks for the Review. I am very busy, and have not had the desirable leisure yet to con it, but I saw some good things. I hope indeed that the public will like this venture of mine better than the last, else you much eschew me.

I enclose a proof of the page of phonetic which will come out in Daniel's volume, which is now all set up and ⅔ printed.

My rhythmical studies have been wading on through various pedantic works—prospering. Everything comes out straight to the confusion of a good deal of pedantry, and I find that some of my discoveries are new to scholars.

yours ever

RB

My wife expects to arrange for another visit from your family this summer. Our kindest remembrances to Mrs. Newbolt—

409: TO HENRY NEWBOLT

Yattendon
February 2, 1903

My dear Newbolt

I posted a line of acknowledgement to you yesterday. Since then I have dined out and had hot coppers—partially recovered, and amused myself with the Monthly. So I am writing again (that my letter may go by the after breakfast collection tomorrow morning) to say how pleased I am with the Review. I should think it must be making its way well with such good and attractive stuff in it, though I grieve to see so few advertisements.

But what I wish to congratulate you on are your admirable editorial "heroic" couplets.—The verse is most excellent, and lots of good things in it. Best perhaps the Science passage which is all fine especially the opening "of our eyes".—I don't think I should have guessed it was by you, though I might have suspected. It is a very good thing for you to have done, for it will show the critics of your rhythm that you can "iambic" with them if you choose.—It is also a very amusing contrast to my couplets for you are able to use openly all the tricks which I had to avoid or disguise—Did you know the line by Bloomfield describing a Suffolk cheese

"Too big to swallow & too hard to bite"?

But of course there are many like that.

It was really too bad of Kipling, or rather of the $E^{d.}$ of the Times, though perhaps he knew what he was about—for the thing seems to have served a good turn as far as I can see—It was very cleverly put.

yours sincerely
R Bridges

410: TO HENRY NEWBOLT

Yattendon
February 3, [1903]

My dear Newbolt

Many thanks for the cheque which is most handsome. I sent you a second note, which you may have received after writing yours, saying how I admired your 'parody'.—My facsimile was chosen out of the poem for the sake of the illustration of the phonetics.—I had to choose some passage which could not shock the reader too much, and could contain all the symbols. I did not consider it from the point of view of literary or poetic interest. Though the line

Noisily in the shallows splashing and disporting uninspired

is I think as good a description of our Walter Crane* style of art as the generation is likely to get.

yours ever
RB

*Insufficient example.

411: TO LIONEL MUIRHEAD

Yattendon
February 27, 1903

My dear Lionel

We are delighted with your proposition to come on Monday, and hope you may be able to stay some time. We have been to the Slade lectures. HEW shut up, was ill (between lectures) and Daniel read the second for him. He went off to London. I am anxious about him, but know nothing. M^rs W also seems to be ill. The lectures were very good indeed, and all very new—on painting in Rome in the Augustan age. I did not know that some really first class things existed.

yours ever

RB

I am ½ way through a 2nd Epistle, on Socialism.
Will send to meet the arrival 3.20 on Monday

412: TO HENRY NEWBOLT

Yattendon
March 12, [1903]

My dear Newbolt

I see by papers that Andrew Carnegie is starting phonetic improvement of spelling, and has endowed a committee in New York with 10,000 dollars a year to work the reform.

Will you enquire about this and tell me whether you would under the circumstances be inclined to print a paper fully descriptive of my system in the Monthly.

Carnegie may frighten the public into consideration of the question.

yours ever

RB

I think it could be managed with a *very* few types, some 10 at most, and 2 pages of facsimile—
P.S.
I have written a note to Andrew Carnegie. Can you address it for me kindly? It's worth venturing.

413: TO HENRY BRADLEY

Yattendon
March 12, [1903?]

My dear Bradley

I wonder whether you or Dr. Murray or some one *in authority in Oxford* could say or write something publicly to make these people, if there is anything in it, pay attention to my system. My interest is, as you know, *calligraphic* and *conservative* and I believe that if our language were spelt properly it would be very like Greek.

It would be of no use for me to write—for every one will have notions of their own.

I think you agree with me that it is only on lines like mine that anything dignified and reasonable can be done.

yours truly

RB

414: TO HENRY NEWBOLT

Yattendon
March 15, 1903

My dear Newbolt
   Thanks for forwarding my letter to the great A.C. I thought it worth trying.
   You say "Certainly I am hoping for a paper on rhythm from you". This rhythm affair will come in due time. I am getting on. But what I asked you was whether in view of Carnegie's disturbing the public mind with his scheme for destruction of the hard g—there would not be a real opening for an article on my phonetic way of writing.

This is quite a different affair and you could have the article (quite short) as soon as the people could print off the facsimiles for it would take no time to write—
   I am glad that you will come at Easter.
   I want a book on tiger hunting in India. I have to do tiger shooting in a poem which I am writing on Socialism, and I require some names of places where there are good shooting jungles, etc. With hexameter metre I like to be able to choose some fine sounding ones.
   No hurry, but you might bring such a book down here with you at Easter.
   The poem promises better than the last.

yours ever

RB

415: TO SAMUEL GEE

Yattendon
March 24, [1903]

My dear Gee
   Thank you for your letter. Your description of metaphysical science was delightful. You know I think there is something in it, though I can't ever understand such things. It always seemed to me that the space difficulty would be more or less got over if we could ever come *round again* to the *same spot*. But I don't know that one would be much better off.
   I am glad that you think my scientific outburst fairly successful. I think the contrast of art with nature at the end is what has never been done so plainly. But

we think differently of art—except that all of your high philosophy is art in a sense which forbids outward expression. I did not quite hope that you would find the hexameters run. I am in an awkward predicament with *all* scholars— and I must write a book on the subject. *No one reads Greek poetry* rightly. They attend neither to the accent nor the quantity—and they say that if they put the right accent on the words (ie the Greek accent), then the verses don't run.—The reason is that they do not read according to the artificial quantities which the Greeks imposed on their syllables in order to get rid of their unfixed various quantities, and enable them to make up rhythms which should be fixed, and which they could rely on to stand alone.

Now if Homer be read according to quantity the accents are nearly all right; it really does not matter where they come—

If you were to take the same liberties with English pronunciation which scholars do with Greek my verses would scan in the same way as Homer's do to you.

Of course my Epistle is not in heroics. While the model of my versification is Greek, the level of it is aimed at Horace's Epistle.

—I hope *some* of the lines pleased you, where they are "accentual". I am now ⅔ through a second Epistle on Socialism. If you could find time to read it and criticise its arguments before it is printed I should be grateful to you. As for the phonetics, if they interest you I will make you a copy of my alphabet. Of course it is only meant to be a helpful tentative. I was most proud of my **ꞓ** (the **ꭰ** of slavery. **sꞯꞇꞓƦy.**) It is made of the **Ɛ** of bed, and the **ɩ** of hit. As correctly given in *vein*. And as **y** = **ɩ** in my alphabet, I get these forms

ꞇнƐy ꭰƐy. ᴠƐɩn sꞯꞇᴠƐƦy . All of which may of course be correctly written alike— Glad of good news of family

yours ever

RB

416: TO HENRY NEWBOLT

Yattendon
April 3, [1903]

My dear Newbolt

What seems to me to have happened is thus: I asked if you would like a *phonetic* article. You replied. Yes of course I am expecting your article on *rhythm*. I replied. I meant *phonetics*—to this *no response*. I therefore thought no more of it.

(1) PHONETICS. The question is whether Carnegie's move is likely to call people's attention to Phonetics, enough to make it worth while to launch mine.

(2) Rhythm. This subject has a way of developing in all directions. Better wait till you come down here. I am getting on *very* well with it, but there is no hurry. I have written nothing.

I am nearly at the end of my 2nd hexameter Epistle (on Socialism), I think it is better than the 1st. I look forward to reading it to you. I have omitted 20 lines in which I want to describe a tiger hunt. For this I want *names of jungles*. You will see that it is a fine opportunity for getting some Indian names in—and there is almost poetical necessity for them. This is why I asked you to bring down some Indian book on tiger hunting. It is only the *places* that I want, but they must be the *right ones:* as I need not tell you.

Don't bother about the Phonetics. It will give me only 2 or 3 days work at any time. Any delay will be in the reproduction of say 2 pages or one plate—I could manage very well with that I should think. There is no hurry—I shall most likely facsimile the whole of my next Epistle, with a translation into newspaper English spelling—You will be here so soon that I shall not write more or again.

yours sincerely
RB

417: TO SAMUEL GEE

Yattendon
April 13, [1903]

My dear Gee

Thank you for your letter, and for saying that you will read my epistle. I am within 40 lines of the end, and had better finish it now before I send it, especially as I am expecting a visitor this week who will be wanting to see it. It is better than the 1st Epistle, and I hope very much that you will think the argumentation on a great scale. It is full of poetry. When I wrote my 1st Epistle I thought that, having Horace's vehicle, I could put more *poetry* into an Epistle than he did. In this 2nd Epistle I have done better than I expected.

I have copied it out in common spelling but shall henceforth *print* in my new phonetic.

I agree with you about democracy. You should have come down here for quiet.

My wife joins in kindest regards to Mrs Gee.—Did Edith leave a little glass "salts" bottle when she was here? One has lately turned up with "Edith" on it.

Yours ever
RB

418: TO LIONEL MUIRHEAD

Yattendon
May 4, 1903

My dear Lionel

I was very glad to hear from you. Sorry for Anthony's mishap. I hope his eye is all right again. We had the Newbolt's with their children staying here during a week of the Easter holidays and the children enjoyed themselves very much. I have been well till the last fortnight. I have now a rather unusual bronchitis, which should have gone away before, but it sticks to me, and I don't know why except that I suppose I am a little "below par".—I have been working harder than usual of late, am now trying to finish Epistle II for the June number of the Monthly Magazine. I think it is better than Ep. I. By the way those Wintry Delights have got me in hot water with Mrs. Daniel and Stuckey Coles. When last I was at Oxford Mrs. D. was quite unlike herself. I shall have to keep away for a bit, especially as my Epistle II won't mend matters. —Daniel is bringing out my "Peace Ode" (16 stanzas of alcaics) on the anniversary June 1, and it may appear simultaneously with the Epistle II in the Monthly. —I am glad to hear that Willert liked the Hexameters. Did you see the notice which the Times 'Literary Supplement' gave them? A whole page and that the first. That is really a very important alliance against the old fashioned idiot.

I will not forget to send you copies of the lener experiments for your blank leaves. In case of their never being printed I shall be glad to be sure of their existing somewhere. I have only about a dozen lines to do to finish my 2nd Epistle and should do them any day if I was quite fit. Still they may be knocked off at any moment and then I shall be at liberty. —We think (my wife and I) of taking Margaret up to the Beethoven Festival in London in the mid of this month from 17th I think for one week.

This next Wednesday we go to Oxford to hear Joachim in an afternoon concert. I don't know if it is possible for you to come in for it. It will be good. Quartetts etc.—

Hanbury's sudden death was a blow to me. Though I did not see much of him he was an old friend with real sympathies—and a very true friend. He will also be a great loss to the country. He was one of the best of our statesmen, and should have had the war office instead of that minion Brodrick. The fact is Salisbury was afraid of him. He likes to have men who will do as he tells them. Hanbury was independent and would have cleaned out the war office.

yours ever
R Bridges

419: TO HENRY NEWBOLT

Yattendon
May 5, [1903]

My dear Newbolt

Thinking you wished for the Epistle, I have been working hard at it, and am glad to say have finished it. It runs to 422 lines. I had left 20 for the tigers etc. and found I wanted 30. I shall be very glad to keep it by me for a month, as no doubt I can improve a word or two here and there.

As for Peace Ode. Daniel has already set it up: so I have written to him for my 'copy' or for a strike off to save me trouble of copying again, and I will send it you when I get it in 2 or 3 days. You can allow space for it, as it is just 16 stanzas of 4 lines each, and it will not bear any introductions or explanation. I think that had better be reserved for the Epistle; it would be too heavy for the ode.

I think however that I might *advertise "Wintry Delights"* in the number of the Monthly that contains the *Peace ode*. So that anyone might see that they can get an explanation if they want it.*

Mackail approves of the Hexameters. Another man, who is fastidious, writes most enthusiastically. There will be a public of some sort.

I am glad that you enjoyed your visit here, and got on well at Birmingham. Your visit was a great pleasure to us, and did me a lot of good, but I have 'contracted a bronchitis' which annoys me very much. It seems rather better today.

We keep note of our dinner invitation. I hope we shall all be alive and well.

yours ever
RB

*¼ or ⅓ of a page advertisement would do. I will send copy with poem—am busy today.

420: TO LOGAN PEARSALL SMITH

Yattendon
May 8, [1903]

My dear Pearsall Smith

Your letter was a great pleasure to me, and it is very good of you to have purchased the Daniel volume. I think that what you say about the fresh opportunities that these classical metres give to English poetry is very much to the point. It is what makes me wish to use them—and I think that my 2nd Epistle, which I have just finished, must convert a good many people to the same opinion.

Newbolt is going to print my "Peace Ode" in the June number of the Monthly Magazine, and (I hope) the 2nd Epistle in the July number. This should give the experiment a fair start, and I shall look forward to publishing a little volume of them.

By the way the Literary Supplement to the Times gave me a full page of approval!!! And that the first page. The article was by an expert, and very good, except that he would for some reason talk of Latin rather than of Greek.

I have been making a lot of small discoveries—

I have done nothing more with Iambics, which is the reason why I have never sent you your little ode. I am not satisfied with my first attempts in that measure, and I think I begin to see where the difficulty lies.

Some of us hope to go up to town for the Beethoven Festival next week. After that we should be at home (from May 23) till August, when we go to the seaside. I shall hope to be up occasionally in Oxford during summer term—

It is very kind of you to ask us to visit you at Haslemere, but I see no chance of that. We must look forward to seeing you here.

You do not say how your work is going on—

Please let me know if you go for any stay in Oxford—

[no signature]

421: TO SAMUEL GEE

Yattendon
May 9, [1903]

My dear Gee

I sent you my Socialistic or Anti-socialistic Epistle yesterday. I hope that the copy is readable. I thought that you would prefer it to the original magnificent phonetics.

I want you to read it for me.—I am coming up to London if all is well on Saturday, for a week; and I will call and have a chat with you.

Several people have read the Epistle, and my conclusion is that it needs a different winding up. I hope that this task of criticising it for me will not be uncongenial.

yours ever
R Bridges

422: TO HENRY NEWBOLT

Yattendon
May 27, [1903]

My dear Newbolt

I enclose you a letter from Daniel. His arrangement for publishing Ode (150 copies at 5/-) seems all right, but a line from you would gratify him, I suspect.

The Provost of Worcester being deceased, Daniel should reign in his stead. But I think there is division amongst them—

I have just been all through (I mean my wife has) one of the most generally used and advanced books on phonetic spelling of English: and I find nothing which my system has overlooked—and I am really almost as much surprised as gratified.

I have been, and am, rather seedy and quite unable to do any work, and unless I recover myself within a few days I shall not be able to *promise* you the Epistle and all its paraphernalia in time for your July number—I think that it is very unlikely that I shall not be on time: but you will want to be warned, so that you may have something else ready.

I find that I must rewrite the last ten lines—I know what I want to end up with:

but it will be difficult to put shortly and clearly, and I shan't do it unless I am in the mood.

I should be disappointed to miss the month—and will write to you as soon as I know. I suppose that if I sent MS by 15th of June it would be in time.

yours ever

RB

423: TO HENRY NEWBOLT

Yattendon
June 11, [1903]

My dear Newbolt

I am glad to be posting you the Epistle on Socialism.—I have done the best I could about the prosody rules. They have been done for me, and I think extremely well, and very briefly.

I have written a short note to be printed after the title of the poem, as you did with the peace ode, for the reader to read before he reads the poem. The prosody is to follow the poem.

Of course if you wish to nip all the prose out you can do so.

There is one line of the poem which I expect to amend before I get the proofs and I will change in correction.

Some syllables have to be marked with /, Some with $\cup$ and $^-$. Otherwise there is nothing to cause printer any difficulty.

You will see at foot of first page of copy a statement that "Wintry Delights" is advertised in your Mag. I should be very glad if you would give it ¼ or ⅓ of a page advertisement, and charge same to me.—You might copy the Daniel press advertisement enclosed.

yours ever

RB

If there is anything in my scheme which you dislike pray alter it—Put my name in somewhere—where you will—and direct printer how to print.

424: TO HENRY NEWBOLT

Yattendon
Friday morning. [Late June 1903]

My dear Newbolt

I am just posting off the corrected proof to Ballantyne Press, the MS with your card arriving this morning *after* I had corrected.

I had no difficulties, but some alterations in the summary at end will want your revision (to see that the corrections are rightly made) or the last pages had better be returned to me.

There is of course nothing that you would not see to as well as I could.

Your insertion of the final Note *before* the Summary was a stroke of genius. I have pointed out to printer the hideousness of his huge line-numeration.—I do not see how to guide the reader to place the footnotes without some numbers—daggers and stars in the text are really more annoying to the eye in a poem. But I do not see why the figures should be so big. Little figures would do just as well, and I rather like them.

The printers, seeing that they have to copy my curious spelling have also copied my MS ampersand. I have had to correct this in places where it does not read well. I do not object to it generally. My wife likes it. But if you don't, please understand that it is an accident, and not my intention.

I have written some instructions to printer on a loose sheet.—Make them send this to you with revise. Make any minor corrections in spelling or punctuation that you wish.

We are having string quartetts. The weather is worse than winter, but we are all pretty well—The Calligraphist Johnston was here the other day and I think the phonetic script is now practically settled. I have made one or two changes.

yours ever
RB

425: TO HENRY NEWBOLT

Yattendon
July 23, [1903]

My dear Newbolt

At your leisure tell me how my Epistle suited the business of your Monthly—and whether you think the public would stand any more of that sort of thing. A man told me yesterday that the Daily Mail pronounced me to be an "idiot"—I want to know for practical purposes. If you are not likely to print any more I shall get rid of the things elswhere as soon as I can.

I hope you are all well. I was at Horris Hill one day, but we marched out of dinner without any opportunity of speaking to your chap.

yours ever
RB

426: TO HENRY NEWBOLT

St. Helens
Ryde
Isle of Wight
August 1, 1903

My dear Newbolt

We are here for the month. Thank you for sending the cuttings. It is of course quite a chance what sort of a man or woman does these things. The only point that comes out is that Stone's Prosody is *difficult* reading for the average man.

Daniell said the same. "Oh! (he said to me) it is most awfully stiff reading." On the other hand Henry Bradley said, that whatever might be thought of Stone's system it was in my hands fluent and forcible. So I suppose it needs a sort of expert to tackle it. The critics all go wrong in saying that I advocate the system. I don't do anything of the kind. At least the only advocacy that I shall ever give it is the exhibition of experiments. The Church Times man by the way did not make this mistake. He chose to think the whole thing an elaborate joke.

Has the Duchess of Sutherland written to ask you to write something for a "Garland" (not her name for it) which she seems to be undertaking for some charitable purpose? And can you tell me—if you should be writing—what sort of person she is.

I have no news except that the flora here amuses the children—and that they try to swim—and that I am reading some revelations about English speech in the 16th century—and that I had a most amusing dream last night which I must try and remember more of.

yours ever

RB

Returning the cuttings, which "please find" enclosed.

427: TO LIONEL MUIRHEAD

S^t. Helens
Ryde
Isle of Wight
August 11, 1903

My dear Lionel

We were glad to hear from you. Already $\frac{2}{5}$ of our stay here is over. We go home in the 1st week of September. I hope that when Antony has gone back to school you will run over and spend a few days at Yattendon, if all is well. Edward is going to school about the 15th September and we shall probably stay at home till end of month, when Monica and I hope to be able to get away to pay a few visits. The notion here is swimming, and it gets on pretty well. I ought to be enjoying myself: but I can't say that I am. I have got into an indescribable condition of mind, which no doubt is very poetic, but it is mere wretchedness—and I can only hope that it may pass off as it came.—I will not suggest it to you by describing it.

There are some Oxford people here, with their children. The weather just now seems rather broken up—and we do not suffer from extreme heat. Indeed it is a difficulty some times to get completely warm again after bathing. Walking and cycling fill up the rest of the day, and I am often more fatigued than I like. I have got Mantell's geological guide with me. It is rather old fashioned now, but it is a good book, and helps the children to pick up geological ideas, and also encourages them to pick up stones which they do not always carry home for themselves. We do not see any newspaper here just now. So I don't know what is going on—but I suppose someone would tell me, if there was anything to tell.

I am looking forward to a few days' visit from Henry Sweet, the phonetic authority. If he stays here, as he intends, I shall get a lot of talk with him.—I expect to learn a good deal from him, and also hope to bring him into line with me on one or two matters—or if this should not be, I shall discover why people think certain extraordinary things that I believe to be rot. I fancy however that we shall agree. I don't find that I get on very well with this letter, and the pen makes my writing so horrid that I will do no more.

With our love

yours ever
RB

I am glad to hear that you enjoyed the hay-carting. What kind of physical ailment it was that profited by it I don't quite satisfactorily diagnosticate. I hope it has passed off.

428: TO MRS. CARRIE GLOVER

St Helens
Ryde
Isle of Wight
August 22, [1903]

Dearest Carrie

I was *very much* surprised to hear that you liked my Socialistic or anti socialistic Epistle. If you really did find it readable you might like to read Epistle I on Science & Art. If so I will send you my copy to read when I get home. I quite understand your thinking that I was hard on the priest, but I don't think I am. I believe that the priests are destroying religion, i.e. making the Christian religion impossible, and the way in which I speak of them is the way in which most people speak of them behind their backs, (except of course their own class) and those also are such enemies to religion that they would like to see the whole thing destroyed.—The main point of my poem is my attempt to get scholars to read Greek properly, by showing them what the Greek system of prosody really was. Greek and Latin are (incredible as it may seem) both pronounced like English in all our schools and universities—whereas it is very well known how they were pronounced in a quite different manner. But I cannot expect you to interest yourself in this, though if you read my verses aloud dwelling a little on the long syllables, and making the short syllables very short you will get a fair idea of Greek hexameters. The accents of the speech do not make syllables long, and it is difficult for an English reader to see this. The best way is to read quite naturally.

I am sorry about Butler's book. He was a very strange fellow. I met him first at Rochdale just before he went to New Zealand, and we made friends. He had then a good deal of charm about him, being always clever earnest and kindhearted.—When, on his return to England, he came to London I met him there, and used often to go in and sit half an hour with him in his chambers. He was a very interesting talker, and I learned a good deal from him. I had a sort of pity for his solitary hardworking life. But one day when I was with him he revealed to me a side of his nature with which I had no sympathy, but rather a strong disgust for it, and from that day I avoided him. We met at times, now and then in the British Museum chiefly, and never had any open break—and I have a good many letters from him, some of the last year of his life, and he sent me all his books. His extreme kindness of heart and his enthusiasm for any work which he undertook made his friends much attached to him; and his literary executor,— who was his last acquirement of that sort,—is a very nice fellow, and a man of considerable literary faculty.—I know him pretty well. But S. B. was both vain and ugly in mind. There was a meanness in his general mental attitude towards humanity, as in his actual social habits and personal appearance.—I do not care to speak more in detail about him, for he was familiarly unreserved towards me, and there is no use in dissecting out the badness of any one. It is very difficult to reconcile his wide charity of disposition with his bitter onesided almost venomous regard towards his own family, nor can I understand how he, who cannot possibly be suspected of anything like hypocrisy, can have, in his intercourse with them, maintained himself in their affection and good opinion (so far as family relations were concerned) till the last. I have not seen this last book, but I suppose from what you say that they have now got the riddle before them.

We are getting on all right here. I am in low spirits; otherwise I suppose all is well. The children enjoy themselves.—Ed can now swim, to his great delight.— The girls swim very well. They swim good long distances from the shore. Yesterday we went to hear the French Benedictines (who came to the Island 2 years ago when expelled from France) sing plain chant. It was very odd to see all their old fashioned elaborate ritual in a corrugated iron building.—The absence of the magnificence of architecture made the whole affair seem incredibly foolish.—It might have looked fine in a beautiful ancient abbey. The prior was a charming old man. While he was chatting to us before the service all seemed attractive, the thing itself as exhibited in the chapel ridiculous beyond conception.—One sees how necessary it is to detach them from these old buildings, at least if they will not move forwards—which returns to the beginning of my letter.

your affectionate brother

RB

I fear there is little chance of my being able to get to Chichester from here.

429: TO LOGAN PEARSALL SMITH

Yattendon
September 14, [1903?]

My dear Pearsall Smith

Thank you very much for sending me the extract from Pattison. It is very good as a grammatical example, though it altogether lacks the grandeur of Leslie Stephen's tour de force—or the inimitable 'flea-bite in the ocean'.

The other extract is most interesting—It is so like my Brazilian forest—I ought to belong to a library—for there are many books that I miss seeing and should never hear of it, if it were not for my friends.

It pleases me very much that you like the *matter* of my Epistles. I always thought that there was splendid matter to work on if one had only got a form for it. There is really no English metre which makes poetry of such subjects; it is like versified prose. —Whether Stone's prosody will come to anything I can't say, but it is worth while trying. I have no convictions. —The most promising things that I have done are Elegiacs—

My wife begs me to thank you for your promise about your Mother's book. We enjoyed your visit—though I was sorry to be so unceremonious the last day.

yours sincerely
R Bridges

430: TO HENRY NEWBOLT

Yattendon
September 14, 1903

My dear Newbolt

In Oxford the other day I told Blackwell to get some copies of the July Monthly (which contains my Epistle) to sell when term begins. He told me that he had already had orders for it. It struck me that Murray's agent in Cambridge might do the same there. If you cannot manage this, I could get some one there to make Macmillan order it. I fancy theirs is the chief book shop for the University men. The new Cambridge Review had asked me to send them something for their first number. I have offered them a poem in Stone's prosody (scazons).—I do not know whether they will buy. If they do, it will advertise the Epistle in a footnote.

I was very much amused with your *Last Voyage of Gulliver*—it is full of good things.—We wondered whether Mary Coleridge had a finger in it—or rather my wife did. —It seemed to me to be yours, as you have lately been revealing yourself.

Edward goes to school on Wednesday—he is looking forward to it eagerly—having been sadly without boy company here. I hope he will not be disappointed.

I was at the Austrian cafe the other day. You no doubt were after the partridge somewhere, or maybe the tastier grouse.

My children all enjoyed their swimming in the sea during August, and so did my wife, who got ever so much stronger than she has been for a long while. I got worn out—and have been for the most of this summer in low spirits. —The gale did a lot of damage to trees about here but our little territory escaped.

yours sincerely
RB

Send me a postcard if you can't manage the Review at the Cambridge shops—

431: TO LIONEL MUIRHEAD

Yattendon
September 29, 1903

My dear Lionel

Margaret is not yet any better; on the other hand she is no worse. She was worse the day you left and I followed you into Oxford and Whitelocke came over this morning. He can find nothing wrong, and supposes that she will soon be better.

I have copied my hendecasyllables carefully out, the latest version, and send them. If the writing does not please you I shall be glad to do them again. My reason for not fulfilling my promise of supplying your blank pages is that almost all the things will be better for treatment. —I shall be going at them now.

I finished off Pearsall-Smith's Iambics yesterday.

I hear this morning that one of the 2 hymns at the diocesan festival at Wells this year from the Yattendon Hymnal is to be your *61*. So if you wish to hear your hymn sung by all the Parish quires of Somersets you had better go. I will find out the day.

yours ever
RB

432: TO LIONEL MUIRHEAD

Yattendon
October 2, 1903
Concerning enclosure see end of letter

My dear Lionel

Thank you for your excellent letter. The anxiety, that I told you I had been such a prey to for something like 3 months, had quite passed off before your visit, and it must have been my natural disquiet of mind caused by my child's sudden sickness that made you think me still to be suffering from it. I can't explain to you what it was. There is no reason why it should ever recur, but it was very dreadful; and I suppose there may be other things like it. I do not think that I worry exactly about myself. I have come to dread nothing but moral disgrace: and my sorrows and anxieties are such as I called in my epistle No 2 "heartache and compassionate grief". The words end a hexameter line, but that was not their only title to a place in my poem. I wish that you had been longer with me: for you would have done me good: but you did well to be off—and we have now a nurse in the house whom we should never have engaged if we could have seen her first. I wish she were in Bavaria with your late governess. Margaret is not any better: but she does not seem any worse. The illness looks as if it might go on for some time. I hope I may get one of my old London friends down, but they won'

ook at anyone who is not in the very jaws of death. If you recover after calling
hem in, you in some sort owe them an apology. I have no fault to find with your
fatalism, except the personal objection that it happens to have been "fated" that I
should have "free-will" and it is no use to strive against this destiny.

I got as far as this last night, and I do not feel disposed to write any philosophy
tonight. But I think the next remark should be that, as I have liberty to turn
round on my heel or not turn round, so I could from and at this moment accept
any fatalistic or optimist theory and live by it. To the objection that such behaviour would not imply belief, and would therefore, lacking conviction, bring
me no comfort, I answer that I can comand [sic] my conviction, and that if
anyone thinks that his conviction is of a diferent [sic] *kind,* he is mistaken. All are
really at times sceptical, and few do more than accept an hypothesis, and fix it by
habit and conduct, and the more thoroughly sceptical one is, the more able one is
thoroughly to accept a chosen hypothesis, because nothing can shake it. Why
then not accept the optimistic hypothesis, so full of comfort as it is? I have
written more than I intended to write and am going to bed. Today has brought
no real change in the child: though she does not seem worse, and the fever has
not been quite so high. The nurse is not so bad when at her work.

Another day. I must send this off. Margaret no worse—we think her a little
better.

Please post enclosed post card with your own letters. It is convenient to me that
the addressee should not know that I am at home.
yours affectionately

RB

433: TO G. LOWES DICKINSON

Yattendon
October 14, [1903]

My dear Dickinson
Thousand thanks for your book. It came at breakfast, and I have already read
it through. 9.30. This is an unmistakably sincere compliment for I very seldom
read a book at all. I am very much of your opinion. At least I mean that I see
those insoluble problems much from your point of view, i. e. with your feelings
and sympathies—and as for that Chinese question—well I feel that I should like
to go to China to help the Chinese to drive out the missionaries. I hope we shall
meet again ere long. I had a long letter from Fry the other day. We had hoped to
get him to pay us a visit just about this time, but one of my children had a
feverish attack of such magnitude as to make visitors impossible. I hope that
your gift was not a peace-offering in atonement for the rejection of my poem by
the Independant [sic] Review. Not that it would matter if it were. Only I was not
offended. Perhaps I ought not to have asked money. It was very Western, but I

have contributed by request to several first numbers of new Magazines and had made a sort of promise to myself that I would in future exact 'something' of my due. The poem was no doubt of questionable popularity. I am going to Oxford today for a college gaudy—which is why I am writing at once.

I saw the new Review in the shop there the other day. It looked to me mighty serious—The name of Canon Barnet is not attractive to me. But I suppose you can't write the whole magazine yourself. By the way it may interest you to know that to my sense of what is agreeable you omit the relative pronoun much too frequently. On page 47 "questions (which) your" I did not understand the sentence at all, and had to read it over 3 or 4 times. —In my opinion it is a colloquialism, I mean a liberty of common speech, which can only be used in good prose with extreme care. There are I think some natural rules for it. One cannot forbid it as Hume did entirely. —On page 72—"habitual belief on which".—It seemed to me on reading that the expression might be charged as conveying the impression of a contradiction—for would not the Chinaman suppose that the stability of English society really did depend on its belief? It could be so very easily altered to obviate this jar (which I felt) that it might be worth your consideration.

yours sincerely
RB

434: LIONEL MUIRHEAD

Yattendon
October 14, 1903

My dear Lionel

Margaret after 15 days fever settled down to a normal temperature and seems to be convalescing satisfactorily but she is very weak.

I went to Oxford yesterday to a college gaudy, returning today, and I hear that Edward is in bed at school with 'a bilious attack'.—I don't like thinking that he may be going to be ill. We saw him the other day, and he seemed very fit and jolly, and to be enjoying himself.

I wrote just what came the other day to you. Perhaps it was not all sense—and one has various moments of different kinds of self deception. I will not rashly commit myself to another.—I send you a copy of the Elegiacs that you liked. I am at odd times now correcting the things which I first wrote—and getting them right by degrees. Experientia docet. I have another article or letter to Editor, on the Latin pronunciation question in the forthcoming Number of the Oxford Point of View. I think it hits pretty hard—but I do not get much encouragement from the Dons.—I shall continue to go at them. We all send our love.

I saw Willert. I think my tirades must bring some of them over.

yours ever
RB

435: TO LIONEL MUIRHEAD

Yattendon
November 6, 1903

My dear Lionel

How are you? We have been getting on pretty well—made use of that awful rain-time for turning out cupboards etc.—staining floor of big room in barn—making new shelves, etc. I did a lot of sawing and planing. Now the 3 females are all abiding with the maternal grandam, and I am alone. I have come to a full stop in my work, and I thought I would write one or [two] letters as I lie on the sofa in the study by the fire, with Ben snoring on the rug. I thought of writing to you because I have been working lately in bed at those early attempts of mine in longs and shorts, and I have got some 25 of them as good as they will ever be, and would write them out for you if I knew for certain which you have already got. I expect that I really know, but I don't like the chance of writing out the same thing twice. I should be glad to send them to you, as I want there to be a duplicate of them somewhere.

I wrote a Causerie for the Speaker the other day, and am hoping to be able to do so again every now and then. If you think of a good subject for me, let me know of it. Unfortunately I must not mention a living wight.

Just at present I am finally polishing up a long 3 barrelled article for the Athenaeum, which will I hope finally justify my *"Milton's Prosody"*, give a fillip to the book and exterminate all adversaries.

Margaret seems to have got quite well, but we may have to go to the sea with her for a week. By the way there should be another paper by me on Latin Pronunciation in the current number of "the Oxford Point of View"—I have not seen it.—It will amuse you if you see it.

Good night

yours ever
RB

436: TO LIONEL MUIRHEAD

Yattendon
Xmas Eve 1903

My dear Lionel

Happy and merry Xmas to you all, and thanks for your greetings just received. I am very glad to hear that Antony's eyes are stronger, and that he is "fat and well-liking". All my 3 children are together again—but I am sorry to say that Margaret has not nearly recovered yet from her fever. I took her up to see Barlow the other day, and he thinks she will be got well in about another month.

Meanwhile she is not able to fiddle or enjoy herself at all and can only take very moderate exercise. This is a nuisance to Edward as it blights his spree. He enjoyed school very much; he even declared that the term was not at all long. He takes a great deal of interest in his class places: and he has I fancy done pretty well, but I have not his "report". He seems to be prodigiously bad at Latin grammar, but though he is almost last in that he was far above his contemporaries in the test of translating really difficult Latin at sight!!! which I think says something for my method.—Yet when asked to "decline veru and Ogos potami" his imagination leads him woefully astray.

The weather is so filthy that our after-tea whist is about the most successful diversion. We have a game of hockey however promised for this afternoon.

Brahms is now the favourite musician and Margaret occupies her sofa leisure in doing counterpoint and harmony. I hope she means to get about again as usual ere long.

I have just heard of the death of a nephew Guy Bridges. I do not know if you ever met him. My brother Tom's eldest boy. He was a parson near Salisbury, a very good and popular fellow. I have just sent off a sonnet of greetings to the Wethereds at Teneriffe. I have not seen them for ever so long.—And here endeth my epistle to you. Xmas salutations from us all!

your affectionate

RB

437: TO ROGER FRY

Yattendon
Berkshire
January 3, 190.

My dear Roger

I am sorry that you cannot come and see us. I was surprised at your writing from Lyme: we were only the other day at Seaton; we did not get over to Lyme as the Listers were away. I hope that the change will do your wife good. Low spirits is a terrible infliction as I know. I had 3 or 4 months of it last summer, and only just got better when Margaret's illness came on—and now my days are consumed in trying to bring her strength back. It is a tedious operation: and the Xmas holidays are not at all what we had hoped.

It is difficult to write about all the things that I should wish to talk of; indeed it seems impossible. I was very much interested in your having wrestled with my hexameters, and naturally wish to show you all my experiments, many of which have more pretensions to beauty than the Epistles. The Elegiacs are I think really successful, but I get tired of copying them out. Then you were also patiently kind about the phonetics. (By the way I have omitted to say that I thought your suggestion of more frequent spondaic endings is really the correct solution of

he English hexameter. It is better than the frequent repetition of the accent on
he last syllable, which very soon comes to be as marked a rhythm as the Virgilian
iímtidy túmtee.)—To return to phonetics. As my system is a compromise, it is
)pen to various improvements, and it has improved in certain particulars since I
vrote the sample in "Wintry Delights". I am quite ready to bring it out now; and
Newbolt was willing to have it in the Monthly Review, but I am not sure that my
1exameters have not rather prejudiced his public, in which case he might not be
,o ready to publish it. In any case there is the difficulty of getting the symbols
)rinted, and I think I may very likely write it all out and get it facsimiled—
)robably lithographed, in the form of a pamphlet. I should like very much to
know more of your friend (in the Education office)'s views—and whether he
knows of any numerable persons who would be likely to attend to it.

Then I am making a fuss at Oxford about the pronunciation of Latin, and this
,ubject is not unconnected, for it is literally true that the present way of teaching
_atin is a chief means of teaching to mispronounce English. And this subject is
:onnected with the movement against the present system of making a useless
ninimum of bad Latin the test of upper education. I am in favour of abolishing
_atin and Greek except as class subjects—or at least of discouraging them as pass
ubjects. I contend that the result of such a reform would be such an im-
)rovement in the teaching of Latin (which at present is extravagantly mis-
nanaged) as would lead to a better pronunciation of English. Are there any of
our Cambridge friends who think as I do in these matters, and could help to
nove things about?

I am doing nothing now, but if I do anything it will most likely be controversy
)n the Latin pronunciation etc. I find the eyes of the younger men are opening.
'iscals will however rule for a time yet. It will be amusing to see how much
onger people will stand the subject.

I guess from your last letter but one that you did not approve of the doctrines
n my Socialistic epistle. I don't either, but they must be met by Socialists before
hey can win the confidence of the world. I was very much annoyed with myself
hat in my 1st Epistle, where I spoke of the solar system and the atoms I adopted
he current scientific view, rather than my own—for as a matter of fact I should
ave made the most explicit prophecy of Radium!! Wasn't it a sell?—It is very
urious how the regular recurrence of a period in an artificial decimal chronol-
·gy disposes the mind to receive new ideas. It looks as if we should soon have a
iew view of the solar system. I am now wandering so I will close my letter written
·y the fireside in an armchair, some of the family being at church on a wet
norning. Wind South and all things miserably grey and cheerless. I hope the
rost may return.

With love from Monica and the children

your affectionate

RB

'lease give our greetings and best wishes for the new year (from all of us) to your
·ife—and do not forget us if you can ever come and see us.

438: TO HENRY NEWBOLT

Yattendon
Berks
January 13, 1904

My dear Newbolt

The notion of your coming cheers me much.

If you should still have that book of Mayor's on English Prosody bring it with you, as I intend to publish in 'pamphlet form' some letters which I am now sending to the Athenaeum, and of adding copious notes in the pamphlet wherein I can dispose of all the intruders.

Also if you have any of William James' philosophical books, I have never seen one—I don't want to buy.

I read the last number of "The Veil of the Temple". I think the *sense* of the writer *very good.*—I didn't quite like his literary attitude.—I don't guess who it is. I dipped once into H. G. Wells, and he couldn't write such good English—

We shall have plenty to talk of—

yours ever
RB

439: TO ROBERT BRIDGES

Haseley Court
Wallingford
January 31, 1904

My dear Robert

The days are surely enough to dispirit the most optimistic, and one is only partially cheered by Anthony's announcement that the sun has a hole in it which will cause the ensuing ten years to go on getting worse and worse in the matter of rain! As it is I quite recognize the profound truth of Heraclitus' maxim πάντα δεεῖ , and I long, vainly, to be transported to any place where falls not rain nor hail nor any snow—

Our Xmas holidays have been much spoilt by the sudden death of our foreign governess who was a very clever lady and suited us admirably, but she was struck down by a paralytic stroke and expired in 2 days. This combined with the fact that a former French governess (30 years ago) went mad in the house, and had to be transported to a maison de santé at Paris, has caused us to pause awhile before embarking on anybody else out of sheer fright as to what may happen to the next one.

In order to console myself I took down my Volume of Crabbe of whom I knew but little: he writes very neatly and graphically but the tales he recites are often so grievously sordid that after following him through his Borough I thought I had read enough, but perhaps you know more of him and can tell me whether to try again: my edition is in double columns of small print which require to be attacked with a predetermined attention.

I see in the S^t. James' Gazette (where the literary editor always writes well about you) that you are sending letters to the Athenaeum about Milton's Prosody: I hope you will smite the Dutchman (whose name I forget but who I remember said some very odd things about scanning Milton's verse according to Vulgar pronunciation) hip and thigh, but I have not sent for the Numbers of the Athenaeum, not feeling sure what you were elucidating.

My children gave me at Xmas "A little book of Life & Death" edited by Mrs Waterhouse: it contains some things very characteristic of her but I am chiefly delighted with it because the first thing in the book is a poem by Dolben: it is a great disappointment to me to think I shall die without reading more of what he wrote.

I hope you are all well and with kindest regards to Monica

I am

yours affectionately
Lionel Muirhead

440: TO LIONEL MUIRHEAD

Board of Guardians
Bradfield
February 2, 1904

My deal Lionel

Your letter this morning reminds me of the thousand apologies which I owe you for not acknowledging and thanking you for your Latin elegiac address. I have not been in the humour to write letters, and I don't think that I am now— but the minutes of the last meeting are being read and confirmed: and I have a dullish hour or more ahead before I walk home 5 miles in the mud to lunch. Margaret has been trying a long course of absolute rest, which is however relieved from the burden of the 'absolute' by her natural restiveness. We think that there is a little improvement beginning to show. This morning I hear that Edward is isolated at school on suspicion of measles. On this last subject I feel a fatalist you will be glad to hear. There is a queer little book on 'human Immortality' by James the American philosopher which I came across the other day which I think it would amuse you to read, I am thinking of sending it to you—it is not polemic against fatalism. The Newbolts have been staying with us, and I have much enjoyed having such a pleasant companion. He cheered me up a good deal: but, as you say, the weather is so abnormally depressing that no sort of tonic has a very durable effect. We have on these rainy days taken to painting the walls and ceiling of the big loft in the barn. The scheme is original and is coming out well. It is rather exciting to see the effect gradually coming out: and it is a sort of fun to sit up on the platform under the roof, daubing. Sometimes we have 3 or 4 workers all daubing together. I have three reds, a white and a brown. I am sorry to hear of your governess tragedy, but I take it from your letter that the accident happened at her home, and not in your house. We have done with governesses. Elizabeth is now working on her own devices. She has a natural taste for algebra (!) which I encourage. If we could afford it we should go to Oxford for one term in the year, and arrange to spend another 3 months in London—and that would do for us admirably. I am trying to make a little odd money for the necessary educational expenses—it was for that reason chiefly that I sent my 3 papers (it came to 3 when divided into the greatest possible admissable [*sic*] parts) on Miltonic elision *on a phonetic basis*. I think the work is pretty solid and final,—and I shall be reprinting it with ample notes as a pamphlet, and subsequently it will make another appendix or so for my "Milton's Prosody" book: which is already, as Monica puts it, suffering from appendicitis. I must make this joke against myself in the volume, lest some one should make it of me. I am now going again at the Latin pronunciation. I intend to have *two* Causeries in the Speaker about it.—If people do not take it up I may publish "a letter to an Etonian" and distribute it amongst the schoolboys and incite them to revolt. I attempt you see to combine usefulness to the public with usefulness to myself. I think the Yattendon Hymnal is gradually asserting itself—outsiders are beginning to find out that there is something in it. The other day a man wrote to me offering me £10 for a single copy of the smaller edition. Unfortunately there are still 4 or 5 copies left at Oxford. He had been informed that it was out of print.— The Master of the Union is now reading his report—"The number of inmates in the house is 109 against 111 of the same week last year." You will not care to hear of the "produce of one cow" or "the 40 pounds of jam" or "The hundred weight of yellow soap, one gross of Haylaces, and the dozen thimbles," etc.

I think the best story by far in Crabbe is the "Frank Courtship". If you don't know that one read it. Very few of them seem to me to be worth reading. I have got a good many of Dolben's verses printed now in different collections, and have myself a fairly complete collection of them in MS. I am sorry that you did not speak of them when you were here, as I could have shown them to you.—

I won't trouble you with any more scrawl. Thanking you again for your verses which I am sorry I was not in a humour to reply to in kind when I got them.

yours ever
RB

441: TO HENRY NEWBOLT

Yattendon
February 3, 1904

My dear Newbolt

I was sorry about your bag. Also I meant to arrange for you to have your Hymnal completed.

The enclosed card can be posted *if you will fill in the Number of the Part which is lacking.*

I enjoyed your visit immensely. We hear that Edward is *isolated* on suspicion of measles. It seems unlikely that it is measles unless some boy returned with it.

yours ever
RB

Monica thanks Mrs. Newbolt for her Collins.
You will tell me if Warren consents to his sonnet being published. I fear it must go alone. My friends would think me a dreadful ass if I *printed* sonnets about them. Could you not stick the Warren sonnet into the Editorial or dodge it somehow so as not to make it seem important?

442: TO HENRY NEWBOLT

Post Card

Yattendon
February 4, [1904]

Someone told me of your editorial verses on Clarke & Pope.—I read them yesterday at Yattendon Court. I shook with laughter over them especially "*Great Gosse*"!! Pray keep us *au courant* in this vein month by month.

RB

The dean of Newburger as equal quantities!!! Lovely. Lovely!! And deserved.

443: TO ROBERT BRIDGES

Haseley Court
February 6, 1904

My dear Robert
   I would come and lend a hand in daubing the rafters with pleasure, but that just now I can't leave my wife alone here: Charis is away for a fortnight; my old aunt is ill in bed, and the upper housemaid was struck down with influenza yesterday morning, a strong attack of it, without however complications so far. If the attack passes and no one else falls ill, Charis is to come back next week, and I will write again as to my possible movements as fate shall determine: if I had free will I would come and daub tomorrow! I wish you would send me a bottle of free will mixture to be taken when required! I was rejoiced to hear that you are going again at the Latin pronunciation in the Speaker. A causerie on Latin pronunciation in the Speaker, sounds indeed a most insistent form of pleading and should be irresistible, but your notion of publishing a letter "to an Etonian" and distributing it amongst the boys inciting them to revolt is too fine a stroke of generalship not to be carried out: Ah! if only you could be in the Upper Fifth

when your letter was distributed—but this unfortunate want of free will stands in the way, I hope things will come right—

I am sorry you missed your £10 for a small copy of the Y. Hymnal by so little, but it is nice to think there is yet such enthusiasm lurking about the world, as the application proves.

your affectionate
Lionel Muirhead

444: TO HENRY BRADLEY

Yattendon
March 17, 1904

My dear Bradley

Thank you very much for the present of your volume. I have no time or inclination to look at it now. We are in great trouble about my musical girl Margaret, who has now a 2nd very serious attack of influenza, and does not get any better. It is of no use writing details. It has kept me away from Oxford, and plunged me in melancholy. My wife says that I have not ¼ of the faith of a grain of mustard seed, and I certainly do lack confidence in obscurities.

My distraction, when I could rise to it, has been writing a masque for the ladies of Somerville to act next term at the opening of their new library.—I have been these last 3 or 4 weeks at it, and it is nearly finished. It will show what sort of work can be done to order under adverse circumstances, though I do not know but that a bit of my feeling may have strayed into the play.

yours sincerely
RB

445: TO LIONEL MUIRHEAD

Yattendon
April 6, 1904

My dear Lionel

I was much grieved to hear from Wooldridge of the death of your brother. He also told me that you were not well. I hope that you are better again by this time, and that nothing serious has been the matter. I don't think that I have written to you since the beginning of February, and towards the end of that month I was visited by the Fates. Margaret fell ill again with influenza, which in her weak condition was in itself a matter of great anxiety, for all through the winter we had been trying to get her strength back after her attack of influenza last autumn. But this was destined to be a much more serious affair. Pleurisy and pneumonia came on—and now nearly 6 weeks since she fell ill the fever has not left her. It is however subsiding, and the chest seems to be coming all right. But

Sir Thomas Barlow who came down to see her made rather a long face, and for nearly 3 weeks I did not much expect her to get well.—

She has however not been so much knocked to pieces as I should have expected, and she has been always cheerful and patient. Poor child, she has been dreadfully disappointed and bored—and of course one cannot tell now whether her recovery may not be incomplete.

Still we are much happier about her.—This has prevented me from writing to anybody. It happened very fortunately for me that I had undertaken to write a play or masque on the subject of Demeter for the girls at Somerville College in Oxford, and had got well settled into the thing when Margaret fell ill. I stuck to it and carried it through in spite of difficulties and was pleased to think that I managed the whole thing in a very few days over the month—interrupted as I was by visits to London and Oxford to get advice for Margaret. It is an interesting piece of work, for I think that I have made the story hang together in a novel and convincing manner. Certainly I never saw how well things all fitted in until I began to think over them—Now I wonder whether *all* the Greek stories would do as well with the same care.

I am now due at the bedside. Send us a line to say how you are.

your affectionate
RB

446: TO LIONEL MUIRHEAD

Yattendon
April 15, 1904

My dear Lionel

On the faith of its 'going to clear up' Monica has gone off to Oxford today with Elizabeth and Edward. I am left at home with the invalid. It has pelted hard all the morning, and my next duty is to make arrangements for getting my family home from the station as dry as possible. I have written seven letters this morning, most of them on useless business, and I thought so much prelude necessary, lest I should suddenly break down over this.

We were so very sorry to hear of your neuralgia and ear trouble, and I hope very much that you are all right by this time. I have had too much anxiety to think of anyone but myself, and though things are a little better now, for Margaret has nearly lost her fever, and is allowed to sit up in bed, yet I don't feel at all in my assiette; indeed I should not be surprised if my temper should prove spoiled for life, what remains of it.—At any rate today I am exceedingly 'cross' and ill disposed towards everything and everybody.

Perhaps it would have been as well to disguise my ill-temper. I made some unsuccessful attempts to mollify myself this morning but to no purpose. My comfort is that I sleep well, and have tea apparatus by my bedside; and really I am very comfortable in bed. I can think of it with satisfaction during the day.

Please thank your wife for being so good as to send us the news of you. I wish it had been better news, but some of it was good.

Reading aloud to Margaret has confirmed me in my contempt for Thackeray and George Eliot. How awfully dull English novelists are. I made a parody on a certain eminent critic the other day—I won't write it all out, else you would know who it was. Here is one stanza—

> A critic by a newspaper
>   Half-hidden from the eye,
> Dull as a pig, when only one
>   Is pining in the stye.

You may imagine the rest. It supposes the critic dead (he isn't, worse luck) and the last line, for which I wrote it

and Oh!

The difference to me—

is really much more fit than in the original poem to Lucy, which I never could see the merit of. But my parody will justify it. I feel that unless you are very bad you will enjoy that stanza. I have nothing more to send today but all our good wishes—with kindest regards to Mrs. L.M.

yours ever

RB

447: TO HENRY BRADLEY

Yattendon
April 24, [1904?]

My dear Bradley

I have just scribbled at my article, and send it to you that you may, as you promised look through it, and tell me if I have said anything which is rot.

You will of course understand that it is written for the Oxford general public, especially the undergraduates, and with the sole purpose of trying to stimulate reform.

I sent you my verses the other day. I hope they came safe. I will be up one day early next week so that you need not trouble to write anything, or send back. I will call and see you. I should send in the article one day next week. I expect I may come up on Monday or Thursday.

yours ever

RB

I will make a good final paragraph to wind up with.

448: TO LIONEL MUIRHEAD

Yattendon
May 5, 1904

My dear Lionel

I am glad to get a good report of you. We are getting on better. Margaret is dressed for an hour or two now every day, and has had 10 minutes at the piano. Yesterday my wife and Elizabeth went to the concert. They did not see your folk. Elizabeth has mathematical tuition in Oxford—twice a month. 2 days ago she and I went to meet Joachim at a house where he lunched and played and we had a good time. Thanks for your newspaper cutting. This morning I am correcting a proof of a Causerie on Sir Thomas Browne. The play will not be printed. From what I hear they will make a success of it—they are much pleased with it.

This weather has been a great delight. Our new rector has daily mass and early services, and has inveigled me into promising to get up the choir again. The bother is that my wife has chronically "lost her voice" and there is little hope of her help for months to come. She can hardly speak now, and has been more or less bad for 3 months.

I have many letters to write this morning so must shut up. By the way I presented Joachim with a full-blown sonnet. I don't yet know how he took it.

yours ever
RB

449: TO HENRY BRADLEY

Yattendon
Berks
May 11, [1904]

My dear Bradley

I have often said that authors should review their own books, and I make this my text for the following request:

I sometimes write a Causerie for the Speaker, and I have one or two in hand on "English"—as it is now written and spoken. They were nearly finished, when I put them aside to write a play for the ladies of Somerville. In taking them up again I thought that I could very easily make my first Causerie on (or professedly about,) your book. It would make a good excuse for my handling of the topic, and I might get you a reader or two.

Now—remembering my text—I want you to tell me what are the points which you would like me to call attention to in your book.

I thought of making out a list of the points which I thought were original in your book and asking you to tell me which were not, but taking up the book again this evening I find this too laborious a process.

I shan't really say very much about the detail of your book—I am not doing a review,—and the sort of thing I shall find convenient to discuss are your estimates of the values of certain peculiarities of the language.

But I should of course like to say what you would like to have said; and if you have time to jot down a few words; or, what would do just as well for me, the *page numbers* where your points occur it would much improve my essay—

I have corrected the proof of a Causerie on Sir Thomas Browne which should be in this week's issue next Saturday. It will interest you I think.—I have been all day in London: a consultation about my wife's throat: which seems to promise us trouble.

I like your book very much.

yours ever
RB

PS. Last number of dictionary goes down to PARGET. I see that Murray derives it from *spargere* with Skeat. I believe that is gammon. If not too late for next number (word is not concluded) I will send him my advocacy for *perjactare* a real word.

450: TO HENRY NEWBOLT

Yattendon
Thursday [May 19, 1904]

My dear Newbolt

I am writing to one of Joachim's friends to tell him that I have given you the sonnet. If there is any objection I will let you know.

The specialist took a very serious line about my wife's throat. He would not however speak decidedly, and both Barlow and I are inclined to think that things are not as bad as he fears. This does not add to my delights.

I don't think I should have written to you now but that I wanted to correct a ridiculous misstatement that I made in conversation. You said that some mathematician had said to you that children could be got up to the integral calculus at 15 years or 16 years of age, and I said that Eliz. had got as far: I don't know what I was thinking of*; as a matter of fact she has not yet begun conic sections, and I don't know really anything about her studies in this department except that she seems to satisfy her teacher for the time—

You will tell me whether that music 'Causerie' will suit you, and whether you will take it for July. I hope you *approve* of it.

I regretted very much missing H. G. W.

yours ever
RB

*I fancy such reckless methods of changing the subject are a sign of advancing age.

451: TO HENRY NEWBOLT

Yattendon
Friday [May 20, 1904]

My dear Newbolt

And the sonnet's in the weekly Times. It seems to me as if the simplest thing was to let it go on—especially as it is set up. Lots of people won't have seen it, and those who have seen it won't have read it, and it carries Warren's.—To print another sonnet will cheapen Joachim's too much. Better than that omit Joachim's.

If you do not mind a footnote I should do this sort of thing. "Mr. Bridges' sonnet to Dr Joachim was written quite independently of his Jubilee which was celebrated the other day in the Queen's Hall, but having been printed with the programme of the music on that occasion has appeared in various newspapers since it was set up by our printers. It is in compliment to Dr Joachim that we break our established rule in offering to our readers anything that they may see elsewhere (ED.)"

Would something of that sort do?

yours ever
RB

Things are not good here. But my wife is expected to come round all right. I saw Evans at the Oxford match yesterday.

452: TO LIONEL MUIRHEAD

Yattendon
WhitMonday [May 23,] 1904

My dear Lionel

If you have two or three days to spare your company would be very welcome here. Monica has gone to Bournemouth ad infinitum. Her brother is with her. She got knocked up I expect with nursing; but she started a bad throat with loss of voice some 3 months ago. It did not get better and all of a sudden the doctors who had considered it of no importance, took a very serious view of it.— However her recovery is considered probable and I believe that she is so far doing well. It is altogether serious—and *I should wish nothing said about it.* I am left to nurse Margaret whose convalescence is of a tedious and "problematical" nature. Both the girls play whist all right: and they are very desirous that you should come, both to take the place of the tedious dummy and to cheer me up.— We live an out-of-doors life; Margaret is allowed one hour at the piano in the day. I have "Causeries" on hand, but nothing goes on here now. We should find a good deal to talk about.

I would send to meet any train at Hampstead Norris or elsewhere,—and will try and get some fresh whiskey in before you come. I have quite run out. The nature of my wife's illness may suggest the notion of infection, but I do not think that there is anything in the way of risk of that sort to prevent your coming. So come if you can with convenience to yourself.

yours ever

RB

I was awfully glad to see you looking all right at Oxford. My misfortunes account for my silence.

453: TO HENRY BRADLEY

Yattendon
May 26, [1904]

My dear Bradley

I send you Demeter. I am afraid that I must ask you not to show it to others. It would damage the interest of the performance, a good deal of which depends on a suspense in the last act. Also the Somervillians might object, but I very much wish you to read it, as your remarks after the performance, if you go to it, will then be of greater value to me.

Thanks for your letter. I won't write philology. I don't know when I shall be in Oxford. Things are really very bad with me, and I may at anytime have to go to my wife at Bournemouth. Else I should be up and have a chat.

yours ever

RB

You will be interested in my use of *small* for *little* (as illustrating your remarks) when you come to it in the play. It no doubt came in as denoting that the nymphs with all their feeling were not quite in touch with human nature.

454: TO HENRY NEWBOLT

Post Card

[early June 1904]

Many thanks for the Monthly. I feel a great swell. Have you ever got *Itamos* reviewed? Didn't M. C. like it? Demeter is on July 11th I think. Do you think you will be in Oxford and want to go. If so write to Miss M. Fry, Somerville College.

RB

The cast of Robert Bridges's masque *Demeter* in front of the Somerville College library, Oxford, June 1904. See letters 444, 445, and 453. Courtesy of Somerville College.

455: TO LIONEL MUIRHEAD

Yattendon
July 5, 1904

My dear Lionel

I have opened a letter to my wife from Miss Wroughton who begs her to let your wife know that her address now is 7. Northmoor Road, Oxford, and that in a few weeks she expects to get into her 'own' house No 13. I think she wants your wife to call on her when she is in Oxford.

I am sorry that I cannot *write* letters about prosody. Those words like recompense are a trouble. The best thing that you can do is *not to use* them. Whatever metre you write in in Greek or Latin there are a lot of words that won't go into the verse anywhere.

I disagreed with Stone about these words, but in writing in his prosody I kept to his laws.

It is a pity that you did not mention this subject when you were here, as I am pretty well up in it now and willing to discuss the matter, and glad to collect opinions, but it is a long business as so much is involved. Perhaps this will show you the point. If you make the 2nd syllable of such words as

Recompense	m
Godalming	l
Carpenter	n
Liberty	r

short, then you must assume that the obscure vowel is non-existent, and that the liquid (z semivowel) is itself the vowel thus

Réc.m̧.pens
God.ļ.ming
Carp.n.ter
lib.ŗ.ty

See Stone's prosody.

yours ever
Robert Bridges

I am going to see my wife tomorrow. She is thought to be doing fairly well. Margaret is much better.

456: TO HENRY NEWBOLT

Yattendon
July 5, [1904]

My dear Newbolt

Thanks for the cheque which is two guineas more than I should have got from the Speaker, and it is very good of you to say such civil things about my contributions. My modesty is fully up to the occasion. I wish that some attention may be given to my proposal about the primary schools. The best men agree with me, but no one will move.—I hope that Somerville will see the paper.

I shall be in London on Monday 18th—(with Elizabeth) and should be glad to arrange a meeting with you if you are unoccupied. I want to see Binyon—and shall write to him. If you are to be at Winchester during the long you must come over here one day—and we must make an excursion there.

I am going tomorrow to visit my wife at her Sanatorium. It is an awful penance for her, but if she will only get well we shall not mind so much.

I was at Horris Hill one day and saw Francis bowling. I thought that he promised to be a cricketer. I also saw Edward bowling in a very different stage of cricket. He seems to have a great liking for games, but no natural facility in physical exercises. He enjoys school thoroughly, and I think it agrees with him wonderfully well.

I do not send receipt for cheque as I gather that Murray must keep his cheques for that purpose

yours ever
R Bridges

A *very good* portrait of Yeats in the Tatler last week.

457 TO HENRY BRADLEY

Yattendon
July 11, [1904]

My dear Bradley

My first impulse is to declare that I will never write to you again if you take so much trouble to answer my letters. But I hope that you felt some satisfaction in pouring out such a stream of learned demonstration. Be sure that it was properly appreciated. Why, when one learned what they called Latin, was not one told these things? And who knows them? A lot of things occur to one to say, but I am afraid that if I make any remarks you will waste your leisure time in replying. I should like a chat with you awfully.

I am also interested in your dissatisfaction with Demeter. It may lead to my improving the play before I print it, which I am in no hurry to do.

I am grieved to hear about your wife. I hope that you may be spared trouble and anxiety. I get fair reports of my invalid, but my life promises to be a muddle of molestiae for years at the best.

I am afraid that with your home trouble you are not likely to be able to pay me a visit in my solitude.

I shall be in Oxford on the 21st. Will you still be there?

It seems to me that as far as teaching Latin pronunciation goes the condition of those syllables that I wrote about might be neglected: or left to the purists.

I have a lot of questions to ask. Meanwhile I shall go on with my crusade.

Your letter was most interesting. I sent it to my wife.

Yours ever
RB

458: TO LIONEL MUIRHEAD

Yattendon
July 30, 1904

My dear Lionel

Thanks for your letter. I should have written before but I have been in uncertainties. However just now things look better. I saw my wife in London 3 days ago. She had an interview with the specialist coming up from her Sanatorium on the Cotswolds and returning the same day. He gave a good account of her and she was allowed the use of her larynx for 30 minutes which she was glad to use in a conversation with me. She is probably to return home in September. She is expected to get practically all right. She looked extremely well, and has I believe put on nearly a stone and a half since her treatment began.

Margaret has been condemned to be suffering from the same bacillus, and she has had another bad bout. However she does not knock under at all—and she is probably to go as soon as possible to join her mother on the Cotswolds.—If this takes place I shall be freer than I have been for a year.

E^d is to come home on Wednesday. The choir promises very well. I have to work hard at it. I wish the rector could sing in tune; he makes things very difficult. There are amusing details. I have no time for them now. I rejoice to think that you will see me in this week's (today's) Speaker on Latin Pronunciation. I feel sure that you will enjoy it. I shall buy a lot of copies and send them about. I hope people will see what it is possible that I may yet say and take warning.

I was glad to hear good news of Anthony. What fun for him to have his friends home. I will write again when I have leisure. This is just an answer to your note.

yours ever

RB

Next time you come you may sit in choir.

459: TO LIONEL MUIRHEAD

Yattendon
September 9, 1904

My dear Lionel

I am forwarding a letter from my wife which comes through me as she apparently did not know your post town. I add a line to say that I have been to see the invalids, and they seem both a little better, and indeed look well. But as for the bacillus—there is nothing miraculous yet in their cure. The Enemy has retreated I suppose to his Mukden—or Kharbin, whether he has reinforcements or no, time only can tell.

Hadow has persuaded me to publish Demeter, and I think that my wife will like doing it when she comes home next month—but I have been wondering whether it is the sort of work that would amuse you. I cannot do it, but I could read the final proofs. I do not think that I shall have any difficulty in finding some one to undertake it: but I should be very happy if you were the person. Hadow says that if it is printed it will be acted "in all the ladies colleges in England and America". If this is so I must of course print it. I should think Bullen would be a good publisher: or Methuen.

I hope all is well with you. I shall be looking out for a new abode. There is little doubt of it. Can you tell me if there would be any chance of finding a roof near Shirbrin Lodge where your sister in law lives? I must take my invalids up to some hill top. Have you any suggestion?

yours ever

RB

Choir doing well. Boys voice quality getting good, and they are good readers.

460: TO E. P. WARREN

Yattendon
October 7, 1904

Dear Mr Warren

I have just sent a P'card to 'my' bookseller telling him to send you a copy of Milton's Prosody.

I think the book will interest you if you will submit to its being written for people who know nothing of phonetics. The fact is that the book grew out of an excursus attached to a school text-book, the object of which was to ensure the verse being read rightly, and not mispronounced in order to make it agree with some pedantic 'scansion' by regular accent. And if I had introduced phonetic formula and symbols not intelligible at first sight to the ordinary reader, no one would have troubled to read it.

My justification is (1) that the book has been a successful teacher; (2) that a phonetic treatment of the subject comes to work out just to the same conclusions. I have done this in 3 papers to the Athenaeum dated this year.

The essay by Stone is the first sound attempt to deal with our language as the Latins dealt with theirs when they threw over their stress prosody and took up with longs and shorts.

I did not share Stone's enthusiasms, but I have no doubt that any experiment in longs and shorts must in English be guided by such rules as he makes. And of course people won't understand English longs and shorts until they read Greek and Latin by quantity, instead of substituting accent for quantity, as they do now.

Stone's essay is very readable. Its value in my book is that it makes the proper distinction between the 3 kinds of verse—(1) the purely quantitative on which the stress or accént is so to say 'counterpoint'; (2) the syllable which is the degradation of the quantitative, always tending to become stressed verse, that is to be governed by stress rather than by counting of syllables; (3) the stressed verse, which I analyse.

I promised Stone that I would one day try his system. But I doubt if I ever should have done so if he had not died. My promise then became sacred and I made a lot of experiments.

In your book of poems I think that you have really succeeded in blending the carnal with the spiritual, and, as I think I said before, it is my 'feeling' that they need to be blended in any satisfying religion. And this is my sympathy with Greek notions. What seems the difficulty to me is that men differ so, and the average runs so low, that such a doctrine is not fitted for all and becomes esoteric. What the true esoteric doctrine is I don't quite know. I don't believe in Patmore's, still less in yours, but I find in your poems something which is very nearly the expression of mine. Your real meaning is therefore a great shock to me, and among all your enemies you will not find a more stubborn foe than me. I wish I could persuade you to confine your verse to controvertible terms. It would then be of the greatest value in my opinion.

Yours sincerely
Robert Bridges

Part III
CHILSWELL
1904–1930

I n October 1904, Bridges and his wife were living in Birdlip on a nine-hundred-foot escarpment overlooking Gloucester and the Severn Vale, a mile and a half from the sanatorium where Margaret was staying. In early February 1905, the family moved to a small furnished house on Foxcombe Hill near Oxford, and spent March and April house hunting. In April Bridges's essay in two parts on Bunyan's *Pilgrim's Progress* appeared in *The Speaker*. In May the family moved to Boar's Hill Heath for about seven weeks, and in this month the Clarendon Press published *Demeter*, Bridges's last dramatic poem. The lyrics and incidental music of the mask were issued in a separate volume. At this time Bridges was preparing a selection of Newbolt's poems with an introductory note for Miles's anthology *The Poets and the Poetry of the Nineteenth Century*. On June 30 Bridges and his wife left England for Switzerland. Before going abroad Bridges introduced his son to his tutor at Eton, but his entering Eton was delayed by objections Bridges raised because he was dissatisfied with the room allocated to him. On August 2 Edward joined his parents in Switzerland. On September 20 Bridges took his son with him to England and put him back in his school for further study before going to Eton. Bridges remained at Yattendon for two weeks to prepare the Manor House for rental and then returned to Switzerland. In October the family went into winter quarters in St. Moritz at Villa Gentiana and rented the Manor House to a "quarum" of old ladies. In October Bridges seriously considered refusing Bullen's request that he write an essay on Shakespeare but he delayed a definite decision. In November Bridges began *Ibant Obscuri*, a paraphrase in quantitative verse of excerpts of the sixth book of the *Aeneid*. *The Last Poems* of Richard Watson Dixon, selected and edited by Bridges, appeared in this month. Edward visited his parents in Switzerland in December and began studying for his entrance exams for Eton.

By the middle of January 1906, Bridges had decided to go ahead with his Shakespeare essay. In March Edward, still in Switzerland, took his examinations for Eton, and Bridges completed the first draft of his essay on Shakespeare, *The Influence of the Audience*, for Bullen's Shakespeare Head edition of the poet's works and sent it to Wooldridge for comment. On March 28 the family returned to London, spent a week or more at Yattendon, and then moved to Bleak House, a small house on Boar's Hill, to await the construction of Chilswell. On May 4 Bridges took Edward to Eton, where he was entered as an Oppidan, and on May 2 Bridges sent his revised Shakespeare essay to Bullen. In June he wrote a review of Morton Prince's *The Dissociation of a Personality*. On August 31 at 9 ..M.,the family laid the first bricks of Chilswell and Bridges wrote a six-line poem in phonetic script for the occasion.[1] In September the family moved to Whitebarn on Boar's Hill, a half a mile from the site of Chilswell. In October Miles's *The Poets and the Poetry of the Nineteenth Century* was published with Bridges's selection of Newbolt's poems and a reprint of Bridges's selection of Hopkins's poems from Miles's *The Poets and the Poetry of the Century* (1892).

In February 1907 Bridges wrote an ode for the Oxford Pageant (June 27–July 3) and by April he had finished a playlet on the beginnings of Oxford University for the occasion, which was published under the title of *Theobaldus Stampensis* by the pageant committee together with the ode in their *Book of Words*. The ode, "An Invitation to the Pageant," was first published in the *Saturday Review*, April 13, 1907. By June Bridges's essay on Shakespeare had been published in the last volume of the Shakespeare Head edition. July 23 the Bridges family moved into Chilswell. On August 25 Mary Coleridge died and Bridges began a critical essay on her for *Cornhill*, completing the final version October 1. It was published in November. In February 1908, Bridges wrote an article on George Darley and in March he was at work on his *Eton Memorial Ode*. In August he and Elizabeth traveled to Scotland for the first time to visit the Wooldridges. On this trip Bridges also visited Dr. Hodgkin at Barwick Castle in Northumberland. *Demeter* was acted three times in Liverpool. On November 12 the Memoir of Richard Watson Dixon was finished. The *Eton Memorial Ode*, set to the music of Sir Hubert Parry, was performed at Eton November 18.

January 1909 in the *New Quarterly*, Bridges published his *Ibant Obscuri*, a paraphrase of excerpts from the *Aeneid*. Smith & Elder brought out his memoir of Dixon as a preface to an edition of Dixon's *Selected Poems*. Bridges and Monica continued their work on their new phonetic script, which was being put into special type by the Clarendon Press. "A Letter to a Musician on English Prosody" appeared in the *Musical Antiquary*, October 1909. The memoir of Digby Dolben was finished by February 1910. In December, Edward won a Demyship at Magdalen College, Oxford. Early in 1911 Bridges was working on a new system of chanting. His "English Chanting" was published in the *Musical Antiquary* in April. In March Margaret went to Dresden and Lionel Muirhead traveled in Italy. Sir William Richmond began painting Bridges's portrait (commissioned by Muirhead) in March and had finished it by July. In July the Bridges family vacationed at Dunwich on the Suffolk coast. Edward entered Magdalen College Michaelmas term, 1911. In October the memoir of Dolben was published as a preface to a selection of his poems. Elizabeth went to Berlin in the fall of this year.

In January of 1912 "Anglican Chanting," Bridges's second article on the subject, appeared in the *Musical Antiquary*. On June 26 Bridges received the degree of D. Litt. from Oxford. Henry James received the same degree on this day, an occasion that gave Bridges and James an opportunity to renew an acquaintance begun in the 1870s. In October the Oxford Press published a one-volume edition of Bridges's *Poetical Works* in large paper and in regular issues.

In January 1913 Bridges, Monica, and Logan Pearsall Smith began laying their plans for organizing the Society for Pure English, and by February Bridges was asking the "adhesion" of Bradley, Abercrombie, Craigie, and Raleigh. Ed ward toured Italy in April. On May 29 *A Tract on the Present State of English Pronunciation* was published—a revision of the first edition, which was issued in 1910. By June Bridges had finished over two hundred lines of a paraphrase in quantitative verse of Book XXIV of the *Iliad,* later published under the title of *Priam and Achilles.* On July 15 Bridges, after some hesitation, accepted the poet laureateship, and then with Monica toured the Avon Valley and Wiltshire, went to Stonehenge and Marlborough, and visited the Newbolts. Edward was studying for Greats, but at the end of August he started with Margaret on a walking tour in Brittany. Elizabeth went alone to western Ireland. In September Bridges visited Lord de Tabley's surviving sister at Tabley Hall, Knutsford, Cheshire, and then went on a tour of Cheshire and Wales. In October the original prospectus of the S. P. E. was printed and circulated. On December 24 Bridges's poem "Noel" appeared in the London *Times* at the command of the King. The poem was one of three that Bridges wrote in this year in Neo-Miltonic syllabics—a new form invented by Bridges in which he was to write nine more poems. This verse form eventually became the medium for *The Testament of Beauty.*

In July 1914, Edward took a first in Greats. On August 4 England declared war on Germany, Elizabeth soon became engaged in hospital service in Dover, returning home in November, and Edward entered the army. In August of this year Bridges received H. J. C. Grierson's edition of the poems of John Donne sent to him by the Clarendon Press at the request of Grierson. By December 4 Bridges had accepted the publisher Longman's invitation to compile an anthology of poetry and prose for wartime reading, *The Spirit of Man,* and also in this month St. John Hornby published a limited edition of *Poems Written in the Year MXMXIII.* Much of 1915 was taken up with *The Spirit of Man.* On June 19 Yeats visited Chilswell for the weekend. Henry Woods died in July. On January 20, 1916, *The Spirit of Man* was published and was widely noticed. Edward was in France during 1916 but was on leave from the front over Christmas. Bridges's sonnet "Lord Kitchener" (written on the occasion of his death) was published in the *Times Literary Supplement,* June 13, 1916, and was also privately printed in twenty copies. *Ode on the Tercentenary Commemoration of Shakespeare* appeared in the *Times Literary Supplement,* July 6, 1916, and it too was privately printed. Bridges's naval ode, *The Chivalry of the Sea,* set to the music of Sir Hubert Parry; *An Address to the Swindon Branch of the Workers' Association;* and *Ibant Obscuri* were also published in this year.

A fire broke out at Chilswell February 6, 1917, which did considerable damage and forced the family to live in the gardener's cottage and elsewhere during reconstruction. The library was untouched. Shortly after the fire, Edward was wounded in the arm in France. In March Bridges and Monica went to London to be near him during his convalescence; by April they were settled in Oxford for the term. Margaret was doing war work in France but came home invalided late in April. On September 7 Bridges requested the permission of Mrs. Hopkins to edit her son's poems. On November 22 he gave an address to the Tredegar and District Co-operative Society on *The Necessity of Poetry.* January 28, 1918, a very successful performance of Psalms was sung by the New College Choir, using Bridges's system of pointing. Much of the year 1918 was taken up with editing and proofreading of the Hopkins edition. *The Necessity of Poetry* was published in June. Edward returned to the Italian front in September. On November 11 the Armistice ended the war with Germany. On November 23 Bridges wrote "Britannia Victrix" and published it in the London *Times* November 25. On December 8 Bridges received an advance copy of his edition of Hopkins's poems (published December 19) and sent it to Mrs. Hopkins.

From June to September 1919 Bridges and his wife took a house at Postmaster's Hall, Merton Lane, Oxford. Margaret Bridges married Horace Joseph on July 3. The plan for the formation of a Society for Pure English, brought to a standstill by the war, was now resumed. S.P.E. Tract No. I, *Preliminary Announcement,* written by Bridges in collaboration with Logan Pearsall Smith, and Tract No. II, *On English Homophones,* by Bridges were published in October. The S.P.E. continued publication of its tracts until 1948. Bridges, the founder of the society, was its leading member until his death in 1930.

In 1920 Edward became a Fellow of All Souls College, Oxford. William Heinemann published *October and Other Poems* in May in regular and limited issues. Bridges's essay "George Santayana" appeared in the *London Mercury* in August. Bridges was a leading member of a group of Oxford men who sought reconciliation with the professors and members of German universities. "Reconciliation: Oxford Letter to German Intellectuals," printed in the London *Times,* October 27, 1920, appears to have been the work of Bridges. It aroused heated and widespread comment.

In 1921 there was a sudden revival of poetic composition, and Bridges wrote a number of poems that were eventually published in *The Tapestry* and in *New Verse.* The revised, final edition of *Milton's Prosody,* with a chapter on accentual verse, was published in 1921, and Bridges contributed "The Dialectical Words in Blunden's Poems" to S.P.E. Tract No. V and also contributed other items to Tracts VI and VII. From now on S.P.E. business consumed a great deal of Bridges's time. In March 1922, S.P.E. Tract No. VIII carried an essay "What Is Pure French?" written by Bridges and his wife under the pseudonym of Matthew Barnes. On May 13 Sir Walter Raleigh died. On June 1 Edward married the Honourable Katharine Farrer.

Bridges's close and honored friend Henry Bradley died May 23, 1923. In July Bridges's expression of strong dislike for the portrait Roger Fry had painted of him almost disrupted their friendship. In November Bridges's daughter Elizabeth married A. A. Daryush and went to Persia to live with him. *Poor Poll,* written in 1921 in Neo-Miltonic syllabics using the twelve-syllable line that was to become the "loose Alexandrine" of *The Testament of Beauty,* was published in this year. *The Chilswell Book of English Poetry,* compiled by Bridges for the use of schools, was issued in March 1924. March 22, 1924, Bridges and Monica sailed for America on the S. S. *Celtic.* They spent about three months in the States, most of it at the University of Michigan, and set sail for their return to England in late June. Bridges contributed "Poetry in the Schools" to S.P.E. Tract No. XVIII, which was published in October. For his eightieth birthday, October 23, 1924, Bridges was presented by his friends with a clavichord made by Arnold Dolmetsch. In November he finished the first section of his memoir of Henry Bradley and sent it to the printer; at this time a strong difference of opinion arose between Bridges and Sir Henry Newbolt as to the kind and degree of American participation in the S.P.E. On Christmas day Bridges wrote fourteen lines of "loose Alexandrines," the first seven of which became the opening passage of *The Testament of Beauty.*

Lionel Muirhead, Bridges's oldest and closest friend, died January 25, 1925. *The Tapestry,* a collection of poems in Neo-Miltonic syllabics designed by Stanley Morison, was issued in November 1925, to be followed the next month by *New Verse,* published by the Clarendon Press, which contained seven poems from *The Tapestry* as well as other poems written in 1921 and a few earlier pieces.

The Memoir of Henry Bradley was published by the Clarendon Press in 1926. Margaret, Bridges's younger daughter, died April 25. On the advice of Monica, Bridges, in an attempt to take his mind off his daughter's death, resumed work on the poem that was to be entitled *The Testament of Beauty,* which he had begun on Christmas Day, 1924. He canceled seven of the fourteen lines written on that day, retaining the first seven. He wrote a few more lines, of which he kept only two. Then he gave it up temporarily and went on vacation to Bognor. After his return he resumed writing on July 8 and finished the first book by the end of the year. He supervised the publication of S.P.E. Tract No. XXIII on English Handwriting, which included a facsimile of Bridges's handwriting from the plate published in *Now in Wintry Delights.*

In 1927 Bridges continued work on *The Testament of Beauty,* finishing the first draft of Book II by the end of July and making a good start on Book III. Elizabeth Daryush and her husband returned to England and settled at Stockwell House on Boar's Hill, a short distance from Chilswell. On July 2 a concert of Bridges's lyrics set to the music of Gustav Holst was performed at Chilswell House in the presence of the composer. In October *The Influence of the Audience,* Bridges's essay on Shakespeare, originally published in 1907, was issued in October, printed in modified phonetic spelling with a preface by Bridges explaining the symbols used in the printing. It was Number I of the *Collected Essays* of Robert Bridges.

January 6, 1928, Bridges published a letter in the London *Times* on "Broadcast English," concerning the pronunciation of English used by the BBC. Also in 1928 Bridges edited S.P.E. Tract No. XXVIII on English Handwriting, a continuation of Tract XXIII. In August Numbers II and III of the *Collected Essays* appeared. He finished the trial text of Book III of *The Testament of Beauty* in March and the trial text of Book IV (except for the tail piece) by the end of the year. Bridges and Monica, under the name of Matthew Barnes, contributed another essay on French words to S.P.E. Tract No. XXX. In September *A Selection from the Letters of Sir Walter Raleigh* was published with an introduction by Bridges.

February 28, 1929, Bridges delivered a lecture entitled "Poetry" for BBC broadcast. On June 3 he was appointed to the Order of Merit. *The Testament of Beauty* was published October 24, 1929, one day after the poet's eighty-fifth birthday. It received widespread acclaim from reviewers and from the public.

Shortly before his death Bridges gave approval for the private printing of "On

Receiving Trivia from the Author." It was issued in an edition of thirty-six copies June 19, 1930. Bridges died at Chilswell April 21, 1930.

Note

1. In Bridges's Manuscript Book (in the Bridges Papers), p. 108.

461: TO LIONEL MUIRHEAD

Birdlip
Gloucester
October 26, 1904

My dear Lionel

Here I am in an old fashioned inconvenient little stone house, in ancient times an inn, just at the top of the steepest highway in England, looking North over Gloucester—trying to get the place comfortable for my wife to inhabit next week. Here she, Elizabeth and I are to make our home until Margaret is well enough to go to Switzerland. And in Switzerland, amid the snows, we are to spend our Xmas, and sing 'Ark the 'erald angels, etc.—I am sure that my wife will be much amused with your newspaper cutting. I have done with these things. I don't know what the H A M committee have accomplished: only that the plain-song music will be all very well edited: because that was done by a good specialist. The word committee was as foolish and incompetent a body as you can imagine, judging that is by the reports which they sent to me—When I consented to take the Yattendon choir 18 years ago I said aloud "I will not do this work for nothing. I will destroy Hymns Ancient and Modern." And now it really looks as if I had. The common folk will never stand the original of Wesley's Xmas hymns. The committees seem to have followed me where they shouldn't—and I know they have not followed me where they should. But I have not seen the book—and I have so far discarded the subject (having done all that I mean to do) that I doubt if I should care to open it, if it were lying on the table.

My patients seem doing well. I have been reading Tolstoi's various essays: trying to make out what he means. I cannot make any good sense of him.—He seems to think that one should discard all family affection, and that everyone should eat rye-bread. I shall know more in a few days.

yours ever
RB

462: TO LIONEL MUIRHEAD

Birdlip
nr Gloucester
November 9, 1904

My dear Lionel

I was glad to read your cheerful letter with its good account of Antony. We hav been settled in here some time. It is a very queer house, though very small it has external doors, and as we live on 'the open door' system the rooms are full of dead leaves and stray cats. Of an evening the lamps blow out and it is impossible

to go about the house with a lighted candle after dark. We are to be here till we
go to Switzerland, and unless we die in Switzerland we shall come back to En
gland in the spring: and that is my view of Switzerland. The patients really seem
to be doing well, but I do not get reconciled to this condition of things: I am quite
ten years older than I was a year ago. I have not been down into Gloucester yet;
hear that the Cathedral organist there is a good musician: so I intend to make hi
acquaintance. The air is lovely up here, and it is a really good place. I should no
at all mind settling here altogether. I wish you could come and see it and th
house is, in spite of the inconvenience of its conveniences very comfortable.
expect that if I was not physically out of sorts, I should be enjoying myself.

Arthur Symons has published a volume entitled 'Studies in Prose and Verse'
It contains a portrait of me and a chapter on my work. You would like to order i
from your library. There is a fair amount of interesting and well-written artisti
criticism in the book. I am reading Cicero! and have been for some time. It is hi
character that interests me. I think him an ass, and I should not be able to read
him but for his style. I think it very likely that some of my depression may be du
to his society. The Prothero who lets us this house is brother to that ilkite wh
was at Merton when we were up at Oxford. He was a member of the brother
hood and is now a parson. The landowner is a Hicks-Beach brother of th
minister: I want to see him for I think he must have been at Eton with us. If Hac
is the perfect tense of Hick, then he is most appropriately named, for he ha
hacked down all the beechwoods and converted them into wretched under
woods. A man wrote to me the other day for an autograph of one of my poems
so I sent him "Lo where the Virgin" (those alcaic stanzas from Blake) written ou
in my phonetic script: the notion of his surprise amused me. When I stop jotting
down these casual remarks to you (my feet are on the mantel shelf over the fire)
am going to look at the American Will James' Talks to Teachers on Psychology
That science is really getting much more reasonable. There is an interestin
article on the Financial condition of the country in the Contemporary Review.
can't think of anything more to tell you, so I will shut this up and turn to James

your affectionate

RB

It is a bright windy night. Gloucester lies below us 7 miles off under the hills
white galaxy of electric lights. There was a fire in that city this evening. W
watched the red patch blazing away till they squirted it out.

463: TO HENRY BRADLEY

Ber
Wel
Somers
December 8, 190

My dear Bradley

I was very glad to hear from you. Your letter was forwarded to me at *Birdl
near Gloucester*, which is my present address, just as I was starting for a 3 day
visit here. I am glad to hear a generally good account of your wife's health.

hope at least that it is really good, and that her being invalided just now is only a temporary setback. My wife is I think also not likely to be of much use till the winter is over, although she spends all her time not in bed but on a couch out of doors in all weathers, and she has put on so much fat that she does not feel the cold. The specialist gives a very good account of her. He says in fact that she is recovered, but she will not be able to talk much, or be generally useful for some time, as the long period of silence has left her throat somewhat irritable, and resentful of exertion. We are wintering on the top of the Cotswolds a mile and a quarter away from the Sanatorium where Margaret (my daughter) is. She has had relapses, but is on the whole doing well, and though her recovery is uncertain yet nothing yet has occurred to forbid it. So much in answer to your kind enquiries.

Robinson Ellis wrote to tell me that he had written something fresh in the 'Point of View' on the Latin pronunciation question. I have not seen it yet. I know about the French movement. One of the men has written to me on the subject. Between ourselves I do not quite trust Ellis in matters of detail, and I could make very little of the Frenchman whose book he seemed to think all right. I don't remember much of it except that it represented some sounds by doubling the consonant where there was no true doubled consonant—and since then the French Academy having advised the exclusion of all false doubling from their orthography I do not suppose that his system will be intelligible.

I expect to be in Oxford for a few days before Xmas, and will try and persuade you to enter this arena. My papers have really had some effect; at least I find that a good many more people are converted—and it will soon be time for me to give them another dig.

I was disappointed at the result of voting on the compulsory Greek. We shall have our way in all these matters in a few years, if we stick to it. It vexes me that they are bothering my boy with Greek. He has only just got over his Latin troubles. The classical master reports him "a sensible translator—inattentive in class". But in mathematics he is "accurate, quick and diligent". This is the whole story. His time is being wasted—and most boys are in the same condition. Fancy your having read (and collected?) 53 reviews of your book. What patience and humility! I suppose that Macmillan sent them to you. I wonder how much you will get out of the canny Scotchmen. I am printing the lst act of my Demeter in "Country Life"! I don't yet know when, but Editor says he has got it into type.

yours sincerely

R Bridges

464: TO LIONEL MUIRHEAD

Birdlip

near Gloucester

December 23, 1904

My dear Lionel

We wish you all a happy Xmas. My invalids have been doing well, but the last event is the return of Edward from school with Influenza. I can't tell what may not be in store for us. I have been two days away at Oxford hunting for houses.

The family very much wish to try Boar's Hill. There are some good people up there, but the general appearance of the settlement is almost as bad as it could be. I had another outing at Wells for 3 days, and enjoyed it; being, that journey, fortunate in the weather. I am cogitating a causerie on "Pilgrim's Progress."—It should be amusing—I suppose that you have not among your books any personal account of John Bunyan, have you? I read that when he retired in his latter days he had a small well-provided house in Bedford, where he collected a lot of old furniture and plate, which the informant suggests may have been presented to him by his admirers.—I should like to know if he had really *bought* anything in "Vanity Fair". It seems most improbable. If you have any life of him look it up and see what you can find. The only one that I have, from which I have quoted is by Froude, in the *Men of Letters* series.—I have not been able to do anything up here. If Edward should be well he will companion Elizabeth, and as they will be glad to be alone I may get a chance. With kindest regards to your wife, and all best seasonable wishes,

> yours ever
>
> RB

465: TO LIONEL MUIRHEAD

> Birdlip
> nr Gloucester
> December 29, 1904

My dear Lionel

Many thanks for your opinion, and William Johnson's about Bunyan. The latter strengthens the impeachment which I have in my head. I am afraid the Speaker is often poor.—It is sometimes very good. Let me thank you for the generous offer in your last letter but one. I am glad to say that I am all right. We even gave away 130£ this Xmas!! My ill luck goes on. Elizabeth had a fall on the ice on Xmas eve, and got a severe concussion of the brain with very alarming symptoms. She seems all right again, but has to keep her bed just when she was wanted to companion Edward, whose cold will not move away in this sunless weather. Today we have driving cloud with a warm West wind. We are in the midst of the clouds. I wish we might have a few sunny days. Excuse this short note. I have many letters.

> your affectionate
>
> RB

466: TO MRS. MARGARET WOODS

> Birdlip
> nr Gloucester
> January 11, 1905

My dear Mrs Woods

I am sorry to hear that 'the Master' is in dock. Among my evil experiences that of hospital patience has not yet befaln me. I sincerely hope that there is nothing wrong with his ears which treatment cannot put right, and I am glad to have your report that he is doing well. I hope he may soon be set free. He will no doubt have perfected some Temple eloquence in his solitude.

As for myself—really I would not answer even your kind letter if I were obliged to tell you of all my misfortunes. I can report that we are alive, and getting broken in to bad fortune, and that we have never been so bad as to wish ourselves in Port Arthur. I have had about 18 months of anxiety and trouble. Our old home is quite broken up, and I don't see how we shall easily make a new one. I am now negociating for a small furnished house (the only possible one) on Foxcombe Hill: where we think to go for February and March, to taste the "neighbourhood". My wife and 2nd daughter must live on a hill of some sort. I am sorry to send you so wretched a letter. I will tell you all about ourselves when we meet. It is really a miracle that I have been able to get anything like written words out of this pen.—I am doing a Causerie on Pilgrim's Progress. I have to find some facts. If you wish it well I should be extremely obliged to you if you would scribble me the shortest possible answers to these questions. (1) Have you read it since you were a child? (2) Do you or did you like it? (3) Has it done you any moral or spiritual good??? The shortest answers suffice my purpose. Also anybody else's ditto will be good for my bootless bene.

yours sincerely
Robt Bridges

I hope that you find London agree with you. We all send kindest regards etc. Good wishes for the New Year.

467: TO LIONEL MUIRHEAD

St Columb's
Foxcombe Hill
nr Oxford
[February 6, 1905]

That's the address, my dear Lionel. Monica Margaret and I are here. Ed has gone back to school and Elizabeth is also making a trial trip at a girls' school at Sherborne but it seems that she dislikes it very much. We sent her only for a change of scene, and to get experience, and she was very keen to go. My two invalids have been doing well, but Monica got overtired with the move. Our house is well situated, looking South over Hingdon. We see the Chilterns on the left of our view, and the Wantage downs on the right. We have no 'garden', and there are other little houses on either side of us. I can get into Oxford on my cycle in about 20 minutes: but it takes 45 to get back. I could meet you in Oxford almost any day. We have taken the house for 2 months: possibly may stay longer. There is to be a good concert on Wednesday evening. The Choral Symphony. I may go to that. I have been absurdly occupied, especially with my family, and I can see that I shall hav no remission yet. My Bunyan paper is sent in. Also I shall have another article in this week's *Saturday*. The calls on my purse have made me acquainted with strange newspapers, and the other day one of them sent me the 2nd and 3rd volumes of Gomperz's *"Greek thinkers"* to review! so I have got the book to read after all, but I haven't the cheek to review it. I have a tiresome piece of work in editing Dixon's posthumous poems. I am recommended to build a house at Garsington!! That would be close to you—but I should be dead before I had seen much of you. E D Stone and his son turned up at lunch in Oxford the other day. I hope you are well. Tell me if you will meet me in Oxford any afternoon.

Our kindest regards to Mrs Muirhead—

your affectionate

RB

468: TO LIONEL MUIRHEAD

Foxcombe Hill

March 8, [1905]

My dear Lionel

Many thanks for your letter. I will come and stay a couple of nights soon. Tomorrow I have to take my wife to Sherborne to visit Elizabeth, shall not be back till Friday evening.

I doubt if Ipsden would do for us as looking in the map, I think it cannot be above the 300 foot line, and if so it would be practically in the "Thames Valley". The house on Turville Heath seems too awfully remote from everything. When I come we will visit Long Crendon and Brill.

Today is the most exciting day of the whole war so far, and we shall not get the morning paper until 2.30.—I cannot tell you how anxious I am that this battle should be a success. If Oyama really bottles the Russians the whole thing may be over, and the notion of the Czar carrying it on for 4 years longer is too awful.

D—n him and all his uncles and starry generals. I will write and tell you when I can come. I should think Monday or Tuesday, if my folk are all right and can be left

yours affectionately

R Bridges

469: TO LIONEL MUIRHEAD

St Columbs

Foxcombe Hill

nr Oxford

March 23 [1905]

My dear Lionel

I send you two articles to smoke over. The Computor Greek was written at request of Editor apropos of the Cambridge vote. I had nothing to say, except to hammer away at the old nail head. The point moves in a bit further each time.

I spend almost all my days house hunting. I had one day at Brill, Long Crendon etc.—another at High Wyccombe, Fingest, Turville Heath etc. The more I see the more I incline to the West of Oxford by Chipping Norton etc. but I have found nothing at all yet.

We get a few visitors up here from Oxford which is pleasant. Demeter has passed first proofs so I can send you a batch of it when you wish.

Love from us all

yours ever

RB

I am afraid that I want the "articles" back as I like to keep a complete set

———

I hope you are doing epigrams.

470: TO LIONEL MUIRHEAD

St Columbs
Foxcombe Hill
April 14, 1905

My dear Lionel

I had quite forgotten about your intention of sending me a Virgil, when his loveliness arrived. I cannot thank you sufficiently for it. Monica is sewing it up in a little silken cover, that it may live safely in my pocket; and I shall hope to carry it about with me on my house hunting expeditions. It will probably make a good deal of difference to my life—

I have not had a moment to write before, indeed I had to get Monica to send you my thanks for the book. I have been out househunting every day, coming home very tired. I find that in this wet weather the damp air rushing through one's room all night makes my clothes quite wet. I dressed in wet clothes this morning and am still trying to get them dry. I don't like it.

I have not had time yet to look carefully at the epigrams. I will attend to them as soon as I can—nor have I yet deciphered the Greek inscription. I look forward to both these entertainments.

I have had several tiresome letters this morning, and am scribbling this before going down to Oxford to meet Elizabeth, who returns home today.

I am glad that you liked the Bunyan. I think that dictum of mine about allegory is right—it never struck me before.

The *Academy* is very promising—last week's issue was readable throughout.

I will write again shortly

your affectionate

RB

I have had to write "notes" to Demeter. I have said a lot of new things about Greek accents, which will give you the opportunity of making a pun about
D__metre

471: TO HENRY NEWBOLT

St. Columbs
Foxcombe Hill
nr Oxford
April 14, 1905

My dear Newbolt

Mr. Alfred Miles has written to me asking if I will write the introductory notice of you and make a representative selection of your work (which he says must be short) for his book of poets. I have told him that I will do it if you can't think of anyone else, and that I am writing to you about it.

I do not really wish to have the responsibility, and am rather hoping that you will be able to find someone else.—Would not Streatfeild do?——But if you really want me to do it I will do my best. In that case you must send me all the biographical particulars which you wish to have inserted—not omitting bibliographical data—as it is necessary to have this sort of information quite correct—

In the case of living authors it is of course better to say as little as possible, so that my task would not be *very* difficult.

I should also like to know which poems you would yourself wish to be represented.

My patients seem to be doing well—I can't however find a house anywhere—I spend all my days cycling about the country.—I like the district about *Churchill.* Do you know Low Morton?

yours ever
RB

I hope you read my papers on John Bunyan in the two last *Speakers.* They would amuse you—

472: TO HENRY NEWBOLT

Boars Hill
nr Oxford
April 19, [1905]

My dear Newbolt

I gather from your letter that you wish me to write this thing—and it would be very easy if we could have a chat in which you could tell me the necessary facts and dates.

The thing is to write something which interests a general reader—criticism is best avoided in the case of a living writer and a friend. I fancy the subjects of your muse might give occasion for reference to pedigree, (which does interest people). With that and the main biographical facts: and some material statistics of bibliographical success there should be no difficulty in making a distinguished and interesting memoir.

We expect to be here till the end of Easter "holidays." I wonder whether you might not get one day in Oxford. It would be very pleasant—if it did not rain too hard.

At this moment Togo excites me. We do not see the morning papers. It seems to me that his war is a very favourable opportunity for persons who have the ear of the public to make a general protest in favour of a European concert for arbitration and mutual reduction of armaments. Do you think that anything could be done?

yours ever

RB

473: TO HENRY NEWBOLT

Boars Hill
nr Oxford
April 27, [1905]

My dear Newbolt

Thanks for your letter. Our plans are more fixed. We leave here on May 5, go for a week to Yattendon, and then return here (not to this house but to a larger and more convenient one) till end of Summer term, i.e. end of June.

It would not do for you to come here when you propose as we shall be busy and disturbed, moving etc.—but you could come to Manor House (where I shall be with Elizabeth) at Yattendon between 5th and 12th, or you could come here when we got back to Boar's Hill. We should have a pleasant term in Oxford.

I am writing to Miles to ask him if he is in any hurry.

yours ever

RB

474: TO HENRY NEWBOLT

Boar's Hill
nr Oxford
May 3, [1905]

My dear Newbolt

I hear from Signor Miles this morning that he wants copy in 3rd week of May.

I shall be at Yattendon from Friday 5 to Friday 12 on which day I return to this Boar's Hill.

We have taken a house furnished called Boar's Hill Heath. I can't well write this affair without seeing you, and I hope that you will spare a day at Yattendon, or else come here for a day as soon as we return.

My moving days will be the Fridays.

Elizabeth and I shall be at the Manor house alone—lots of room.

yours ever

RB

I shall be more at leisure after 12th, and it would be fun to be in Oxford together. At Yattendon I have a lot to do.

475: TO HENRY NEWBOLT

Yattendon
May 12, [1905]

My dear Newbolt

We are going tomorrow to *"Boar's Hill Heath"* and I will meet you any day in Oxford, the sooner the better: as I ought to send this thing off, and cannot possibly do it without your generous assistance. I have reread, and made my selection, but can offer you alternatives, though I don't expect that you will quarrel with my choice.

I shall be househunting, and very much engaged. Therefore you must tell me a day beforehand when you are coming. We are all fairly well.

yours ever
RB

476: TO HENRY NEWBOLT

Boar's Hill Heath
Oxford
May 17, [1905]

My dear Newbolt

I hope the enclosed is all right. I send you the copy which my wife made from my dictation from my notes.

There was no mean allowed between 500 and 1060 words. I thought it best to try 500—but had great difficulty.

I have sent a copy to Mr. Miles for him to get set up, to see if it will go in to the two pages.

I want you to alter not only any inaccuracies, but to tell me whether you would like any thing in the matter changed or differently worded.

yours ever
RB

I forgot "the dead son" is in my list—do you object? I omitted it by accident when I showed list to you.

477: TO WILLIAM SANDAY

Boar's Hill Heath
May 19, [1905]

My dear Sanday

When we stood at the grave yesterday I was wondering about things that I did not dare speak of, and do not now trust myself to write of. But after I got home it struck me that you *might perhaps* like to see the two distichs (epitaphs) which I am sending you. I wrote them now some years ago when I made my first experiments with Stone's prosody. I add a phonetic script of them, which does something to explain—but I am a heretic about the $\begin{Bmatrix} \text{Oxford} \\ \text{Orthodox} \end{Bmatrix}$ way of reading Greek and Latin.

yours ever

RB

478: TO LIONEL MUIRHEAD

Boar's Hill Heath
nr Oxford
May 23, [1905]

My dear Lionel

I hope that you are getting on fast. Mrs. Lionel sent us a good report of you.

The last notion about *us* is that we are ordered all to go to Switzerland at end of June. This is Sir Thomas Barlow's prescription. He thinks both the invalids doing as well as possible. Others do not agree. I don't know yet whether we shall go, but I shall have to find out where to go to—and it struck me that your knowledge of Switzerland would be of the useful sort.

I must come over some day and have a chat with you about it—or will you be able to visit us here before we leave?

I do not say this at all with the idea of saving myself the trouble of visiting you: but we are now very comfortably housed with an acre of wild garden to the South of the house, and the air would probably repay you and help your convalescence.

I have read the whole of Virgil in that little book which you gave me, and a great deal of him 3 or 4 times.

If we really leave England at end of June I have a pretty busy time before me—as I must thoroughly clear out at Yattendon. I do not know when we should return to England, probably not till this time next year.

yours ever

RB

479: TO HENRY NEWBOLT

Boar's Hill Heath
nr Oxford
May 26, [1905]

My dear Newbolt

We are probably going on the Continent at end of June.

Do you think that there is any chance of my being able to meet H. G. Wells before then? Perhaps he might like a day in Oxford.

I have told Mr Miles Esq to hurry on with his proofs and I will correct the introduction according to your wishes. Of course you shall have the proofs—

Have been this afternoon with Elizabeth to a garden party at C.C.C. Sidgwick's Oxford didn't show up very well. I am on (as expert I suppose) in a L L D* degree examination!! I see that the words which I wrote might imply more than was intended.

I think the selection will go into 8 pages.

> Drake
> Medusa
> Gillespie
> Commem[oration]
> the only son
> Fidele

is I think the lot

yours ever

RB

* or Doctor of Letters??
the new thing

480: TO LIONEL MUIRHEAD

Boar's Hill Heath
June 21, [1905]

My dear Lionel

I have just had two days at Yattendon, and find your letter here on my return. We are leaving tomorrow week, and I am therefore awfully busy, but as I did not get my dinner till 9:30 this evening I am sitting up over a pipe and grog, and can write a letter or two. I must thank you for all the kind things that you say about Demeter: and explain *"Zibian" only you must not tell anyone,* it is a puzzle for the learned—indeed I met a specialist on Greek statues, who knew all about the Erycinian Aphrodite, and yet couldn't tell why I called it the Zibian. The facts are that the district about Mt. Eryx was always a country of special preeminence or distinction, and it seems to have been specially so considered by the Phoenicians. Now the early Phoenician coins of the Eryx district have on them the letters I I I = ZIZ. and the Greeks copied this in their Erycian coinage, but (disliking the two Z's I suppose) made ZIB of it, and from ZIB I made Zibian.

It is a very good word—because it seems to me not at all improbable that the name of Σικελοί may have some connection with the Phoenician name which they shortened into Σεπ —but I don't know how possible this may be. At any rate it pleased me to make up a piece of antique language for Demeter talking of Daedelus.—You will think the grog has got into my writing but as a matter of fact I haven't yet begun it. Here goes—It's very strong of the lemon.

You can get Illingworth's Bamptons—I think the book is called *Personality* (some name of that sort) for 6d. It is one of the Macmillan series of cheap novels etc.!! It is well written, and interesting as showing what the modern Englishman reads in that department. But I shouldn't buy a more expensive edition. The 6d one is in good type—quite legible. Slatter and Rose sell it—

We are going to start at Lucerne—or rather just above Lucerne. I will write and tell you how we get on.—Please thank Charis for liking Demeter—I wrote it for young ladies, and I pleased them much. Which is as good a compliment as I wish for—I don't know what could be made of the Perseus legend. I should have to read it all up again—and shall not have any opportunity of doing that. I read all there was ancient about Demeter before I began, and was amazed to find that it made so intelligible and consecutive a story in motives. I really think that people will now remember my version, for I have added nothing. The connection between Demophoön and the Eleusinian mysteries, has never been, so far as I know, hinted at! I can't lay my hand on your letter containing the elegiacs. So excuse my putting them off till another time. I have been constantly occupied with 1000 things to remember. Tomorrow I am going to interview the lawyer about "the site".

your affectionate

RB

481: TO MRS. MANLEY HOPKINS

Boar's Hill Heath
nr Oxford
June 21, 1905

Dear Mrs Hopkins

Thank you very much for writing. It gave me great pleasure to hear that you had got my little book safely, and would read it. I have been thinking of you a good deal lately, for I have had all Gerard's letters to Canon Dixon on hand. I was going to write a long account of Dixon and his poetry, and was intending to make copious extracts from Gerard's letters, and I hope that I may yet do this some day. But now it happens that I am going to Switzerland next week with my wife and two daughters, and we expect to be away for about a year.

I have had great trouble the last 18 months. My wife started with a pleurisy 3 years ago, and though she recovered from it, as it was thought, completely, yet it must have been tubercular, and 18 months ago one of my girls after 3 attacks of what the best physicians considered to be influenza was found to be infected. They both went to a Sanitorium, and have done very well, and it is hoped that a year in Switzerland may complete and establish their cure. At any rate it is the best that we can do, at least we think that it is. You may imagine what a time I have had of it. My wife was forbidden to talk: and did not speak a word for some 6 months!!!

My home is of course broken up, and we shall not return to it. I have let the house, and am now thinking of building a small house in a proper kind of place. Meanwhile all is confusion. But we have much to be grateful for, and are happy in being able to do what is recommended, for it really seems as if the sort of treatment was successful. Both the invalids are now looking very well and my wife weighs quite two stone more than she ever did in her life.

I am sorry that my letter is taken up with this kind of matter; but I console myself with thinking that you have *Demeter* to turn to, for whatever demerits it may have it will be better reading than this letter.

I cannot conclude without saying how bright all my memories are of you, and how happy it makes me to think that you are still interested in my work.

I am yours sincerely
Robert Bridges

I should have replied before but have been away.

482: TO SAMUEL GEE

Boar's Hill Heath
nr Oxford
[Late June 1905]

My dear Gee

Your letter comes in the very nick of time, for we are all off to Switzerland on Friday: Barlow's order: and we shall not return I suppose till next Spring. The two invalids have both done well. They are both very stout, and have had no febrile symptoms for many months. Except for remains of basic pleurisy there are percussion signs, and Barlow could hear nothing in my wife's chest, while Semon says that her palsied chord now acts almost normally. The girl has still crepitant sounds of varying character dispersed about both lungs—that is what I gather at least from what the doctors say—but they regard her improvement in this respect as very marked and promising. It only remains to be seen what that Swiss air and altitude may do. Elizabeth is very well. Edward is at school at top of his class (not a very high class about 2 months below average) and is to follow us out in August. I, myself I, am very thin, and often rather melancholy, but this evening in good spirits. I have been more profoundly vexed and bored by it all than I can say: and those words aren't quite strong enough.

I took Edward down to Eton last Saturday, to introduce him to his tutor, for he was to have gone to Eton next term. However when they showed me the "room" which was destined for him to inhabit, I told them that I could not accept it. To describe it—there was not space enough in it for a small boy to sit or move about comfortably in. It was on the first floor in the corner of a "well". .i.e. a 3 sided well, one side not being built round and beneath the window the "well" was roofed in over ground floor buildings, which were the kitchen and part of the enlarged dining-room of the house. What air could get in at the window being contaminated by the ventilator of the dining room, and the effluvia of the kitchen, and its refuse. Considering what you have to pay at Eton, and that you have to enter a boy ten years beforehand, this is pretty bad: and you may probably guess what is likely to ensue from a man's having had the impudence to offer me this ultimatum. It is perhaps in the man's favour that I am going abroad, but that will not altogether quit him, and it is very much in my favour that there is a new headmaster coming next term.

The reason for my telling you all about this is that I want you to find me some backers among the physicians who must have been from time to time summoned to Eton. Perhaps you yourself have something to say. I am not going to wait for backers: my guns will go off till I have made a breach: but it must be that there are some physicians in London who would be glad of the occasion of speaking out. A doctor who is called in to a special case cannot write to the papers to expose the criminal conduct or neglect of his client. But it must still be on his conscience if he knows of an evil and may not expose it.

Now I think that I shall make a good opportunity for getting this abuse looked into, and I should be of course very much strengthened if I had some R C P allies. Find one or two for me. I shall be here till Friday; after that day a letter addressed to me at Yattendon (franked with 2½d for foreign postage) and marked *to be forwarded,* will reach me in three days.

Referring to your letter. We have been on this hill since February. My papers on Bunyan were in the Speaker, not the Spectator. (I would not write in that paper.) I must send you my last poem. If you go to Switzerland in August *could you escort Edward?* He is going from Folkestone on the 2nd of August, but could wait a day. He will be travelling from Folkestone to Bale or Lucerne and I should like to find a companion for him—send me an answer to this question if you can before I go on Friday—with our love

your affectionate
R Bridges

483: TO HENRY NEWBOLT

"Yattendon
near Newbury
to be forwarded"
June 29, [1905]

My dear Newbolt

We are going off tomorrow. I wrote a fortnight ago to Miles and he said that he could not send me proofs yet. So I have now just written to him to tell him to send the proofs to you and that you will correct the place in the introduction into conformity with truth. I do not propose any form for the correction to take because I condensed the matter to make it go into two pages there being nothing between 2 and 4 allowed—I can not be *certain* that I have not overrun the space by a line though I kept some 40 words below his estimate.—On the other hand you may find that you have a line or two to spare, and that will make all the difference in expressing a matter which it seems is difficult to express. I return you the papers lent for my use—

yours ever

RB

You must keep an eye on Miles and not let him escape you. I have told him there is a mistake to correct—I suppose he will have printed the right poems. This also you will see to. I have not kept a list for I expected the matter to be settled ages ago. But I am certain about these following

> Gillespie
> Drake
> Medusa
> Dead son for only son
> Commemoration
> Fidele

I rather fancy that there was another, but I cant recall it for certain. Of course they are all *in full*. No omissions—
I am on the brink of a row at Eton I think. Edward's prospective tutor told me that he must go into a certain room for his first year, which said room is thoroughly unsanitary. Wherefore I shall load my guns—

484: TO HENRY NEWBOLT

Axenstein
July 7th, 1905

My dear Newbolt

(1) I took Edward down to Eton, with the notion that he was to go there next term, and his tutor showed me an "unsanitary" room as his prospective abode. Hence the devil of a row—I am going to push the matter. I wrote first to the headmaster, and he disclaims any 'jurisdiction'.

Now I am insisting on the Managers investigating the matter and giving a judgement. If they do not support my complaint and condemn the room I shall go for the public.

My difficulty will be my absence from England. I shall write a long letter to the Times. It is probable that the Times would wish to suppress it. If the Editor does not insert it, I shall not know—as I can't be sure of seeing the Times.

So I am asking you to do for me what I in the first instance asked of that free fighter Professor Ray Lanhester, only he is ill of gout and refused to assist through his secretary.

If the Managers shuffle, may I send my letter to the Times in an enclosure to you? And will you forward it to the Editor with a short note saying "my *friend RB has sent me this enclosure from Switzerland asking me to forward it to you for insertion at earliest opportunity*"? Then the Editor will know that there is a witness to the sending of the letter, and that the matter is no secret,—and you will be able to tell me whether or no it is inserted.

If you cannot do this can you find any one who will. It is really a great difficulty in my way—

(2) Edward is coming out to us on the 2nd. He will have to find his way out. I wrote asking Miss Coleridge to give him midday dinner in London and see him into proper afternoon train at Charing Cross and see that his portmanteau was looked through. She says she will be out of London on the 2nd—

It is a very inconvenient thing to ask of any one, but I am asking you if you could do it, if you are in town. Edward would I suppose arrive with Francis, and would eat with him and you might be able to find some one to start him from Charing Cross in the afternoon—If you *can't* do this send me a line. Indeed I want an answer to (1) also.

I hope you got my letter about Miles. We have done well so far despite the rather trying weather.

yours ever
R Bridges

P.S. Please address to me *Yattendon* nr Newbury "To be forwarded." My address is changeful—and will be known at Yattendon—

485: TO HENRY NEWBOLT

Kurhaus
Stoos
Brunnen
Lac Lucerne
Switzerland
[July 11, 1905]

My dear Newbolt

I am most truly grateful to you for your kindness in promising to see Edward off. It will be his first journey of any length alone, and though I have no doubt he would get on all right I should not be able to be quite comfortable about him, especially as he is I am afraid working for his class prize, and may be rather run down by end of term.

I think the boys always get off pretty early from Horris Hill, by the first train—so that as his train leaves Charing Cross at 2.20 there should be plenty of time for him to get a good meal with you before starting. That is one important thing, as he will be in the train until 6:30 the next morning and it is difficult to get food by the present arrangements.—He will be instructed to take sufficient sustenance in his hand-bag. I shall hope to meet him at Basle at 6:30 and have breakfast for him.

Give him a rest if he wants one, and bring him on here in the evening. He has got his ticket—and I shall write him full instructions.—His box must of course be booked right through to Basle.—I was very loth to trouble you, but the people whom I first thought of as being pretty free from engagements (Mary Coleridge was one of them) all responded that they would not be in town—Edward will be much better off in your hands—as you have better knowledge of what the boy will need to be done for him, and the parental sympathy.

I shall be writing to you again before the day—though I don't think there is anything else to say about that.

There should be a meeting of Provost and Fellows at Eton this week, when my complaint will be considered. Of course they will try and shelve it—but I must wait and let them have their chance. It is rather a disaster for me, for I cannot conscientiously let the matter go by, and if I have to attack them publicly it may end in sufficient ill feeling to make it unwise to send Edward to Eton. Now this is of course exactly the sort of thing that they rely on—and I shall not let it stop me.—A review of Demeter in the Athenaeum amused us very much. The compliment was very indirect: but really it could not have been greater.—The reviewer snubbed the poem and made his main point a criticism of the notes about accents!! He praised all my old experiments, which his predecessor damned when they were new—and damned the new ones.—Also a review in the Chronicle in which I am coupled with *Lady Esher* (who is she) and it is said that I write as good blank verse as any one living except YEATS and STURGE MOORE.

"What has become of Swinburne. Where is Philipps [*sic*]?" and where is Binyon for that matter? Funny people these critics. Excuse my stingy paper. Every letter here costs 3d and we have many to write. All send their kindest remembrances.

yours ever

RB

I see notices of your Nelson Book—I hope it is selling well.
[Above the address is written: you can address letters here]

486: TO HENRY NEWBOLT

Luftkurort Stoos
Sommerfrische ob Morschach
Stoos
den July 25, 1905

My dear Newbolt

I am so very much obliged to you for undertaking to look after Edward. He has got a first class ticket so I think it very probable that you may be able to commit him into the charge of some decent fellow going as far as Basle and that would be the best thing. But he will find his way all right. I am pretty sure that the train leaves Charing Cross at 2.20 but I didn't come that way myself—it is 2.20 in the June Bradshaw—

He should have about a sovereign in his purse in case of accidents, and I don't know whether you may not have to give him some cash, or pay for the booking through of his box to Basle. That is of course important—and also to see that he puts the ticket of his registered box into the pocket of his ticket case.

I shall be at *Euler's Hotel—Basle* and shall come to meet the train—

Mrs. Newbolt kindly wrote to my wife about his food. He will be very hungry in the train.—The enclosed is to be given to Edward if you can remember to do so. He will be interested by the mess[age]. I would send it to him—but we have rather pestered him with directions and I think he might lose it or forget it—

We have all had a sharp attack of Hill sickness.—I am not well yet (inside)—or I should have been at Lugano today—where I was going to see a place which we think of spending September in.

with many thanks

yours ever
R Bridges

P.S.   When *you* book Ed's box get change for him in *French money*. I have no doubt you would have done this, but Ed has written to ask what he is to do about foreign money so I write of it.

A note from Eton. The room is to be examined by a "Doctor" and to be condemned or passed. I hope they don't know their doctor too well.

487: TO HENRY NEWBOLT

POST CARD

Stoos
July 28, [1905]

You will have heard from Godlees that they cannot find seats in Ed's train. I took Edward's ticket in June from Cook, and ordered it for August 2. But they dated it for August 1. (as it is available for 15 days from date. I don't know what arrangements the companies make for filling their trains: but I have written to Cook and Son 39 Piccadilly asking them to take any steps to secure Ed his seat, and to communicate if necessary with you. I write to inform you of this, and to suggest that it may be worth while to be early at the station. If you can't get him off, I dare say the Godlees will be in London and will bring him with them. If not he will be on your hands. If you don't get him off, telegraph me at Euler's Hotel Basle as I shall want to know.

yours
RB

488: TO HENRY NEWBOLT

Luftkurort Stoos
Sommerfrische ob Morschach
Stoos
den July 29, 1905

My dear Newbolt

The Godlees difficulty in getting seats in the train has made me worry about Edward being possibly left behind at Boulogne. I wrote to Cook and Son as I told you on a postcard—I have just written to the stationmaster at Boulogne.

But it would be a good thing to get some fellow traveller to *promise to see him into the train at Boulogne*. And tell Edward that if he *should* be left behind at Boulogne he must go to the English Consulate (or whatever it is there) and make the Consul feed him and put him up until he can come on. And on no account is he to eat any uncooked food, or drink *water* on his journey—only Cafe au lait, bread and cooked food.

I wish there were not so many people about.

yours ever
RB

489: TO HENRY NEWBOLT

Stoos ob Morschach
Lac Lucerne
August 5, [1905]

My dear Newbolt

I sent you a grateful telegram from Basel. You did excellently in introducing Edward to those Kebles. He said that they had sent 2 of their party on by the previous boat to secure seats in the train, and but for that precaution he doubts if he should have got a place. The train was 45 minutes late leaving Boulogne. When I got to Bâle station at 6.30 next morning it was credited with 58 minutes of Verspäterung, which it accurately preserved. I kicked my heels. Edward when he at last appeared was all right. We went to hotel and got baths and breakfast, and then reposed a bit and after had a drive in the town, lunched in hotel garden, and took afternoon train on to Lucerne. It was very hot. We pulled through and had ½ an hour at Lucerne before we took shipping.—Then the boat was overcrowded, but we found seats, and in a light head breeze magnified by our headway made a pleasant passage enough. I had reckoned on dining in the boat. That was made impossible by the crowd, on whom the 2 waiters could make no impression; but now came the great success of the whole 'voyage': I wish you could have seen it and my delight at the discovery of the precious remains of your generous provisions for Edward. How much he had already eaten of it I don't know, but his sack when explored still revealed a good part of a roast fowl, bread and butter both brown and white, buttered buns with cress, biscuits, cake, gingernuts, bananas and cheese: all done up in separate papers: also ½ a bottle of excellent lemonade. I can partly account for Edward's not having more reduced this stock by his story that his fellow-travelers had provided themselves with a preservative against seasickness, and the sea being indeed calm and giving them no occasion for proving it, they out of mere good spirits and gratitude to providence administered it to Edward who described it as a stomach twister: and that may have taken away his normal appetite—but indeed you may have given him so good a lunch as to have lasted him out. However I found these treasures and arranged them all in a row on one of the deck-tables, to the great scandal of the correct tourists, english and german-apeing english, who were sipping deleterious iced squashes and waters: I on the other hand ordered a bottle of Veltliner Sassella, and in the face of all the gaping staring fellows and families who never thought how I was playing on them, I took the paper parcels in order. I think my breaking up the cheese ostentatiously with my fingers disgusted them most: but you should know that I had on a hat old enough to take anyone's character away. Imagine how I enjoyed myself! Ed of course assisted, and, when he had finished the lemonade, joined on to the wine, which was good. I watched the horror and contempt of my spectators pass gradually through wonder into natural envy and honest admiration, while the curious miscellany of viands was successively and impartially assimilated and the papers one by one emptied and folded up flat, till nothing was left but the bare bottles and glasses. I seldom enjoyed a meal better: and I narrate it in confidence that *Mrs. Newbolt will like to know that not a crumb of her excellent provender was wasted.* Thus we came happily to Brunnen pier, where on landing we saw a strange sight. There were some American passengers named Pyne, the disbarking of whose baggage employed all the able bodied men of the district. The innumerable boxes and cases as they were piled up on shore made a heap that soon rivalled the neighbouring mountains: and the last thing we saw, as we drove off, was a party of half-tipsy tourists who having come upon this obstacle unexpectedly from the southeast just when they thought they had finished their day were angrily making its ascent with their alpen stocks and knapsacks, and jodelling loudly as they clambered up its precipitous heights.

We had a delightful drive of 2½ hours, getting gradually cooler as we ascended, till we had to put on our greatcoats before we reached home.

I am writing this with my wife's stylo pen, an awful thing, as I sit on a wood-stack on the hillside.

With many thanks

yours ever
R. Bridges

490: TO LIONEL MUIRHEAD

> Chasellas
> Campfer
> Engadine
> September 13, [1905]

My dear Lionel

I am coming home (bringing Edward back) for a fortnight on the 20th and shall be at Yattendon clearing out the house.

This—where I am leaving my females—is a lovely little restaurant in the hills—everything satisfactory. They will remain here till October 15th—when we go into winter quarters at St Moritz.

I think things are going on well. I will write from Yattendon—I am really too unsettled and busy with arrangements to write a decent letter now—Elizabeth says that she is writing to Charis, so you may get some gossip from her.

> your affectionate
> RB

491: TO A. H. BULLEN

> Villa Gentiana
> St Moritz
> Engadine
> Switzerland
> October 15, [1905]

My dear Bullen

My experience of life in Switzerland combined with "open air treatment" is convincing me that it is extremely improbable that I shall be able to do this Essay for you. Indeed I am beginning to doubt whether any kind of consecutive thought is possible when one is cold and uncomfortable. Therefore if my essay is needed to make the back of your tenth volume commensurate with the others I advise you to lose no time in engaging another pen. I have thought a good deal about it, and have made out what seems to me an original and really hopeful line: but to do justice to it will require opportunities for "study" which appear very improbable. However the address at the top of this letter names a house which is "replete with every modern comfort" and we go there in 3 days and it is just possible that I may settle down there in mind as well as in body. I will not give the intention up till I see that the time forbids its fulfilment.

What you said of Venus and Adonis is very interesting. No doubt you have by this time discovered the facts. I do not remember any Italian version. Titian's picture is good.—Give my love to Yeats.

> yours ever
> R Bridges

I hope that you liked the classical metre choruses in Demeter. I do not agree with all Stone's Prosody. If I do anything more in this way I shall try to modify it in a few particulars. The freedom from rhyme is delightful.—I have written a good lot of "Stone's Prosody," but the critics are so unkind to "experiments" that I shall not publish them. Dr Johnson said of Lycidas that it was "peculiar without excellence" and Dryden condemned Milton's blank verse for its lack of rhyme etc. etc.—

492: TO LIONEL MUIRHEAD

Villa Gentiana
St. Moritz
Engadine
October 23, 1905

My dear Lionel

Had I written to you three weeks ago I should have been in better spirits, things seemed going on as well as possible. Now Margaret is in bed with another attack. I had taken Edward to school, and had spent a fortnight in England cleaning out the Manor House,—which is now let, and indeed already tenanted by a "quarum" of old ladies—and all my furniture and chattels are stored in the big barn.—When I got back I found that Margaret had taken cold, and two days after it was evident what was up. We were able to move her here from the little restaurant where we were living, about 2 miles off, and she is not very bad. Still it must throw her back, and I am rather out of heart. I need not however trouble you with my troubles: only nothing could reconcile me to this life but the persuasion that it was good for some of us—to have the "alarms" and the "horrible place" (COWPER) both, is more than I bargained for. Still Monica so far is really well, and regaining her voice. I hate Switzerland as man has made it, and don't really much care for it as created—though I must praise as I enjoy the bright clean air and the beauty of the valleys, where I have spent delightful hours wandering among the rocks and pines and streams and eating the wild raspberries. The mountains to my thinking are merely damnable; though of course such monstrous masses must under the changing atmospheric conditions sometimes make strange and great effects. I have had with me your little Virgil and have already read it through 3 or 4 times. Now I am reading Shakespeare with the notion of writing something about him for a new edition, the last volume of which is to consist of essays by various hands. I don't know yet whether my hand will do what I want. I wrote something on leaving the Manor House, in the form of a sonnet to H.E.W. Here it is, it will at least amuse you. I owed HEW a sonnet.

> Love and the Muse have left their home; now bare
> Of memorable beauty; all is gone,
> The pleasant charm of happy Yattendon,
> Which thou wert apt, dear HEW, to build and share.

> What noble shades are flitting, who while-ere
> Haunted the temple where our life ran on
> In sanctities of joy, by reverence won,
> Music and choral grace, and studies fair.
>
> These on some kindlier field may Fate restore,
> And may the old house prosper, dispossest
> Of her whose equal it can nevermore
>   Hold till it crumble; O Nay! and the door
> Will moulder ere it open on a guest
> To match thee in thy wisdom and thy jest.

Our intention of building on Boar's Hill is in danger of falling through, Lord Abingdon's agents being difficult to deal with. My lawyers will not advise my trustees (without whom I can do nothing) to allow us to build on a site which they cannot get secured from the vulgarest invasion. But we have not quite given it up. Our plan, if Providence and her bacilli are agreeable is to remain here till Easter: and I am thinking of trying to get a tutor for Edward, who will come out to us at Xmas, and of keeping him here till we go home, for he is to go to Eton after Easter. The authorities there behaved well to me, and practically admitted the reasonableness of my complaint. The house we are in here is luxurious, but constructed so that if anything igneous went wrong in the elaborate lighting and heating machinery, we should be all converted to cinders in about 10 minutes. All the houses and hotels being in much the same predicament, and nothing disastrous occurring we take our chance. But the getting safe away will add hugely to the delight of returning to England—"home" I cannot say, for we have no home, nor any prospect of one.

I hope that you are well, and have been well, and all your family. Envy brings me frequent thoughts of my friend in England; and I see you in your lofty and spacious drawing room seated in an armchair by the fire smoking your pipe over an evening paper, or some lovely Aldine or other antique book. We huddle round the stack of ornamental iron pipes that heats our sitting room. Monica calls it "the Incubator". But I cannot say that the house is not a very good advertisement of 'central heating' and altogether comfortable.

You will be glad for me also to hear that we have a good cook. She is somewhat expensive, but we had to take her by cubic measurement, and "die Ursula" is not really diminutive. I have not seen a newspaper of any sort for 3 weeks, so if you are dead pray excuse my writing. Perhaps the king is dead. Who can tell? But I get "cuttings" sent me from the Oxford University Press, reviews of Demeter, and they are amusing enough. The last was almost the best of all. I was reviewed with a lot of other small people under POETAE LEVIORES. Unfortunately there was no quantitative sign over the e of levior, so I don't know exactly what was intended.—What would they have said of Demeter if Tennyson had written it? I ought to tell you that the lawyers say that we shall come in for a pretty large slice of my late Father-in-law's leavings. I would give figures if I had any confidence in them (that is in the lawyers). But there is no doubt that we shall be (or should be) very much better off. Indeed I shall be richer than I ever expected or wished to be, neither desiring nor deserving. It will however get us over the material end of present difficulties. My wife sends love to Mrs. M.

I am yours ever
RB

PS.   I'll try and improve that sonnet. It's not worth much now. It was "made in Switzerland"—

493: TO HENRY NEWBOLT

Villa Gentiana
St. Moritz
Engadine
October 31, [1905]

Private

My dear Newbolt

Your apparition in my dreams last night warned me that [I] owed you a letter, at least I remember your enquiring what had transpired about my rumpus at Eton. It has quieted down. Per ambages non te tenebo. Shortly, I had to wait till Warre had got off: it would have been very bad form to have attacked him when in the throes of his terrestrial glorification—by the way some one has made a bust of him, which, though not always recognisable by those familiar with his mortal appearance, is really like him, and will perpetuate him to posterity as a thinker!—then I was obliged to give the local authorities their chance, and they met my complaint with such courtesy and practical consideration that there was nothing left for me to do. It only remains for me to get at the Council or Committee of Managers, which I am hoping to effect. Though I am very glad not to have the bother of a public correspondence, I do not think that I have been at all influenced by that. I am convinced that nothing would be gained by it.

—I don't like Switzerland any better. The snow is now beginning to fall and it is expected always to go on falling until it is about 6 feet deep. The place is as dreary as possible, and the visitors have not yet begun to arrive. Perhaps you know the routine of these places. We have a very comfortable house: but I have not yet found it possible to do anything. The life does not agree with me at all, and I have not yet found out the way to live. I suppose you may have heard that I have definitely left Yattendon. The house is let: and I have stored all my things in the big barn. We look forward to coming home at Easter: but have no house in prospect, and I can't see where or when or how we shall settle down. If you have ever any time to be charitable write me a letter. I should like to know what you are doing and how you are getting on. I send this enclosed in another so that you will get it with only the English postmarks. We spend about a shilling a day on stamps, and are throwing money away in every direction. I hope some good may come of it:—You will see that I am in a very bad humour today. With our kindest remembrances to your wife—

yours ever
Robert Bridges

494: TO LIONEL MUIRHEAD

Villa Gentiana
St. Moritz
Engadine
November 12, [1905]

Dear Lionel

Deeply grateful for your long letter—Interested about the 330 Epigrams. What a lot! I am myself now doing some Hexameters. So many friends who thought that I had made something of them in the Epistolary vein questioned whether they would do equally well in heroic style. The other day the notion of trying to paraphrase Virgil attracted me; so I plunged at the middle of the 6th book of the Aeneid.—I had also another motive. I never quite agreed with all Stone's rulings. I think his *general* rules all right; but I find that working by them one gets a lot of syllables ruled long which are not long: and I am trying to work out rules for exceptions. This will interest you. I have not yet got far, but I find the definite article a great bore, and mean to use its Miltonic elision (optional) before a vowel. Also I cannot do with *and* being always long: so I hope to allow myself to use *ăn'* before a vowel. I have not done this yet. Then I will write *ŏ'thĕ* for *ŏf thĕ* if I choose, and *i th'* or *ithe* for *ĭn thĕ* —and I tell you these things that you may, if you agree, feel no scruple. Then I think the 3rd syllable of *ăppēar-ancēs* is short. There is no a in it, nor any other vowel than the n, and I should write it *ăppēar n cĕs*. This would make *carpenter* to be *cărp'n̄ tĕr* which I argued for with Stone—but his *general* rule is still right because e.g. *vēngŭnçe* has the second syllable long though it is of the same pronunciation. I do not see my way to making a rule yet: but I shall. The fact is that it is possible and easy to hold on these vocalised liquids Ls and Ns as long as one likes; only under certain conditions one does not do so, and I think one of the conditions is when they are the 1st of 2 syllables following a stress as in *cárp n̄ ter* and *appéar n̄ ces*. I do not know how I shall get on with my Virgil: but I will send you a specimen ere long. It is very curious work. Virgil being untranslatable, and the paraphrase consequently a matter of extreme ingenuity. It is astonishing how long a time one can spend over one line as you no doubt discover with your epigrams. It is a wonderful time killer.

November 13, [1905]   There was an old man of St Moritz
Who said "I don't cáre so much fór it's"—
When they said "For it's *what?*"
He replied "It's all rot:
It's only my rhyme to St Moritz".

This extemporized at dinner aided digestion considerably. Elizabeth immediately capped it thus

> There was an old man of Chasellas*
> Who said "I don't féel half as wéll as . . ."
> When they said "Well as *whén?*"
> He replied "sold agen!
> It's only my rhyme to Chasèllas."

I have done about 20 more lines of Virgil today: so I shall soon have some to send you. I am glad that you liked the sonnet. I improved it before I sent it to HEW. I think the main alterations (and only ones) were line 3 "*The dedicated charm of Yattendon*" and line 6 "*Haunted the ivied walls where 'Time ran on*". You can alter them in your copy if you keep it. HEW was pleased.

November 14, 1905—Virgil has been going on well—Today we have had some jolly skating. You talk of frosts—but we have 20 degrees of frost at 9 a.m. I don't know what it goes to in the night. We sit with open windows. The house is warm. The place all looks much better in the snow.

One of my emendations of Stone's prosody is that I allow an open long vowel to be shortened.—When I say I allow it I mean that I find it is shortened. Stone relied a great deal too much on the quality of the vowels. I find that a pure long vowel often disappoints one very much—it does not come up to its character. The action of consonants is much more reliable, and they affect the vowels. We used to be taught Amō amās amăt amamus amātis amant. But no one ever told us that the 3rd amy was short because t had the property of shortening the preceding vowel, and yet that is the simple account of it, e.g. Audĭt and monĕt have long i and long e — — shortened by t.

November 19, [1905] I meant to have written you a better letter but must send this as it is. I hope my prosodial vagaries won't disturb you. Send me 2 or 3 of the epigrams. I have not ventured any thing like cārp ň tĕr yet.

yours ever
RB

*our last residence

495: TO LIONEL MUIRHEAD

POST CARD

St Moritz
December 11, 1905

You will have been expecting to hear from me. The ἐπιγρ came all right. The skating has however been very good and Maro has absorbed every moment of leisure. As my industrious fit may pass off I am using it while it lasts. The success is extraordinary. You shall have a sample soon, but Elizabeth who undertook to copy has neglected it, and I haven't time yet.

RB

We are all right as I hope this will find you.

496: TO LIONEL MUIRHEAD

Post Card

December 23, [1905]

I hope you got my MS. Send me a postcard and you shall have the rest. I have come to the end of it. I decided only to go to lines 751 and then add the 894–899 at end. I don't think anyone would care for the rest. I am now correcting, and see that I must have sent you several unfinish'd lines. I never knew till I worked at it what Maro intended. His passage on the gates of sleep seems plainly to assert not only that the whole was a vision in the cave—but he very well excuses the awful pessimism of his Hell by sending Aeneas out at the ivory gate. IBANT is therefore almost impossible to translate. It means "They found themselves walking". "They seemed to be walking"—This is a difficulty that I can't get over without spoiling the passage. I very much hope that you like it—shall be grateful for any verbal criticism.

RB

Edward has arrived out here. He seems now quite qualified as a traveller.

497: TO LIONEL MUIRHEAD

St. Moritz
December 24, 1905

My dear Lionel

I am very glad that the Virgil pleases you. Your criticism is most valuable and I will do what I can to get rid of some sibilants. I meant to be careful about them but as every plural and genitive ends in S or Z it is difficult to exclude them without messing one's sentences. You must remember that most of them are soft Z which is not really a very disagreeable sound. Have you ever examined Virgils S's? I have paid a good deal of attention to them, and have wondered at his indifference. He really quite often collides the true S between words, like in foribus stabilant. And his double SS is of course a very harsh sound which we have not got. ferro invasisset praedamque ignara putasset. If you read Virgil with the English pronunciation i. e. with the soft C, saying sircum for kirkum. (circum) Then he has I expect many more sibilants than my translation. And if you only counted his true S's, and in my verses counted all the sibilant sounds i. e. S. Z. (as in his) and the Sh of all words ending in tion like affliction (shon) etc. and of course all the xes in both, then there is very little difference. Virgil's average would work out to about 2.7 a line, mine to 2.8. But I will try and get rid of this difference, if I can. The correction amuses me very much, and as I delayed sending my 2nd batch it will be disfigured by corrections which I have made since I wrote it out.

By the way in words like sécyular and salutátion the accent makes the difference. This is my rule. The accent separates the first consonant from the following y.

I have not written about your epigrams. There were some excellent things among them and I especially liked (as a whole) "I hate all the novels". But I do not think that you manage to conquer the difficulty of getting the sort of expression without which the epigram is not of much account. I find that I have to work very hard at vocabularies before I can do anything, and I have long lists of words for which I have never found any use. Now you don't seem to get the words which lie ready to hand. e. g. in the epigram "One deaf man" you begin one line very awkwardly

> "Fust claimd 5 months' rent was due."

why not

> Plaintif appeal'd for a 5 months' rent.

Of course I know how long it takes to get into the way of thinking in quantity. It nearly drove me mad at first, but it is conquered with patience.

Patience by the way is one of those horrid words which forbid my competition with Virgil; it has *two* sibilants, innocent as it looks, and there innocent has another. But Virgil could say innocens (not in no senz) and patientia.

I will send the rest when it is copied out.

With best Xmas wishes

yours ever

RB

Wife also and all of us join in most hearty good wishes to Mrs. Muirhead and all the family.

498: TO A. H. BULLEN

Villa Gentiana

St. Moritz

Engadine

January 15, 1906

Private

My dear Bullen

Thank you for your letter. I am sorry that lawyers have worried you. I have not escaped them. I saw about the Gentleman's Magazine in the Times. I wish you luck—but I am writing to you about the Shakespeare. The flattering estimation of my unwritten essay is very awkward: and I am sure that I should not write anything to justify your expectation. It would be better for my credit with you (which I cherish) that I should remain contented with the supposition that the essay would have been good if I had written it. On the other hand I do not wish to disappoint you—and I am now quite at leisure, so that I feel rather urged by my duty to have a try at it.

But when I wrote my first postcard the motive which *convinced* me that I had better withdraw was—as follows. My notion of my essay was (I think I said something about it in a letter to you) to make a sort of emotional—i. e. not intellectual, analysis of Shakespeare's work, and separate off all that *offended*. Regard this as a chemical reaction. You have an unknown, miscellaneous and extremely elaborate mixture to analyse. You take a simple reagent, the quality of which is known and determinate, you treat the mixture, which you have to analyse, with this reagent, and get a definite precipitate. Then analyse the precipitate.

Now something very definite ought to come of this. The process is simple and (observe) entirely free from the usual blemish of testing a great *intellect* by a smaller one.

I was pleased with the notion, and went some way towards working it out.

But the result was that I very soon came to the conclusion that my essay would not please you. You will of course know that I share the general opinion of S's preeminence—and I have read him all my life and never tired of him—but there is something very strange about him, and my "precipitate" would lead me to say some very strange things, such as you might not care to put into such a book as you are bringing out.

The length of the essay would not allow me to do more than follow the line of examination proposed, and this (setting aside the bad jokes and bawdry) would initially amount to a tabulation and classification of defects or blemishes which all point one way—at least as far as I thought the matter out they seem to do so.

I do not think that you would like it and I don't see my way to doing anything else.

I doubt if one could say anything in the essay to take the bad taste out. Still it is possible that it will not work out so badly as it promises, but I think it would be thoroughly heterodox and unsuitable to your book. —My lucubrations have not at all changed my opinion of S. nor do I think that I should be able to solve the problem which his extraordinary mixture of "brutality" with extreme, even celestial, gentleness offers, but the examination supposing it to be successful would define the brutality (the word is not mine) and that would be unpleasant to most readers. It has always puzzled me very much: and I shall probably for my own satisfaction see what I can make of it.

I think, after reading this you will not wish for my essay.

yours sincerely

Robt Bridges

499: TO LIONEL MUIRHEAD

Park-Hotel Vitznau
Vitznau
den 22 March, 1906

My dear Lionel

Here we are descended from the Engadine. We came into Midsummer weather, and in half an hour were again plunged into mid winter, a westerly gale with snow, which now lies 6 inches deep under a cielo chiuso. We are sending into Lucerne today to get tickets for England, hoping to arrive in London next Wednesday. Chute, Edward's tutor, has left us for Palermo, where his people now are, and Ed has passed his Examination (I suppose he has passed, having done the papers) for entrance into Eton, converting the billiard room here for 2 days into an Examination chamber. He had some 20 papers to do in two days. Chute turned out to be an excellent teacher, and Ed enjoyed his winter term. He proved a very good skater, and could I think have passed his test at St. Moritz, but the ice broke up and we all had the Influenza. I have not recovered from it. Still having a baddish cough, and being unable to walk more than 100 yards without an unaccountable aching of the legs. I hope to get to England alive, and am really feeling a little better, but you know my impatience of maladies. I was glad of your long letter. It is very good Charis going to Dresden. I hope she will enjoy it. There is nothing more delightful than music. My girls have been learning German and Italian out here and have made a fair start at both. I don't think we have wasted the time. I told you I suppose that I had written an Essay on Shakespeare for Bullen's new edition. It interested me very much. I have never been able to read much Shakespearean criticism just because the commentators all neglect what I consider the true explanation of a lot of difficulties, and the purpose of my essay was to explain and advocate this view of mine. I did not know how it would work out: but it made a much stronger case, when it was all put together, than I had foreseen: so that there is some chance of my contribution to Shakespearean literature being more or less important: and it will be amusing to see how the critics take it. I have really no doubt whatever that I am right, but one may of course be deceived: and I am generally over-sanguine about anything that I am actually engaged in. I sent the Essay to HEW and I think he was persuaded; which is hopeful.

This is a very first rate hotel, and, if only the weather were tolerable, we should be well off. As it is I have to stay indoors all day with my cough and bad leg. —We shall spend one night in London, then be at Yattendon for a week, and then go to Boar's Hill for the summer, where you must come and see us, and stroll about Oxford. Monica looks very well. She is said to be quite well: but she has not got back much voice strength. Margaret is pronounced recovered. But we wait for what the London doctors will say. She seems quite well: so that there is some chance of better times. We have not yet found water on our site at Boar's Hill: which is annoying, and may cause us delay: but I think it is impossible that there should not be water there. We have passed the plans of the house, and if we find water shall probably begin to build immediately on our return. Meanwhile we are very fortunate in having found a small house up there in which we can live while we are building. We have been 9 months away, and the children are wild to get back. We think of spending one night at Arnicus. We could not make use of any of your delightful suggestions of stopping places, as we had to bring Edward's examination off. He is going to Byrne's house. Lyttelton gives a good account of it, but I know nothing of him. Chute thought well of him. By the way Chute is going to Eton as Geographical and Mathematical master after the long. It is a new appointment.

Farewell. Please post enclosed.

yours ever

RB

500: TO A. H. BULLEN

Boar's Hill
nr Oxford
April 7th, 1906

My dear Bullen

The extension of time should be valuable, and I hope to make use of it. Perhaps you may find time to read the essay yourself. I should welcome any suggestions from you.

About the ecclesiastical paper—Can it be this? Some years ago my old friend Dr Sanday—Regius professor of divinity at Oxford—started a new theological Quarterly, and flattered me by asking me to write him something for his first number. I wrote a paper on Church Hymns (music), and I believe that the 'article' was thought buoyant: when afterwards reprinted alone it sold out freely: and is still sometimes enquired for.

Blackwell tells me that he has his own publisher's copy which he would lend you if you wish to read it.—I am houseless and all my books stored. We shall be here all the summer I expect.

The object of my paper was to advertise the Yattendon Hymnal. Thereby hangs a very long tale. I believe that the only hope for national taste in music is to banish bosh from Church and school—I have also written to this effect in the Monthly Review.

If you care to read the Hymn paper, no doubt Blackwell will send you his copy. Then if you should think it worthy of your press I should be glad enough that it should have a third airing. (I might wish to change a word or two). But I am afraid you would not think much of it as a piece of prose, for it must be somewhat deficient in ornament.

yours sincerely
Robt Bridges

501: TO HENRY NEWBOLT

Boar's Hill
Oxford
April 25, [1906]

My dear Newbolt

Margaret tells me that you will be in town today. I enclose you a letter from my fighting nephew Tom. He is a major in Royal Artillery. I have written to him to tell him I have written to you. You will see that he is leaving town tomorrow night.

He is worth knowing, and I should think his friends must be interesting and worthy. If you can't do anything for them introduce Miss B to someone who has leisure. I have told Tom to call on you if he has time. He may come before you get this letter.

yours ever
R. Bridges

We shall hope to see you this summer. We are setting about building.

502: TO A. H. BULLEN

Boar's Hill
May 12, 1906

My dear Bullen

I send Essay by this Post. I shall like to hear that it duly arrives, and if you read it do not forget that I am really somewhat anxious to know how you like it and whether it will suit your book.

It has given me almost as much pleasure as trouble.

yours sincerely
Robt Bridges

There is by the way a timorously friendly allusion to you in the opening which could be omitted if you preferred.
P.S.
Perhaps I had better be more explicit. I do not think that I should say anything in my Essay which I might not have 'said' in conversation any time these 30 years, but it is one thing to say casually that one does not think (e.g.) Macbeth's character a psychological study, and another to trace its inconsistencies to an indifference of S to certain moral distinctions. This is the sort of thing that I expect would come about.

503: TO LIONEL MUIRHEAD

Boar's Hill
May 26, 1906

My dear Lionel

I have been longing to hear how you were getting on, but too unsettled to write a letter, which is very unsettled. Yesterday I was in London, visiting a cousin who, too old to visit me, was up there for a few days. Today Monica and Margaret have gone to see Edward at Eton in the pouring rain, added to which inconvenience they missed their train, and the necessary telegrams etc. were enough to make one wish that one lived on a desert island. I have not got rid of my sciatica, but am generally better. But this new houselet that we are in proves abominable, and so far from its being, as we hoped, a possible abiding place for us till our own is built, it would be intolerable in any weather but the most propitious. The wretched wintry days have so thoroughly exposed its insufficiencies that we shall clear out of it as soon as we can. This makes our plans more uncertain than ever. We are thinking of making up a party for the North of France in August and September. This is only in the dream-stage.

I have been a good deal down in Oxford. What they call Eights-week was dreadful. I never saw such crowds of useless-looking people anywhere. They can't have enjoyed themselves much, for the sun scarcely shone at all, and a bitter wind blew all through their festival.—There was much talk of "bumps"— which seemed an insufficient compensation. I have attended all the Organ-recitals at New. They are every Tuesday at 4. pm. You would find me in the Quad there at 3.50 next Tuesday and the Tuesday after.

Please send me my Virgil MS some day. I altered it so much that I do not like the old version to exist. If I can't alter the MS I will rewrite it for you.

I got rid of my Shakespeare essay before we left our last abode. I don't know what Bullen thinks of it: and hardly what I think of it myself, except that it is a careful piece of prose, and interesting reading.

I long to be doing something but have no energy to get to work.—Please let us know how you are.

your affectionate
RB

504: TO LIONEL MUIRHEAD

Boar's Hill
May 29, 1906

My dear Lionel

I have corrected the MS and return it. Many thanks. I do not know whether I shall print it yet and therefore wished the copy to be correct.

I am sorry that you have had so much trouble with your eye, and am afraid that it may have been set going by something in your visit here. Still I rejoice that it is better.

I am somewhat better of my sciatica, and have lost my cough. I *hope* to meet you at Eton on the 6th. I am not certain.

yours ever

RB

505: TO A. H. BULLEN

Boar's Hill

June 7, [1906]

My dear Bullen

I saw your Gentlemen's Magazine the other day—and therein an advertisement of the Shakespeare. Wherefore I guessed that you won't be printing volume X yet—

When I get proofs I shall want to add a footnote of some 6 lines about midway in Essay. So I write to say that if MS has not gone to press it will probably save trouble (and put off expence) in shifting type, if you would send it me again—when I will write the note in its proper place so as not to give trouble—

I do not suppose that I shall make any other alteration (that involves derangement) on the proofs so that it is worth while to have none at all.

yours truly

R. Bridges

506: TO LIONEL MUIRHEAD

Boar's Hill

June 22, 1906

My dear Lionel

I hope that by this time you are really feeling more comfortable. We were very sorry to think how much pain and trouble you had to go through, but I was immensely relieved to hear from your wife's letter that it was really over and that you were none the worse for the operation.

You must have been spared a good deal of awful anticipation, by being compelled to capitulate unexpectedly: and I hope that you discovered that the pain was most in apprehension.

As I guess you will not be allowed to read, I won't write much today. If you need a unique and very entertaining book order "The dissociation of a personality" by Morton Prince. It amused me so much that I have written a review of it for a London Weekly if I can get one to take it. I have been telegraphing this morning to an Editor who didn't answer my postal enquiry.

I am no better of my leg. I sometimes wish that I could get it cut off, but then probably the other would go bad, and when it does not actually ache it works well enough for its years.

I find that if ever I complain of this or that to a Doctor, in hope of getting a suggestion, he treats me as an imposter or hypochondriac, which I believe myself to be, but I can't believe that anyone of my age has such a pain in his leg.

With our kindest regards to Mrs. Lionel.

yours affectionately

RB

Please let us have an occasional bulletin.

There is an account of my dowser in Country Life correspondence—just come.

507: TO LIONEL MUIRHEAD

Boar's Hill

Sunday

June 24, 1906

My dear Lionel

It was very satisfactory to see your hand-writing again: a full assurance of your recovery—and I am glad that the business gave so little trouble.

I wonder if you had your share of our mighty thunder-storm last night—it kept us awake nearly an hour, with its incessant hurlyburly just over our heads.

We had had a pleasant dinner with Evans—to meet Richmond who is going to paint his portrait; and was as amusing as ever. Evans told me that he had lately been in Spain where he had seen cave *paintings* in 3 colours, supposed to be about 100,000 years old. At any rate in what is considered the prehistoric geological period. I am hoping to learn some details from him about his new language, which seems to imply an alphabet some hundreds of years earlier than anything yet discovered. I had heard nothing about it.

I expect to go up to town for a few days next week, and to Eton for a day the week after. But I do not get better of my leg; it is a most annoying hindrance to activity.

With congratulations from us all

yours affectionately

RB

508: TO LIONEL MUIRHEAD

Boar's Hill

September 5th, 1906

My dear Lionel

I told applicant whose applications are enclosed, that I didn't know whether you desired to be annotated, and that therefore I left the matter in your hands.—It seems to me that he will have considerable trouble with the Y. H.

Edward does not know what day he has to return to Eton, nor what hour is usual. He says that there is a different day stated in the school list from what was on the Almanack. I think Elizabeth has written to Charis for Anthony's advice.

I wonder how you have got through the dog days.—We are now beginning to worry about our next move. On September 29 we migrate to Whitebarn, an unfurnished house, and have to get all our furniture up from Yattendon.

We laid the first brick of the house on August 31st. Everything, especially the road, is in a dreadful mess with brick cartage.

I have been amusing myself with Virgil.

The President of Magdalen was highly gratified by your attentions when he was at Haseley.

yours ever
RB

509: TO A. H. BULLEN

October 10, 1906

My dear Bullen

I have received proof of my Essay, and will return corrections (if I find anything to correct) in a day or two.

Meanwhile I should be very glad to hear from you (1) whether you are satisfied with my contribution and (2) whether there is anything in it which you would desire to be altered.

There is in the first section a reference to yourself—personal—and at the end a "moral". I should really be very curious to know what your impression of the whole was when you read it—as I assume you now have since it is in print.

yours sincerely
Robt Bridges

510: TO A. C. BENSON

Boar's Hill
Oxford
October 17, 1906

My dear Benson

You will be surprised by a letter from me, but since you left Eton I have always been expecting to meet you, and in my two years wanderings seem to have met everyone else. I left Yattendon finally last year, and have just got housed here, 5 miles from Oxford, and half a mile from the site of a new house that I am building. My small boy who was to have been your pupil is now in his 2nd term at Eton, and my renewed relations with the school always remind me of you—and last night as, among the duties of changing my home I was clearing out 20 years accumulation of papers, I came on an old letter of yours, which revived our short acquaintance very warmly. This has set me writing. I am hoping that you may be

persuaded to pay Oxford and us a visit this term. Is it possible? and if so when?—
I get down to the University in 25 minutes on a cycle, and it takes about 45 to
return up the hill. If you brought your cycle, supposing that you still ride one,
you might not find us inconveniently out of the way up here. These are the
material conditions, which sometimes require a waterproof, and I should add
that you would not like to come unless you are accustomed to open windows.
The house is absolutely quiet and homely: and the air fresh. It would be very
delightful to us if you should come.

yours sincerely
Robert Bridges

511: TO A. C. BENSON

Boar's Hill
nr Oxford
October 21, [1906]

My dear Benson

I am very sorry that there is no chance of your paying us a visit this term. I had
no kind of right to expect that you would: but it is a disappointment; and it was
very kind of you to attempt to mitigate it by saying so many magnificently
gracious things. Many thanks for them. Be assured that they were truly appreciated, and plants do really need watering in some seasons.

What you say about your getting to Oxford for the inside of a day might result
in a very pleasant day, and if you settled your visit a few days beforehand, I could
make arrangements that your time should not be wasted. But it would not be
likely that we should get much continuous talk—and I think that there are
several subjects which it might be fruitful for us to discuss: and I really hope that
when you have finished with Victoria you will have leisure for the problematical—when I wrote problematical I thought it was quite the right word, and now I
can't finish the sentence. It does not want finishing.

Since you launched forth into criticism I have been a good deal out of England: but I have seen reviews of your books which have always interested me
very much and I am now getting the books to read—

My boy is not at Macnaughtons'. His name was down for his house, but at the
last moment there was a 'difficulty' which ended in the Head Master making me
a vacancy at Byrne's. I do not really know either MacN or B. The boy seems
contented. My wife lunched with Mrs. Cornish the other day, who seemed to be
in unusually good form.

If you think of coming for a day to Oxford you may wish to make appointments yourself, or if you tell me whom you wish to meet I will try and drive them
together for you, but I should have a day or two's notice.

yours sincerely
Robt Bridges

Please don't address me as Mr B.

512: TO LIONEL MUIRHEAD

Whitebarn
Boar's Hill
November 10, 1906

My deal Lionel

I have been all the morning planting in our herbaceous border, and have filled about ⅑ of it, 10 feet wide. The sun was bright and I enjoyed myself immensely, though the wind being bitter, and one E. gave us a sample of what the most severe conditions will be in our new house.—I am writing to say that we can take any odds and ends which your gardener would have "no use of" as they say in Berkshire—a hamper or old box stuffed full of roots and committed to the G W R will be brought up by our carrier and duly planted out. But I should be sorry if you were to send anything either tender or valuable. Pray reserve such kindnesses for a more suitable occasion. We only want hardy things to plant on our waste and exposed site. We shall not be able to get any shelter for some time. The house will provide a good deal, and the Southward terraces below it, but though the house is going on well, we shall not be free to work the ground about it till late in the Spring. The man whom we took on as gardener turns out to be a very exceptionally practical and intelligent fellow; he is doing very well for us. We are now scheming our gardener's cottage—

Enough about us. I was in town the other day and saw HEW, indeed slept at his house. He did not seem very fit, and Mrs W was in bed with a bad cold. He says that he persuades her to stay in bed when she has a cold.—He can't come and see us because of our open windows. He is to sit and poison himself in London all the winter, and recruit in Scotland in the summer.—I don't believe that they really much like the Scotch house, for they get no company, and it seems to me that he was better off before he took it. It all made me rather melancholy on his behalf.—If you see Country Life you will not miss the photograph of the nebula in Andromeda. It is wonderful. It looks a picture made-up to illustrate La Place's theory. I am sorry that I wrote Laplace wrong.

Evelyn Wood's life—from Midshipman to Field Marshal is exceptionally good. I do not know that I have anything else to recommend except a new book on handwriting by Johnson of which I will send you a copy.

With kindest regards to your wife

yours ever
RB

513: TO A. H. BULLEN

November 14, 1906

My dear Bullen

I am glad that you are getting on, and hope that you will soon be well. I did not know what influenza was till this year, when after a moderate attack of it in Switzerland I was unable to walk for 4 or 5 months.

I do not like the quotation from Horace, as title. I think a motto is out of place, and this one not quite apposite: at least I understand it as applying to the *shiftiness* of popular favour, which is not exactly to the point.

Influence of the Audience is just right, but the accidental awkwardness of the verbal terminations requires one of the words to be changed—and as it [is] better not to change audience, we need a substitute for Influence. I do not like *Ear* because it does not cover enough ground, and is therefore not descriptive of the matter of the Essay.

I should be satisfied with *"The Pleasure of the Audience"*. That seems to me almost as good as Influence of the Audience. Will that suit you?

Did I ever send you a copy of my *Demeter*? If you havn't read it I will send you one. I fancy that you might like it better than Achilles which I was flattered to hear that you had been looking at again. I had a better "influence of the audience" than W. S.

yours sincerely

RB

Silly things words are [RB's note]

P.S.
My wife, who is better than I am at this sort of thing, suggests

    (1) *"Shakespeare and his audience"*
    (2) *"The pleasure of the million"*
         taken from his words "it pleased not the million"
    (3) *"The influence of the million"*

I have no objection to any of these. So now you have 4 to choose from. She also likes my other suggestion

    (5) *The will of the audience*

and it strikes me that his own words "My project . . . was to please" (Temp epilogue) might give a title.

    (6) *The project to please.*

Now you have 6

514: TO HENRY NEWBOLT

Whitebarn
Boar's Hill
November 21, [1906]

My dear Newbolt
The worst thing about you is that you are too friendly and well-disposed a critic towards me. Still I was gratified.—Your book came from the Times the day

after you left, so that we have now 2 copies—I shall read it at once. Elizabeth is taking one copy in the train with her today on an expedition to Eton—whither, if the rain does not descend violently before we start, we are bound. Thank you for saying kind things about the children. I might have done as well by you, but now it would seem constrained, and really I saw as little of Celia as you did of Margaret. We all enjoyed your visit immensely, and wished that you could have stayed longer. Is it impossible that you should come and live up here? You could have this house when we leave it next year, and the landlord would be glad to improve it where it needs improvement. It has a great many advantages and the Macans wept to leave it. Monica wishes me to thank your wife and Celia for their kind letters.—Now I am off to Oxford.

yours ever
RB

515: TO A. H. BULLEN

Whitebarn
Boar's Hill
Oxford
November 21, 1906

My dear Bullen

I really hope that you are feeling better, and regaining your strength.

There was a part of your letter to which I did not reply.

You said that you hoped I would *'expand'* my Essay so that you might publish it separately.

I expect that, when your volume is published, critics will pay very little attention to my contribution. There are only one or two men who are likely to tackle it.—But if it should arouse any discussion, the different things that were said about it might provide the skeleton of an interesting book. At least it seems to me now that if I could get a lot of definitely expressed opinions on the questions that I have raised, the ground that they would cover would give a fine opportunity.

If you think there is anything in this, perhaps you will promote the scheme by filing the "reviews" as they appear. Also if you could inveigle *Bernard Shaw* and *Chesterton* to commit themselves, the tilting ground would be expanded. If you see your way to helping in this, the more the better. *Swinburne,* and *Sidney Lee,* and *Dowson,* and A. C. Benson.

What a vision of glorious critics!! I fear however that it is too good to be true.

yours sincerely
Robert Bridges

Bradley is sure to answer in the Times, if that journal has not by that time had to drop literature—

516: TO HENRY NEWBOLT

Whitebarn
Boar's Hill
Oxford
November 23, [1906]

My dear Newbolt

I have this moment finished your book—and must write at once to tell you how delighted I have been. It is first rate; I congratulate you. I was intensely interested—and that is the only fault that I find with it—for I did not want to read anything.—I will write about it more intelligently when I have the opportunity. At present I am struck most by your modesty, for in your letter you did not seem at all confident that I should like the book.

No more now—I am going out. Was at Eton with Elizabeth yesterday and got very tired.

I think the public will like it (although it is far too good for them) if they can be got to read it, and it will do infinite good

yours ever
RB

517: TO A. C. BENSON

Boar's Hill
nr Oxford
December 8, 1906

My dear Benson

I have read the two pamphlets which you gave me with great interest. I think that your verdict on the dulness of boys' imagination is rather too general. No doubt it is your genuine experience, but I should add it to the evidence against our scholastic methods: and what is not due to that, but brought from home, I should think may be partly traceable to the education of the boys' parents.

Details of possible practical reform are difficult: but it seems to me that two things might be unhesitatingly agreed upon, and enforced at once.

First, that no boy should begin Greek before he was about 16 years old—Secondly—the wretched *scholarship examinations*, which now set all the rival private schools at their cramming, should be arranged so as to baffle unwholesome preparation.—I have excluded Greek. Such modern languages as were examined in, should be tested in viva voce examination, by natives, and not by those who cannot (as they often cannot) talk with certainty and fluency and without "accent".—Grammatical papers for boys under 14 should be confined to translation into the foreign language (Latin or French or German), and to the analysis or explanation of the sentences actually occurring in the 'seen' and 'unseen' passages set for translation into English.

Besides these precautions there should be good miscellaneous papers, involving original application of elementary mathematical and scientific methods, in order to bring out ingenuity and practical intelligence: and also, (if this were not enough) optional papers which might exhibit any special aptitude whether—e.g. for music or drawing or mechanics.

It seems to me absolutely inhuman to set boys of 10 to 12 to learn the grammar of two dead languages, which their teachers cannot themselves speak or even pronounce. Boys of 10 can learn any language rapidly and almost without effort by ear. This faculty is *entirely neglected:* they are taught languages by those who do not speak them, in a method which is both unnatural and difficult. I believe that nothing more foolish could well be invented.

yours sincerely
Robert Bridges

518: TO LIONEL MUIRHEAD

[Boar's Hill]
December 22, 1906

My dear Lionel

Many thanks for the shrubs and things which duly arrived and were soon in their places. I should have written to thank you for them before. Now I send you all our Xmas good wishes. You will be rejoicing in Anthony's society. I hope that he came home in good health. Ed seems all right, but he says that the weather was very bad at Eton.

The roof timbers are nearly all on the house, and the gables built up, and faced with stone so it seems possible that the house may be done as soon as we hoped. The planting has I think been a success—I am dreadfully bored with it all—and Xmas coming on the top of it is depressing. The carol singers from all the neighbouring villages, and the mummers, and the hand bell ringers visit us every evening. They began after the 2nd Sunday in Advent. We are trying to get up some young hockey for the children. House dealers also annoy me. I am in a very bad temper with everybody. Having no astronomical book to distract me I read Greek syntax. When I am in a better mood I will try and write you a letter— All our good wishes to Mrs Muirhead and Anthony.

your affectionate
RB

519: TO G. E. P. ARKWRIGHT

Whitebarn
Boar's Hill
Oxford
January 2, 1907

My dear Arkwright

First let me send you the compliments of the season with our best wishes to you and to your sister for this new year.

Then to the purpose of my letter. I have undertaken to edit Campion's verse for the University Press. They are bringing out a series of Tudor reprints.

I naturally want to know whether your investigations of Campion led to anything more than you have given to the public. It struck me that you might have come upon something later—and be able perhaps to give me a hint as to probable fields of enquiry. Unfortunately all my books are in packing cases and I cannot at present refer to your edition of the Ayres—and I have quite forgotten what you said about him.

Is there any chance of being able to get at a MS or portrait?

I shall be much obliged to you if you would write and communicate any useful information.

We are getting on with our new home, and I think it is probable that we shall be able to move our furniture into it in June, even though it may not be quite ready for domestic habitation—

We have except for colds been fairly well so far—our present house is not lovely, but the situation is pleasant. And now we have a pony and chaise in which my wife can get to Oxford whenever she wishes.

I hope that you have been well. I heard of you last from Wooldridge when I slept one night at his house—Mrs W was in bed with influenza or some thing. He did not seem very fit. I am afraid that his house in Scotland will prevent his leaving London.

You will I hope come and see us as soon as we are settled. This house is not impossible for a cyclist in better weather.

yours sincerely
R Bridges

I shall have of course no difficulty in getting to see your account of Campion— But I can't refer to it today—

520: TO HENRY NEWBOLT

Whitebarn
Boar's Hill
Oxford
January 25, 1907

My dear Newbolt

You owe this letter to my being laid by to mend after an accident of the purely gravitational kind, in which one of my ankles got sprained: but it is a muscular neuralgia of the *other* leg, produced I supposed by some strain or contusion, which fetters me to the inkpot.—You will have been expecting me to keep my promise of writing to you about your book. The difficulty of formulating all that I wished to say fortified my indolence.—Now today I feel quite incapable. The book seemed to me altogether successful and beautiful. After I had read it I enjoyed reading it aloud to the family, who all enjoyed it. I admired the skill by which you rendered the dream-part of the story the more real. This was essential and well mastered. There may have been more elaboration of detail between the parts than I observed—or perhaps more elaboration would have spoiled the effect. It struck me that the perfect form would have contained a correspondence between the drampers of the two parts. I did not look for it* at the time: and cannot now find the book. I suppose that the power implied is mesmeric. Only one exp[ression] struck me as out of date, somewhere the Bishop I think says that the heretic should be passed over from the physician to the surgeon. The antithesis between drugs and knives is of course universal, but that between the classified professions is surely not known till early 16th century.

I have had an amusing correspondence with Mr Scott of the Board of Education about an anthology that you wot of. The net result was 6£6s. He objected to my title "The Fair brass" on the score of *Brass* being ambiguous and suggesting quite irrelevant ideas. I replied that I did not know of any definite object that was called a *brass* except that which I intended. I knew well of coppers of two kinds and of irons of various kinds and of tins also, but not of golds or of silvers, nor of brasses other than my sort. He answered after some further mystification on my part, that there were *two* somewhat slangy uses of the word, which might denote impudence or money: and he made no charge or deduction from my fee for this information, out of a proper consideration, no doubt for the salary that he draws from His Majesty's Government. He seemed an agreeable fellow: but I doubt whether he'll make much of an anthology. It is possible I find to say that he has got "The brass" in 3 senses.—Holidays passed very quickly. Ed went back yesterday.—Clarendon Press has invited me to edit Campion. I have been reading Bullen's Edition of his Latin poems.—I never was so bored in my life.

yours ever

RB

*The correspondence

521: TO LOGAN PEARSALL SMITH

Boar's Hill
January 28, [1907?]

My dear Pearsall

I looked through Shakespeare's sonnets last night and came to the opinion that if I were to select eleven, five of those eleven would be sonnets that are not in the Golden Treasury.—Considered as perfect poems I am not nearly as enthusiastic about S's sonnets as I once was.—Perhaps you will like to see my list.
(l) CXXIX The expense of spirit.

(About this sonnet. I think it the most powerful one that S wrote: and therefore I should not like to exclude it from any book of English poetry on account of its lack of beauty. Except for the commanding diction of the first line, it does not appear to me to have any purely poetic beauty, and this might exclude it from your selection)

(2) XC Then hate me when thou wilt.

(This sonnet again is not distinguished by any special beauty of diction: but it seems almost of the same value, and direct expression as the last. It is of the most convincing sincerity of passion.)

(3) XXXI. Thy bosom is endeared.

(I have long thought this the most beautiful in meaning of all the sonnets— and it is through its Platonism allied to the non-typical sonnets whereas S's usually are supposed to stand apart)

Next come four that Palgrave and Tennyson took

(4) XXX. When to the sessions. GT.

(5) LXXI. No longer mourn. GT.

(6) LXXIII. That time of year. GT.

(7) XCVII. How like a winter. GT.

Then I have

(8) XCVIII From you have I been absent.

(9) CII. My love is strengthened.

(The 2nd and 3rd quatrains I think of the greatest beauty, and the whole sonnet convincing.)

Then two more which are in the Golden Treasury

(10) Let me not to the marriage. CXVI GT.

(11) Poor soul. CXLVI GT.

(This last sonnet being the only "religious" poem that S wrote has as much claim to quotation as that other exceptional one "The expense of spirit." It also lacks beauty, but the couplet at the end is of extraordinary value in S's mouth)

I was somewhat disappointed with this result. The sonnets are excellent poetic reading, but they very seldom satisfy one throughout, and it is perhaps for that reason that I have put among those which I select some which in their general strength argument and intention are complete, although these are deficient in the poetic beauty for which some more imperfect sonnets are conspicuous.

I suppose that your choice would depend on the purpose of your anthology. I think that (1) If you wish to make a book which shall contain the poems which poets would like to have handy, then some such selection as mine would be right. But if (2) you wish to have only specimens of the highest poetry, in which the diction shall be as high as the subject will carry, then the question will arise whether it will not be necessary to take some parts only of some of the sonnets.

Other of the better sonnets are to my thinking

> XII When I do count the clock.
> XXIX When in disgrace.   G.T.
> XXXII. If thou survive.
> LII So am I as the rich.
> * LX Like as the waves.   GT
> LXVI Tired with all these.   GT
> LXXV So are you to my thoughts.
> LXXXVII Farewell thou art too dear.   GT

CIV To me fair friend.   GT
* CVI When in the chronicle.   XXXXX. GT
CVII Not mine own fears.
CX Alas, 'tis true.

I daresay that if we were to talk over this matter I should be disposed to revise my judgement.—I feel in such matters as if I were a little stale. Of course there is some advantage in this, because I still like some things as much as ever, and it is probable that the things which outlast are the best. On the other hand this sort of criticism would not make a book for the young, and they are the readers of poetry.

yours sincerely

RB

*I do not think these should be omitted, though LX is marred by obscurities.

522: TO RICKMAN GODLEE

Whitebarn
Boar's Hill
Oxford
February 3, 1907

My dear Godlee

I was delighted on impatiently tearing open an unpromising parcel to discover your illustrated lecture. It groups so many associations. I remember the blessed vision of you and Mrs. Godlee in the Bodleian, when you were searching into the history of the texts. Then there are the ground plans and elevations of my father-in-law's unique building: and others by my brother-in-law, and rural views of extinct London, and portraits of the old fashioned notables of my youth, and the millionaires of today, and then a bit of my poem on "the splendid ship" quoted and most ingeniously worked in to your topic, and the proposal for a seal: on the motto of which I congratulate you. It reminds me that the authorities of St. George's Hospital once asked me to give them a motto for their seal, and when I gave it them, they would not use it. They were bound to use an intaglio of St. George killing the dragon: and I explained to them that that forbade a classical motto, because the serpent and his kin were sacred to Aschilepius: wherefore they must have a Christian motto, and I suggested Novissima inimica destinetur Mors. I thought it happy but they didn't. May you have better luck with yours. Your humour is excellent. It is an odd coincidence that for the last two days I have been designing a ship, and a cross between a seaserpent and a dolphin. With what purpose? To illustrate the knight's tour on a chess board!! As those curling monsters in a map of the skies figure the constellations. But I have been laid up with a sprained ankle, and various contusions from a fall in our new house, which while it demonstrated me to be an ass, did some credit to my future, for that resisted the effects of gravitation better than might have been expected. The said house is roofed in and most of the rooms are floored.—I can't say what the severe frost may not have done to our plantings. We are well and hope you both are also. The weather has been lovely but our open windows deter visitors, and though I can now hobble about I shall not profit by any chances of skating.

The main drawback of your subject is of course the difficulty of getting outsiders to differentiate the conflicting interests and ideals that have competed for the dignity and service of education in London. You can hardly imagine how confused my ideas are on this matter. It has been fruitlessly explained to me from time to time. I shall now study your lecture with hope of enduring enlightenment.

With our kindest regards

yours truly
Robert Bridges

523: TO LIONEL MUIRHEAD

Whitebarn
Boar's Hill
Oxford
February 12, 1907

My dear Lionel

It was raining and blowing when your letter came so that I expected your telegram. If tomorrow is propitious come then. You will find all things ready any fine day that disposes you to the excursion. I wish you could have been up here yesterday and seen the Chilterns from our new house. It is a joy to us to fix our eyes on the spot where Haseley lies, though naturally we cannot see it, and have not yet brought a glass to bear on it. Monica begs me to say that the bed is always aired. —I am glad to hear better news of your Aunt, though I suppose that life is not very desirable for her any longer.

If you come, take a cab at the station, if no one is there to meet you. We cannot always get down. On Sunday we drove the ponycart to New College at 8.20 pm and heard the Papae Marcelli Mass most beautifully sung—We did not know of its coming on till just before.

yours ever
RB

524: TO LIONEL MUIRHEAD

Boar's Hill
Oxford
February 19, 1907

My dear Lionel

We enjoyed your visit very much—and I was greatly cheered, and sorry when you left. I apologise for not bidding you Farewell properly.—I walked too far for my ankle on Sunday and have been resting since and trying to get on with the

Ode. I am sure that everyone will wish it to rhyme, so I am worrying myself with these useless appendages—which are terrible obstacles in the way of one's saying exactly just what one wants to say. Today the South wind is raging up here, and the windows are so constructed as to give a great variety of notes according to the force of the blast. One of them is whistling like a blackbird. Hope all is well with you. We have just heard that some of our new house windows have arrived—and will I expect be put in tomorrow. All send their salutations.

yours ever
RB

525: TO HENRY BRADLEY

Whitebarn
Boar's Hill
Oxford
February 22, 1907

My dear Bradley

I am very sorry to hear that you are laid up with the Influenza. I hope it will soon pass off. It is in any case better than "the spotted Fever" from what I hear of it.

I am sorry that you troubled to write me a letter, and I am very sorry that I can't come and see you. I never had the Flu but once, and that was this time last year in Switzerland—and it retreated to my right fore leg, whence I did not drive it for 4 or 5 months.

If you are disposed to read gossip I will tell you that the Pageant people asked me to write all the Charles I scenes for their show. When I had thought about it for a few days I declined, because I found out that I didn't at all understand Charles. It is very odd how needful it is to have one's attention drawn to any matter before one really thinks about it. Lucubrating over this made me wish to read all the private memoirs and letters of the time, and I should have been at the Bodleian now if it had not been for my ankle. However, next thing was that they asked me to write an *ode* for them, generally about Oxford and the Pageant. This I accepted for it is a magnificent subject, though I don't think I have made much of it. I have written the ode this week, and should like to show it you, and get the advantage of your criticism. When you are well enough I will send it to you. Next they asked me to write them the introductory scene of the pageant: which I have begged them to find someone else to do. —Don't you think that I ought to feel very much flatter'd?— No doubt it is easily explained: they have entered on this thing without sufficient preparation, and cannot now find any-one to write their dialogues for them.

I hope you rest yourself completely and do not attempt to do any work. I shall be anxious to hear of you, how you are getting on. Do let Mrs Bradley send me a Post card. When I hear I will write again.

yours ever
R Bridges

526: TO HENRY BRADLEY

Whitebarn
Boar's Hill
Oxford
March 12, 1907

My dear Bradley

We were glad to hear of you, and that you are better. My boy got influenza badly at school, and they thought there that it was measles, of which there was some in the house. I went down and fetched him away here, and he is all right, except that there is a chance of his having got infected with measles through his attendants, so that we are not altogether out of the wood. And this accounts for my not having written. By the way (No: this is really what set me writing tonight) my boy had dreadful headach in convalescence. It would come on early in the morning, and we found that it yielded immediately to a small dose of phenacetine. I believe that it is a *cardiac depressant,* so that it might not suit you, but if a doctor is attending you it might be worth while to try it. It is commonly given with caffeine.

We have always found it very useful for various algias.

I have written my Ode for the Pageant players, and am writing the First Scene of the Pageant which I think should be interesting. I wish I could show them to you.

My mother in law is coming to stay with us, which is a great event for everybody concerned.

The house is going on well. Let me know when you return. I am just beginning to walk and shall I hope be soon able to cycle.

With kindest remembrances to your wife, and all our good wishes for your speedy recovery.

yours very sincerely
R Bridges

527: TO LIONEL MUIRHEAD

Whitebarn
Boar's Hill
Oxford
April 15, 1907

My dear Lionel

I hope all has gone on well with you. I have not written since you told me of the death of your Aunt—and I did not see any occasion to trouble you with a letter when you must have had so much to attend to. You knew all my sentiments—and though I could not without quite an affectionate regret think of the dear old lady whom I had known for so many years as being now no more, the regret and sorrow were merged in the general ἀνάγκη , and I could not have wished her more of that useless trouble of life, which I should wish myself to be spared.

I find that Monica has not yet written to your wife. You must both take this as an index of the superabundant worry and fuss which has daily occupied her,— and we have had some extra domestic complication, which I might tell you of if you were here, but which are not fit matter for recapitulation.

I am sending you a copy of the ode which I wrote for the Oxford Pageant programme. I also wrote them a short scene which I think will come first or second on the programme.

The ode must serve me for a better. I hope you will like some of it. I was sorry that I could not make more of so fine an opportunity.

Please return me the copy some day.

With our kindest remembrances and a promise that my wife is writing and will write to yours "in the course of ages" as the children say.

your affectionate

RB

528: TO MRS. HUMPHRY WARD

Whitebarn
Boar's Hill
Oxford
April 16, 1907

Dear Mrs Ward

If this matter is merely an ancient boredom do not trouble yourself about it.

Cornish of Eton came in casually to tea the other day and asked me about your uncle's tree. —What I replied resulted in his stating in the Morning Post on my authority that it could not be identified. —That is not my opinion, at least I should not have published such a statement, and his doing so induced me to look into the matter for myself. Having lived up here for many months one is able to make very decided negative arguments and these really exclude decisively the false claimants, and point to a very strongly probable conclusion.

I have heard what Mr Claridge Druce* (the botanist) has to say, and he appears to allege the authority of Dr Jackwell. Arthur Evans tells me that he has it from you that you questioned the poet on the subject, and that he was not very clear on the identification of the spot.

It is necessary for me to write something on the matter: in order to clear myself from misrepresentation, and I think I can make out a very strong case. What I write to you about is to ask you whether you care to make any statement to me. I should of course be very sorry not to have the advantage of anything which your uncle may have said. Still if you had rather say nothing do not be beguiled by compassion.

I think that if I knew what Mat Arnold really said himself I should be able to be irrefutable. I dare say you know that we are building a house up here on the very beloved spot.

Hoping you are well

yours sincerely
Robert Bridges

*Druce's contention is ridiculous [RB's note]

I have sought to honour Mat. A. in my ode for the Oxford pageant. Evans agrees with me.

529: TO MRS. HUMPHRY WARD

[Boar's Hill]
April 26, 1907

Dear Mrs Ward

Thank you for writing me so full a letter on the tree. Those two elegies will, I think, be always chief favourites, and I love them. It was only an accident that set me on the prosaic enquiry into facts, but when I wrote to you I was held by the idea that since there is an actual definite walk—fulfilling the literal requirements of the poem—to a definite spot, whence the picture of the "youthful Thames" etc can be seen, it was a pity that the poem should be attached to another walk, to another place, neither of which corresponded.—Now I incline to think that it is better that the mystification should be complete. The fault of the poem is the ethical importance of the tree: and if the tree is imaginary, the fault is in a manner dissipated: for a purely poetic intangible object may better bear the burden. Who can say then what it means? And a mystery will satisfy a good many minds.

Though I should wish to keep your letter, I will destroy it if you would rather not have your pronouncement registered. But perhaps, if you agree with the above remarks, you might wish your witness to remain.

How could I, if you can not, suggest the personality of the *wisest one?* He must, I suppose, be an Englishman; and your uncle's intimate appreciations are concerned. I never knew them. Personally,—but there are our natural differences.—I dislike the man's attitude, and do not heartily sympathise with the poet. But I do not quarrel.

I was delighted by your handwriting, remembering the days when your right arm was unnerved. Your script now is without trace of impairment.

"Fenwick's Career" was read by all the family: and I questioned whether I ought not to write and thank you, or rather I knew that I ought to do so, but argued the duty off until it wasted. Time has not helped me. For now, when I have really forgotten, you round on me: and it is impossible for me to recall all the natural delicacy of my actual emotions. I must ask you to believe that they existed in full force, and that it is only the fluxious quality of my brain that forbids my attempting more than a vague record of the pleasure which your book gave me.

It would be very pleasant to meet again, and, if we ever get through with our housebuilding, of which I often despair, I hope that the site may tempt you to pay us a visit.

Your kind enquiries—Monica, who sends love and thanks, is very well. Her voice has never recovered its full strength; but, though easily fatigued, does not much trouble her. Margaret, the other invalid, looks to be quite reestablished, but these things are uncertain. Elizabeth is grown up. Edward is in 5th form at Eton. I play the lean and slipper'd pantaloon.

At the risk of boring you I enclose a copy of the ode that I wrote for the Oxford Pageant at request of their committee. I hope it may interest you enough to justify my troubling you to return it. (You need not add a *single word* of appreciation.) At any rate old Oxford days will excuse it to your husband who has always been kind to my Muse—to him my kindest remembrances—

yours sincerely
Robt Bridges

530: TO LIONEL MUIRHEAD

Whitebarn
Boar's Hill
Oxford
May 8, 1907

My dear Lionel

Monica orders me to write to you. She remembers that you said that the parapet work in your South garden was recent, and made of concrete, and she thinks that she would like something of the same sort on the parapets of our South lawn. Therefore I am to ask you whether you got yours done (that is manufactured) on the spot, or whether the pieces were carted like stones. We should like to make ours on the premises.

Also I am to tell you that there is a general consensus of opinion that we ought to get away from here for a day or two while we can, and that it would be possible for us next Monday till Wednesday, and she wishes me to take my cure at Haseley. She will probably go to Yattendon. My mind is not fully awake to the full consequences of this proposal, and I do not even know that you have returned from Germany, but I would come at least for a day and be slothful at Haseley if it suited you and nothing here prevented. This offhand suggestion is prepared for any answer, and it is possible enough that I shall be kept here. Still it is unlikely that I could not get off for a day.

Sanday and Coles both told me that they could not *understand* my ode: from which I gather that I have not pleased the churchmen. On the other hand Warren told me that it had delighted some less rigid minds.

A lady who came in to tea here the other day said that the Warrens had taken Great Milton Rectory for the latter part of the summer this year. She also told me that it was impossible to "read the lessons" better than you did. I shall cycle over some Sunday when there is a fine bit of Old Testament for you to declaim: but though I went 20 miles the other day I am obliged to recognise that my legs are not altogether what they used to be.

> "And now I cannot wear my shoes
> Upon my feats of arms."

I always liked that pun, it is so indefensibly bad, and makes the orthodox pun maker quite angry. I am afraid that it is dragged in here somewhat wildly: but it will excuse itself. I address this to Mrs. Lionel in case you should be away. The uncertainty as to who will read my salutations makes it impossible for me to express them with the proper pronouns, so bless yourselves for me.

yours affectionately

RB

531: TO SAMUEL GEE

[Boar's Hill]

June 13, 1907

My dear Gee

I was glad to hear from you. I was thinking of you all last Tuesday afternoon. I did not realise that you had retired.

Your leisurely visits to Milton's statue and the British Museum remind me of Lamb's Essay on the Superannuated man. Of course you know it. If not do so at once. By the way there is a recent handy and very readable edition of the Essays of Elia in Harmsworth's Shilling Library. But above all this leisure of yours suggests the possibility of your visiting ME, which I take it is one of the chief advantages of your retirement.

I cannot *write* about myself. There is too much, but I would talk to you for days. You know that we are building ourselves a new house: It is probable that we move into it on the 25th.—After that day I shall be unvisitable for a long while. This is a delightful and healthy place, among woods on a hill which overlooks the counties of Berks and Oxford for 20 miles on all sides. We have a pony-cart which could take you into Oxford, 5 miles by road, whenever you wished: and a footpath through the fields is only 3 miles—a pleasant stroll in summer. But is this summer? There is snow on the hills in Cumberland.

My answer to your letter has two main objects (1) To get you to say when you will visit us—(2) Apropos of Birch and Shakespeare—to send you an Essay which I wrote for the Stratford on Avon Edition of Shakespeare which is now out. 10 volumes price £10. You will prefer to read my proof copy of the Essay. If my contention is true I take it that Shakespearian criticism has to readjust itself. I wonder what you will say. The critics will of course only hum and haw and say nothing either one way or the other, and 10 years hence will have assimilated my contribution.—You will see that I pretend to prove my position, which is a different thing from mere conjectural opinion.—Tell me what you think.

> yours ever
>
> RB

532: TO LIONEL MUIRHEAD

> Boar's Hill
> August 4th, 1907

My dear Lionel

If I do not write tonight I don't know when I shall—we came in here last Tuesday week, and are very much pleased with the house. Our days are of course fully occupied in getting things straight: but though there seems no end to this we are comfortable enough, and all the machinery works well. I shall be anxious for you to come and see us ere long, but I am writing to say that I do not see any probability of my writing letters for a month at least. You will be pleased to hear that the builders are all going off *next Saturday*. The gardener's house, and the first section of the stables being finished. Edward has come home all right, and is enjoying his freedom from study.

If you ever go into Oxford let me know. It would be pleasant to meet there even if you did not get up here. There will be no rest for me for ever so long.

With kindest messages from us all

> your affectionate
>
> RB

533: TO HENRY NEWBOLT

> Boar's Hill
> Oxford
> August 31, 1907

My dear Newbolt

My wife, who read your kind letter, made two spontaneous remarks upon it (1) That it expressed very much what she had been feeling (2) That she wished that you lived nearer: and these are exactly the two things that were uppermost in my own thoughts; except that I was very much touched by your friendship, and can hardly write quite as I feel about it: for I am getting so *very* old (you talk of yourself as turning) that I am accustoming myself to friends falling away, and am almost humourously surprised at anyone drawing nearer. It is ridiculous to find how the friends of one's life seem to shrivel and get absorbed in their immediate surroundings and occupations when the 60th year comes on them.

Mary Coleridge's death was a great blow to us, and I know how much worse it must be to you. I felt very sympathetic towards her: and she had such a fine free imaginative spirit that her "Limitations" (as they say) did not count for anything but a queer side of her fancy. I was also particularly grateful to her for the encouragement which I always got from her liking of my work: since she instinctively disliked the sort of poetry which a good many critics assert mine to be—and I could trust her natural temperament in such a matter. You will have a great deal to tell me about her when we meet. When that may be, should be for you to decide. We are now settled in the new house, and though when all the children are with us we have only one absolutely vacant bedroom, yet we have built so as [to] have some elasticity. We mean to have a bed in the bungalow, and I shall sleep when I like in the library.

Things have gone pretty well: and I wish that you had not determined that the place would not suit you. There is so much to do here that it is unlikely that we shall be going away except for a few days at a time for ever so long. My old friend and cousin Moñt Cashell is coming to see us today, and I am writing this before the day's occupations begin. The pen that I selected has a curve in the quill which prevents my holding it properly as I lie on the sofa—the attitude being assumed for mental convenience—so that I am afraid you may have difficulty in reading. As our respective wives (it is mine's birthday) correspond, I will leave them to arrange any visit that you may be able to make us. I am very grateful for your letter, and hope that circumstances will allow us to meet more frequently. The situation here near Oxford is very congenial to me. If you had all been here today Mrs. Newbolt could have played a violin part in a scratch overture this afternoon. We have also a boat on the upper river.

yours very sincerely

R Bridges

534: TO HENRY NEWBOLT

Boar's Hill
Oxford
September 4, 1907

My dear Newbolt

I have sent your letter on to de la Mare because I had a letter by same post as yours from Reginald Smith offering me 12 pages of the Cornhill and I think that would suit me better, and that I should not write both notices.

I know what I should wish to say about the poetry and I don't suppose that there is anybody who would venture (or perhaps desire) to say so much. But I feel that I shall have great difficulty in satisfying my conscience in almost all the other matters: and I shall want your assistance.

As you are not going to write anything yourself, I wish you would consider what you would like to have said, and make a few notes. I shall not want to write about that side of her life which I knew nothing or very little about, and shall therefore confine myself to the literary side as much as possible—but I shall send you a lot of questions.

I do not know at all how she used to spend her days, and so little of her intimate friendships that I feel I am really unpardonably venturesome in undertaking to write any sort of memoir, but this scruple is perhaps sufficient safeguard, and my motive is solely the wish to do justice to the poems.

When I have turned the matter over I shall know what I wish to ask you. Perhaps it would suit me best to be able to *quote* from a letter of yours such a description of her London Life as you might send me. Could you write such a picture for me?

yours ever
RB

E G.   I have never read the K with 2 faces! and don't want to!!!

535: TO HENRY NEWBOLT

Boar's Hill
September 14, 1907

My dear Newbolt
Thank you very much for writing. My "article" is wanted by October 1 for the November number of The Cornhill. I have been thinking about it a good deal—and the more I think the more difficult it seems. I am glad to see Mr de la Mare's appreciation. Violet Hodgkins is going to send me a copy of the later poems. I will send them on to you as you request. I am curious to see them.—It is good of you to wish to use my paper again in preface to the edition of her poems. You had better wait until you see it: I doubt if it will be of any service: but I will try and make it so as to call serious attention to the poems. Really what I am afraid of now is that a miscellaneous collection may not justify the expectations which the Daniel volume might arouse. As literary executor you will be able I suppose to decide whether all the poems should be printed or only a selection. I should be inclined to publish them *without* any introduction or comment. I will write again and tell you how I get on. I had seen the "news" about Menander. It was rather sad.

yours ever
RB

536: TO HENRY NEWBOLT

Boar's Hill
Oxford
September 23, 1907

My dear Newbolt
I have written about ⅔ of my paper. Reginald Smith wants it sent to him on October 1. I should very much wish you to look through it and tell me if there is anything which you think would be better altered.

If you could send me word where you will be up to October 1 I will try and send you the MS

I have confined myself entirely to trying to get serious attention to the poems, but am afraid I shall not please anybody more than I do myself.

yours ever
Robt Bridges

537: TO HENRY NEWBOLT

Boar's Hill
Oxford
September 25, 1907

My dear Newbolt

Thank you for your postcard. There is no pen here better than this. I have sent the "Essay" to my wife, and if she returns it in time I will send it to you on Friday—to Orchardleigh. Then if I get it back on Monday morning I can do what is requisite to it before sending it to Smith Younger and Company.—

I have tried to make it of *general* literary interest, in order to attract readers.

I will send you the poems. I have not yet read the new ones! I shall do so this evening. When they came I looked at about 4 or 5 and they did not seem to me as good as the ones selected in Fancy's Following. I therefore determined to write my paper before I read more, lest they should hamper me in saying what I wished to say. My wife read them all, and her verdict was that there were not (This is of course privately said to me) more than a dozen at most which could go in same rank as Daniel's book. I think that you will have a difficult task: There were 48 poems in Daniel's book.—If you cannot get more than 20 or 30 more without lowering the standard it will be difficult to determine whether you will print a small book with a high standard maintained: or whether you will include *everything*, from the autobiographical, psychological, anthropological and religious standpoint. I am of course very much in favour of the select plan: and it would prevent others being printed at some future time. But I confess that writing my appreciation has led me to sympathize with the other point of view.—Perhaps you know what her actual wishes were. I hope you will not dislike what I have written. After you have read it and I have read the new poems we can write again.

Is there any chance of your being able to come here on your way westward? I could meet you in Oxford any day, and put you up.

yours ever
R Bridges

538: TO HENRY NEWBOLT

Boar's Hill
evening
September 25, [1907]

My dear Newbolt
I have read all the poems. There are more than my wife thought. Towards the end the good ones come pretty thick. I did not count them but I should think there would be quite 25 first class—not all very finished, but excellent in their way. These, with the 48 of Fancy's Following—and say some 15 more from the earlier book and say 10 doubtful ones—would make near 100—and I am *very* strongly of opinion that these should not be diluted with poorer stuff. It is so exceedingly beautiful. She speaks out pretty plainly in some of these last ones, and I am glad to find that there is nothing wrong in my paper. I have really hit on the main point.

I shall hope for an answer to my letter this afternoon to say that you are coming here. Then you can take the 2 volumes of poetry with you.

Else tell me if I am to send them to Orchard Leigh. One of the volumes appears to be extremely precious—and it is—

Excuse horrid writing with back of a bad quill.

Thursday morning [September 26]

My wife does not ½ like my paper so I may have to keep it here a bit when she returns it—and so be unable to submit it to you—

[unsigned]

539: TO HENRY NEWBOLT

Boar's Hill
October 1, 1907
but late for this day's post

My dear Newbolt
I am very glad that there will be so many poems, and I quite agree that they should be all in one volume, and if this compels you to print them continuously, instead of always beginning a fresh page, I am glad of this. I very much object myself to buying a lot of blank paper: and bad paper. It is the cheapness of the paper that has ruined the book.

A good many of the poems in that common Heine have titles and these do not seem much in the way. They are set below the number thus

3
Zwei Brüder
Oben auf der Bergespitze
Liegt das Schloss in Nacht gehüllt

which looks well enough. It implies a good strong figure for the numeration, and is of course best when the title is short. If the titles are generally long it might be well to make a rule for them that they shall not exceed a certain length and so drive them into lines rather closely.

82
The man who fol-
lowed his nose
The ways of man are dark and sad
etc.—

There is sure to be some way out of it.

About the subscribers' edition. I think the chief interest in it will be the list of subscribers, so that I should not let *any* one subscribe, but I do not see why we should not let any bona fide admirer have a copy. I think you should fix the price of this at once—and if no one is in want of money I should think 10 shillings would be ample to ask. The subscribers' copies need not be struck off till the printing of the main edition. I will beat up Oxford for subscribers if you agree about the cost. One must name the price, and it would be well to have a printed slip, in form of prospectus, though that is not necessary. It would probably be a means of reaching people whom we might otherwise miss. What would you say to a morocco binding with a price at £1. I rather like that notion.

It is very nice having Celia here. I hope she won't be dull. I have just looked up a train for her to Salisbury; it is only 2 hours journey.

I finished copy of essay this morning and have sent it off (you assisted me very much by your talk.) I hope that it will give satisfaction and help the book.

In case of the book not selling the subscribers edition ought to be arranged to cover *printing* expenses.

yours ever

RB

540: TO LIONEL MUIRHEAD

Chilswell
Oxford
Sunday, October 6th, 1907

My dear Lionel

I was sorry that you have been having trouble of such a nature as to strain your philosophy. I do not exercise myself in vain conjecture: but hope that it is not of irretrievable ill. I should have written to you during the last 3 weeks, but have had more than usual on my hands, entailing daily letters etc. chiefly on account of, Monica's absence. She is with Elizabeth at Harrogate. It was thought that Harrogate would suit Elizabeth: and that she needed something. It will take a whole month to accomplish the amelioration which I understand is progressing well: and that Elizabeth enjoys her bath and riding exercise. They are to return about the 17 inst. or prox. I never knew which was which in futures.

Another occupation which I may have told you about. I undertook to write an Essay for the Cornhill Magazine on Mary Coleridge's poems. It gave me much trouble. It should be in the November number. I hope it may interest and amuse you. No doubt you heard the lamentable news of her death. She is a great loss to us. We have indeed been enjoying the lovely weather. Now it is over. Possibly we may have another bright spell: but yesterday was windy, and today is as damp as autumn can be. I have lit the dining room fire and set the heater on, for the walls not being yet really dry show moisture in a good many places in this condition of the 'atmosphere'. Whenever I have hung any pictures (except where they are just above a heater) I have put crumpled brown paper between them and the wall. This is a most satisfactory device, for it increases the draft between the picture and the wall, and the paper betrays the presence of any moisture at once, and also takes up what there is. I was glad to find that so far the paper has remained pretty crisp.

There are a hundred things that need or "want" doing everywhere. Our present fuss is the drive up to the house, which is just now impassible for carriages, as we have put all the big stone down, and have not got the gravel on top. We have fortunately found a very good gravel deposit quite handy, and hope to get this right before the end of the week.

We have also sown as much lawn as we have made, and in another fortnight ought to be putting in trees. I had an offer two days ago of an oriental plane from the temple of DIANA of EPHESUS! You will think me very lucky.—I do not know how big the tree is, nor whether the tree-fancier who offers it will hear of the lower greensand.

The surprise about this house is that it is somewhat *beautiful!* Not in the manner of the temple of Diana: but in a fitness and propriety, and absence of mere appearances, while the detail is generally extremely competent and harmonious. All the main devices which could be foreseen have turned out effective. The rooms also are very comfortable. The sitting room and dining room combining comfort and absence of draughts with a complete airiness and great varieties of ventilation.

You must come over some day when you get a chance. Let me know if I can meet you in Oxford. I do not know if you like walking, but a cab to Ferry Hinksey ½ mile from the station brings you within a 1¾ mile walk of the house.

I must not go on chatting. I am glad that Charis thinks she will like Dr Walker. Since I saw you Margaret's pianoforte teacher (the German) has returned to his Vaterland, so that Margaret now goes to Walker for her lessons.

yours ever

RB

I dreamed last night that I saw Keble—he was a bishop, and quite naked except for a pair of gaiters. He had the most enormous leg muscles, which I felt and examined, and wondered how a man with such muscles could ever have died: for he was dead. I think it all came from some steel engraving in Scott's Waverleys: which I have been reading of late.

541: TO HENRY NEWBOLT

Boar's Hill
October 11, 1907

My dear Newbolt

Thanks. I return you the proof.

I would gladly use Stevenson extract, but there are two objections (1) The pagination would give fresh trouble (2) He goes on to say exactly what I go on to say—viz. that its interest is the main thing above all other considerations.

So I propose to let my text stand, and (if you will allow me) write a letter to Athenaeum after the Cornhill is out, saying that you have sent me the exact words. This will have a doubly good effect in keeping the ball rolling (and also strengthening my dicta about romance).—If I put it in my essay it would seem as if I had got my opinions from RL Stevenson.

———

Another matter

I have struck the accent off the word *forgèd* in my copy. It is accented in Daniel. It seems a pity, whether Mary Coleridge intended it to be accented or no, not to let the reader read it as a monosyllable if he prefers it such, as I do. I hope you will follow me.

RB

542: TO A. H. BULLEN

Chilswell
nr Oxford
October 15, 1907

My dear Bullen

Many thanks for answering my letter, and for sending the review which I return to you. The reviewer honours me by giving my Essay so much space in his criticism, and then confessing that he "has no space" etc. He really does not face the matter, and his assumption that I do not sympathize with Shakespeare and am overlaid with modern refinement is I think wrong. "Refinement" is not modern in the only sense in which it can be alleged that I appeal to it. There were plenty of "refined" minds in Shakespeares day, and *always have been everywhere*. And did Shakespeare read the gospels or no? And if he did was his mind incapable of understanding? On the other hand there are always plenty of brutes, and the London audiences do more harm to the drama today than they did in Shakespeare's time—but in a different manner. They are however the chief cause of the badness of the art.

You must come here when you visit Oxford. At present we are unapproachable, for the torrential rain has made havoc of our attempts to make a road.

Thank you for promising to read my paper on Mary Coleridge. She was an

example of a character which it would have delighted Shakespeare to drama-
tise—almost incredible contradictions.

I wonder if you liked Professor Raleigh's book.

yours sincerely
Robt Bridges

543: TO WILLIAM BUTLER YEATS

Chilswell
nr Oxford
November 15, 1907

My dear poet

I have not heard that you have got married since I saw you last, therefore you
must rely on your dramatic imagination to tell you what you would do if your
mother-in-law were an anthologist and she were to ask you to make use of the
slight friendship between us (which you have so selfishly neglected) to persuade
me to allow her to print some of my poems in her anthology. It is as you may
have guessed Mrs. Waterhouse of Yattendon who insists on approaching you in
this roundabout way, and I enclose her request. She anthologises for Methuen
who gives her a good price for her work and agrees to pay fees for copyright
poems up to a certain limit. The anthology is a religious "day-book". I have now
done my duty—and I leave her in your hands. If you look through the list (which
I have not done) you will be able to see whether you can fix any price for
Methuen to pay. I do not wish that out of kindness to me you should do anything
unusual. I have a great abhorrence of these anthologists, though I now and then
get something out of them. But I believe that the multiplication of their poetry
books does really hinder the sale of poems.

I have built a home up here. Everything is new. It was a barren waste. If ever
you should feel at all kindly disposed to me we should be glad to see you, but
Summer is better than Winter. It is a pleasant place, very near Oxford on a hill,
solitary.

yours very sincerely
R. Bridges

You can reply to me or to Mrs. Waterhouse
Yattendon Court.

544: TO LIONEL MUIRHEAD

Chilswell
nr Oxford
November 15, 1907

and very nearly November 16th, My dear Lionel, as I sit by the last embers of the
diningroom fire smoking your favourite baccy. Monica has gone off to Yattendon for Sunday to swear to the creed in behalf of Amyas' firstborn who is her

godchild. Wherefore I am alone, at least after the girls are gone to bed, and I should have gone to my couch also, but the wind after a still day has just sprung up and the engine is filling up the cisterns, and in an hour I shall go and turn it off before tuning in. That's the sort of joke that you make; I hope it pleases you. We have got our road a bit better, and are planting on the banks. By the way the reason I am writing to you is that I have just been writing to a German Professor on the subject of "Wintry delites". That brought you into my thoughts, and I thought I should like a chat with you. This week now ending I have spent mostly in reading and reviewing a book of poetical Essays for the Times. My review has amused me much (though it was a bore) and I am looking forward to its amusing you and Wooldridge. When it comes out I will send it you. It was a most luscious topic. I did not get down to Palestrina on Friday. I had one day to go to London to see my fighting nephew married. His chums were splendid. One day we had a sort of rehearsal of the unfinished symphony, which was great pleasure. The Library is a very good music room. Our final building-accounts have come in, and are more favourable than we had dared to hope: So Monica (who does all these things) says that we ought to be able to finish up the Library at once. This will be delightful for me, as it is my room, and at present it cannot be said to be comfortable, though it is a great luxury when we wish for music. We have got the designs completed for the bookcases: and we find that we must have the corridor which connects the house with the library glazed in from the wind for when there is any wind it collects at high pressure in the corridor, and makes great efforts to get into the house.—I have not heard from you since the boys went back to school—yes I think your last letter was later than that but I don't know whether Anthony is with you or at Eton. We think of going down to Eton on Thursday. Is there any chance of your going there on that day? I hear from HEW in London, and wish that he could pay us a visit. But he is afraid of the cold, and I don't know what we should do to amuse Mrs. HEW in this weather. I hope that you are well and amusing yourself. I am pretty well, though some days very lame. The girls went down to hear the Romanes lecture (Curzon) and one of them caught the inevitable cold which open-air folk catch in a crowded room, and gave it to me so that I am sniffling and sneezing. The doctors will have to find out that colds are good for one. That really would be an optimistic discovery. I have been fairly optimistic for a few days lately. You no doubt are in your everlasting seat.

with kind regards to Mrs M and Charis

yours ever

RB

545: TO HENRY NEWBOLT

Chilswell
Oxford
December 15, [1907]

My dear Newbolt

Thank you for your letter. I am looking forward to seeing the book, and it will make a very good sort of Xmas present, useful as well as dolce.

I write to send you my fighting nephew's address; it is Fittleton Manor Salisbury.

Mrs Tom I have only seen once. She was Mrs. Wilfred Marshall, and my nephew's friends were all pleased. She seemed to be a musical person and I expect she can play the piano, so that if Fittleton is near you, she may be a good neighbour. We all of us liked her. My nephew is still Major R.A. but is going to join the Cavalry I believe. I need not recommend him to you. But if Fittleton is near I hope that Mrs. H.N. will call on Mrs. T. B.

Margaret enjoyed her visit to you very much.

yours ever

RB

546: TO HENRY NEWBOLT

Chilswell
nr Oxford
December 18, 1907

My dear Newbolt

The "poems" has arrived. I like your introduction and the general appearance of the book. I hope it may be successful. I can't imagine how you managed to do it so quickly. I have not had time to read in it much yet.

My nephew tells me that he is 10 miles out of Salisbury, so that Mrs. Newbolt cannot be expected to call, but if you will let them they will motor over to see you when they have got a motor.

This carries our best Xmas wishes. I am making Xmas gifts of Mary Coleridge's poems.

With our salutation to all your party.

yours ever

RB

I must thank you for the compliment implied in your quotation.

547: TO BRUCE RICHMOND

Chilswell
nr Oxford
January 30, 1908

Dear Mr Richmond

I was glad to hear from you.

As for Ben Johnson or Jonson. I have to confess that when I was an undergrad I bought the rare one's works—and it was one of the severest disappointments in my life. Ergo I have never read him, and do not know him, and do not wish to. Of course I read one or two plays very carefully, and have had the conscience to give him another chance now and then: but if I wrote about him you would not wish to print it. Hume seems to me quite right when he says of him he had all the learning which Shakespeare lacked, but none of his genius.

As for Darley. I finished reading him—which was no joke—about a week ago, and can send you the paper on him at any time. I have written about ⅔ of it—

I hope that I have not made an error of judgment in thinking that, as his work is quite unknown to the public, it would be best to write very explicitly and somewhat separately about the different plays and poems. I would send you the article one day early next week, and if you had time to look through it I should have no trouble in recasting it if you thought it advisable.

Also I am in some doubt about the length. I calculate now that I shall not be far short of 3500. *I should be very glad to know if you think this too long.* Whatever tether you give me I shall use up in quotations from the poems.

I will of course cut down to any length that you prescribe.

I remember reading the article on Thompson, and I enjoyed it and thought the comparison with Tennyson very just.

Remember your promise to come up here some day.

yours very truly
Robt Bridges

548: TO HENRY NEWBOLT

Chilswell
February [2]7, 1908

My dear Newbolt

We were all very sorry for this disappointment, but glad to hear that Celia does not seem seriously ill. I had been looking foward to talking with you, especially as I never wrote you any worthy congratulations on Mary Coleridge's poems coming out. As those who live near the church do not attend it—I have to confess that I have not yet come to any full acquaintance with those of the poems that are new to me. But I am getting on. I like your preface the oftener I look at it: although it is my vanity and affections rather than my judgement that approve of that extract from my paper in the Cornhill. Someone told me (Father Stone) that Swinburne had praised the poems. This is very satisfactory to me for I feared that my advocacy must have done them injury in that quarter.—I have an article on Darley in this week's Times Literary Supplement—and a good paper on "Abercrombie" in the Nation—at least it should be in, as it was written to date by request. The cares of this world and the deceitfulness of a limited riches choke the word and have choked it now for a good while. I am so ungrateful for the many great blessings that are showered upon me that I have taken to reading "The general Thanksgiving" at family prayers.

Hope to see you soon

yours ever
RB